DESIGN GUIDE
TO THE 1997
UNIFORM
BUILDING CODE

DESIGN GUIDE
TO THE 1997
UNIFORM BUILDING CODE

Richard T. Conrad, FAIA, CBO
Steven R. Winkel, FAIA, PE

JOHN WILEY & SONS, INC.
New York • Chichester • Weinheim • Brisbane • Singapore • Toronto

This book is printed on acid-free paper. ♾

Published simultaneously in Canada.

Library of Congress Catalog Card Number 90-86363

ISBN 0-471-23641-1
ISSN 0897-7097

10 9 8 7 6 5 4 3 2 1

PREFACE TO THE FOURTH EDITION

This fourth edition of the Design Guide will be the last covering the Uniform Building Code (UBC). The International Conference of Building Officials (ICBO) has suspended publication of the UBC with the 1997 edition to focus on the development of the International Building Code (IBC), scheduled to be published in the year 2000, in conjunction with the Southern Building Code Congress and the Building Officials and Code Administrators International.

This edition of the Guide will be the first to address the UBC since the adoption of the "common code format" by ICBO and the other model code organizations. This reformatting resulted in a reorganization of the UBC provisions. We have maintained the organization of the Guide found in the third edition and incorporated the changes in the text reflected in the UBC. We will not provide a discussion of the reformatting other than to reference appropriate sections of previous editions of the UBC. Readers with experience using the 1994 UBC will be able to follow the adjustments easily.

Of special note will be the revisions to the means of egress provisions of Chapter 10. This chapter has been rewritten in its entirety. It is now organized around the format used by the other model code organizations and will be the format of the corresponding chapter in the IBC. We have given special attention to our interpretation of these new provisions. We hope they will be beneficial to the readers in understanding the concepts of this important chapter. Be aware that these interpretations may vary from those provided by local building officials since they have not been tested in practice.

There have been changes to the accessibility provisions since the third edition as well. These are reviewed and analyzed for the reader.

Because of the changes associated with the reformatting of the code in 1994, we have not provided a reference to changes to the UBC incorporated since the 1991 edition. This would be a complex and confusing exercise due to the reorganization and renumbering of the code sections. We hope our discussions will overcome this need.

We extend our appreciation to Sondra Jarvis for her assistance in the new graphics for this edition. We also extend our special thanks to John Canestro, P.E. for his support and encouragement in taking on this endeavor and to the staff of the ICBO; Cheryl Melendez in the publication department and Jay Woodward in the education department.

CONTENTS

ARTICLE 1
BACKGROUND FOR THE READER AND THE DESIGNER AND THE LOCAL OFFICIALS

1. BACKGROUND FOR THE READER

A. Presentation of Material in This Guide

This Guide is based on the 1997 Uniform Building Code (UBC). Generally, the 1997 code text of a provision is followed by a discussion of the provision. The entire text of a referenced code section may not be printed in its entirety, and the code text may be interrupted by a discussion of a relevant portion of the section.

Uniform Building Code text will appear as shown in this sentence.

Although the authors have permission to reprint code provisions from the UBC, it should be clearly understood that the discussions of the code's intent and the interpretations of the provisions are solely those of the authors. They do not necessarily have the support or backing of the International Conference of Building Officials (ICBO).

Certain of the technical material that was in the body of the previous editions of the Guide have been relocated into the Technical Appendix portion at the end of this Guide.

The purpose of the UBC is to protect the public by regulating the construction, alteration and maintenance of structures. The UBC establishes certain minimum criteria that define the code intent. The criteria set forth for accomplishing the code's goals are stated in specific language because codes are legal ordinances adopted by government and are ultimately enforced by the courts. However, the code language is meant not to exact a specific method of meeting the code but to establish the code intent.

The emphasis in the discussions of the code provisions is on providing the reader with an explanation of the intent behind the provision. In some instances, historical precedent is used to establish this intent. In other instances, the established intent is represented as the author's opinion. In these latter situations, the opinion may be at variance with an ICBO position or may cover an item for which there is no formal opinion. When this is the case, the rationale for the opinion is provided so that the reader can formulate an independent judgment on the matter.

The modern approach to codes is to strive for performance rather than specificity. The reader is advised that there may be several different ways to meet a particular provision. Where it will help in clarifying a provision, sketches and diagrams are provided in this Guide. A description or diagram should not be viewed as the only solution, but rather one of several possible solutions. Careful attention should be given to the reasoning provided in the interpretations because understanding that reasoning can lead to other solutions to problems involving the particular provision.

The building code should not be used as one would use a dictionary or encyclopedia. The various provisions do not function alone, but together comprise part of a regulatory outline of public safety philosophy. Although many designers and others tend to use the code as a catalog of isolated requirements, doing so limits the design flexibility essential to many projects. Therefore, understanding the intent of the code provisions as a whole is a critical initial step in the process of properly applying the code.

The approach used in this Guide does not offer a section-by-section explanation of the UBC or an examination of set problems and their solutions in meeting a specific code provision. Instead it provides

- overviews of the intent of the major design provisions,
- the background to the concepts involved where relevant to the explanation and
- examples of the types of solutions the designer might consider in meeting that intent.

When a particular provision of the UBC is discussed, the discussion also covers

- the less obvious implications of the provision and
- how the provision ties in with the code concept being expressed.

The 1994 edition of the UBC was reformatted to be consistent with the "common code format" developed jointly by the three model code organizations. There have been significant changes in the code provisions since the 1991 edition, the last edition for which the Guide was published. We will not try to identify these changes, rather they will be discussed in the appropriate sections of the Guide. We will make special reference to the changes to Chapter 10, Means of Egress, in Article 7. This UBC chapter has been completely revised in the 1997 UBC.

The reader should understand, in regard to Articles 3 through 10 of this Guide, that each article presents an integrated discussion of the provisions of the particular chapter(s) of the UBC being reviewed. The discussion will provide the philosophy or intent of the code as represented by that chapter of the code.

An illustration of how one could relate to the code intent, instead of only the specific requirement, may help clarify the concept.

> **Example:** The code might require two buildings on the same lot to be separated from one another by 20 feet if both buildings are to have operable plain glass windows instead of fixed wired-glass fire windows. The intent is to prevent fire from spreading rapidly from one building to another, i.e., concern with the prevention of conflagration.
>
> It may be that only one building needs to have operable windows. The facing wall of the other building could have
>
> - no openings in it or
> - openings with fixed wired-glass windows.
>
> The distance between the buildings could be reduced to as little as 10 feet. For a detailed discussion on this matter, see Figure 5-5 and the analysis in Article 5 of Section 503.3.
>
> Another possible way of satisfying the code might be to equip both buildings with fire sprinkler systems not otherwise required by the code. These systems, along with an adequate water supply, can be accepted by the enforcement official as an alternative method of meeting the intent of the code in preventing conflagration by suppression of fire. That acceptance would allow a closer spacing of the buildings. The acceptance of alternative methods of construction will be discussed in more detail with regard to the provisions of Section 104.2.8.

Essentially, there are different ways to satisfy the code's intent. Knowledge and understanding of that intent provides the designer with the ability to choose a solution that will both meet the code and best serve the design.

Many building code requirements relate to the prevention of conflagration and the providing of structures in which the occupants are protected against the hazards of fire and panic. Besides the siting requirements for conflagration control, the building code also regulates the type of construction permitted based on the degree of life and property hazard a proposed use may present to the occupants and the structure.

There are many subjects addressed by the UBC; this Guide deals with the primary concerns of fire and panic. We will be examining these areas of concern through the following provisions of the code:

- occupancy,
- height of building,
- areas of occupancy,
- separation between buildings and other properties,
- fire-resistive requirements and
- means of egress.

These subjects, contained in Chapters 3, 5, 6, 7 and 8, and 10 of the UBC, will be given detailed discussion in Articles 5, 6, 7 and 8 of this Guide.

Requests for additional coverage of certain code provisions, together with increasing numbers of code changes to other portions of the code that affect life safety and the work of the designer, have resulted in additions to the Guide. The Guide has been expanded in regard to the other chapters of the UBC in Article 9 of this Guide, which covers provisions in Chapters 3, 4 and 6; and Article 10, which covers provisions in Chapters 8, 9, 11, 14, 15, 23, 26, 35 and Appendix Chapter 29.

The structural, general construction and other provisions of the UBC will be discussed only as they relate to aspects of the design process that involve the primary concerns of fire and panic.

B. Model Building Codes in the United States

The background to codes in the United States, and to the model codes in particular, may assist the designer in understanding the development of the UBC provisions and the processes involved in amending that code.

The regulation of building construction in the United States is generally handled through a building permit process. This process establishes minimum construction criteria to protect life and property. These criteria are contained in various documents, primarily the building code. Other documents are supplemental to the building code and usually are used to establish the criteria for electrical, plumbing, mechanical, fire prevention and elevator construction in buildings.

Building codes are normally enforced at the lowest level of government, i.e., the city or town. When enacted into law, these codes are legal documents in the same manner as are traffic laws and the multitude of other laws at the local or state level. In some instances, the building code enforced in a jurisdiction is one adopted by the state legislature and required to be enforced by the local government. The enforcement official may have any of a variety of titles ranging from building inspector to manager of a public safety department.

There has been a long-standing trend to reduce the number of differences among the various codes. The main method for doing this has been through the use of "model codes." A model code is a document developed by knowledgeable people in the field of that code's activity. It is reviewed and amended by a body of enforcement officials on an annual basis to keep it reasonably current with construction and design technology and materials.

The model code serves the same purpose as a model house: that of a complete and functional structure one views when planning to buy a new home. The model represents the home a buyer may wish to purchase rather than having an architect or builder develop drawings and then build a home to those specifications.

A model code is a complete document that can be adopted into law, by reference, without the jurisdiction having to write it. The term "by reference" means that a law or ordinance enacted by the legislative body need only refer to the name and edition of the code and need not print the code in its entirety.

The three model codes in general use in the United States are

1. The Uniform Building Code published by the International Conference of Building Officials: This is the most widely used model building code in the United States. It is used by over 1200 jurisdictions in all parts of the country and is almost the exclusive code west of the Mississippi. In some states it is the state code.

2. The Basic National Building Code published by Building Officials and Code Administrators International (BOCA). It is used primarily in the northeastern part of the country.

3. The Standard Building Code, published by the Southern Building Code Congress International (SBCCI): It is used almost exclusively in the southeastern part of the country.

A jurisdiction, which may be a town, city or state, adopts the code into law. That adoption may include amendments to portions of the code or simply be the code as written, since the code's form permits direct adoption. The jurisdiction also adopts into law the companion codes needed to provide a full range of regulations for construction. Except for the electrical code, these companion code documents are published by each of the model code bodies. The model electrical code most in use in this country is the National Electrical Code published by the National Fire Protection Association.

In addition to the codes in effect in a jurisdiction, state and federal laws also apply to building construction. Some, but not all, of these other laws may be enforced by the local enforcement official. These other laws include

- Occupational Safety and Health Administration (OSHA) regulations,
- environmental regulations,
- planning and zoning laws,
- energy conservation,
- security,
- accessibility and
- other special laws too numerous to list.

With the passage in 1990 of the Americans with Disabilities Act (ADA), the federal government has in effect mandated substantial changes in the model codes as they relate to accessibility provisions.

The provisions in Chapter 11 and Appendix Chapter 11 to the code have been a major step toward meeting the ADA requirements. It is suggested that the designer also obtain a copy of the Americans with Disabilities Act Accessibility Guidelines (ADAAG) to ensure compliance with those requirements.

> In the authors' opinion, the designer and the enforcement official should insist on the adoption of both Chapter 11 and the Appendix Chapter 11 simultaneously in order to avoid impacting existing buildings by the egress requirements of Chapter 11. See the more detailed discussions in Article 10 of this Guide.

This Guide does not deal with most of these other laws and regulations, except to point out that they exist and vary from jurisdiction to jurisdiction. The impact of the "accessibility" provisions of Chapter 11 on the exiting requirements in Chapter 10 will be discussed in Part 7 of this Guide.

Codes are ordinances adopted by local or state governments and are generally enforced at the local level. Enforcement involves a permit of one type or another, issued to the owner or agent, by the local jurisdiction. The process by which the permit is issued involves one or more of the codes in effect in that jurisdiction.

The permit process may vary from one jurisdiction to another, but all have a basic similarity that warrants understanding by anyone who must use the process. The details of the typical permit process are discussed in Appendix A1. The designer should be familiar with the procedure in the jurisdiction under consideration and coordinate the design with both the codes and local officials.

2. DESIGNER AND LOCAL OFFICIALS

A. Relationship of the Designer to the Enforcement Official

It is important to understand the relationship between the designer and the government official who will review the design for code compliance and building permit issuance. The designer sets the parameters that determine the review process. The designer has control over all phases of the design and therefore over which provisions of the code will apply.

The designer decides

- the location of the building on the site,
- the type of construction to be used,

- the layout of the interior of the building,
- the occupancy type,
- the relationships between different occupancies within the building and
- all the other elements of a design.

The function of the building official is to review and verify the designer's decisions. That review will determine the compliance of the submitted documents with the various code requirements pertaining to

- the type of construction and
- the site location and occupancy relationships.

The official's review is a verification of the code compliance of the designer's documents. The official is not charged with the responsibility for the design of the building. The official is charged with the responsibility of determining or verifying that all proposed construction meets the local code or its intent.

A designer may decide that a particular building and its use should be classified as a Hazardous Occupancy—a Group H, Division 2 or 3 (H-2 or H-3) Occupancy, rather than a Business Occupancy—Group B Occupancy. The permit documents must be reviewed by the building official under the H-2 or H-3 Occupancy provisions (provided the designer's selected occupancy reflects the "most restrictive" use the actual construction and use warrant).

On the other hand, if the occupancy chosen by the designer is "less restrictive" than that reflecting the true use or occupancy proposed for the building, the building official can and must require that the proper occupancy be used. For example, assume that the designer has designated a use to be B when in fact it should be the more restrictive H-2. The building official will require that all documents reflect the H-2 Occupancy. The official will then review those documents using the H-2 requirements of the code.

The official cannot require compliance with code provisions that relate to other occupancy classifications unless the designer has chosen an occupancy less restrictive than the correct one for the intended use.

The terms "more restrictive" end "less restrictive" must be defined to enable the designer and the officials to evaluate design decisions on a common basis. Using the provisions of Table 5-B, the restrictiveness can be established based on the allowable areas and heights permitted for a particular use or occupancy in the same type of construction.

For example, a comparison, using Table 5-B, of a Type III One-hour building with an H-2 Occupancy to the same building with a B Occupancy reveals a difference in their allowable areas:

H-2 Occupancy = 5600 square feet and
B Occupancy = 18,000 square feet.

Similarly, referring to Table 5-B, the number of stories allowed are

H-2 Occupancy = one story and
B Occupancy = four stories

These comparisons readily show that the code is more restrictive regarding the H-2 Occupancy than it is for the B Occupancy.

The same general concept holds true for the type of building construction proposed by the designer, for example, Type I versus Type V One-hour. This concept is contained in Sections 302 and 601, which will be discussed further in Articles 5 and 6, respectively, of this Guide.

B. Preliminary Plan Check

To obtain a permit with a minimum of delay or problem, the designer should use techniques that are encouraged by local building officials. They want to facilitate the issuance of permits, a task that can be accomplished most easily when the submitted documents comply with the code.

Within a particular jurisdiction, some form of preliminary plan check procedure is usually provided and made available by the staff of the local agencies. This procedure is recommended to be used at the earliest conceptual stage of the design when there are sufficient details developed to show the following:

- general overall size of the building,
- arrangement of the occupancies within the structure and
- arrangement of the exits.

The purpose of the preliminary plan check meeting with the local officials during the early schematic design phase is

- to familiarize them with what you intend to do and
- to determine their concerns with the design and to have them indicate potential problem areas.

An early meeting is necessary to avoid substantial redesign later and to reduce excess work in coordinating the several design disciplines if changes are found necessary. The meeting should be arranged by the principal design professional with the building official of the jurisdiction. A request should be made to have the fire department represented at the meeting, so that any items involving their responsibilities or concerns can be addressed at the same time.

The design professional should bring others who can add technical information and facilitate understanding at the meeting. Extra copies of the design drawings should be made available for both the building official and fire official.

During the discussion it will be the responsibility of the design professional to keep notes or minutes of the discussion. This is an extremely important step, since the results of the meeting will form the basis of the detailed design and because it will be the only recorded summary. If no such summary of the meeting is made and no copy sent to the jurisdiction for confirmation, there will be no record of the meeting ever having taken place or of any conclusions having been reached. *Do not assume that a representative of the jurisdiction will make notes of the meeting.*

Note that there may actually be a series of preliminary plan check meetings, especially as more detailed information is developed or revisions are made as a result of prior meetings or owner needs.

Again, it is imperative to document the discussions and conclusions of all such meetings. At the end of each meeting, the designer should indicate that officials will receive copies of the designer's understanding of the discussions' outcomes for review and concurrence, so that work on the drawings can confidently proceed.

At such meetings, alternatives to be evaluated should be presented and explained by the design professional. To provide design flexibility, the designer should seek acceptance of as many alternatives as necessary. At the meeting, the building official may make a decision based on some provision of the code or an interpretation thereof. The decision may prevent an alternative from being accepted. When this happens, the designer should note the section of the code involved for later verification and, if necessary, redesign to comply.

The designer is responsible for

- initiating the request for acceptance of an alternative to the code requirements and
- providing the documentation for demonstrating the equivalence of the alternative to the code.

The designer must demonstrate, per Section 104.2.8, the obvious equivalence or superiority of the design to the code requirements.

C. Summarizing the Meetings—Confirmation Letter

After the meeting with the officials, the design professional should send a copy of the notes or minutes to both the building official and the fire marshal (or the head of the fire code enforcement agency in the jurisdiction if that agency had a representative at the meeting).

It is suggested that courtesy copies be sent to all actual attendees at the meeting, together with any drawings discussed at the meeting if these were not previously left with them.

The agreements and conclusions reached at the meeting should be summarized in the confirmation letter. To expedite review of the letter, citations of the relevant code sections that were discussed should be provided therein. Doing this will also create a detailed record of the areas discussed and the compliance sought and received.

Similarly, the designer should document an understanding of any unaccepted design or concept along with the relevant sections of the code pertaining to that disapproval. If the designer believes that the interpretation of these sections was incorrect, this would be a good time to request reconsideration of the item. In Appendix A3, an example of such a letter is provided.

If an alternative design or system was discussed and accepted, the confirmation letter should provide the rationale behind the request and its acceptance to make clear in the record that the code was met as a result of the alternative presented.

The cover letter for these notes should request written confirmation that the summary meets the attendee's understanding of the discussions.

Do not use either of the following approaches in the confirmation letter because they may result in problems:

> "Unless I hear from you within days, I will presume that you concur with my summary."
> "Please sign at the bottom of this letter indicating you accept the summary."

The designer should not assume anything; the designer alone has the responsibility to create a written record in the jurisdiction's files. To expect that such a record of the meeting will be created by simply mailing or delivering a letter to the local jurisdiction is presumptuous. The letter could be lost or misrouted.

If no record exists in the files, the meeting is assumed never to have occurred. The officials cannot be bound to the agreements that may have been reached. By the time the final design drawings are completed, the individuals who attended the meeting may no longer be in the same responsible positions and their successors may know nothing about their oral agreements.

Therefore, the designer should request written confirmation. Make sure the letter was received. If there is no response after a reasonable time, the designer should write a follow-up letter indicating when the original letter was sent and enclose a copy of it therewith. The designer should emphasize the desire for an early written reply; he or she is entitled to one. If no reply is received after a month, the building official should be contacted personally by phone and reminded of the meeting and the need for an immediate reply.

The reason for waiting a reasonable time before calling is to avoid giving the official the impression of being harassed. The building official has a great many other jobs to deal with, the designer's being only one of them. By proceeding at a reasonable pace in awaiting the response, the designer is in a position to suggest that the official look into the matter as a possible internal communications breakdown.

The preliminary plan check phase is the time for all parties to become familiar with the building in question. Both applicant and official must become knowledgeable in the particular project, and this is best done with all parties present. Written records must be kept.

The value of this procedure for all concerned cannot be overemphasized. A successful preliminary plan check will expedite the future building permit review. It will reduce the impact and number of code problems that may arise during the actual plan check for permit issuance because most will have been corrected in the earlier plan check stages. Finally, it will usually mean an earlier start of construction.

ARTICLE 2
UNIFORM BUILDING CODE OVERVIEW

This article outlines the Uniform Building Code (UBC) development process and the main elements affecting the design of buildings. This article generally familiarizes the reader with the code and its philosophy in major areas, so that the detailed provisions can be understood in their proper context. The main design provisions of the UBC will be reviewed in greater detail in Articles 3 through 10 of this Guide.

A. Code Amendment and Adoptive Procedures

The Uniform Building Code is the product of the International Conference of Building Officials (ICBO), the largest of the three model building code organizations. Previous to the 1997 edition of the UBC, the code was amended annually at ICBO's Annual Business Meeting with the amendments issued as supplements in the year following that meeting. Every third year the code is published as a complete new edition.

The International Conference of Building Officials suspended publication of the UBC following the 1996 Annual Business Meeting. It, along with the other model code organizations, are in the process of developing the International Building Code (IBC) under the International Code Council (ICC). A discussion of the ICC and its development processes can be found in Appendix A2 of this Guide.

The most recent code available at the time of the writing of this Guide is the 1997 edition. Unless otherwise stated, all references to sections or chapters in this Guide are to those in the 1997 Uniform Building Code. Certain provisions of that edition are new and of particular concern to the designer. They will be emphasized where they appear in the discussion herein.

The code may be adopted locally or on a statewide basis. The adoption may be by ordinance or by a legislative act depending on whether the state has, by law, preempted the field of building codes. In the latter case, a local jurisdiction enforces the state-adopted version of the UBC rather than adopting its own version.

In most jurisdictions, the UBC is adopted with few amendments except in the administrative part of the code. The adoptive process is the same as for any other legislation involving hearings and a vote by the legislative body of the jurisdiction. The code is usually enforced by an official and staff members of the local governmental department or agency legally charged with building code enforcement. In this Guide, the head of the enforcement agency will be referred to as the building official.

The adoptive ordinance may include the appendix provisions of the code. Unless the ordinance so specifies, the appendix has not been adopted, since to do so requires a specific act on the part of the jurisdiction.

Section 101.3 paragraph 4
Wherever in this code reference is made to the appendix, the provisions in the appendix shall not apply unless specifically adopted.

Because the adoptive process is time-consuming, the jurisdiction may not choose, as a general practice, to adopt the supplements that are issued each year. However, the building official can either

- consider the provisions in a supplement as equivalent to the code in effect in the jurisdiction by using the provisions of Section 104.2.8 or
- recommend to the legislative body the adoption of all or part of the supplement.

B. Organization of the Code

The UBC is organized into three volumes. Each volume contains chapters oriented for the same purpose. Volume 1 contains administrative, fire- and life-safety provisions, Volume 2 contains structural engineering provisions and Volume 3 contains material, testing and installation standards.

This Guide will deal with the provisions contained in the following chapters in Volume 1:

Chapter 1 Administration

Chapter 2 Definitions and Abbreviations

Chapter 3 Use or Occupancy

Chapter 4 Special Use or Occupancy

Chapter 5 General Building Limitations

Chapter 6 Types of Construction

Chapter 7 Fire-resistant Materials and Construction

Chapter 8 Interior Finishes

Chapter 9 Fire Protection Systems

Chapter 10 Means of Egress

Chapter 11 Accessibility

Chapter 12 Interior Environment

Chapter 14 Exterior Wall Coverings

Chapter 15 Roofing and Roof Structures

Excerpts from Chapter 23—Wood

Chapter 24 Glass and Glazing

Chapter 25 Gypsum Board and Plaster

Chapter 26 Plastic

Chapter 34 Existing Structures

Chapter 35 Uniform Building Code Standards

The designer must understand the entire code as it affects a particular project. However, for preliminary design purposes the main code considerations are Chapters 3, 5, 6, 7 and 10. This Guide will concentrate primarily on these chapters. Other chapters and sections of the UBC will be discussed to a lesser degree.

C. Occupancy Classifications

The occupancy classification is one of the primary regulatory criteria in the code. A building is assigned a classification based on its proposed use or occupancy. Other key code criteria include

- the type of construction to be used for the building and
- the height and areas of the proposed building.

The various occupancy classifications are listed and defined in Table 3-A. They are divided into 10 major classes or occupancy groups:

A —assembly,
B —business,
E —educational,
F —factory and industrial,
H—hazardous,
I —institutional,
M—miscellaneous,
R —residential,
S —storage and
U—utility.

These occupancy groups are further subdivided into categories called divisions. The divisions distinguish specific subtypes of the occupancy from one another. For example, Group R, Division 1 refers to an occupancy having a large number of dwelling units (three or more), and Division 3 refers to a single- or two-family dwelling. There is no Division 2 at present.

NOTE: The above examples of these divisions have been chosen by the authors merely as a means of highlighting their differences. The reader is referred to Chapter 3 and Table 3-A for the more complete, detailed descriptions of each occupancy.

Although a considerable number of occupancies are listed in the code, they do not represent the large range of occupancies possible. Section 301 of the code provides the building official with the means for classifying a use that does not fit any specific code description with the one it most nearly resembles, the criteria being based on life safety and fire hazard.

This code provision does not preclude the designer electing a "higher" hazard (more restrictive) classification for the building's use. The building official, in reviewing the permit documents, may bring this higher than necessary classification to the designer's attention. The building official would be overstepping legal authority if the designer's choice was not honored. Though one cannot predict the action of an individual official, it is likely that most building officials will recognize the validity of this concept.

By applying the method established in Table 5-B, the occupancy class, together with the type of building construction, is used to determine the allowable floor area and permitted number of stories This method will be discussed in detail in Chapter 5.

When there is more than one occupancy in a structure, the relationship of these occupancies within the building is a code concern because the hazards of fire, explosion or panic in one occupancy can endanger another. To reduce the dangers the code requires that different occupancies be separated from each other by the level of fire-resistive construction determined in Table 3-B.

A final regulatory concern based on occupancy is the relationship of a building, housing one or more occupancies, to the adjacent property line. The setback and fire-resistive requirements of the exterior walls, which vary depending on proximity to the property line, are contained in Section 503 and Table 3-B.

D. Types of Construction

Five general types of building construction are defined by the code and are designated by the roman numerals I through V. All but Type IV are divided into two or more subtypes, each based upon the degree of fire resistance required for the building elements. The types of construction are described in detail in Chapter 6. The required level of fire resistance of the building elements for each type is provided in Table 6-A.

The construction types range, in the degree of requisite fire protection, from unprotected wood frame buildings (Type V-N) such as the typical home, to the fire-resistive type (Type I) such as the high-rise buildings found in downtown areas of major cities. As the fire resistance of a building increases, so does the allowable floor area and the number of stories permitted by the code, as shown in Table 5-B.

A designation "N" following the roman numeral designation for the type of construction means that minimum construction provisions do not require any general level of fire resistance. However, the N-type building may have individual fire-resistive requirements for certain building elements based on:

- Table 6-A,
- proximity to a property line,

- required occupancy separations,
- stairway and shaft enclosures and
- area separation walls.

A designation of "One-hour" following the type of construction means that the building has fire-resistive construction of at least a one-hour rating for all elements as required in Table 6-A. In general, these elements in a building include

- floors,
- roof,
- columns,
- beams,
- exterior walls,
- bearing walls and
- shaft enclosures.

The general concept behind establishing the various types of construction involves compartition of the fire hazard. As a building becomes larger in either floor area or height, its elements require a higher degree of fire resistance. The public is thereby afforded a degree of safety from fire in one part of the building by the fire-resistive compartments formed by the building's walls and floors. In the same sense, the building itself forms a compartment to confine a fire and prevent it from spreading from one building to another. This will be discussed in greater detail in Article 6.

D.1. Chapter 6 Types of Construction

The provisions in Chapter 6 address the specific construction requirements for the five general types of construction. These are used in conjunction with the provisions Table 6-A. In Article 6 we discuss the different types of construction and the rationale behind Chapter 6 and Table 6-A.

In Chapter 6, the intent is to set out the philosophy of that building construction type insofar as the types of materiels that are permitted for the building envelope and specific portions within the building; it provides the accepted types of materials that may be used for the structural elements of that building. It further states which of the building's structural elements may be combustible. For Types I and II all the structural elements must be noncombustible; only certain nonload-bearing walls may be combustible.

It is important to recognize that the requirements of Sections 602.1 and 603.1 do not prevent the use of interior finishes or combustible insulation on or within the building elements as permitted in Section 2605.2

Sections 602.3, 603.3, 604.3, 605.3 and 606.3 (the ".3" sections) provide for the various types of construction, the permitted exterior wall constructions insofar as fire-resistive ratings and materials permitted. In particular one should note that for Types III and IV buildings, where Table 6-A requires 4-hour fire-resistive rating, these ratings may be substantially reduced based on distance to adjacent property lines. Furthermore, these sections permit certain combustible materials where noncombustibility is essentially otherwise required.

In using the .3 provisions, the designer should first check the "openings in walls" sections requirements for the opening protection requirements that generally determine the permissible wall construction. This reversal of normal code reading will facilitate the designer in determining the applicable requirements.

For additional explanatory material on the detailed application of the .3 provisions, see Article 5 of this Guide.

The .4 and .5 provisions provide for the types of materials permitted for the stair and roof construction, respectively.

The special high-rise provisions of Section 403 are discussed generally in Article 9 of this Guide.

In preparing the preliminary design, designers must interrelate two critical code criteria with the space requirements of their clients:

- the occupancy class and
- the type of construction.

These criteria are under designers' control in the design process and are their responsibility when it comes to deciding what best applies to a particular building.

E. Means of Egress

The main panic control provisions in the building are the exiting requirements in Chapter 10, Means of Egress. The purpose of these provisions is to provide a means for the public to reach a protected area and progress to the outside of the building in a reasonably short period of time. This aim is accomplished by limiting the distance a person must travel before reaching a fire-resistive enclosure, i.e., a corridor or stairway.

The width of these protected segments of the exit path is based on the following:

- occupancy class served,
- occupant load factor per square foot for that occupancy,
- size of the occupancy served,
- minimum width permitted by the code and
- minimum width in lineal feet for the occupancy served based on the calculated occupant load of the occupancy.

The relationship of width to numbers of people is based on studies of the movement of large numbers of people in confined spaces.

Having entered the fire-protected exit system, the occupant must remain protected until reaching the exterior of the building. The code establishes the fire-resistive requirements for the walls, floors and ceilings of these enclosures and the doors and windows opening into or adjacent to them.

The arrangement of the exit ways is another critical element of the preliminary design. The exit ways should be given detailed study by the designer in that stage of the design. The preliminary plan check meeting with the local officials will usually lead to consideration of that item before others. The exit arrangement involves

- the length of travel (travel distance) on a floor to reach a stairway or other higher level exit facility and
- the concept of requiring access to at least two exits separated from one another.

The Chapter 10 means of egress provisions will be discussed in greater detail in Article 7 of this Guide.

F. Fire Resistance

The fire-resistive requirements of buildings are defined in Table 6-A according to the types of building construction. Details of how the hourly fire-resistive ratings can be obtained for the various building elements are provided in Chapter 7. That chapter contains two tables that provide descriptions of assemblies with the required hourly rating. These assemblies have all been prequalified by the code as complying with the fire test standards set forth in Chapter 7. There are numerous other assemblies that can also qualify for use but either are proprietary or for other valid reasons have not been placed in the tables.

The ICBO Evaluation Reports also furnish listings of assemblies deemed by that organization's Evaluation Committee as satisfying the equivalency requirements of Section 104.2.8. It is important to understand the difference between the tables in Chapter 7 and an Evaluation Report. The listings in the code are legally a part of the code and must be accepted and are binding on the building official. On the other hand, an Evaluation Report is just that: an evaluation that may or may not be accepted by a building official.

A building official has to make a specific acceptance or approval of an Evaluation Report for it to be used in a jurisdiction.

The listings in the Gypsum Association's "Fire Resistance Design Manual" have been accepted by the UBC (see footnote a of the Chapter 7 tables). Therefore, the designer has available many ways of satisfying the code fire resistance requirements without making an extended review by the officials necessary.

The designer may propose assemblies not described in one of the references noted. Any assembly can be submitted for review and approval by the official. However, the designer is cautioned that a job undertaken to obtain such acceptance may become time-consuming and require more information and expertise than the designer is able to provide. Due to the demands involved in the process, it is best left to the manufacturer and the technical staff to pursue such approvals.

The use of generally referenced assemblies will speed up the permit review.

The code intends that the support elements of fire-resistive construction have at least the same or greater fire resistance rating than the element being supported. Although this is not stated in Chapter 6 or 7, this intent is clearly stated in Section 302.2 relating to occupancy separations.

Where the occupancy separation is horizontal, structural members supporting the separation shall be protected by equivalent fire-resistive construction.

This limitation of the support continuity to horizontal occupancy separations does not provide a consistency that is requisite to the code.

> In the authors' opinion, to achieve both a consistency in the code and the development of designs that provide logical fire resistance to a building, the general principle previously stated should be used: A fire-resistive element shall be supported by elements of the same or greater fire resistance.

For an example of these occupancy separation wall fire rating requirements, see Figures 2-1 and 2-2.

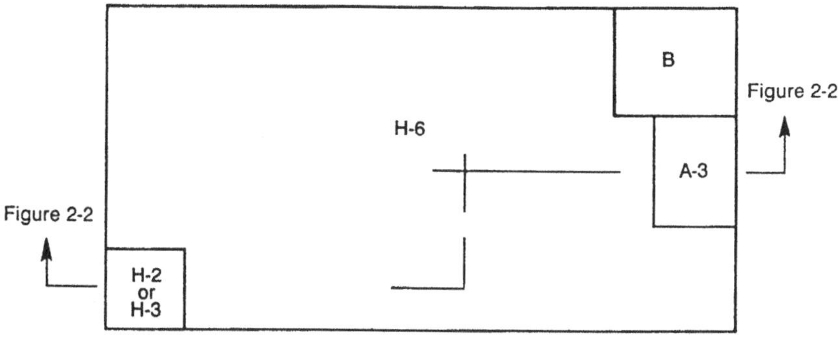

PLAN 1st FLOOR

ASSUME:
Type II One-Hour Building
Two Story
First Floor as Shown
Second Floor all H-6 and B

Occupancy Separation Requirements

Second Floor	B/H-6	1-Hour
Between Second & First Floor	B/H-2	2-Hour
	B/H-3	1-Hour
	H-6/A-3	3-Hour
First Floor	H-6/H-2	2-Hour
	H-6/H-3	1-Hour
	H-6/A-3	3-Hour

Because the building is Type II One-hour, separation requirements are readily met.

The B/H-2 and H-6/H-2 two-hour requirements mean that the floor of the second floor and its supports for the segment over the H-2 Occupancy must have two-hour fire resistance to the ground. The three-hour requirement between the H-6/A-3 Occupancies similarly must have three-hour rated supports to the ground.

REFERENCE: SECTION 302.4 and TABLE 3-B

FIGURE 2-1 FIRE-RESISTIVE SEPARATION WALLS

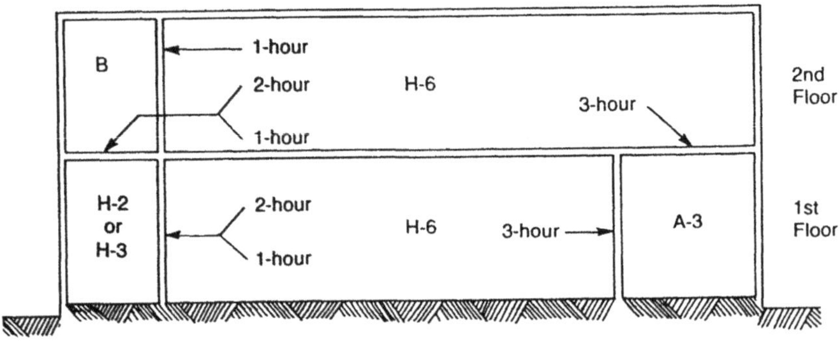

Occupancy Separations per Table 3-B

1st Floor	H-6/H-2	2-Hour	1½-Hour
	H-6/H-2	1-Hour	1-Hour
	H-6/A-3	3-Hour	3-Hour
	B/A-3	N	N
2nd Floor	H-6/B	1-Hour	1-Hour
Between 1st Floor & 2nd Floor	Depending on Location of Occupancies on each floor		
	H-6/H-2, H-3, A-3, B	Same as First Floor	
	Floor B/A-3, H-6, H-2, H-3	Same as First Floor Except B/H-2 = 2-Hour	1½-Hour
		B/H-3 = 1-Hour	1-Hour

N - No fire rating required

NOTE: Where the second floor separations are required to have fire-resistive ratings greater than one-hour, the wall/floor construction involved must have the same higher rating for all support members down to the ground. See Figure 2-1.

REFERENCE: SECTION 302.2, TABLE 3-B

FIGURE 2-2 FIRE-RESISTIVE SEPARATION SUPPORTS

ARTICLE 3
ADMINISTRATIVE PROVISIONS OF THE UBC

CHAPTER 1 ADMINISTRATION
CHAPTER 34 EXISTING STRUCTURES

The administrative provisions of the UBC are contained in Chapter 1, certain sections of which, being of particular interest to the designer, are discussed in this article. Similar administrative provisions relating to existing buildings are contained in Chapter 34. These sections are reprinted, followed by an analysis and discussion.

Chapter 1 Administration

This chapter defines the overall philosophy of the code as it pertains to public welfare and safety. It sets the parameters for changes of use or occupancy, alterations, maintenance, approval of new materials and methods of construction and, in special cases, variances.

> **101.2 Purpose.** The purpose of this code is to provide minimum standards to safeguard life or limb, health, property and public welfare by regulating and controlling the design, construction, quality of materials, use and occupancy, location and maintenance of all buildings and structures within this jurisdiction and certain equipment specifically regulated herein.
>
> The purpose of this code is not to create or otherwise establish or designate any particular class or group of persons who will or should be especially protected or benefitted by the terms of this code.

The code establishes the minimum criteria for the protection of the public and of property. Although the code's primary emphasis is on life safety, property, to a lesser degree, is also a concern. The code provides the minimum requirements, representing the least one is required to do; it is not and should not be considered a handbook for design. There are many construction concerns, of building owners or occupants, not addressed by the code; these are the responsibility of the design professionals involved in the process.

The code is a legal document, usually adopted by ordinance in the local jurisdiction. All its provisions, therefore, have legal implications and are not simply a collection of minimum standards. An example of the enacting ordinance can be found on page 1-xix of the Uniform Building Code (UBC).

Section 101.2 mentions maintenance of structures. This is an important matter that will be discussed later in Chapter 34; for the time being it is sufficient to note that the code's legal requirements apply for the life of the building.

101.3 Scope. The provisions of this code shall apply to the construction, alteration, moving, demolition, repair and use of any building or structure within this jurisdiction, except work located primarily in a public way, public utility towers and poles, mechanical equipment not specifically regulated in this code, and hydraulic flood control structures.

For additions, alterations, moving and maintenance of buildings and structures, see Chapter 34. For temporary buildings and structures, see Section 3103 and Appendix Chapter 31.

Where, in any specific case, different sections of this code specify different materials, methods of construction or other requirements, the most restrictive shall govern. Where there is a conflict between a general requirement and a specific requirement, the specific requirement shall be applicable.

Wherever in this code reference is made to the appendix, the provisions in the appendix shall not apply unless specifically adopted.

Section 101.3 states that the code governs all construction of buildings in the jurisdiction, whether new or alteration work. That is, the same code requirements as they relate to new buildings will apply to alteration work done on an existing building and to the part of the building in which a change of occupancy occurs.

The third paragraph of this section establishes the relationship of the code's general provisions to its specific ones. For example, a general requirement such as that for a Type V 1-hour building requires that such a building be constructed as 1-hour fire-resistive throughout as stated in Section 606.

However, there are special provisions that either increase or decrease that 1-hour general standard:

- An occupancy separation may require a 2-hour fire rating per Section 302.4.
- Within a dwelling unit in an apartment house, the nonbearing walls may be of nonfire-rated construction per Section 601.5.2.

SECTION 104—ORGANIZATION AND ENFORCEMENT

104.2.1 General. The building official Is hereby authorized and directed to enforce all the provisions of this code. For such purposes, he shall have the powers of a law enforcement officer.

The building official shall have the power to render interpretations of this code and to adopt and enforce rules and regulations supplemental to this code as he may deem necessary in order to clarify the application of the provisions of this code. Such interpretations, rules and regulations shall be in conformity with the intent and purpose of this code.

This section establishes the authority of the building official as the enforcement officer for the code. Because the official is directed to enforce the code, the official has no option whether or not to enforce the code.

The second paragraph allows the official to develop interpretations, rules and regulations to implement the enforcement process by helping to clarify the provisions of the code. It is most important that these interpretations, rules and regulations be put in writing, even when there is only one project to which a particular determination applies.

The official and the designers must work together to develop interpretations, rulings or regulations to assure that the intent of the code is not sacrificed. It would be prudent for the building official to use the criteria in Section 104.2.8 in making an interpretation, ruling or regulation.

When they will have broad application to many projects, these documents should be available to the designers and the public. The building official should use the locally available methods for distributing these documents to those interested in the code. Some resources are the local chapters of the American Institute of Architects, the local builders' exchange or similar builder or contractor organization, the local newspaper and other public access media.

The reason given for this section was that administrative policies must be established for the building official to carry out the assigned function properly. The authority to promulgate rules and regulations was partially intended to cover that area of the enforcement activity.

The authority extended by the second paragraph is couched in language reflecting the requirement that the official must clarify the code within the intent of the code. Thus, this authority is not to be used in place of Section 104.2.7 or to authorize a departure from the code but is the authority to make reasonable application of the code provisions to a particular project within the overall intent of the code. The criteria in Section 104.2.7 are good touchpoints in developing an interpretation.

An important provision of the UBC, contained in Section 105, provides for the establishment of a Board of Appeals, which can review new construction methods and materials and which has the authority to interpret the code. This provision conceives of a board made up of individuals knowledgeable in building construction. Unfortunately, many jurisdictions either do not have such appeals boards or their respective legislative bodies assume the role of an appeals board without the members possessing the requisite construction knowledge. In either instance the intent is lost.

Jurisdictions having such boards have found them to provide an excellent means of bringing the design professionals and others in the construction industry into the code process. The resulting interchange benefits both the public and private sector. It makes available to the official the expertise that often is needed to evaluate complex new products or systems. Organizations of architects, engineers and contractors are usually willing to recommend qualified members to serve on the board. It is advised that the appointments be based on these recommendations rather than on politics.

The right of appeal to a qualified technical board strengthens the code and the enforcement process.

104.2.7 Modifications. Whenever there are practical difficulties involved in carrying out the provisions of this code, the building official may grant modifications to individual cases, provided he shall first find that a special individual reason makes the strict letter of this code impractical and that the modification is in conformity with the intent and purpose of this code and that such modification does not lessen any fire protection requirements or any degree of structural integrity. The details of any action granting modifications shall be recorded and entered in the files of the code enforcement agency.

This section provides the building official with the authority to allow modifications of or variances from code compliance when practical problems prevent strict code compliance. The use of this provision places great responsibility on the official. To use the latitude afforded, the official has to find that

- there are unusual circumstances to warrant consideration of the matter and
- the modification does not lessen the fire protection or structural integrity.

These criteria are substantial and must be justified in writing for permanent retention in the code agency's records.

It is the authors' opinion that all parties consider the use of this provision with care and avoid its use unless absolutely necessary. Its use and the resultant waiving of code provisions may place the parties involved in legally exposed positions. A strong, well-documented case must be prepared whenever the provision is used, so that the designer and the official can fully substantiate the modification.

104.2.8 Alternate Materials and Methods of Construction. The provisions of this code are not intended to prevent the use of any material or method of construction not specifically prescribed by this code, provided any alternate has been approved and its use authorized by the building official.

The building official may approve any such alternate, provided he finds that the proposed design is satisfactory and complies with the provisions of this code and that the material, method or work offered is, for the purpose intended, at least the equivalent of that prescribed in this code in suitability, strength, effectiveness, fire resistance, durability, safety and sanitation.

The building official shall require that sufficient evidence or proof be submitted to substantiate any claims that may be made regarding its use. The details of any action granting approval of an alternate shall be recorded and entered in the files of the code enforcement agency.

Section 104.2.8 permits the development of alternative arrangements and constructions other than those specifically cited in the code. The burden of demonstrating the equivalence of the proposed alternative system is placed on the person desiring the alternative's acceptance. The second paragraph establishes the criteria for the building official's evaluation of the suggested equivalence.

To use this section, the designer or owner has to be assured that the enforcement official is both willing and capable of reviewing the alternative. The official can use the International Conference of Building Officials (ICBO) conference headquarters staff to assist in the evaluation. The staff is not usually available to a designer or owner for such review. The ICBO policy is that its staff will respond only to a building official's request.

Another method of obtaining the acceptance of new materials is to proceed through the Evaluation Committee of the conference. This involved process is usually the province of the manufacturer and should not be undertaken by the designer. The procedure will not be detailed in this Guide.

If the local official is willing to evaluate the request or to refer it to ICBO staff, the designer or owner should fully prepare the case for the alternate design so that its obvious equivalence to the code is demonstrated. The request should be documented and a written response requested so that a clear record is made of the process and the acceptance.

The purpose of this section is to provide the code with flexibility that permits innovation and ingenuity. This flexibility enables the designer to develop a design that fits the needs of the owner and meets the code's intent, if not its precise letter. This concept is at the heart of modern codes and code enforcement.

SECTION 106—PERMITS

106.1 Permits Required. Except as specified In Section 106.2, no building or structure shall be erected, constructed, enlarged, altered, repaired, moved, improved, removed, converted or demolished unless a separate permit for each building or structure has been obtained from the building official.

The intent of this section is to require a building permit when virtually any construction work in a building is to be done. Specific items exempt from permits are listed in Section 106.2. Except for low (5′9″) partitions and painting, almost any work in an occupancy requires a building permit.

The less obvious intention of this section is to establish a record for the operation of the facility in compliance with the code. Were some untoward event to occur, the owner would be in a poor legal position if it were found that work was being done without a permit. Whether or not that work was code compliant would not be the issue. The owner would be a scofflaw and presumed to be in the wrong. The burden would then rest on the owner to prove innocence. The owner would have a self-made credibility problem.

One benefit of obtaining permits is the assistance local officials can provide the designer or owner in meeting the intent, though not necessarily the letter, of the code. If contact is not opened with them via permits, this assistance will be unavailable. In most instances, given the opportunity, the officials are cooperative, knowledgeable and will provide assistance in solving problems.

106.3 Application for Permit.

106.3.1 Application. To obtain a permit, the applicant shall first file an application therefore in writing on a form furnished by the code enforcement agency for that purpose. Every such application shall:

1. Identify and describe the work to be covered by the permit for which application is made.

2. Describe the land on which the proposed work is to be done by legal description, street address or similar description that will readily identify and definitely locate the proposed building or work.

3. Indicate the use or occupancy for which the proposed work is intended.

4. Be accompanied by plans, diagrams, computations and specifications and other data as required in Section 106.3.2.

5. State the valuation of any new building or structure or any addition, remodeling or alteration to an existing building.

6. Be signed by permittee, or his authorized agent.

7. Give such other data and information as may be required by the building official.

Section 106.3.1 lists the several items required on a building permit application. The designer should be particularly concerned with item 3. The proposed use should be carefully and properly identified, preferably by the code designation for the occupancy or occupancies in the building. The reason for carefully and fully describing the use(s) is that in the future the decision of whether a change of occupancy may be allowed in an alteration or new tenancy will in great part be based on the original use(s) entered in the permit records.

106.3.3 Information on Plans and Specifications. Plans and specifications shall be drawn to scale upon substantial paper or cloth and shall be of sufficient clarity to indicate the location, nature and extent of the work proposed and show in detail that it will conform to the provisions of this code and all relevant laws, ordinances, rules and regulations.

Plans for buildings more than two stories in height of other than Group R, Division 3 and Group U Occupancies shall indicate how required structural and fire-resistive integrity will be maintained where a penetration will be made for electrical, mechanical, plumbing and communication conduits, pipes and similar systems.

The designer should be sure that the plans comply to this section. Items often overlooked in regard to the first paragraph include the following:

1. All fire-resistive assembly details must fully cover the requirements for the project. These include details for
   - walls,
   - floor-ceiling and roof-ceiling assemblies,
   - area separation walls including the foundation and roof intersections and proximity to openings,
   - occupancy separations and their supporting elements and

- structural members and the method of protecting them including materials, attachments and the conditions associated with their use.

2. In the second paragraph, the code requires that the plans indicate how the fire-resistive and structural integrity is maintained where certain penetrations are made. The designer should consider the following:
   - Utility lines and how they are brought to and from each floor. Included in these items are telephone, waste and vent lines, electrical and duct systems, computer and other services.
   - Poke-thru, and how it is to be avoided. See Article 8 for further discussion of this subject.
3. Weather tightness is not specifically regulated in this section. It is implied by the phrase in the first paragraph:

"the work proposed will conform to the provisions of this code . . ."

See discussion of Section 1402 in Article 6 for the minimal code provisions on this subject. The only other reference in the code to weather protection is in Section 1503, second paragraph.

The designer should be sure the weather tightness details are sufficient and drawn to a large enough scale to be clear to the contractor. This is an area in which the designer, not the official, carries the prime and almost total responsibility. Included in this subject area are flashings for the roof, windows and doors, exterior intersections and penetrations.

106.4 Permits Issuance.

106.4.1 Issuance. The application, plans, specifications, computations and other data filed by an applicant for permit shall be reviewed by the building official. Such plans may be reviewed by other departments of this jurisdiction to verify compliance with any applicable laws under their jurisdiction. If the building official finds that the work described in an application for a permit and the plans, specifications and other data filed therewith conform to the requirements of this code and other pertinent laws and ordinances, and that the fees specified In Section 107 have been paid, he shall issue a permit therefore to the applicant.

When the building official issues the permit where plans are required, he shall endorse in writing or stamp the plans and specifications "APPROVED." Such approved plans and specifications shall not be changed, modified or altered without authorizations from the building official, and all work regulated by this code shall be done in accordance with the approved plans.

The building official may issue a permit for the construction of part of a building or structure before the entire plans and specifications for the whole building or structure have been submitted or approved, provided adequate information and detailed statements have been filed complying with all pertinent requirements of this code. The holder of a partial permit shall proceed without assurance that the permit for the entire building or structure will be granted.

This section sets forth the requirements for issuing a permit after review of the drawings and related submissions in conformity with the laws in the jurisdiction. The provision contained in the second paragraph stating "where plans are required" relieves the building official of the responsibility for enforcing the entire contents of the approved plans; the enforcement official will be responsible only for those contents of the approved plans that are regulated by the code. As a result, the designer and the owner cannot rely on the enforcement agency to back up their intentions with regard to noncode-regulated items shown on drawings.

Among the typical noncode-regulated items usually found on the drawings are

- decorative items such as paint, wall papering and other coverings not subject to Chapter 8 regulation,
- nonfire-rated windows and doors,
- methods of flashing and waterproofing,
- floor coverings and
- types of hardware other than those regulated by Chapters 7 and 10.

The designer and the owner must provide for the enforcement of items on the approved plans hereafter.

106.4.3 Validity of Permit. The issuance or granting of a permit or approval of plans, specifications and computations shall not be construed to be a permit for, or an approval of, any violation of any of the provisions of this code or of any other ordinance of the Jurisdiction. Permits presuming to give authority to violate or cancel the provisions of this code or of other ordinances of the Jurisdiction shall not be valid.

The issuance of a permit based upon plans, specifications and other data shall not prevent the building official from thereafter requiring the correction of errors in said plans, specifications and other data, or from preventing building operations being carried on thereunder when in violation of this code or any other ordinances of this Jurisdiction.

Notwithstanding the previous discussion regarding the value of a permit to the owner, important caveats exist with regard to what the permit does or does not grant the owner. The substance of this subsection can be stated as follows:

The issuance of a permit or the issuance of a final completion for the building does not legalize noncompliance if

- there are elements in the design that do not comply with the code or
- the construction does not follow the design or code requirements.

This section emphasizes the need for honest communication among the designer, the owner and the local officials. Do not presume that getting past the building official or obtaining the permit closes the matter. There have been numerous successful suits against the owners and the design professionals based on code violations in a building for which a building permit and Certificate of Occupancy had been issued.

The jurisdiction has covered itself in this section. The responsibility of being in legal compliance with the code remains with the designer and owner. In some states, the statute of limitations for latent defects, such as code violations, begins at the point when the violations are discovered and not from the date of permit issuance. The design professional and the owner are bound by law to follow the code and will be looked to at some future time for recompense if corrections need to be made.

The second sentence in the first paragraph extends the statement relating to a permit not authorizing any violation of the code to include any other ordinance of the locality. This extension of the intent of the paragraph has been necessitated by the increasing amount of litigation involving the codes and ordinances of the localities.

The reason presented for this code provision contained the following language that clearly indicates that permits, inspections and Certificates of Occupancy will not legalize the violation of the code or any other ordinance: "the issuance of an inspection approval of a Certificate of Occupancy does not imply, nor is intended to imply, that violations which may surface after the fact have been sanctioned or approved."

For no other reason than that stated in this section, the permit process must be an open interchange of ideas and knowledge. Documentation should be presented at the conclusion of the discussions for equivalence on which the permit will subsequently be issued. The written record of the decisions will provide testimony in the future of why and how code equivalence was established. Such equivalence, however, should be obvious and not the result of the parties ignoring the problem.

SECTION 108—INSPECTIONS

108.5 Required Inspections.

108.5.1 General. Reinforcing steel or structural framework of any part of any building or structure shall not be covered or concealed without first obtaining the approval of the building official.

Protection of joints and penetrations in fire-resistive assemblies shall not be concealed from view until inspected and approved.

The building official, upon notification, shall make the inspections set forth in the following sections.

108.5.2 Foundation inspection. To be made after excavations for footings are completed and any required reinforcing steel is in place. For concrete foundations, any required forms shall be in place prior to inspection. All materials for the foundation shall be on the job, except where concrete is ready mixed in accordance with approved nationally recognized standards, the concrete need not be on the job. Where the foundation is to be constructed of approved treated wood, additional inspections may be required by the building official.

108.5.3 Concrete slab or under-floor inspection. To be made after all in-slab or under-floor building service equipment, conduit, piping accessories and other ancillary equipment items are in place but before any concrete is poured or floor sheathing installed, including the subfloor.

108.5.4 Frame inspection. To be made after the roof, all framing, fire blocking and bracing are in place and all pipes, chimneys and vents are complete and the rough electrical, plumbing, and heating wires, pipes and ducts are approved.

108.5.5 Lath or gypsum board inspection. To be made after all lathing and gypsum board, interior and exterior, is in place but before any plastering is applied or before gypsum board joints and fasteners are taped and finished.

108.5.6 Final inspection. To be made after finish grading and the building is completed and ready for occupancy.

The required inspections in this section are usually overrated by most people. They assume that the building inspector who visits the job site will reveal and note for correction any deficiencies that may exist.

The required inspections are only minimal inspections. They relate to specific areas of the work and do not represent an inspection of all work that has been done. Ideally, these inspections are made as the code lists them. Unfortunately, due to the workload of the inspectors, for the most part only some of the work will be seen at a time when all the elements needing verification are visible.

For example, consider a three-story wood-frame office building with the framing completed and the wallboard installation in progress. When will the inspector be called? If the wallboard is up and cannot be taped until the inspector sees all the fasteners and their spacings, then the wallboard subcontractor will be unable to phase the job efficiently. Therefore, the wallboard will probably be installed with the taping to proceed sequentially. The inspector will only see a portion of the fasteners at the time of the "called" inspection.

The purpose of this discussion is to point out that the designer should not rely completely on the building inspector for assurance that the construction by the contractor has adhered to the designer's drawings. The designer has a responsibility to determine whether or not the design is being properly followed because any future noncompliance noted may come back to haunt all parties.

If deviations from the design are sought by the contractor, the designer should be aware that the design may be compromised. Although the inspectors are legally responsible for seeing that the approved drawings are followed, their workload usually prohibits them from adequately doing so. In such instances it is up to the designer to ascertain compliance.

This process will no doubt be costly in time and effort to the designer. If the designer does not want to be held responsible, the designer can, at best, formally advise the jurisdiction and the owner of the fact that the designer is not responsible for the construction and that field changes will not be reviewed or approved by the designer.

As a result, the jurisdiction will be required to place responsibility on the owner for designating a design professional who will be responsible for any changes proposed. Unless a design professional is designated by the owner, there should be no changes permitted from the original approved drawings. If a design professional is named, that person should be required to take on the full responsibility for the original design and the construction phase so as to avoid divided responsibility for the building.

SECTION 109—CERTIFICATE OF OCCUPANCY

109.1 Use and Occupancy. No building or structure shall be used or occupied, and no change in the existing occupancy classification of a building

or structure or portion thereof shall be made until the building official has issued a Certificate of Occupancy therefore as provided herein.

EXCEPTION: Group R, Division 3, and Group U Occupancies.

Issuance of a Certificate of Occupancy shall not be construed as an approval of a violation of the provisions of this code or of other ordinances of the jurisdiction. Certificates presuming to give authority to violate or cancel the provisions of this code or of other ordinances of the jurisdiction shall not be valid.

In many situations alterations are made within a building that result in a change of occupancy from the previous legal use to a new one. This may involve a complete change in the use of a structure, the change of one office or the extension of one area's use into space previously used for other occupancies.

Note, however, that the second paragraph to this section reiterates the similar provisions in Section 106.4.3; i.e., that a Certificate of Occupancy (CO) may be issued for buildings that may contain code violations. The issuance of such a certificate in no way validates, cancels or sanctions the violation. When discovered, the code violations will require correction to the requirements of the code in effect at the time of original construction.

In all these instances, and in any other of a similar nature, the obtaining of a CO at the conclusion of the permit work is as much a safeguard for the designer and the owner as is the filing for the building permit. The CO represents the final step by the jurisdiction in determining legal compliance. Although the caveat previously stated regarding Section 106.4.3 still applies, the CO can establish a reasonably safe position for the designer and the owner in that they have complied with the code.

Chapter 34 Existing Structures

SECTION 3401—GENERAL

Buildings in existence at the time of the adoption of this code may have their existing use or occupancy continued, if such use or occupancy was legal at the time of the adoption of this code, provided such continued use is not dangerous to life.

Any change in the use or occupancy of any existing building or structure shall comply with the provisions of Sections 109 and 3405 of this code.

For existing buildings, see Appendix Chapter 34. See also Section 101.3

For a comprehensive code and guidelines on the treatment of existing buildings, see the *Uniform Code for Building Conservation.*

Existing installations are covered by this section as remaining legal uses. So long as an existing use or occupancy in the building was permitted by the code in effect at the time the use or occupancy was installed, it can remain. Thus, new code provisions do not have retroactive application to an existing use.

The reference to Appendix Chapter 34 applies only in those jurisdictions that have specifically adopted the Appendix provision in their enacting ordinance or where the state has adopted it, or other specific retroactive requirements. See Article 12 of this Guide for detailed discussion of what code applies to existing buildings.

SECTION 3402—MAINTENANCE

All buildings and structures, both existing and new, and all parts thereof, shall be maintained in a safe and sanitary condition. All devices or safeguards which are required by this code shall be maintained in conformance with the code edition under which installed. The owner or his designated agent shall be responsible for the maintenance of buildings and structures. To determine compliance with this subsection, the building official may cause any structure to be reinspected.

The UBC's purpose includes maintenance. Section 3402 requires the owner to be responsible for maintaining the building. In particular, all safeguards and devices required by the code in effect at the time of the construction or alteration of the facility must be maintained in conformance with that code.

Under this code provision, the owner has the responsibility of continuing to maintain the building henceforth in compliance with the earlier code.

In this section the term "safeguards and devices" includes, in part, fire-resistive assemblies, fire doors, sprinklers and detectors.

When alterations or additions are contemplated for an existing building, the designer has the responsibility of determining whether the building is in compliance with the maintenance provision. The designer should ascertain that either

- the original construction complied with the code then in effect or
- the work now contemplated will satisfy both the original code and the present one as it effects the new work.

The designer is often faced with the situation in which a major alteration is contemplated for an old building. The second sentence of Section 3402 clearly indicates that the building must conform at least to the code in effect at the time of original construction. All too often the designer assumes that the construction in place was compliant with the code and then proceeds to duplicate that construction.

The designer has the responsibility to determine whether compliance existed, so that the owner can be notified to correct the preexisting violations and thus have the structure comply with both the prior and the present code.

The alteration work must meet the present code. If only the new work was done, the existing deficiencies not checked and corrected, and an incident occurred, the possible ensuing litigation could cite the present designer for failing to correct obvious preexisting deficiencies. For this reason, any alteration work should be preceded by a check of the area of the proposed work for potential noncomplying construction.

> In the authors' opinion the designer should undertake certain necessary protective steps when dealing with existing buildings. The designer may incur legal liability for the failure to identify and correct a prior violation if
>
> - the designer does not determine that the building was in compliance with the code at the time of original construction and
> - in the new work encounters construction that does not conform to that earlier code and fails to advise the owner.

The designer should contact either an attorney or professional liability insurance carrier to provide for this contingency. A suggested approach, for consideration, is outlined hereafter.

The designer should specify in the service contract documents that the designer be held harmless by the owner for all preexisting code violations. In the absence of a hold-harmless provision, the designer should notify the owner in writing of any code violation findings, recommending that they be corrected. If the owner does not want to correct the violations, then the owner takes full responsibility for the violations and all claims and legal costs that may subsequently be incurred by the designer regarding those violations.

There have been cases in which the alteration designer has been brought into a suit for just such a failing, even though the designer's work may have been code complying. To avoid such a situation, the designer should review both the records of the original construction and the requirements that were then applicable. This information can be obtained from the building inspection agency's files and should be checked by the designer.

SECTION 3403—ADDITIONS, ALTERATIONS OR REPAIRS

3403.1 General. Buildings and structures to which additions, alterations or repairs are made shall comply with all the requirements of this code for new facilities except as specifically provided in this section. See Section 310.9 for provisions requiring installation of smoke detectors in existing Group R, Division 3 Occupancies.

This provision restates the basic requirement that the alteration work must meet the new construction regulations except as specifically stated otherwise in the section.

A reference to Section 310.9 is provided as that section contains the only retroactive provision in the code. The smoke detector requirement in Section 310.9.1.2 is triggered when any work proposed to be done in an existing dwelling (R-3 Occupancy) has a permit valuation "in excess of $1,000." In all other respects, the code, unless the Appendix Chapter 34 is specifically adopted in the jurisdiction, is not retroactive.

Although the UBC is not a retroactive document except as noted, many states and some jurisdictions have legislated portions of the UBC as being retroactive. The designer should determine early in the preliminary design phase whether the Appendix Chapter 34 or other retroactive provisions are in effect in that locality. See Article 12 for further discussion of this important subject.

3403.2 When Allowed. Additions, alterations or repairs may be made to any building or structure without requiring the existing building or structure to comply with all the requirements of this code, provided the addition, alteration or repair conforms to that required for a new building or structure.

Additions, alterations or repairs shall not be made to an existing building or structure which would cause the existing building or structure to become unsafe. An unsafe condition shall be deemed to have been created if an addition or alteration will cause the existing building or structure to be stuct-urally unsafe or overloaded; will not provide adequate egress in compliance with the provisions of this code or will obstruct existing exits; will create a fire hazard; will reduce required fire resistance or will otherwise create conditions dangerous to human life. Any building so altered, which involves

a change in use or occupancy, shall not exceed the height, number of stories and area permitted for new buildings. Any building plus new additions shall not exceed the height, number of stories and area specified for new buildings.

Additions or alterations shall not be made to an existing building or structure when such building or structure is not in full compliance with the provisions of this code except when such addition or alteration will result in the existing building or structure being no more hazardous based on life safety, fire safety and sanitation, than before such addition or alterations are undertaken. (See also Section 207.11.3 for Group H, Division 6 Occupancies.)

EXCEPTION: Alterations of existing structural elements, or additions of new structural elements, which are not required by Section 3401 and are initiated for the purpose of increasing the lateral-force-resisting strength or stiffness of an existing structure, need not be designed for forces conforming to these regulations provided that an engineering analysis is submitted to show that

1. The capacity of existing structural elements required to resist forces is not reduced,

2. The lateral loading to required existing structural elements is not increased beyond their capacity,

3. New structural elements are detailed and connected to the existing structural elements as required by these regulations,

4. New or relocated nonstructural elements are detailed and connected to existing or new structural elements as required by these regulations, and

5. An unsafe condition as defined above is not created.

3403.3 Nonstructural. Alterations or repairs to an existing building or structure which are nonstructural and do not adversely affect any structural member or any part of the building or structure having required fire resistance may be made with the same materials of which the building or structure is constructed. The installation or replacement of glass shall be as required for new installations.

These sections are a further restatement of the principle that the alteration work meet the present code requirements. The entire existing building in which the work is to be done need not be brought into compliance with the present code.

A further latitude is afforded in this section for proposed construction work that neither involves a structural element nor adversely affects the structural capacity or fire resistance of the building. In such instances the materials for the new work may be the same as those previously in place. The new work, in this case, need not conform to the present code.

It should be understood that the provision in the last paragraph of Section 3403.2 does not permit the use of the same material with which the building was originally constructed if that original material and construction failed to comply with the earlier code.

SECTION 3405—CHANGE OF USE

No change shall be made in the character of occupancies or use of any building which would place the building in a different division of the same group of occupancy or in a different group of occupancies, unless such building is made to comply with the requirements of this code for such division or group of occupancy.

EXCEPTION: The character of the occupancy of existing buildings may be changed subject to the approval of the building official, and the building may be occupied for purposes in other groups without conforming to all the requirements of this code for those groups, provided the new or proposed use is less hazardous, based on life and fire risk, than the existing use.

No change in the character of occupancy of a building shall be made without a Certificate of Occupancy, as required in Section 109 of this code. The building official may issue a Certificate of Occupancy pursuant to the intent of the above exception without certifying that the building complies with all provisions of this code.

This section requires that when a change in building use occurs, the building must be brought up to the requirements applicable to the new use under the provisions of the current code. It must be understood that many changes do not involve what the code defines as a change in use. For example, a change in a building's original use from a bank to an office is not considered a change in use because all these uses are classified under Group B Occupancy. (See Table 3-A.)

The change in use provisions apply only when the new use belongs to another occupancy group or another division of the original occupancy group.

In the authors' opinion, and contrary to an ICBO interpretation, a change in the character of an occupancy within the same occupancy division does not constitute a change of occupancy under the provisions of Section 3405.

Section 3405 also states that it is the code's intent to allow a change in the occupancy or use in an existing building without requiring full compliance with the code. The code stipulates in the exception, however, that for such an allowance the proposed use must be "less hazardous" than the previous one. In the Article 1 discussion in this Guide, it is recommended that Table 3-B be used to determine whether one use is more or less hazardous than another.

The designer should note that according to the last sentence of the second paragraph cited above, the issuance of a CO for an existing building does not require the building official to certify that the entire building meets the code. Clearly, the intent of the code is to have the official determine the relative hazard of the proposed use and then to require only those code provisions be met that relate to an increased hazard of the proposed use.

The latitude expressed in this section places a judgmental responsibility on the official to evaluate the existing building and determine whether the proposed use is more or less hazardous than the previous use. Thus, Section 3405 permits the determination of the life and fire hazards of a proposed use on basis more realistic than one of invoking the literal provisions of the code.

ARTICLE 4
DEFINITIONS, ABBREVIATIONS AND GLOSSARY

Chapter 2 Definitions and Abbreviations

Certain specialized terms used in the code either are not in the 1986 edition of *Webster's Third New International Dictionary of the English Language,* to which the UBC refers for generally accepted definitions, or have meanings different from those found in that dictionary. Chapter 2 provides the code's intended meanings for such terms.

However, there are additional specialized terms not defined anywhere in the code. To understand these terms, the reader must either rely on general construction knowledge or infer meanings from the context of the provisions. This Guide provides definitions for some of these terms where they appear in this review of the code.

The designer should clarify with the enforcement official any term encountered that is either ambiguous or otherwise lacking adequate definition.

In our review of Chapter 2 we will address only selected terms of special importance to the designer.

SECTION 202—A

ADDITION is an extension or increase in floor area or height of a building or structure.

This term forms one subgroup of the activities generally included in the overall term "alteration." It involves the vertical or horizontal extension of a building. All work has to be in compliance with the current Uniform Building Code (UBC).

ALTER or ALTERATION is any change, addition or modification in construction or occupancy.

This is the general term for any work on an existing building. The code requirements for such work are set forth in Section 3403.

APARTMENT HOUSE is any building or portion thereof which contains three or more dwelling units and, for the purposes of this code, shall include residential condominiums.

This definition, together with that of a dwelling, establishes the two classes of residential occupancies, namely

- the multifamily Group R, Division I Occupancy and
- the single- or two-family dwelling, Group R, Division 3 Occupancy.

There is no Group R, Division 2 Occupancy at present.

The designer should understand the distinctions between the two residential occupancy divisions and also the code requirements that regulate these differences.

A frequently encountered problem is that of determining which type of occupancy is involved in a project. What may look like a group of single-family dwellings may be either

- a series of one- or two-family dwellings or
- an apartment house.

Such situations often arise with townhouse construction, which could be in the form of side-by-side, one- or two-family row houses. These could be separated into Group R, Division 3 segments, with each pair of units bounded by property line walls. An alternative method of segmentation would be the use of area separation walls to define the pairs of dwelling units.

Without either of these means of separation, the building would be defined as multifamily because there would be three or more dwelling units within the building. The building would be defined as an apartment house, R-1.

This confusion arises from the real estate industry's desire to sell property. The terms used by the realtor or the developer do not precisely fit into the categories the code establishes for residential uses. The designer and enforcement officials are confronted with such terms as "townhouse," "condominium" and "garden apartment." Any of these uses could be defined as a Group R, Division 1 Occupancy.

Residential condominiums come in a variety of dwelling unit arrangements. The building official and designer must ignore the promotional hype of the developer and determine the occupancy classification from the configuration and based on the code's criteria.

In Figure 4-1, for example, four townhouse condominium arrangements are shown.

Detail A is a typical townhouse-configured apartment house, two or three stories in height.

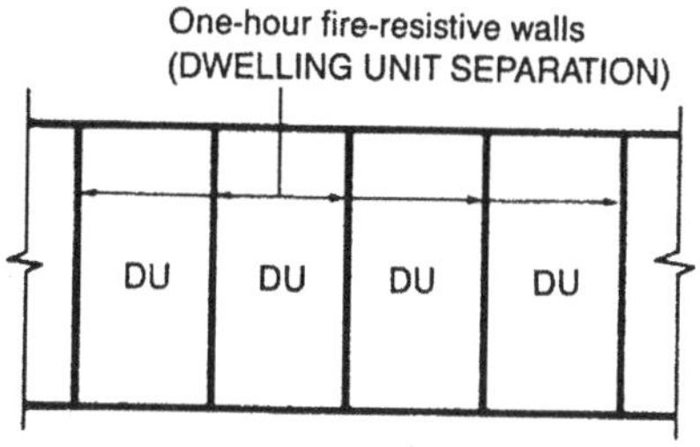

Detail "a"

PLAN VIEW

APARTMENT BUILDING
Group R, Division 1 Occupancy

ONE BUILDING

ONE-HOUR TENANT WALLS BETWEEN DWELLING UNITS (DU) Per Sec. 310.2.2

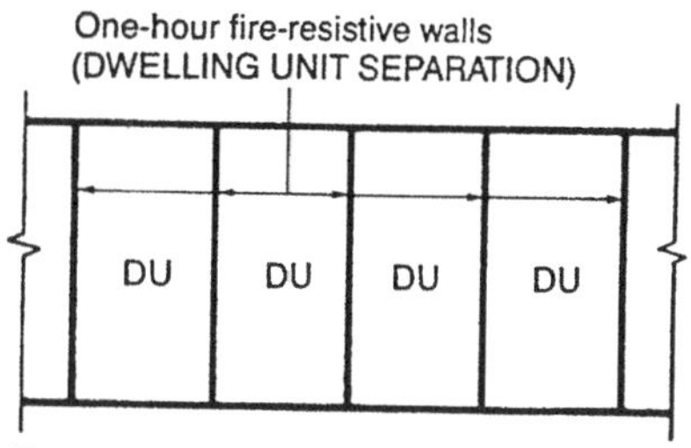

Detail "b"

PLAN VIEW

TOWN HOUSES (CONDOS)
Group R, Division 1 Occupancy

ONE BUILDING

ONE-HOUR TENANT WALLS BETWEEN DWELLING UNITS (DU) Per Sec. 310.2.2

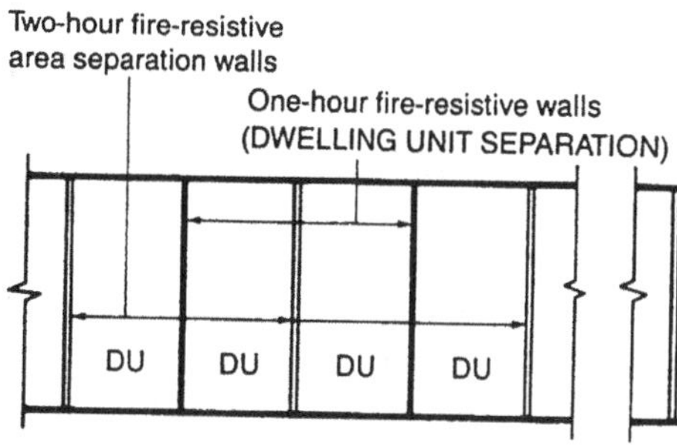

Detail "c"

PLAN VIEW

TOWNHOUSES (CONDOS)
Group R, Division 3 Occupancy

MULTIPLE BUILDINGS WITH AREA SEPARATION WALLS BETWEEN PAIRS OF DWELLING UNITS

ONE-HOUR TENANT WALLS BETWEEN ALTERNATE DWELLING UNITS (DU) Per Section 310.2.2

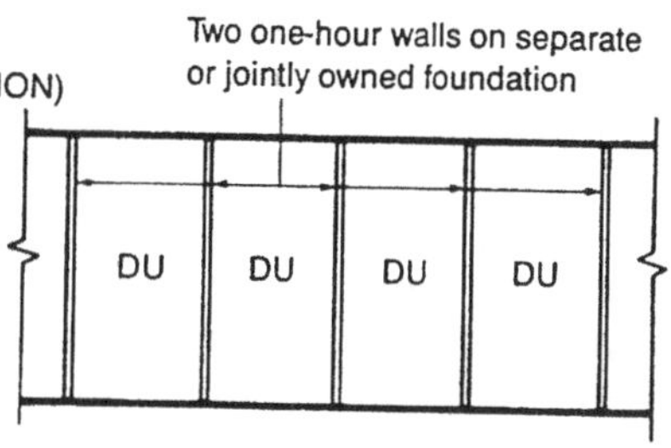

Detail "d"

PLAN VIEW

TOWNHOUSES AS Group R, Division 3 Occupancy

ROW HOUSING

TWO ONE-HOUR WALLS

ONE EACH SIDE OF PROPERTY LINES

REFERENCE: SECTION 202, 310.2.2

FIGURE 4-1 APARTMENT HOUSE DEFINITION–COMPARISON OF ARRANGEMENTS, TOWNHOUSES, CONDOMINIUMS & GROUP R, DIVISION 3 OCCUPANCY

Detail B is the same townhouse arrangement but because it is an Group R, Division 1 Occupancy (apartment house) condominium, it is shown with property lines between the units.

Detail C is also the same townhouse arrangement, but this time the pairs of dwelling units are separated from each other by area separation walls creating Group R, Division 3 Occupancy buildings. The units still have property lines between them to define the condominium ownership limits.

Detail D shows a typical single-family row house arrangement. For this example it is part of a condominium, and unless the dwelling units are constructed as for Group R, Division 3 Occupancy, it may be a Group R, Division 1 Occupancy building. The Group R, Division 3 Occupancy requirements, which must be in the Caveats, Covenants and Regulations (CC&Rs) that govern the condominium, must include

- two 1-hour walls, one on each side of the property line between each unit,
- access to each owner for future repair of the property line walls,
- title to the shared foundation if this is present,
- proper roof-ceiling construction to avoid a parapet at the property line where a parapet is required,
- noncontinuous side walls and roof construction, and
- separate utilities for each unit without common lines crossing the property lines.

Furthermore, the CC&Rs must clearly place on each owner the responsibility for the maintenance of that unit's building envelope. Otherwise, as in most condominiums, the enclosing envelope (exterior walls, tenant walls, roof, etc.) form a single building entity that may be a Group R, Division I Occupancy building and not a series of Group R, Division 3 Occupancy buildings.

The designer should not be confused as to what type of occupancy is involved and should be prepared to discuss this subject with the owner. All parties should be aware of the code requirements applicable to each residential occupancy and type of construction and of the means by which the occupancy classification may be changed.

A designer who applies for a building permit and uses terms such as "townhouse" in place of R-1 or R-3 designations is creating a problem for both the designer and the official. The building official should determine whether the designer fully understands the code and how it may be applied to the proposed structure and use.

Several important exiting and fire protection requirements apply to a multifamily Group R, Division 1 Occupancy structure, including the allowable areas and heights of such structures. Therefore, in the design process it is important that the designer use code-recognized terminology and phraseology. Doing so leads to proper design decisions and will avoid having to adapt the building to the code later when the building official brings the problems to the designer's attention.

The term "condominium" was added to the 1985 UBC. The definition of an apartment house was also amended to include a condominium when there are three or more condominium dwelling units in the building.

At the time this code change was adopted, another change proposing to add the term "townhouse" was denied inclusion in the R-1 apartment house definition because townhouse construction was considered by many building officials to be row housing containing either a single- or two-family dwelling and by others to be an apartment house.

When a building contains three or more dwelling units connected without either property line or area separation walls between groups of two units, by definition it is an apartment house.

In some jurisdictions the building official has encountered only townhouses built as true row housing of one or two dwelling units and has not seen them in groups of three or more, as would constitute apartment houses. It is probable that as more problems are experienced by building officials with the townhouse concept, construction and the misapplication of occupancy requirements, the term "townhouse" will be added to the apartment house definition.

APPROVED, as to materials and types of construction, refers to approval by the building official as the result of investigation and tests conducted by the building official, or by reason of accepted principles or tests by recognized authorities, technical or scientific organizations.

Throughout the code there are occasions when a material or method of construction is accepted "when approved." The term "approved" requires the application of the criteria in Section

104.2.8. Section 104.2.8 provides the basic concept of acceptance of alternative methods and materials and the evaluation to be made by the enforcement official. It provides latitude to the official to accept variations of design and materials other than those set forth in the code.

The building official can use any of the following means for granting approval:

1. The Evaluation Reports promulgated by the International Conference of Building Officials (ICBO).
2. A building official can request the ICBO staff to assist in review of designs that may be too complex or novel for the building official to evaluate alone.
3. If the jurisdiction has a technical review body such as the Board of Appeals described in Section 105, said body can assist the building official.

All these approaches are aimed at making the code flexible and receptive to new materials and designs.

ASSEMBLY BUILDING is a building or portion of a building used for the gathering together of 50 or more persons for such purposes as deliberation, education, instruction, worship, entertainment, amusement, drinking or dining or awaiting transportation.

An assembly occupancy or building is one with an occupant load of 50 or more. This occupant load cutoff is a distinction that places the building in either

- a Group A Occupancy when the occupant load is 50 or more or
- a Group B Occupancy when the occupant load is less than 50.

The occupant load is determined by the floor area of the building or the space in the building and not by the actual number of occupants that will use the facility. This is discussed more fully in Article 7 of this Guide (Chapter 10).

Thus a room or space with a 49-person maximum occupant load will have an area of either

- less than 750 square feet, where there are tables and seats, or
- less than 375 square feet, where there are no tables, such as in a bar.

When these areas are exceeded, the designer will have an A Occupancy, not a B Occupancy.

Group A Occupancies are rigorously regulated and often subject to state law enforced by state and local fire marshals. Examples of uses considered to be assembly-type occupancies, besides restaurants, bars and theaters, include

conference rooms,
libraries,
gymnasiums
churches,
bus, railroad and airport facilities,
museums and
bowling alleys

ATRIUM is an opening through two or more floor levels other than enclosed stairways, elevators, hoistways, escalators, plumbing, electrical, air-conditioning or other equipment, which is closed at the top and not defined as a mall. Floor levels, as used in this definition, do not include balconies within assembly occupancies or mezzanines that complying with Section 501.

The designer should be aware that an atrium is subject to code requirements only when the opening exceeds two stories in height. It is possible for a two-story building with an opening between the two stories not to be subject to the atrium provisions. This is true because the atrium provisions apply only to openings that go through two or more floors, i.e., connect three or more levels.

The designer should avoid using the term "atrium" unless the space truly meets the definition of an atrium. This will avoid considerable difficulty and the imposition of restrictive provisions that should not apply to nonatrium spaces.

AUTOMATIC, as applied to fire protection devices, is a device or system providing an emergency function without the necessity of human intervention and activated as a result of a predetermined temperature rise, rate of rise of temperature or increase in the level of combustion products.

In the code this term is well-defined. It appears at different points throughout the code, often in conjunction with another term, "self-closing," relating to fire door operation.

Although it may appear that an automatic closing door would be preferable, in the parlance of the fire protection field an automatic door is one that is normally found in the open position. It is the normal position of the door that may be of concern in a specific situation and not the means of activating the closing device.

Thus, a self-closing door is one that is normally found in a closed position. It will self-close after each opening through the presence of a door closer and the absence of a hold-open device. In many situations, the preference may be for the self-closing feature in order to provide a better smoke barrier.

SECTION 203—B

BALCONY is that portion of the seating space of an assembly room, the lowest part of which is raised 4 feet (1219 mm) or more above the level of the main floor and shall include the area providing access to the seating area or serving only as a foyer.

This definition of balcony is only a partial one. The term is also applied in the code to nonassembly uses as well. For instance, residential and office balconies may be recreational or serve purposes other than assembly uses. Thus, the definition given here, referring to a public assembly such as a theater, is not one exclusively so used in the body of the code. The dictionary definition also applies.

BASEMENT is any floor level below the first story in a building, except that a floor level in a building having only one floor level shall be classified as a basement unless such floor level qualifies as a first story as defined herein.

Determining whether a level is a basement requires more than simply reading the definition. It requires recourse to other definitions including those of "grade" and "story." Once it is found that a definition is applicable to the level in question, other sections of the code are affected. For example, an area defined as a basement is not, as specified in Section 504.5 to be included as part of the total allowable area calculation.

The definition of story states that the determination of whether a level is to be a story is based on the relationship of the level to adjacent grade. Once a level is determined to be a basement, it could not be a story and would not be counted in the allowable floor area calculation.

According to the definition of story, if a finished floor is less than 6 feet above adjacent grade, that level would be considered the first floor of the building; by the code definition of "basement," the area below would be a basement. The determination of grade would have to satisfy the criteria of Section 208.

The purpose of the code provisions cited above is to reduce the overall height of a building and to count only those levels that are mainly above ground.

The height limits are based on the difficulty the average fire department faces in fighting fires when it is necessary to reach, with hose streams and ladder, the upper levels of tall, minimally fire-resistant buildings.

This discussion points out the considerable degree of interrelationship that exists between code concepts, requirements and definitions. The designer can greatly benefit from understanding the intent of the code and the relationships permitted or required to exist in order to make a provision operative.

BUILDING is any structure used or intended for supporting or sheltering any use or occupancy.

This is the basic definition of what constitutes a building. It is all inclusive and encompasses every type of structure and any use or occupancy.

The designer or owner should assume in all instances that any structure contemplated is a building and is thus subject to the building code regulations.

BUILDING, EXISTING, is a building erected prior to the adopting of this code, or one for which a legal building permit has been issued.

There is considerable distinction between whether a design applies to a building not yet constructed or to one already in existence. If the building is in existence, no code requirements will apply until alteration work is contemplated, as long as the following is true:

- The use is determined to be the same as originally intended in the building permit for its construction.
- The use is found to be in compliance with any subsequent building permit covering the change in use or occupancy.

No code requirements will apply until alteration work is contemplated. This subject was discussed earlier in relation to Section 3403. 1 in Article 3. The key point to remember is the importance of the building permit that establishes the legal status of the building.

- The jurisdiction has not adopted Appendix Chapter 1 or there are no locally or state-mandated retroactive regulations. See Article 12.

SECTION 204—C

CONDOMINIUM, RESIDENTIAL. See "Apartment House."

The term "condominium" was added for the first time to the 1985 UBC. The cross reference to "apartment house" was used to avoid any misunderstanding or misapplication of the code when this form of unit ownership is involved in a building. When three or more condominium dwelling units are in the building, it is an R-1 apartment house.

It should be noted that legally a condominium owner does not own a portion of the structure but really owns a portion of the airspace within the structure that defines the dwelling unit. The unit owner shares the ownership of the building's common areas with the other owners. These common areas include the actual structure as well as all the spaces that are in common use. All the walls, floors and roofs are actually owned by the condominium association. The condominium owner is merely a shareholder in that association.

The term added is "residential condominium." There are also commercial condominiums. These latter condominiums are B Occupancies. Therefore the qualification of the term included in the code is necessary to differentiate the R-1 from the B condominiums.

SECTION 205—D

DRAFT STOP is a material device or construction installed to restrict the movement of air within open spaces of concealed areas of building components such as crawl spaces, floor-ceiling assemblies, roof-ceiling assemblies and attics.

This definition relates to the requirements of the new provisions primarily found in Section 711.

The definition of draft stop henceforth will differentiate between materials that are to limit air movement and those for fire stops that are to resist passage of flame, heat and hot gases. The provisions in Section 708 that relate to "Fire Blocks and Draft Stops" avoid the semantics problems previously experienced when fire stops meant two different things.

DWELLING is any building or portion thereof which contains not more than two dwelling units.

This is one definition for a Group R, Division 3 Occupancy. The designer should be sure that an R-3 is constructed and not an R-1 without its required safeguards.

SECTION 207—F

FAMILY is an individual or two or more persons related by blood or marriage or a group of not more than five persons (excluding servants) who need not be related by blood or marriage living together in a dwelling unit.

This definition is a carryover from the one- and two-family dwelling definition previously used for the Group R, Division 3 Occupancy concept. It is now more accurate to refer to a Group R, Division 3 Occupancy as one containing one or two dwelling units.

FIRE RETARDANT-TREATED WOOD is any wood product impregnated with chemicals by a pressure process or other means during manufacture, and which, when tested in accordance with U.B.C. Standard No. 8-1 for a period of 30 minutes, shall have a flame spread of not over 25 and show no evidence of progressive combustion. In addition, the flame front shall not progress more than 10 1/2 feet (3200 mm) beyond the centerline of the burner at any time during the test. Materials which may be exposed to the weather shall pass the accelerated weathering test and be identified as Exterior type, in accordance with U.B.C. Standard No. 23-4. Where material is not directly subject to rainfall but exposed to high humidity conditions, it shall be subject to the hygroscopic test and identified as interior Type A in accordance with U.B.C. Standard No. 23-4.

All materials shall bear identification showing the fire performance rating thereof. Such identification shall be issued by an approved agency having a service for inspection of materials at the factory.

A general misinterpretation of the definition of fire-retardant-treated wood is that it means fireproof wood. This is not the case: The fire retardant chemicals merely reduce the rate by which flame-spread travels over the surface of the wood.

For a better understanding of flame-spread and fire resistance, refer to the discussions in Article 8 of this Guide.

The BTU fuel content of fire retardant wood and untreated wood is essentially the same.

FLOOR AREA is the area included within the surrounding exterior walls of a building or portion thereof, exclusive of vent shafts and courts. The floor area of a building, or portion thereof, not provided with surrounding exterior walls shall be the usable area under horizontal projection of the roof or floor above.

The floor area of a building is of great importance to the owner and the designer since it is a key determinant of the type of construction that has to be used for the building. This will be discussed in detail in Article 5 in relation to Sections 504, 505, 506 and Table 5-B. The floor area definition requires the measurement of the area to include everything within the exterior walls except for vent shafts and courts.

There is a difference of opinion among building officials whether the exterior wall thickness is to be included or excluded from the computation. That is, is the measurement to be made from the outside of the exterior wall or from the inside? Early in the design stage, the designer should determine the prevailing method in the jurisdiction and confirm it in writing if it is an important consideration in the particular building.

The area calculation is a gross figure. Items such as elevators, stairways and utility or mechanical shafts are not to be deducted. Where there is an overhang covering a portion of the floor area without enclosing walls, as might be found in a loading dock or a balcony, the floor area must be calculated to the outside edge of the overhang. (See Figure 4-2.)

The floor area calculation is of such importance that the designer should establish this figure early in the preliminary discussions with the local enforcement agency.

SECTION 208—G

GARAGE is a building or portion thereof in which a motor vehicle containing flammable or combustible liquids or gas in its tank, is stored, repaired or kept.

GARAGE, PRIVATE, is a building or a portion of a building, not more than 1,000 square feet (93 m^2) in area, in which only motor vehicles used by the tenants of the building or buildings on the premises are stored or kept. (See Section 312)

GARAGE, PUBLIC, is any garage other than a private garage.

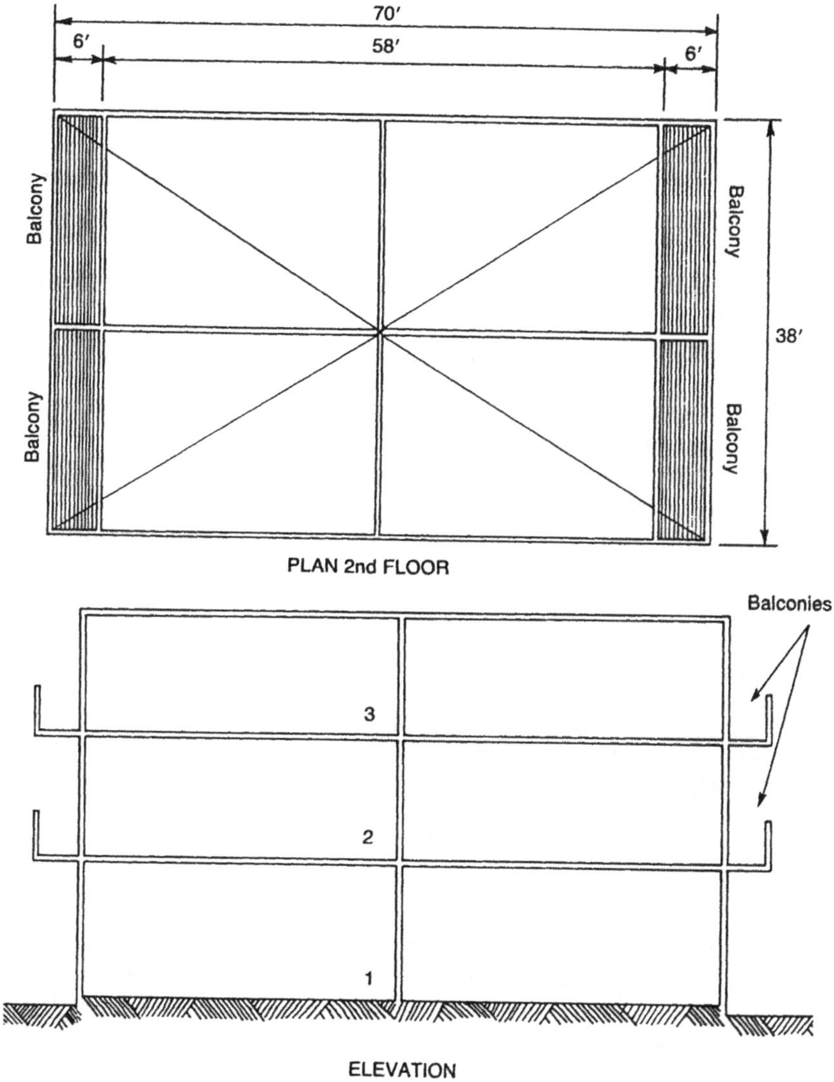

Floor Area of 1st and 2nd Floors is shown by diagonal lines, i.e., $70 \times 38 = 2660$ square feet.
Floor Area of 3rd floor $= 58 \times 38 = 2204$ square feet, since the 3rd floor balcony is not covered by a roof.

REFERENCE: SECTION 207

FIGURE 4-2 FLOOR AREA CALCULATION WITH BALCONY

There are several definitions, and three different classifications, of garages. The least restrictive definition refers to a garage in conjunction with a dwelling or a small office building: a private garage. It is classified as a Group U, Division 1 Occupancy.

When the garage is larger, or if it is in a larger building or serves occupants other than those in the building, it is called a public garage. This garage is classified as a Group S, Division 3 Occupancy.

The third class of garage is a repair garage classed as a Group S, Division 4 Occupancy.

The reason for the three different garage classes is illustrated in Table 5-B. In a Type III-N building, a Group S, Division 3 Occupancy allows a floor area of 12,000 square feet. In a similar building, a Group S, Division 4 Occupancy is not allowed. Per Table 5-B and Table 3-H, a Group S, Division 4 Occupancy is not permitted in a Type III-N building.

On the other hand, the Group U, Division 1 private garage is limited to 1000 square feet with a maximum of 3000 square feet in any one building. The provisions in Section 312.2.2 enable the private garage to reach the maximum of 3000 square feet in the building.

GROUND (Adjacent Ground Elevation) is the lowest point of elevation of the finished surface of the ground, paving or sidewalk within the area between the building and the property line or, when the property line is more than 5 feet (1524 mm) from the building, between the building and a line 5 feet (1524 mm) from the building.

This definition requires that the elevation of the ground surface to be used be either

- the level between the building and the property line or
- where the property line is more than 5 feet from the building, the lowest point within a distance of 5 feet from the building.

The code intent is to establish what would be a natural ground line and to prevent someone from piling soil up against the foundation of the building and claiming that it represents the grade. By requiring the measurement to be the lowest elevation within 5 feet of the building, the code establishes a 5-foot width to represent grade and not simply a mound of earth against the foundation. A retaining wall can be used to establish this 5-foot level width.

The determination of the grade level is important to the designer for several reasons, including the qualification of a level as a basement and the measurement of the allowable overall height of the building. (See Figure 4-3.)

SECTION 209—H

HEIGHT OF BUILDING is the vertical distance above a reference datum measured to the highest point of the coping of a flat roof or to the deck line of a mansard roof or to the average height of the highest gable of a pitched or hipped roof. The reference datum shall be selected by either of the following, whichever yields a greater height of building:

1. The elevation of the highest adjoining sidewalk or ground surface within a 5-foot (1524 mm) horizontal distance of the exterior wall of the building when such sidewalk or ground surface is not more than 10 feet (3048 mm) above lowest grade.

2. An elevation 10 feet (3048 mm) higher than the lowest grade when the sidewalk or ground surface described in Item 1 above is more than 10 feet (3048 mm) above lowest grade.

The height of a stepped or terraced building is the maximum height of any segment of the building.

Height of building discussed in this definition relates to the provisions in Chapter 5 for considering the maximum height for a given type of construction and number of stories in a building. (See Figure 4-4.)

Height and stories are interdependent in Table 5-B wherein the limitations for the height in feet and the number of stones are established. The provisions for measuring the height require reference to the ground surface. The 5-foot horizontal width in item 1 is comparable to the 5-foot width measurement for determining grade.

The concern with the method of height measurement is based on the fire and panic hazards presented by taller structures or those with more levels of occupancy. Many times the misinterpretation or misapplication of the height and story measurement has been the result of a desire to avoid the added exit and fire protection requirements that apply when a building is three or more stones in height.

The designer is cautioned that any error in this part of the design can produce considerable repercussions; hence, the designer should use a conservative approach to the height measurement.

HOTEL is any building containing six or more guest rooms intended or designed to be used, or which are used, rented or hired out to be occupied, or which are occupied for sleeping purposes by guests.

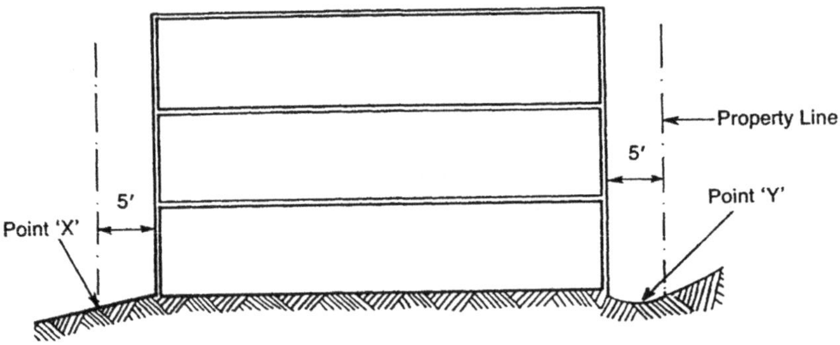

ELEVATION 'A'

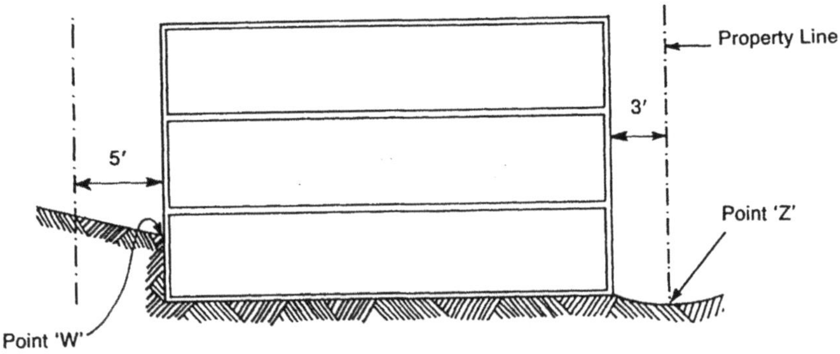

ELEVATION 'B'

The "lowest" grade elevation to be used in connection with the definition of "story" are, for the 2 examples above:

Elevation A

Points 'X' and 'Y' show how to determine the lowest point within 5′ of the building.

Elevation B

Points 'W' and 'Z'; Point 'Z' is the grade at the property line which is used when that line is less than 5′ from the building.

Points 'W' is the grade used when it is the lowest point within 5′ of the building.

REFERENCE: SECTION 208

FIGURE 4-3 GRADE DETERMINATION

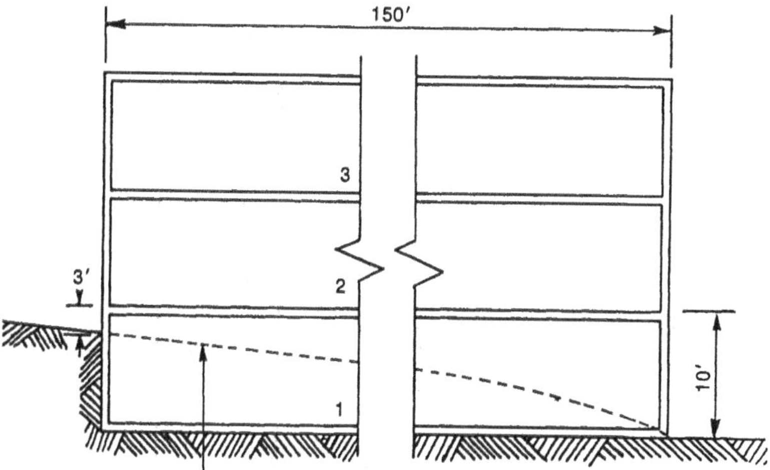

Level 1 is a story if the floor of the level above is more than 6′ above grade for more than 50% of the total perimeter of the building or more than 12′ above grade at any point.

Grade is the level of the lowest point of the adjacent ground finished surface within 5′ of the building or if the property line is less than 5′ from the building, the elevation along that property line. See Figure 4-2.

In the example above, assuming the building to be 150′×300′, and the 6′ elevation of the 2nd level of one end is 90 feet back from the 10′ high side and at the other end is 75 feet back from the 10′ high side, the percentage of the perimeter that is more than 6′ above grade is:

$$\frac{300 + 90 + 75}{300 + 300 + 150 + 150} = \frac{465}{900}$$

Percentage > 6′ = 52%

Therefore, Level 1 is a story.

REFERENCE: SECTIONS 203, 208, 220

FIGURE 4-4 RELATIONSHIP OF GRADE FOR STORY DETERMINATION

The hotel is another subgroup of the Group R, Division 1 Occupancy, multifamily usage. The controlling criterion is the number of guest rooms rather than dwelling units (as is used in the apartment house definition).

SECTION 214—M

MECHANICAL CODE is the *Uniform Mechanical Code* promulgated by the International Conference of Building Officials, as adopted by this jurisdiction.

One of the codes referenced in the UBC provisions is the Mechanical Code, in particular the Uniform Mechanical Code (UMC). It is adopted by a jurisdiction in a similar manner as is the UBC.

MEZZANINE or MEZZANINE FLOOR is an intermediate floor placed within a room.

The construction provisions for mezzanines are contained in Section 507. The key determinant in whether a level qualifies as a mezzanine is stated in item 3 of Section 507, which reads:

3. The aggregate area of mezzanines within a room shall not exceed one third the area of the room in which it is located.

SECTION 215—N

NONCOMBUSTIBLE as applied to building construction material means a material which, in the form in which it is used, is either one of the following:

1. Material of which no part will ignite and burn when subjected to fire. Any material conforming to U.B.C. Standard No. 2-1 shall be considered noncombustible within the meaning of this section.

2. Material having a structural base of noncombustible material as defined in Item 1 above, with a surfacing material not over 1/8 inch (3.2 mm) thick which has a flame-spread rating of 50 or less.

"Noncombustible" does not apply to surface finish materials. Material required to be noncombustible for reduced clearances to flues, heating appliances or other sources of high temperature shall refer to material conforming to Item 1. No material shall be classed as noncombustible which is subject to increase in combustibility or flame-spread rating, beyond the limits herein established, through the effects of age, moisture or other atmospheric condition.

Flame-spread rating as used herein refers to rating obtained according to tests conducted as specified in U.B.C. Standard 8-1.

The term "noncombustible" is used to define the basic burning characteristic of a material. It is not a term applicable to interior finish materials but rather applies to components of the building and to fire-resistive assemblies.

The primary requirement for a material to be classed as noncombustible is that it meet the UBC Standard 2-1, which is derived from the national standard ASTM E-136. This standard requires that the test specimen not raise the temperature of the test furnace by more than 54°F after the test sample is inserted into the preheated furnace. The initial test furnace temperature is 1382°F.

Therefore, the material has to have a high resistance to ignition or a low BTU content in order to maintain the temperature at or below the permissible limit. Another test criteria is that, after 30 seconds exposure in the furnace, the test sample does not flame.

The purpose of requiring a material to be noncombustible is to prevent it from contributing to a fire as would a combustible material. This requirement serves as a means of reducing the available fire load in an area.

Examples of some of the common building materials regarding their combustibility follow:

	NONCOMBUSTIBLE	COMBUSTIBLE
Chipboard, with or without FR treatment		X
Fiberglass or mineral insulation if paperbacked	X	
Gypsum wallboard	X	X
Plastics, with or without FR treatment		X
Plywood, regular or FR treated		X
Steel studs and other members	X	
Plaster	X	
Wood studs and other members		X
Wood studs, FR treated		X

FR, fire retardant.

The term "incombustible" is often used synonymously with noncombustible.

SECTION 216—P

OCCUPANCY is the purpose for which a building, or part thereof, is used or intended to be used.

The term "occupancy" encompasses one of the main criteria in the design of a building. The occupancy of a building is, by code, to be assigned by the building official per Chapter 3. Regardless of the use that may be proposed for the building, the building official has to assign it to a general occupancy class: the one which it most nearly resembles.

The occupancy or use may vary from time to time. However, whenever the occupancy or use changes from one occupancy group or division to another, as defined in Chapter 3, the code requires a building permit be obtained to legalize that change of occupancy. There is no such requirement when the change is within the same occupancy division, such as a doctor's office changing to a barber shop, both being Group B Occupancies. (See the discussion of Section 302 in Article 3.)

OWNER is any person, agent, firm or corporation having a legal or equitable interest in the property.

This term includes more than one might think on first reading the definition. The phrase "having a legal or equitable interest" refers also to a lessee or tenant of the property. Once a building or portion thereof is leased, the improvements to the premises often are made by the tenant or lessee; in fact, most lease agreements stipulate that this be the case.

The code often refers to the responsibilities of the building permit applicants. Because any action regarding a permit involves the legal status of a building, it can readily be seen that the applicant for the permit has the power to affect this status.

In the leasing agreements between owners and tenants, the lessee is usually required to comply with local codes and ordinances. Usually there is no provision in the lease coveting the possible affect that a tenant applied-for building permit might have on the owner's investment.

For example, assume that a tenant files for a permit. To lower the cost of the intended work, the tenant may request that the building type of construction be changed from Type I to Type V One-hour. That change, along with the subsequent work, will result in a legal change in the city's records for that building. Any future use of the building could involve substantial expense to the owner. These changes can occur without the owner being aware of them until much later.

The owner might also be unaware of a change in the building's occupancy classification. A tenant could apply for a permit, indicate a less hazardous occupancy will be involved than previously, and thereby change the occupancy of the building from that previously recorded to the new use. The tenant may have arranged this change in occupancy in order to reduce the code requirements applicable to the proposed alteration. In the future the owner may find that, if the building's original occupancy classification were to be reestablished, it would have to conform to the requirements for that occupancy in the most recent building code. This could prove to be costly. See Sections 3401 and 3405.

The tenant or lessee is accepted, in the code and by the local jurisdiction, as acting for the owner. The tenant or lessee, in proposing to make improvements to the building or changes in the occupancy classification thereof, should be required to provide the owner with written notification of that intention. The tenant would thus be subject to future liability as a result of having taken action without first advising the owner.

SECTION 217—P

PROTECTIVE MEMBRANE is a surface material which forms the required outer layer or layers of a fire-resistive assembly containing concealed spaces.

This definition relates to the requirements of the penetration provisions primarily found in Chapter 7.

SECTION 219—R

REPAIR is the reconstruction or renewal of any part of an existing building for the purpose of its maintenance.

The code regards repair work as an "alteration." All repairs, except for minor ones such as filling holes in walls, require a building permit per Section 106.1. Before doing repair work, it is best to determine whether that jurisdiction requires a permit for that class of repair work.

SECTION 220—S

SHAFT is an interior space, enclosed by walls or construction, extending through one or more stories or basements which connects openings on successive floors, or floors and roof, to accommodate elevators, dumbwaiters, mechanical equipment or similar devices or to transmit light or ventilation air.

SHAFT ENCLOSURE is the walls or construction forming the boundaries of a shaft.

These definitions relate to the requirements for "Shaft and Exit Enclosures" found in the sections (i.e., 303.6 for Group A Occupancies, 304.6 for Group B Occupancies, etc.) covering the specific occupancy provisions in Chapters 3 and 7.

SMOKE DETECTOR is an approved listed device that senses visible or invisible particles of combustion.

There are two general categories of smoke detectors, the ionization type and the photoelectric type. A smoke detector containing both means of detection provides maximum protection. Each detection means has a different reaction time in response to varying fire and smoke conditions.

In Section 310.9.1.2 the code stipulates that when alterations of $1000 or more are done in Group R Occupancies, a smoke detector must be installed. Some jurisdictions also require that smoke detectors be provided upon changes in ownership.

STORY is that portion of a building included between the upper surface of any floor and the upper surface of the floor next above, except that the topmost story shall be that portion of a building included between the upper surface of the topmost floor and the ceiling or roof above. If the finished floor level directly above a usable or unused under-floor space is more than 6 feet (1829 mm) above grade as defined herein for more than 50 percent of the total perimeter or is more than 12 feet (3658 mm) above grade, as defined herein, at any point, such usable or unused under-floor space shall be considered as a story.

The most important part of this definition lies in the second sentence. Together with the definitions of "grade" and "basement," this provision determines whether there is an extra level included in the count of the floor area and in the overall number of stories in a building. This, in turn, will affect the choice of the building construction type. (See Figure 4-5.)

STREET is any thoroughfare or public way not less than 16 feet (4877 mm) in width which has been dedicated or deeded to the public for public use.

A "public way" is one form of frontage or separation and is thus acceptable in determining whether the allowable floor area may be increased. (See Section 505). Because at least one building line may front on a street, the requirements of Table 5-A will apply to that line.

This allowance is usually not a problem unless the street or public way is narrow. In such a situation, the application of Section

505 and Table 5-A could result in a requirement for protection of the wall and/or openings on that part of the building.

SECTION 222—U

UBC STANDARDS are those standards published in Volume 3 of the *Uniform Building Code* promulgated by the International Conference of Building Officials, as adopted by this jurisdiction. (See Chapter 35.)

Throughout the code there are references made to the "U.B.C. Standard X-X." These standards are contained in a separate document, Volume 3 of the UBC. The standards are listed in Chapter 35 of the UBC with the source document identified. With some exceptions, the bulk of the UBC Standards are derived from existing national standards. Appropriate editing makes them enforceable as legal documents.

The numbering system of the UBC Standards is such that the first number corresponds to that of the primary chapter to which the standard relates. The second number is sequentially assigned. Thus, UBC Standard 7-1 is the first standard cited in Chapter 7. A check of the Chapter 35 provisions reveals that Standard 7-1 is derived from source document of the American Society for Testing and Materials: Fire Tests of Building Construction and Materials. Standard Methods ASTM E-119-83 of the ASTM.

The standards are as much a part of the code as is any section or chapter contained therein, as is specifically stated in Section 3501:

The Uniform Building Code standards referred to in various parts of this code, which are also listed in Part II of this chapter, are hereby declared to be a part of this code and are referred to in this code as a "UBC standard."

SECTION 224—W

Walls shall be defined as follows:

Bearing Wall is any wall meeting either of the following classifications:

1. Any metal or wood stud wall that supports more than 100 pounds per lineal foot (0.445 kN per lineal meter) of superimposed load.

2. Any masonry or concrete wall that supports more than 200 pounds per lineal foot (0.89 kN per lineal meter foot) superimposed load, or any wall supporting its own weight for more than one story.

Exterior Wall is any wall or element of a wall, or any member or group of members, which defines the exterior boundaries or courts of a building and which has a slope of 60 degrees or greater with the horizontal plane.

Faced Wall is a wall in which the masonry facing and backing are so bonded as to exert a common action under load.

Nonbearing Wall is any wall that is not a bearing wall.

Parapet Wall is that part of any wall that is entirely above the roof line.

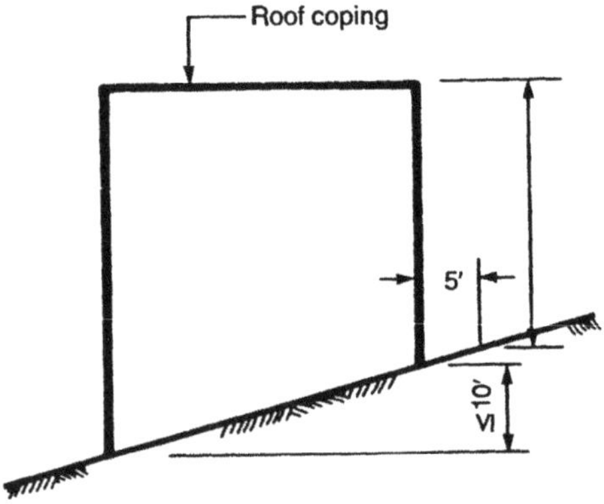

CASE 1

GROUND @ UPPER WALL
MORE THAN 10 FEET ABOVE GRADE
OF GROUND @ LOWER WALL OF BUILDING

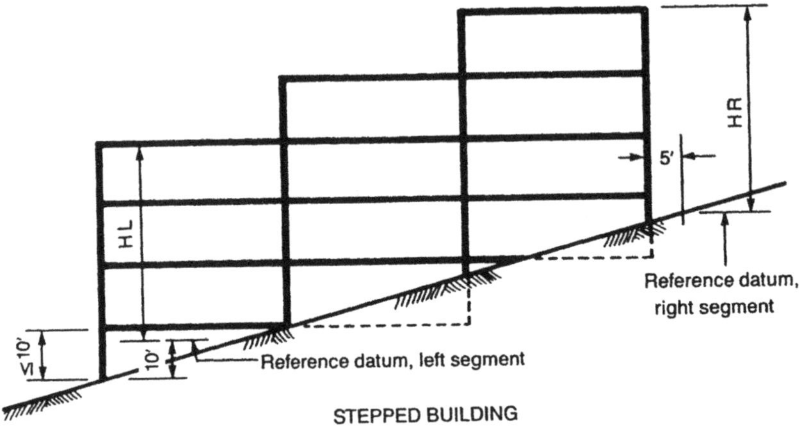

STEPPED BUILDING

REFERENCE: SECTION 209

FIGURE 4-5 HEIGHT OF BUILDING MEASUREMENT

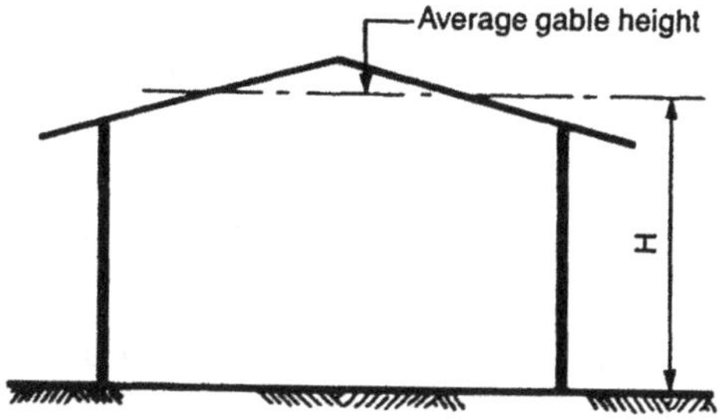

PITCHED ROOF

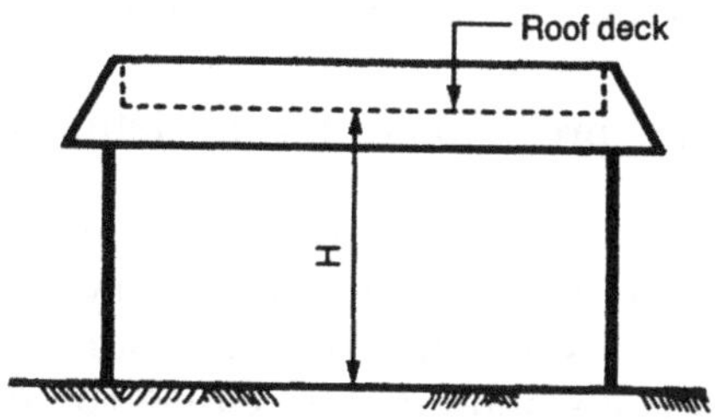

MANSARD ROOF

H = Height of Building

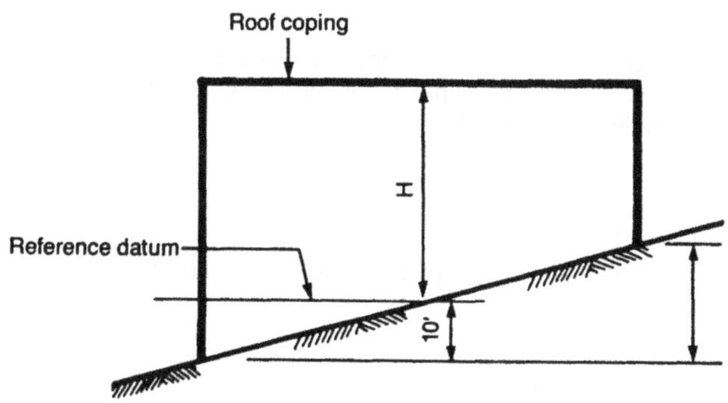

CASE 2

GRADE OF GROUND @ UPPER WALL
10 FEET OR LESS ABOVE GRADE
OF GROUND @ LOWER WALL OF BUILDING

Retaining Wall is a wall designed to resist the lateral displacement of soil or other materials.

The definition of "exterior wall" should be noted. An A-frame building with a slope of more than 60 would be a wall; however, a surface of less than 60, as might be found in a mansard, could be considered a roof.

WEATHER-EXPOSED SURFACES are all surfaces of walls, ceilings, floors, roofs, soffits and similar surfaces exposed to the weather, excepting the following:

1. Ceilings and roof soffits enclosed by walls or by beams which extend a minimum of 12 inches (305 mm) below such ceiling or roof soffits.

2. Walls or portions of walls within an unenclosed roof area, when located a horizontal distance from an exterior opening equal to twice the height of the opening.

3. Ceiling and roof soffits beyond a horizontal distance of 10 feet (3048 mm) from the outer edge of the ceiling or roof soffits.

For illustrations of the provisions of this definition, see Figure 4-6.

The three criteria in the above definition may not be sufficient because topography and climatic conditions vary. The designer should be aware that he or she could be liable for failing to take into account these conditions should they cause the deterioration of the surfaces or the materials they cover. The designer is responsible for the design and should know the site conditions to which the surfaces may be subjected.

SECTION 226—Y

YARD is an open, unoccupied space, other than a court, unobstructed from the ground to the sky, except where specifically provided by this code, on the lot on which a building is situated.

A yard is another of the specific frontages or separations that may be used in whether the allowable area may be increased per Section 505. For most occupancies, the parking lot around a building can be considered a yard.

GLOSSARY

The following are terms that are used in this Guide but that have special meanings not usually found in the dictionary. These

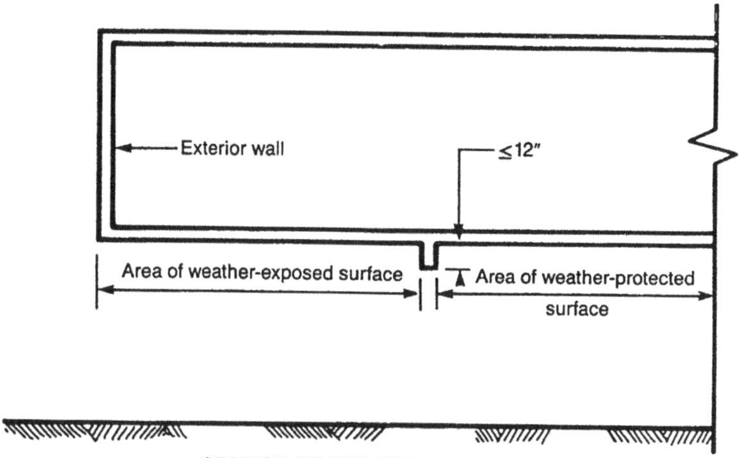

SECTION OF BUILDING
WITH UNENCLOSED EXTERIOR OPENING
ITEM 1
SECTION 224 WEATHER-PROTECTED SURFACES

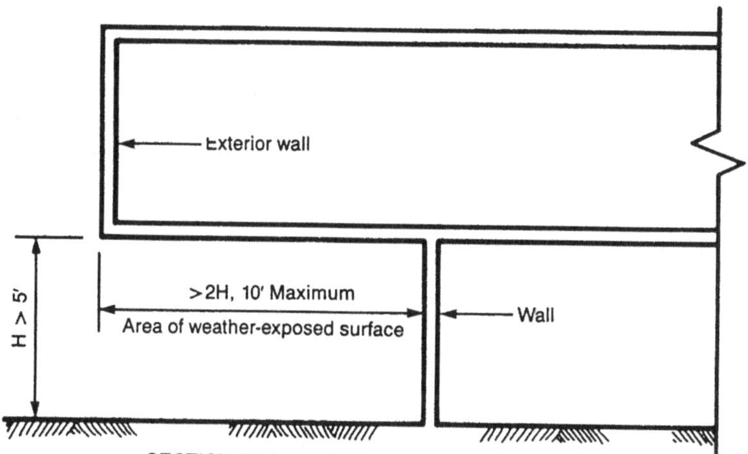

SECTION OF BUILDING
WITH UNENCLOSED EXTERIOR OPENING
ITEM 2 AND 3
SECTION 224 WEATHER PROTECTED SURFACES

NOTE: When 2H = 10′, regardless of the height of the opening, any surface more than 10′ from the outer edge is considered as a weather-protected surface.

REFERENCE: SECTION 224

FIGURE 4-6 DEFINITION OF WEATHER-EXPOSED SURFACE ILLUSTRATED

terms are supplementary to the definitions in the Uniform Building Code:

ADA. Federal law Americans with Disabilities Act.

ANSI. American National Standards Institute.

ASTM. American Society for Testing and Materials.

ENFORCEMENT AUTHORITY OR OFFICIAL. The enforcement authority referred to in this Guide is the building inspection agency that enforces the building code in its locality and the fire service enforcement official (usually the fire marshal) or the fire prevention agency of the fire department that is charged with enforcing the fire code.

ICBO. The International Conference of Building Officials is the organization that publishes several model codes including the Uniform Building, Fire, and Mechanical Codes.

JURISDICTION. This term is used as a blanket reference to the legal governmental entity that enacts and enforces the code. It includes any level of government from town, city, county or state. It has the legal power and responsibility to adopt the laws and to prosecute violations thereof. (See also the definition in the UBC.)

MAINTENANCE. This term has two slightly different meanings, one relevant to the UBC and another, broader term used in the Uniform Fire Code (UFC). As used in the UBC, it refers to the maintaining, by the owner of the building, of all devices and safeguards in conformance with the requirements in effect when the building was constructed.

The UFC, on the other hand, is concerned with the overall maintenance of the safety features including the materials in use within the building and its exit paths. Thus the building, once it has been built, is subject to periodic fire service inspections performed to assure that the use and occupancy has not been made more hazardous than intended under the original building permit, and that exits as well as other safety features are operational.

In short, one builds under the requirements of the building code and one maintains and operates under those of the fire code.

NFPA. National Fire Protection Association.

OFFICIAL. As used herein, this term refers to one of the enforcement officials, usually the building official.

UBC. Uniform Building Code.

UFAS. Uniform Federal Accessibility Standards.

UFC. Uniform Fire Code.

UHC. Uniform Housing Code.

UL. Underwriters Laboratories, Inc.

ARTICLE 5
OCCUPANCY PROVISIONS

CHAPTER 3 USE OR OCCUPANCY
CHAPTER 4 SPECIAL USE AND OCCUPANCY
CHAPTER 5 GENERAL BUILDING LIMITATIONS

Chapter 3 Use or Occupancy

As mentioned in Article 2, Chapter 3 provides the occupancy requirements for the design of a building. The pertinent sections of Chapter 3 are discussed in this Guide in the same sequence as they appear in the Uniform Building Code (UBC). Each analysis and discussion is preceded by all or a portion of the code text.

SECTION 301—OCCUPANCY CLASSIFIED

Every building, whether existing or hereafter erected, shall be classified by the building official, according to its use or the character of its occupancy, as set forth in Table 3-A, as a building of one of the following occupancy groups

Group A	**Assembly (see Section 303.1.1)**
Group B	**Business (see Section 304.1)**
Group E	**Educational (see Section 305.1)**
Group F	**Factory and Industrial (see Section 306.1)**
Group H	**Hazardous (see Section 307.1)**
Group I	**Institutional (see Section 308.1)**
Group M	**Mercantile (see Section 309.1)**
Group R	**Residential (see Section 310.1)**
Group S	**Storage (see Section 311.1)**
Group U	**Utility (see Section 312.1)**

Any occupancy not mentioned specifically or about which there is any question shall be classified by the building official and included in the group that its use most nearly resembles, based on the existing or proposed life and fire hazard.

For changes in use, see Section 3405.

This section charges the building official with two responsibilities:

1. To designate the occupancy classification for an existing or proposed use in a building.

2. If a use does not fit into one of the existing occupancy groups or divisions listed in Table 3-A, to place the use in the group and division it most nearly resembles, based on life and/or fire hazard that would exist with that use.

Early in the design process, the designer should ascertain the categories for uses that do not fit into predefined groups. The categorizing is done to avoid problems resulting from a difference of opinion with the building official. If the official does not agree with the designer's choice of the classification, the official could place the use in an entirely different and possibly more restrictive classification. Such an action could necessitate the redesign of the proposed structure or of the alterations planned for an existing building.

SECTION 302—MIXED USE OR OCCUPANCY

302.1 General. When a building is used for more than one occupancy purpose, each part of the building comprising a distinct "Occupancy," as described in Section 301, shall be separated from any other occupancy as specified in Section 302.4

EXCEPTIONS: 1. Where an approved spray booth constructed In accordance with the Fire Code is installed, such booth need not be separated from other Group H Occupancies or from Group B Occupancies.

2. The following occupancies need not be separated from the uses to which they are accessory:

2.1 Assembly rooms having a floor area of not over 750 square feet.

2.2 Administrative and clerical offices and similar rooms which do not exceed 25 percent of the floor area of the major use when not related to Group H, Division 2 and Group H, Division 3 Occupancies.

2.3 Gift shops, administrative offices and similar rooms in Group R, Division 1 Occupancies not exceeding 10 percent of the floor area of the major use.

2.4 The kitchen serving the dining area of which It is a part.

2.5 Customer waiting rooms not exceeding 400 square feet (41.8 m^2) when not related to Group H Occupancies and when such waiting rooms have an exit directly to the exterior.

3. An occupancy separation need not be provided between a Group R, Division 3 Occupancy and a carport having no enclosed uses above, provided the carport Is entirely open on two or more sides.

4. A Group B, Division 1 Occupancy used exclusively for the parking or storage of private or pleasure-type motor vehicles need not be separated from a Group B, Division 3 Occupancy open parking garage as defined In Section 709.

When a building houses more than one occupancy, each portion of the building shall conform to the requirements for the occupancy housed therein.

An occupancy shall not be located above the story or height set forth in Table No. 5-B, except as provided in Section 506. When a mixed occupancy

building contains a Group H, Division 6 Occupancy, the portion containing the Group H, Division 6 Occupancy shall not exceed three stories nor 55 feet (16 764 mm) in height.

A. General

Most buildings contain one or more occupancy in addition to the main occupancy or use. An office building, Group B, often contains parking facilities (S-3), a canteen or cafeteria (A-2.1 or A3), and conference or meeting rooms (A-2.1 or A-3). These other uses within the office building are not unusual and represent a mixed occupancy regulated by this section.

This section requires that when there are different occupancies in a building, they must be separated from each other by fire-resistive construction in accordance with Section 302.4. It further limits the location of each particular occupancy, vertically within a building, to no higher than the number of stories and height stated in Table 5-B.

In Exception 3 reference is made to a carport. The code does not have a definition of a carport or what differentiates it from a garage. This exception provides such a definition; i.e., a carport is a facility that is open on at least two sides used for storing an automobile or similar vehicles.

It is important that the designer be aware of this characteristic of a carport to avoid inadvertently considering a space with only one open side as a carport.

B. Mixed Occupancy and Effect of Change in Type of Construction

In certain circumstances, a change proposed for a portion of a building warrants a reexamination of the building. The results can be surprising. For example, assume there is a one-story Type III-N building (typical tilt-up warehouse) of Group B or M Occupancy with an area of 110,000 square feet, sprinklers and side yards of 60 feet or more all around. With these qualifications, the B or M Occupancy is permitted to use the unlimited area provisions of Section 505.2.

Assume there is now a proposal to use 27,000 square feet of the building for Group H, Division 6 Occupancy (semiconductor facility). The code does not permit an H-6 Occupancy to have the unlimited area benefits. It is therefore necessary to reassess the building under the provisions of Section 302, Table 5-B together with the separation and sprinkler credits allowed. (See Figure 5-1.)

The B Occupancy will now occupy an area of 13,000 square feet of the building with the H-6 Occupancy at 27,000 square feet.

Per Table 5-B, a B or M use in a Type III-N building is allowed:

A basic floor area of	12,000 square feet
The separations on four sides permit a 100% increase	24,000 square feet
The one-story building is allowed sprinkler credit of 300%, or a total allowable for the B or M	72,000 square feet

Because the B or M and H-6 are both allowed the same basic floor areas in Table 5-B, for the floor area determinations the building can be considered as if it were a single type of occupancy.

The B or M and H-6 areas aggregate 110,000 square feet. The Type III-N construction cannot be used because the building exceeds the code allowables.

If the fire resistance in the building is increased to Type III One-hour:

The basic allowable area increases to	12,000 square feet
The separations then allow	36,000 square feet
The sprinkler credits (300%) raise the allowable area to	108,000 square feet

Because the overall size of the building is 110,000 square feet, increasing the fire resistance to Type III One-hour is still not sufficient.

A solution to the problem created in this example may be to add an area separation wall to either the Type III-N or III One-hour construction. Such a wall must be of 4-hour construction. Because the roof of either of these two types of construction will be of either nonrated or 1-hour combustible construction, the area separation wall must penetrate the roof and form a parapet above the roof. The alternative to a parapet does not apply when a 4-hour area

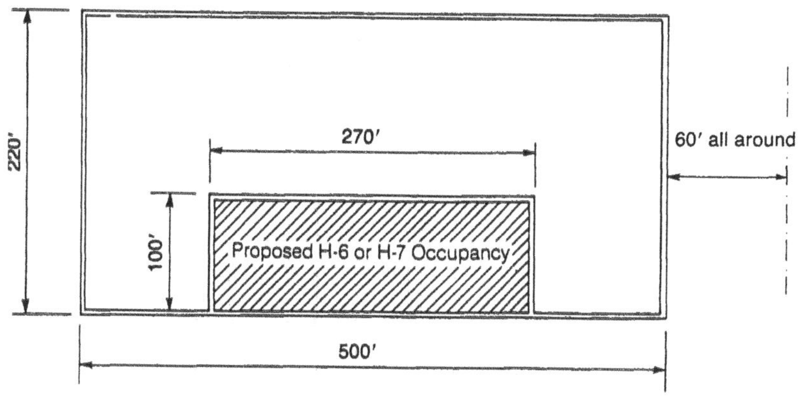

This example relies on material to be discussed in other portions of the Guide. However, it does meet the change of occupancy intent of Section 3405.

Section 3405 requires a change in use meet the requirements for the new use or occupancy. However, the type of construction requirements must similarly be satisfied. Thus the Table 6-A provisions apply.

This example illustrates a possible means for satisfying the code by downgrading the building's type of construction from Type III-N to Type V One-hour and the benefit that could derive.

ASSUME:
Type III-N Building, One story
B Occupancy, 110,000 S.F.
Fully sprinklered, 60-foot separations all around

a) B and H-6 in Type III-N, 4 separations and sprinklered
B and H-6 allowable area - 1 story building = 12,000 x 2 x 3 = 72,000 S.F.,
since building overall area = 110,000 S.F., it exceeds allowable area.

b) If Type III=N were changed to Type V One-hour,
H-6 and B allowable area = 18,000 x 2 x 3 = 84,000 S.F.; 83,000 S.F. desired.
Use one area separation between B and H-6; two-hour construction
H-6 allowable area = 14,000 x 3 = 42,000 S.F.; the 27,000 S.F. desired is O.K.

Thus by reducing the construction type and adding an area separation wall of two-hour construction (which need not have a parapet), the proposed mixed occupancy building meets the code.

REFERENCE: SECTIONS 3405, 302, 505.2 AND TABLE 5-B

FIGURE 5-1 CHANGE IN USE/CHANGE IN BUILDING CONSTRUCTION TYPE

separation wall is involved. The construction of such an area separation wall and parapet is costly and may not be acceptable to the building owner because it precludes future flexibility.

Another alternative for the designer to consider is to downgrade the original building's construction type from Type III-N to Type V and to add 1-hour fire resistance throughout.

If the Type V One-hour building with the B occupancy has three separations as shown in Figure 5-1:

The basic allowable area is	14,000 square feet
Separation increase (100%)	28,000 square feet
Sprinkler increase (300%)	84,000 square feet

Therefore, the total allowable size for the B is 84,000 square feet.

If the same building contains the H-6 Occupancy as shown in Figure 5-1 with only one area separation:

The basic allowable area is	14,000 square feet
Sprinkler increase (300%)	42,000 square feet

Total allowable area of the H-6 is 42,000 square feet. Thus, the allowable area for the H-6 Occupancy exceeds the 28,000 square feet of H-6 space needed.

The downgrading of type of construction and the addition of the 1-hour fire resistance enables these two occupancies to meet the code in a Type V One-hour building that could be permitted to be up to 126,000 square feet in size (84,000 + 42,000 = 126,000).

Furthermore, using this design is more feasible than attempting to accomplish the same results in a Type III building due to

- the lesser fire rating required of the area separation wall (2-hour) for Type V buildings and
- the termination at the roof of the area separation wall by use of Section 504.6.4 Exception 3 for the parapet alternative permitted in the Type V building.

The designer should explain the options to the owner before proposing to downgrade the construction of a building. As shown in this example, there are some advantages that may be worth exploring with the owner before deciding on a course of action.

The exceptions in Section 302.1 recognize that there are inherent ancillary or auxiliary uses in addition to the primary use or occupancy. These include the following:

- Offices in connection with public garages, for example, where the parking fees are paid and the record of the vehicle location is kept: These offices are normally small rooms.
- Administrative offices for principals in schools: These Group B Occupancies need not be separated from the Group E Occupancy, provided they do not have excessive floor areas. Similarly for B uses in hotel lobbies or the administrative offices in hotels.

The 25 percent limitation is the code's means of recognizing the relationship the related activities have to the major use.

In the authors' opinion, the general rule to use is that the auxiliary space should

- be less hazardous, as evaluated from the Table 5-B allowables and
- involve a larger occupant load factor from Table 10-A, i.e., 100 square feet/ person vs. 20 square feet/person.

302.2 Forms of Occupancy Separations. Occupancy separations shall be vertical or horizontal or both or, when necessary, of such other form as may be required to afford a complete separation between the various occupancy divisions in the building.

Where the occupancy separation is horizontal, structural members supporting the separation shall be protected by equivalent fire-resistive construction.

The various occupancies within a mixed occupancy building can generally exist located in almost any spatial relationship to one another. The occupancy separation may be vertical or horizontal or a combination of both. (See Figure 5-2.)

The supports for an occupancy separation are required to have at least the same fire-resistive rating as that of the member being supported. (See Figure 5-3.)

Assume the occupancy separation is a wall requiring a 2-hour rating by Table 3-B, such as between an H-2 and a B Occupancy. See Figure 5-3. That wall is supported by a floor system that rests in turn on a bearing wall directly beneath the 2-hour wall. The

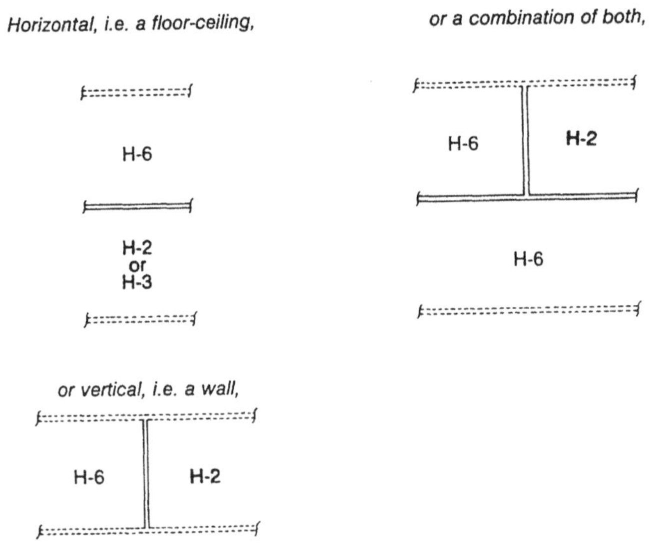

An occupancy separation may occur either in the horizontal or vertical plane. In some instances there will be both a vertical and horizontal component to the separation. Note that in addition to the fire-resistive rating of the wall or floor as required in Section 302.3 and Table 3-B, there are specific limits set in Section 302.3 for openings in the separation. These limits include the fire-resistive rating for the opening protection as well as percentage limits for the amount of opening permitted in a given surface.

REFERENCE: SECTION 302.2

FIGURE 5-2 FORMS OF OCCUPANCY SEPARATION

lower wall separates H-3 and B Occupancy areas located directly below the respective H-2 and B Occupancies.

Because the lower wall need only have a 1-hour rating by Table 3-B (H-3/B in the matrix) and because the floor between the H-2 and H-3 Occupancies similarly need only be 1-hour rated, both the floor system and the upper wall could fail in just over one hour from a fire located in the H-3 area. Were this to happen, the 2-hour wall between the H-2 and B areas would collapse because the supporting wall below it would have failed. Fire, therefore, would attack the upper-level B Occupancy and expose it to the hazards of the H-2 Occupancy in 1 hour, instead of the 2 hours intended by the code.

302.3 Types of Occupancy Separations. Occupancy separations shall be classed as "four-hour fire-resistive," "three-hour fire-resistive," "two-hour fire-resistive," and "one-hour fire-resisitve."

1. A "four-hour fire-resistive occupancy separation" shall have no openings therein and shall be of not less than four-hour fire-resistive construction.

2. A"three-hour fire-resistive occupancy separation" shall be of not less than three-hour fire-resistive construction. All openings In walls forming such separation shall be protected by a fire assembly having a three-hour fire-protection rating. The total width of all openings in any three-hour fire-resistive occupancy separation wall in any one story shall not exceed 25 percent of the length of the wall in that story and no single opening shall have an area greater than 120 square feet.

All openings in floors forming a "three-hour fire-resistive occupancy separation" shall be protected by vertical enclosures extending above and below such openings. The walls of such vertical enclosures shall be of not less than two-hour fire-resistive construction and all openings therein shall be protected by a fire assembly having a one and one-half-hour fire-protection rating.

EXCEPTION: When the walls of such enclosure extending below the three-hour fire-separation to the foundation are provided with a fire-resistive rating of not less than three hours with openings therein protected as required for walls forming three-hour occupancy separations, the enclosure walls extending above such floor used as the three-hour fire-resistive occupancy separation may have a one-hour fire-resistive rating, provided:

1. The occupancy above is not required to be of Type I or II fire-resistive construction, and

2. The enclosure walls do not enclose an exit stairway, a ramp or an escalator required to have enclosure walls of not less than two-hour fire-resistive construction.

3. A "two-hour fire-resistive occupancy separation" shall be of not less than two-hour fire-resistive construction. All openings in such separation shall be protected by a fire assembly having a one and one-half-hour fire-protection rating.

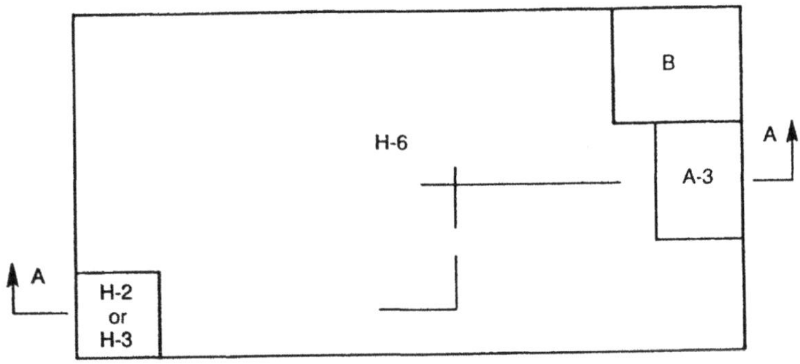

PLAN 1st FLOOR

OCCUPANCY SEPARATIONS PER TABLE NO. 5-B

		Wall Requirement	Opening Protection
On 1st Floor	B /A-3	N	N
	H-6/A-3	3-hour	3-hour
	H-6/B	1-hour	1-hour
	H-6/H-2	2-hour	1½-hour
	H-6/H-3	1-hour	1-hour
Between 1st and 2nd Floor	B /A-3	N	N
	B /H-2	2-hour	1½-hour
	B-2/H-3	1-hour	1-hour
	H-6/A-3	3-hour	3-hour
	H-6/H-2	2-hour	1½-hour
	H-6/H-3	1-hour	1-hour
On 2nd Floor	H-6/B	1-hour	1-hour

N = No fire rating required

In this figure, the hourly rating of the various occupancy separation are tagged on the sectional view.

The table indicates the several fire resistive ratings for the various occupancy separation in accordance with Table 3-B. Also shown are the corresponding opening protection in accordance with the provisions of Section 502.3.

Since the building is of Type II one-hour fire-resistive construction, the one-hour requirements are met. The B/H-2 and H-6/H-2 two-hour requirement mandates the floor of the second story and its supports for the segment over the H-2 occupancy must have two-hour fire resistance to the ground. The three-hour occupancy separation of the second floor over the A-3 Occupancy and its supports similarly must have that rating carried to the ground.

REFERENCE: SECTION 302.2, 302.3 AND TABLE 3-B

FIGURE 5-3 OCCUPANCY SEPARATION REQUIREMENTS

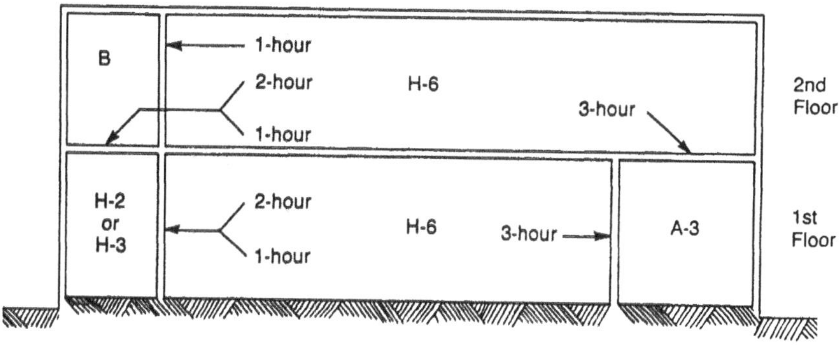

SECTION A-A

ASSUME:
Type II One-hour Building
2 Story
1st Floor as Shown
2nd Floor all H-6 and B

4. A "one-hour fire-resistive occupancy separation" shall be of not less than one-hour fire-resistive construction. All openings in such separation shall be protected by a fire assembly having a one-hour fire-protection rating.

The fire rating of an occupancy separation is determined through the use of Table 3-B. Once the fire-resistive time period is determined, the fire rating and construction limitations for openings in that separation can be located in Section 302.3.

The fire-resistive construction requirements for the elements of the occupancy separation are listed in Chapter 7. The construction requirements for fire assemblies for opening protection in the occupancy separation are found in Section 713. (See Figure 5-3.)

It is important to note that where a 4-hour occupancy separation is required, no openings are allowed in the occupancy separation.

TABLE OF OCCUPANCY SEPARATION PROVISIONS

RATING	OPENING PROTECTION REQUIREMENT HORIZONTAL	VERTICAL
4-hour	No openings allowed	No openings allowed
3-hour	3-hour Aggregate width max. 25%	2-hour vertical enclosure with $1\frac{1}{2}$ hour opening protection
2-hour	$1\frac{1}{2}$ hour	$1\frac{1}{2}$ hour
1-hour	1 hour	1 hour

302.4 Fire Ratings for Occupancy Separations. Occupancy separations shall be provided between the various groups and divisions of occupancies as set forth in Table No. 5-B.

EXCEPTION: 1. A three-hour occupancy separation may be used between a Group A, Division 1 and a Group S, Division 3 Occupancy used exclusively for the parking or storage of private or pleasure-type motor vehicles and provided no repair or fueling Is done. A two-hour occupancy separation may be used between a Group A, Division 2, 2.1, 3 or E or I Occupancy and a Group S, Division 3 Occupancy that Is used exclusively for the parking or storage of private or pleasure-type motor vehicles provided no repair or fueling is done.

2. Unless required by Section 311.2.2, the three-hour occupancy separation between Group R, Division I Occupancy and a Group S, Division 3 Occupancy used only for the parking or storage of private or pleasure-type vehicles with no repair or fueling may be reduced to two hours. Such occupancy separation may be further reduced to one hour where the area of such Group S, Division 3 Occupancy does not exceed 3,000 square feet (279 m^2).

3. In the one-hour occupancy separation between a Group R, Division 3 and U Occupancy, the separation may be limited to the installation of materials approved for one-hour fire-resistive construction on the garage side and a self-closing, tight fitting solid wood door $1\frac{3}{8}$ inches in thickness or a self-closing tightfitting door having a fire-protection rating of not less than 20 minutes when tested in accordance with Part II of U.B.C. Standard 7-2 will be permitted in lieu of a one-hour fire assembly. Fire dampers need not be installed in air ducts passing through the wall, floor or ceiling separating a Group R, Division 3 Occupancy from a Group U Occupancy, provided such ducts within the Group U Occupancy are constructed of steel having a thickness not less than 0.019 inch (0.48 mm) (No. 26 galvanized sheet gage) and having no openings into the Group U Occupancy.

4. Group H, Division 2 and Group H, Division 3 Occupancies need not be separated from Group H, Division 7 Occupancies when such occupancies also comply with the requirements for a Group H, Division 7 Occupancy.

When two different occupancies are adjacent to each other, either horizontally or vertically, a fire-resistive occupancy separation is usually required. The Table 3-B matrix provides the required fire-resistive time rating for the occupancy separation.

The constructions required to meet the time period are found in Tables 7-B and 7-C. These tables list various constructions and their respective fire-resistive time values. As stated in Article 8 of this Guide, other listings and means of obtaining acceptance of assemblies are available to be used.

The occupancy separation must completely separate the two different occupancies.

- If the occupancies are side by side, the separation takes the form of a wall.
- If one occupancy is below the other, the separation involves a floor-ceiling assembly. See Figure 5-2.

In either case, the supporting structure for the occupancy separation must have a fire-resistive rating at least equal to that of the occupancy separation as was stated in the discussion of Section 302.2 in this Guide. (See Figure 5-4.)

Exceptions 2 and 3 of this section relate to the garages in residential buildings. It should be clearly understood that Exception 2 relates to Group U-type garages and not to all public garages, (Group S, Division 3). That limitation is indicated by the 3000 square foot area allowed.

This is consistent with both the Section 309.2 and Table 3-B provisions that allow Group R, Division 1 buildings to contain Group U garages with a reduction in the fire-resistive separation. This reduction is warranted due to the limitation of

- the overall size of the garage and
- the type of vehicles, the ones allowed being passenger cars generally owned by tenants of the building.

In Exception 3, the code refers to the garage attached to a single- or two-family dwelling. The requirement for the separation between garage and dwelling considers the general nonfire-resistive construction of the building and requires only that the garage side surface be covered with a type of material used to make a fire-resistive assembly, for example, $\frac{5}{8}$-inch Type X wallboard and a $1\frac{3}{8}$-inch solid core door with closer.

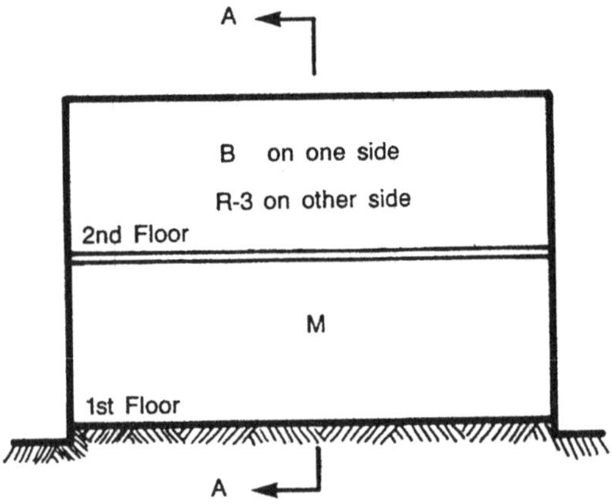

ELEVATION

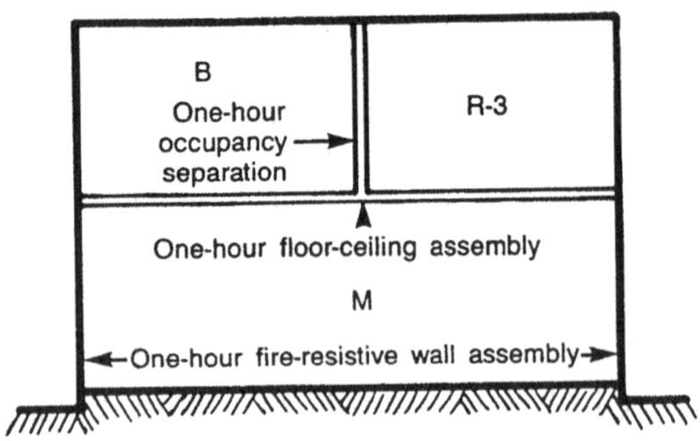

SECTION A-A

In Section A-A, the floor ceiling occupancy separation between the Group B and the U occupancies has to be one-hour fire rated construction. Similarly, there must be a one-hour occupancy separation wall between the B and R-3 Occupancies per Table 3-B.

The supports for the floor-ceiling assembly, per section 302.2 must be one-hour construction. This requirement is more restrictive than the Group R-3/U separation requirement. Thus, the entire floor-ceiling assembly over this garage arrangement ans its supporting walls must have at least one-hour construction.

REFERENCE: SECTIONS 302.2, 310.2.2 AND TABLE 3-B

FIGURE 5-4 OCCUPANCY SEPARATION REQUIREMENTS, GROUP R, DIVISION 3 & GROUP B AND U OCCUPANCIES

This required protection applies not only to the ceiling in the case of a room above the garage but also to the following situations:

- Walls providing the support of the ceiling, because a fire in the garage would attack both the ceiling and walls: If the walls were unprotected, a failure of the wall would cause a breach of the protection formed by the ceiling.
- Piping, tubing and duct work that penetrate the required separation: These elements are required to be fire-stopped so that a fire cannot bypass the surface of the membrane.

Exception 3 was clarified to permit a tested and labeled smoke and draft-stop door meeting the UBC Standard 7-2 test requirements for use in this location without regard to the door's thickness or material of construction.

The prior code text appeared to have precluded the acceptance of a tested door that met the performance requirements in lieu of an untested door of stated thickness. The door that meets the UBC Standard 7-2 requirements will be a gasketed door satisfying the tight-fitting provision.

Table 3-B

In Table 3-B the requirement for a 1-hour occupancy separation between Group B Occupancy and a Group R, Division 3 Occupancy is more restrictive than the occupancy separation between Group R, Division 3 and a Group U Occupancy.

In the case of a Group R, Division 3 building with a dwelling unit being used for an office or business purpose (Group B use) as now required in Table 3-B, there must be an occupancy separation between the two occupancies. Per Section 302.4, Exception 3 and Table 3-B, the code does not require a full 1-hour occupancy separation, however, between the Group R, Division 3 and a Group U garage occupancy. Per Section 302.4, Exception 3, the separation and the supporting structure need only have the covering of a 1-hour assembly. Openings therein may have a solid-core door with closer instead of a 1-hour fire assembly.

The Group B Occupancy must be separated from both the Group U and the Group R, Division 3 Occupancies by 1-hour fire-resistive construction. As shown in Figure 5-4, the entire horizontal separation and its supporting structure must be of at least 1-hour fire-resistive construction. Per Section 302.2, the horizontal occupancy separation must be supported by 1-hour fire-resistive construction. These more restrictive provisions take precedence over the exceptions for the Group R, Division 3 Occupancy.

Chapter 4 Special Use and Occupancy

SECTION 402—ATRIA

402.1 General. Buildings, of other than Group H, with automatic sprinkler protection throughout may have atria complying with the provisions of this section. Such atria shall have a minimum opening area and dimension as set forth in Table 4-A.

The designer should note that an atrium exists only when the opening is through two or more floors and not when through a single floor. Floor penetrations are permitted through a single floor for shafts, stairs and escalators, without special requirements, by the provisions in Sections 711 and 1005.3.3.1. (See Figure 5-5.)

The requirements for atria are

- an automatic sprinkler system throughout the building,
- a smoke control system so that the building does not get smoke-logged and
- compliance with the provisions of Section 403 (the high-rise life safety requirements) for
  a. stand-by power and
  b. handling of the smoke control system within the occupied spaces of the building.

Exit balconies may be open to the atrium without any separation between the balcony and the atrium space provided the balconies

- are sprinklered and
- have smoke-tight doors into the tenant spaces, either self-closing or automatic-closing by a smoke detector-operated release device.

The minimum spatial criteria for the atrium is set forth in Table 4-A and is dependent on the height of the atrium in stories. These minimum limits are required in order to provide a sufficiently large volume for dissipation of smoke to be handled by the smoke control system. The combustibility of the atrium furnishings is regulated under the Fire Code. The designer should discuss these regulations

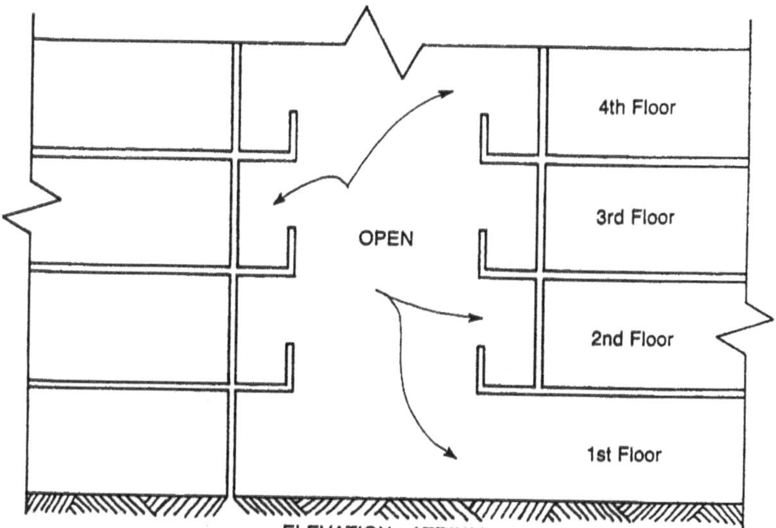

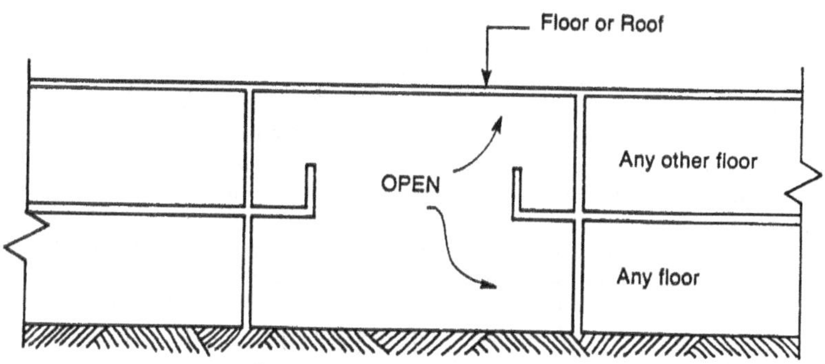

REFERENCE: SECTION 402

FIGURE 5-5 ATRIUM, DEFINITION

with the fire service to assure that the combustible loading and smoke generation limits of the furnishings are not exceeded. The atrium smoke control provisions are detailed and specialized and will not be discussed in detail in this Guide.

402.2 Smoke-control System. A smoke-control system meeting the requirements of Section 905 shall be provided within the atrium and areas open to the atrium. The smoke-control system shall operate automatically upon actuation of the automatic sprinkler system within the atrium or areas open to the atrium as required by Section 905.9.

Smoke control systems, an integral part of the atriun design, should be left to a qualified fire protection engineer or mechanical engineer. The requirements adopted in the 1994 UBC were a major departure from the previous smoke control provisions. The new requirements require a "designed" system.

402.3 Enclosure of Atria. Atria shall be separated from adjacent spaces by not less than one-hour fire-resistive construction.

EXCEPTIONS: 1. The separation between atria and tenants spaces that are not guest rooms, congregate residences or dwelling units may be omitted at three floor levels.

2. Open exit balconies are permitted within the atrium.

Openings in the atrium enclosure other than fixed glazing shall be protected by smoke- and draft-control assemblies conforming to Section 1004.3.4.3.2.

EXCEPTION: Other tight-fitting doors which are maintained automatic closing, in accordance with Section 713.2, by actuation of a smoke detector or self-closing may be used when protected as required for glazed openings in Exception 2 below.

Fixed glazed openings in the atrium enclosure shall be equipped with fire windows having a fire-resistive rating of not less than three-fourths hour and the total area of such openings shall not exceed 25 percent of the area of the common wall between the atrium and the room Into which the opening is provided.

EXCEPTIONS: 1. In Group R, Division I Occupancies, openings may be unprotected when the floor area of each guest room, congregate residence, or dwelling unit does not exceed 1,000 square feet and each room or unit has an approved exit not entering the atrium.

2. Guest rooms, dwelling units, congregate residences and tenant spaces may be separated from the atrium by approved fixed wired glass set in steel frames. in lieu thereof, tempered or laminated glass or listed glass block may be used subject to the following:

2.1 The glass shall be protected by a sprinkler system equipped with listed quick-response sprinklers. The sprinkler system shall completely wet the entire surface of the glass wall when actuated. Where there are walking surfaces on both sides of the glass, both sides of the glass shall be so protected.

2.2 The tempered or laminated glass shall be in a gasketed frame so installed that the glazing system may deflect without breaking (loading) the glass before the sprinkler system operates.

2.3 The glass block wall assembly shall be installed in accordance with its listing for a three--fourths-hour fire-resistive rating and Section 2110.

2.4 Obstructions such as curtain rods, drapery traverse rods, curtains, drapes or similar materials, shall not be installed between the sprinkler and the glass.

Section 402.3 provides the requirement for the atrium enclosure walls. The key provision in the exception to the first paragraph permits use of open exit balconies facing the atrium. The third paragraph permits the use of glazed walls fronting directly onto the atrium. The requirements for the glazing are stated with the details of the permitted construction.

Plain glass is allowed, in the exception to the third paragraph, for Group R, Division 1 Occupancies with specific limitations.

The use of quick-response sprinklers is required by the present code to protect the plain glass, provided the heads are listed. Prior codes had a temperature designation for the sprinkler heads adjacent to the atrium glazing. The availability and preferability of the listed quick-response sprinkler heads take precedent over the temperature characteristic.

Thus, the deletion of the temperature designation in favor of the quick-response characteristic results from an improved performance requirement. The listed requirement is defined in Exception 2.1 to the third paragraph of Section 402.3. The new heads must have been tested by an accredited independent agency.

This reflects the increasing emphasis on the use of the new generation of sprinkler heads. Prior to the development of the quick-response head, the usual method for obtaining fast action from a sprinkler head was to require a lower temperature actuation mechanism.

The new sprinkler head is constructed in such a way that it reduces the heat sink lag time and thereby accelerates the action of the release mechanism. These heads are tested and manufactured by several sprinkler companies.

The allowance of plain glass is a less restrictive provision that recognizes the suites now popular in atrium construction. The code allows guest rooms, dwelling units and tenant spaces to face directly on the atrium, provided the openings are protected by any of the following (see Figure 5-6):

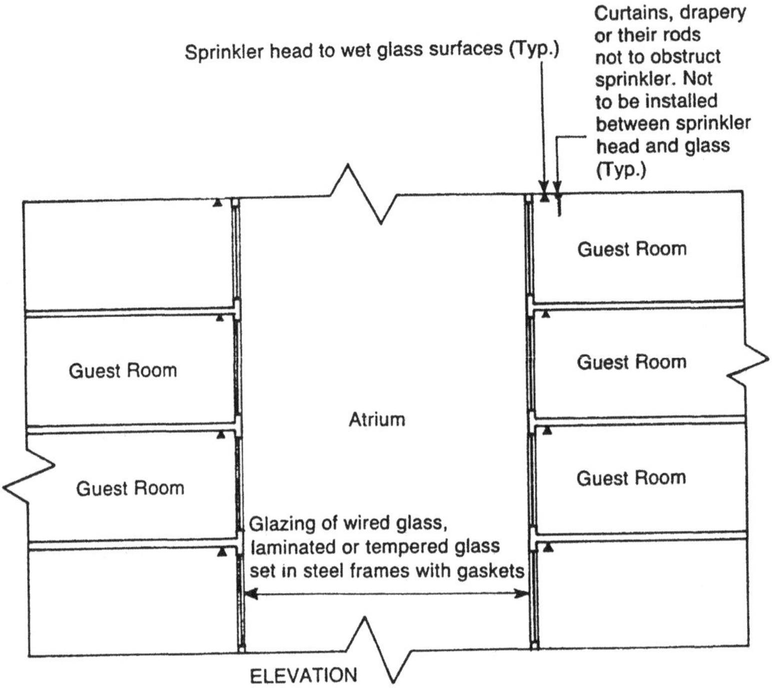

REFERENCE: SECTION 402.3, PARAGRAPH 3, EXCEPTION 2

FIGURE 5-6 ATRIUM AND ADJACENT ROOMS

- Fixed wired glass set in steel frames,
- Tempered glass set in steel frames and
- Laminated glass set in steel frames.

When any of the glazing cited above is used, the criteria governing the glazing as described in Items 2.1, 2.2 and 2.3 of Exception 2 apply.

The exception to Section 402.3 permits the omission of the otherwise required opening protection on not more than three floor levels, provided all other floors have the required protection. This provision is consistent with the covered-mall provisions in Section 404.

SECTION 409—PEDESTRIAN WALKWAYS

409.1 General. A pedestrian walkway shall be considered a building when determining the roof covering permitted by Table 15-A. Pedestrian walkways connecting separate buildings need not be considered as buildings and need not be considered in the determination of the allowable floor area of the connected buildings when the pedestrian walkway complies with the provisions of this section.

.
.
.

409.7 Required Means of Egress. Pedestrian walkways at other than grades shall not be used as a means of egress. Pedestrian walkways at grade level used as required means of egress shall be unobstructed and shall have a minimum width in accordance with Chapter 10.

EXCEPTION: Pedestrian walkways conforming to the requirements of a horizontal exit may be used as a required means of egress.

This section regulates the connections between buildings, including those that may be on different properties. The provisions include ground-level connections, such as covered arcades, and elevated connections or bridges. The "skyways" in Minneapolis are examples of the latter type.

The intent of this section is to permit such facilities, but not to include them, in the floor area calculations for the buildings to which they are attached and to require the necessary construction to protect buildings and users of the walkways.

The exception in the provisions in Section 409.7 allows the use of a passageway between buildings, i.e., a connecting bridge, to be used as an exit way provided it conforms to the requirements for a horizontal exit.

This type of construction, where two or more buildings are interconnected via bridges, has increasingly been used as a design tool. All too often, however, the designer and the building official have failed to realize that additional protection is required when the bridge is used as an exit way. Section 409.7 makes a clear statement of what has logically been the legal requirement for such use.

Chapter 5 General Building Limitations

SECTION 502—PREMISES IDENTIFICATION

Approved numbers of addresses shall be provided for all new buildings In such a position as to be plainly visible and legible from the street or road fronting the property.

This provision may seem to be an odd requirement to be placed in a building code. However, to provide emergency services, the fire department must be able to identify the location of the building.

Often when an alarm is phoned in and an address given, the fire in question may not be visible from the fire department's approach side of the building. The only means of identifying the location of the fire is the building address. It is for such emergency reasons that the code mandates that the address be visibly located.

SECTION 503—LOCATION ON PROPERTY

Section 503 contains the siting requirements applicable to individual buildings.

503.2 Fire Resistance of Walls.

503.2.1 General. Exterior walls shall have fire resistance and opening protection as set forth in Table 5-A, and in accordance with such additional provisions as are set forth in Chapter 6. Distance shall be measured at right angles from the property line. The above provisions shall not apply to walls at right angles to the property line.

Projection beyond the exterior wall shall not extend beyond:

1. A point one-third the distance to the property line from an assumed vertical plane located where fire-resistive protection of openings is first required due to location on the property; or

2. More than 12 inches into areas where openings are prohibited.

503.2.2 Area of Openings. Where openings in exterior walls are required to be protected due to distance from property line, the sum of the area of such openings shall not exceed 50 percent of the total area of the wall in each story.

The requirements of Section 503.2 relate to the proximity of the building to adjacent property lines. The intent is to avoid the hazard of conflagration—fire spreading from one property to the next.

The required fire resistance of an exterior wall is dependent on the distance that wall is from the adjacent property line and on the use or occupancy of the building in question. The farther away, the lesser the degree of required fire protection.

The fire-resistive time ratings required are set forth in Table 5-A for all buildings of Type II One-hour, II-N and V construction. The wall and opening protection requirements for buildings of Type I, II-FR, III and IV construction are outlined in Sections 602.3, 603.3, 604.3, 605.3 and 606.3—the .3 sections referred to hereinafter.

For most occupancies, the Table 5-A provisions require the exterior wall to be fire-rated when the wall is less than 10 feet from the property line. If the wall is more than 10 feet from the property line, it may have unprotected openings (i.e., plain glass windows).

For other occupancies, however, the specific provisions vary from these general 10-foot distances.

There are instances when the "fixed" property line of a lot can be "moved" to accommodate the exterior wall fire protection requirements for a building.

1. The adjacent property is permanently and legally declared open space (cannot be built on), such as railroad rights-of-way, green belts or parks, streets and alleys.
2. A permanent deed restriction, acceptable to the enforcement authority, declaring that a specific width of the space on the other property is to be kept free of buildings or structures, based on rulings made by the enforcement authority to meet code requirements of the jurisdiction. When such deed restrictions require that any changes in the restrictions must have the approval of the enforcement authority, there is assurance that public concern is protected.

This method of determining the exterior wall construction requirements has been used many times, but it does require individual approval by the enforcement authority. The text of the deed restriction must provide clear and permanent assurance of the equivalence of the movement of the property line involved. (See Figures 5-8 and 5-9.) Note that any change in the location of the moved property line will require a reassessment of the effect on the two buildings.

The eave projection provision of Sections 503.2 and 1204 limits the projection where openings in the exterior wall are prohibited to not more than 12 inches. See Case A and B of Figure 5-7.

In using these two criteria, the first provision involves the establishment of an assumed vertical plane parallel to the property line and at a distance equal to the dimension specified in Table 5-A or the -03 sections referenced above at which opening protection is first required.

For example, for a Group B Occupancy in a Type V building, Table 5-A requires protection of openings when the exterior wall is 5 feet from the property line. Section 503.2.1, Item 1, therefore, allows a projection of 20 inches (60/3 = 20). Thus, this criterion would allow the edge of the roof overhang to be within 40 inches (3 feet 4 inches) of the property line. However, openings are prohib-

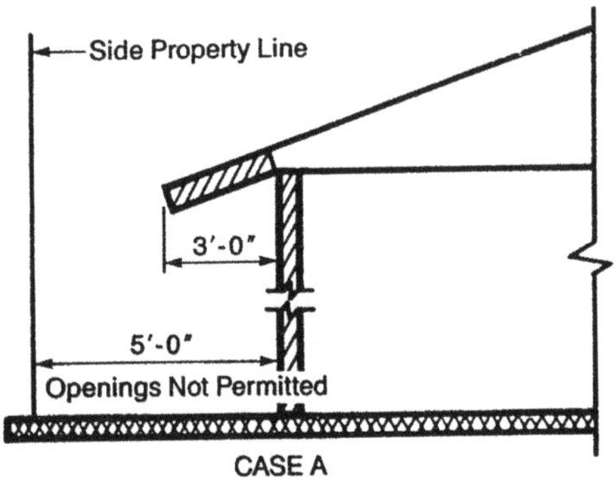

CASE A

ASSUME: 3'-0" Eave desired

VERIFY: Is eave code complying?

Type V Building, Group R, Div.1 Occupancy

Distance to property for unprotected openings = 5'-0" (60")

1/3 x 60" = 20"

Maximum eave projection may not exceed 20". However, as eave projects into space where openings are not permitted, maximum projection is 12". Eave must be reduced to 12".

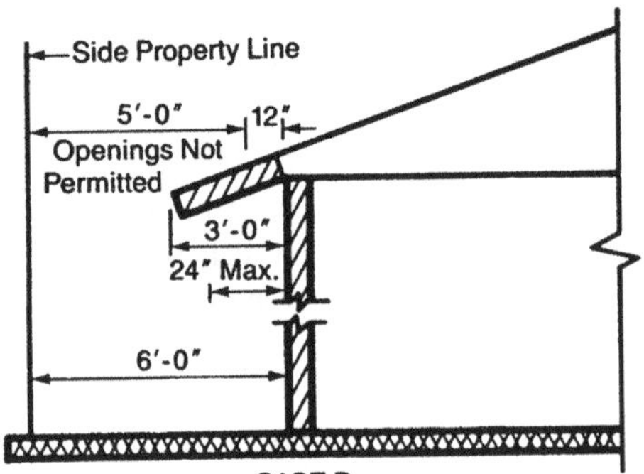

CASE B

ASSUME: 3'-0" Eave desired

VERIFY: Is eave code complying?

Type V Building, Group R, Div. 1 Occupancy

Distance to property for unprotected openings = 5'-0" (60")

1/3 x 60" = 20"

Maximum eave projection may not exceed 20". However, as eave projects into space where openings are not permitted, maximum projection is 12". Eave must be cut back to 24" from exterior wall.

REFERENCE: SECTION 503.2

FIGURE 5-7 PROJECTION BEYOND EXTERIOR WALL (EAVE)

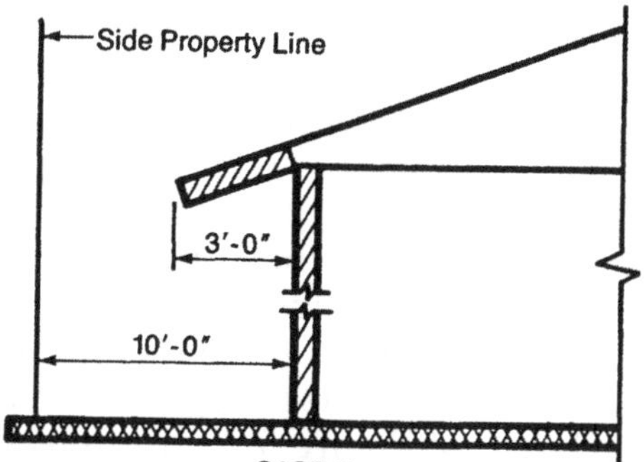

CASE C

ASSUME: 3'-0" Eave desired

VERIFY: Is eave code complying?

Type V Building, Group B Occupancy

Openings not permitted within 5'-0" of property line.

Distance to property line for unprotected openings is 10'-0".

As maximum setback of exterior wall is 10', the maximum eave projection may be 3'-4"; (10'/3). Therefore, the 3'-0" eave projection is OK.

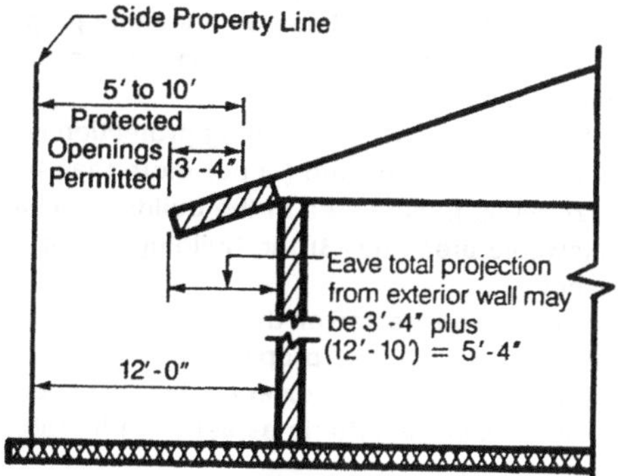

CASE D

ASSUME: Type V Building, Group B Occupancy

DETERMINE: Maximum permitted eave projection

10'/3 = 3'-4"

However, as the exterior wall is 12' from the property line, the total eave projection may be 3'-4" + 2' = 5'-4".

ited in Table 5-A when the exterior wall is within 5 feet of the property line. Item 2 of this section limits the projection in such instances to not more than 12 inches. Because this is more restrictive, Item 2 controls, and the projection therefore cannot exceed 12 inches.

With the exterior wall when openings are prohibited within 3 feet of the property line, the effect of either provision will be the same.

The benefit of Item 1 occurs when the building is located a greater distance than the minimum for prohibited openings. Using our example building and locating the exterior wall 8 feet from the property line, we get the following permissible projection:

The assumed vertical plane of when opening protection is first required from Table 5-A is 10 feet from the property line. Because the exterior wall of the building is 8 feet from the property line, Item 1 allows 10/3 or 3 feet 4 inches projection from the assumed plane. As shown in Case C of Figure 5-7, this allows the projection to be 3 feet 4 inches from the exterior wall toward the property line.

If the exterior wall of the building was located 12 feet from the property line, the projection allowed would again be 3 feet 4 inches (10/3) and the overall projection could be 5 feet 4 inches. This is the 3 feet 4 inches plus the greater setback of 2 feet 0 inches for the building's exterior wall. See Case D of Figure 5-7.

503.3 Buildings on the Same Property and Buildings Containing Courts. For the purposes of determining the required wall and opening protection and roof-covering requirements, buildings on the same property and court walls of buildings over one story in height shall be assumed to have a property line between them.

EXCEPTION: In court walls where opening protection Is required such protection may be omitted, provided (1) not more than two levels open Into the court, (2) the aggregate area of the building including the court is within the allowable area and (3) the building Is not classified as a Group I Occupancy.

When a new building is to be erected on the same property with an existing building, the location of the assumed property line with the relation to the existing building shall be such that the exterior wall and opening protection of the existing building meet the criteria as set forth in Table No. 5-A and Chapter 6.

EXCEPTION: Two or more buildings on the same property may be considered as portions of one building if the aggregate area of such buildings is within the limits specified In Section 504 for a single building.

When the buildings so considered house different occupancies or are of different types of construction, the area shall be that allowed for the most restricted occupancy or construction.

In Section 503.3, the requirements relate to the proximity of one building to another on the same property or site.

The designer should be aware that the requirements of Sections 503.2 and 503.3 must not be intermixed or misapplied.

The property line of the lot to which the Section 503.2 provisions apply is fixed on the record and not "movable." As stated in the discussion of that section, that property line can be "moved" on paper for fire protection considerations. That line lies between separate properties and buildings.

On the other hand, the assumed property line in the first paragraph of Section 503.3 applies to multiple buildings on the same property.

The more restrictive provisions are mandatory in their application to the building's relationship to the fixed property line of an adjacent property and not to the building line of an adjacent structure on the same property. The provisions of Section 503.3 permit the designer, not the enforcement official, to locate the "movable assumed" property line between two buildings on the same lot. (See Figure 5-8.)

For conditions whereby the "fixed" property line may be "moved," see the discussion in Section 503.2.

Except for the wall requirements relating to a court, in no instance are the exterior wall requirements ever applicable to a wall or occupancy within a building as it relates to another wall or occupancy within the same building. The exterior wall requirements apply only to a wall as it relates to another building or property line of an adjacent property.

The key provision in this section, stated in the second paragraph, allows the placement of a theoretical property line between the buildings on the same property. This flexibility permits the designer to determine the exterior wall construction that best suits the design. The designer can make use of the existing construction of the adjacent building to assist in that design.

For example, assume the existing building is a Type V One-hour warehouse with nonbearing concrete walls and no openings near the new building, as shown in Figure 5-9.

In the examples listed in Figure 5-9, the new building, Type III-N, can be located in relation to the assumed property line as if the line were a real property line.

For siting of a new Group B building, where the wall of the existing building has a 4-hour rating, the property line can be assumed to lie at the face of the wall; where the wall has a 2-hour

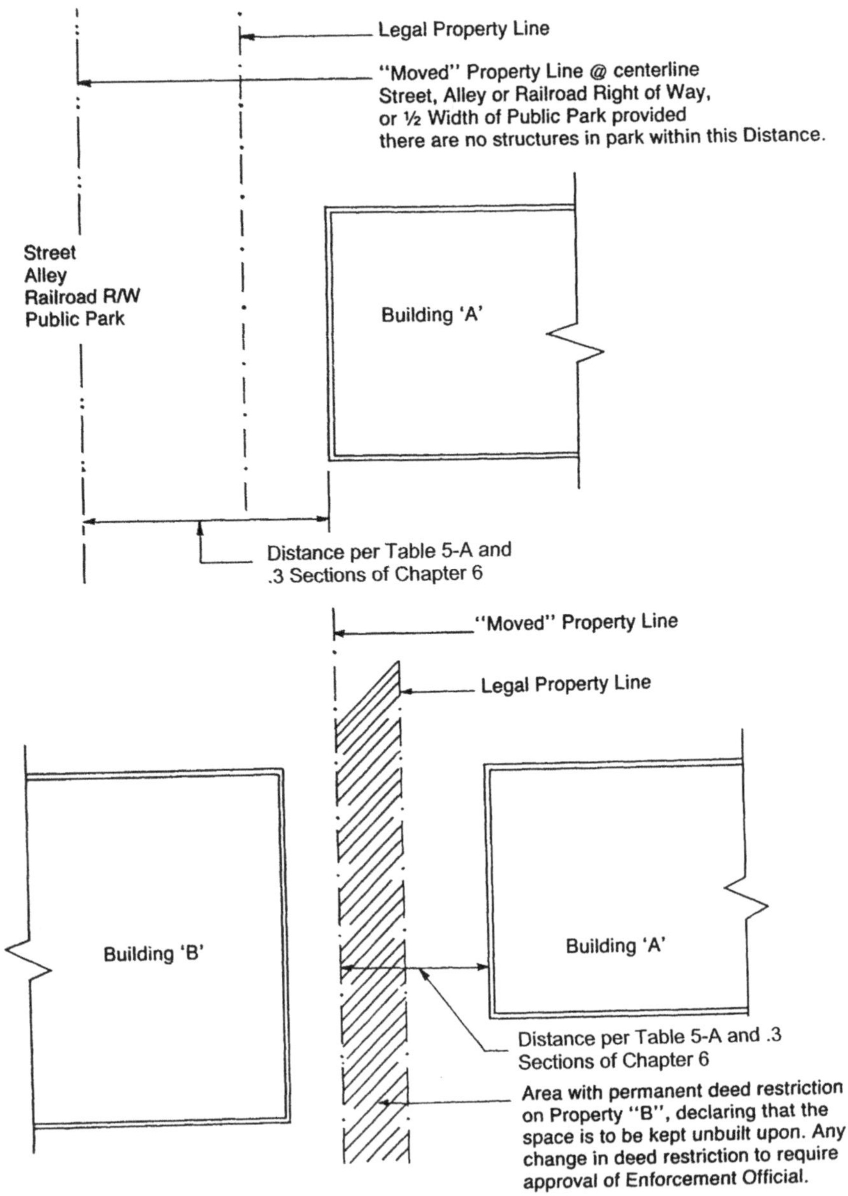

REFERENCE: SECTIONS 503.3, 602.3, 603.3, 604.3, 605.3, 606.3 and TABLE 5-A

FIGURE 5-8 EXTERIOR WALL REQUIREMENTS–ADJUSTMENT OF PROPERTY LINE

rating, the property line can be assumed to be 5 feet from that wall; where the wall has a 1-hour rating, the property line can be assumed to be 20 feet from the wall.

NOTE: If the existing building has walls at least 7.5 inches thick, then per Table 7-B Item 6-1.1 the wall has a 4-hour fire-resistance rating; if at least 5.5 inches thick it has a 2-hour rating; if at least 4 inches thick, it has a 1-hour rating.

Other variations of siting are possible, and are limited only by the imagination of the designer and the physical conditions present.

SECTION 504—ALLOWABLE FLOOR AREAS

504.2 Areas of Buildings Over One Story. The total combined floor area for multistory buildings may be twice that permitted by Table No. 5-C for one-story buildings, and the floor area of any single story shall not exceed that permitted for a one-story building.

The basic allowable floor area for a one story building is provided in Table 5-B. When there is a multistoried building, the aggregate basic allowable area is not to exceed two times the Table 5-B values. Thus, if there is a two-story building, each story can have the area permitted in Table 5-B. When the building contains more than two stories, the maximum area of any one story is still limited to the value in Table 5-B; however, the sum of the areas of all stories still must not exceed two times the Table 5-B value.

Therefore, in a three-story building with equal floor areas on each floor, and notwithstanding any allowable area increases for separations or sprinklers, each floor cannot have more than two times the basic allowable floor area per Table 5-B divided by three. If the basic allowable floor area for a Type V 1-hour building with a Group B Occupancy is 14,000 square feet, a three-story Group B Occupancy building can have three stories of $14{,}000 \times 2/3 = 9333$ square feet per story. If the building had four stories, the maximum allowable area per floor would be 7000 square feet. (See Figure 5-10.)

504.3 Allowable Floor Area of Mixed Occupancies. When a building houses more than one occupancy, the area of the building shall be such that the sum of the ratios of the actual area for each separate occupancy divided by the allowable area for each separate occupancy shall not exceed one.

EXCEPTIONS: 1. The major occupancy classification of a building may be used to determine the allowable area of such building when the major

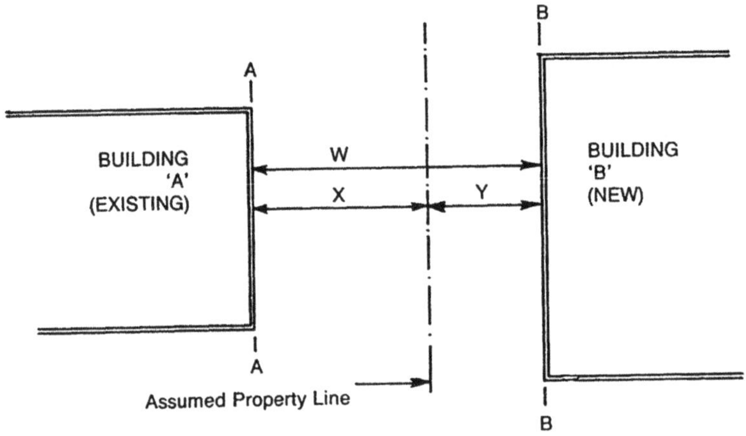

Property line may be located at any distance from the two buildings, depending on the most advantageous distances to the designer.

Distances X + Y = W.

The respective distances X and Y will be based on the provisions of Table 5-A and the .3 section in Chapter 6. There are a large number of variables which will permit the width "W" to vary from about o' to 40' depending on the types of construction and occupancies involved in each building. See also Section 503.

Example: Building A = Type V One-hour, Group B Occupancy
Building B = Type III-N, Group B Occupancy

To illustrate the large number of possibilities the designer may have in any particular instance, the following example is used. For illustrative purposes the "X" and "Y" dimensions have been assigned letter designations. Thus, a combination of 'C + G' is the "X" designated 'C' dimension of 20' and the "Y" designated 'G' dimension of 20' with a total width of 40'. Similarly the combination of 'C + P' has a "Y" dimension of 1" resulting in a total dimension of 20'-1", which is noted as 20'+

For each different occupancy and combination of occupancies there will be a different set of dimensions possible. The designer can readily develop similar tables of variables for any particular project.

FIGURE 5-9 EXTERIOR WALL–PROPERTY LINE RELATIONSHIP, BUILDING ON SAME PROPERTY

Property Line

Existing Bldg. 'A' Type V One-Hr, B WALL 'A-A'				New Bldg. 'B' Type III-N, B WALL 'B-B'			
"X" Comb.	Fire-Resistant Rating	Opening Protection	Setback from PL	"Y" Comb.	Setback from PL	Fire-Resistant Rating	Opening Protection
C	N	N.O.	20′+	G	20′+	N	N.O.
D	N	N	20′+	H	20′+	N	N
E	1-Hr.	N.O.	1″±	J	10′+	1-Hr.	N.O.
F	1-Hr.	¾ Hr.	5′+	K	10′+	1-Hr.	¾ Hr.
				L	5′+	2-Hr.	N.O.
				M	5′+	2-Hr.	¾ Hr.
				P	1″±	4-Hr.	N.O.

Comb. = Assigned reference combination for X or Y
N.O. = No Openings
N = No Rating Required

TOTAL COMBINATION OF POSSIBILITIES

Comb.	X	Y	W	Comb.	X	Y	W
C+G	20′+	20′+	40′+	E+G	1″±	20′+	20′+
+H	"	"	"	+H	"	"	"
+J	"	10′+	30′+	+J	"	10′+	10′+
+K	"	"	"	+K	"	"	"
+L	"	5′+	25′+	+L	"	5′+	5′+
+M	"	"	25′+	+M	"	"	"
+P	"	1″±	20′+	+P	"	1″±	2″±
D+G	"	20′+	40′+	F+G	5′	20′+	25′+
+H	"	"	"	+H	"	"	"
+J	"	10′+	30′+	+J	"	10′+	15′+
+K	"	"	"	+K	"	"	"
+L	"	5′+	25′+	+L	"	5′+	10′+
+M	"	"	"	+M	"	"	"
+P	"	1″±	20′+	+P	"	1″±	5′+

REFERENCE: SECTION 503.3, 604.3.1, 604.3.2 and TABLE 5-A

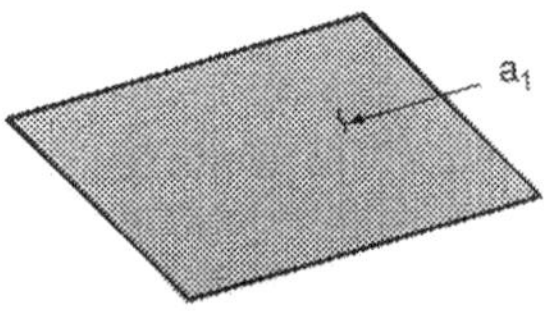

Basic Floor Area
One Story Building
Maximum a_1 = Value per Table No. 5-B
= 14,000 s.f. maximum

EXAMPLE 1

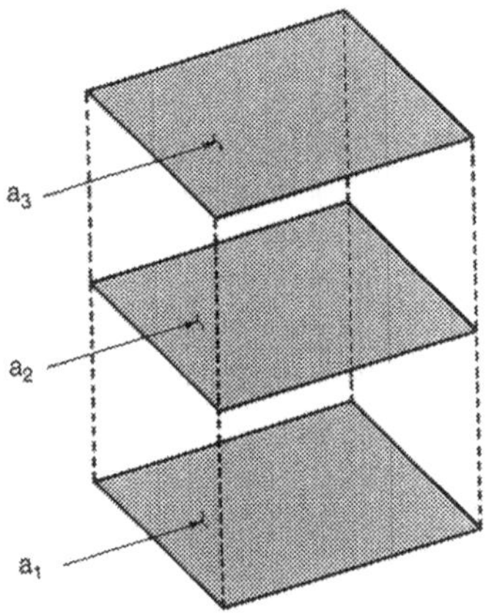

Multistoried Building
$a_1 + a_2 + a_3 => 2 \times a_1$
$=> 2 \times$ value per Table No. 5-B

EXAMPLE 3

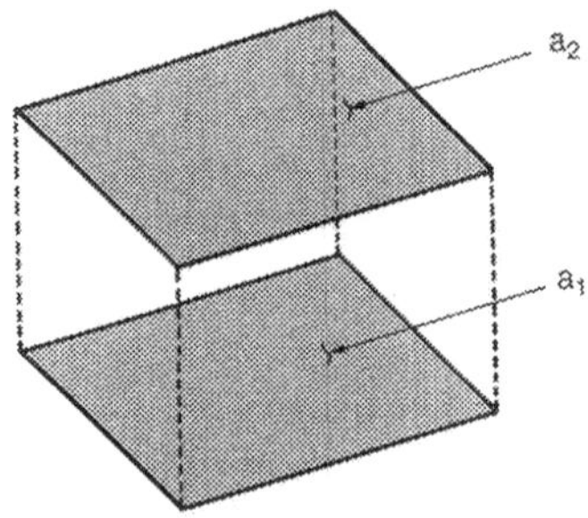

Two Story Building
Maximum area building = $2 \times a_1$
= $2 \times$ value in Table No. 5-B

EXAMPLE 2

For any number of storied building
$a_1 + a_2 + a_3 + a_n => 2 \times a_1$
where a_1 = value from Table No. 5-B

Assume a Type V One-hour Building, Group B, Division 2 Occupancy with each floor of the same area
To obtain the maximum size of each floor
In Example 1: a_1 = 14,000 s.f. maximum
In Example 2: $a_1 + a_2$ = 14,000 s.f. maximum each
In Example 3: $a_1 + a_2 + a_3 = 14{,}000 \times 2/3 = 9{,}333$ s.f.
If there were six stories in the building, the maximum floor area per floor
= 14,000 s.f. $\times$ 2/6 = 4,667 s.f. each

REFERENCE: SECTION 504.3

FIGURE 5-10 ALLOWABLE AREA CALCULATIONS WITHOUT AREA INCREASES OR SEPARATIONS OR SPRINKLERS

use occupies not less than 90 percent of the area of any floor of the building and provided that other minor uses shall not exceed the basic area permitted by Table 5-B for such minor uses and that various uses are separated as specified in Section 302.4.

2. Groups B, F, M and S and Group H, Division 5 Occupancies complying with the provisions of Section 502.2 may contain other occupancies provided that such occupancies do not occupy more than 10 percent of the area of any floor of a building, nor more than the basic area permitted in the occupancy by Table 5-B for such occupancy, and further provided that such occupancies are separated as specified in Section 302.4.

Where minor accessory uses do not occupy more than 10 percent of the area of any floor of a building, nor more than the basic allowable area permitted in the occupancy by Table 5-B for such minor use, for the purpose of determining allowable area the major use of the building shall determine the occupancy classification, provided the uses are separated as specified in Section 302.4.

Section 504.3 establishes two general criteria or rules. These are:

1. *The Unity Rule.* This is contained in the first paragraph of the section. Its application is to buildings when the minor uses exceed 10 percent of the floor area of the floor of the building on which the minor uses are located. The sum of the ratios of the various actual floor areas for each use, divided by the allowable area for that use, cannot exceed one (1). (See Equation 5-1.)

$$\frac{a_1}{A_1} + \frac{a_2}{A_2} + \cdot \cdot \cdot + \frac{a_n}{A_n} \leq 1.0 \qquad (5\text{-}1)$$

where a_1 = Area of one use
a_2 = Area of a second use
a_n = Area of any other use
A_1 = Maximum allowable area of first use per Table 5-B and allowable increases
A_2 = Maximum allowable area of second per Table 5-B or infinity if Section 505.2 applies
A_n = Maximum allowable area of any other use per Table 5-B and allowable increases

2. *The 10 Percent Rule.* This is contained in the second paragraph of this section. Always check if the aggregate of the minor uses on any floor is equal to or less than 10 percent of the floor area of that floor. In conjunction with this rule is a key stipulation

that the basic allowable area of the minor uses cannot exceed that permitted in Table 5-B. See Figures 5-11 and 5-12 for examples of calculations of these two criteria.

Because of the importance of this section of the code, the author provides a detailed analysis of the intent of these criteria and the rationale that must be used in Technical Appendix TA-1.

504.6 Area Separation Walls.

504.6.1 General. Each portion of a building separated by one or more area separation walls which comply with the provisions of this subsection may be considered a separate building. The extent and location of such area separation walls shall provide a complete separation.

When an area separation wall also separates occupancies that are required to be separated by an occupancy separation, the most restrictive requirements of each separation shall apply.

504.6.2 Fire resistance and openings. Area separation walls shall be not less than four-hour fire-resistive construction in Types I, 11-F.R., III and IV buildings and two-hour fire-resistive construction in Types II One-hour, II-N or V buildings. The total width of all openings in such walls shall not exceed 25 percent of the length of the wall in each story. All openings shall be protected by a fire assembly having a three-hour fire-protection rating in four-hour fire-resistive walls and one- and one-half-hour fire-protection rating in two-hour fire-resistive walls.

504.6.4 Terminating. 3. Area separation walls shall extend vertically from the foundation to a point at least 30 inches (762 mm) above the roof.

EXCEPTIONS: 1. Any area separation wall may terminate at the underside of the roof sheathing, deck or slab, provided the roof-ceiling assembly is of at least two-hour fire-resistive construction.

2. Two-hour separation walls may terminate at the underside of the roof sheathing, deck or slab, provided:

2.1 Where the roof-ceiling framing elements are parallel to the walls, such framing and elements supporting such framing shall be of not less than one-hour fire-resistive construction for a width of not less than 5 feet (1524 mm) on each side of the wall.

2.2 Where roof-ceiling framing elements are not parallel to the wall, the entire span of such framing and elements supporting such framing shall be of not less than one-hour fire-resistive construction.

2.3 Openings in the roof shall not be located within 5 feet (1524 mm) of the area separation wall.

2.4 The entire building shall be provided with not less than a Class B roof covering as specified in Table 15-A.

3. Two-hour area separation walls may terminate at the underside of noncombustible roof sheathing, deck or slab of roofs of noncombustible construction provided:

3.1 Openings In the roof are not located within 5 feet (1524 mm) of the area separation wall.

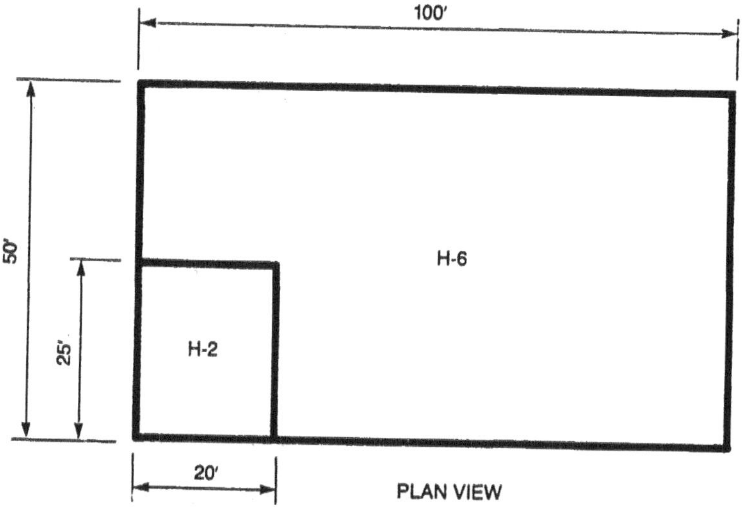

One-HOUR Occupancy Separation
Per Table 3-B

Given: Type V-N Building, one story

Group H, Div. 6 space = 4,500 s.f.; consider as area a_1
Group H, Div. 2 space = 500 s.f.; consider as area a_2

Allowable areas per Table 5-C are:
Group H, Div. 6 8,000 s.f.; consider as allowable area A_1
Group H, Div. 2 2,500 s.f., consider as allowable area A_2

Check for Unity Rule

$$\frac{a_1}{A_1} + \frac{a_2}{A_2} = \leq 1.0$$

$$\frac{4{,}500}{8{,}000} + \frac{500}{2{,}500} = .56 + .2 = .76 < 1.0 \quad \text{OK}$$

Check for 10% Rule

Minor use (H-2) is less than 10% of the floor area and less than the Table 5-B basic allowable area. Building is therefore a Group H, Div. 6 occupancy with the Group H, Div. 2 occupancy as a minor use.

REFERENCE: SECTION 504.3

FIGURE 5-11 MIXED OCCUPANCY CALCULATION OF ACCEPTABILITY–TWO OCCUPANCIES

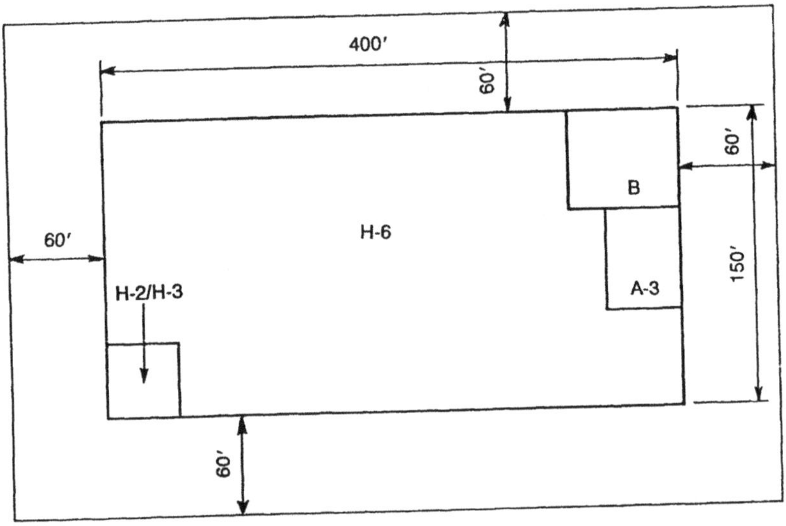

Given:
Type II 1-Hour, 2 Story Building—60,000 s.f. overall
Fully Sprinklered; 60′ clear all around building (4 separations)

Group H-6 space	=	50,000 s.f.
Group H-2/H-3 space	=	1,500 s.f.
Group B space	=	5,500 s.f.
Group A-3 space	=	3,000 s.f.
		60,000 s.f.

(Note: Arrangement of Occupancies within building shown schematically only.)

Allowable Areas

	Basic Allowable (Table No. 5-C)		Sprinkler Increase		Separation Increase*		Gross Allowable Area
H-6	18,000	×	2	×	2	=	72,000
H-2/H-3	5,600	×	-	×	2	=	11,200
B	18,000	×	2	×	2	=	72,000
A-3	13,500	×	2	×	2	=	54,000

*Separation increase for 60′ all around = (60 − 20) × 2.5% = 100%

Mixed Occupancy Calculation Per Sec. 302.1

$$\frac{\text{Actual Area}}{\text{Allowable Area}} \leq 1.0$$

$$\underset{\text{H-6}}{\frac{50{,}000}{72{,}000}} + \underset{\text{H-2/H-3}}{\frac{1{,}500}{11{,}200}} + \underset{\text{B}}{\frac{5{,}500}{72{,}000}} + \underset{\text{A-3}}{\frac{3{,}000}{54{,}000}} \leq 1.0$$

$$0.69 + 0.13 + 0.08 + 0.06 = 0.96 < 1.0 \quad \text{O.K.}$$

REFERENCE: SECTION 504.3

FIGURE 5-12 MIXED OCCUPANCY EXAMPLE

3.2 The entire roof is covered with not less than a Class B roof covering as specified in Table 15-A.

504.6.5 Parapet faces. Parapets of area separation walls shall have noncombustible faces for the uppermost 18 inches (457 mm), including counterflashing and coping materials.

The use of area separation walls (ASWs) permits a structure to be considered as divided into separate buildings. An illustration of how an area separation wall is installed in a two-story Group R, Division 1 Occupancy building is shown in Figure 5-13 both with and without a parapet. The parapet requirements and the conditions to be met if a parapet is to be omitted are contained in this section.

Each subdivided area can have the maximum allowable areas per Table 5-B for its occupancy and construction type.

The second sentence in the first paragraph requires that the choice of the location and the extent of the ASW must achieve a complete separation of the structure. This provision will enable the enforcement official to assure that the ASW is located where it is effective in creating the intended separation.

The second paragraph combines the requirements of occupancy separation and ASW. This is a new interpretation of the code, although some enforcement officials may have made similar interpretations of the code in the past.

The second paragraph appears to contradict the longstanding provisions in the opening paragraph, namely, that an ASW creates separate buildings. In that concept there is no need for an occupancy separation between the "buildings."

If this principle, as contained in this subsection, were, in fact, of long standing, then the addition of this new sentence simply repeats Section 101.3, third paragraph. There has been a great reluctance on the part of the International Conference of Building Officials (ICBO) to repeat provisions for emphasis.

> It is therefore the authors' opinion that this is not just emphasis of an accepted principle but a new provision and thus changes the ASW concept.

The *Handbook to the Uniform Building Code* discusses ASWs on pages 79 and 80. That discussion emphasizes the separate building concept and does not mention the occupancy separation aspect as

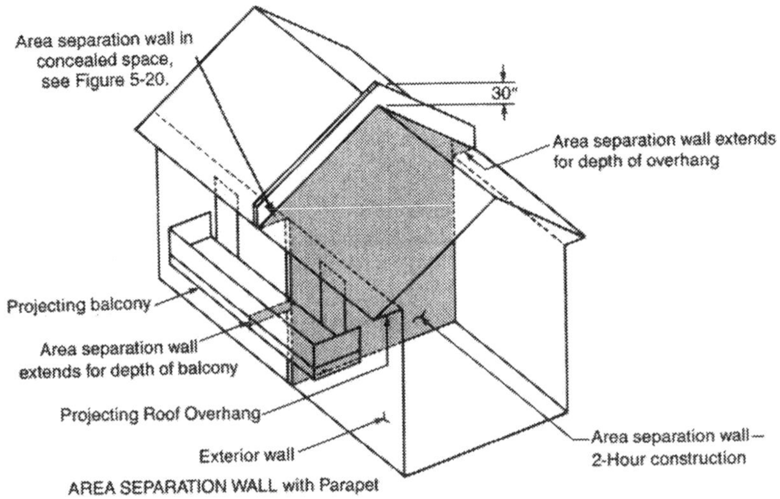

AREA SEPARATION WALL with Parapet

Given:
Type V-N Building, Group R, Division 1 Occupancy

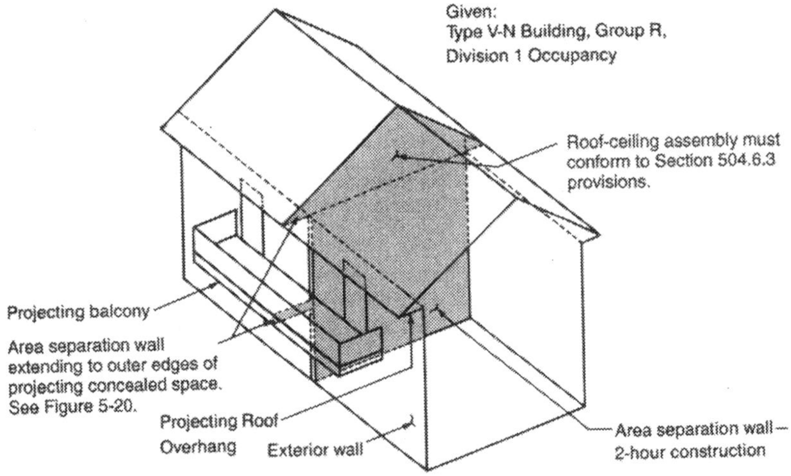

AREA SEPARATION WALL without parapet

See also Figures (5-16 thru 5-18).

NOTE: Under projections (i.e. roof overhang or balcony), unless the wall at right angles to the ASW is of one-hour fire-resistive construction for a length at least equal to the depth of the projection on each side of the ASW, the ASW must extend to the edge of the projection.

REFERENCE: SECTION 504.6

FIGURE 5-13 AREA SEPARATION WALL EXAMPLE WITH & WITHOUT PARAPET GROUP R, DIVISION 1 BUILDING

applying. We must conclude that up to this time the separate building concept was the intent of the code and this new change reverses that concept.

In Figure 5-14, the several specific requirements governing the construction of the ASW are shown and listed. The provisions in Exception 2 of Section 504.6.3 apply based on the 2-hour ASW criteria.

> In the authors' opinion, there is an inconsistency in invoking the ASW and occupancy separation requirements under the two examples shown in Figure 5-15.

Figure 5-15 demonstrates, in Plan View B, that with an unrated building on each side of a property line, only 1-hour fire-resistive walls are required alongside the property line: one on each side. Therefore, there would be only a 2-hour fire-resistive rating provided under that condition as against the 3-hour fire-resistive rating required by Section 504.6.2 for the occupancy separation of Plan View A.

The walls alongside the property line would not be permitted to have any openings; however, the ASW or occupancy separation provision in Section 504.6 does not allow a reduction in the occupancy separation provision (3-hour rating) if there are no openings in the separation. For most conditions of mixed occupancies, the new provisions in Section 504.6 will not cause problems. That is because the ASW requirement of 2-hour construction usually exceeds the occupancy separation requirements of Table 3-B. However, in some special mixed occupancies, this interpretation-into-code provision may cause considerable problems.

> In the authors' opinion, there has been a trend to erode the ASW provisions. In particular, changes have recently been made that violate the "separate building" concept. The fire alarm provision in Section 403.3, 403.5 and 403.6 was the first such erosion, and this is the second. All parties should be aware of this tendency to make the code unnecessarily restrictive and to downgrade the use of ASWs, an important design tool.

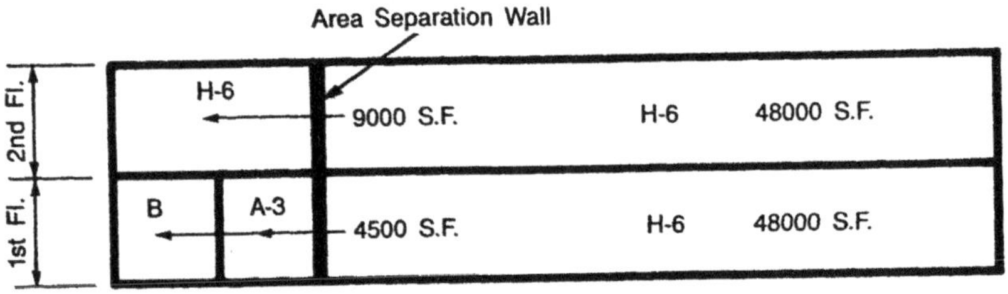

ELEVATION

GIVEN: Type II-N Building
Two Story Sprinklered
Group A, Div. 3, Group B and Group H, Div. 6 Occupancy on First Floor
Group H, Div. 6 Occupancy on Second Floor

ASSUME: Area separation wall required due to maximum allowable area calculated per Sec. 302.1

The walls between the Group A, Division 3 Occupancy and the Group H, Division 6 Occupancy on the first floor and the Group B Occupancy and the Group H Division 6 Occupancy on the second floor serve as both an area separation wall and an occupancy separation wall. This is in accordance with the provisions of Sec. 504.6.1 first paragraph, second sentence.

Per Table 3-B, the occupancy separation required is 3 hour. Per Sec. 504.6.1, first paragraph, a Type II-N building may have a two-hour area separation wall.

The second paragraph of Sec. 504.6.1 requires that the most restrictive provision applicable to an area separation wall and an occupancy separation wall shall apply. Therefore, the wall will have to meet the following conditions as a minimum:

a) Fire-resistive rating–3 hour.
b) Extend from foundation to a point at least 30 inches above the roof. (Parapet to comply with area separation wall requirements.)
c) Openings to have a fire assembly with three-hour rating. (Occupancy separation provisions.)
d) Maximum area of single opening limited to 120 S.F. (Occupancy separation Provisions.)

The Sec. 302.2 requirements also apply to the separation between the first floor and the second floor. The Group A, Division 3 Occupancy and the Group H, Division 6 Occupancy above require a three-hour fire-resistive floor-ceiling assembly with the supports for that assembly to be of at least three-hour fire-resistive construction.

REFERENCE: SECTIONS 101.3, 302.2, 504.6 AND TABLE 3-B

FIGURE 5-14 MIXED OCCUPANCY BUILDING, OCCUPANCY SEPARATION AND AREA SEPARATION WALL REQUIREMENT, TYPE II-N BUILDING

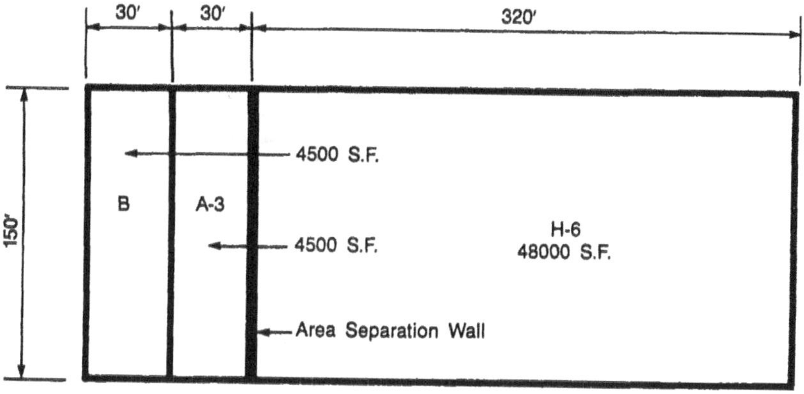

PLAN VIEW—FIRST FLOOR

The fire-resistive requirements for ASWs are contained in Section 504.6.2 as are the opening protection criteria. A four-hour ASW may have openings in the wall, whereas a 4-hour occupancy separation wall is not permitted to have any openings.

Section 504.6.5 requires only the uppermost 18 inches of the parapet to have noncombustible faces. This is a companion to the Section 709.4.2 parapet provisions. The intent behind the section is to prevent fire spread over the parapet by the surfacing material and to permit the roofing to be effectively flashed to the parapet.

Opinions differ in regard to the intent and applicable requirements for ASWs in such matters as

- street frontage for the segments of the building created by the ASW,
- exiting through an ASW,
- utilities through the walls and
- accessibility of fire department equipment to building segments.

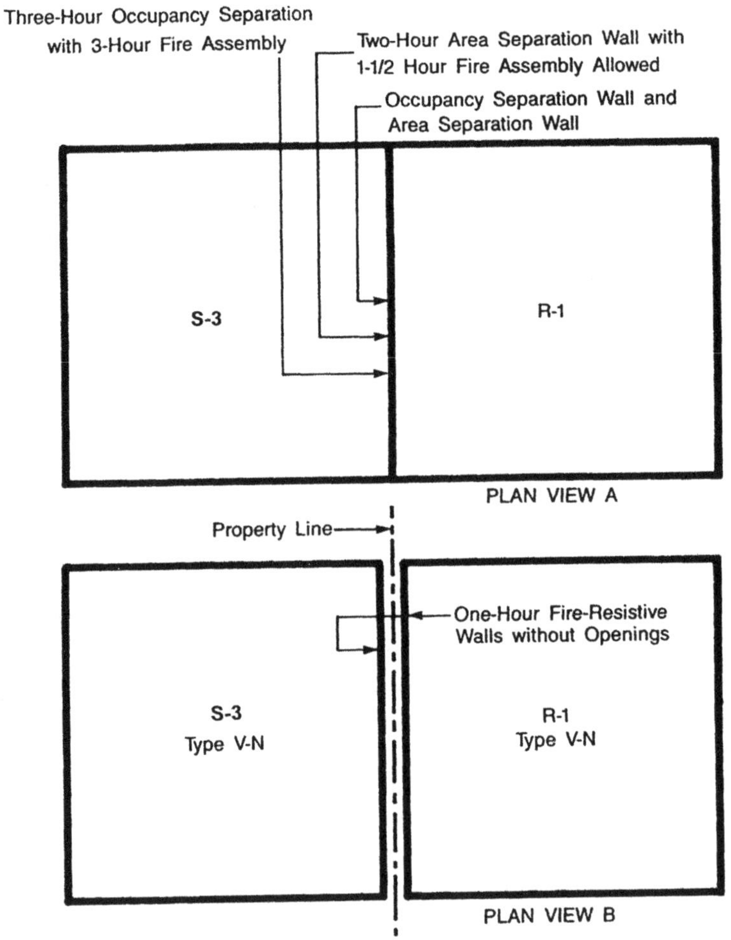

ASSUME: Building Type V-N with Group S, Division 3 Occupancy and Group R, Division 1 Occupancy (See Note).

NOTE: This is an illustration of how the Section 504.6.1 first and second paragraph apply to two different but comparable situations.

In Plan View A, where a single building is involved, both the area separation wall and occupancy separation wall requirements apply.

In Plan View B, where the individual occupancies of Plan View A are in separate buildings on different properties, only one-hour fire-resistive walls are required on the property line.

REFERENCE: SECTION 504.6.1

FIGURE 5-15 COMPARISON OF AREA SEPARATION WALL/ OCCUPANCY SEPARATION WALL/PROPERTY LINE WALL REQUIREMENTS-SAME TYPE OF CONSTRUCTION & OCCUPANCIES

The designer is urged to discuss with the enforcement official the use of ASWs and should obtain written confirmation from the official of the official's understanding of that jurisdiction's regulations governing the ASWs being considered in the project.

> In the authors' opinion, each segment of the building created by the ASW should have its own street frontage and access.

The computation of the allowable floor areas for each segment depends on the number of streets or yards on which any given segment of the building fronts, as provided in Section 505. (See Figures 5-16 through 5-18.)

Each segment should have its own exits. However, an ASW can be considered to provide a horizontal exit per Section 1005.3.5, thereby reducing the total number of exits. See discussion of horizontal exits in Section 409.7 hereinafter and Article 7 of this Guide.

ASWs are useful devices, provided one understands their limitations as well as their benefits. The ICBO staff interpretations regarding ASWs clearly limit them to vertical elements with no horizontal offsets; that is, the ASW cannot be offset laterally, using a floor/ceiling assembly as part of the area separation. (See Figure 5-19.)

The prohibition against use of an offset ASW, as shown in Figure 5-19, applies to projecting building elements such as cantilevered upper levels of a building. (See Figure 5-20, Section A-A.) Where such projections of upper-level floors are desired, the projection must be eliminated at the location of the ASW.

Of equal importance to where and how to design an ASW are the methods allowed by the code for the roof termination of the ASW. The basic requirement is that the ASW penetrate the roof, terminating in a parapet above the roof.

However, Section 504.6.4, Exception 3, refers to those situations when an ASW may terminate at the underside of the roof sheathing. (Section 504.6.6 contains similar provisions for roofs of buildings of different heights.)

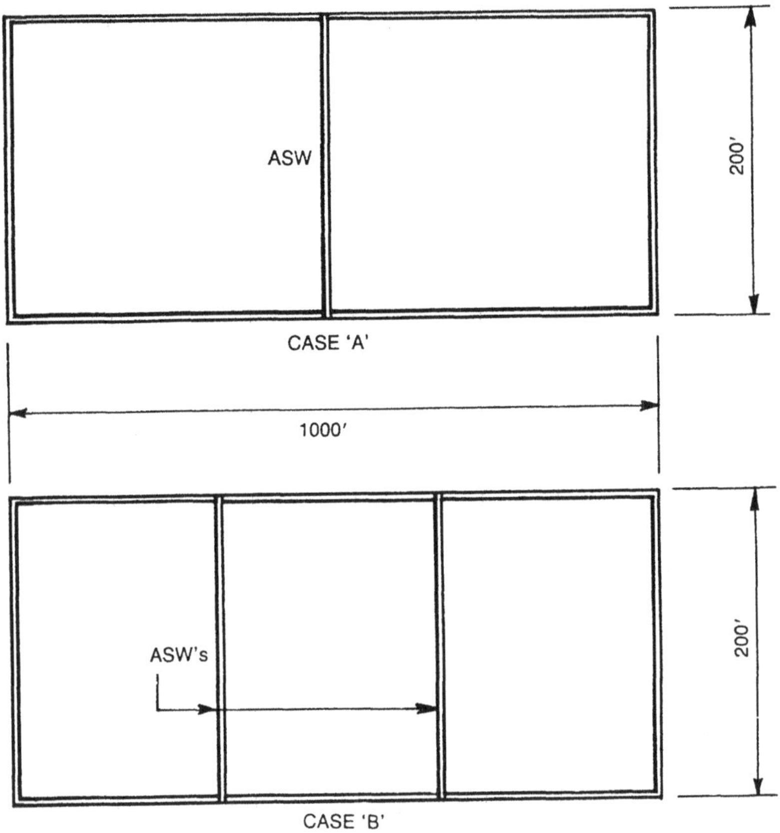

REFERENCE: SECTION 504.6.1, 505.1 and 505.3

FIGURE 5-16 AREA SEPARATION WALLS FOR AREA INCREASES

NOTE: See page 121 for Cases A and B of Figure 5-16. See page 123 for Case C.

ASSUME:
Type III One-Hour Building, One Story
Sprinklered, H-6 Occupancy
200,000 S.F., 40-foot separations all around

Allowable Area per Table 5-B	18,000
Increase for separation (40 – 20) × 5% = 100%	18,000
	36,000
Increase for Sprinklers = (300%)	108,000 (not sufficient, proposed building over area)

Illustrative building is 200,000 sq. ft., therefore either the type of construction will have to be upgraded to Type II-F.R. or an area separation wall (ASW) installed. Since one-ASW will establish 2 separate buildings in effect; each will have only 3 sides with separations of 40′. Therefore the allowable increase for separations will be (40 – 20) × 2½% = 50%. Unless the width of the separations is increased there will have to be more ASW's in order to reach the 200,000 sq. ft. of the building. The separations can be increased up to 60′ to allow a 100% area increase (60 – 20) × 2½% = 100%

The following example of the calculations can illustrate the effect of increasing the number of ASW's in a one-story building (assume 200,000 sq. ft. building).

Case A

One ASW - 40′ separations all around

Basic allowable area	18,000
Separation increase (40 – 20) × 2½% = 50%	9,000
	27,000
Sprinkler increase - 300% - 1 Story	81,000

Total allowable area w/one ASW = 2 × 81,000 = 162,000 S.F. (not sufficient)

Case B

Two ASW's - 40′ separation all around

	3 sides	2 sides
Basic allowable area	18,000	18,000
Separation increase - 3 sides = 50%	9,000	
2 sides = (40 – 20) × 1¼% = 25%		4,500
	27,000	22,500
Sprinkler increase 300% - 1 Story	81,000	67,500

Total allowable area 2 × 3 sides + 1 × 2 sides
= 162,000 + 67,500 = 239,500 OK exceeds 200,000 S.F. proposed

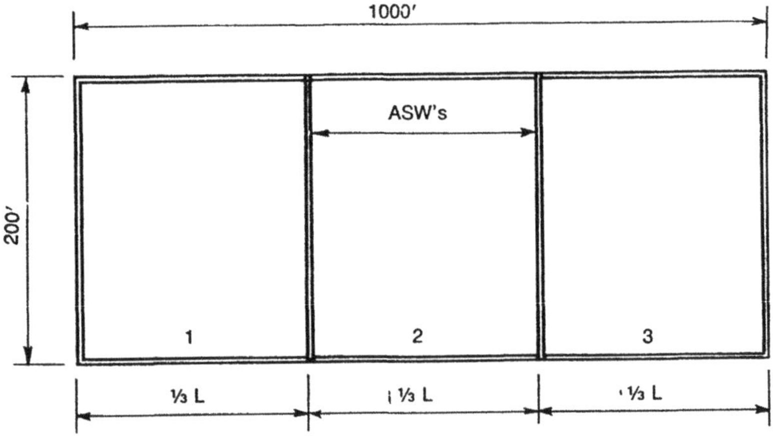

ASSUME:
Type III 1-Hour Building
B Occupancy; 200,000 S.F.
2 stories, 40′ yards all around (parking lot)

For all Segments

Basic Allowable Area	18,000	18,000
For Segments 1 and 3: Separation credit = (40 − 20) × 2 ½% = 50% =	9,000	
For Segment 2: Separation credit = (40 − 20) 1¼% = 25% =		4,500
Allowable: Segements 1 and 3 = 18,000 + 9,000 =	27,000	
Allowable: Sprinkler increase Segments 1 and 3 = 200% =	54,000	
For Segment 2: allowable area w/separation increase = 18,000 + 4,500 =		22,500
Allowable sprinkler increase Segment 2 = 200% =		45,000

Total building, Segments 1 + 2 + 3 = 54,000 + 45,000 + 54,000
Maximum Allowable Area = 153,000 sq. ft. NG
Another ASW is needed (total 3 ASW) = 2 × 54,000 + 2 × 45,000
+ 108,000 + 90,000 = 198,000 sq. ft.

Reduce overall size if possible to 198,000 sq. ft. or increase separation width 1′ to 41′ which will result in a 2.5% increase in the 3 separation credits (450 sq. ft. each) and a 5% (2 × 2.5) increase in the sprinkler credits (900 sq. ft. each) for total allowable increase of 2,700 sq. ft., 198,000 + 2,700 = 200,700 sq. ft., OK each story.

REFERENCE: SECTION 504.6.1, 505.1 and 505.3

FIGURE 5-17 AREA SEPARATION WALLS–SEPARATION CREDITS TWO STORY EXAMPLE

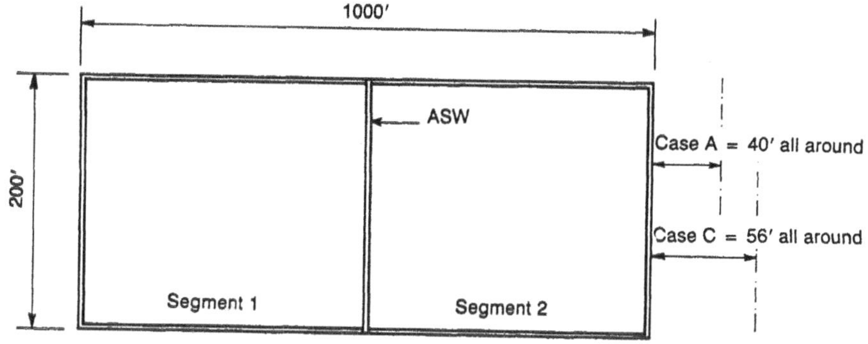

NOTE: Building same as Figure 5-16 Case A.

Case C

Another way to increase the allowable area other than by using the second area separation wall (ASW) is to increase the width of the separation. If we use one ASW and increase the separation width to 56′ all around:

Basic Allowable area for segment	18,000
Separation increase (56 − 20) × 2½% = 90% × 18,000 =	16,200
(3 sides per segment)	34,200
Sprinkler increase 300% - (1 Story Building)	102,600 per segment
Total allowable area-building = 2 × 102,600 =	205,200 OK

REFERENCE: SECTION 504.6.1, 505.1 and 505.3

FIGURE 5-18 AREA SEPARATION WALL AND INCREASE IN SEPARATION WIDTH

These exceptions apply only to ASWs of 2-hour fire-resistive construction. The designer should understand that, where a parapet cannot be constructed due to conditions beyond the control of the client,the designer must look to the types of building construction that will allow the use of a 2-hour and not a 4-hour ASW.

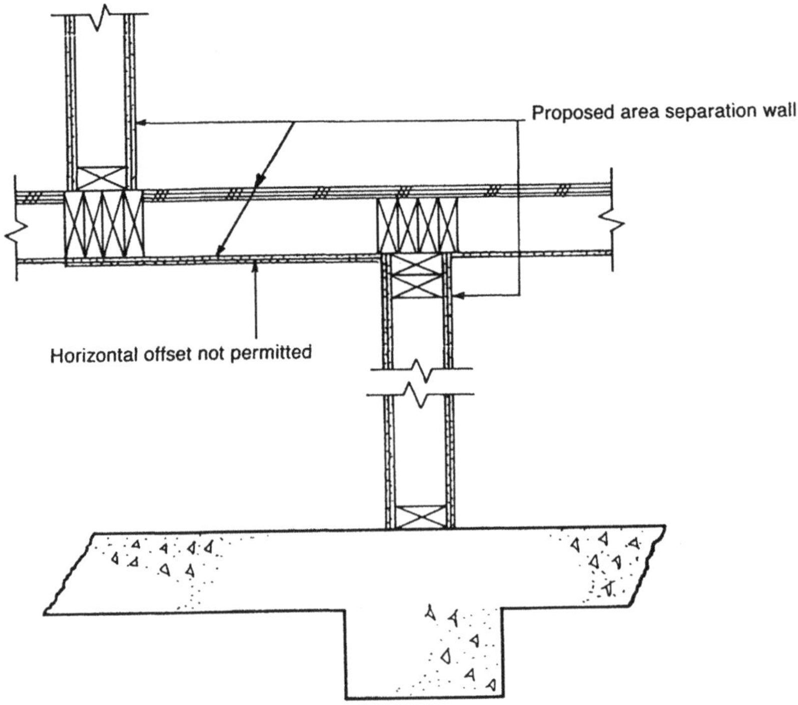

REFERENCE: SECTION 504.6.1

FIGURE 5-19 AREA SEPARATION WALL WITH HORIZONTAL OFFSET

In Exception 3, for omission of a parapet, the entire roof must have roof covering as specified in Table 15-A. The intent is to reduce the spread of fire across both the roof covering and the ASW and to restore the effectiveness of the ASW where the Section 504.6.4 provision is used. When the roof is required to be of noncombustible construction, the intent is that the noncombustibility encompass the entire roof including the framing and decking.

When an ASW terminates at the underside of the roof sheathing, the method of framing the roof supports determines how much of

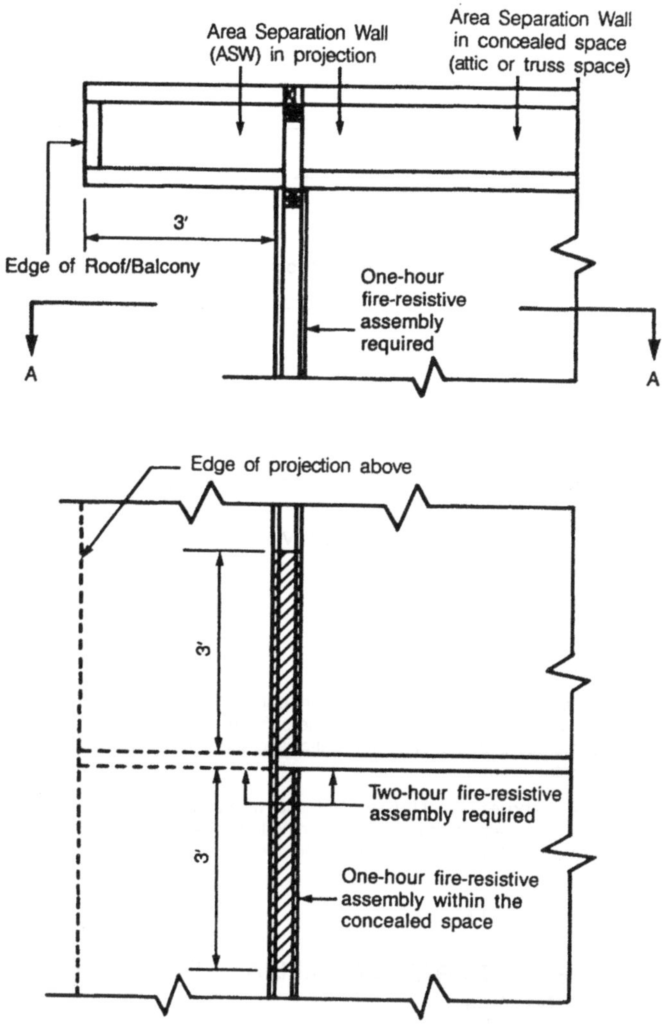

Section A-A

NOTE: The one-hour fire-resistive assembly within the concealed space may be omitted when the entire length of the projecting element is constructed as a one hour fire-resisistive assembly.

REFERENCE: SECTION 504.6.2

FIGURE 5-20 AREA SEPARATION WALL–ROOF/CEILING SUPPORT REQUIREMENTS; "N" BUILDING, NO PARAPET

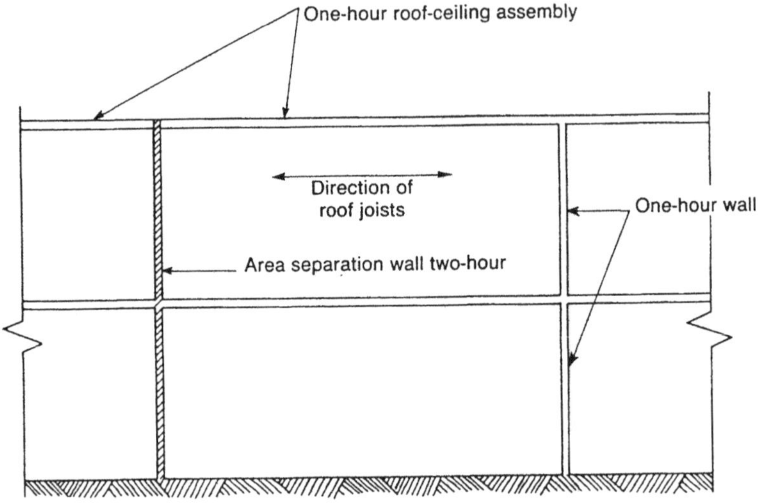

Where joists, adjacent to area separation wall (ASW) are parallel to the ASW, the roof-ceiling assembly need only be one-hour fire-resistive for distance of 5 feet from the ASW. However the support walls and other members for that one-hour roof-ceiling segment will also require at least one-hour fire-resistance to the ground.

The above requirement also applies to roof trusses. Note that where the joists or trusses are parallel to the ASW and there is no parapet, the walls supporting the ends of the joists or trusses within five feet of the ASW must also be of at least one-hour fire-resistive construction down to the ground.

REFERENCE: SECTION 504.6.3

FIGURE 5-21 AREA SEPARATION WALL AT PROJECTING ELEMENTS

that roof-ceiling must comply with a 1-hour fire-resistive rating: (See Figure 5-21.)

- When the supporting members are at right angles to the ASW, 1-hour construction is required for the entire span of the roof-ceiling assembly.

- When the supporting members are parallel to the ASW, the 1-hour construction is required only for a minimum of 5 feet on each side of the ASW.

> In the authors' opinion, the support elements for the roof-ceiling assembly, other than the ASW itself, must in turn also be supported by not less than 1-hour fire-resistive construction. When this support condition occurs on an upper floor of a building, the same degree of fire protection must be used for all applicable construction down to the ground or to such point where it rests on a level of at least 1-hour fire-resistive protection.

This is similar to the requirements for occupancy separations discussed in Section 302.2 and shown in Figure 5-3.

This concept is of importance particularly in a building that may otherwise be of nonfire-resistive construction. It requires that the far end of the roof system span be supported all the way down to the foundation by minimum 1-hour fire-resistive construction. The designer should take care to note that this requirement is often overlooked when using an ASW. The fire-resistive construction for these roof-ceiling support elements should be designed as complete fire-resistive assemblies and not simply as protection for the side of the wall facing the ASW. (See Figure 5-22.)

Two prerequisites must be met to allow the permissible termination of the 2-hour ASWs at the underside of noncombustible roofs:

1. No openings in the roof within 5 feet of the ASW are allowed.
2. Roof covering of the entire building must be provided with not less than a Class B roofing assembly.

These provisions are identical to the provisions for combustible roofs in Exception 2, Items 2.3 and 2.4. The purpose of this is to exclude the roof covering from the noncombustible limitation of the general provision and at the same time restrict the roofing assembly to at least Class B.

Because many Class B roofing assemblies contain combustible components, the latter provision allows such roof coverings to be

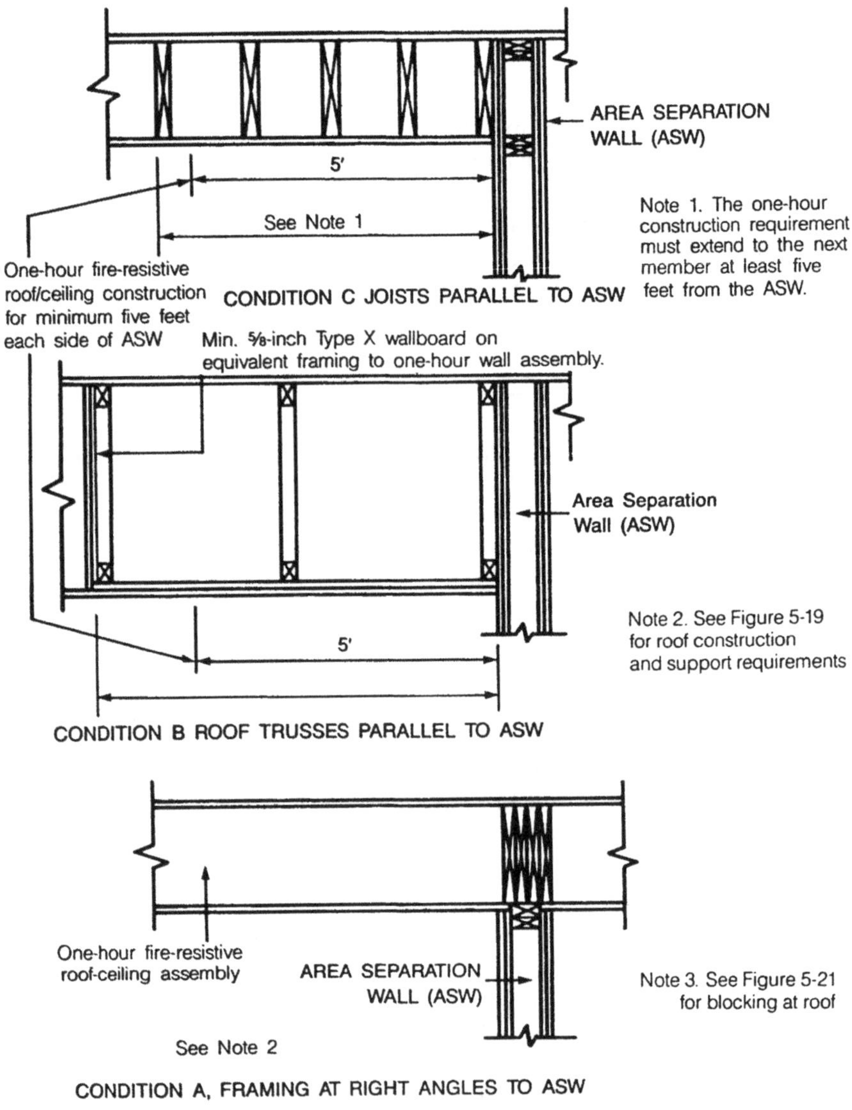

REFERENCE: SECTION 504.6.3

FIGURE 5-22 ROOF-CEILING PROTECTION AREA SEPARATION WALL, BASED ON DIRECTION OF FRAMING

used in conjunction with the noncombustible roof construction and to qualify for termination of the ASW at the underside of said roof.

The designer is advised to trace the support elements for the roof-ceiling framing down to the ground, because in some buildings these support elements are not vertically aligned. The actual support elements to which the 1-hour fire resistance apply may include walls, floor-ceiling assemblies and possibly beams and columns.

As previously noted, when the roof support framing is parallel to the wall, the framing need only be protected with 1-hour construction for a distance of 5 feet on both sides of the ASW. There is no method through which that fire-resistive rating can be achieved by placing wallboard directly under the roof sheathing or metal or ⅝-inch Type X wallboard above the roof sheathing. Unfortunately, such constructions have been frequently used by designers, apparently on the advice of someone who has misunderstood the intent of the code or who is unaware of the type of construction that qualifies as a 1-hour assembly.

As is discussed in Article 8 of this Guide, a fire-resistive roof-ceiling assembly consists of two elements separated by an air space. The ceiling of the room or space under the roof framing is one part of the fire-resistive membrane of the assembly.

In warehouses, due to the type and spacing of the roof framing used, it is unlikely that only a 5-foot strip of the framing, adjacent to the ASW and supporting the roof sheathing, would need the 1-hour protection. In most residential and office building construction, to keep the plane of the ceiling flat, the entire roof-ceiling probably must be of 1-hour construction for the length of its span within the room adjacent to the ASW.

It should be noted that the ASW must continue to the underside of the roof sheathing. Therefore, the wall extension, in the space above the ceiling membrane, must be equivalent to the 2-hour ASW. This can be accomplished by any of the following methods:

1. continuing the two-hour wall above the ceiling line,
2. in wood construction, solid blocking with a minimum of four layers of 2x material for the full height of the intervening space and
3. in steel construction, installing several layers of wallboard in the space. (See Figure 5-23.)

On the drawings, these ASW details should be fully delineated, so that in discussions with the building official they can be reviewed

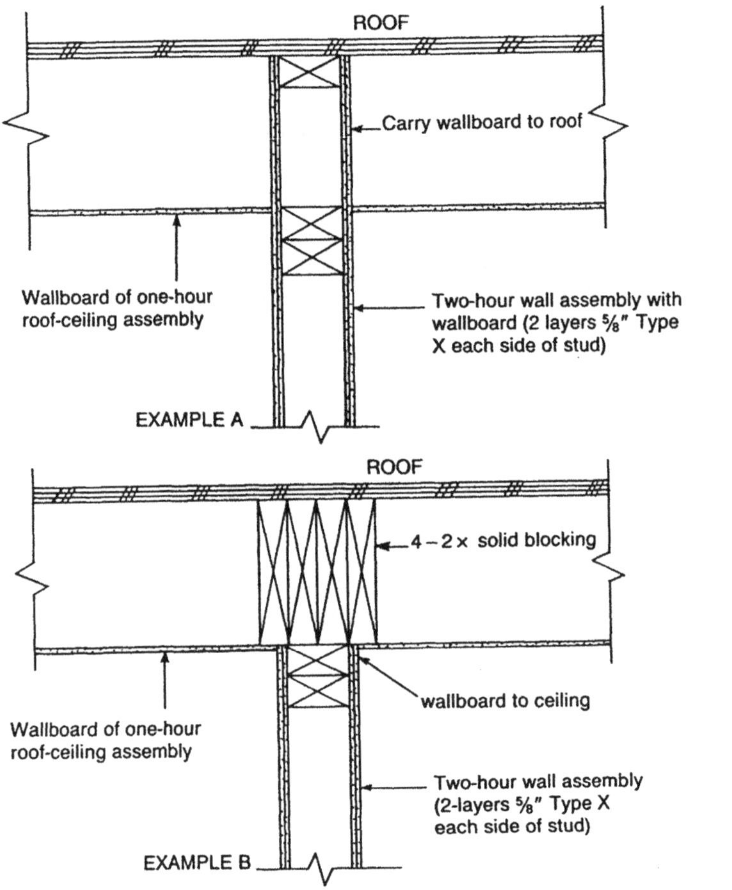

REFERENCE: SECTION 504.6.3

FIGURE 5-23 AREA SEPARATION WALL–ROOF/CEILING (NO PARAPET) TYPICAL CONSTRUCTION

and accepted as equivalent to the code-accepted construction. Examples of intermediate floor intersection details are shown in Figure 5-24.

When an ASW extends below the first floor, usually in a crawlspace or basement area and to the foundation, it must be of the same fire-resistive rating as required for the main segments of the ASW. (See Figure 5-25.)

Other projecting elements such as roof overhangs, balconies and similar architectural projections are covered in Section 504.6.3. When there are concealed spaces in the projecting element, such as are created by joists or trusses, the ASW must extend through the projection to the outer edge of the projection. (See Figure 5-20.)

There are exceptions to extending the ASW in the concealed space of the projection. The essential requirements for use of these exceptions are provided below.

The projection must be a 1-hour fire-resistive assembly for a distance on each side of the ASW equal to the depth of the projection. Thus, in Section A-A (Figure 5-20), with a three-foot roof overhang the one-hour construction must extend at least three feet on each side of the ASW. See Plan View in Figure 5-20.

- Openings in the exterior wall below the projection and within a distance of the ASW equal to the depth of the projection must be protected by fire assemblies with at least $\frac{3}{4}$-hour fire resistance rating.
- The protection of the exterior wall below the projection must continue down to the foundation to avoid a premature failure of the wall section directly below the projection.
- When the concealed space in the projection contains openings parallel to the exterior wall, as would be the case if trusses were involved or where architectural treatment frames an open concealed area, the 1-hour protection for the projection must be carried up, within the concealed space, to the point of termination of the 1-hour projection construction. If the entire length of the projection was constructed with a 1-hour fire-resistive rating, this internal cutoff within the concealed space is not required. See Plan View in Figure 5-20.

Separation walls are of such importance that the designer must be assured that the contractor carries out the intent of the code

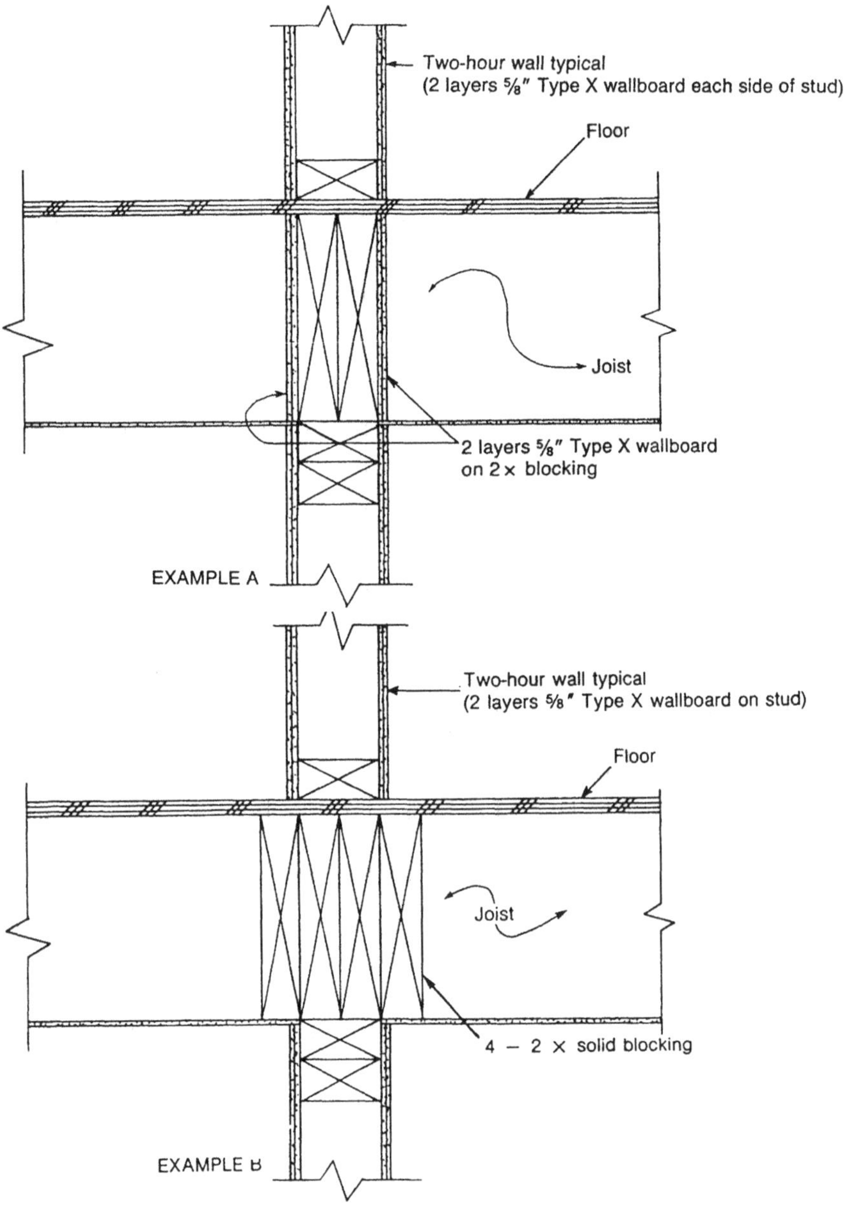

FIGURE 5-24 AREA SEPARATION WALL–INTERMEDIATE FLOOR DETAILS

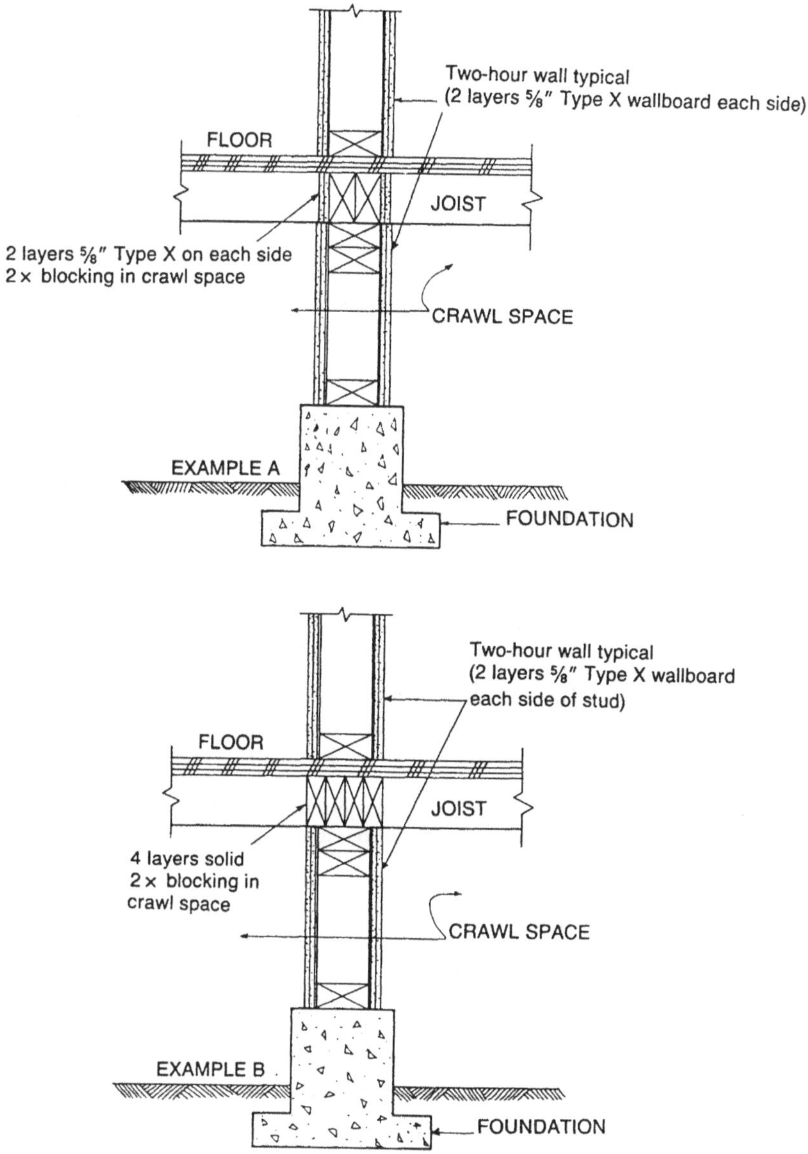

FIGURE 5-25 AREA SEPARATION WALLS–FOUNDATION DETAILS

requirements. The designer's drawings should fully detail the ASWs so that the contractor does not confuse the ASWs with other walls of the building. They are not the same. ASWs have the validity and importance of an exterior wall located at a property line and hence, except for protected openings, must be constructed in an unbreached manner.

Site visits by the designer are essential to assure that the ASWs are constructed properly. An improperly constructed ASW will be difficult or impossible to correct without great expense and can jeopardize the validity of that building's entire occupancy.

SECTION 505—ALLOWABLE AREA INCREASES

505.1 General. The floor areas specified in Section 504 may be increased by employing one of the provisions of this section.

505.1.1 Separation on two sides. Where public space or yards more than 20 feet in width extend along and adjoin two sides of the building, floor areas may be increased at a rate of $1\frac{1}{4}$ percent for each foot by which the minimum width exceeds 20 feet, but the increase shall not exceed 50 percent.

505.1.2 Separation on three sides. Where public space or yards more than 20 feet In width extend along and adjoin three sides of the building, floor areas may be Increased at a rate of $2\frac{1}{2}$ percent for each foot by which the minimum width exceeds 20 feet, but the Increase shall not exceed 100 percent.

505.1.3 Separation on all sides. Where public space or yards more than 20 feet in width extend on all sides of a building and adjoin the entire perimeter, floor areas may be increased at a rate of 5 percent for each foot by which the minimum width exceeds 20 feet. Such increases shall not exceed 100 percent, except that greater increases shall be permitted for the following occupancies:

1. Group S, Division 5 aircraft hangers not exceeding one story in height.
2. Group S, Division 2 of Group F, Division 2 Occupancies not exceeding two stories in height.
3. Group H, Division 5 aircraft repair hangers not exceeding one story in height. Area increases shall not exceed 500 percent for aircraft repair hangers except as provided in Section 505.2

The basic floor area for a given occupancy and type of construction is indicated in Table 5-B. This area may be increased depending on the number of streets, yards or equivalent open spaces that bound the building.

The code's intent is to permit a building to have larger allowable areas when wide separations exist

- between it and the property lines or
- between it and other buildings on the site.

The increases are based on the amount of separation in excess of a 20-foot minimum. Where there are several separations of differing widths around the building, the minimum width is used in the calculations. The separation must extend for the entire length of the building.

The percentages used to calculate the increase are based on

- the number of frontages and
- the minimum width of separation in excess of 20 feet for the frontages involved.

NUMBER OF SEPARATIONS	MAXIMUM PERCENTAGE INCREASE	MAXIMUM PERCENTAGE PERMITTED	MINIMUM DISTANCE FOR MAXIMUM
1	0	0	—
2	1.25	50	60
3	2.5	100	60
4	5.0	100	40

NOTE: Distance calculation based on total separation is as follows:

Allowable = % Increase × (total width of separation − 20 feet)

In some instances, the designer might do better to use the larger separations and eliminate a smaller one, thereby obtaining a greater percentage increase than otherwise. For instance, assume a building has three separations of 60 feet and one of 30 feet.

Either

a. four separations can be used, with a 30-foot width used in the calculations, or
b. three separations with a 60-foot width could be used.

Thus

a. four separations: 5% (30 − 20) = 50% increase allowed or
b. three separations: 2.5% (60 − 20) = 100% increase allowed.

The effect of using the larger separations on a multistoried building would be to increase the allowable area for the building as a whole. The percentage increase applies to the overall allowable for the building per Section 504.2 which is two times the basic area per Table 5-B. Thus, for a multistoried building, two times the separation percentage increase is also permitted. An exaxnple of these calculations is shown accompanying Figure 5-26.

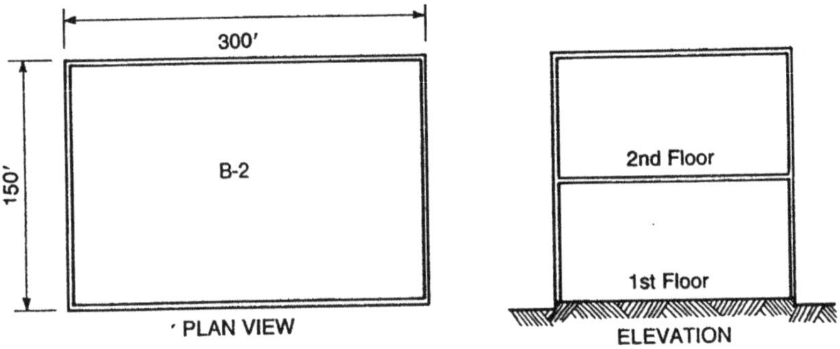

ASSUME:
Type III-N Building
B Occupancy, Sprinklered
2 story, 40′ separations all around (4 sides)
Each story = 45,000 S.F., Gross area = 90,000 S.F.

Allowable area per Table 5-B =	12,000
Increase for separations (4) = (40 − 20) × 5% = 100%	12,000
	24,000
Increase for sprinklers (2 Story Bldg.) = 200% =	48,000
Total allowable area in building = 2 × 48,000 =	96,000

Each story is allowed the 48,000 sq. ft. area
Actual area = 45,000 sq. ft. per story O.K.

NOTE: The 96,000 sq. ft. total allowable area is also the maximum area allowed for a B Occupancy in a Type III-N building *regardless* of the number of additional stories. Therefore, a 3 story B-2 Type III building can have only 48,000 sq. ft. max/story and 96,000 sq. ft. maximum for the entire building.

REFERENCE: Section 504.2, 505.1 and 505.3

FIGURE 5-26 ALLOWABLE AREA CALCULATIONS–MULTI-STORIED BUILDING

Where there are different occupancies in the building, the basic area is computed based on the Section 504.3 calculations. When there are ASWs in the building, each of the segmented areas has the percentage increase computed based on that area's frontages, without regard to the frontages of the building as a whole.

It must be noted that the provisions of these increases only apply to separations in the form of streets, yards and public ways. Parking lots are considered yards.

The definition of these terms are taken from Chapter 2:

> **STREET is any thoroughfare or public way not less than 16 feet (4877 mm) in width which has been dedicated or deeded to the public for public use.**
>
> **YARD is an open unoccupied space, other than a court, unobstructed from the ground to the sky, except where specifically provided by this code, on the lot on which a building Is situated.**

In calculating the area increases, a court is not considered to be a yard and thus does not qualify as a separation. The definition of yard clearly precludes a court from being considered as a yard. As stated in Section 505.1, only public way, streets or yards qualify as separations.

> In the authors' opinion, the concept of the increases includes an unstated prerequisite for qualifying a space for the frontage: The ability for the fire service to access the building for fire fighting.

An acceptable space would provide fire service access as well as have the required width and extent of separation to qualify for the area increase. In keeping with this concept of access, parking lots and their driveways that meet the minimum width and open to the sky requirements are usually accepted as yards, thereby meeting the separation requirements.

On the other hand, if the yard to be used for separation credits is a storage yard or other such obstructed use with limited access by the fire service, then it fails to satisfy the access criteria and also presents a greater fire hazard than does a parking lot. Thus, a storage yard or other obstructed space, in the author's opinion, should not be credited for separation area increases.

505.2 Unlimited Area. The area of any one- or two-story building of Groups B; F, Division 1 or 2; M; S, Division 1, 2, 3, 4 or 5; and Group H, Division 5 Occupancies shall not be limited, If the building is provided with an approved automatic sprinkler system throughout, as specified In Chapter 9, and entirely surrounded and adjoined by public space, streets or yards not less than 60 feet (18 288 mm) in width.

The area of a group S, Division 2 or Group F, Division 2 Occupancy in a one-story Type II, Type III One-hour or Type IV building shall not be limited if the building is entirely surrounded and adjoined by public space, streets or yards not less than 60 feet in width.

Section 505.2 permits an unlimited area building to be built of any type of construction, including Type V-N, provided the building is

- a one- or two-story structure,
- used for Group B or H, Division 5 occupancies,
- fully sprinklered and
- is entirely surrounded and adjoined by public space, streets or yards not less than 60 feet in width.

This section is probably the most liberal provision in the code. It permits shopping centers, markets, warehouses and factories to use their parking areas, usually required for their day-to-day operation, together with standard sprinkler protection in lieu of all built-in fire protection. See the Technical Appendix TA-1 discussion for additional detailed commentary on the unlimited area building with mixed occupancies.

The designer should be aware of both the benefits and liabilities to the owner in making use of these provisions. The large cost savings possible when not using fire-resistive construction are offset to a degree by a total reliance on the sprinkler system to protect the property.

The designer should consider increasing the reliability of the sprinkler system by

- requiring all shut-off valves and the water-flow detectors to be supervised by a central station and not simply relying on locks to keep the valves open and
- providing a second source of water either by connection to another main or by providing on-site water storage.

The supervision alone will raise the reliability level of sprinkler performance to 99.9+ percent.

505.3 Automatic Sprinkler Systems. The areas specified in Table 5-B and Section 504.2 may be tripled in one-story buildings and doubled in buildings of more than one story if the building is provided with an approved automatic sprinkler system throughout. The area increases permitted in this subsection may be compounded with that specified in paragraphs 501.1, 505.1.2 or 505.1.3 The increases permitted in this subsection shall not apply when automatic sprinkler systems are installed under the following provisions:

1. Section 506 for an increase in allowable number of stories.
2. Section 904.2.6.1 for Group H, Divisions 1 and 2 Occupancies.
3. Substitution for one-hour fire-resistive construction pursuant to Section 508.
4. Section 402, Atria.

This section provides another method for increasing the allowable area of a building: the installation of a complete fire sprinkler system in the building. The area increases allowed with the sprinklers is either three times or two times the basic allowable area depending on whether the building is a single or multistoned structure, respectively.

Section 505.3 is not applicable when sprinklers are required for any of the four provisions specifically listed in this section:

1. The designer may compound the sprinkler increase with that from separations in Section 505.1 but cannot compound the sprinkler increase with both area increases and increase in the number of stones per Section 507.
2. When a sprinkler installation is required in Section 904.2.6.1 Group H, Divisions 1 and 2 Occupancies.
3. When the sprinklers are used as a substitute for the structural fire resistance of a 1-hour building per Section 508.
4. When a sprinkler installation is required in Section 402 for atria.

The area increases for sprinklers may be compounded with the percentage increases obtained based on Section 505.1 separations.

Examples of the method used to compound sprinkler credits and the separation credits for street, yard or public space are shown in Figures 5-16 through 5-18.

In short, separation and sprinkler credits can be added together but sprinkler credits alone cannot be used to gain both area and height increases. With the exception of those described in Section

904.2.6.1, all the required fire sprinkler installations cited in Chapter 9 can be used for the sprinkler credits as specified in Chapter 5, provided the entire building is sprinklered. Therefore, the designer may use sprinkler credits to obtain area increases even when the sprinklers are required by a provision of Chapter 9.

SECTION 506—MAXIMUM HEIGHT OF BUILDINGS AND INCREASES

The maximum height and number of stories of every building shall be dependent upon the character of the occupancy and the type of construction and shall not exceed the limits set forth in Table 5-B, except as provided in this section and as specified in Section 302.1 for mixed occupancy buildings.

.
.
.

The story limits set forth in Table 5-B may be increased by one story if the building is provided with an approved automatic sprinkler system throughout. The increase in the nurnber of stories for automatic sprinkler systems shall not apply when the automatic sprinkler systems throughout are installed under the following provisions:

1. Section 904.2.6 for Group H, Divisions 1, 2, 3, 6 and 7 Occupancies.

2. Section 505 for an increase in allowable area.

3. Substitution for one-hour five-resistive construction pursuant to Section 508.

4. Section 402, Atria.

5. Section 904.2.7 for Group 1, Division I, Division 1.1 and 1.2 Occupancies used as hospitals or nursing homes or health-care centers in Type II One-hour, Type III One-hour, Type IV or Type V One-hour construction.

See Chapters 3 and 4 for special occupancy provisions.

This section provides the requirements for the number of stories and overall height in feet for each type of construction and occupancy. The matrix in Table 5-B contains these limitations.

The increase permitted in the number of stories, under the condition that fire sprinklers are installed, is not permitted for the three provisions cited.

Sprinklers may be used to increase, by one story, the number of stories allowed in a building. For example, a Type V One-hour building of Group R, Division 1 per Table 5-B is limited to three stories. If fully sprinklered, the same building type and occupancy can be four stories.

Where there is more than one occupancy in the building, and these occupancies are located on different floors, the maximum level a particular occupancy may be in the building is regulated by Table 5-B provisions.

For example, consider a building that is proposed to have a Group B Occupancy on the first and second floors, an A-3 Occupancy on the third floor, and a Group R, Division 1 Occupancy on the top floor. The overall height of the building is four stories. The designer would like to use a building of either 1-hour or Type IV construction.

In this example, checking Table 5-B, we note that the limits for a Type II One-hour, III One-hour and IV for the three occupancies are

B, four stories;
A-3, two stories and
R-1, four stories.

A Type V One-hour building would allow the B and R-1 Occupancies no higher than the third story.

The A-3 Occupancy cannot be located on the third floor in any of these four types of buildings because the maximum height permitted for that use is two stories. Thus the proposed arrangement is not allowed.

If the A-3 use were to be located on the second floor and the B Occupancy in a basement and first floor, the mixed uses would be allowed on the levels desired in any of these types of construction except for the Type V One-hour.

Another solution could be to provide sprinklers for the entire building. Doing this would allow the various occupancies to be located one floor higher than that shown in Table 5-B.

Thus, the building could be constructed as Type V One-hour with the arrangement of the occupancies as originally intended. The A-3 use could be on the third floor and the R-1 Occupancy on the fourth floor.

SECTION 507—MEZZANINES

A mezzanine need not be counted as a story for determining the allowable number of stories when constructed in accordance with the following:

1. The construction of a mezzanine shall be consistent with the requirements for the type of construction in which the mezzanine is located, but the fire-resistive time period need not exceed one hour for unenclosed mezzanines. The clear height above and below the mezzanine floor construction shall be not less than 7 feet (2134 mm).

2. There shall be not more than two levels of mezzanines in a room. However, there is no limitation on the number of mezzanines within a room.

3. The aggregate area of mezzanines within a room shall not exceed one third the area of the room in which it is located.

4. All portions of a mezzanine shall be open and unobstructed to the room in which it is located, except for columns and posts and protective walls or railings not more than 42 inches (1118 mm) in height.

EXCEPTIONS: 1. Partitioning may be installed if either of the following conditions exist:

1.1 The aggregate floor area of the enclosed space does not exceed 10 percent of the mezzanine area.

1.2 The occupant load of the enclosed space does not exceed 10.

2. Mezzanines having two or more exits need not open into the story in which they are located, provided at least one of the exits gives direct access to a protected exit corridor, an exit court, enclosed exit stairway, exterior exit, exterior exit balcony or exit passageway.

3. In industry facilities, mezzanines used for control equipment may be glazed on all sides.

5. Two means of egress shall be provided from a mezzanine when two are required by Table 10-A.

6. If any required means of egress enters the room below, the occupant load of the mezzanine shall be added to the occupant load of the room in which it is located.

The provisions for mezzanines are grouped together into this section. The basic criterion for a mezzanine is that it not occupy more than one-third the floor area of the room in which it is located. If this limitation is met, the mezzanine cannot be considered as constituting a story of the building. Thus, the mezzanine level avoids being added to the other stories of the building in determining compliance with Table 5-B.

A mezzanine generally is unenclosed on the side facing the room below. However, this requirement is not mandatory if the provisions of subsection 4 Exception 2 are met. This exception requires that there be two exits from an enclosed mezzanine with at least one exit providing direct access to an enclosed stairway, protected exit corridor (i.e., 1-hour corridor) or similar protected exit enclosure.

When the mezzanine is used only for the control equipment of an industrial operation, as in a F-2 factory, the mezzanine can be enclosed with glazing on all sides without having to meet the exit provisions just cited. (See Figures 5-27 and 5-28.) The other provisions of the section require:

- The mezzanine area must be added to that of the floor below for determination of occupant load. The occupant load of the mezzanine is to be added to that of the floor into which it exits. Thus, a mezzanine's occupant load will be added to that of the floor below it. If there are two exits required, as in Exception 2 above, one-half the

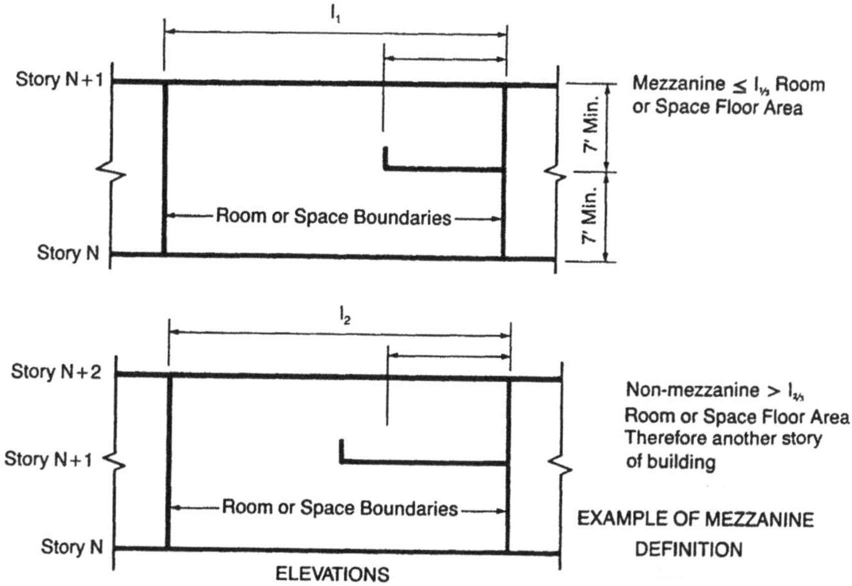

Assume intermediate floor level extends to other boundaries of room or space in elevations

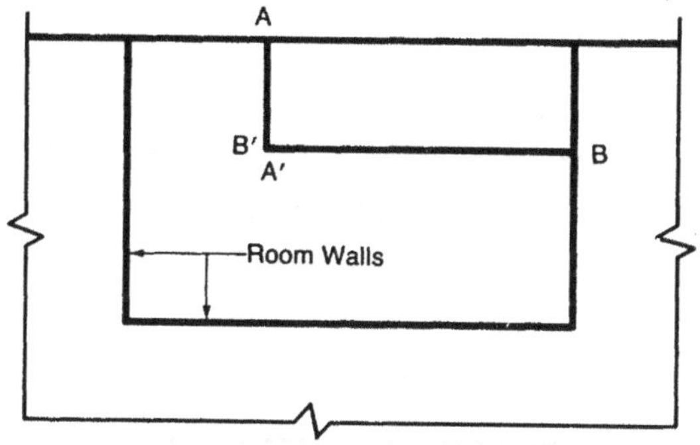

AA′ and BB′ essentially unenclosed

LIMITATIONS FOR UNENCLOSED MEZZANINES

1. Total of mezzanine areas in a room or space shall not exceed ⅓ the floor area of that room or space.
2. Construction of the mezzanine shall be the same as for the room or space in which it is located. Fire-resistive construction need not exceed one-hour.
3. Ceiling clear height above and below mezzanine to be 7 feet minimum.
4. Open sides may have columns, posts and 42" high wall or railing.
5. Two exits required per Table 10-A when mezzanine area exceeds 2,000 square feet.

REFERENCE: SECTION 214 and 507

FIGURE 5-27 MEZZANINE–UNENCLOSED

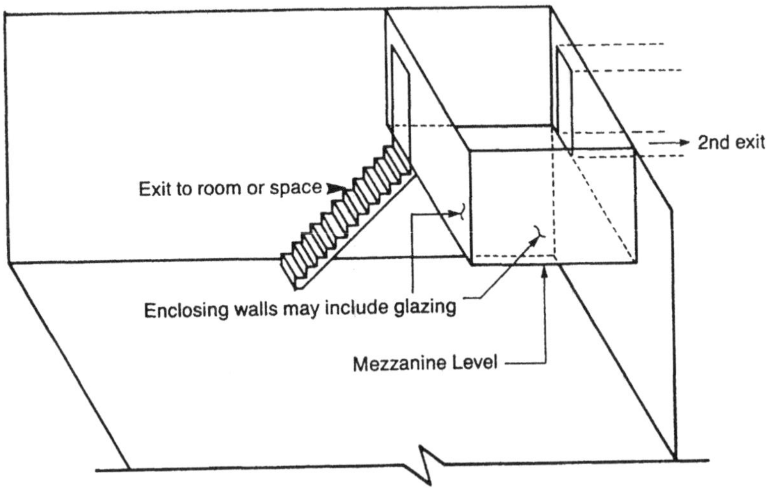

Isometric View

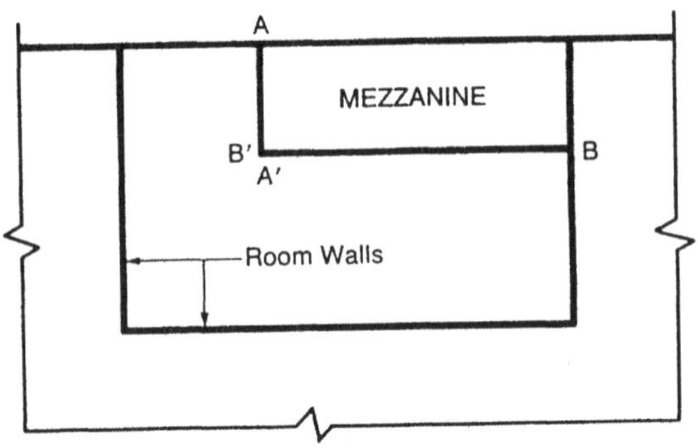

AA′ and BB′ may have enclosing walls

LIMITATIONS FOR ENCLOSED MEZZANINES

1. Figure 5-27, Items 1-3: these items also apply to enclosed mezzanines.
2. Every enclosed mezzanine must have two exits. One exit must go directly to an exit, not an exit access. (See Article 7 for detailed discussion of exit requirements.)

REFERENCE SECTION 214 AND 507

FIGURE 5-28 MEZZANINE–ENCLOSED

mezzanine occupant load will exit as stated and the other may go to the floor below it and be added to that floor's occupant load.

- The construction of the mezzanine must be comparable to that of the building in which it is located, with the further limitation that the fire-resistive rating of the mezzanine need not exceed 1 hour.
- There must be two exits for any mezzanine when required by Table 10-A provisions or when the mezzanine area is greater than 2000 square feet. The more restrictive criteria shall govern. If the mezzanine is enclosed, the provision cited in Subsection 4 Exception 2 takes precedence over this provision.

SECTION 508—FIRE-RESISTIVE SUBSTITUTION

When an approved automatic sprinkler system is not required throughout a building by other sections of this code, it may be used in a building of Type II One-hour, Type III One-hour and Type V One-hour construction to substitute for the one-hour fire-resistive construction. Such substitution shall not waive or reduce required fire-resistive construction for:

1. Occupancy separations (Section 302.3).

2. Exterior wall protection due to proximity of property lines (Section 503.2).

3. Area separations (Section 504.6).

4. Dwelling unit separations (Section 310.2.2).

5. Shaft enclosures (Section 711).

6. Corridors (Sections 1004.3.4.3.1 and 1004.3.4.3.2).

7. Stair enclosures (Section 1005.3.3).

8. Exit passageways (Section 1005.3.4).

9. Type of construction separation (Section 601.1).

10. Boiler, central heating plant or hot-water supply boiler room enclosures (Section 302.5).

The substitution of fire sprinklers for structural fire-resistive construction is permitted for buildings in which *only 1-hour fire-resistive construction throughout* is required by the code. These types of buildings are Type II One-hour, Type III One-hour and V One-hour. The section does not therefore apply to any other type of building or to any building not required to be of 1-hour resistive construction throughout.

Certain specific limitations to this substitution in the three types of building are listed. In addition, the substitution is not permitted when sprinklers throughout are required by other provisions of the code. Thus, for example, the substitution would not be permitted in Group H Occupancy buildings or in three- (or more) story Group R, Division 1 Occupancy buildings.

> In the authors' opinion, this section provides the opportunity for enforcement officials to permit the use of sprinklers as an alternative for certain other code provisions or limitations. For example, in a Group B Occupancy, Type V One-hour building, the designer may be willing to provide the 1-hour fire-resistive construction but may want to increase the percentage of protected glazing in an exit corridor.

The designer may offer to provide closely spaced fire sprinklers on both sides of the wired glass area. By using Section 104.2.8, the enforcement official can accept increased glazing area and fire sprinklers as providing equivalent or greater protection to the corridor and not be in violation of this section.

The provisions of this section do not limit the use of sprinklers in lieu of 1-hour fire-resistive construction in Type I or Type II-FR buildings for elements of those buildings. For example, if the designer offered to fully sprinkler a floor of a building that otherwise did not require sprinklers, the enforcement official could permit a wall required for a 1-hour occupancy separation to be of unrated construction.

This provides opportunities for designers and enforcement officials to reach innovative solutions to design problems without sacrificing safety.

SECTION 509—GUARDRAILS

509.1 Where Required. Unenclosed floor and roof openings, open and glazed sides of stairways, aisles, landings and ramps, balconies or porches, which are more than 30 inches above grade or floor below and roofs used for other than service of the building shall be protected by a guardrail.

EXCEPTION: Guardrails need not be provided at the following locations:

1. On the loading side of loading docks.

2. On the auditorium side of a stage or enclosed platform.

3. Along vehicle service pits not accessible to the public.

509.2 Height. The top of guardrails shall be not less than 42 inches in height.

EXCEPTIONS: 1. The top of guardrails for Group R, Division 3 and Group M, Division 1 Occupancies and interior guardrails within individual dwelling units, Group R, Division 3 congregate residences and guest rooms of Group R, Division 1 Occupancies may be 36 inches in height.

2. The top of guardrails on a balcony immediately in front of the first row of fixed seats and which are not at the end of an aisle may be 26 inches in height

3. The top of guardrails for stairways, exclusive of their landings, may have a height as specified in Section 3306 a) for handrails

Where an elevation change of 30 inches (762 mm) or less occurs between an aisle parallel to the seats (cross aisle) and the adjacent floor or grade below, guardrails not less than 26 inches (660 mm) above the aisle floor shall be provided.

EXCEPTION: Where the backs of seats on the front row of the cross aisle project 24 inches (610 mm) or more above the adjacent floor of the aisle, a guardrail need not be provided.

The top of guardrails at the ends of aisles terminating at the fascia of boxes, balconies and galleries shall extend for the width of the aisle and be no closer than 42 inches (1067 mm) to the closest surface of the aisle where there are steps and 36 niches (914 mm) otherwise.

509.3 Openings. Open guardrails shall have intermediate rails or an ornamental pattern such that a sphere greater than 4 inches in diameter cannot pass through.

EXCEPTIONS: 1. The open space between the intermediate rails or ornamental pattern of guardrails in areas of commercial and industrial-type occupancies which are not accessible to the public may be such that a sphere 12 inches in diameter cannot pass through.

2. The triangular openings formed by the riser, thread and bottom element of a guardrail at the open side of a stairway may be of such size that a sphere 6 inches (152 mm) in diameter cannot pass through.

For guardrail requirements at grandstands, bleachers or other elevated seating facilities, see Section 1008.5.7.

311.2.3.5 Vehicle Barriers. In all parking garages where any parking area is located more than 5 feet above the adjacent grade, vehicle barriers shall be provided.

EXCEPTION: Parking garages of Group U, Division 1 Occupancies.

Vehicle barriers shall have a minimum vertical dimension of 12 inches (457 mm) above the parking surface. See Table 16-B for load criterion.

Section 509 regulates guardrails; Section 311.2.3.5 regulates vehicular barriers. The guardrails and barriers referred to in these sections are only those that are part of a building or structure. Furthermore, although not stated in the code, numerous exceptions are traditionally applied in addition to those cited in the section.

In the authors' opinion, some additional exceptions should include

- play structures such as slides, jungle gyms, diving platforms, etc.,
- walks and ramps outside the building or structure,
- stairs and walls in gardens not within a building,
- show windows,
- trap doors in stages and other locations and
- attic access openings.

The previous requirements of this section were designated as Subsection (a) with the third paragraph of that subsection amended to require that a sphere greater than 4 inches must not pass through the intermediate rails or pattern. This reduction in the spacings permitted from the 6-inch sphere was predicated on considerable data obtained by the American Academy of Pediatrics on the physiognomy of young children.

A second exception was added to this paragraph to permit the triangular space formed on a stairway by the bottom rail of a guardrail, the riser and the tread. (See Figure 5-29.) This exception permits the size of the opening to prevent passage of a 6-inch sphere.

Although the code provisions refer to rails and ornamental patterns, there is no prohibition of the use of tempered glass or other solid or partially solid materials in constructing the guardrails.

Section 311.2.3.5 contains regulations for vehicle barriers in garages for those parking levels more than 5 feet above grade. Group U, Division 1 garages are exempted from these requirements.

The design force provision assumes a 1-square-foot area of impacting force on the guardrail, i.e., 6000 pounds on 1 square foot of guardrail. With this loading, the designer can design a vehicle barrier that will perform properly.

The barrier design may be a part of the guardrail or an independent element. In either design, the code requires that the forces be carried down to the structural framing. This provision mandates a properly thought out design carried to the support framing. (See Figure 5-30.)

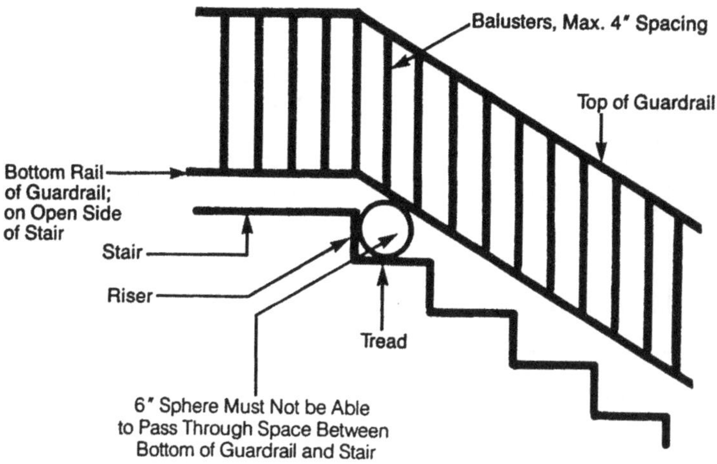

REFERENCE: SECTION 509.3

FIGURE 5-29 GUARDRAIL, OPENING BETWEEN BOTTOM RAIL AND STAIR

The minimum design elements of the barrier are set forth in the code provision; however, the design can incorporate these minimums within a design that serves the function of the barrier and satisfies the building design parameters of the project.

The barrier provision is the result of accidents and deaths resulting from barrier failures and recommendations of national groups in the parking garage field.

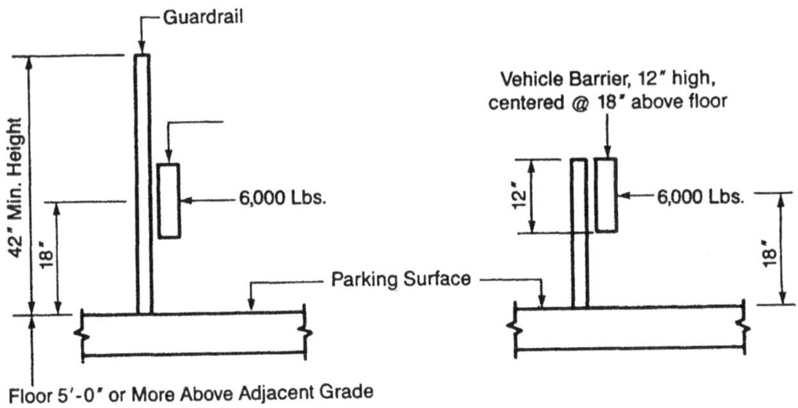

When the parking surface is more than 5'-0" above adjacent grade, there must be a vehicle barrier provided. The barrier can be either on the guardrail at the edge of the parking surface or can be a separate element.

The barrier must be capable of resisting a horizontal force of 6,000 pounds applied at 18" above the parking surface over a one square foot area of the barrier.

REFERENCE: SECTION 311.2.3.5, TABLE 16-B

FIGURE 5-30 VEHICLE BARRIER–MINIMUM DESIGN CRITERIA

ARTICLE 6
TYPE OF CONSTRUCTION

Chapter 6 Types of Construction

Chapter 6 contains the requirements relating to the type of construction for buildings. Included are the fire-resistive requirements of the building elements (the structural framing, roofs, shaft enclosures and bearing walls), insulation and weather protection.

The main fire-resistive construction requirements are described in Section 601.1 and Table 6-A. The remainder of Chapter 6 covers

- specific fire-resistive requirements,
- clarifying details for certain fire-resistive requirements and
- miscellaneous provisions for other aspects of the building construction that do not readily belong in another chapter.

The concept contained in Table 6-A, used in the model codes for the majority of buildings, is compartition. Compartition is defined as the dividing of a space into compartments. As discussed in Article 5 of this Guide in regard to the provisions of Chapter 3, control of conflagration from building lot to building lot is achieved through compartition of the building site according to the exterior wall and setback requirements for each building.

Within a building, the compartition is primarily created by

- the floor system,
- the stair and shaft enclosures and
- the protection of the structural load-bearing members (columns, beams, walls).

These building elements prevent both fire spread from floor to floor and the type of collapse that would break down the compartment formed by the floor system.

A fire is confined to a floor by these fire-resistive compartments. Floors with corridors serving different tenants or occupants generally have fire-rated walls. These walls further subdivide a floor into smaller compartments.

Within a tenant space, be it an apartment or an office, there are no specific requirements for compartition since these would

- be difficult to maintain,
- hamper operations within the space and
- not afford more than token safety in the event of fire due to inability to enforce the door closer, width of aisles, height of partitions and similar enforceability factors.

The less restrictive tenant provisions are contained in Section 601.5, Exceptions to Table 6-A, for the partitioning and nonload-bearing walls within apartments and offices.

The compartition concept also includes regulating the materials of construction and their combustibility for the compartment envelope, based on the building's type of construction. The materials in the envelope should not provide potential fire loading in a Type I building. In a Type V building, however, they are permitted to be combustible and could contribute to the fire load once the protective membrane on the structural element (the stud) has been breached.

Chapter 6 provisions cover a wide range of construction requirements for buildings. The primary emphasis of this article of the Guide is on the fire-resistive provisions: Other items in Chapter 6 such as weather protection, solar collectors and guardrails will be discussed to a limited degree.

The materials and fire-resistive requirements in Table 6-A are related to the occupancies in the buildings, as discussed in Article 5 of this Guide. This interrelationship must be recognized because the mandated requirements in Table 6-A and Section 504.5 may influence the designers decision.

For example, assume the building under design consideration is required to have an area separation wall, but that a fire-resistive rating is not required for its roof. Unless a parapet is constructed, the roof-ceiling assembly and its supporting structure must have at least a 1-hour fire rating. For this to be achieved, the entire building may have to be upgraded to at least a 1-hour fire-resistive rating. (See Figure 5-21.)

SECTION 601—CLASSIFICATION OF ALL BUILDINGS BY TYPES OF CONSTRUCTION AND GENERAL REQUIREMENTS

601.1 General. The requirements of this chapter are for the various types of construction and represent varying degrees of public safety and resistance

to fire. Every building shall be classified by the building official into one of the types of construction set forth in Table 6-A. Any building which does not entirely conform to a type of construction set forth in Table 6-A shall be classified by a building official into a type having an equal or lesser degree of fire resistance.

A building or portion thereof shall not be required to conform to the details of a type of construction higher than that type which meets the minimum requirements based on occupancy even though certain features of such building actually conform to a higher type of construction.

When specific materials, types of construction or fire-resistive protection are required, such requirements shall be the minimum requirements and any materials, types of construction or fire-resistive protection which will afford equal or greater public safety or resistance to fire, as specified in this code, may be used.

For additional limitations or allowances for special uses or occupancies, see the following;

SECTION	SUBJECT
402	Atria
403	High-rise office buildings and Group R, Division 1 Occupancies
404	Malls
405	Open parking structures
307.11	Group H, Division 6 Occupancies
411	Aviation control structures
413	Agricultural buildings
3111	Membrane structures

This section provides for the building official to determine the type of construction classification for a building. The classification is to be made based on the construction requirements for the particular type as set forth in Table 6-A. If the designer desires the building to be classified into a lesser type of fire-resistive construction, the building official can do so. The official must determine that, for the proposed building size and occupancy, Chapter 5 of the code permits a type of construction of equal or lesser fire resistance than that assigned to the building in Table 6-A. The evaluation of the "equal or lesser degree of fire resistance" is based on the proposed fire resistance of the building elements.

For example, if the proposed construction, as shown on the drawings, meets the type of construction known as Type II-FR, the designer could request that the building be classified as Type II One-hour, Type V One-hour or Type V-N. If such a lower type of construction is chosen by the designer, the height and area limitations of that class of construction, per Chapter 5, would govern.

The other provisions of this section include

- repeating the concept stated in Section 104.2.8, i.e., acceptance of equivalent construction to that required in Table 6-A and
- permitting the use of area separation walls per Section 504.6 so that each segment may be constructed as if it were a separate building, provided each segment created by the area separation walls meets the requirements for its particular type of construction.

601.5 Exceptions to Table No. 6-A

601.5.1 General. The provisions of this section are exceptions to the construction requirements of Table No. 6-A, Chapter 3 and Sections 602 through 606.

601.5.2 Fixed Partitions.

601.5.2.1 Stores and offices. Interior nonload-bearing partitions dividing portions of stores, offices or similar places occupied by one tenant only and which do not establish a corridor serving an occupant load that would require it to be of fire-resistive construction under the provisions of Section 1004.3.4.3.1 may be constructed of:

1. Noncombustible materials.
2. Fire-retardant treated wood.
3. One-hour fire-resistive construction.
4. Wood panels or similar light construction up to three fourths the height of the room In which placed; when more than three fourths the height of the room, such partitions shall have not less than the upper one fourth of the partition constructed In glass.

601.5.2.2 Hotels and apartments. Interior nonload-bearing partitions within Individual dwelling units in apartment houses and guest rooms or suites in hotels when such dwelling units, guest rooms or suites are separated from each other and from corridors by not less than one-hour fire-resistive construction may be constructed of:

1. Noncombustible materials or fire-retardant treated wood in buildings of any type of construction; or
2. Combustible framing with noncombustible materials applied to the framing in buildings of Type III or V construction.

Openings to such corridors shall be equipped with doors conforming to Section 1004.3.4.3.2 regardless of the occupant load served.

For use of plastics in partitions, see Section 2603.10.

The exceptions outlined in this section were discussed earlier. The designer should also note the provisions of Section 1005.3.3.2

for consideration along with Section 601.5.2 relating to nonload-bearing interior partitions in offices and stores.

Where there are sprinklers provided on an entire floor, the occupant load may be as great as 100 before fire-rated corridor walls are required within a tenancy. Where the partitions are less than 5 feet 9 inches high, the occupant load criteria does not apply. In fact, there is no maximum occupant load in such an office facility. (See the extensive discussion, in Article 7 of this Guide, regarding the Chapter 10 corridor requirements.)

NOTE: See comments at the end of Section 601.5.5 discussion.

601.5.4 Walls fronting on streets or yards. Regardless of fire-resistive requirements for exterior walls, certain elements of the walls fronting on streets or yards having a width of 40 feet may be constructed as follows:

1. Bulkheads below show windows, show-window frames, aprons and show-cases may be of combustible materials, provided the height of such construction does not exceed 15 feet above grade.

2. Wood veneer of boards not less than 1-inch (25 mm) nominal thickness or exterior panels not less than $\frac{3}{8}$-inch (9.5 mm) nominal thickness may be applied to walls, provided the veneer does not exceed 15 feet (4572 mm) above grade and further provided such veneer shall be placed either directly against noncombustible surfaces or furred out from such surfaces not to exceed $1\frac{5}{8}$ inches (41 mm) with all concealed spaces fire blocked as provided in Section 708. Where boards, panels and furring as described above comply with Section 207 as fire-retardant treated wood suitable for exterior exposure, the height above grade may be increased to 35 feet (10,688 mm).

See the discussion regarding Section 708.

601.5.5 Trim. Trim, picture molds, chair rails, baseboard, handrails and show window backing may be of wood. Unprotected wood doors and windows may be used except where openings are required to be fire protected.

Foam plastic trim covering not more than 10 percent of the wall or ceiling area may be used, provided such trim (1) has a density of no less than 20 pounds per cubic foot (320.4 kg/m^3), (2) has a maximum thickness of $\frac{1}{2}$-inch (12.7 mm) and a maximum width of 4 inches (102 mm) and (3) has a flame-spread rating no greater than 75.

Materials used for interior finish of walls and ceilings, including wainscoting, shall be as specified in Chapter 8.

The designer should be aware that these code provisions for foam plastic trim can be misapplied. During construction, the determination of these percentages will be made by field personnel whose decision may differ from that of the designer as represented in his drawings. The materials can then be used in actual constructions that are outside the control of the designer unless the designer, through field observations, becomes actively involved in the construction phase.

Technically, in cases of litigation, the designer may truly have no responsibility for any misapplication or for extension beyond the allowed percentages. However, the litigation process would probably involve the designer in some capacity. Because of this possibility, the designer should consider avoiding use of materials that rely on "bookkeeping" controls, unless the designer has the authority during the construction phase to prevent misuse of this code section.

> In the authors' opinion, foam plastic materials present a serious hazard potential of generating considerable quantities of smoke in the event of a fire. This potential hazard therefore warrants the designer to carefully evaluate the use of these materials.

NOTE: In the following comments regarding Sections 601.5.2.2 and 601.5.5, this Guide offers conservative recommendations that should result in lesser likelihood of field errors and, hence, a safer building. When the designer is confident that the field work will be properly controlled, the use of these code provisions is warranted.

To avoid misapplication of materials, the designer should consider whether his or her involvement in the project, after the design phase is completed, will allow adequate field control of the construction. It is unlikely that the level of field supervision or materials control on a large project will be adequate enough to avoid these field errors. It is best that such avoidance begin during the design process.

When considering the use of Section 601.5.2.2 for Group R, Division 1 Occupancy, it is important to anticipate the possible results from the use of nonrated construction within the dwelling units. For example, assume that a designer proposes to have the load-bearing elements in the Group R, Division I Occupancy building covered with $\frac{5}{8}$-inch Type X wallboard and the interior nonload-bearing partitions covered with $\frac{1}{2}$-inch standard (nonfire-rated) wallboard. There is a strong possibility that when the carpenters install the wallboard, they may mix the materials and use whatever is on hand at that particular location.

Unfortunately this has repeatedly been the case. Nonrated construction has been found installed in locations that were to have fire-rated construction. The designer should consider whether to accept the probability of misapplication or, for the nominal additional cost involved, use only the $\frac{5}{8}$-inch Type X wallboard in the building. Doing this would avoid the possibility of misapplication by the workers of the required wallboard.

Since the code requirements set only the minimum acceptable standard, good practice to avoid field errors would be to design to a higher-than-minimum level.

Table 6-A Types of Construction—Fire-Resistive Requirements

Table 6-A is used with the provisions of

- Sections 302.4 and 504,3 for occupancy separation and area separation walls, respectively,
- Section 1004.3.4 for corridors and
- Section 1003.3.3 for stairways.

The table provides the overall construction requirements of the basic building elements and systems.

Chapter 5 addresses the two main fire concerns of the code provisions:

1. prevention of a conflagration spreading from building to building and
2. prevention of fire spread within a building to avoid either collapse of the structure or fire moving from floor to floor.

The details for achieving the degree of fire resistance indicated in Table 6-A are outlined in Chapter 7. There are, in addition, other reference documents including the Evaluation Reports of ICBO, the Underwriters Laboratories Inc. *Fire Resistance Directory* and the Gypsum Association *Fire Resistance Manual,* to name a few of the most common sources.

The concepts of fire protection, allowable areas and heights are represented in the hourly ratings in this table. An examination of the elements of the table is of assistance in visualizing this code approach. For an analysis of this table and the types of construction therein, see Technical Appendix TA-2.

Table 6-A includes stairway construction as a building element. Although the item appears to simply be a listing of the cross references to the Chapter 6 provisions, the intent is to clarify the fire protection requirements, particularly for Type V One-hour buildings.

Stairways in Type V One-hour buildings may have exposed wood stair treads, risers and stringers. The enclosure provisions of Section 1005.3.3 apply to the separation requirements of the stairway from the rest of the building.

Thus, the stairway construction provision of Table 6-A is consistent with the Chapter 10 provisions and provide cross references for the stairway construction requirements only insofar as the materials and riser/tread/stringer construction are concerned. The stairway enclosure and occupancy separation requirements, when applicable, would still apply per Chapters 10 and 5, respectively.

The method for determining the exterior structural frame rating is illustrated for Type I and II buildings in Figure 6-1 for Group B Occupancy. Similar rationale can apply to other occupancies and types of construction.

Type of Construction Analysis

This section discusses the provisions of Table 6-A regarding the types of construction and the relationship of the provisions therein.

Type V Construction

Starting with the least fire-resistive type of building construction, Type V-N building in Table 6-A, no building elements other than shaft enclosures require hourly fire ratings. A check of Section 711.3 indicates that there are exceptions to this requirement:

- In other than Group I Occupancies, openings that penetrate only one floor and are not connected with other

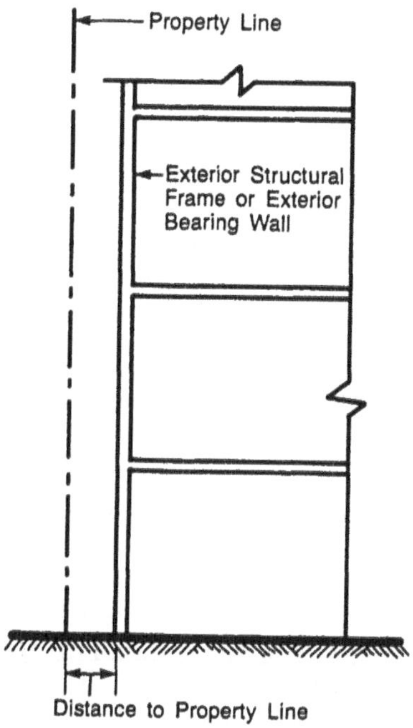

GIVEN: Type II-FR Building
Group B Occupancy

When the exterior wall is located so that, per Table 5-A or the .3 sections of Chapter 6, openings are either not permitted or require protection, the structural frame must be protected for the time period cited in Table 6-A for the exterior bearing walls or for the "structural frame" requirements, whichever is the higher hourly rating.

Thus for a Type I or II-FR building within 20 feet of the property line, the structural frame must be protected for four hours. When the exterior wall is more than 20 feet from the property line, the structural frame need only be protected for two hours. See Sections 602.3 and 603.3 and Table 6-A.

REFERENCE: TABLE 6-A, FOOTNOTE 1 AND SECTIONS 602.3, 603.3, 604.3, 605.3, 606.3

FIGURE 6-1 FIRE-RESISTIVE RATING FOR STRUCTURAL FRAME EXTERIOR WALL

openings communicating with other stories or basements need not be enclosed.

- In one- and two-story buildings other than Group I Occupancies, gas vents, piping and factory-built chimneys that extend through not more than two floors need not be enclosed.

In the review of the concepts of Table 6-A, we will address only the major requirements and not those special items whose exceptions are cross referenced to other parts of the code, as with Type V shaft enclosures.

The Type V-N building is assigned the lowest allowable area, number of floors and building height in Table 5-B for each occupancy group. Thus, the least fire-resistive building has the smallest allowable areas and the lowest allowable heights. These limitations mean that a fire in such a building would affect only a limited number of stories and occupants.

Type II-N and III-N Construction

Presumably, the other two nonfire-rated building types, Types II-N and III-N, would have similar restrictive heights and areas per Chapter 5. This, however, is not the case. The Table 6-A requirements—and the character of the buildings these two types of construction represent—will be discussed in light of the two main fire spread criteria of the code concept.

All Type II buildings are required to be constructed of noncombustible materials, i.e., the structure will not provide fuel to a fire. With the noncombustible requirement satisfied, the allowable area, but not the number of stories of the Type II-N building, is permitted to be increased. A comparison of these two types of construction with the Type V-N building, using Table 5-B, shows the greater allowable area afforded to Type II buildings as a result of their noncombustible construction materials.

The noncombustible characteristics theoretically will limit the intensity of the fire and thus reduce the overall conflagration potential. Therefore, the allowable area for the Type II-N building is increased over that allowed for the Type V-N building. However, the lack of fire separations and protection for building support members within the building permits fire spread from floor to floor or collapse, if a bearing member were attacked by a fire. Thus, the number of allowable stories remains the same in the Type II-N buildings as in the Type V-N building for all occupancies except for H-6 and H-7.

The Type III-N building, however, has fire-resistive requirements for the exterior walls of the building. Although this type of building can be constructed internally of any type of material, combustible or noncombustible, the exterior wall has to be noncombustible.

The fire-resistive requirements of the exterior wall elements will assist considerably in limiting conflagration potential from a fire either within the structure or from another building. Accordingly, the Type III-N building is considered on a par with the Type II-N building for allowable area. However, the exterior wall protection does not provide any additional safety within the building from either the fire spread or internal collapse if interior support members are attacked by a fire. The number of stories for the Type III-N building is therefore the same as the Type II-N and V-N buildings, again, with the exception of the H-6 and H-7 occupancies.

Type II One-Hour, III One-Hour and V One-Hour Construction

The three building types having at least a minimum 1-hour fire-resistive requirement, Types II One-hour, III One-hour and V One-hour, are substantially more fire-resistive than nonfire-rated types. The Table 5-B provisions indicate that both the conflagration hazard and the internal fire spread or collapse hazard are mitigated by the 1-hour construction requirement.

Accordingly, their allowable areas are greater than for the comparable nonfire-rated buildings. The three types of 1-hour buildings are not considered equal to one another in their limitation of the conflagration hazard. The Type V One-hour building has neither the degree of exterior wall protection required for the Type III One-hour building nor the limitation of combustibility for the materials used to construct the Type II One-hour building. Therefore, the Type V One-hour building is permitted a lesser allowable floor area than the other two 1-hour building types.

Type I and II-FR Construction

The component of the Type I and II-FR buildings are required to have substantially greater fire-resistive ratings than those of the 1-hour buildings. Except for the roof and the interior nonbearing partitions, all the fire-resistive ratings for the Type II-FR buildings are for the most part double those of the 1-hour structures. The allowable area is generally at least double those allowed for the 1-hour buildings.

The hazard of interior fire spread or collapse is sharply reduced due to the minimum 2-hour requirement for the floors and the structural and interior bearing walls. As a result, for many of the occupancies the allowable number of stories for the Type II-FR building is greatly increased over that allowed for the 1-hour buildings. The danger to the occupants and fire fighters in such a building is reduced because more time is available for evacuation and fire fighting.

The Type I building represents the highest type of fire-resistive construction because the fire rating for the entire structural support system is raised to 2 or 4 hours. The resultant reduction of the building collapse hazard is considerable. The code allows unlimited area and height of the Type I building for almost all occupancies because of the substantial fire resistance of the building.

The only exception to this unlimited allowable area applies to the Group H-1 and H-2 Occupancies. The code considers that the hazards associated with the H-1 and H-2 Occupancies could be such that even the fire-resistive requirements of the Type I building are insufficient to permit more than a 15,000 square-foot basic allowable area.

Type IV Construction

The remaining type of construction, Type IV, is an anomaly insofar as our prior rationale is concerned. This building is also known as a Heavy Timber, or HT type. It represents a construction type common for factories at the turn of the century: the mill building. This was a structure built with exterior walls of masonry and exterior openings protected by steel shutters. The interior was all wood of very heavy and substantial dimensions. The columns, beams and girders were massive timbers. The floors, because they had to support a heavy load of equipment or storage, were of heavy planking usually at least 3 inches thick and tightly joined.

The fire experience with these buildings indicated that a fire was usually contained within the structure. In most instances the heavy floor members helped slow the fire's spread from floor to floor and allowed evacuation and fire fighting to proceed. The massive columns and beams were slow to burn through and cause collapse.

For these reasons, the Type IV or HT building is permitted the same allowable areas and stories as the Type II and III One-hour buildings.

However, the system of establishing fire-resistive ratings using the ASTM standard E-119 fire test procedure does not equate HT with 1-hour construction, nor does the code. In this instance we are guided by experience rather than scientific rationale.

ARTICLE 7
MEANS OF EGRESS PROVISIONS OF CHAPTER 10

CHAPTER 10 MEANS OF EGRESS

NOTE: This UBC chapter has been revised in its entirety.

Overview

Chapter 10 of the Uniform Building Code (UBC) contains the requirements for designing exiting systems, now known as "means of egress." A means of egress provides a continuous, unobstructed and undiminished path of exit travel from any occupied point in a building to a public way.

> **1001.1 Scope. Every building or portion thereof shall be provided with a means of egress as required by this chapter. A means of egress is an exit system that provides a continuous, unobstructed and undiminished path of exit travel from any occupied point in a building or structure to a public way. Such means of egress system consists of three separate and distinct elements:**
>
> **1. The exit access,**
> **2. The exit, and**
> **3. The exit discharge.**

The term "means of egress" is used in all of the other model codes and is the general term now applied to ways of getting out of a building. *Webster's Third New International Dictionary of the English Language* is the reference noted in Section 201 of the code for ordinarily adopted meanings. This defines egress as "1: the act or right of going or coming out." This term has been chosen to encompass all of the parts, or components, of the system for getting people out of a building in an emergency.

This new set of definitions allows such common terms as "exit" or "exit discharge" to take on more specific, code-defined meanings as components of a "means of egress," which is the complete system for escape. Pay close attention to nomenclature as you familiarize yourself with this totally new chapter. This is one chapter where past experience with the code may actually be a hindrance to successful application of the chapter requirements. Terms with old, familiar meanings from prior editions of the code take on wholly different meanings in the new chapter. As one example, the definition of "corridor" has always been problematic for the developers of the UBC. The new connotations and relationships of corridors to other means of egress components in this new chapter unfortunately do not clear up past conflicts and may add new ones to the problem of defining and designing egress systems. Those with some familiarity with the UBC should not assume that this chapter is just a rearrangement of old words and concepts. Old words take on new meanings in this revision to Chapter 10. See Figure 7-1 for a depiction of the basic elements of a means of egress.

The chapter is divided into segments based on the progression of design of a means of egress:

a. The basic criteria for determining the number and width of exits required [1001, 1002, 1003]
b. The Exit Access [1004]
c. The Exit [1005]
d. The Exit Discharge [1006]

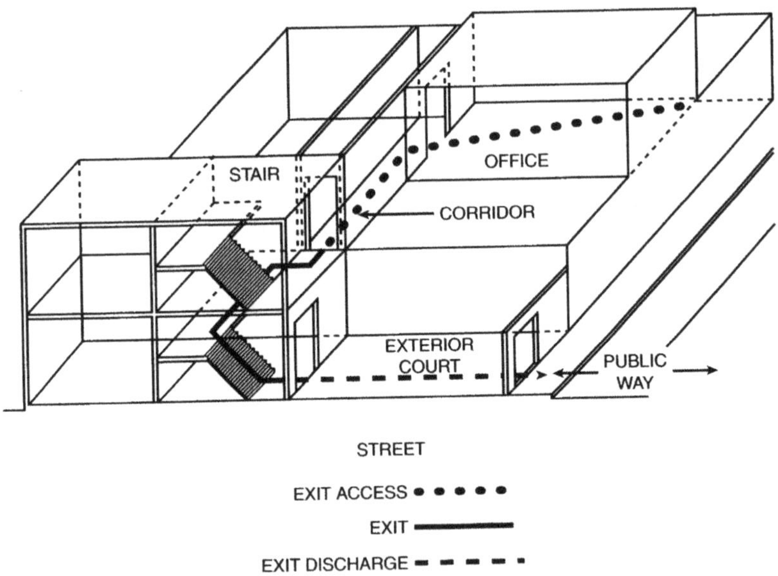

REFERENCE: SECTION 1001.1

FIGURE 7-1 ELEMENTS OF EXIT PATH

e. Specific Means of Egress Requirements Based on Occupancy [1007]
f. Requirements for Reviewing Stands, Grandstands, Bleachers, and Folding and Telescoping Seating [1008]
g. Building Security [1009 and Appendix Chapter 10]

Subsections are arranged logically. The .2 sections address the design requirements (the "what") and the .3 sections address the components to be used in that particular portion of the means of egress (the "how").

The means of egress for every occupancy in a building must meet the provisions of this chapter. The requirements are driven by the occupancy of the area to be provided with egress and the occupant load calculated per Table 10-A. A building may contain several occupancies. The designer has to consider all of the uses, present or contemplated, so that adequate numbers and widths of exits are provided. The occupant load is typically calculated as if each area is occupied at the same time to determine the maximum possible number of occupants to be accommodated by the means of egress. There are specific and narrow exceptions to the requirements for calculating occupant load, which will be discussed later. The basic design principal for a means of egress is to get all of the potential number of occupants out of the building in a safe and expeditious manner. The best analogy to remember is that of water courses. Small streams lead to creeks, which feed rivers, which then lead to the sea. Rivers get larger as they go downstream and carry more water as tributaries feed into them. So should the conceptual design of a means of egress. There is a direction of flow to every means of egress, leading from an occupied space to a final safe outside area, away from any hazard or emergency in the building. The means of egress should lead from areas of lesser safety to areas of greater safety and must remain the same size or get larger as the building occupants proceed "downstream" in the means of egress.

Certain definitions have important application for the designer. The term "exit" is obviously one such term. The essential feature of an exit is a continuity of unobstructed traverse to the public way outside the building. The exit door from the exterior of the building should provide access to the public way in compliance with the definitions of exit and exit discharge. This means that the exit discharge should meet the criteria for access to the public way, open to the sky and available for public use.

There are many ways of obtaining such access to the public way. The designer should determine early in the design process that the proposed means of egress satisfies the intent of the code, particularly when it does not show a clear path, but may require traversing courts, yards or obstructed spaces.

Another basic exiting principle is that at least two different exit paths should lead from the interior of a building to the outside at ground level. The rationale is that if one path is blocked or endangered by a hazard then the other path will be available. There are minor exceptions to this rule based on relatively small numbers of occupants, but the designer should begin with the basic design concept that two ways out of any space should be provided for emergencies.

Two sections of the exit path are required to provide fire-resistive protection to the occupant. These components start at the access door to a corridor, then lead to an exit, extend in the exit enclosure down through the building and then to the exit discharge leading to the exterior. Once in the corridor or exit stairway, the occupant is to remain protected until the building exterior is reached.

The general objective of exiting, that of providing a continuous path of protection to the outside of the building, is basic to the code and must be thoroughly understood. It must also be understood that when the exit path from a major occupancy of the building passes through an area containing another occupancy, possibly a public assembly or a garage area, the exit path retains the occupancy class designation and fire protection requirements of the main use. The provisions of Section 1004 apply to these locations.

In some instances occupancy separation requirements may exceed the egress enclosure rating requirements. For example, if the path of travel is through a tunnel, corridor or exit passageway from a stairway to the street, the separation may be required to have a greater hourly rating than the 1- or 2-hour rating of the stair enclosure. If a higher degree of protection is required for the occupancy separation between the occupancy on the floor and the occupancy whose exit way is traversing the floor, the higher protection requirement will apply.

Definitions and Basic Concepts

SECTION 1002—DEFINITIONS

For the purpose of this chapter, certain terms are defined as follows:

EXIT (1005.1) is that portion of the means of egress system between the exit access and the exit discharge or the public way. Components that may

be selectively included in the exit include exterior exit doors, exit enclosures, exit passageways and horizontal exits, in addition to those common means of egress components described in Section 1003.3.

EXIT ACCESS (1004.1) is that portion of the means of egress system between any occupied point in a building or structure and a door of the exit. Components that may be selectively included in the exit access include aisles, hallways and corridors, in addition to those means of egress components described in Section 1003.3

EXIT DISCHARGE (1006.1) is that portion of the means of egress system between the exit and the public way. Components that may be selectively included in the exit discharge include exterior exit balconies, exterior exit stairways, exterior exit ramps, exit courts and yards, in addition to those common means of egress components described in Section 1003.1.

EXIT DOOR (1003.3.1.1) shall mean all of those doors or doorways along the path of exit travel anywhere in a means of egress system.

MEANS OF EGRESS (1001.1) is an exit system that provides a continuous, unobstructed and undiminished path of exit travel from any occupied point in a building or structure to a public way.

HORIZONTAL EXIT (1005.3.5.1) is a wall that completely divides a floor of a building into two or more separate exit-access areas to afford safety from fire and smoke in the exit-access area of incident origin.

PUBLIC WAY is any street, alley or similar parcel of land essentially unobstructed from the sky to the ground that is deeded, dedicated or otherwise permanently appropriated to the public for public use and having a clear width of not less than 10 feet (3048 mm).

The exit path normally consists of three components or sections. Since this concept is new to the Uniform Building Code it is worth reiterating some of the basic definitions set forth above. The components are listed in the order that a building occupant would encounter them in exiting the building:

1. *The Exit Access.* This is typically that portion of the path of exit travel leading from an occupied room or space to a door giving access to a fire-rated, protected enclosure (the "exit"); for example, an exit stairway. In the typical exit path from a room or space, one may encounter aisles, hallways, corridors or other rooms before gaining access to the protected enclosure. The distance to be traversed is limited by the code, as will be covered in the Section 1004 analysis. The basic concept of the exit access it that it is the part of the building where the occupants of the building are engaged in the functions for which the building was designed. It allows the occupants the most freedom of movement, but conversely parts of the exit access offer the lowest level of life safety protection of any of the components of the means of egress. This is the space to be gotten out of in an emergency. This corresponds to the portion of a building where travel distance was measured under previous

editions of the code. Typical components of exit access include rooms, aisles, hallways, doors and corridors.

2. *The Exit.* The exit portion of the means of egress is defined as that portion of egress travel between the exit access and the exit discharge. This is a path of exit travel through a protected enclosure. Where the enclosure is an exit passageway, as in an upper level of a building, it will connect to at least one, and usually two, stairways. The distance one may travel within a protected exit enclosure is not limited by the code. This part of the egress path may be very long, for example, the stairways in a high-rise building. This is the protected portion of the means of egress that allows the occupants to be in a protected environment from the area where a hazardous event is occurring to a place where they may finally escape the building. Exits include exterior exit doors, exit enclosures, exit passageways and horizontal exits.

3. *The Exit Discharge.* This is the connection from the exit to a public way, including exterior exit balconies, exterior stairs, exterior exit ramps, exit courts and yards. Many of these are building-related components, but this also includes site elements. This portion of the means of egress is typically assumed to be at grade and open to the atmosphere. The occupants are able to clearly see where an area of safety outside the building lies and are able move toward it. Travel distance is limited at other than grade level, but not limited at grade. Exit discharge includes exit courts, exterior exit stairways/ramps, yards and exterior exit balconies. There are potential problems associated with exit balconies, which are most likely not at grade, being considered part of the exit discharge. This will be discussed at greater length later in the chapter.

It is important that components be integrated with the requirements for accessible means of egress stated in Chapter 11. Some provisions of Chapter 11 may supersede those of Chapter 10. These chapters must be considered together.

The basic elements of an egress system are shown in Figures 7-2, 7-3, and 7-4.

The means of egress for a small one-story building is usually simple, since the second and third sections of the exit path are often combined. A corridor may extend to the exterior wall and open onto a street, yard or other public space. This simultaneously provides the exit access, the exit and the exit discharge to the exterior public way of the building at ground level. In many one-story buildings, such as retail stores and banks, only the first portion of the means of egress exists. The room or space opens directly

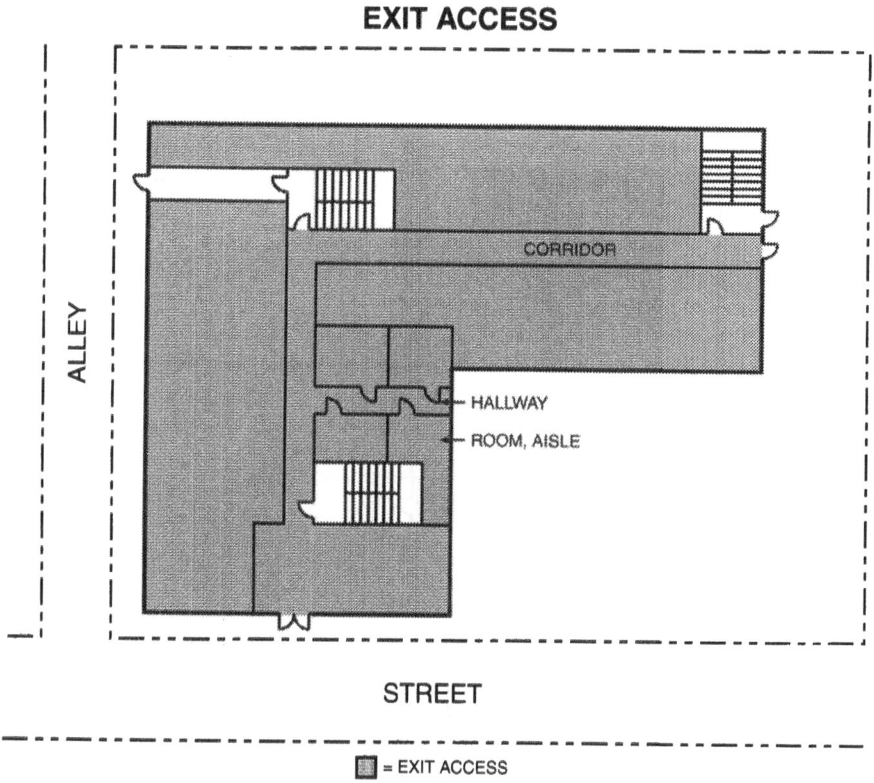

REFERENCE: SECTION 1004

FIGURE 7-2 TYPICAL EXIT ACCESS COMPONENTS

to the building's exterior without the need of protected corridors or stairways. It is important to remember that the distance one may travel in an exit access, from the most remote point in the room or space to the exterior doorway, is regulated by the code. It may be necessary to provide a fire-rated passage, such as a corridor, for larger floor areas that may exceed the travel distances for various other means of egress components. Travel distances are not restricted in exits or in the portion of the exit discharge located at grade.

The general requirements that there be two exit paths available has as its determinants

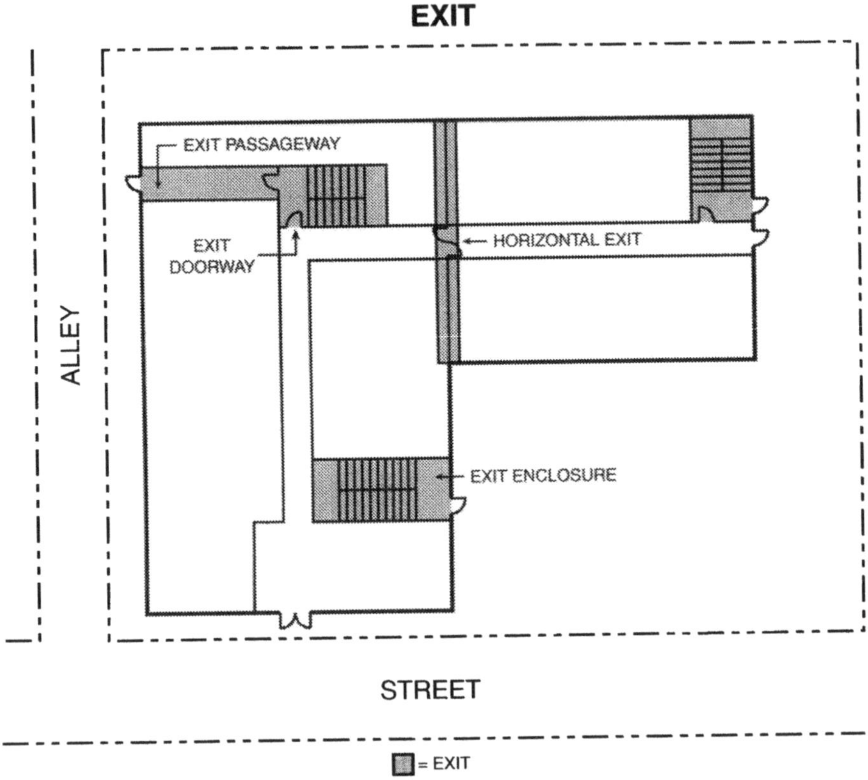

REFERENCE: SECTION 1005

FIGURE 7-3 TYPICAL EXIT COMPONENTS

- the number of people that may be in a room, space or floor and
- the number of stories in the building

If the maximum number of occupants in a space is small, the code does not require that two paths be provided. Although this allowance may at first seem to reflect a callous disregard for people's lives, one must consider that a building code has to take into account the cost/benefit involved in such a requirement. It would be impractical to require a two-story building, with a 500-square-foot apartment on both floors, to provide two separate exits for each unit. On the other hand, the larger and taller the building, the greater

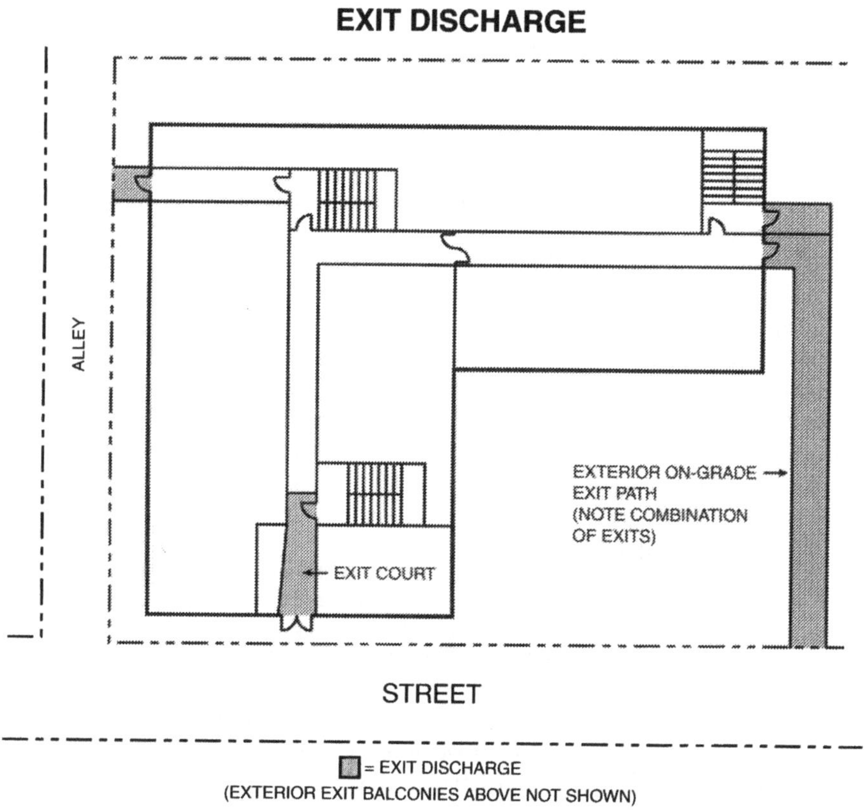

REFERENCE: SECTION 1006

FIGURE 7-4 TYPICAL EXIT DISCHARGE COMPONENTS

the number of occupants. As the number of occupants increases, so does the potential danger to them, thus warranting the multiple-exit requirement.

If a space is used as a warehouse, the probable number of occupants would be low since the majority of the space would contain stored material. On the other hand, if a space is used as a bar, in a popular location, the number of occupants could at times be very large in relation to the relatively small area of the space. The occupant load factors in Table 10-A are based on such assumptions regarding the number of occupants associated with various uses. Although one might want to challenge the seemingly arbitrary numbers established by the code, there is sufficient empirical evidence to sustain their validity.

General

1003.2.1.2 Change in use. No change in use or occupancy shall be made to any existing building or structure unless the means of egress system is made to comply with the requirements of this chapter for the new use or occupancy. See Section 3405.

As specified in Section 1003.2.1.2 the requirements of Chapter 10 are triggered when a change in use or occupancy occurs. It is important to remember that this section is applicable even if no remodeling is intended to occur. When such a change in use or occupancy occurs, the means of egress that serves the affected area should be analyzed for compliance to the current code.

1003.2.2 Occupant load.
1003.2.2.1 General. The basis for the design of the means of egress system is the occupant load served by the various components of such system.
1003.2.2.2 Determination of occupant load. Occupant loads shall be determined in accordance with the requirements of this section.

The term used for describing the code-related space assigned per occupant for the different occupancies is "occupant load." In Table 10-A, Minimum Egress Requirements, it is called the "occupant load factor," but the simpler term will be used hereafter due to its general use in both the UBC and other references. The occupant load for a space is the floor area of that space divided by the occupant load factor from Table 10-A for the particular occupancy. Note that these factors are to be used only for determining occupant loads for means of egress. Footnote 3 to Table 10-A states: "This table shall not be used to determine working space requirements per person." It is not necessary that every office worker have a 100-square-foot office even though the occupant load factor is 100. As previously indicated, these values and numbers are based not on the actual physical situation within any building, but, for code purposes, on probabilities. The values are codified so that they can be used by anyone in determining the exit details; i.e., the number and width of the exit components. They are not intended as design program guidelines.

The exit quantity requirements apply to all parts of the means of egress design. However they do not appear until Section 1004, which describes the *exit access*. Note that even though these requirements occur in the exit access section they have application throughout Chapter 10. See the discussion regarding Section 1004.2.3 in detail, which appears later in this article. The basic concepts will be introduced here in general and discussed in detail later. (See Figure 7-5.)

The criteria for determining the basic number of exits required typically applies to the whole of one-story buildings and also to individual spaces located within any building. Additional determinants apply to multistory buildings. Note that at least two exit paths must be provided for all basements and all floors above the first floor. Exceptions allow one exit from the second floor or basement under specific circumstances where there are fewer than 10 occupants. The same calculations are used to determine the number of exit doorways from a room or space anywhere in a building required to give access to a protected corridor, stairway or the exterior of a building. At least two exit doorways are required when the occupant load of the room or space equals or exceeds the number for that use according to Table 10-A. To assure that such doorways remain accessible in the event of fire or panic, they must be separated from each other by a distance equal to at least one-half the diagonal dimension of the space involved. (See Figure 7-6.)

> **1003.2.2.2.1 Areas to be included.** In determining the occupant load, all portions of a building shall be presumed to be occupied at the same time.
>
> **EXCEPTION:** Accessory use areas that ordinarily are used only by persons who occupy the main areas of an occupancy shall be provided with means of egress as though they are completely occupied, but their occupant load need not be included when computing the total occupant load of the building.

As noted above, the requirements for design of a means of egress are driven by occupant load. Each space is to be considered as fully occupied when designing the means of egress. The only exception is for areas that are considered "accessory uses." If persons can be considered to be in either space A *or* space B, then the total occupant load would be the largest of either A or B. It is important to remember that even for accessory uses the exit access from each space must still be designed to accommodate the anticipated number of occupants for each space. The occupant load may be located in either space. The number of exits required from each space is determined by anticipated occupant load based on the occupant load factor for each. (See Figure 7-7.)

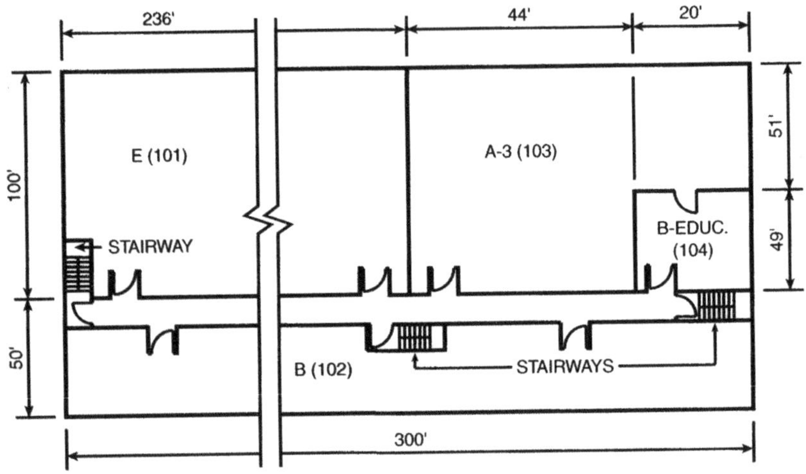

Occupancy	Room. No.	Size	Area - Square Feet	Occupant Load per Square Foot	Occupant Load
B	101	100 x 236	23,600	100	236
B	102	50 x 300	15,000	100	150
A-3	103	44 x 100	4,400	15	294
		51 x 20	1,020	15	68
B(Education)	104	49 x 20	980	20	49
				TOTAL OCCUPANT LOAD =	797

Note that servant spaces such as corridors and stairs are not counted since they serve the occupied spaces.

Number of exits per Section 1004.2.3. 3 exits required per Section 1004.2.3.4 since the occupant load is greater than 500. All rooms require a minimum of 2 means of egress since each has an occupant load of more than 50, except for the small B educational occupancy in Room 104.

Width of exits required per Section 1003.2.3.2 and Table 10-B. Exit widths calculated as below:

Total Occupant Load:	797
Corridor Width in inches:	797 x 0.2 = 159.40″
Divided among 3 exits:	159.40″/3 = 53.13″ = 4.43 feet width for each corridor (may be adjusted among exits as long as minimum widths are maintained)
Stair widths:	797 x 0.3 = 239.10″
Divided among 3 stairs:	239.10/3 = 79.70″ = 6.64′ width for each stair (may be adjusted among exits as long as minimum widths are maintained)

REFERENCE: SECTION 1003.2.2 AND SECTION 1004.2.3

FIGURE 7-5 OCCUPANT LOAD CALCULATIONS & NUMBER OF EXITS BASED ON OCCUPANT LOAD

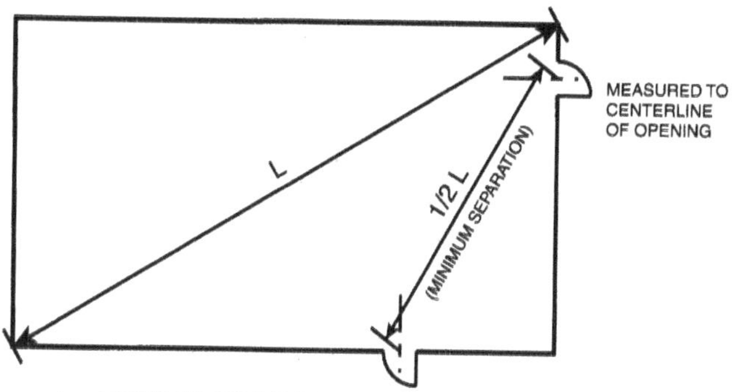

L = LENGTH OF DIAGONAL DISTANCE
1/2 L = ONE-HALF LENGTH OF DIAGONAL DISTANCE

REFERENCE: SECTION 1004.2.4

FIGURE 7-6 DIAGONAL DISTANCES FOR EXIT SEPARATIONS

The exceptions for accessory uses do not apply to corridors, toilet facilities, storage areas and other rooms used by the public. These public areas are to be included in the occupant load determination.

> **1003.2.2.2.2 Areas without fixed seats.** For areas without fixed seats, the occupant load shall not be less than the number determined by dividing the floor area under consideration by the occupant load factor assigned to the use for such area as set forth in Table 10-A.
>
> The occupant load for buildings or areas containing two or more uses or occupancies shall be determined by adding the occupant loads of the various use areas as computed in accordance with the applicable requirements of Section 1003.2.2.2.
>
> Where an individual area has more than one proposed use, the occupant load for such area shall be determined based on that use that yields the largest occupant load.

Occupant loads for areas with fixed seats are set by the number of seats. In areas without fixed seats the occupant load is determined by using the occupant load factor for the open area. For pews 18 inches is assigned per occupant. For booths used for dining the length assigned per occupant is 24 inches. Note that the distance

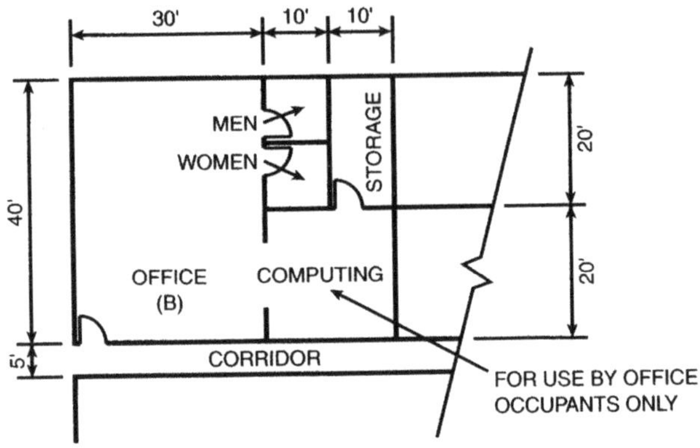

A.

OCCUPANT LOAD:

Occupancy	Dimensions	Area in square feet	Occupant Load Factor	Occupant Load
B - Office	30 x 40	1200	100	12
Computing	20 x 20	400	Accessory	---
Toilets - Men	10 x 10	100	Accessory	---
Toilets - Women	10 x 10	100	Accessory	---
Storage	10 x 20	200	Accessory	---
		TOTAL OCCUPANT LOAD		12

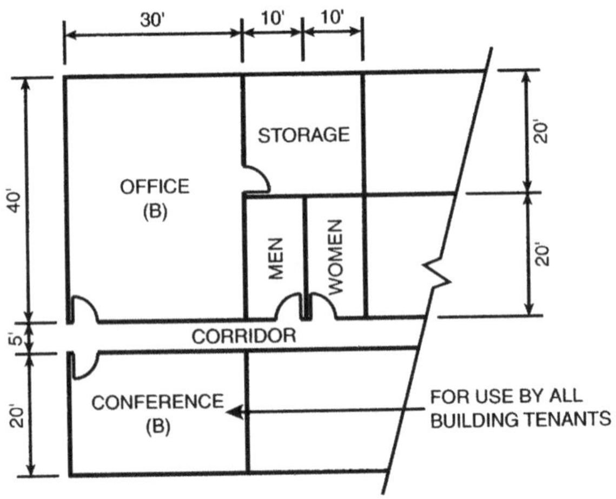

B.

OCCUPANT LOAD:

Occupancy	Dimensions	Area in square feet	Occupant Load Factor	Occupant Load
B - Office	30 x 40	1200	100	12
Conference	30 x 20	600	15	40
Toilets - Men	10 x 20	200	Accessory	---
Toilets - Women	10 x 20	200	Accessory	---
Storage	10 x 20	200	Accessory	---
		TOTAL OCCUPANT LOAD		52

REFERENCE: SECTION 1003.2.2.2.1

for measuring curved booths is to be the longest radius. This will lead to a higher number of occupants than will actually be able to sit at the booth since the inside radius determines how people's knees fit together. This is a minor additional element in determining occupant load, but one that could impact requirements for more than one exit in smaller dining areas.

The second paragraph of 1003.2.2.2.2 referenced above is of importance in any building with more than one occupancy. A B-2 office building, for example, may have within it several other uses. Each of the other areas of use will have its occupant load determined individually and the exit requirements for each space will be based on the occupant load on the space. The aggregate occupant load will then be applied to the design of the rest of the means of egress system. (See Figures 7-5 and 7-7.)

Where the use of a space may vary, the third paragraph of this section requires the occupant load to be based upon the occupancy with the highest occupant load factor. This will generate the maximum number of potential occupants and result in the means of egress being designed to accommodate the worst-case occupant loading.

1003.2.2.2.4 Outdoor Areas. The occupant load of yards, patios, courts and similar outdoor areas shall be assigned by the building official in accordance with their anticipated use. Such outdoor areas accessible to and useable by the building occupants shall be provided with a means of egress as required by this chapter. Where an outdoor area exits only through a building, the occupant load of such outdoor area shall be considered in the design of the means of egress system of that building.

This provision in the code requires exits for outdoor areas. Unless the areas are secured, or otherwise made inaccessible and unusable by the building occupants, the provisions must apply. (See Figure 7-8.) The section requires consideration of the occupant load "where an outdoor area exits *only* through a building". This implies that where two exits are required from an exterior space the exit through the building does not contribute to the occupant load calculations.

FIGURE 7-7 ACCESSORY USES & OCCUPANT LOAD CALCULATIONS

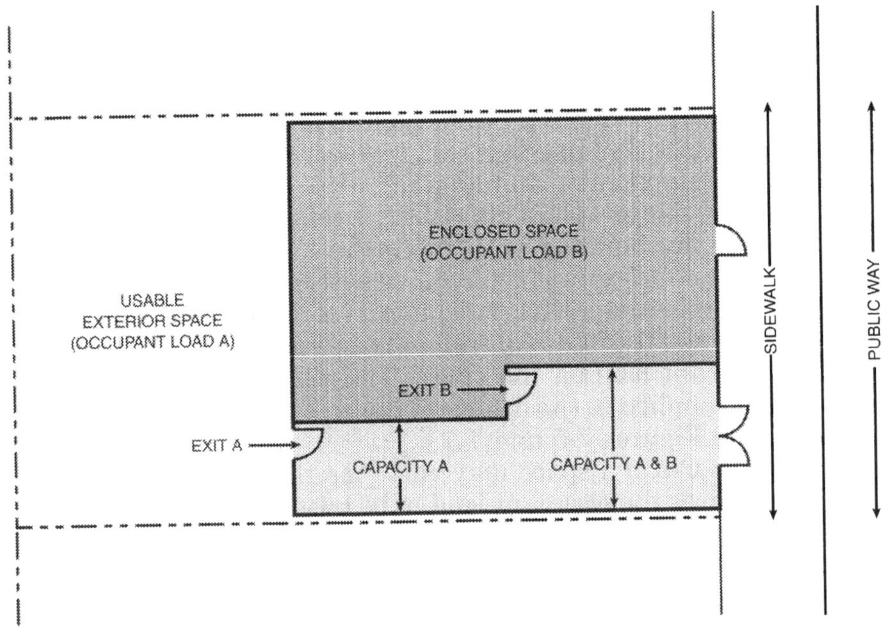

REFERENCE: SECTION 1003.2.2.2.4

FIGURE 7-8 EXITING AT OUTDOOR AREAS

This section presumes that all accessible outdoor areas will contain occupant loading and will not be accessory uses per the exception to Section 1003.2.2.2.1. Outdoor seating areas used by the occupants of the building are to be counted as part of the total occupant load of the building. They are also are to be provided with exits based on their individual occupant load. Large open areas may be dictated by the topography or easements or other sources beyond the control of the owner or the designer. Larger outside areas located in the interior of city blocks may have trouble providing two means of egress when they lead through the main spaces. The only means of minimizing the exiting provisions rests with the building official. The reasoning given during the debate over adoption of this provision was related to Group A Occupancies, i.e. large restaurants. However, the code provision is not occupancy limited.

In the authors' opinion, this provision should be limited as to occupancy. The intent of the proponent and the code change committee was with regard to Group A Occupancy and Group B, Division 2 restaurant occupancies. It should not apply to all occupancies as does the present wording. The building official should recognize this and provide relief from an onerous provision of the code. In the event the building official cannot provide that relief, the owner and designer should consider physically limiting access to the outdoor space.

1003.2.3.2 Minimum width. The width, in inches (mm), of any component in the means of egress system shall not be less than the product determined by multiplying the total occupant load served by such component by the applicable factor set forth in Table 10-B. In no case shall the width of an individual means of egress component be less than the minimum required for such component as specified elsewhere in this chapter.

Where more than one exit or exit-access doorway serves a building or portion thereof, such calculated width may be divided approximately equally among the means of egress components serving as exits or exit-access doorways for that area.

The required width of means of egress components is determined by both the occupant load and the occupancy. Tying the width requirement to occupancy is a new addition to the code. The width of the exit is determined by multiplying the occupant load by the factors listed in Table 10-B. Note the factors for stairs are larger than those for other components of the means of egress. This recognizes that people travel more slowly on stairs than through other means of egress components. (See Figure 7-9.)

TABLE NO. 10-B—Egress Width per Person Served

Use	Stairways (Inches per Person)	Other Egress Components (Inches per Person) (× 25.4 for mm/Person)
Hazardous: H-1, H-2, H-3 and H-7	0.7	0.4
Institutional: I-1	0.3	0.2
Institutional: I-2	0.4	0.2
All other uses	0.3	0.2

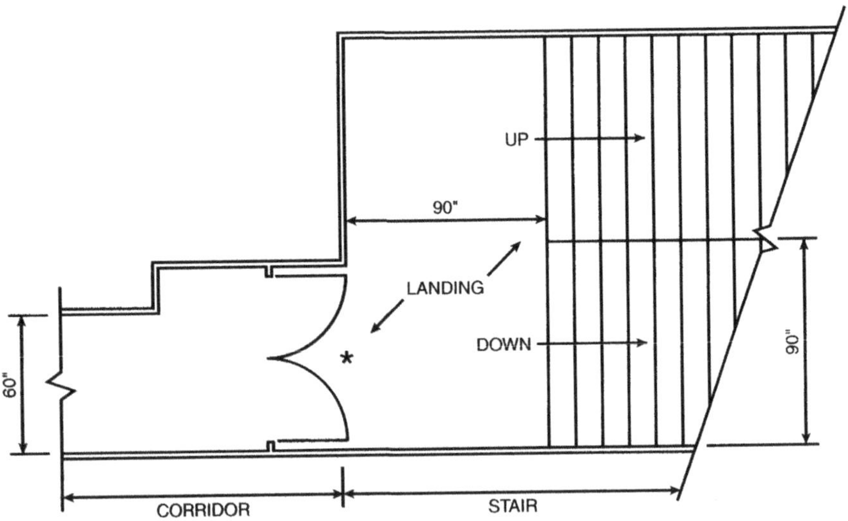

Diagram shows typical, see table for variations

Assume 300 person occupant load:

	Minimum Stair Width	Minimum Corridor Width
Typical Conditions & I-1 Occ.	300 x 0.3 = 90″	300 x 0.2 = 60″
Hazardous Occupancies	300 x 0.7 = 210″	300 x 0.4 = 120″
I-2 Occupancy	300 x 0.4 = 120″	300 x 0.2 = 60″

* Note that a pair of doors, each 3′ wide must be used to achieve the 60″ minimum egress width from the corridor. Section 1003.3.1.3 requires a minimum door width of 3′ and Section 1003.3.1.4 allows a maximum 4′ door leaf width.

REFERENCE: SECTION 1003.2.3.2, 1003.3.1.3, 1003.3.1.4 AND TABLE 10-B

FIGURE 7-9 EGRESS WIDTH RELATIVE DIMENSIONS

Certain occupancies also have higher requirements. Schools, hazardous occupancies and certain institutional occupancies have larger factors than typical. This is based on the assumption that various occupancies require differing occupant load capacities. Some factors are related to the need to facilitate evacuation for populations with different capabilities than those in typical occupancies, for example, children or the elderly. Other factors are related to the anticipated higher exposure to hazardous conditions in H Occupancies and the resultant need to exit quickly and easily.

1003.2.3.3 Maintaining width. If the minimum required width of the means of egress system increases along the path of exit travel based on cumulative occupant loads served, such width shall not be reduced or otherwise diminished to less than the largest minimum width required to that point along the path of exit travel.

There is a directional nature to the flow of a means of egress. Thus a corridor can be relatively narrower than the stair into which it empties. For example, 200 occupants using a corridor will require 200 × 0.2, or 50, inches of corridor width. This same occupant load would require a stair width of 200 × 0.3, or 75, inches of stair width.

Based on a strict interpretation of the requirements of Section 1003.2.3.3, an exit passageway leading *from* a stair may be reduced to the minimum *required* width based on Table 10-B. However, this may be subject to varying interpretation by the building official. It should be verified that there is not an expectation that the exit width, once established, not be reduced, based on Table 10-B. See also the provisions of the following section.

1003.2.3.4 Exiting from adjacent levels. No cumulative or contributing occupant loads from adjacent building levels need be considered when determining the required width of means of egress components from a given level.

Where an exit from an upper floor and a lower floor converge at an intermediate floor, the width of the exit from the intermediate floor shall be based on the sum of the occupant loads of such upper and lower floors.

Previous editions of the code required portions of the occupant loads of floors exiting through adjacent floors be added together to determine the required widths of exiting. This is no longer required. The width calculations are based on the premise that persons move through the exit system at a more or less constant rate and that as the persons on the lower floor leave the means of egress, the persons from floors above will follow them without congestion. Note that if there is a larger occupant load upstream of a given floor then the requirement that the exit path be undiminished will govern, and thus the width of exits at lower floors may be larger than that required for a particular level. When multiple exit paths converge into one, then the exit path width must increase based on the sum of the two occupant loads.

Strictly speaking, the authors' believe the letter of the code allows reduction of exit component widths based on whether the component is a stair or flat passage. This is consistent with the reasoning for widening stairs to facilitate free flow when not on a flat surface. Conversely, a narrower flat passage downstream of a stairway will not impede persons coming from the stair. Thus it may be possible to have a narrower exit passageway downstream of an exit stair. Any assumptions regarding designing a means of egress with such a configuration *must* be discussed with the building official to determine how this will be interpreted by a particular jurisdiction.

1003.2.4 Height. Except as specified elsewhere in this chapter, the means of egress system shall have a clear height of not less than 7 feet (2134 mm) measured vertically from the walking surface to the lowest projection from the ceiling or overhead structure.

The minimum height of the means of egress is 7 feet, except that stairs may have clear height of 6 feet 8 inches per Section 1003.3.3.4. Note that this requirement applies to all portions of the means of egress unless specifically modified by another section. For example, exit discharge areas outside the building must comply with this requirement.

1003.2.5 Exit continuity. The path of exit travel along a means of egress shall not be interrupted by any building element other than a means of egress component as specified in this chapter. Obstructions shall not be placed in the required width of a means of egress except projections permitted by this chapter. The required capacity of a means of egress system shall not be diminished along the path of exit travel.

The widths of means of egress are based on the stream analogy. Once set, the required width of the means of egress is not to be diminished as it proceeds downstream. The widths should be set by the minimum widths of components such as stairs, corridors or passageways. Thus, if a column or other structural element projects into a means of egress, then the width is determined by the new clear space available for exiting. Passages must be laid out to allow the widths determined by the occupant load to be maintained throughout the egress system.

In some instances, the fire-resistive enclosure may pass by other occupancies. In the process of exiting, the occupant cannot move out of the protected environment into these occupancies to get to the next portion of the egress or to the exterior because doing so would necessitate removing the protection the exit enclosure is required to provide. This concept of protection is specifically indicated in Section 1003.2.5 where the requirement for exit continuity is delineated. (See Figures 7-10 and 7-11.)

1003.2.6 Changes in elevation. All exterior elevation changes and interior elevation changes of 12 inches (305 mm) or more along the path of exit travel shall be made by steps, stairs or stairways conforming with the requirements of Section 1003.3.3.3 or ramps conforming with the requirements of Section 1003.3.4.

Interior elevation changes of less than 12 inches (305 mm) along the path of exit travel serving an occupant load of 10 or more shall be by ramps conforming with the requirements of Section 1003.3.4.

EXCEPTIONS: 1. In Group R, Division 3 Occupancies and within individual dwelling units of Group R, Division 1 Occupancies.

2. Along aisles adjoining seating areas.

Note that changes in elevation inside the building of less than 12 inches are to be by ramps. Stairs must have a rise greater than or equal to 12 inches. This is especially true when designing an accessible means of egress per the provisions of Section 1104.1. (See Figure 7-12.)

> While this section implicitly permits the use of steps in the exterior (exit discharge) where grade changes are less than 12 inches this should be avoided. One or two step stairs are often a surprise to users and can lead to falls. It is always desirable to avoid elevation changes in the egress path wherever possible. If they are necessary, ramps should be used. Grade changes of less than 1:20 slope are even better since these are not ramps and do not require handrails.
>
> Notwithstanding the fact that 1:8 ramps are permitted under certain circumstances, it is the authors' opinion that ramps should be designed to be 1:12 as required for accessible means of egress wherever possible. Ramps that are 1:8 are not compatible with Chapter 11 or the Americans with Disabilities Act (ADA).

1003.2.7 Elevators or escalators. Elevators or escalators shall not be used as a required means of egress component.

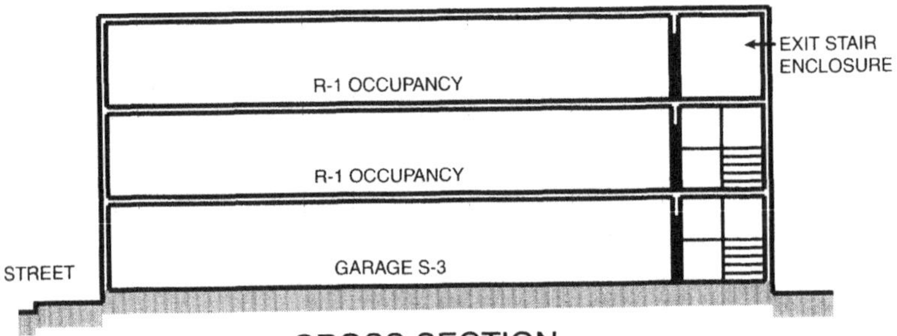

CROSS SECTION

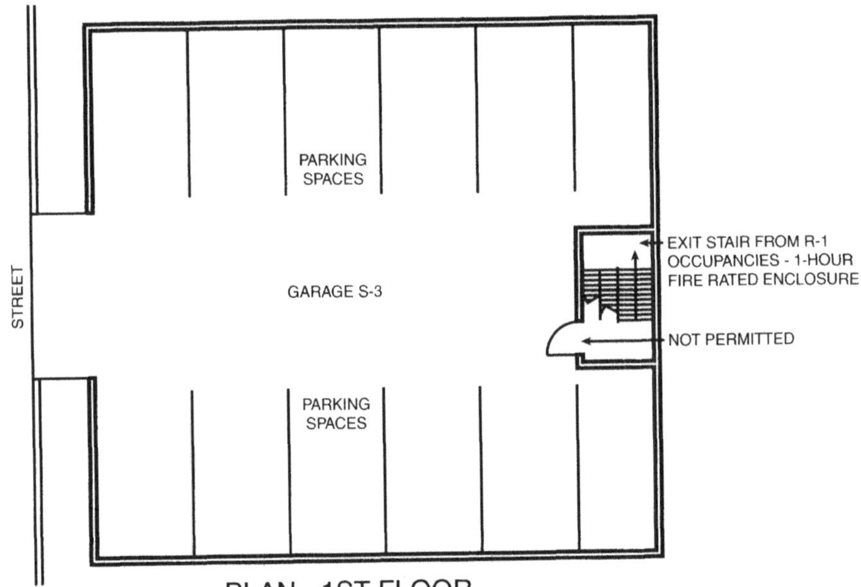

PLAN - 1ST FLOOR

NOTE: Exit stair from upper floor R-1 Occupancy exits into garage space through the S-3 Garage without proper occupancy separation. This is not permitted. See Figure 7-11 for an acceptable modification.

REFERENCE: SECTION 1003.2.2.2.4

FIGURE 7-10 NON-PERMITTED EXIT ENCLOSURE LEADING FROM ONE OCCUPANCY INTO ANOTHER

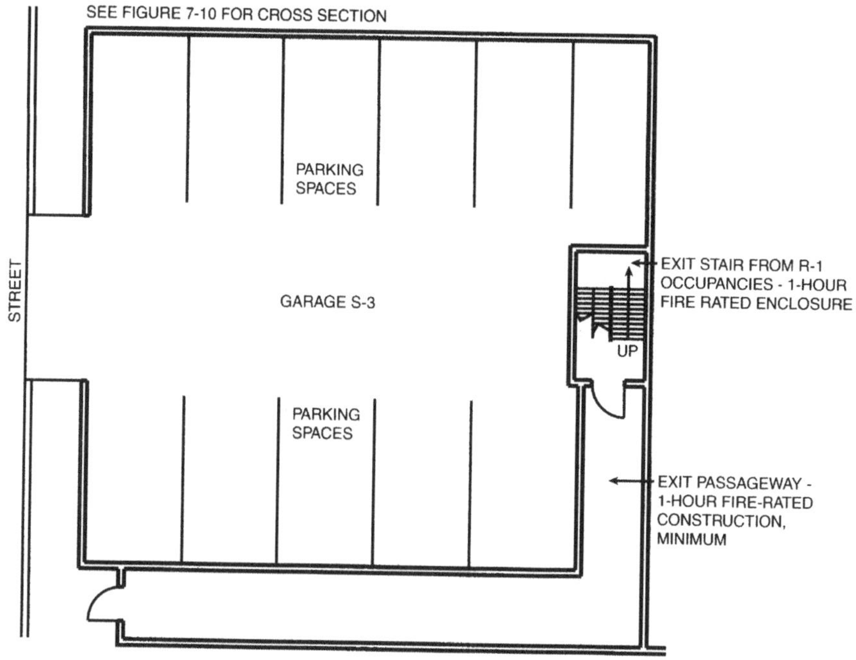

NOTE: Exit stair from upper floor R-1 Occupancy exits into an exit passageway separated from the S-3 Garage.

REFERENCE: SECTION 1003.2.5

FIGURE 7-11 ACCEPTABLE EXIT ENCLOSURE LEADING FROM ONE OCCUPANCY PAST ANOTHER

Elevators or escalators are not to be considered as part of the means of egress. The prohibition of elevators must be reconciled with the requirements of Section 1104.1.3 for accessible means of egress. Any use of elevators for accessible means of egress should be carefully discussed with the building official and a determination recorded.

1003.2.8.2 Where required. The path of exit travel to and within exits in a building shall be identified by exit signs conforming to the requirements of Section 1003.2.8. Exit signs shall be readily visible from any direction of

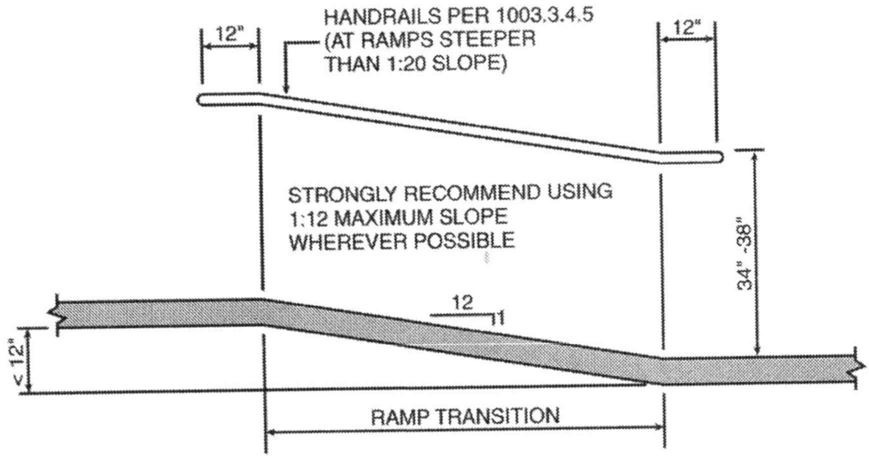

- No stair transitions are to be used for less than 12 inch grade changes, a ramp is to be used
- Where possible, avoid grade changes of any kind in exit paths
- If grade changes are required use slope of less than 1:20 where possible to avoid needing ramp handrails and landings.
- Avoid using a ramp slope in excess of 1:12 to avoid potential conflicts with access regulations.

REFERENCE: SECTIONS 1003.2.6 AND 1003.3.4.5

FIGURE 7-12 CHANGES IN ELEVATION AT INTERIOR PATH OF EXIT TRAVEL

approach. Exit signs shall be located as necessary to clearly indicate the direction of egress travel. No point shall be more than 100 feet (30 480 mm) from the nearest visible sign.

EXCEPTIONS: 1. Main exterior exit doors that obviously and clearly are identifiable as exit doors need not have exit signs when approved by the building official.

2. Rooms or areas that require only one exit or exit access.

3. In Group R, Division 3 Occupancies and within individual units of Group R, Division 1 Occupancies.

4. Exits or exit access from rooms or areas with an occupant load of less than 50 where located within a Group I, Division 1.1, 1.2 or 2 Occupancy or a Group E, Division 3 day-care occupancy.

Exit signs are required unless the exit is clearly obvious as noted under the exceptions to Section 1003.2.8.2. Note that additional floor-level exit signs are required by Section 1007.6.2 as part of occupancy-specific requirements for R-1 hotel occupancies. (see Figure 7-38.)

> The first paragraph speaks about signs "within exits." It would seem the intent here relates to exit passageways and that exit signs would not be required in exit stairs. The 100-foot maximum requirement for exit signs may lead to nonuniform interpretation in large rooms more than 200 feet wide. Will this require signs suspended in the interior of large rooms?

1003.2.9.1 General. Any time a building is occupied, the means of egress shall be illuminated at an intensity of not less than 1 foot-candle (10.76 lx) at the floor level.

EXCEPTIONS: 1. In Group R, Division 3 Occupancies and within individual units of Group R, Division 1 Occupancies.

2. In auditoriums, theaters, concert or opera halls, and similar assembly uses, the illumination at the floor level may be reduced during performances to not less than 0.2 foot-candle (2.15 lx), provided that the required illumination be automatically restored upon activation of a premise's fire alarm system when such system is provided.

The means of egress is to be illuminated with a minimum of 1 foot-candle at the floor level. This illumination is to have emergency power where there are more than 100 occupants and in I 1.1 and 1.2 occupancies. This applies to all parts of the means of egress except as noted. Design of emergency lighting for exit access will require that certain light fixtures throughout occupied spaces be on emergency power to provide the minimum illumination. Most jurisdictions will test the emergency lighting operation and intensity prior to final occupancy and will not grant occupancy if the lighting does not meet the minimum criteria.

1003.2.10 Building Accessibility. In addition to the requirements of this chapter, means of egress, which provide access to, or egress from, buildings for persons with disabilities, shall also comply with the requirements of Chapter 11.

With the enactment of the federal Americans with Disabilities Act (ADA) in 1990 and the subsequent adoption of accessibility requirements in the code, building accessibility for the disabled has become an important consideration for buildings. Chapter 11's egress requirements are frequently more restrictive than their counterparts in this chapter. (See the discussion of Chapter 11 in Article 10 of this guide.) The provisions of Appendix Chapter 11 should be used when undertaking a proposed alteration to an existing building.

Note that if the locality does not adopt Appendix Chapter 11 provisions for existing buildings, the designer and enforcement official must use Chapter 11 provisions without any means for ameliorating the severe impact of such requirements on an existing building.

In the authors' opinion, in buildings without sprinkler systems the stair width requirements of Section 1104.1.2 take precedence over the provisions in Section 1003.3.3.2 (44 inches) in those areas required to be accessible. Therefore, the minimum gross width of stairs is 55 inches instead of 44 inches, as has long been the criteria. See Figure 7-13. Note that this applies only in buildings that are not fully sprinklered per Exception 2 to 1104.1.2.

The 55-inch width is premised on a clear width between handrails of 48 inches mandated in Section 1104.1.2 and the 7-inch handrail incursion into the stairway permitted in Section 1003.3.3.2. It is recommended that a cross reference to 1104.1.2 be added to Section 1003.3.3.2 so that this important requirement is not overlooked in buildings without sprinkler systems.

1003.3 Means of egress components. Doors, gates, stairways and ramps that are incorporated into the design of any portion of the means of egress system shall comply with the requirements of this section. These means of egress components may be selectively included in the exit access, the exit or the exit discharge portions of the means of egress system.

Items such as doors, gates, stairways and ramps may occur in any of the three portions of a means of egress. These components are required to comply with the design requirements of Section 1003. The term "exit door" is used for doors no matter in which portion of the means of egress the door occurs. It is essential to

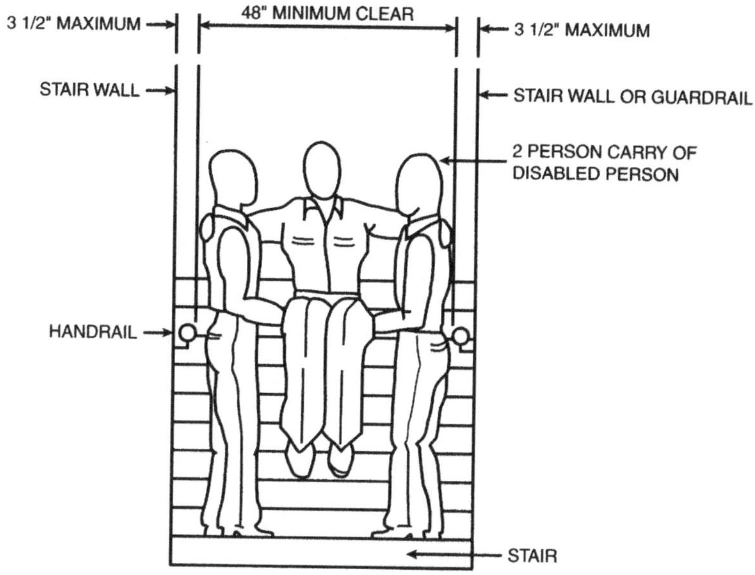

EVACUATION OF DISABLED PERSON DOWN STAIR, TWO PERSON CARRY

REFERENCE: SECTION 1104.1.2

FIGURE 7-13 MINIMUM WIDTH OF STAIRWAY BASED ON TWO PERSONS CARRYING DISABLED PERSON DOWN STAIRWAY (NON-SPRINKLERED BUILDINGS)

understand this nomenclature. There may be certain areas of each of the three parts of a means of egress where only certain elements can occur. In those cases the text will call out the relationship to the particular means of egress. For example, a hallway can only occur in the exit access. Corridors too are mentioned only in the exit access section. Exit passageways occur in the exit section. On the other hand, exit doors may occur in any and all of the three parts of the means of egress.

1003.3.1 Doors

1003.3.1.1 General. For the purposes of Section 1003.3.1, the term "exit door" shall mean all of those doors or doorways along the path of exit travel anywhere in a means of egress system.

1003.3.1.3 Width and height. Every required exit doorway serving an occupant load of 10 or more shall be of a size to permit the installation of a door not less than 3 feet (914 mm) in nominal width and not less than 6 feet 8 inches (2032 mm) in nominal height. Where installed, exit doors shall be capable of opening such that the clear width of the exit is not less than 32 inches (813 mm). In computing the exit width as required by Section 1003.2.3, the net dimension of the doorway shall be used.

1003.3.1.4 Door leaf width. A single leaf of an exit door serving an occupant load of 10 or more shall not exceed 4 feet (1219 mm) in width.

1003.3.1.5 Swing and opening force. Exit doors serving an occupant load of 10 or more shall be of the pivoted, balanced or side-hinged swinging type. Exit doors shall swing in the direction of the path of exit travel where the area served has an occupant load of 50 or more. The door shall swing to the fully open position when an opening force not to exceed 30 pounds (133.45 N) is applied to the latch side. For other door opening forces, see Section 905.3 and Chapter 11. See Section 3207 for doors swinging over public property.

Exit doors serving an occupant load of 10 or more are to be 3 feet wide (32 inches clear exit width) and 6 feet 8 inches high. Door leaves are to be a maximum of 4 feet wide so that doors do not get too large and become unwieldy in emergencies. Doors are to swing in the direction of exit travel when serving an occupant load of 50 or more. There may be a conflict between the 30-pound opening force required by Section 1003.3.1.5 and the opening force requirements of the technical requirements specified in Chapter 9 and Chapter 11. Door opening forces may also be impacted by pressurization requirements for buildings with smoke control systems. The design of the smoke control system must not put such force on doors that they become inoperable when the smoke control system is in operation. The smoke control system is designed to be in operation in just the kind of emergency situation when the egress system will be used.

> The wording of Section 1003.3.1.3 does not specify the width of exit doors serving fewer than 10 persons. In the authors' opinion, due to access requirements in addition to the requirements for exit doors, no doors of less than a 3-foot width should ever be used in a means of egress or in any area accessible to the public and not in a residence.

Doors are to have landings on each side of the door except in residential occupancies. The maximum landing elevation difference between the door threshold and the landing is typically 1 inch, however, this is reduced to $\frac{1}{2}$ inch at landings on accessible routes per Chapter 11.

1003.3.1.8 Type of lock or latch. Regardless of the occupant load served, exit doors shall be openable from the inside without the use of a key or any special knowledge or effort.

EXCEPTIONS: 1. In Groups A, Division 3; B; F; M and S Occupancies and in all churches, key-locking hardware may be used on the main exit where the main exit consists of a single door or pair of doors where there is a readily visible, durable sign on or adjacent to the door stating, "THIS DOOR MUST REMAIN UNLOCKED DURING BUSINESS HOURS." The sign shall be in letters not less than 1 inch (25 mm) high on a contrasting background. When unlocked, the single door or both leaves of a pair of doors must be free to swing without operation of any latching device. The use of this exception may be revoked by the building official for due cause.

2. Exit doors from individual dwelling units; Group R, Division 3 congregate residences; and guest rooms of Group R Occupancies having an occupant load of 10 or less may be provided with a night latch, dead bolt or security chain, provided such devices are openable from the inside without the use of a key or tool and mounted at a height not to exceed 48 inches (1219 mm) above the finished floor.

Manually operated edge- or surface-mounted flush bolts and surface bolts or any other type of device that may be used to close or restrain the door other than by operation of the locking device shall not be used. Where exit doors are used in pairs and approved automatic flush bolts are used, the door leaf having the automatic flush bolts shall have no doorknob or surface-mounted hardware. The unlatching of any leaf shall not require more than one operation.

Exit doors must be openable from the inside (or in other words, from the direction of exit travel) without a key or any special knowledge or effort. It is acceptable to have the main doors in occupancies such as retail shops be locked after hours if they are unlocked during operational hours and signs posted to that effect. In any case, even such lockable doors should be openable by employees after hours without any great effort, to avoid trapping people in emergencies. See the prohibition in the final paragraph on manual flush bolts and "any other type of device that may be used to close or restrain the door other than by operation of the locking device." The intent is that exit doors be openable with one operation, that it not require multiple independent steps to release a lock mechanism.

1003.3.3 Stairways.

1003.3.3.1 General. Every stairway having two or more risers serving any building or portion thereof shall comply with the requirements of Section 1003.3.3. For the purposes of Section 1003.3.3, the term "stairway" shall include stairs, landings, handrails and guardrails as applicable. Where aisles in assembly rooms have steps, they shall comply with the requirements in Section 1004.3.2.

1003.3.3.2 Width. The width of stairways shall be determined as specified in Section 1003.2.3, but such width shall not be less than 44 inches (1118 mm), except as specified herein and in Chapter 11. Stairways serving an occupant load less than 50 shall not be less than 36 inches (914 mm) in width.

Handrails may project into the required width a distance of $3\frac{1}{2}$ inches (89 mm) from each side of a stairway. Stringers and other projections such as trim and similar decorative features may project into the required width $1\frac{1}{2}$ inches (38 mm) from each side.

1003.3.3.3 Rise and run. The rise of steps and stairs shall not be less than 4 inches (102 mm) nor more than 7 inches (178 mm). The greatest riser height within any flight of stairs shall not exceed the smallest by more than $\frac{3}{8}$ inch (9.5 mm). Except as permitted in Sections 1003.3.3.8.1, 1003.3.3.8.2 and 1003.3.3.8.3, the run shall not be less than 11 inches (279 mm) as measured horizontally between the vertical planes of the furthermost projection of adjacent treads or nosings. Stair treads shall be of uniform size and shape, except the largest tread run within any flight of stairs shall not exceed the smallest by more than $\frac{3}{8}$ inch (9.5 mm).

Exceptions: 1. Private steps and stairways serving an occupant load of less than 10 and stairways to unoccupied roofs may be constructed with an 8-inch-maximum (203 mm) rise and a 9-inch-minimum (229 mm) run.

2. Where the bottom or top riser adjoins a sloping public way, walk or driveway having an established grade (other than natural earth) and serving as a landing, the bottom or top riser may be reduced along the slope to less than 4 inches (102 mm) in height with the variation in height of the bottom or top riser not to exceed 1 unit vertical in 12 units horizontal (8.3% slope) of stairway width.

1003.3.3.4 Headroom. Every stairway shall have a headroom clearance of not less than 6 feet 8 inches (2032 mm). Such clearances shall be measured vertically from a plane parallel and tangent to the stairway tread nosings to the soffit or other construction above at all points.

1003.3.3.5 Landings. There shall be a floor or a landing at the top and bottom of each stairway or stair run. Every landing shall have a dimension measured in the direction of travel not less than the width of the stairway. Such dimension need not exceed 44 inches (1118 mm) where the stair has a straight run. At least one intermediate landing shall be provided for each 12 feet (3658 mm) of vertical stairway rise measured between the horizontal planes of adjacent landings. Landings shall be level except that exterior landings may have a slope not to exceed $\frac{1}{4}$ unit vertical in 12 units horizontal (2% slope). For landings with adjoining doors, see Section 1003.3.1.7.

EXCEPTIONS: 1. In Group R, Division 3, and Group U Occupancies and within individual units of Group R, Division 1 Occupancies, such length need not exceed 36 inches (914 mm) where the stair has a straight run.

2. Stairs serving an unoccupied roof are exempt from these requirements.

Any stair of two or more risers must comply with exiting requirements. The stairs are to be a minimum of 44 inches wide except stairs serving an occupant load of less than 50 may be 36 inches wide. The rise and run is typically 7 and 11 inches. This can be reduced for certain occupancies serving fewer than 10 occupants. The variations in tread and riser dimensions are $\frac{3}{8}$ inch maximum. This must be monitored closely by the designer in the field as this is a source of potential liability for accidents on stairs. Stairs are the source of a large number of residential and commercial accidents due to steep stairs or poor uniformity of treads and risers. Note that stairs may have 6 feet 8 inches height clearance per Section 1003.3.3.4, whereas other components of the means of egress are required to have 7 feet clear height per Section 1003.2.4. Landings are to be provided at the top and bottom of each run with a minimum length equal to the stair width and a maximum required run of 44 inches for straight stairs. An intermediate landing must be provided in straight run stairs at every 12 feet of vertical rise. The intent of the code, based on previous editions, would require that intermediate landings be provided where the rise equals or exceeds 12 feet. (See Figure 7-14.)

> In the authors' opinion stairs should be designed with 7-inch risers and 11-inch treads wherever possible, even in residential occupancies, to minimize stairway accidents.

1003.3.3.6 Handrails. Stairways shall have handrails on each side, and every stairway required to be more than 88 inches (2235 mm) in width shall be provided with not less than one intermediate handrail for each 88 inches (2235 mm) of required width. Intermediate handrails shall be spaced approximately equally across with the entire width of the stairway.

EXCEPTIONS: 1. Stairways less than 44 inches (1118 mm) in width or stairways serving one individual dwelling unit in Group R, Division 1 or 3 Occupancy or a Group R, Division 3 congregate residence may have one handrail.

2. Private stairways 30 inches (762 mm) or less in height may have a handrail on one side only.

3. Stairways having less than four risers and serving one individual dwelling unit in Group R, Division 1 or 3, or a Group R, Division 3 congregate residence or Group U Occupancies need not have handrails.

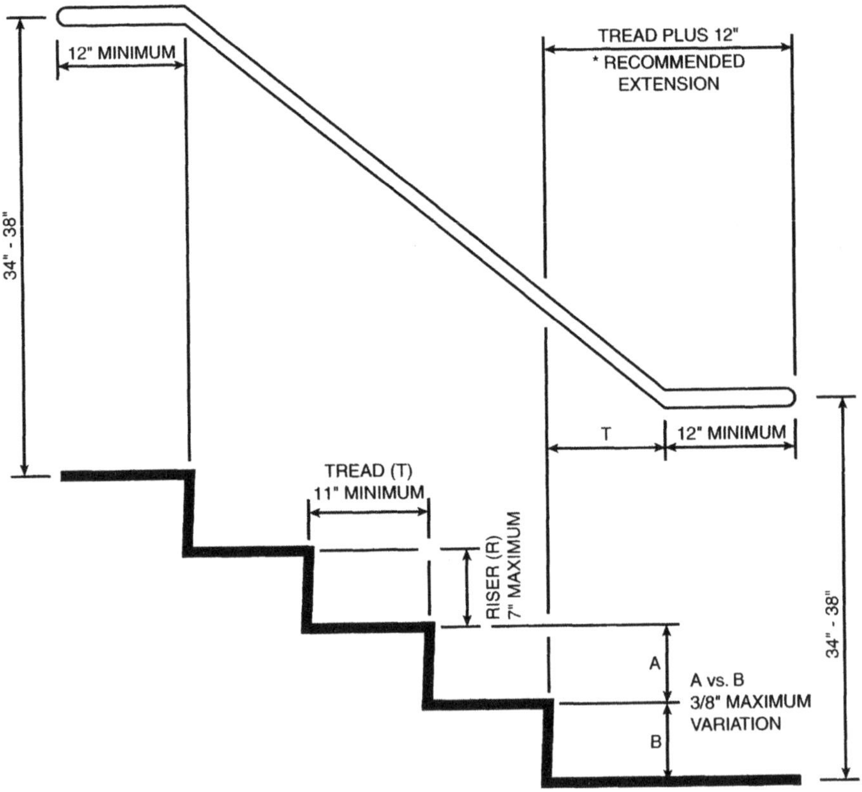

TYPICAL STAIR

Note the recommended handrail extension is greater than that required by Section 1003.3.3.6. This is based on the requirements of the ADA and most state accessibility regulations and also upon ANSI A117.1-1992 which is adopted by reference by Chapter 11, Section 1101.2.1.

Note also the recommendation to use 7″ and 11″ stairs where possible. This is based on evidence that stairs steeper than these dimensions are less safe than those designed using 7/11 criteria. Note also that the draft of the new International Building Code (as of the writing of this book) requires 7/11 stairs in all applications, with no exceptions. It may be worthwhile to get ahead of the trend and begin using 7/11 stairs now.

REFERENCE: SECTION 1003.3.3

FIGURE 7-14 STAIR AND HANDRAIL DIMENSIONS

> The top of handrails and handrail extensions shall not be placed less than 34 inches (864 mm) nor more than 38 inches (965 mm) above landings and the nosing of treads. Handrails shall be continuous the full length of the stairs and, except for private stairways, at least one handrail shall extend in the direction of the stair run not less than 12 inches (305 mm) beyond the top riser nor less than 12 inches (305 mm) beyond the bottom riser. Ends shall be returned or shall have rounded terminations or bends.
>
> EXCEPTIONS: 1. Private stairways do not require handrail extensions.
>
> 2. Handrails may have starting or volute newels within the first tread on stairways in Group R, Division 3 Occupancies and within individual dwelling units of Group R, Division 1 Occupancies.
>
> The handgrip portion of handrails shall not be less than 1¼ inches (32 mm) nor more than 2 inches (51 mm) in cross-sectional dimension or the shape shall provide an equivalent gripping surface. The handgrip portion of handrails shall have a smooth surface with no sharp corners. Handrails projecting from a wall shall have a space of not less than 1½ inches (38 mm) between the wall and the handrail.

Rails are to be provided on each side of stairs where stairs are required to be wider than 36 inches. The next exit width increment is 44 inches, thus any exit stair required to be greater than 36 inches must be at least 44 inches and must have two rails. Note that if stairs are *"required"* (emphasis added) to be more than 88 inches in width per occupant load/width calculations, only then must intermediate rails be provided.

The basic increment of exit width is 22 inches based on one person. Thus, 44 inches is the width required for one person to pass another in a hall. 44 inches is also the required width for two persons to travel a corridor side by side or to descend a stair side by side in an emergency. The 88-inch requirement comes from the intent that persons needing rails to assist their egress be able to reach the rails in an emergency without crowding against the side rails. The stair widths for large occupant loads thus need intermediate rails to contain crowds moving down stairs and to provide rails for those needing them when the stairs are full of persons moving out of a facility in an emergency. Wide, ornamental stairs, where the stair width is not set by the occupant load and the *required* width of the stairs is less than 88 inches, will not need the extra rails as the stair use will not exceed the capacity of the side rails to serve the anticipated load.

The UBC requires handrails to extend 12 inches beyond the top riser and 12 inches beyond the bottom riser. This is in direct contravention to the requirements of the ADA for 12-inch extensions at the top and 12 inches plus the tread at the bottom. (See Figure 7-14.)

> The stair rail projection requirements are for persons with visual impairments and apply to all stairs, not just those on the accessible means of egress defined in Chapter 11. The designer should *never use the standard handrail projection provisions of the UBC at stairs outside of private residences* as this will result in stairs that do not comply with the ADA. Stair rails noted in the exceptions to Section 1003.3.3.6 are generally not covered by the ADA and should therefore be usable.

Exception 2 to the second paragraph of Section 1003.3.3.6 allows the use of traditional starting newels as often used in residential stairs. This allows the use of volutes in the first tread and solves what has been a long-standing interpretation and enforcement problem with traditional style residential stairs.

Handrails are to be $1\frac{1}{4}$ inches minimum and 2 inches maximum in cross section. Note that many traditional residential and ornamental commercial rails do not comply with these criteria. These requirements are subject to wide variations in interpretation by local building officials. The definition of "equivalent gripping surface" is open to interpretation. A $1\frac{1}{4}$-inch square rail has a total perimeter length of 5 inches. A 1 by $1\frac{1}{2}$-inch bar has the same perimeter area but is less than the $1\frac{1}{4}$ inches mininimum. Is this an "equivalent gripping surface?" This has been an ongoing argument for several code adoption cycles with various proponents of differing anthropometric criteria battling over rail dimensions. With so much background controversy the designer, if in any doubt, should verify acceptance of the rail cross section by the building official during plan review and not risk being found in noncompliance during a field inspection after the rail is installed. Documents should clearly call out the size and cross-section configuration of the rails for the plans examiner to review. (See Figure 7-15.)

Various stair configurations for circular, winding and spiral stairs are discussed in the code. Without going into detailed analysis of the variations of each, the best advice we can give is that since almost all of these types of stairs are manufactured items, the designer should ask the manufacturer for written documentation of acceptance of the stair by the authorities having jurisdiction. This advice holds true for all manufactured products. Specification

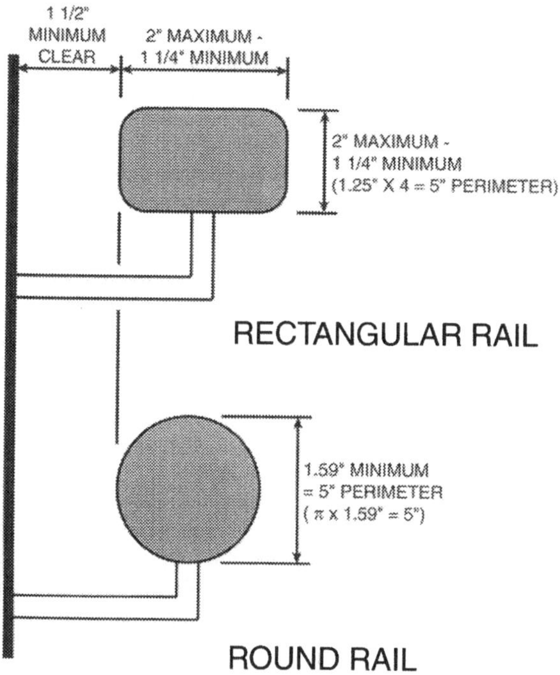

Recommended minimum dimensions based on the sum of perimeter dimensions. The sums assume the minimum of 1-1/4″ x 4 = 5″. The maximum dimension is 2″. Note that many traditional handrails available from manufacturers may not strictly meet these criteria, but may be acceptable as providing "an equivalent gripping surface". Use of any handrail which does not fall within the specified maximum and minimum dimensional criteria should be verified with the Building Official at the time of plan review, prior to installation in the field.

REFERENCE: SECTION 1003.3.3.6

FIGURE 7-15 HANDRAIL DIMENSIONS

should require manufacturers to submit documentation to assure the designer of code compliance for all products and systems.

1003.3.4 Ramps.

1003.3.4.1 General. Ramps used as a component in a means of egress system shall conform to the requirements of Section 1003.3.4.

EXCEPTION: Ramped aisles within assembly rooms shall conform to the requirements in Section 1004.3.2.

1003.3.4.2 Width. The width of ramps shall be determined as specified in Section 1003.2.3, but shall not be less than 44 inches (1118 mm), except as

specified herein and in Chapter 11. Ramps serving an occupant load of less than 50 shall not be less than 36 inches (914 mm) in width.

Handrails may project into the required width a distance of $3\frac{1}{2}$ inches (89 mm) from each side of a ramp. Other projections, such as trim and similar decorative features, may project into the required width $1\frac{1}{2}$ inches (38 mm) from each side.

1003.3.4.3 Slope. The slope of ramps required by Chapter 11 that are located within an accessible route of travel shall not be steeper than 1 unit vertical in 12 units horizontal (8.3% slope). The slope of other ramps shall not be steeper than 1 unit vertical in 8 units horizontal (12.5% slope).

1003.3.4.4 Landings. Ramps having slopes steeper than 1 unit vertical in 20 units horizontal (5% slope) shall have landings at the top and bottom, and at least one intermediate landing shall be provided for each 5 feet (1524 mm) of vertical rise measured between the horizontal planes of adjacent landings. Top landings and intermediate landings shall have a dimension measured in the direction of ramp run of not less than 5 feet (1524 mm). Landings at the bottom of ramps shall have a dimension in the direction of ramp run of not less than 6 feet (1829 mm).

Doors in any position shall not reduce the minimum dimension of the landing to less than 42 inches (1067 mm) and shall not reduce the required width by more than 7 inches (89 mm) when fully open.

Where ramp access is provided to comply with the requirements of Chapter 11 and a door swings over a landing, the landing shall extend at least 24 inches (610 mm) beyond the latch edge of the door, measured parallel to the door in the closed position, and shall have a length measured in the direction of travel through the doorway of not less than 5 feet (1524 mm).

1003.3.4.5 Handrails. Ramps having slopes steeper than 1 unit vertical in 20 units horizontal (5% slope) shall have handrails as required for stairways, except that intermediate handrails shall not be required. Ramped aisles serving fixed seating shall have handrails as required in Section 1004.3.2.

1003.3.4.6 Guardrails. Ramps open on one or both sides shall have guardrails as required by Section 509.

1003.3.4.7 Construction. Ramps shall be constructed as required for stairways.

1003.3.4.8 Surface. The surface of ramps shall be roughened or shall be of slip-resistant materials.

Any sloped surface in excess of 1 : 20 is considered a ramp. Conversely, any sloped surface shallower than that slope is not a ramp and thus no landings or rails are required. No ramp should ever have a greater slope than 1 : 8, but most ramps should be 1 : 12 due to access regulations. Width, railing and landing requirements for ramps correspond to those for stairs.

> Because of the requirements for accessibility, ramps in public areas should not have slopes greater than 1:12 and should comply with the landing, width and handrail requirements for accessible ramps. Ramp handrail requirements are referenced from those for stairs. As noted previously the stair requirements do not match those from Chapter 11 or the ADA, but when applied to ramps the Chapter 10 requirements do match the ramp access requirements of Chapter 11 and the ADA.
>
> While sloped surfaces of less than 1:20 may be used, long runs at any slope in excess of 1:50 (approx. ¼ inch per foot, or 2%) should be avoided. Typically, sloped conditions should be essentially flat, using only the minimum slope required for positive drainage to allow easy movement by persons with disabilities. Note also that the ADA requires the use of "the least possible slope" for any ramp.

The Exit Access

1004.1 General. The exit access is that portion of a means of egress system between any occupied point in a building or structure and a door of the exit. Components that may be selectively included in the exit access include aisles, hallways and corridors, in addition to those means of egress components described in Section 1003.3.

The exit access is defined as the portion of a means of egress that includes travel through occupied areas on a path leading to a door that then enters into the exit. Portions of means of egress systems that have been in the past considered as "exits," such as corridors, are now typically considered parts of the exit access. There are no automatic rating requirements for portions of the exit access. Ratings must be deduced from the relationships of various parts of the exit access. Note that many of the components of the exit access are not defined in the code and may be subject to wide ranges of interpretation. There is a hierarchy of protection contained in the terms used for parts of the exit access even though the terms are undefined other than by the context of their use. Occupied rooms or spaces are the lowest unit, aisles next, then hallways, then corridors.

1004.2.1 General. The exit access portion of the means of egress system shall comply with the applicable design requirements of Section 1004.2. For

the purposes of Section 1004.2, the term "exit-access doorway" shall mean the point of entry to one portion of the building or structure from another along the path of exit travel. An exit-access doorway occurs where access to all exits is not direct (see Section 1004.2.3). An exit-access doorway does not necessarily include a door. When a detailed requirement specifies an "exit-access door," however, then a door shall be included as a portion of the doorway.

An exit access doorway marks the passage from one part of the exit access to another. This is in the direction of exit travel, downstream toward the exit and the exit discharge. Note that an exit access doorway need not have a door. However, if the term "exit access *door*" is used, then a door is required.

1004.2.2 Travel through intervening rooms. The required access to exits from any portion of a building shall be directly from the space under consideration to an exit or to a corridor that provides direct access to an exit. Exit access shall not be interrupted by intervening rooms.

EXCEPTIONS: 1. Access to exits may occur through foyers, lobbies and reception rooms.

2. Where access to only one exit is required from a space under consideration, exit access may occur through an adjoining or intervening room, which in turn provides direct access to an exit or to a corridor that provides direct access to an exit.

3. Rooms with a cumulative occupant load of less than 10 may access exits through more than one intervening room.

4. Where access to more than one exit is required from a space under consideration, such spaces may access one required exit through an adjoining or intervening room, which in turn provides direct access to an exit or to a corridor that provides direct access to an exit. All other required access to exits shall be directly from the space under consideration to an exit or to a corridor that provides direct access to an exit.

5. In a one- or two-story building classified as a Group F, Group S or Group H, Division 5 Occupancy, offices and similar administrative areas may have access to two required exits through an adjoining or intervening room, which in turn provides direct access to an exit or to a corridor that provides direct access to an exit, if the building is equipped with an automatic sprinkler system throughout and is provided with smoke and heat ventilation as specified in Section 906. Such areas shall not exceed 25 percent of the floor area of the major use.

6. Rooms within dwelling units may access exits through more than one intervening room.

Hallways shall be considered as intervening rooms.

Interior courts enclosed on all sides shall be considered as interior intervening rooms.

EXCEPTION: Such courts not less than 10 feet (3048 mm) in width or less than the width determined as specified in Section 1003.2.3 and

providing direct access to the exit need not be considered intervening rooms.

In other than dwelling units, a means of egress shall not pass through kitchens, storerooms, restrooms, closets or spaces used for similar purposes.

A means of egress serving other than Group H Occupancies shall not pass through rooms that contain Group H Occupancies.

The path from the exit access to the exit cannot pass through intervening rooms except as specifically allowed by the exceptions. This is a case of the exception proving the rule. The exceptions to 1004.2.2 are quite broad and in effect allow the use of intervening rooms for exiting under a wide variety of conditions. However, note that the exceptions do have specific conditions. For example, Exception 3 states "less than 10." If the calculated occupant load is 10, then this exception cannot be used unless the room size is adjusted to have 9 or fewer occupants. The primary intent of this section is expressed by Exception 4, which allows exit access to pass through one intervening space when two exits are required. Only one of the exit access paths may pass through an intervening room. Note also that hallways are considered as intervening rooms, so they may not be used for exiting without using the exceptions to 1004.2.2. (See Figures 7-16 and 7-17.)

Interior courts surrounded on all sides are in essence "rooms" and are considered as intervening rooms unless they are at least 10 feet wide and provide direct access to an exit. A court that is open on one side is considered an exit court and is considered part of the exit discharge.

1004.2.3 Access to exits.

1004.2.3.1 General. Exits shall be provided from each building level. Additionally, access to such exits shall be provided from all occupied areas within building levels. The maximum number of exits required from any story, basement or individual space shall be maintained until arrival at grade or the public way.

This is an area where the location of requirements and the terminology can be somewhat confusing. The number of "exits" to be provided is determined by the requirements located in the "exit access" section of the chapter. Once the number of exits is determined, then that number must be maintained until safe arrival at a dispersal point away from the building or at the public way. Just as widths, once established, must be maintained downstream on the exit path, so too must the number of exits. Even though individual

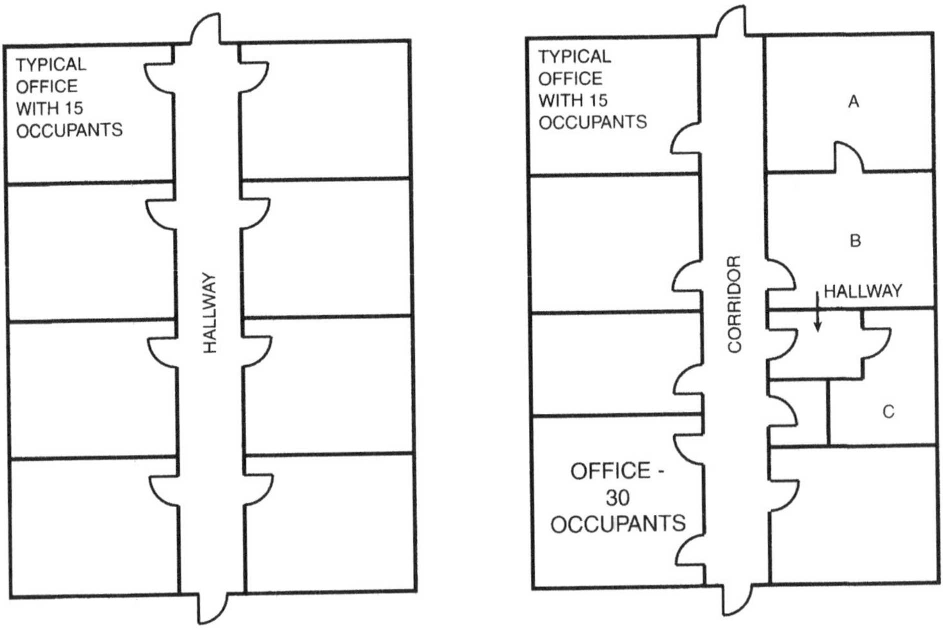

Where only one exit is required from a space, the exit access may pass through an intervening room. (Section 1004.2.2, Exception 2). Hallway are considered as intervening rooms. (Sections 1004.2.2 and 1004.3.3.1)

Rooms with a cumulative occupant load of less than 10 may have exit access passing through more than one room. Thus a series of rooms with 2 occupants could be lined up 3 deep before reaching a hallway. The hallway must then access a corridor or an exit. Note that this applies to "less than 10" so a cumulative load of 10 or more would require access through only one intervening space. (Section 1004.2.2, Exception 3)

Hallways are considered as intervening rooms so that where two exits are required from a space only one may pass through a hallway (Section 1004.2.2, Exception 4) Spaces requiring two exits cannot have both exits pass through a hallway (intervening room).

A hallway may be used if all spaces served by it comply with the intervening room requirements, otherwise a corridor will be required.

Hallways in Group R-1 or Group I Occupancies with an occupant load of 10 or more must comply with corridor requirements (Sections 1007.5.3 and 1007.6.1)

REFERENCE: SECTIONS 1004.2.2 AND 1004.3.3

FIGURE 7-16 HALLWAYS AND TRAVEL THROUGH INTERVENING ROOMS

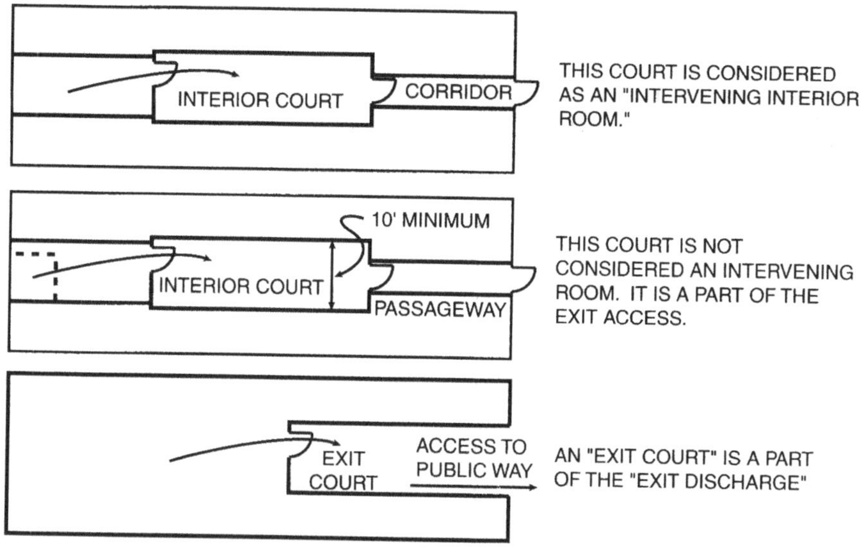

Interior courts enclosed on all sides are considered as intervening rooms except as illustrated above. (Section 1004.2.2)

When courts are more than 10 feet wide and provide direct access to an exit they are not considered intervening rooms, but are part of the exit access and are included in travel distance calculations.

When a court which is part of the egress systems is not bounded on all sides it is considered as a portion of the exit discharge.

REFERENCE: SECTION 1004.2.2

FIGURE 7-17 TRAVEL THROUGH INTERVENING ROOMS

spaces downstream of other larger spaces may require fewer exits, the number of exits must be maintained to allow the upstream contribution of occupants to flow through the means of egress system to the end of the exit discharge and thus safely out of the building.

This section permits multiple exits to be combined at grade, before they reach a public way. Thus two exit enclosures may empty into a single on-grade exit discharge leading to the public way. This is a change from previous code editions that required that the exits be continuous and separate until reaching the public way.

In the authors' opinion the provisions of the older code, which required separate means of egress to extend to the public way, should be used whenever possible. It is good practice to keep exits well separated until the occupants can complete their exit travel at a safe public way some distance from the building.

1004.2.3.2 From individual floors. For the purposes of Section 1004.2, floors, stories, occupied roofs, mezzanines, and similar designations of building levels other than basements shall be considered synonymous.

Every occupant on the first story shall have access to not less than one exit and not less than two exits when required by Table 10-A. Every occupant in basements and on stories other than the first story shall have access to not less than two exits.

EXCEPTIONS: 1. Second stories having an occupant load less than 10 may be provided with access to only one exit.

2. Two or more dwelling units on the second story or in a basement may have access to only one exit where the total occupant load served by that exit does not exceed 10.

3. Except as provided in Table 10-A, access to only one exit need be provided from the second floor or a basement within an individual dwelling unit or a Group R, Division 3 congregate residence.

4. Where the third floor within an individual dwelling unit or a Group R, Division 3 congregate residence does not exceed 500 square feet (46.45 m^2), access to only one exit need be provided from that floor.

5. Occupied roofs on Group R, Division 3 Occupancies may have access to only one exit where such occupied areas are less than 500 square feet (46.45 m^2) and are located no higher than immediately above the second story.

6. Floors and basements used exclusively for the service of the building may have access to only one exit. For the purposes of this exception, storage rooms, laundry rooms, maintenance offices and similar uses shall not be considered as providing service to the building.

No cumulative or contributing occupant loads from adjacent levels need be considered when determining the number of required exits from a given level.

The second paragraph of Section 1004.2.3.2 states the basic proviso, discussed earlier, that there be at least two exits provided in most buildings. (See Figure 7-18.) The intent is that if one exit is

FIGURE 7-18 EXCEPTIONS TO THE REQUIREMENTS FOR TWO MEANS OF EGRESS

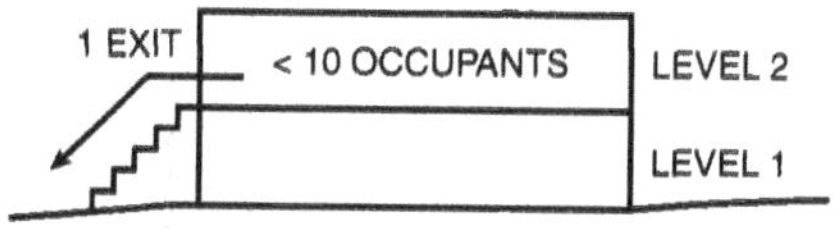

EXCEPTION 1 - SECOND STORY WITH LESS THAN 10 OCCUPANTS

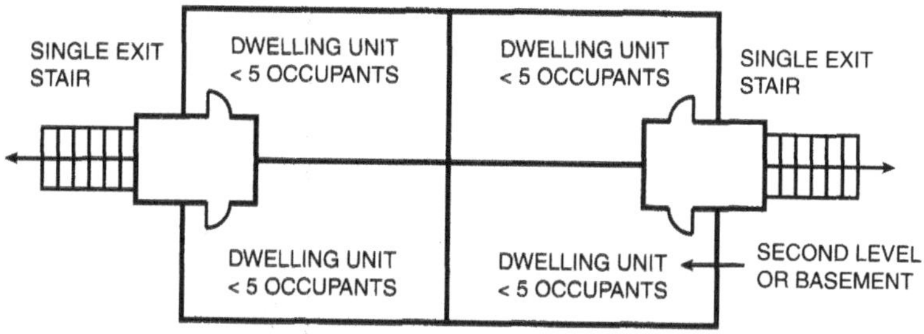

EXCEPTION 2 - DWELLING UNITS ON SECOND STORY OR BASEMENT WITH 10 OR FEWER TOTAL OCCUPANTS

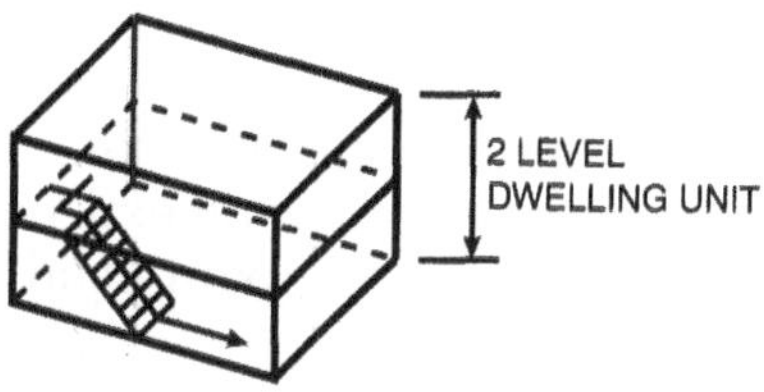

EXCEPTION 3 - ONE EXIT FROM SECOND LEVEL WITHIN A DWELLING UNIT

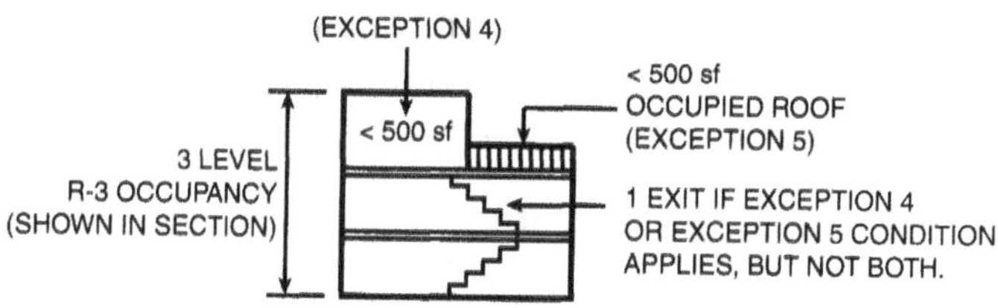

EXCEPTIONS 4 AND 5

Note: It is the author's opinion that the intent of the code is that *either* Exception 4 or Exception 5 be used and that they not be used together. Thus the illustration for the Exception is not permitted for *both* an occupied roof and an occupied third level space.

REFERENCE: SECTION 1004.2.3.2

blocked or otherwise not usable the other should be available. This requirement is invoked in paragraph 2 under two conditions:

- based on occupant load, which is determined by the area and occupancy of the floor in question per Table 10-A and
- location in the building, either in a basement or on stories above the first level.

The requirements are specific in these paragraphs and their exceptions. The second floor of a building must have two exits when the occupant load exceeds 10, with the exceptions for the special cases noted. Thus for a building with a B-2 (office) occupancy with an occupant load factor of 100, this exit requirement will apply when the floor area exceeds 1000 square feet. The exceptions are intended to be for special cases for low occupant load uses. Note also that additional means of egress provisions may appear in other chapters of the code. For example, the egress criteria for mezzanines are also noted in Section 507.

Unusual situations can arise as a result of using the exception criteria. For example, if an R-1 building has 2400 square feet per floor, only the third floor must have two exits. The second floor, by these criteria alone, need have only one exit per Exception 2. This determination is based on the occupant load of the second floor being 8 (2400/300 = 8 occupants).

> The general rule is that regardless of the size of the floor, there must be two means of egress from occupied spaces on all floors above the second, except under very specific and very limited circumstances. When in doubt, provide two exits.

For example, consider a B office occupancy. The occupant load factor is 100 and two exits are required when there are more than 30 occupants. Therefore, the allowable area will have to exceed (100 × 30 =) 3000 square feet before two exits are required. Conversely, taking the size of a space and dividing it by the occupant load factor of Table No. 10-A results in the occupant load for the area. For example, a 6000-square-foot locker room space with a Table 10-A occupant load factor of 50 square feet per occupant would have an occupant load of 6000/50 = 120 occupants. Note that two means of egress would be required from the locker room in question since 120 occupants exceeds the 30-occupant threshold.

The escape window required in Section 310.4 cannot substitute for one of the required exits. Such windows are in addition to the number of exits required by the other provisions of Chapter 10.

The designer should be aware of all these criteria and their applications. If the third-floor stairway ends at the second floor, the occupant loads of both floors must be considered, even if the occupant load of the second floor alone warrants only one exit. This is a commonly overlooked exiting provision.

1004.2.3.3 From individual spaces. All occupied portions of the building shall have access to not less than one exit or exit-access doorway. Access to not less than two exits, exit-access doorways or combination thereof shall be provided when the individual or cumulative occupant load served by a portion of the exit access is equal to, or greater than, that listed in Table 10-A.

EXCEPTIONS: 1. Elevator lobbies may have access to only one exit or exit-access doorway provided the use of such exit or exit-access doorway does not require keys, tools, special knowledge or effort.

2. Storage rooms, laundry rooms and maintenance offices not exceeding 300 square feet (27.87 m^2) in floor area may be provided with access to only one exit or exit-access doorway.

The number of exits, or exit access doorways, required from individual spaces in the exit access are to be determined using the criteria set forth in Table 10-A. There may be a number of rooms in the exit access. Each of these may require two exits or exit access doorways. These must lead in turn into multiple exits when these paths leave the area considered to be the exit access and enter the exits.

1004.2.3.4 Additional access to exits. Access to not less than three exits, exit-access doorways or combination thereof shall be provided when the individual or cumulative occupant load served by the exit access is 501 to 1,000.

Access to not less than four exits, exit-access doorways or combination thereof shall be provided when the individual or cumulative occupant load served by the exit access exceeds 1,000.

1004.2.4 Separation of exits or exit-access doorways. Where two or more exits or exit-access doorways are required from any level or portion of the building, at least two of the exits or exit-access doorways shall be placed a distance apart equal to not less than one half of the length of the maximum

overall diagonal dimension of the area served measured in a straight line between the center of such exits or exit-access doorways. Additional exits or exit-access doorways shall be arranged a reasonable distance apart so that if one becomes blocked, the others will be available.

EXCEPTION: The separation distance determined in accordance with this section may be measured along a direct path of exit travel within a corridor serving exit enclosures. The walls of any such exit enclosure shall not be less than 30 feet (9144 mm), measured in a straight line, from the walls of another exit enclosure.

Occupant loads of greater than 501 persons require three exits and more than 1000 occupants requires four exits. The minimum separation of exits when two exits are required is one half of the maximum diagonal dimension of the area in question measured in a straight line. When more than two exits are required, they are to be distributed evenly around the space to meet the intend expressed in this section: if one exit path becomes blocked, then other alternative paths will still be available without traveling great distances. Note also that there are additional occupancy-specific requirements for location and sizes of multiple exits contained in Section 1007 of Chapter 10. These are discussed later in this article. Note that separation is measured to the center of the doorway, not to the nearest edge of the opening. This only becomes critical in situations where the separation is very close to the minimum. (See Figures 7-19, 7-20 and 7-21.)

> It is the authors' opinion that the intent of the code is that the separation measurements are to doorways entering into corridors or exit enclosures. The measurements should be to the centerline of openings, not to the center of the area of an exit enclosure treated as a two-dimensional object in plan. Measuring to the center of such objects could result in inadequate exit separations.

Note that the 30-foot minimum separation requirements for exit enclosure walls is triggered only when the exception to Section 1004.2.4 is used. No minimum is specified otherwise, although good practice should dictate that separate means of egress systems be kept as far apart as possible in the interest of safety. Also note that there are no requirements stated in the exception regarding

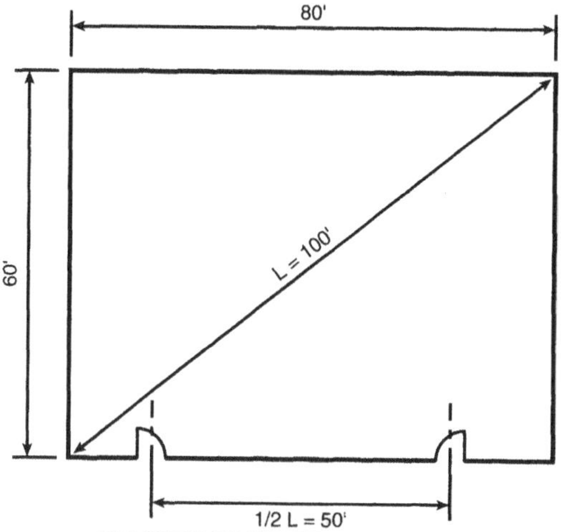

EXAMPLE: Office, B Occupancy

Occupant Load Factor Per Table 10-A: 100 sf per occupant

Area: 60′ x 80′ = 4,800 sf

Number of Occupants: 4,800/100 = 48 occupants; greater than 30, therefor two exits are required

Separated by 1/2 the length of the diagonal distance (L)

L = 100′ : L/2 = 50′

REFERENCE: SECTION 1004.2.4

FIGURE 7-19 MEASUREMENT OF DIAGONAL DISTANCES

the fire rating of the corridor, although for most purposes the corridor will most likely be rated for other reasons.

The determination of the maximum diagonal distance should use a worst-case scenario for establishing the distance. Also, note that the requirements use the center of exits or exit access doorways, not the jamb. As can be inferred from Section 1004.2.5.1 following, the intent of this section is that movable elements are not to be considered as interfering with the straight-line measurement. When determining exit separation distances that are close to the

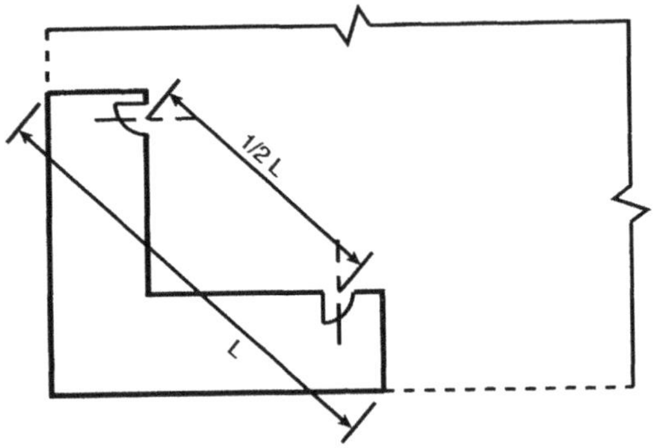

PLAN "A"

PLAN "A"

Shown is a common corner configuration for a building's partial floor. In all these examples only a portion of a building is shown. The concept remains the same whether for a portion of a floor or the entire floor. The exits have to be separated by not less than the length of one-half the diagonal distance measured across the longest diagonal of the area served.

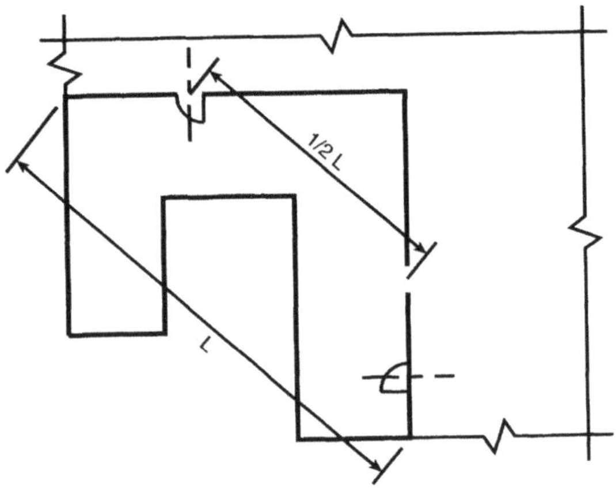

PLAN "B"

PLAN "B"

The shape of the area for which the separation of exits is to be determined can wrap around space outside of the area under consideration. The length of the longest diagonal may extend through the outside space. Thus, the measurement is unchanged by the configuration or the presence of outside space. The method remains the same, i.e., the longest diagonal is used.

REFERENCE: SECTION 1004.2.4

FIGURE 7-20 MEASUREMENT OF DIAGONAL DISTANCES WITHIN IRREGULARLY SHAPED SPACES

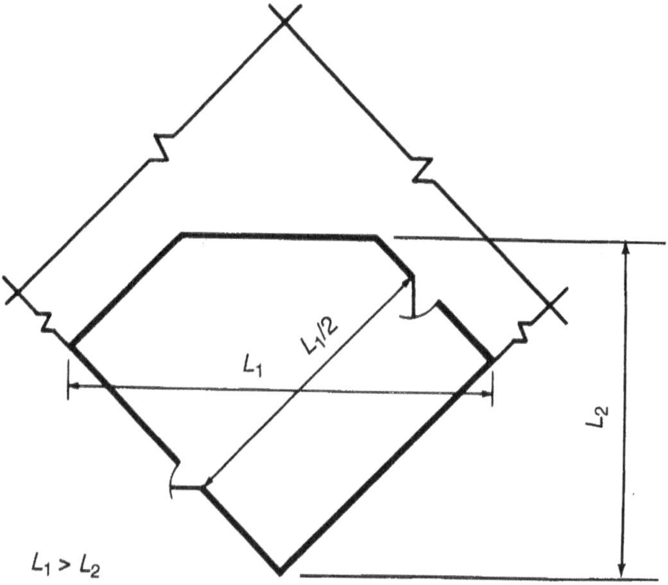

PLAN "C"

PLAN "C"

When the area served is irregular in shape with more than four sides, the longest diagonal must be used to determine the required separation of exits. Assuming $L_1 > L_2$ then 1/2 of the longest diagonal is $L_1/2$ which will set the minimum exit separation.

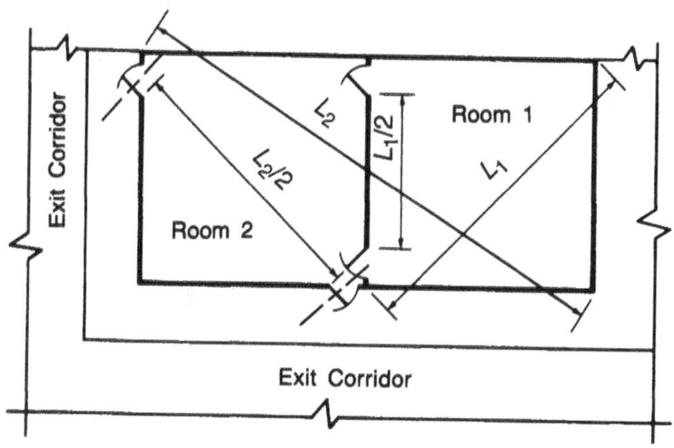

PLAN "D"

PLAN "D:"

Room 1 exits into Room 2. In Room 1 the separation of exits uses as its longest diagonal that of the room being served. The Room 2 measurement of the separation of exits has to include Room 1 as it is part of the total area served.

For example, in a suite of offices the longest diagonal will be that which crosses the entire suite, not just that of the last area leading to a corridor. The space should be measured to include the entire area of the suite and the exits then arranged accordingly.

REFERENCE: SECTION 1004.2.4

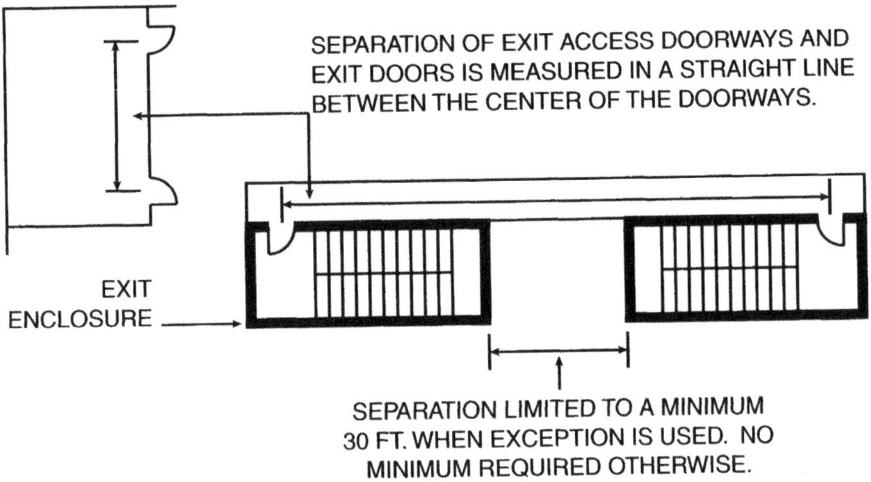

Exit separations are measured to the center of the doorway, not the nearest edge. This only becomes critical where it is difficult to meet the minimum 1/2 the diagonal separation criteria. The criteria also calls for multiple exits to be distributed in a reasonable pattern to minimize the danger of more than one exit being blocked simultaneously by an emergency. Ideally 3 exits will each be roughly a third of the perimeter apart, 4 exits a quarter of the perimeter and so on.

Where a corridor is used to meet the exit separation requirements, per the exception to Section 1004.2.4, then the distance is to be measured within the corridor. If this method is used then the walls of the exit enclosures are to be a minimum of 30 feet apart. Note that this separation requirement only applies if the exception is used.

Per Section 1004.2.3.1 the exit separation need only be maintained until grade is reached at the exit discharge. This section seems to allow joining of exits in the exit discharge.

In the author's opinion separate exit paths should be maintained to the public way whenever possible. If exits must be combined at the exit discharge, careful attention must be paid to make certain that required exits widths are maintained.

REFERENCE: SECTIONS 1004.2.4 AND 1005.2.1

FIGURE 7-21 SEPARATION OF EXITS OR EXIT ACCESS DOORWAYS

specified minimum, such seemingly minor variations as missing a beveled corner in a room or mismeasuring to the edge of a pair of exit doors can result in a time-consuming redesign of the space if the separations are miscalculated. Another issue to verify when calculating diagonal distances within spaces is that the building official concurs that such unoccupied spaces as mechanical rooms or storage areas are not considered part of the larger exit access space.

1004.2.5 Travel distance.

1004.2.5.1 General. Travel distance is that distance an occupant must travel from any point within occupied portions of the exit access to the door of the nearest exit. Travel distance shall be measured in a straight line along the path of exit travel from the most remote point through the center of exit-access doorways to the center of the exit door. Travel distance shall include that portion of the path of exit travel through or around permanent construction features and building elements. Travel around tables, chairs, furnishings, cabinets and similar temporary or movable fixtures or equipment need not be considered as the normal presence of such items is factored into the permitted travel distance.

Unless prohibited elsewhere in this chapter, travel within the exit access may occur on multiple levels by way of unenclosed stairways or ramps. Where the path of exit travel includes unenclosed stairways or ramps within the exit access, the distance of travel on such means of egress components shall also be included in the travel distance measurement. The measurement along stairways shall be made on a plane parallel and tangent to the stair tread nosings in the center of the stairway.

1004.2.5.2 Maximum travel distance. The travel distance to at least one exit shall not exceed that specified in this section.

Special travel distance requirements are contained in other sections of this code as follows:

1. For atria, see Section 402.5.
2. For Group E Occupancies, see Section 1007.3.
3. For Group H Occupancies, see Section 1007.4.
4. For malls, see Sections 404.4.3 and 404.4.5.

1004.2.5.2.1 Nonsprinklered buildings. In buildings not equipped with an automatic sprinkler system throughout, the travel distance shall not exceed 200 feet (60 960 mm).

1004.2.5.2.2 Sprinklered buildings. In buildings equipped with an automatic sprinkler system throughout, the travel distance shall not exceed 250 feet (76 200 mm).

1004.2.5.2.3 Corridor increases. The travel distances specified in Sections 1004.2.5.2.1, 1004.2.5.2.2, 1004.2.5.2.4 and 1004.2.5.2.5 may be increased up to an additional 100 feet (30 480 mm) provided that the last portion of exit access leading to the exit occurs within a corridor. The length of such corridor shall not be less than the amount of the increase taken, in feet (mm).

1004.2.5.2.4 Open parking garages. In a Group S, Division 4 open parking garage as defined in Section 311.9, the travel distance shall not exceed

300 feet (91 440 mm) in a building not equipped with an automatic sprinkler system throughout and 400 feet (121 920 mm) in a building equipped with an automatic sprinkler system throughout. The travel distance may be measured to open stairways, which are permitted in accordance with Section 1005.3.3.1.

1004.2.5.2.5 Factory, hazardous and storage occupancies. In a one-story building classified as a Group H, Division 5 aircraft repair hangar, or as a Group F or Group S Occupancy, the travel distance shall not exceed 300 feet (91 440 mm) and may be increased to 400 feet (121 920 mm) if the building is equipped with an automatic sprinkler system throughout and is also provided with smoke and heat ventilation as specified in Section 906.

It is essential to have an understanding of the criteria for determining travel distance and knowing to which elements of the means of egress travel distance limits apply. (See Figures 7-22, 7-23 and 7-24.)

Travel distance is measured in a straight line, regardless of temporary obstacles such as cabinets or furnishings, but mindful of permanent obstacles such as walls or columns. The distances are measured through the center of exit access doors and then to the center of exit doors. It is acceptable to have open, unprotected elements such as stairs or ramps, connecting multiple levels of the exit access. However, all travel distances on such elements must be added together as part of the total travel distance measurements.

The exit access can be considered as one large element with level changes, open stairs and interconnecting levels as long as the distance traveled on any path on any of those elements to get to the exit is accounted for in calculating the travel distance. Specific measurement criteria are noted for open stairways. The occupants are given a domain to wander in, relatively less protected in the exit access. However, there is a maximum distance they are expected to traverse to reach a contained and protected exit that will conduct them to the exit discharge. Travel distances are measured to the "nearest exit." Where two or more exits are required, the occupant need only reach the nearest exit within the allotted travel distance. Other exits may exceed the travel distance from a given point as long as one meets the travel distance criteria.

Figure 7.22 graphically compares exit access travel distances. Travel distances apply only to the exit access, there are no travel distance limitations for exits. Note that the corridor increases permitted under Section 1004.2.5.2.3 do not specify that the corridor be rated. Thus these increases are permissible in nonrated corridors

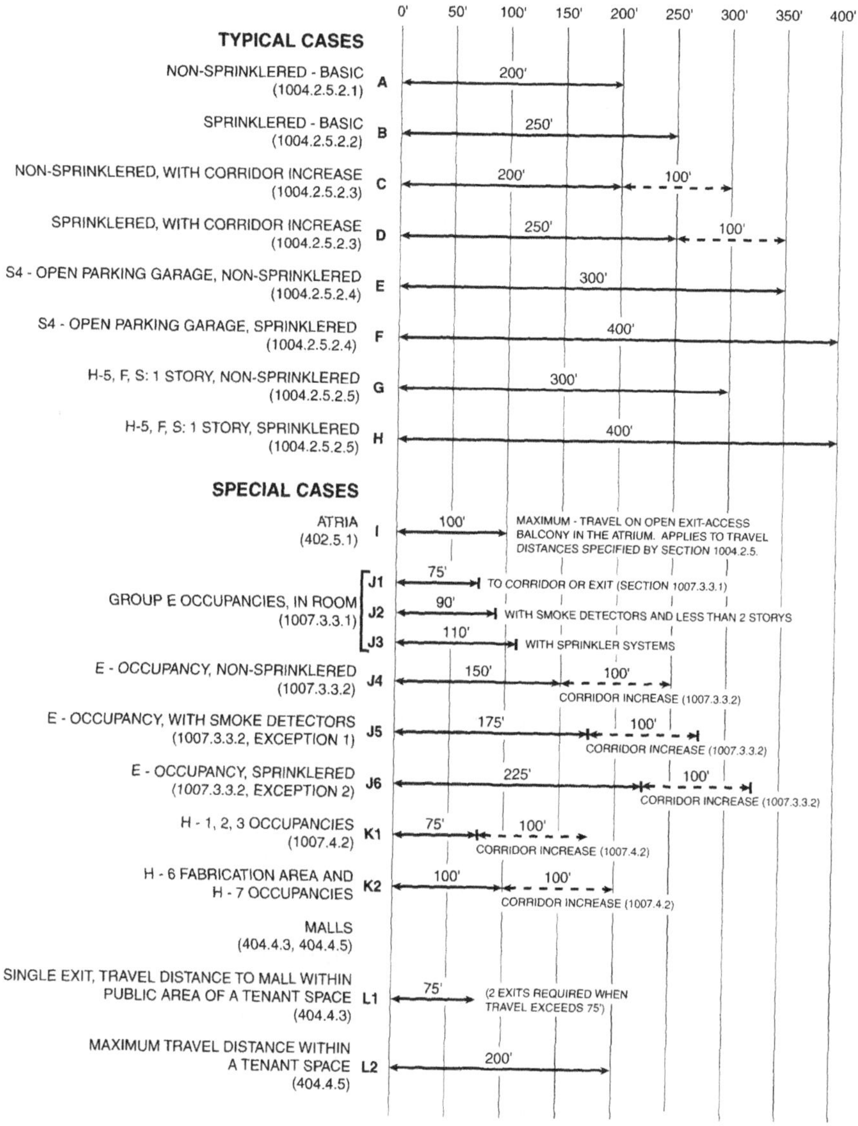

REFERENCE: SECTION 1004.2.5

FIGURE 7-22 EXIT TRAVEL DISTANCES GRAPHICALLY ILLUSTRATED

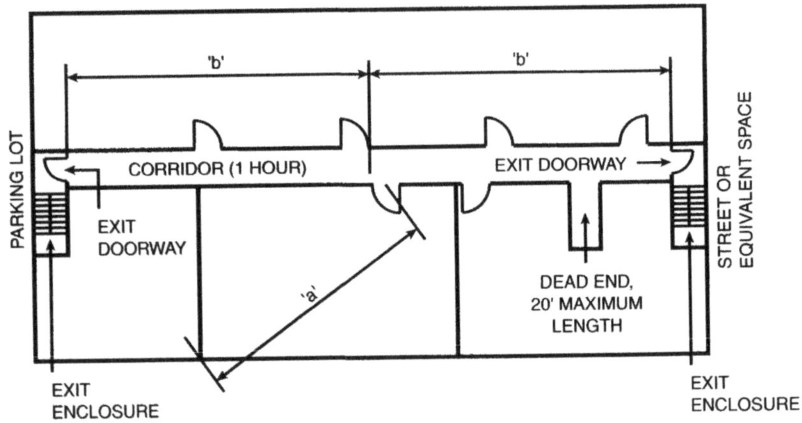

Unsprinklered Building:

'a' = Travel distance to reach one hour corridor = 200′ maximum
'b' = Travel distance within one hour corridor to reach exit = 100′ maximum

Sprinklered Building:

'a' = 250′ maximum
'b' = 100′ maximum

REFERENCE: SECTION 1004.2.5

FIGURE 7-23 EXIT TRAVEL DISTANCES

that comply with the exceptions to Section 1004.3.4.3 as discussed later.

Where choices of travel exist and where more than one exit or exit access doorway is required, the maximum length of a dead-end corridor is 20 feet. This is intended to apply to those side passages that do not lead to an exit or exit access doorway. This provision is intended to prevent occupants from traveling off of the egress pathway and finding a blank wall or a locked door that does not lead to the egress path. The maximum distance to retrace steps to get back on a path leading to egress is set at 20 feet by the UBC. The allowable dead-end distance varies in the various model codes and is somewhat arbitrary, but is nonetheless the regulation and must be complied with. It is acceptable to have 20-foot runs of passageways when the occupant will not be required to retrace

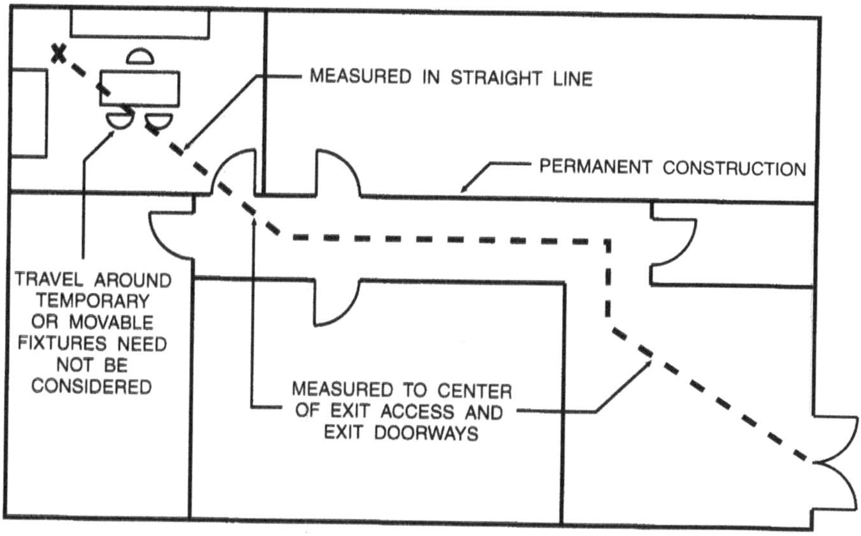

Travel distance is to be measured in a straight line along the accessible path. The path need not take into account movable objects or fixtures such as desks or tables. The path must include distances around permanent construction such as walls or fixed partitions.

Basic travel distances are 200 feet in non-sprinklered buildings and 250 feet in sprinklered buildings.

The 100 foot corridor increase is allowable even in unrated corridors construction in accordance with the exceptions to Section 1004.3.4.3

REFERENCE: SECTION 1004.2.5

FIGURE 7-24 EXIT TRAVEL ILLUSTRATED

steps in order to proceed toward the ultimate end of a means of egress. Thus, when there is a potential dead-end corridor where two paths of egress intersect, it is permissible to put a door in one passageway that opens in the direction of exit access for one passage and reduces the dead end for the other passage to less than 20 feet.

> **1004.3 Exit-access Components.**
> **1004.3.1 General. Exit-access components incorporated into the design of the exit-access portion of the means of egress system shall comply with the requirements of Section 1004.3.**

These components are intended to be those portions of the means of egress that may be included in the exit access portion of the means of egress. They are listed logically more or less in ascending order of protection for occupants of the exit access. Protection requirements for fire resistance and thus life safety tend to increase for each listed component. Again, note that "corridors" are listed in this portion of the means of egress, not in the "exit" portion.

As previously noted, these terms are not defined for the purpose of their use in the chapter, so the designer must assume that they are defined as noted in Section 201.1 in terms of the context in which they are used per *Webster's Third New International Dictionary of the English Language.*

1004.3.2 Aisles.

1004.3.2.1 General. Aisles serving as a portion of an exit access in the means of egress system shall comply with the requirements of Section 1004.3.2. Aisles shall be provided from all occupied portions of the exit access that contain seats, tables, furnishings, displays, and similar fixtures or equipment.

1004.3.2.2 Width in occupancies without fixed seats. The width of aisles in occupancies without fixed seats shall be determined in accordance with the following:

1. In areas serving employees only, the minimum aisle width shall be 24 inches (610 mm), but not less than the width determined as specified in Section 1003.2.3.

2. In public areas of Groups B and M Occupancies, and in assembly occupancies without fixed seats, the minimum clear aisle width shall be 36 inches (914 mm) where seats, tables, furnishings, displays and similar fixtures or equipment are placed on only one side of the aisle and 44 inches (1118 mm) where such fixtures or equipment are placed on both sides of the aisle.

The required width of aisles shall be unobstructed.

EXCEPTION: Handrails and doors, when fully opened, shall not reduce the required width by more than 7 inches (178 mm). Doors in any position shall not reduce the required width by more than one half. Other nonstructural projections such as trim and similar decorative features may project into the required width $1\frac{1}{2}$ inches (38 mm) from each side.

Aisles in this context are defined in *Webster's* as " a passage between sections of seats." The section also notes that the term "aisle" applies where there are tables, furnishings and fixtures in addition to seats. Aisle widths are set, step relationships are set and rails are specified, but there are no requirements for enclosures or fire-protective construction for aisles. The intent and implication of these requirements is that aisles are open to the exit access domain. They are to provide a clear and unobstructed pathway leading to the next level of exit access component, such as to an exit access doorway, or to an exit. Widths are set by the same basic criteria as doors and stairs and once set must not diminish in the direction of flow toward the exit. Heights defining aisle pathways are noted under "hallways" in Section 1004.3.3.3. (See Figure 7-25.)

There are numerous detailed provisions for aisle configurations and slopes in assembly areas that are beyond the detail of a basic text such as this. Do remember that the same underlying watercourse analogy of increasing size of channels as one proceeds downstream applies to aisles too.

1004.3.3 Hallways.

1004.3.3.1 General. Hallways serving as a portion of the exit access in the means of egress system shall comply with the requirements of Section 1004.3.3. Hallways may be used as an exit-access component unless specifically prohibited based on requirements specified elsewhere in this chapter.

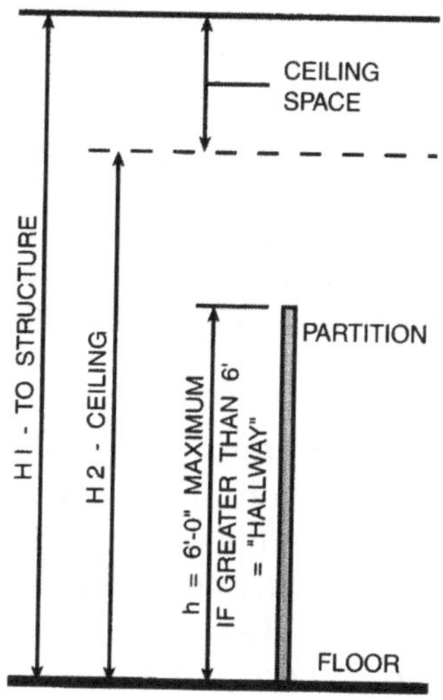

Aisle partitions may be 6′-0″ high within any occupancy regardless of the floor to ceiling height of the room or area. Partitions any higher are to be construed as hallways.

REFERENCE: SECTION 1004.3.3.3

FIGURE 7-25 HEIGHT OF NON-FIRE RESISTIVE PARTITIONS FORMING AISLES OR HALLWAYS WITHIN TENANT SPACE

For exit-access design purposes, hallways shall be considered as intervening rooms.

1004.3.3.2 Width. The width of hallways shall be determined as specified in Section 1003.2.3, but such width shall not be less than 44 inches (1118 mm), except as specified herein. Hallways serving an occupant load of less than 50 shall not be less than 36 inches (914 mm) in width.

The required width of hallways shall be unobstructed.

EXCEPTION: Doors, when fully opened, and handrails shall not reduce the required width by more than 7 inches (178 mm). Doors in any position shall not reduce the required width by more than one half. Other nonstructural projections such as trim and similar decorative features may project into the required width $1\frac{1}{2}$ inches (38 mm) from each side.

1004.3.3.3 Construction. Hallways are not required to be of fire-resistive construction unless a building element of the hallway is required to be of fire-resistive construction by some other provision of this code.

Hallways in buildings of Types I or II construction shall be of noncombustible construction, except where combustible materials are permitted in applicable building elements by other provisions of this code. Hallways in buildings of Types III, IV or V construction may be of combustible or noncombustible construction.

Hallways may have walls of any height. Partitions, rails, counters and similar space dividers not over 6 feet (1829 mm) in height above the floor shall not be construed to form a hallway.

1004.3.3.4 Openings. There is no restriction as to the amount and type of openings permitted in hallways, unless protection of openings is required by some other provision of this code.

1004.3.3.5 Elevator lobbies. Elevators opening into hallways need not be provided with elevator lobbies unless smoke- and draft-control assemblies are required for the protection of elevator door openings by some other provision of this code.

A hallway is defined in *Webster's* as "an entrance hall." The intent here is that a hallway is a confined space, similar to a corridor, but with lesser requirements for protection. Hallways are treated similarly to rooms since they are considered intervening spaces per Sections 1004.2.2 and 1004.3.3.1. Hallway widths are basically 44 inches for more than 50 occupants and 36 inches for fewer than 50. They are not required to be of fire-resistive construction.

Note also the requirements for door swing clearances at hallways, corridors and similar passageways. Where doors do not meet these clearance criteria the doors will need to be recessed into a pocket to keep the door swing from encroaching too far into the passage. The minimum exit and accessible door width should always be at least 36 inches. If this door swings out into a typical 44-inch hallway, it will encroach into the passage by more than half the width of the passage. Thus a pocket will be required. (See Figure 7-26.)

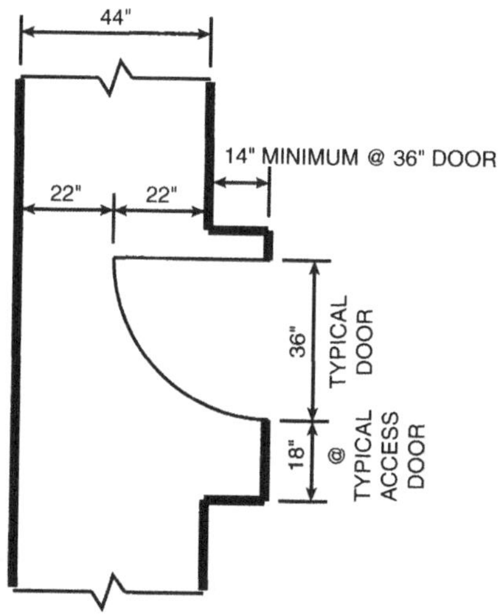

Width restriction requirements for the relationship of door swings to passage width apply to hallways, corridors, exit passageways and exit discharge.

Typical door recess depicted, based on the following assumptions:

Passage serving more than 50 occupants = 44′ minimum width

Door is typical 36″ minimum passage door

Door cannot encroach more than one-half passage width in any position and not more than 7 inches when fully open. The intent regarding the 7″ projection is that this apply to doors opening 180 degrees and resting against the wall. If this were not the intent then for doors opening 90 degrees the recess would need to be 36″ - 7″, or 29″ deep to keep the door from projecting into the corridor when it is "fully opened". This does not agree with the other provision in the paragraph which allows encroachment upon one half the passage width.

It is the author's opinion that outswinging doors should be recessed fully to prevent the door from opening into to required exit path. This allows the exit path to remain open under any conditions and also prevents the door from being a hazard to persons moving through the passage under normal circumstances.

REFERENCE: SECTIONS 1004.3.3.2, 1004.3.4.2, 1005.3.4.2, 1006.3.2.2

FIGURE 7-26 PROJECTION OF DOORS INTO MEANS OF EGRESS

The only fire-resistive requirements for hallways relate to those dictated by the building type classification. Hallways may be of any height, but partitions, such as in an open office, less than 6 feet in height are not construed to form a hallway. Openings into the hallway from rooms are not restricted. Elevator lobbies need not be provided at hallways unless required by some other section of the code. (See also Figure 7.28.) Basically, given the intervening room criteria and the lack of protection criteria, hallways are best considered as long, narrow intervening rooms. A hallway is permitted if all space it serves comply with the intervening room provisions of Section 1004.2.2.

1004.3.4 Corridors.

1004.3.4.1 General. Corridors serving as a portion of an exit access in the means of egress system shall comply with the requirements of Section 1004.3.4.

For restrictions on the use of corridors to convey air, see Chapter 6 of the Mechanical Code.

1004.3.4.2 Width. The width of corridors shall be determined as specified in Section 1003.2.3, but such width shall not be less than 44 inches (1118 mm), except as specified herein. Corridors serving an occupant load of less than 50 shall not be less than 36 inches (914 mm) in width.

The required width of corridors shall be unobstructed.

> **EXCEPTION:** Doors, when fully opened, and handrails shall not reduce the required width by more than 7 inches (178 mm). Doors in any position shall not reduce the required width by more than one half. Other nonstructural projections such as trim and similar decorative features may project into the required width 1½ inches (38 mm) from each side.

Corridor is an undefined term in the UBC. There have been numerous attempts over the years to write a definition of corridor that the membership of the International Conference of Building Officials (ICBO) would accept, but none has been adopted. *Webster's* defines corridor variously as: "1a: a usually covered passageway; especially one into which compartments or rooms open . . . 2a: a usually narrow passageway or route." Corridors are not required to be considered as intervening rooms as hallways are. This is deduced since this requirement is not mentioned in the corridor sections of 1004.3.4. Also 1004.3.4.4 notes that corridors are not to be interrupted by intervening rooms. A corridor will thus be used where the configuration of spaces can not comply with the hallway intervening room requirements for means of egress design.

Width requirements for corridors follow the now familiar 44 inches for 50 or more occupants and 36 inches for less than 50 occupants. Corridors are basically required to be fully enclosed, with walls, floors, a ceiling and protected openings.

> **1004.3.4.3 Construction.** Corridors shall be fully enclosed by walls, a floor, a ceiling and permitted protected openings. The walls and ceilings of corridors shall be constructed of fire-resistive materials as specified in Section 1004.3.4.3.1.
>
> EXCEPTIONS: 1. One-story buildings housing Group F, Division 2 and Group S, Division 2 Occupancies.
>
> 2. Corridors more than 30 feet (9144 mm) in width where occupancies served by such corridors have at least one exit independent from the corridor. (See Chapter 4 for covered malls.)
>
> 3. In Group I, Division 3 Occupancies such as jails, prisons, reformatories and similar buildings with open-barred cells forming corridor walls, the corridors and cell doors need not be fire-resistive.
>
> 4. Corridor walls and ceilings need not be of fire-resistive construction within office spaces having an occupant load of 100 or less when the entire story in which the space is located is equipped with an automatic sprinkler system throughout and an automatic smoke-detection system installed within the corridor. The actuation of any detector shall activate alarms audible in all areas served by the corridor.
>
> 5. Corridor walls and ceilings need not be of fire-resistive construction within office spaces having an occupant load of 100 or less when the building in which the space is located is equipped with an automatic sprinkler system throughout.
>
> 6. In Group B office buildings of Type I, Type II-FR and Type II-one-hour construction, corridor walls and ceilings need not be of fire-resistive construction within office spaces of a single tenant when the entire story in which the space is located is equipped with an approved automatic sprinkler system and an automatic smoke-detection system is installed within the corridor. The actuation of any detector shall activate alarms audible in all areas served by the corridor.
>
> Corridor floors are not required to be of fire-resistive construction unless specified by some other provision of this code.

Corridors are to be constructed of fire-resistive materials per Section 1004.3.4.3. These basic requirements are offset by numerous exceptions. The exceptions deal primarily with certain occupancies, such as offices, that occur with great frequency where literal enforcement of the basic requirements would impact greatly. These occupancy configurations have good loss records when the spaces have sprinklers. Thus Exceptions 4, 5 and 6 allow relaxation of the corridor requirements in trade for increased sprinkler and life safety system protection. Wide corridors, over 30 feet in width, are excepted as well. This is a vestige from older editions of the code that was developed to accommodate covered mall buildings. Section 1004.3.4.3, Exception 2 refers to the mall section of Chapter 4.

Other exceptions deal with low hazard manufacturing, storage and jails.

For general design purposes corridors are required when a space has more than 30 occupants. Two exits are required for this occupant load and only one such exit can go through an intervening space, thus a corridor is required to serve at least one exit door from the space. Corridors are typically 1-hour construction other than as noted in the exceptions to Section 1004.3.4.3, or as required by the building construction type.

> **1004.3.4.3.1 Fire-resistive materials. Corridor walls shall be constructed of materials approved for one-hour fire-resistive construction on each side. Corridor walls shall extend vertically to a floor-ceiling or roof-ceiling constructed in accordance with one of the following:**
>
> **1. The corridor-side fire-resistive membrane of the corridor wall shall terminate at the corridor ceiling membrane constructed of materials approved for a one-hour fire-resistive floor-ceiling or roof-ceiling assembly to include suspended ceilings, dropped ceilings and lay-in roof-ceiling panels, which are a portion of a fire-resistive assembly.**
>
> **The room-side fire-resistive membrane of the corridor wall shall terminate at the underside of a floor or roof constructed of materials approved for a one-hour fire-resistive floor-ceiling or roof-ceiling assembly.**
>
> **EXCEPTION: Where the corridor ceiling is an element of not less than a one-hour fire-resistive floor-ceiling or roof-ceiling assembly at the entire story, both sides of corridor walls may terminate at the ceiling membrane.**
>
> **2. The corridor ceiling may be constructed of materials approved for a fire-resistive wall assembly. When this method is utilized, the corridor-side fire-resistive membrane of the corridor wall shall terminate at the lower ceiling membrane and the room-side fire-resistive membrane of the corridor wall shall terminate at the upper ceiling membrane.**
>
> **Corridor ceilings of noncombustible construction may be suspended below the fire-resistive ceiling membrane.**

Those corridors not excepted from fire-resistive construction requirements per the exceptions are to have 1-hour fire-resistive materials on each side per the requirements of Section 1004.3.4.3.1. See the accompanying illustrations (Figure 7-27) for the configurations of code-required fire protection at corridors.

> **1004.3.4.3.2.1 Doors. All exit-access doorways and doorways from unoccupied areas to a corridor shall be protected by tightfitting smoke- and draft-control assemblies having a fire-protection rating of not less than 20 minutes when tested in accordance with UBC Standard 7-2, Part II. Such doors shall not have louvers, mail slots or similar openings. The door and frame shall bear an approved label or other identification showing the rating thereof, followed by the letter "S," the name of the manufacturer**

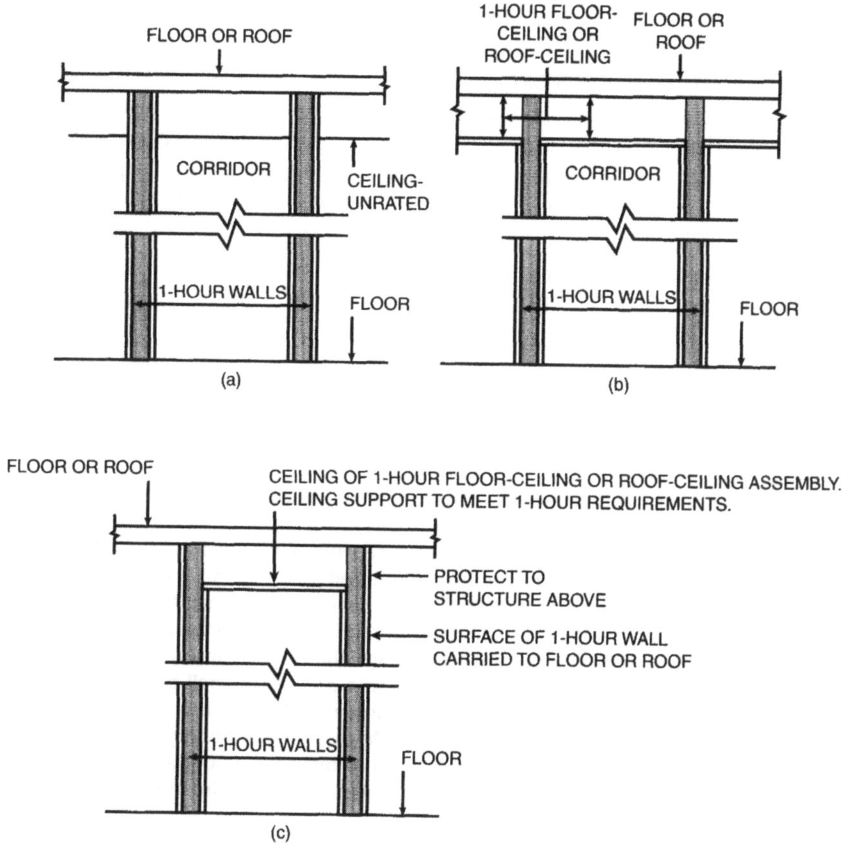

REFERENCE: SECTION 1004.3.4.3.1

FIGURE 7-27 ONE-HOUR EQUIVALENT CORRIDOR CONSTRUCTION DETAILS

and the identification of the service conducting the inspection of materials and workmanship at the factory during fabrication and assembly. Doors shall be maintained self-closing or shall be automatic closing by actuation of a smoke detector in accordance with Section 713.2. Smoke- and draft-control door assemblies shall be provided with a gasket installed so as to provide a seal where the door meets the stop on both sides and across the top.

Openings into corridors such as exit access doorways are to be protected by 20-minute doors with an S rating. Rated doors are not required at corridors excepted from fire-resistive requirements by the exceptions to Section 1004.3.4.3. These requirements apply to doors leading into the corridor from other exit access components. In other words, doors opening into the corridor from "upstream" in the means of egress are to be 20-minute doors. Doors opening from the corridor into a "downstream" exit are to be rated per the exit enclosure requirements. See the door provisions for exit components in Section 1005.3. Doors into exit components have a temperature rise limitation of 450°F at the end of 30 minutes of testing. Windows in rated corridors are to be three-quarter hour listed with an area not to exceed 25 percent of the common wall with a room.

1004.3.4.4 Intervening rooms. Corridors shall not be interrupted by intervening rooms.

EXCEPTIONS: 1. Foyers, lobbies or reception rooms constructed as required for corridors shall not be construed as intervening rooms.

2. In fully sprinklered office buildings, corridors may lead through enclosed elevator lobbies if all areas of the building have access to at least one required exit without passing through the elevator lobby.

1004.3.4.5 Elevators. Elevators opening into a corridor shall be provided with an elevator lobby at each floor containing such a corridor. The lobby shall completely separate the elevators from the corridor by construction conforming to Section 1004.3.4.3.1 and all openings into the lobby wall contiguous with the corridor shall be protected as required by Section 1004.3.4.3.2.

EXCEPTIONS: 1. In office buildings, separations need not be provided from a street floor elevator lobby, provided the entire street floor is protected with an automatic sprinkler system.

2. Elevators not required to meet the shaft enclosure requirements of Section 711.

3. Where additional doors are provided in accordance with Section 3007.

Elevator lobbies shall comply with the requirements of Section 3002.

The intervening room requirements for corridors are much more stringent than those for hallways. There are far fewer exceptions. This is in keeping with the idea that a corridor has higher requirements for life safety and protection of occupants than does a hallway.

Elevator lobby requirements have been the subject of ongoing debate for many code cycles. Lobby requirements have appeared and disappeared with such frequency that many designers and code officials are quite confused about the current requirements.

The requirements for provision of elevator lobbies at corridors has changed with every recent edition of the code. This is the source of much confusion, even for relatively new office buildings, especially when remodeling. There are numerous buildings built without elevator lobbies that are noncompliant under today's code. A small remodeling in such a building may have a large impact on the design of the means of egress. This will be further exacerbated by the new reformatting of Chapter 10 as designers and code officials struggle to absorb the new definitions, relations and interpretations of such items as corridors, hallways and exit passageways. This is an area where the designer must consult early on with the building official to determine the jurisdiction's policy for treating elevator lobby requirements. (See Figure 7-28.)

Elevators opening into a corridor are required to have elevator lobbies that will separate the elevators from the corridor. Construction and opening protection is to be the same as for the rest of the corridor. This does not apply to the entry lobby level in office buildings where the ground floor is sprinlklered. Also elevators that are excepted from shaft enclosure requirements under Section 711 are not required to have lobbies. Section 711.3 does not require shaft protection for openings serving only one adjacent floor. However, this section also states that this applies only to those openings "that are not concealed within building construction assemblies." Does not the elevator shaft and door conceal the opening? Additional doors or listed closures may be provided in addition to the hoistway doors of the elevator itself. These doors are to be self-closing or automatic closing and cover the elevator door to prevent smoke from escaping from the shaft. These assemblies must be openable from the elevator side per Section 3002 to allow persons on the elevators to escape into the corridor in an emergency.

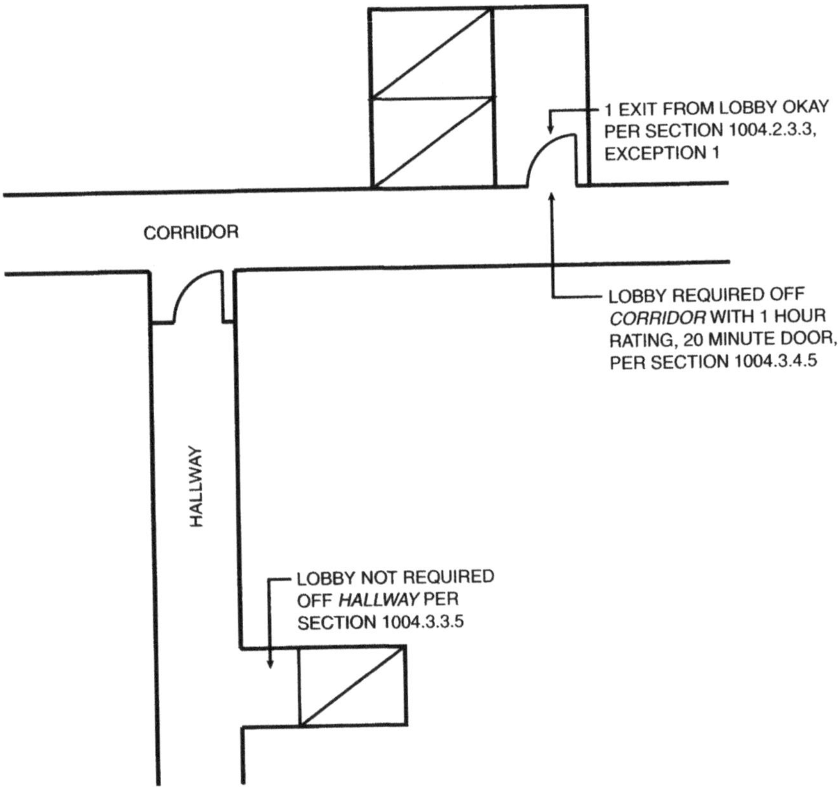

Note that lobbies are not required at the street floor of office buildings when the street floor is sprinklered, per Section 1004.3.4.5, Exception 1.

REFERENCE: SECTIONS 1004.2.3.3, 1004.3.3.5 AND 1004.3.4.5

FIGURE 7-28 ELEVATOR LOBBY REQUIREMENTS

In the authors' opinion the current elevator lobby provisions, as we interpret them, are overly restrictive. These seem to apply to almost all elevators, even in low-rise buildings. The purpose of elevator lobbies is to prevent the spread of smoke to other floors through the elevator shaft way doors. These hoistway doors, while fire rated, are not smoke tight due to opening and closing clearances required for operation. The lobby doors are to close in the event of fire and close off the shaft way from the corridor. This idea has merit in taller building where the convective currents generated by the "stack effect" of tall shafts and by movement of the elevators can force smoke to migrate with great speed. This is not the case in lower buildings and this requirement seems overly restrictive. It is not clear what, if any, elevators are excepted by the reference to Section 711.

Note also that even relatively new buildings may not be compliant with the newest edition of the code. Verify the interpretations regarding elevator lobby requirements with the local authorities having jurisdiction.

The Exit

1005.1 General. The exit is that portion of the means of egress system between the exit access and the exit discharge or the public way. Components that may be selectively included in the exit include exterior exit doors, exit enclosures, exit passageways and horizontal exits, in addition to those common means of egress components described in Section 1003.3.

The exit is defined by exclusion. It is that which is not the exit access or the exit discharge. It may include exterior exit doors, exit enclosures, exit passageways and horizontal exits. Note that corridors are not included on the list. The so-called common means of egress components are described in 1003.3 and include doors, gates, stairways and ramps.

1004.2.4 Separation of exits or exit-access doorways. Where two or more exits or exit-access doorways are required from any level or portion of the building, at least two of the exits or exit-access doorways shall be placed a distance apart equal to not less than one half of the length of the maximum overall diagonal dimension of the area served measured in a straight line between the center of such exits or exit-access doorways. Additional exits

or exit-access doorways shall be arranged a reasonable distance apart so that if one becomes blocked, the others will be available.

EXCEPTION: The separation distance determined in accordance with this section may be measured along a direct path of exit travel within a corridor serving exit enclosures. The walls of any such exit enclosure shall not be less than 30 feet (9144 mm), measured in a straight line, from the walls of another exit enclosure.

The requirements for exit separations are contained in Section 1004.2.4 of the exit access section, as discussed previously in this article and repeated above. The criteria for exit access doors and exits are thus the same. The intent of these sections is that exit access doors and exit doors be separated by at least one half the diagonal dimension of a space. Also critical is the requirement contained in the exception to Section 1004.2.4 that the walls of exit enclosures be a minimum of 30 feet apart. It is not permissible to separate the exit access doors in each corner of the space and then have exit passageways located adjacent to each other leading to separate exit discharges. The intent of means of egress exit design where two or more exits are required is that these exits be safe havens for occupants and that each exit will be as far as possible from the other. The goal of means of egress design is that any problems with one means of egress will not impact any others.

1005.2.2 Travel distance. Travel distance shall not be limited within an exit enclosure or exit passageway, which complies with the applicable requirements of Section 1005.3.

1005.2.3 Travel through intervening rooms. Exits shall not be interrupted by intervening rooms.

EXCEPTIONS: 1. Horizontal exits may lead to an exit-access element complying with the requirements of Section 1004.

2. In office buildings, and Group I, Division 1.1 hospitals and nursing homes, a maximum of 50 percent of the exits may pass through a street-floor lobby, provided the entire street floor is protected with an automatic sprinkler system.

Note that there are no travel distance restrictions for exit enclosures or exit passageways. However, exit components must be of fire-resistive construction as discussed in 1005.3. Note that the fire-resistive requirements for exit passageways vary with the length of the passageway. Also note that temperature rise limitations apply to all interior doors into the passageway as required to all exit components. Exits may not pass through intervening rooms except that half of the exits may pass through street floor lobbies of office buildings, hospitals and nursing homes when the street floor is fully sprinkled.

As in the requirements for exit widths, once a given level of fire resistance is set for an exit that level of fire resistance must be maintained until arrival at the exit discharge. The only exception is for horizontal exits that may lead to an exit access element. This is in keeping with the concept that a horizontal exit creates, in effect, two separate buildings.

The fire-resistive construction requirements for the major exit components: exit enclosures, exit passageways and horizontal exits are summarized in Table 7-1.

1005.3.3 Exit enclosures.

1005.3.3.1 General. Exit enclosures serving as an exit in a means of egress system shall comply with the requirements of Section 1005.3.3. Exit enclosures shall not be used for any purpose other than as a means of egress.

Interior stairways, ramps or escalators shall be enclosed as specified in this section.

EXCEPTIONS: 1. In other than Groups H and I Occupancies, an exit enclosure need not be provided for a stairway, ramp or escalator serving only one adjacent floor. Any two such atmospherically interconnected floors shall not communicate with other floors. For enclosure of escalators serving Group B or Group M Occupancies, see Sections 304.6 and 309.6.

2. Stairways in Group R, Division 3 Occupancies and stairways within individual dwelling units in Group R, Division 1 Occupancies need not be enclosed.

3. Stairs in open parking garages, as defined in Section 311.9, need not be enclosed.

Exit enclosures are required to be provided at stairs, ramps or escalators. They are to be continuous and fully enclose all portions of the stairway or ramp. Escalators are permitted to be open with draft stops and sprinklers in B or M Occupancies, per Sections 304.6 and 309.6. Escalators are not permitted to be used as part of the means of egress so it is unclear why they are mentioned here. Provision of an enclosure still does not allow the use of an escalator as part of a means of egress. Enclosures need not be provided for stairs and ramps serving only one adjacent floor. Exit enclosures are to connect with exit passageways leading to the exit discharge or to the public way. Exit passageways are not required where exit enclosures are not required, such as unenclosed stairs, or at places where exits are not required to be enclosed, as at one half the exits through lobbies described in 1005.2.3 Exception 2 and 1005.3.3.3 Exception 2.

TABLE 7-1—Exit Component Fire Ratings[a]

Const. Type	C/NC	Exit Enclosure[b]/Openings		Exit Passageway/Openings		Horizontal Exit/Openings/Const.
		<4 stories	>4 stories	<400 ft	>400 ft	
I	NC[c]	2 hr/1.5 hr	2 hr/1.5 hr	1 hr/1 hr	2 hr/1.5 hr	2 hr/1.5 hr/NC
II-FR	NC[c]	2 hr/1.5 hr	2 hr/1.5 hr	1 hr/1 hr	2 hr/1.5 hr	2 hr/1.5 hr/NC
II	NC[c]	1 hr/1 hr	2 hr/1.5 hr	1 hr/1 hr	2 hr/1.5 hr	2 hr/1.5 hr/NC
III	C/NC	1 hr/1 hr	2 hr/1.5 hr	1 hr/1 hr	2 hr/1.5 hr	2 hr/1.5 hr/NC
IV	C/NC	1 hr/1 hr	2 hr/1.5 hr	1 hr/1 hr	2 hr/1.5 hr	2 hr/1.5 hr/C/NC
V	C/NC	1 hr/1 hr	2 hr/1.5 hr	1 hr/1 hr	2 hr/1.5 hr	2 hr/1.5 hr/C/NC

[a]C-combustible construction; NC-noncombustible construction.
[b]See exception to 1005.3.3.2 for glazing in enclosure of parking garages.
[c]Except as permitted elsewhere in the code.

1005.3.3.5 Openings and penetrations. Openings in exit enclosures shall be limited to those necessary for egress from normally occupied spaces into the enclosure and those necessary for egress from the enclosure.

EXCEPTION: Exit enclosures on the exterior walls of buildings may have unprotected openings to the exterior when permitted by Table 5-A.

Openings into exit enclosures are to be limited and should be intended for exiting, not for access to other spaces. The openings should be protected as noted in Table 7-1. Penetrations are prohibited except for utilities serving the enclosure itself. Note that unprotected openings may occur in the exterior walls where they are permitted by location on the property.

Exit enclosures at high-rise buildings (having an occupied floor more than 75 feet above the lowest level of fire department access) are to be pressurized. They are also to have pressurized vestibules. The vestibules are to be 2-hour construction with $1\frac{1}{2}$-hour rated doors, in keeping with the fact that they are in all likelihood in a building of more than four stories.

1005.3.4 Exit passageways.

1005.3.4.1 General. Exit passageways serving as an exit in a means of egress system shall comply with the requirements of Section 1005.3.4. Exit passageways shall not be used for any purpose other than as a means of egress.

Exit passageways have the same width criteria as corridors and similar hallways noted in other sections. The minimum width is 44 inches except where serving less than 50 occupants, when the passageway may be 36 inches wide. Note also that the same door swing clearance criteria apply as for hallways and corridors noted under exit access.

Openings in exit passageways are limited as are those in exit enclosures. In addition it is noted that elevators may not open into exit passageways. Thus, elevator lobbies are required at exit passageways to separate elevator doors from the exit passageway. Openings are to be protected as noted in Table 7-1. Penetrations are prohibited except for utilities serving the passageway itself. Passageways may not be interrupted by intervening rooms except at office buildings where 50 percent of the exits may discharge through a street floor lobby if the street floor is protected with an automatic sprinkler system. Note that this exception to the exit passageway section is different than that for exit enclosures and for exits in general, in that Exception 2 in 1005.2.3 and Exception

2 in 1005.3.3.3 mentions offices, hospitals and nursing homes while the exception to 1005.3.4.5 mentions only office buildings. Exit passageways over 400 feet in length are required to be of 2-hour construction.

Exit passageways have the same requirements as corridors regarding dead ends. Where two exits are required, it must be possible to go in either direction from any point in the exit passageway except for dead ends not exceeding 20 feet.

> **1005.3.5 Horizontal exits.**
>
> **1005.3.5.1 General. Horizontal exits serving as an exit in a means of egress system shall comply with the requirements of Section 1005.3.5. A horizontal exit is a wall that completely divides a floor of a building into two or more separate exit-access areas to afford safety from fire and smoke in the exit-access area of incident origin.**
>
> **It is permissible for a horizontal exit to serve as an exit for each adjacent exit-access area (e.g., a two-way exit), providing that the exit-access design requirements for each exit-access area are independently satisfied.**
>
> **A horizontal exit shall not serve as the only exit from the exit access. Where two or more exits are required from the exit access, not more than one half of the total number of exits or total exit width may be provided by horizontal exits.**
>
> **1005.3.5.2 Construction. The wall containing a horizontal exit shall be constructed as required for an occupancy separation having a fire-resistive rating of not less than two hours. The horizontal exit wall shall be continuous from exterior wall to exterior wall and shall extend from the floor to the underside of the floor or roof directly above so as to completely divide the floor that is served by the horizontal exit. Structural members supporting a horizontal exit shall be protected by equivalent fire-resistive construction.**
>
> **Horizontal exits in buildings of Type I, II or III construction shall be of noncombustible construction. Horizontal exits in buildings of Type IV or V construction may be of combustible or noncombustible construction.**

This is a unique concept for exiting because it provides an area of refuge rather than a means of egress to grade. The concept is that by providing a high degree of fire-resistive separation between two segments of a building, one can pass through the separation, which is essentially an area separation wall, and be safe from the danger that caused the egress.

The essential characteristics of a horizontal exit are as follows:

- The separation must be of at least 2-hour construction.
- There must be no interconnection of the ductwork or utilities that would permit fire or smoke to enter the refuge area.
- It may be only used for one of the required exits.

The construction provisions require that support of the horizontal exit have the equivalent rating and assure complete separation both horizontally and vertically. The wall of the horizontal exit is thus to be supported by structure of equal or higher rating. (See Figure 7-29.)

For many buildings, using this concept enables the omission of one stairway. (See discussion in Article 5 regarding Section 509.) If a building exceeds the allowable area and an area separation wall is used, only one stairway need be provided for each segment,

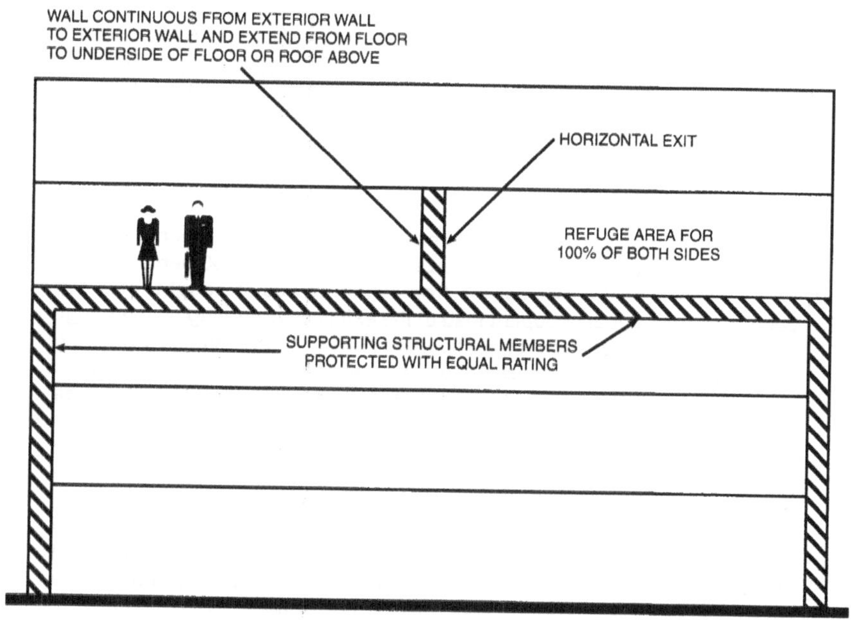

Construction requirements state that horizontal exit supports are to have equivalent rating to the horizontal exit.

Refuge area requirements are specified. The intent is that the refuge area be comprised of the "net clear floor area of aisles, hallways and corridors". Rooms such as offices or toilet rooms should not be counted as contributing to the refuge area.

REFERENCE: SECTION 1005.3.5

FIGURE 7-29 HORIZONTAL EXITS

and the horizontal exit can be used as the second exit for each segment. (See Figure 7-30.)

When the occupant load is 50 or more in each segment, the door in the area separation wall must swing in the direction of exit travel. In such instances there must be two doors in the horizontal exit, one swinging into each segment per Section 1003.2.3.5. Each door leaf must be at least 36 inches wide, thus necessitating that the designer provide at least a 6-foot wide corridor at the location of the horizontal exit.

As discussed in Article 5 of this Guide, the integrity of the area separation wall is dependent on its construction and details. The designer must give more detailed consideration when the area separation wall is used as part of a horizontal exit.

As noted previously, a horizontal exit is intended to essentially create separate buildings on each floor level to allow exiting to occur from one protected area into another without entering exit enclosures or exit passageways. The horizontal exit may not be the only exit from the exit access area served. See Fig 7-30 describing horizontal exit layout.

1005.3.5.4 Refuge area. The floor area of the exit access to which a horizontal exit leads shall be of sufficient size to accommodate 100 percent of the occupant load of the exit access from which refuge is sought, plus 100 percent of the normal occupant load of the exit access serving as the refuge area. The capacity of such refuge floor area shall be determined by allowing 3 square feet (0.28 m^2) of net clear floor area of aisles, hallways and corridors per occupant. The area of stairs, elevators and other shafts shall not be used. In Group I, Division 1.1 Occupancies, the capacity of the refuge area shall be determined by allowing 15 square feet (1.4 m^2) of net clear floor area per ambulatory occupant and 30 square feet (2.8 m^2) of net clear floor area per nonambulatory occupant.

The design of the exit access serving as the refuge area shall comply with the requirements of Section 1004.2 based on the normal occupant load served and need not consider the increased occupant load imposed by persons entering such refuge area through horizontal exits.

The theory underlying the horizontal exit involves moving occupants from an area impacted by an emergency to another safe area of refuge. A building designed with a horizontal exit has two adjacent areas that may serve as both exit access and horizontal exit. In order to accommodate the anticipated number of occupants, the area to be considered as a horizontal exit must accommodate its own occupant load plus 100 percent of the load of the area being exited. The area is to be calculated using the net clear floor area

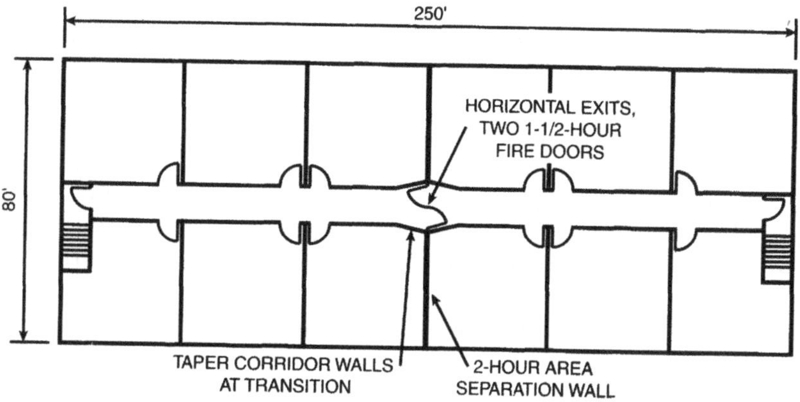

PLAN VIEW

Assume:
R-1 Occupancy, Type V One-hour Building
Three story over Type I garage

60′ separation all around

Proposed area per floor = 80 x 250 = 15,000 sf
Proposed area of building = 3 x 20,000 = 60,000 sf

Allowable area, Type V, One-hour = 10,500 sf
Separation four sides, increase 100% = 10,500 sf

Allowable area with separation increase = 21,000 sf

TOTAL ALLOWABLE AREA = 21,000 x 2 = 42,000 sf

As the proposed area exceeds the allowable area, an area separation wall will be used

Occupant load, 1/2 floor = 125 x 80/200 = 50 persons

Therefore two 1-1/2 hour fire doors are required for the horizontal exit, each swinging in the direction of exit travel.

REFERENCE: SECTIONS 504, 505 AND 1005.3.5

FIGURE 7-30 HORIZONTAL EXIT EXAMPLE WITH AREA SEPARATION WALL

of "aisles, hallways and corridors." The intent of this clause is that such areas as enclosed offices and restrooms are not to be used in calculating available areas for refuge. This additional occupant load is calculated at 3 square feet per occupant of net clear area for other than hospitals. This recognizes that in an emergency people can be in tighter quarters and still egress safely. Where there may be nonambulatory patients the floor area requirements are 15 square feet per occupant to allow more space for beds and wheelchairs. The application of the design criteria takes into account the direction of exit flow. The downstream area, receiving the occupants from upstream must be the larger area. Only when a horizontal exit may function in both directions must both areas have more exit capacity than normally required just for the area itself. A two-way exit is allowed when the exit access design requirements are independently satisfied for each exit access area.

The Exit Discharge

1006.1 General. The exit discharge is that portion of the means of egress system between the exit and the public way. Components that may be selectively included in the exit discharge include exterior exit balconies, exterior exit stairways, exterior exit ramps, exit courts and yards, in addition to those common means of egress components described in Section 1003.3.

EXCEPTION: When approved by the building official, the exit discharge may lead to a safe dispersal area on the same property as the building being exited. The proximity and size of such safe dispersal area shall be based on such factors as the occupant load served, the mobility of occupants, the type of construction of the building, the fire-protection features of the building, the height of the building and the degree of hazard of the occupancy. In any case, such safe dispersal areas shall not be located less than 50 feet (15 240 mm) from the building served. (See Section 1007 for means of egress from safe dispersal areas.)

The general intent of the definition of exit discharge is that it be the final portion of the means of egress leading to a safe place away from a building. The exception allows the discharge to lead to a safe dispersal area not at the public way. This recognizes that buildings on large sites, especially with surface parking lots, may not need to conduct occupants all the way to the public way for them to be safely away from the building. (See Figure 7-31.)

A frequent question that arises, primarily after an accident, is: Where does the exit path terminate? This concern arose because of some previous misapplications of Chapter 10 provisions, which have been erroneously applied to areas outside the building or

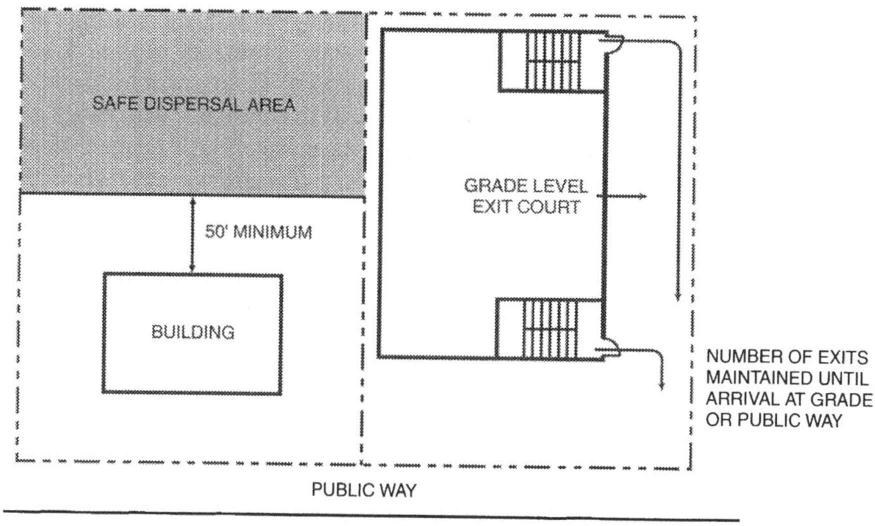

The number of exits must be maintained until they reach grade. (Section 1004.2.3.1). See Figure 7-21 for a discussion regarding maintenance of exit paths at grade.

The use of a safe dispersal area requires the approval of the Building Official (Section 1006.1, Exception)

REFERENCE: SECTIONS 1004.2.3.1 AND 1006.1

FIGURE 7-31 EXIT DISCHARGE ACCESS TO SAFE DISPERSAL AREA

structure. For example, the handrail provisions of Sections 1003.3.3.6 and 1003.3.4.5 have been applied to ramps in shopping centers where there are curb cuts for wheeling shopping carts from a store to one's car. In other instances, where there are paths containing stairs at some distance from a building, the requirements of Section 1003.3.3.6 have been applied to the stairs.

If we look at the areas on a property, aside from the building, we find numerous areas that can have paths, stairs, ramps and other features comparable to certain Chapter 10 regulated exit elements. That does not mean that Chapter 10 provisions apply. These only apply to areas considered as a means of egress. A terraced garden would have to have some means of reaching each terraced level. The stair or ramp need not have a minimum width rise and run of step, handrail or guardrail per Section 1003.3.3.

Many cities have relatively steep streets, exceeding a slope of 1 in 8. In some cities such as San Francisco, streets of slopes 1 in 5 are not uncommon. In these cities, there are no handrails along such streets. When the street's sidewalk is provided with a stairway, we find no handrail or minimum width of stair involved because these areas are not part of the exit path within a building or structure. In fact, because they are primarily in the public way, they are not subject to the code at all. (See Figure 7-32.)

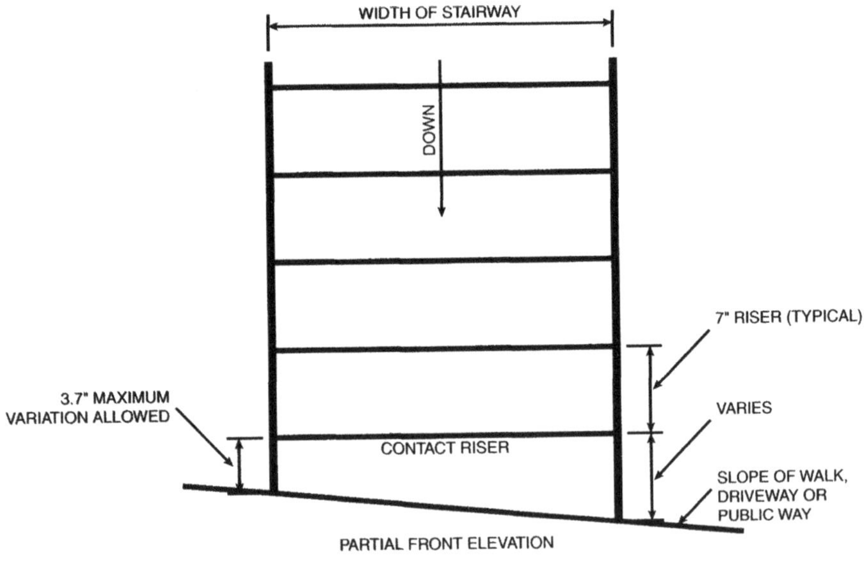

ASSUME: Stair width = 44″. Walk, driveway or public way slope = 10% (1″ in 10″). Variation in riser required to match the slope of the walk, driveway or public way for 44″ width of stair/10 = 4.4″, required parallel to the walk, driveway or public way. See Detail "A".

Allowable variation in riser height of contact step is 3″:36″ (1″ in 12″) for 44″width of stair/12 = 3.7″ maximum variation allowed.

Therefore the contact step cannot exactly match the walk, driveway or public way slope. The slope adjacent to the stair will have to be shaped to conform to the maximum allowable variation of 3/7″ rather than maintain the 10% slope unbroken across the stairway frontage. See Detail "B".)

REFERENCE: SECTION 1003.3.3.3 AND 1006.3.3.4

FIGURE 7-32 RISER VARIATION PERMITTED FOR STAIRWAYS ON SLOPING WALKS, DRIVEWAYS AND PUBLIC WAYS

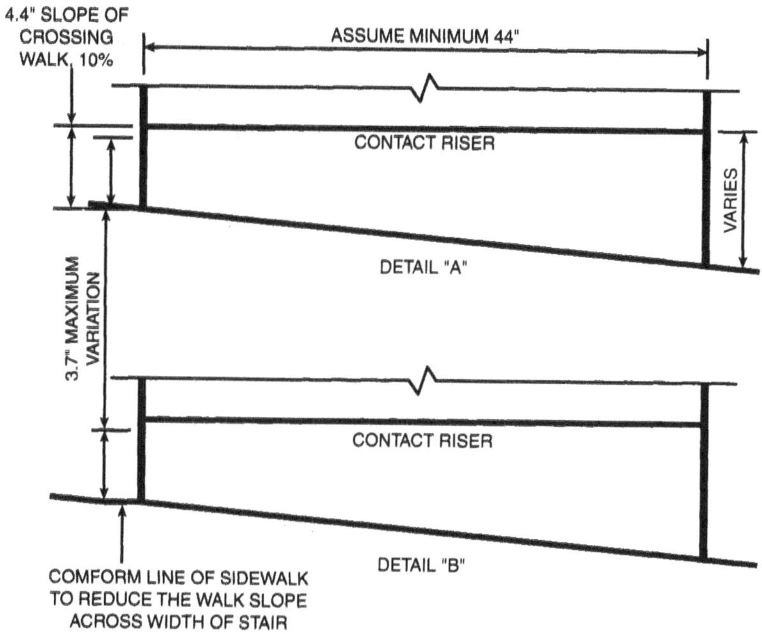

REFERENCE: SECTION 1003.3.3.3 AND 1006.3.3.4

There is a decided difference between a mandatory code requirement applicable to a situation and a situation when the choice of construction criteria rests with other agencies, e.g., the public works department, or with the property owner. The use of an exit path within a building is predicated on that element being involved in an emergency. Outside the building, the use is generally in a nonemergency mode, with the user having the time and choice of direction and speed of travel.

Until Chapter 10 was rewritten, there was no clear delineation of the limitations of applicability of Chapter 10, and this has led to the problems previously described. The logical interpretation of Section 1006.1 suggests that the path of exiting extends all the way from the building to the street, regardless of how long that path may be. Thus the exception becomes an important issue to resolve with the building official when designing for large sites.

The question of the exit path termination beings with Section 1001.1:

Every building or portion thereof shall be provided with a means of egress as required by this chapter. A means of egress is an exit system that provides a continuous, unobstructed and undiminished path of exit travel from any occupied point in a building or structure *to a public way.* (emphasis added)

Thus, while the exiting provisions of Chapter 10 relate only to buildings and structures, they clearly extend to *a public way* as defined in Section 1002. This has been a problem under previous editions of the code. It seems to be remedied by the exception to Section 1006.1, which allows the building official to designate a "safe dispersal area." While it is not explicitly stated in Section 1003, it must be presumed that the intent of the code is that exit discharge components are to be hard surfaced paving materials. This is the only interpretation that would allow the exit discharge to comply with the requirements that it be "continuous, unobstructed and undiminished" as well as conforming to ramp gradient and stair rise and run requirements.

1006.2.1 Location. The exit discharge shall be at grade or shall provide direct access to grade. The exit discharge shall not reenter a building. Exterior exit balconies, exterior exit stairways and exterior exit ramps shall not be located in areas where building openings are prohibited or openings are required to be protected by Table 5-A.

1006.2.2 Access to grade. Where the exit from a building discharges at other than grade level, there shall not be less than two separate paths of exit travel to grade level. Such paths of exit travel shall be arranged so that there are no dead ends more than 20 feet (6096 mm) in length.

EXCEPTIONS: 1. Where the occupant load served by such exit is less than 10, only one path of exit travel to grade level need be provided.

2. Where exits discharge to an exterior exit stairway, such stairway may serve as a single path of exit travel directly to grade.

1006.2.3 Travel distance. Travel distance in the exit discharge at grade level shall not be limited.

Travel distance in the exit discharge at other than grade level shall not exceed the following:

1. In buildings not equipped with an automatic sprinkler system throughout, the travel distance to grade shall not exceed 200 feet (60 960 mm).

2. In buildings equipped with an automatic sprinkler system throughout, the travel distance to grade shall not exceed 250 feet (76 200 mm).

Where the path of exit travel includes unenclosed stairways or ramps within the exit discharge, the distance of travel on such means of egress components shall also be included in the travel distance measurement. The measurement along stairways shall be made on a plane parallel and tangent to the stair tread nosings in the center of the stairway.

The underlying assumption regarding the exit discharge is that it is at grade. The clause in the second line of Section 1006.2.1

regarding not reentering the building is problematic for exterior exit balconies, as will be discussed later. This will probably be construed to allow reentry into a protected exit enclosure or exit passageway, which would still meet the underlying intent that the means of egress be separate from the building occupancy. The intent is that an equal or higher level of protection than being outside of the building must be provided. This would not be provided by an exit access, but an exit would provide such protection.

It also is problematic in the example noted above where an exit passageway is downstream of an exit court. Where an exit discharges at other than grade level, there are to be two separate paths of exit travel to grade without any dead ends over 20 feet. Travel distances in such a situation are as noted below. The distance is to be measured from the exit to grade and includes distance traveled on unenclosed balconies, stairs or ramps.

Travel distance is not restricted in an exit discharge *located at grade.* Where an exit discharge is at other than grade, the travel distance requirements are as follows. This distance is to be measured to grade, including unenclosed stairways and ramps. Once at grade, the travel distance is not restricted since this now becomes an exit discharge at grade. (See Figure 7-33.)

These criteria would seem to allow the use of the exit passageway noted in the first example above since the passage is of equal or higher protection than other exit discharge components. However, the exit passage is an exit component, not an exit discharge component, since the passageway does not meet the openness requirements of Section 1006.3.1. See Table 7-2.

1006.3 Exit Discharge Components.

1006.3.1 General. Exit discharge components incorporated into the design of the exit discharge portion of the means of egress system shall comply with the requirements of Section 1006.3. In all cases, components of the exit discharge shall be sufficiently open to the exterior to prevent the accumulation of smoke and toxic gases.

The basic distinction between the exit component of a means of egress and the exit discharge component is the assumption that exit discharge components are open to the exterior.

1006.3.2 Exterior exit balconies.

1006.3.2.1 General. Exterior exit balconies serving as a portion of the exit discharge in the means of egress system shall comply with the requirements of Section 1006.3.2. An exterior exit balcony is a balcony, landing or porch

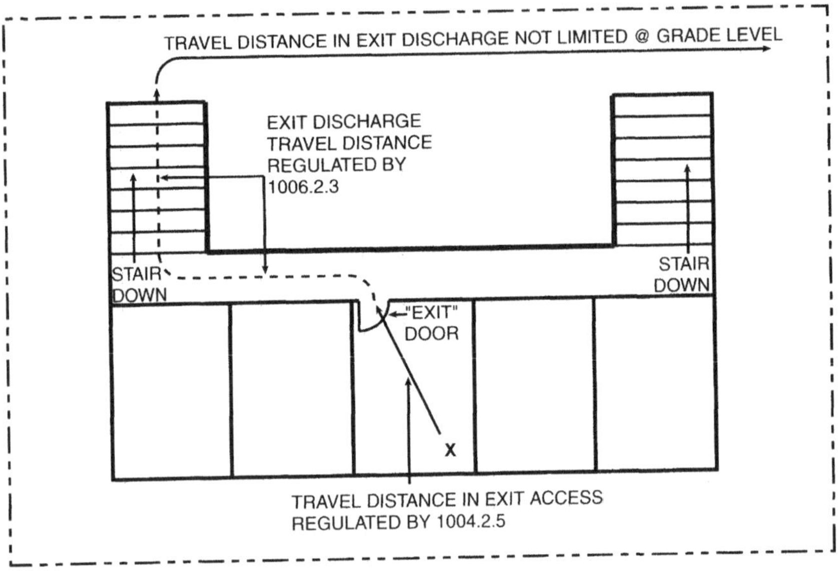

Exit discharge at other than grade (as at an exterior exit balcony) requires at least two paths of travel

Travel distance is regulated at other than grade. Travel distance in such cases is 200 feet in unsprinklered buildings and 250 feet in sprinklered buildings. The distance is measured from the exit to grade and includes distance traveled on unenclosed stairs or ramps.

There are no travel distance regulations for the exit discharge at grade.

Exit discharge is not permitted to re-enter the building per Section 1006.2.1

(This leaves an open question of whether one can re-enter a protected exit stair after using an exterior exit balcony. This is subject to interpretation and may be enforced non-uniformly.)

REFERENCE: SECTIONS 1006.2.2 AND 1006.2.3

FIGURE 7-33 ACCESS TO GRADE AND TRAVEL DISTANCE AT THE EXIT DISCHARGE

TABLE 7-2—Exit Discharge Not at Grade

Sprinklers	Travel Distance to Grade
No	200 feet
Yes	250 feet

projecting from the wall of a building and serves as an exit discharge component in a means of egress system.

1006.3.2.3 Construction. Exterior exit balconies projecting from the walls of buildings of Type I or II construction shall be of noncombustible construction. Exterior exit balconies projecting from the walls of buildings of Type III, IV or V construction may be of combustible or noncombustible construction.

Walls of exterior exit balconies serving a Group R, Division 1 or Group I Occupancy having an occupant load of 10 or more shall not be less than one-hour fire-resistive construction and ceilings shall not be less than that required for a one-hour fire-resistive floor or roof system.

EXCEPTIONS: 1. Exterior sides of exterior exit balconies.

2. In other than Type I or II construction, exterior exit balcony roof assemblies may be of heavy-timber construction without concealed spaces.

1006.3.2.4 Openness. The long side of an exterior exit balcony shall be at least 50 percent open, and the open area above the guardrail shall be distributed to prevent the accumulation of smoke or toxic gases.

Balconies are to meet the same width criteria as other similar passages in the means of egress. The balcony is to be of fire-resistive construction per Section 1006.3.2.3 and are to be at least 50 percent open on the exterior, long side of the balcony. It is not required to be at grade, in fact it is implied that it is not at grade. (See Figure 7-34.)

Note that there are openness requirements for each exit discharge component in keeping with the underlying philosophy that this portion of the means of egress is at the downstream end of the means of egress system and is nearing the safety of the public way or a safe dispersal area. Another aspect of this philosophy are requirements that the walls adjacent to the discharge components be fire protected to keep the exit discharge components safe for egress.

Walls and ceilings at the closed sides of exterior exit balconies are required to be of 1-hour construction in R-1 or I occupancies when serving more than 10 occupants. Where openings in exterior walls are within 10 feet of an exterior exit stair or ramp, the openings are to be protected by $\frac{3}{4}$-hour assemblies except in R-3 Occupancies and where the stairs or ramps are served by a common exit balcony.

The most controversial part of the definition of exit discharge is the inclusion of exterior exit balconies in the exit discharge. It is conceivable that in temperate climates exterior balconies will be used. They are allowed to be open on the exterior side away from the building. These balconies may then lead to enclosed stairs.

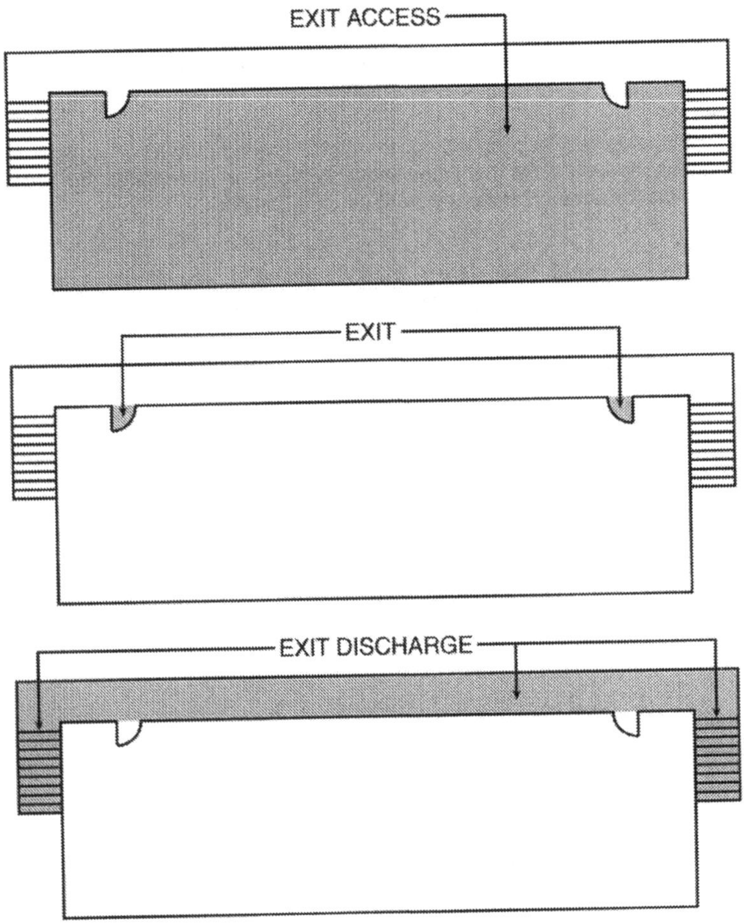

REFERENCE: SECTIONS 1006.3.2

FIGURE 7-34 RELATIONSHIP OF MEANS OF EGRESS COMPONENTS AT EXTERIOR EXIT BALCONIES

Thus one can go from the exit access through an exit door to an open balcony to the exit discharge and then back into an "exit" stair meeting the exit section enclosure criteria and then leading to another exit discharge.

> One possible interpretation of the exterior exit balcony requirements could require any stairs downstream of an exit balcony to be open, to be considered a part of the exit discharge. Thus the travel distance restrictions on travel to grade would be applicable. It may be acceptable to have a closed stair, thus considered an exit with no travel distance restrictions, but that would place the exit downstream of a portion of the exit discharge, which runs counter to the overall organization of the chapter. Section 1006, and especially 1006.3.2 regarding exterior exit balconies, should be approached with great caution and only after close consultation with the building official. The discussions regarding this section during the code development process generated widely differing opinions regarding its interpretation. It is to be expected that this will also generate varying interpretations in the field.

1006.3.3 Exterior exit stairways.

1006.3.3.1 General. Exterior exit stairways serving as a portion of the exit discharge in the means of egress system shall comply with the requirements of Section 1006.3.3. An exterior exit stairway serves as an exit discharge component in a means of egress system and is open on not less than two adjacent sides, except for required structural columns and open-type handrails and guardrails. The adjoining open areas shall be either yards, exit courts or public ways; the remaining sides may be enclosed by the exterior walls of the building. Any stairway not meeting the definition of an exterior stairway shall comply with the requirements for interior stairways.

Exterior exit stairs and ramps are also assumed to be open. Note that Section 1006.3.3.1 requires exterior stairs to be open on not less than two *adjacent* sides. This means that a "breezeway" or tunnel-style stairway, open on opposite ends, is not acceptable under this definition. This also applies to ramps as noted in Section 1006.3.4.1. (See Figure 7-35.)

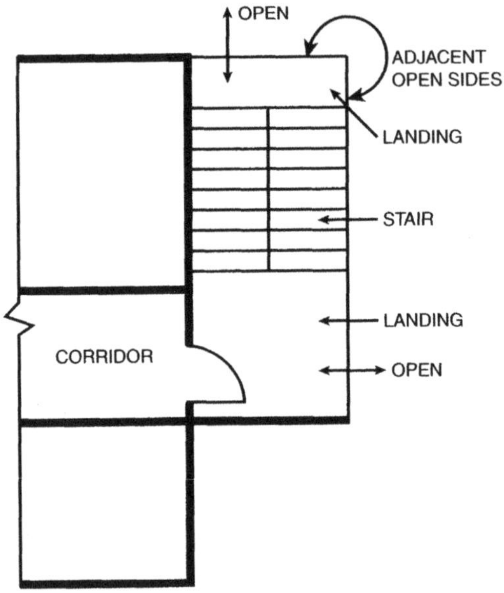

Permitted exterior exit stair:

Open on 2 adjacent sides

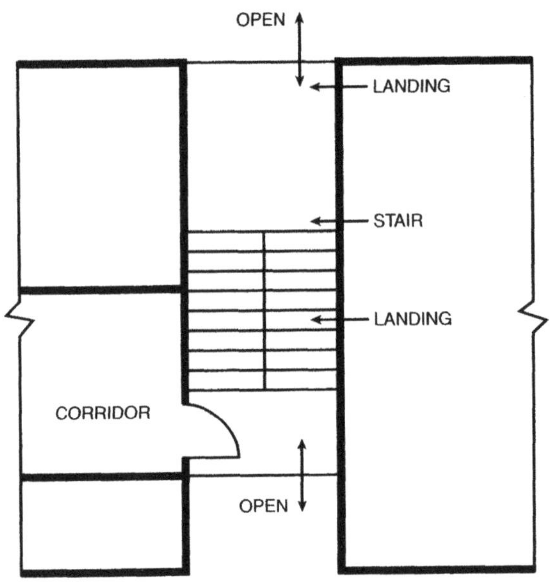

Non-permitted exterior exit stair:

Stair is open on 2 sides, but sides are not adjacent

REFERENCE: SECTIONS 1006.3.3.1

FIGURE 7-35 OPEN SIDE REQUIREMENTS AT EXTERIOR EXIT STAIRS

> In the authors' opinion this requirement is overly restrictive and places an unreasonable burden on the designer. While there is a clear requirement that there be two sides open on stairs to allow venting of gases to occur, there is no overriding concern that these two sides be adjacent. A tunnel-type stair arrangement that allows free air movement is no more likely to be contaminated by smoke than a stair with two adjacent sides open. See Figure 7-35.

1006.3.3.3 Protection of exterior wall openings. All openings in the exterior wall below and within 10 feet (3048 mm), measured horizontally, of an exterior exit stairway serving a building over two stories in height or a floor level having such openings in two or more floors below shall be protected by fixed or self-closing fire assemblies having a three-fourths-hour fire-protection rating.

EXCEPTIONS: 1. Group R, Division 3 Occupancies.

2. Openings may be unprotected where two separated exterior stairways are served by a common exterior exit balcony.

3. Protection of openings is not required for open parking garages conforming to Section 311.9.

See Figures 7-36 and 7-37 for opening protection requirements relative to the relation of exterior exit stairs to openings.

Means of Egress Requirements Based on Occupancy

1007.1 General. In addition to the general means of egress requirements specified elsewhere in this chapter, the detailed requirements of this section shall apply to those occupancies described herein.

After determining the basic requirements contained in the previous sections of Chapter 10, the designer must examine the occupancy-based requirements. These requirements may significantly alter critical design elements such as travel distance and fire-resistive ratings of the means of egress. No design is complete without verifying whether any of these specific additional provisions apply to a project. These provisions are supplementary to those in previous sections of this chapter and will supersede other requirements. In the event of any perceived conflict, the most restrictive should be applied to assure that fire and life safety requirements are not compromised.

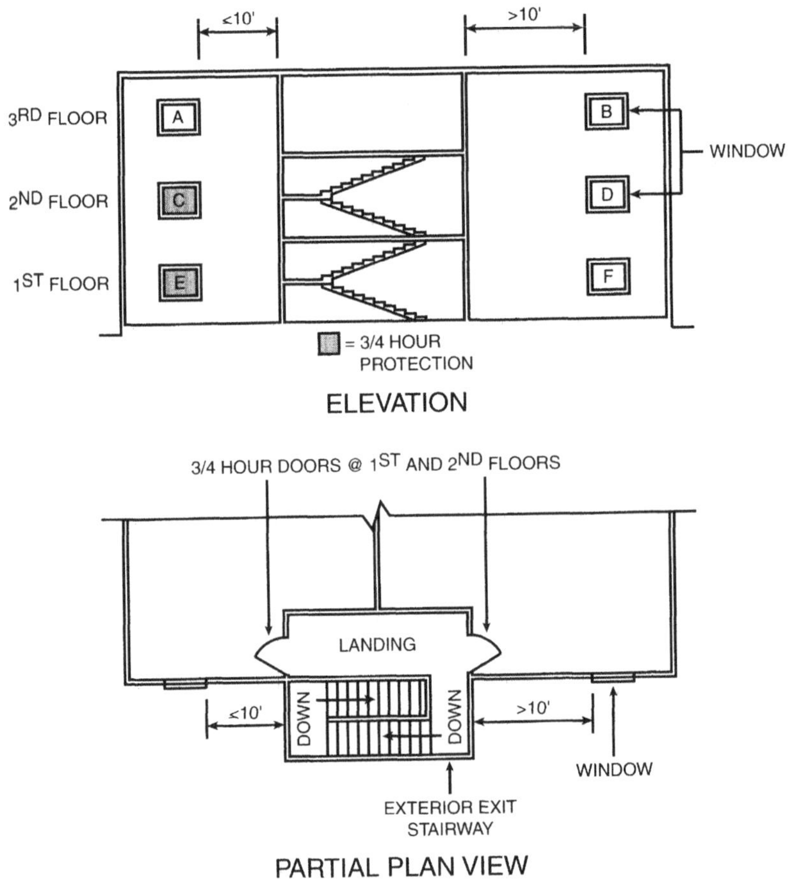

REFERENCE: SECTIONS 1006.3.3.3

FIGURE 7-36 OPENING PROTECTION REQUIREMENTS AT EXTERIOR EXIT STAIRWAY

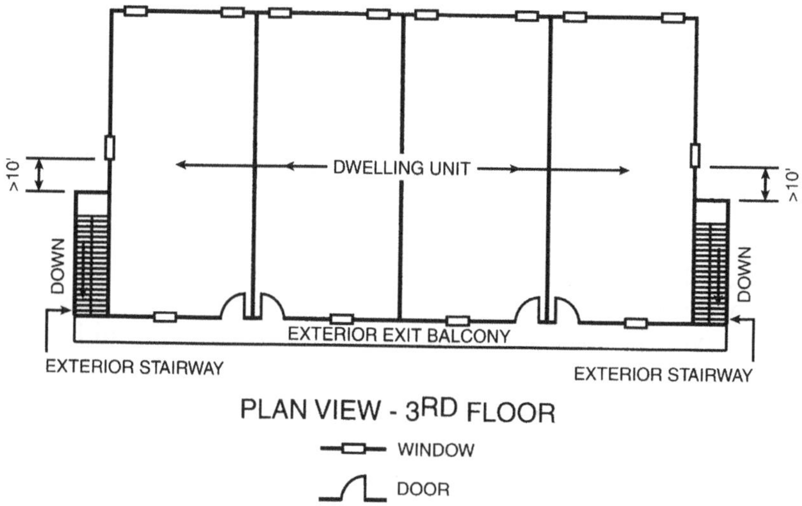

Exterior exit balconies are permitted to have unprotected openings on exterior wall provided the balcony is set back sufficiently from adjacent buildings and property lines. The wall construction of the balcony, however must be per Section 1006.3.2.3.

Openings within proximity of exterior stairways may have to have protection per Section 1006.3.3.3. See Figure 7-36. The exterior stairway may be constructed of any material permitted for that building's type of construction.

ASSUME: Group R-1 Occupancy
Type V-One Hour Building
Four Dwelling Units per Floor
Three Stories

Two exits are required per 1004.2.3.
Exterior exit balcony openings "D" and "W" may be unprotected per Section 1006.3.3.3

Openings in side walls are below, but more than 10 feet away from, exterior stairs and need not be protected per Section 1006.3.3.3.

REFERENCE: SECTIONS 1006.3.2.3 AND 1006.3.3.3.3

FIGURE 7-37 EXTERIOR STAIRWAY AT R-1 OCCUPANCY, TYPICAL CONFORMING DESIGN

1007.2 Group A Occupancies.

1007.2.1 Main exit. Group A, Division 1, 2 and 2.1 Occupancies shall be provided with a main exit. The main exit shall be of sufficient width to accommodate not less than one half of the total occupant load, but such width shall not be less than the total required width of all means of egress components leading thereto.

1007.2.2 Side exits. Auditoriums, theaters and similar assembly rooms of Group A, Division 1, 2 or 2.1 Occupancies shall be provided with exits on each side. The exits on each side of such assembly rooms shall be of sufficient width to accommodate not less than one third of the total occupant load served. Side exits shall open directly to a public way or into an exit or exit discharge leading to a public way. Side exits shall be accessible from a cross aisle.

1007.2.4 Multitheater complex. The main exit from a multitheater complex shall be of sufficient width to accommodate one half of the total occupant load of such complex.

Section 1007.2.1 calls for a main exit that can accommodate at least one half of the occupancy load of the space. In large occupancies with over 500 occupants three exits are required, and four exits are required for more than 1000 occupants. This section requires that the sizes of those exits not be evenly distributed, but weighted toward the main exit. This is based on the theory that in an emergency occupants will first attempt to leave the space on the path they used for entry. Thus the main entrance path and the main exit path must coincide and must be larger than the other, less obvious exits.

Note also that these sections may result in provision of a greater number of exits than may be generated by the occupant load provisions of 1004.2.3.4. Sections 1007.2.2 and 1007.2.4 impact the location and distribution of exits in addition to the width requirements of 1007.2.1. Section 1007.2.2 would seem to cover a wider group of occupancies than in previous code. This will probably result in the provision of auditorium-style exiting schemes in a broader range of assembly areas than before.

1007.2.5 Panic hardware. Exit and exit-access doors serving Group A Occupancies shall not be provided with a latch or lock unless it is panic hardware.

Panic hardware, per Section 1003.3.1.9, is required in Assembly, Educational, Hazardous and Institutional occupancies. Note that these requirements are occupancy-group dependent, not just occupant load dependent. See Table 7-3.

TABLE 7-3—Panic Hardware Criteria

Occupancy	Section	Occupant Load	Panic Hardware Required
Group A: Exit, Exit-access*	1007.2.5	No minimum	Yes, Exception 1 @ A-3*
Group E: Exit, Exit-access	1007.3.10	50 or more	Yes
Group E: From Corridor	1007.3.10	Not specified	Yes
Group H: Div. 1,2,3,6,7	1007.4.5	Not specified	Yes
Group I: Exit, Exit-access	1007.5.8	50 or more	Yes

***EXCEPTIONS: 1. In Group A, Division 3 Occupancies and in all churches, panic hardware may be omitted from the main exit where the main exit consists of a single door or pair of doors. A key-locking device may be used in place of the panic hardware, provided there is a readily visible durable sign adjacent to the doorway stating, "THIS DOOR MUST REMAIN UNLOCKED DURING BUSINESS HOURS." The sign shall be in letters not less than 1 inch (25 mm) high on a contrasting background. When unlocked, the single door or both leaves of a pair of doors must be free to swing without operation of any latching device. Manually operated edge- or surface-mounted flush bolts and surface bolts or any other type of device that may be used to close or restrain the door other than by operation of the locking device shall not be used. The use of this exception may be revoked by the building official for due cause.**

It is possible to have a large occupant load in an office or retail occupancy without triggering a requirement for panic hardware. The application of the requirement for panic hardware in other than the specified occupancies may be subject to local amendments or nonuniform interpretation by some building or fire officials.

Panic hardware is so named because it will open the door when occupants are pushed against the door, depressing the bar and opening the door. The hardware is always mounted such that the door swings away from the side of the door on which the hardware is mounted.

1007.3 Group E Occupancies.

1007.3.1 Definitions. For the purpose of Section 1007.3, certain terms are defined as follows:

INTERIOR ROOM is a room whose only exit access is through an adjoining or intervening room and not a corridor.

ROOM is a space or area enclosed on more than 80 percent of the perimeter of such space or area. When determining the enclosed area, openings less than 3 feet (914 mm) in clear width and less than 6 feet 8 inches (2032 mm) high need not be considered.

SEPARATE MEANS OF EGRESS SYSTEM is not less than two paths of exit travel, which are separated in such a manner to provide an atmospheric

separation that precludes contamination of both paths of exit travel by the same fire.

1007.3.2 Separate means of egress systems required. Every room with an occupant load of 300 or more shall have one of its exits or exit-access doorways lead directly into a separate means of egress system. Not more than two required exits or exit-access doorways shall enter into the same means of egress system.

In buildings used for educational and day-care occupancies the means of egress requirements are higher than for other buildings. The intent is that children receive a higher degree of protection than that specified for the basic means of egress.

1007.3.3 Travel distance.

1007.3.3.1 In rooms. The travel distance from any point in a room shall not exceed 75 feet (22 860 mm) to a corridor or an exit.

EXCEPTIONS: 1. In buildings not more than two stories in height and protected throughout by smoke detectors, the travel distance may be increased to 90 feet (27 432 mm).

2. In buildings equipped with an automatic sprinkler system throughout, the travel distance may be increased to 110 feet (33 528 mm).

1007.3.3.2 From any location. In buildings not equipped with an automatic sprinkler system throughout, the travel distance shall not exceed 150 feet (45 720 mm).

EXCEPTIONS: 1. In buildings not more than two stories in height and protected throughout by smoke detectors, the travel distance may be increased to 175 feet (53 340 mm).

2. In buildings equipped with an automatic sprinkler system throughout, the travel distance may be increased to 225 feet (68 580 mm).

The travel distances specified above may be increased up to an additional 100 feet (30 480 mm), provided that the last portion of travel leading to the exit occurs within a corridor. The length of such corridor shall not be less than the amount of the increase taken.

Travel distance criteria for E Occupancies vary from those for other occupancies. The typical criteria increases for sprinklers are accommodated. Also additional distances are allowed when portions of the means of egress are in a corridor. See Table7-4.

1007.3.5 Hallways, corridors and exterior exit balconies. The width of hallways and corridors in a Group E, Division 1 Occupancy shall be determined as specified in Section 1003.2.3, plus 2 feet (610 mm), but shall not be less than 6 feet (1829 mm).

EXCEPTION: Where the total number of occupants served is less than 100, such hallway or corridor may be 44 inches (1118 mm) wide.

Any change in elevation of less than 2 feet (610 mm) in a hallway, corridor or exterior exit balcony shall be by means of a ramp.

TABLE 7-4—Travel Distances at E Occupancies

Criteria	From Room to Corridor or Exit	From Any Location
Basic, without sprinklers	75 feet	150 feet
Two stories maximum, with smoke detectors	90 feet	175 feet
With sprinklers throughout	110 feet	225 feet
Increase when last portion is in a corridor leading to exit	NA	100 feet

1007.3.6 Stairways. The width of stairways shall be determined as specified in Section 1003.2.3, but stairways serving an occupant load of 100 or more shall not be less than 5 feet (1524 mm) in width.

In buildings primarily serving children all of the width requirements for exit components are increased. Widths larger than the minimum, as generated by occupant load, are still calculated based on occupant load criteria, but the minimum widths are larger than for other occupancies.

1007.4 Group H Occupancies.

1007.4.1 Access to exits. Every portion of a Group H Occupancy having a floor area of 200 square feet (18.6 m²) or more shall have access to not less than two separate exits or exit-access doors.

EXCEPTION: Group H, Division 4 Occupancies having a floor area of less than 1,000 square feet (92.9 m²) may have one exit or exit-access door.

1007.4.2 Travel distance. In Group H, Divisions 1, 2 and 3 Occupancies, the travel distance specified in Section 1004.2.6 shall not exceed 75 feet (22 860 mm).

In Group H, Division 7, and within fabrication areas of Group H, Division 6 Occupancies, the travel distance specified in Section 1004.2.6 shall not exceed 100 feet (30 480 mm).

These provisions are significantly higher than those for other occupancies. They assume that the likelihood of an emergency in a hazardous occupancy is much higher than in other occupancies. The low threshold requirements for two means of egress assume that in an emergency one of the exits is likely to be blocked by fire, toxic fumes or gases.

1007.5 Group I Occupancies.

1007.5.1 Minimum size of means of egress. The clear that of [*sic*] means of egress components in areas serving bed or litter patients shall be such to allow ready passage of beds, gurneys and similar equipment, but shall

not be less than 44 inches (1118 mm). Other aisles shall have a clear width of not less than 32 inches (813 mm).

1007.5.2 Travel distance. All portions of Group I, Division 1.1 or 3 Occupancies shall be within 200 feet (76 200 mm) of an exit.

1007.5.3 Hallways. Hallways in Group I Occupancies that serve an occupant load of 10 or more shall comply with the requirements of Sections 1004.3.4 and 1007.5.4 for corridors.

1007.5.4 Corridors. Corridors serving any area caring for one or more nonambulatory persons shall not be less than 8 feet (2438 mm) in width.

EXCEPTION: Corridors serving surgical areas of Group I, Division 1.2 Occupancies shall not be less than 6 feet (1829 mm) in width.

There are significant modifications to the basic means of egress criteria for I Occupancy means of egress components. These criteria are based on the assumption that beds, gurneys and wheelchairs will occupy the passages of the means of egress in such occupancies. Thus wider passages are necessary to allow for emergency exiting in means of egress components that may contain large obstacles such as beds.

There are additional detailed requirements for hospital and nursing home corridors in I Occupancies. These are contained in Section 1007.5.4. A detailed discussion of these requirements is beyond the scope of this book as a basic text. However, a designer dealing with this occupancy must be aware of the modifications to the basic means of egress criteria contained in Section 1007.4. No design of an I Occupancy can be completed without a detailed review of the additional provisions for means of egress design contained in 1007.5

1007.6 Group R Occupancies.

1007.6.1 Hallways. Hallways in Group R, Division 1 Occupancies which serve an occupant load of 10 or more shall comply with the requirements of Section 1004.3.4 for corridors.

1007.6.2 Floor-level exit signs. Where exit signs are required by Section 1003.2.8.2, additional approved low-level exit signs that are internally or externally illuminated, photoluminescent or self-luminous, shall be provided in all corridors serving guest rooms of hotels in Group R, Division 1 Occupancies.

The bottom of such sign shall not be less than 6 inches (152 mm) nor more than 8 inches (203 mm) above the floor level and shall indicate the path of exit travel. For exit and exit-access doors, the sign shall be on the door or adjacent to the door with the closest edge of the sign within 4 inches (102 mm) of the door frame.

Hallways and corridors are to be considered in the same way in R-1 Occupancies. The major implication of this requirement is that hallways serving fewer than 10 occupants, in R-1 Occupancies, will be of 1-hour rated construction.

Note also the occupancy-specific requirements for floor-level exit signage at R-1 Occupancies. This is further limited by the code text to apply only to hotel corridors serving guest rooms. This requirement is based on the assumption that such corridors may become contaminated by smoke in an emergency. This smoke will fill the upper part of the corridor first and may obscure exit signs mounted above the doors. Low-level signs will be visible to persons crawling on the floor to escape smoke in the corridor. There have been several attempts to insert additional exit path markings into the code, with little success. The code requirement applies only to hotel corridors and requires only additional exit signs, not other lighting. (See Figure 7-38.)

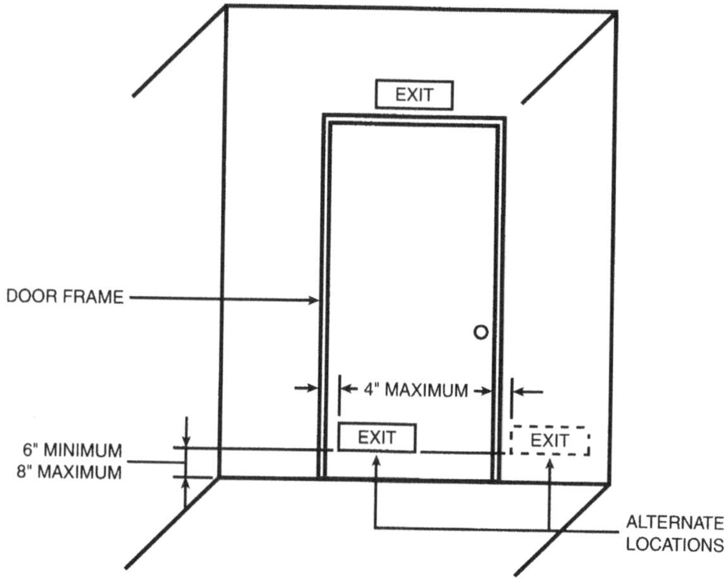

Low-level exit signs must be provided in Group R, Division 1 hotels wherever exit signs are required in interior exit corridors.

The code provision does not provide guidance for pairs of doors, doors in area separation walls or horizontal exits. It should be assumed that low-level signs would be required in all such cases in R-1 hotels.

The low-level exit sign may be internally or externally illuminated.

REFERENCE: SECTION 1007.6.2

FIGURE 7-38 LOW-LEVEL EXIT SIGNS IN EXIT CORRIDORS OF GROUP R, DIVISION 1 OCCUPANCY-HOTELS

Chapter 10 has been completely reorganized and the new concept of means of egress and its components has been introduced. This will be new territory for many designers and building officials who may be familiar with the old UBC, but not with the new organization and philosophy. The designer should consult early with the building official regarding the design of all means of egress to be certain that the interpretation of Chapter 10 by the building official is in concert with the designer's interpretation. It is to be expected that a variety of possible interpretations will continue to be made as this new chapter is put into practice in the field.

ARTICLE 8
FIRE-RESISTANT MATERIALS AND CONSTRUCTION AND INTERIOR FINISHES

Before discussing the next provisions, it is necessary to place Chapters 7 and 8 in perspective. Both chapters relate to fire regulations of building construction materials.

The provisions of Chapter 7 regulate the capacity of building elements such as walls, floors, beams and columns and doors and windows to withstand an attack by fire and prevent fire penetration through, or collapse of, the element within a specified period of time period of up to 4 hours.

The provisions of Chapter 8 regulate the surface burning characteristics of materials used to decorate, sound deaden or insulate the walls and ceiling of a room or space in a building. The purpose of these regulations is to control the rate of fire spread along the surface of the material.

The Chapter 8 regulations trace their roots back to the early 1940s when the tragic Boston Coconut Grove fire claimed over 400 lives. A major cause of those deaths was traced to the wall and ceiling coverings. The covering materials permitted the fire to spread rapidly, cutting off access to exits. The subsequent investigations resulted in Underwriter's Laboratories, Inc. (UL) developing a test procedure for surface burning characteristics.

The 1952 Uniform Building Code (UBC) contained the first flame-spread regulations. The regulations were based on the test procedure, UBC Standard 42-1 (ASTM E-48), commonly called the tunnel test.

Materials used for floor coverings are not presently regulated in the UBC. However, under state and federal regulations, certain occupancies such as hospitals are so regulated.

Flooring materials, where they are presently regulated, are tested using an evaluation procedure that differs from the tunnel test. In the tunnel test, a sample of material 20 inches wide and 24 feet long is placed at the top surface of a "tunnel" that is 12 inches high, 18 inches wide and 25 feet long. The sample is exposed to a $4\frac{1}{2}$-foot flame tongue at one end with a prescribed air flow, gas supply and pressure. The test period for the burn is 10 minutes. The furnace is initially calibrated with asbestos cement board and red oak samples before testing the particular material.

A row of glass view ports along one side of the furnace allows the flame front's rate of progress for the two calibration samples to be observed and noted during the test period. The rate of flame spread for the asbestos cement board and red oak is rated 0 and 100, respectively.

Chapter 7 Fire-Resistant Materials and Construction

Chapter 7 regulates the capacity of building elements such as walls, floors, beams and columns and doors and windows to withstand an attack by fire and prevent fire penetration through, or collapse of, the element within a specified period of time period of up to 4 hours. These regulations include specific listings of materials and assemblies for particular uses and fire ratings.

Unless the material or assembly has been previously fire tested and listed in an acceptable reference document, a fire test must be conducted to determine the fire-resistive rating of a material or assembly.

Acceptable references include

- UBC Tables 7-A, 7-B and 7-C,
- International Conference of Building Officials (ICBO) evaluation reports,
- Gypsum Association *Fire Resistance Design Manual* and
- many Underwriters Laboratories, Inc. listings in its *Fire Resistance Directory*.

The fire resistance of a material or assembly is determined by a fire test such as the UBC Standard 7-1 (ASTM E-119). This test procedure involves placing a sample of the material or assembly in a furnace and subjecting it to a fire source that exposes the sample to temperatures in accordance with a prescribed time–temperature curve. That curve requires a furnace temperature, 5 minutes after the start of the test, of 1000°F. At the end of 1 hour of the test exposure, the furnace temperature reaches 1700°F. (See Figure 8-1.)

For a detailed discussion of the fire testing procedure see Technical Appendix 4.

In the use of Chapter 7, some important common misconceptions arise regarding fire-resistive assemblies. These erroneous concepts need clarification:

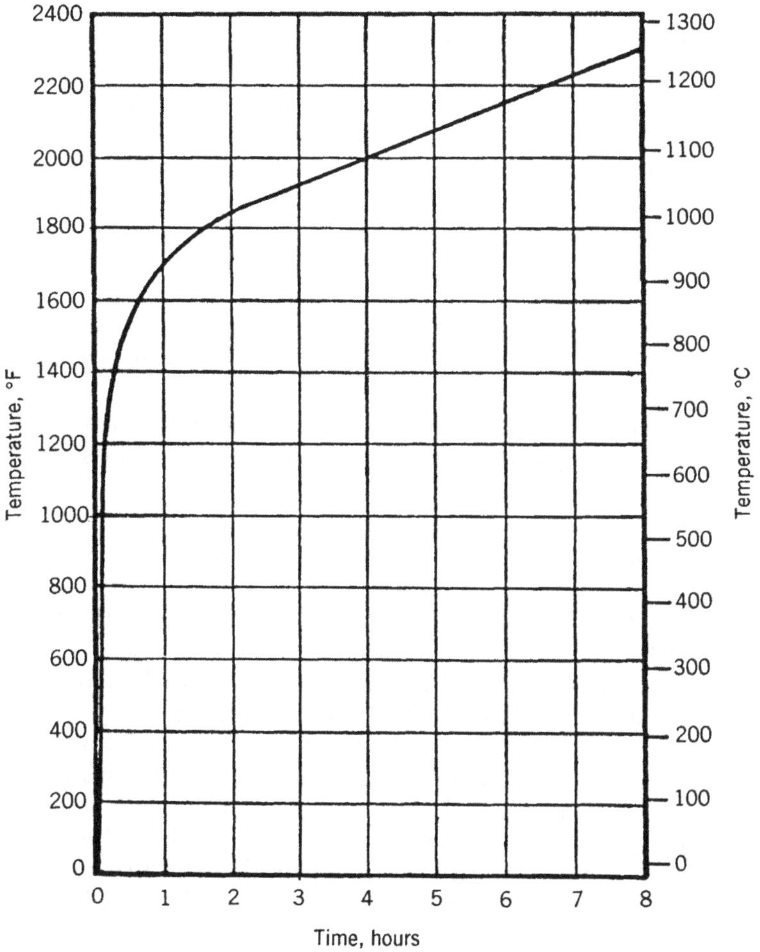

REFERENCE: UBC STANDARD 7-1, FIGURE 7-1-1, ASTM E-119

FIGURE 8-1 STANDARD FIRE TEST TIME-TEMPERATURE CURVE

1. *Suspended ceilings.* The ceiling usually contains steel framing members that are attached by wire or other hangers to the floor assembly above it.

The tile or board ceilings often used for both acoustical and fire resistance ratings are assumed to be 1-hour or 2-hour rated elements. But it is the assembly, incorporating the ceiling as a part of the fire barrier, that has the rating and not the suspended ceiling by itself. The tiles or boards, as well as the framing members, bear labels of the inspection agency. These labels are required in order to assure that their fabrication meets the approved fire test criteria.

In addition to the various components that make up the overall assembly, often the relationship of the elements within the assembly is important in achieving the desired hourly rating. The distance between the floor and the ceiling as well as the clearance between any beams or girders in the cavity and the ceiling protection have bearing on the rating.

There are no 1-hour suspended ceilings: There are only 1-hour suspended ceilings as part of floor-ceiling assemblies. (See Figure 8-2.)

2. *Gypsum wallboard.* (The trade name that is usually used for this material is Sheetrock, the product of the U.S. Gypsum Company, one of several manufacturers of this generic building material.)

It is often assumed that $\frac{5}{8}$-inch-thick wallboard with the designation of Type X, Type XXX, Type C, or a similar label by Underwriters Laboratories, Inc., means that the wallboard is 1-hour fire rated. The special designation Type X, or one of the other similar designations, derives from ASTM C-36. In that standard, a wood stud wall assembly, consisting of one layer of $\frac{5}{8}$-inch wallboard placed on each side of a 2 × 4 wood stud, is tested under the fire test criteria of the code (UBC Standard 7-1, which is based on ASTM E-119). If the assembly can pass a 1-hour fire test, the wallboard is given the Type X designation. The manufacturer can use another name for the product and still market it for use in 1-hour assemblies.

It is the combined assembly of the two layers of Type X wallboard with the stud that achieves the fire rating: There is no such thing as 1-hour wallboard by itself. (See Figure 8-3.)

This background discussion has provided a brief overview of a complex subject. It has been abbreviated to avoid getting weighed down in the details of individual tests and passage criteria. If the reader wishes to further study the tests discussed herein, UBC

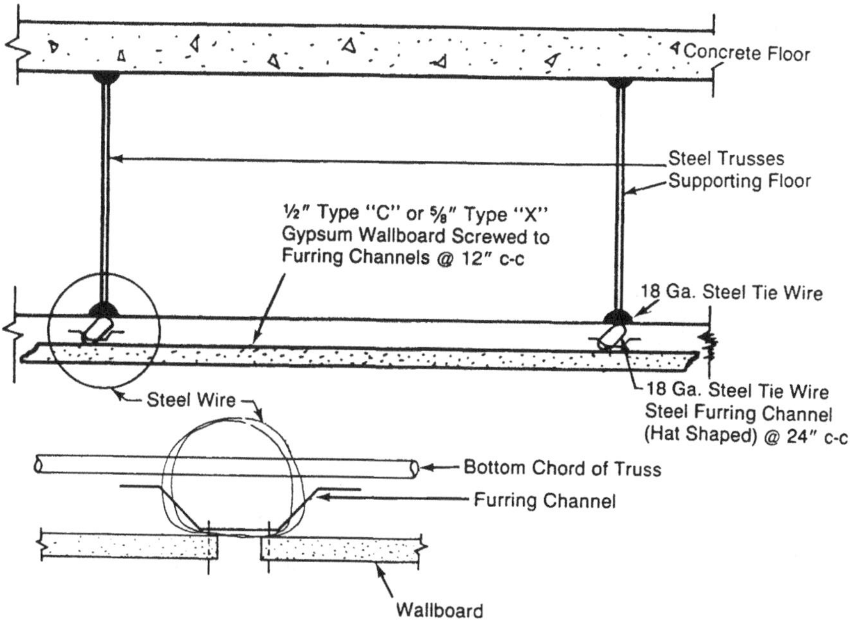

A floor-ceiling assembly consists of several items in most projects, unless the floor is of concrete slab construction that meets the thickness requirements of Table 7-C, Items 1 through 4. When a suspended ceiling is used as part of the rated floor-ceiling assembly, the elements of that assembly must all be present for the assembly to replicate the approved and tested configuration.

Gypsum wallboard that is customarily used in fire-resistive assemblies is not, by itself, adequate to provide the required hourly rating. Usually there are airspace and attachment requirements and minimum requirements for the floor portion of the assembly, If a tile or lay-in board suspended or directly attached ceiling is part of the floor-ceiling assembly, that ceiling is not, by itself, capable of providing the required fire-resistive rating.

REFERENCE: TABLE 7-C

FIGURE 8-2 FLOOR-CEILING ASSEMBLY

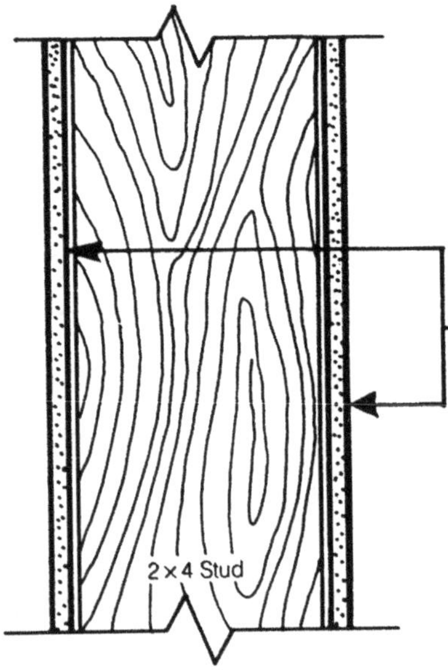

NOTE: Details of attachments and finishes not shown.

The use of gypsum wall board to provide a one-hour fire-resistive wall assembly, in the configuration shown above, replicates the fire test requirement on which the ASTM Type X conformance is based. That requires a wood stud with wallboard on each side of the stud. The wallboard is not, by itself, adequate to provide the required hourly rating. The airspace and attachment requirements are essential for the fire-resistance rating.

REFERENCE: TABLE 7-B

FIGURE 8-3 GYPSUM WALLBOARD ONE-HOUR WALL ASSEMBLY (ASTM C-36)

Standards 7-1, 7-2 and 7-4, and the ASTM fire test standards on which they are based are suggested reading. The ASTM standards contain Appendices explaining many of the requirements.

SECTION 702—DEFINITIONS

F RATING is the time period the penetration firestop system limits the passage of fire through the penetration when tested in accordance with UBC Standard 7-4.

T RATING is the time period that the penetration firestop system including the penetrating item, limits the maximum temperature rise to 325°F (163°C) above its initial temperature through the penetration on the nonfire side, when tested in accordance with UBC Standard 7-5.

The sections dealing with the penetration of rated systems has been reorganized. The 1994 UBC had the definitions for membrane penetration fire stop and through-penetration fire stop located in Chapter 4. Those definitions are now located in Section 702, Definitions. The penetration requirements are now separated by element; Section 709, Walls and Partitions and Section 710, Floor Ceilings or Roof Ceilings.

SECTION 703—FIRE-RESISTIVE MATERIALS AND SYSTEMS

703.1 General. Materials and systems used for fire-resistive purposes shall be limited to those specified in this chapter, unless accepted under the procedure given in 703.2 or 703.3.

The materials and details of construction for fire-resistive systems described in this chapter shall be in accordance with all other provisions of this code except as modified herein.

For the purpose of determining the degree of fire resistance afforded, the materials of construction listed in this chapter shall be assumed to have the fire-resistance rating indicated in Table 7-A, 7-B or 7-C.

As an Alternative to Table 7-A, 7-B or 7-C, fire-resistive construction may be approved by the building official on the basis of evidence submitted showing that the construction meets the required fire-resistive classification.

This section stipulates that a fire resistive assembly is one that is either contained in the Chapter 7 tables or that has been accepted under the procedures referenced in UBC Volume 3, Material, Testing and Installation Standards. The tables' listings were all derived from fire tests conducted over a period of many years. It is therefore given that a fire-rated assembly must have been tested in accordance with the established test criteria and accepted or approved by a responsible agency.

An assembly must conform not only to the construction details contained in the tables, but to the general construction requirements of the code as well. For example:

> Plywood installations, when used as diaphragms to resist lateral forces, must meet the provisions of Chapter 23. The nailing of plywood that is part of a fire-resistive floor and that is also being used as a lateral force-resisting diaphragm must meet

the nailing requirements of Table 23-II-H and Table 7-C, Item 21.

The last paragraph of Section 703.1 allows any person to submit the evidence of the equivalent fire-resistive performance to the building official. In the code prior to 1991, the requirement was for the person responsible for the structural design to submit the evidence. Although the change applies generally via 703.1, the specific requirement in Section 703.2 remains relating to restrained assemblies; i.e., the structural designer is the only one who can submit the restrained evidence of equivalent performance.

The original intent for adding the criteria for the structural designer was for the restrained assemblies due to the critical nature of the evaluation of these assemblies that may combine structural and thermal restraint.

703.2 Qualified by Testing. Material or assembly of materials of construction tested in accordance with the requirements set forth in UBC Standard 7-1 shall be rated for fire resistance in accordance with the results and conditions of such tests.

EXCEPTION: The acceptance criteria of UBC Standard 7-1 for exterior-bearing walls shall not be required to be greater with respect to heat transmission and passage of flame or hot gases than would be required of a nonbearing wall in the same building with the same distance to the property line. The fire exposure time period, water pressure and duration of application for the hose stream test shall be based on the fire-resistive rating determined by this exception.

Fire-resistive assemblies tested under UBC Standard 7-1 shall not be considered to be restrained unless evidence satisfactory to the building official is furnished by the person responsible for the structural design showing that the construction qualifies for a restrained classification in accordance with UBC Standard 7-1. Restrained construction shall be identified on the plans.

This section refers to the UBC Standard 7-1, which is based on the national fire test standard ASTM E-119. It further indicates that any assembly submitted to the building official may be accepted if the person responsible for the structural design submits proper evidence that the assembly meets the required fire rating. Considerable responsibility is placed on both the building official and the structural design professional.

In the authors' experience there are few structural design professionals knowledgeable in the area of fire testing and qualification of assemblies per UBC Standard No. 7-1 or ASTM E-119.

> We recommend that the design professional who is unfamiliar with the subject of fire-resistant design proceed with caution when planning to undertake the certification required for new assemblies by the second paragraph of this section for new assemblies.

The third paragraph indicates that the preferred method of evaluating a fire-resistive assembly, such as a fire-resistive floor system, is that based on unrestrained conditions. To accept fire test values for an assembly based on the restrained conditions requires evidence approved by the building official and provided by the structural design professional. Furthermore, the restrained constructions must be detailed on the drawings.

The concept of restraint as it applies to fire-resistive assemblies is discussed below. The code citations are in Section 703.2.

The temperature of the structural elements such as columns, beams and girders is used to determine the endpoint of the test. This became a generally required condition for horizontal structural elements after it was noted that several tests had been deemed successful even though they had "structurally" failed. An evaluation of the many fire tests conducted in the 1950s and 1960s clearly indicates that the main structural members in these tests had expanded under the heat of the furnace and were subjected to very high compressive thermal restraint from the test furnace.

The horizontal fire test furnace has two heavy steel beams enclosing the top of the furnace, which form a box-shaped ring that resists the forces that occur when a floor system expands during a test. These heavy furnace beams are capable of exerting sufficient reaction of the expansion of the test assembly to cause, shortly after the start of the fire test, what originally was to be a simple beam, i.e., a pin-ended member, to become a fix-ended member. The fire test protocol requires that the member must be loaded to produce stresses comparable to the field conditions. When the end support and fixity conditions of the structural member change, the loading condition no longer meets that test criteria. The change from pin-end to fix-ended conditions substantially reduces the test loading condition, particularly the maximum bending moment.

The solution to this fire test problem was to establish a two-track system of rating an assembly based on one fire test.

1. The first method uses the endpoint temperature of 1100–1300°F. This method and the resultant test value is called the unrestrained value for the assembly. It is a conservative value, independent of how the assembly is installed in the field.
2. The second method allows a restrained or higher hourly rating to apply, but requires that the method of providing the thermal restraint of the assembly in the actual building be certified by the structural engineer as meeting the conditions attendant to such assemblies in the standard.

One further comment is necessary regarding the latter test condition of passage. The restraint that develops in the fire test and for which the structural design must provide evidence is not the restraint associated with continuous members or similar standard structural restraint. The fire test restraint is thermally induced and therefore will exist in addition to any structural design values that result from the normal design calculations. The structural designer should be aware of this difference and how to deal with it.

> In the authors' opinion, unless the designer is confident that both the design and field installations can be satisfied, the unrestrained fire resistance ratings should be used.

It is difficult for the designer to properly control the actual conditions in the field or the personnel responsible for installing the fireproofing. The cost of the additional fireproofing may not be sufficient to warrant the designer taking the responsibility for any design or field deficiencies and the possible resultant liability.

SECTION 704—PROTECTION OF STRUCTURAL MEMBERS

704.1 General. Structural members having the fire-resistive protection set forth in Table 7-A shall be assumed to have the fire-resistance ratings set forth therein.

Section 704.1 refers to the first of the three tables in Chapter 7. Table 7-A contains predetermined fire protection thicknesses for individual structural members. These members include beams and columns and similar isolated members rather than systems such as floor-ceiling or wall assemblies.

Table 7-B contains the details of fire-resistive wall assemblies of the following types:

- solid,
- hollow,
- combustible and
- noncombustible.

Table 7-C contains the details of the following fire-resistive assemblies:

- floor,
- roof,
- floor-ceiling and
- roof-ceiling.

704.2 Protective Coverings.

704.2.1 Thickness of protection. The thickness of fire-resistive materials required for protection of structural members shall be not less than set forth in Table 7-A, except as modified in this section. The figures shown shall be the net thickness of the protecting materials and shall not include any hollow space back of the protection.

704.2.2 Unit masonry protection. Where required, metal ties shall be embedded in transverse joints of unit masonry for protection of steel columns. Such ties shall be as set forth in Table 7-A or be equivilent thereto.

704.2.3 Reinforcement for cast-in-place concrete column protection. Cast-in-place concrete protection for steel columns shall be reinforced at the edges of such members with wire ties of not less than 0.18 inch (4.6 mm) in diameter wound spirally around the columns on a pitch of not more than 8 inches (203 mm) or by equivalent reinforcement.

704.2.4 Embedment of pipes. Conduits and pipes shall not be embedded in required fire protection of structural members.

704.2.5 Column jacketing. Where the fire-resistive covering on columns is exposed to injury from moving vehicles, the handling of merchandise or other means, it shall be protected in an approved manner.

704.2.6 Ceiling membrane protection. When a ceiling forms the protective membrane for fire-resistive assemblies, the assemblies and their supporting horizontal structure members need not be individually fire protected except where such members support directly applied loads from a floor and roof or more than one floor. The required fire resistence shall not be less than that required for individual protection of members.

704.2.7 Plaster application. Plaster protective coatings may be applied with the finish coat omitted when they comply with the design mix and thickness requirements of Tables 7-A, 7-B and 7-C.

704.2.8 Truss protection. Where trusses are used as all or part of the structural frame and protection is required by Table 6-A, such protection may be provided by fire-resistive materials enclosing the entire truss assembly on all sides for its entire length and height. The required thickness and construction of fire-resistive assemblies enclosing trusses shall be based on the results of full-scale tests or combinations of tests on truss components or on approved calculations based on such tests that satisfactorily demonstrate that the assembly has the required fire resistence.

Section 704.2.1 requires the thickness of the materials in Table 7-A to be the net thickness. Hollow spaces behind the protection are not to be included in the measurement. For example, if two inches of protection are required and there is a furring space between the main member to be protected and its protective coating, only the thickness of the protective coating is to be used for the 2-inch measurement; the width of the furring space is not to be considered.

The several cautions and specifications in Sections 704.2.2 through 704.2.8 relate to Table 7-A fire-protective coatings. However, some cautions and specifications also have application to materials not in this table, but which are used in a similar manner, such as spray-applied fireproofing. Sections 704.2.4 and 704.2.5 should be applied by the designer to such materials to obtain proper and long-lasting assemblies.

Section 704.2.6 is frequently misunderstood. A ceiling of a floor-ceiling assembly can be used to protect both the flooring and the structural members therein, provided the structural members are not supporting more than one floor or the roof.

For example, assume there is an intermediate column placed so that a beam on the fourth floor is carrying not only the fourth floor load but also a portion of the fifth floor load via the intermediate column. This beam must have individual fire protection and could not rely on the membrane fireproofing. (See Figure 8-4.)

704.3 Protected members.

704.3.1 Attached metal members. The edges of lugs, brackets, rivets and bolt heads attached to structural members may extend to within 1 inch (25 mm) of the surface of the fire protection.

704.3.2 Reinforcing. Thickness of protection for concrete or masonry reinforcement shall be measured to the outside of the reinforcement except where that stirrups and spiral reinforcement ties may project not more than $\frac{1}{2}$ inch (12.7 mm) into the protection.

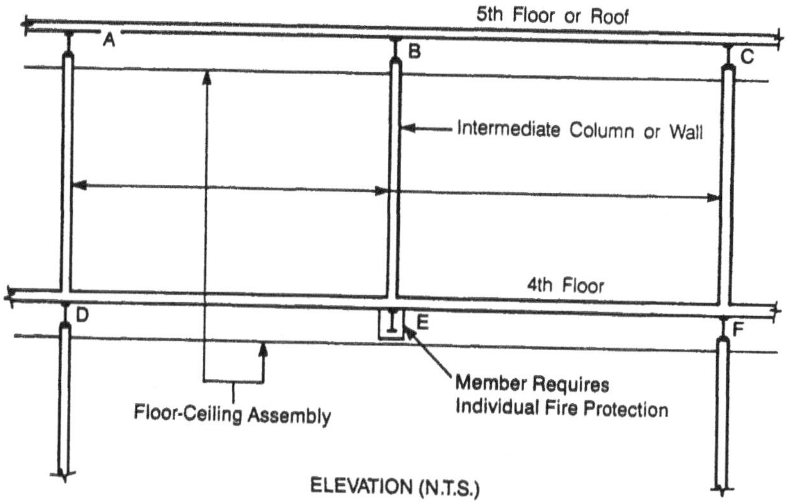

Members A, B, C, D, and F may be fire protected by the fire-rated membrane ceiling of the floor-ceiling assembly.

Member E, which carries its own floor load and that from member B, via the columns, requires individual fire protection.

REFERENCE: SECTION 704.2.6

FIGURE 8-4 INDIVIDUAL BEAM PROTECTION/MEMBRANE PROTECTION

704.3.3 Bonded prestressed concrete tendons. For members having a single tendon or more than tendon installed with equal concrete cover measured from the nearest surface, the cover shall not be less than set forth in Table 7-A.

For members having multiple tendons installed with variable concrete cover, the average tendon cover shall not be less than that set forth in Table 7-A provided:

1. The clearance from each tendon to the nearest exposed surface is used to determine the average cover.

2. In no case can the clear cover for individual tendons be less than one half of that set forth in Table 7-A. A minimum cover of ¾ inch (19.1 mm) for slabs and 1 inch (25.4 mm) for beams is required for any aggregate concrete.

3. For the purpose of establishing a fire-resistive rating, tendons having a clear covering less than that set forth in Table 7-A shall not contribute more than 50 percent of the required ultimate moment capacity for members

less than 350 square inches (0.226 m^2) in cross-sectional area and 65 percent for larger members. For structural design purposes, however, tendons having a reduced cover are assumed to be fully effective.

Section 704.3.2 cautions that the protective covering for reinforcement is to be measured to the outside of the reinforcement. To avoid field problems, the designer should include such information in the details of the contract drawings. The steel reinforcement in concrete is subject to loss of load-carrying capability when heated in a fire. To reduce the rate loss of strength in fire, the proper thickness of coverage of the steel is necessary.

The coverage requirements for prestressed tendons are similarly specified due to the tendon's loss of strength at relatively low temperatures. Prestressed tendons lose strength when their temperature reaches the 800°F range as contrasted to the 100–1300°F range for carbon steel.

704.4 Members Carrying Masonry or Concrete. All members carrying masonry or concrete walls in buildings over one story in height shall be fire protected with not less than one-hour fire protection or the fire-resistive requirement of the wall, whichever is greater.

This section requires that supporting members for masonry or concrete walls have at least 1-hour fire resistance. This is aimed at both wood and unprotected steel members in particular. The language was changed to reflect the concept outlined in Article 5 of this Guide regarding support elements. If the wall is required to have a fire-resistive rating greater than 1 hour, the support member must have at least that higher rating as well. (See Figure 8-5.)

Thus, if a wall is required to be of 2- or 4-hour construction, as may be the case with an occupancy separation wall or an exterior building wall near a property line, all the support elements for that wall must be of at least the same rating down to the ground. Previously, the code provision had only the 1-hour minimum requirement.

Under prior codes, a designer could err in providing only a 1-hour fire-resistive support for a 2- or 4-hour concrete or masonry wall. In the event of a fire in such a situation lasting just over 1 hour, the wall could collapse at a much earlier time than its own required fire rating, after the support element failed.

The designer should be aware that whenever a rating is required, regardless of whether it is for an area separation wall, occupancy

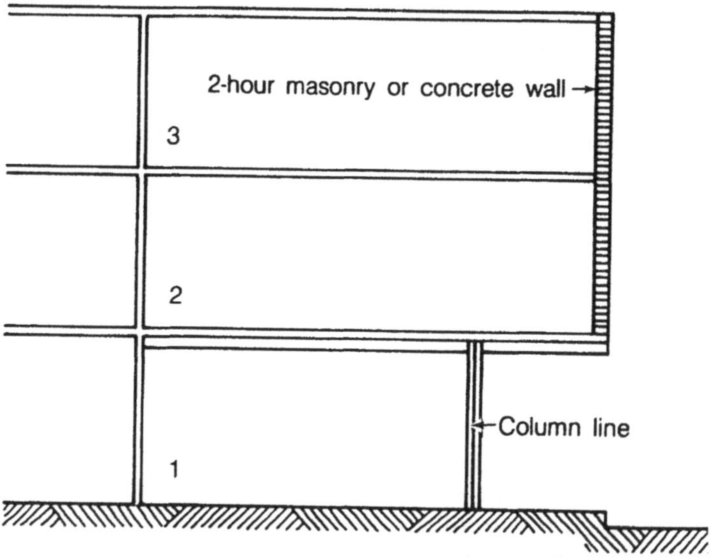

ASSUME: TYPE III One-Hour building, 2-Hour masonry or concrete exterior wall.

Floor-ceiling assembly of 2nd floor is 2-Hour or greater.

Columns on 1st floor supporting 2-Hour masonry or concrete wall is 2-Hour or greater.

REFERENCE: SECTION 704.4

FIGURE 8-5 FIRE RATING FOR MEMBERS SUPPORTING RATED MASONRY OR CONCRETE WALLS

separation, or if a structural element is involved, the support for that construction must have equivalent or greater fire resistance than the supported item. This degree of fire resistance for the support must be carried down to the ground, so that the support member will not fail sooner than the time period required of the supported element.

The designer should clearly understand this concept of tracking the support system. Tracking should become a standard procedure during the design and contract document preparation stages.

704.6 Spray-applied Fire-resistive Materials. The density and thickness of spray-applied fire-resistive materials shall be determined following the procedures set forth in UBC Standard 7-6.

Section 704.6 relates to spray-applied fireproofing. The designer should be aware that the protection afforded by this type of material is a function of

- the application density and
- its thickness.

Unfortunately, when spraying large areas of decking, it is difficult to control the number of hollow spaces or holidays that may occur. It is therefore recommended that the designer consider a minimum thickness of one-half inch for spray-applied fireproofing.

In fire tests, a $\frac{1}{4}$-inch fireproofing thickness may be sufficient on a given assembly for a particular fire rating. However, in the field it is difficult to control the application of fireproofing to that degree. The recommendation for a thicker installation will therefore provide a margin of safety for the field installation. With this procedure, any holidays will usually be less than $\frac{1}{4}$ inch.

Section 710.3 contains another often misunderstood provision. Openings are permitted in the ceiling membrane of a floor-ceiling assembly. The openings described in the exceptions to this section are for such things as light fixture outlet boxes and fire sprinklers.

These openings should not penetrate to the floor above. They are permitted only in the membrane ceiling. The code previously contained the phrase "ceilings shall form a continuous membrane." This is still the code's intent, requiring a through penetration as specified in Section 710.2 to be a fire-resistive shaft enclosure, thereby maintaining the integrity of the membrane. If the openings in the membrane are larger that 100 square inches in 100 square feet, they must be tested assemblies. This may include larger light fixtures, ducts and other ceiling penetrations or access hatches. (See Figure 8-6.)

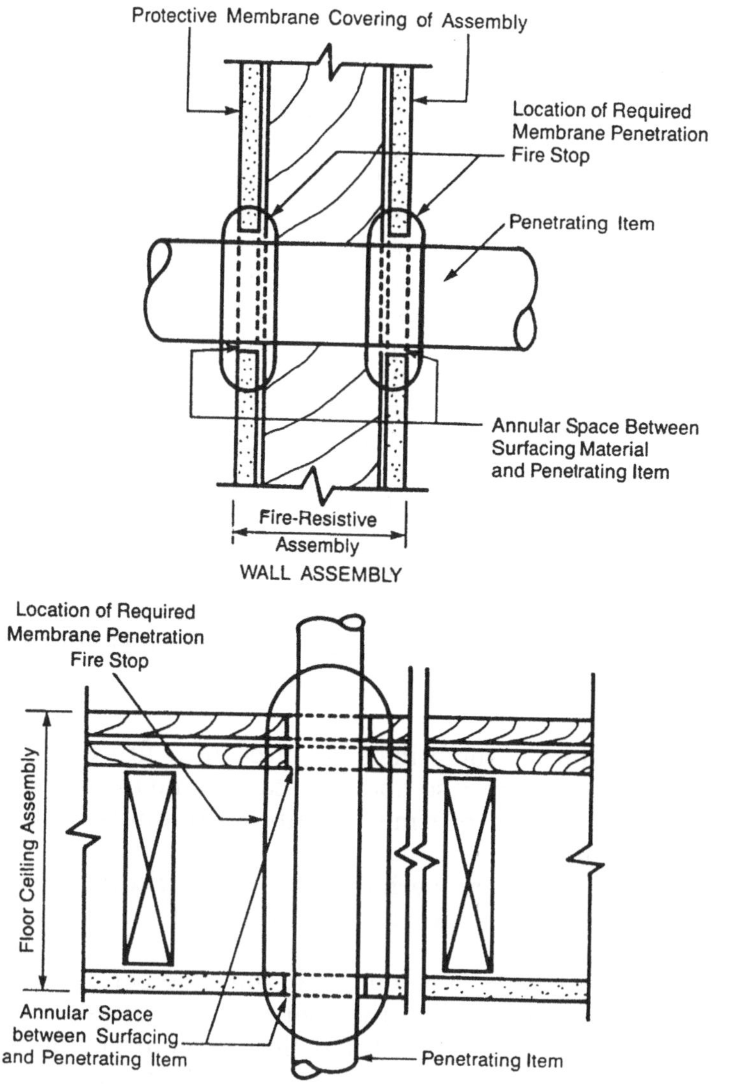

FIRE-RESISTIVE FLOOR-CEILING ASSEMBLY

NOTES:
1. See Section 710.2, Exceptions and 710.2.3
2. The annular space around the membrane penetrations shall be not more than 1/8-inch wide unless a greater width is permitted by the approved listing.
3. Note #2 also applies to penetration of plates.

REFERENCE: SECTIONS 709.6.3 AND 709.7

FIGURE 8-6 ILLUSTRATION OF THE USE OF A THROUGH-PENETRATION FIRE STOP

There are no specific references to access doors or hatches in the code as there once was. However, Section 710.1 states that "when materials are incorporated into an otherwise fire-resistive assembly that may change the capacity for heat dissipation, fire test results or other substantiating data shall be made available to the building official to show that the required fire-resistive time period is not reduced." Therefore, if an access door or hatch is listed by an approved testing agency such as UL, or covered by an ICBO evaluation report for the required time period, they may be installed as part of a floor- or roof-ceiling assembly.

The term "approved horizontal access door assembly" is not defined in either Chapter 2 or 7 of the code. Thus it is necessary to determine what the requirements are for such an assembly to be "approved." The key criteria for a fire-resistive element, such as a door, are that they

- withstand fire for a period of time,
- stay in place, i.e., remain latched and hinged and
- be closed at the time of fire attack.

Another criterion sometimes required of a fire door is that it prevents temperature rise above a stated amount on the back of the door for a period of time, usually 30 minutes. This is not a mandatory criterion.

Therefore, certain and perhaps all of these criteria are not applicable because the code provision does not refer to a "fire-door assembly."

For the access door to be effective, the time period and stay-in-place criteria must apply for the floor-ceiling or roof-ceiling assembly in which the door is located. The closure requirement, therefore, must be the criterion that is not satisfied by the term "access door assembly."

> In the authors' opinion, a closing device is not required; the access door need not be self-closing or automatic closing. The horizontal access door assembly required should meet all the fire door assembly requirements, with the exception of the need for an automatic or self-closing mechanism.

SECTION 706—FIRE-RESISTIVE JOINT SYSTEMS

706.1 General. Joints installed in or between fire-resistive walls, fire-resistive floor or floor-ceiling assemblies and fire-resistive roof or roof-ceiling assemblies shall be protected by an approved fire-resistive joint system designed to resist the passage of fire for a time period of not less than the required fire-resistive rating of the floor, roof or wall in or between which it is installed. Fire-resistive joint systems shall be tested in accordance with Section 706.2

EXCEPTION: Fire-resistive joint systems are not required for joints in the following locations:

1. Floors within a single dwelling unit.
2. Floors where the joint is protected by a shaft enclosure in accordance with Section 711.
3. Floors with atriums where the space adjacent to the atrium is included in the volume of the atrium for smoke-control purposes.
4. Floors within malls.
5. Floors within open parking structures.
6. Mezzanine floors.
7. Walls that are permitted to have unprotected openings.
8. Roofs where openings are permitted.

Such material or construction assembly shall be securely installed in or on the joint for its entire length so as not to dislodge, loosen or otherwise impair its ability to accommodate expected building movements and to resist the passage of fire and hot gasses.

706.2 Fire-resistive Joint Systems. Fire-resistive joint systems shall be tested in accordance with UBC Standard 7-1 under the following conditions:

1. Joint systems shall be installed full height in wall assemblies and full length in floor and roof assemblies.
2. Floor and roof assemblies shall be tested with a minimum positive pressure differential of 0.01 inch of water column (2.5 Pa).
3. Wall assemblies shall be tested with a minimum positive pressure differential of 0.01 inch of water column (2.5 Pa) measured at the mid-height of the wall assembly.
4. Joint systems shall contain a splice. For wall assemblies, the splice shall be located above the mid-height of the wall assembly.
5. Joint systems shall be tested at the maximum joint width for which they are designed. Joint systems designed to accommodate movement shall be expanded to the maximum joint opening width for which they are intended to function.
6. Joint systems designed to be load-bearing shall be loaded to the maximum design load in accordance with their intended application.
7. Joint systems designed to accommodate movement shall be preconditioned by cycling between the minimum and the maximum joint opening width for which they are intended to function for the number of cycles specified in Table 7-D
8. Nonsymetrical wall joint systems shall be tested in accordance with Sections 706 and 709.5.

This section is part of the requirements relating to penetrations of fire-resistive wall, floor-ceiling and shaft wall assemblies. It is the result of experiences in fires such as at McCormick Place in Chicago and the MGM Grand Hotel in Las Vegas. In both instances the spread of fire, smoke and hot gases was facilitated by expansion, wind or seismic joints in fire-resistive assemblies.

The common method of providing for these joints disregards the fire resistance requirement and usually simply uses a sliding joint cover as shown in Figure 8-7. Such a joint cannot provide the required fire resistance of the floor or wall assembly because the materials will buckle, open or melt out.

Some examples of fire-resistive methods for providing for such movements and retaining the fire resistance of the assembly are shown in Figure 8-8.

The designer should be aware that there are numerous configurations of methods for maintaining the fire-resistive integrity for openings through fire-resistive assemblies. Many can be adapted from the assemblies used for protecting pipe penetrations. Other systems are in the Underwriters Laboratories, Inc. *Building Materials Directory*.

When a material is to be used to provide both watertightness and fire resistance, it is important that the material be compressible so that, as shown in Detail D of Figure 8-8, it will permit the movement of the joint and still stay in place. The gap must be designed to provide for the amount of movement expected and must be based on the compressibility of the material inserted within the space to avoid binding.

Where the fire resistance is to be provided by either a material that bridged the gap, as in Detail C of Figure 8-8, or on the intumescent action of the material such as the intumescent tapes shown in Details A and B of Figure 8-8, the amount of fire-resistive material will be determined by

- the amount of the expanded material required to provide the degree of fire resistance needed and
- the amount of expanded material needed to close off the gap. See Details A and B of Figure 8-8.

The enforcement official should be aware that the great variety of conditions the designer may have in a building will require the official to apply judgment when evaluating the system the designer chooses. That judgment should be based on requiring that the system is a listed one and one that has comparable applicability to the materials on the project. In other words, a system designed

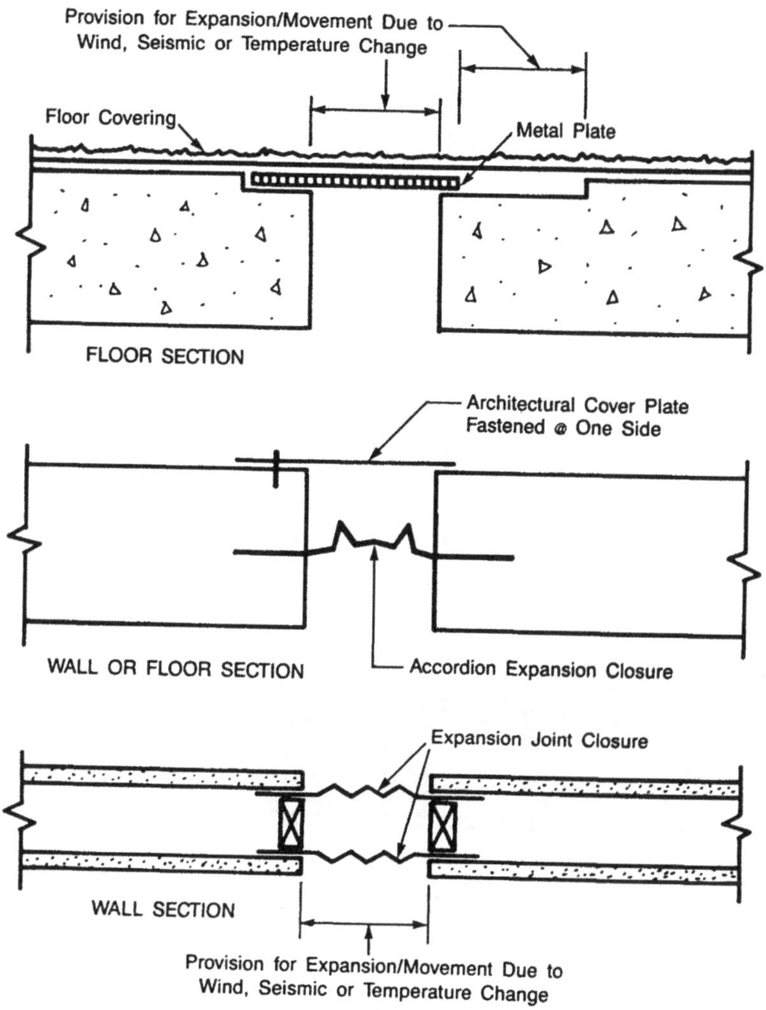

TYPICAL UNPROTECTED JOINTS IN FIRE-RESISTIVE ASSEMBLIES

REFERENCE: SECTION 706

FIGURE 8-7 TYPICAL UNPROTECTED JOINTS IN FIRE-RESISTIVE ASSEMBLIES FOR WIND, SEISMIC OR EXPANSION MOVEMENTS-NOT ACCEPTABLE

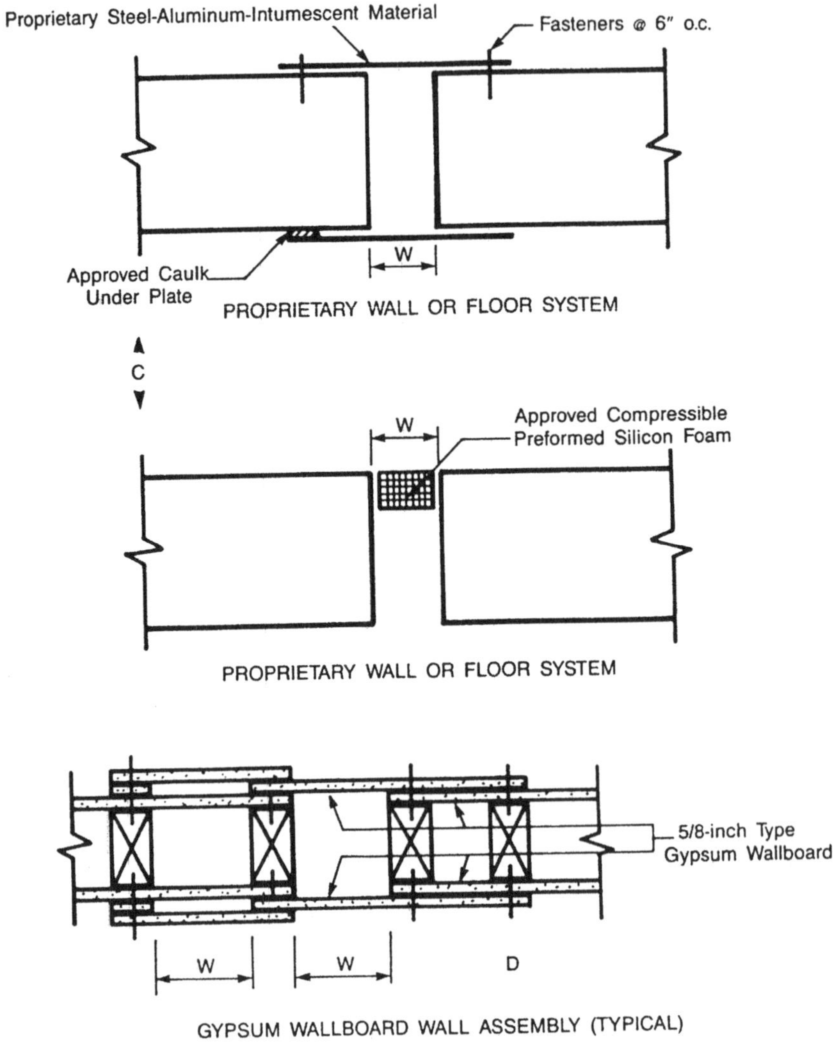

$$W = \text{Width of Gap} = \frac{\text{Amount of Expansion/Movement Required}}{\text{Compressibility Coeficient of Compressible Gasket}}$$

REFERENCE: SECTION 706, U.L. BUILDING MATERIALS DIRECTORY

FIGURE 8-8 TYPICAL METHODS OF PROTECTING JOINTS TO PROVIDE FOR WIND, SEISMIC OR EXPANSION MOVEMENT

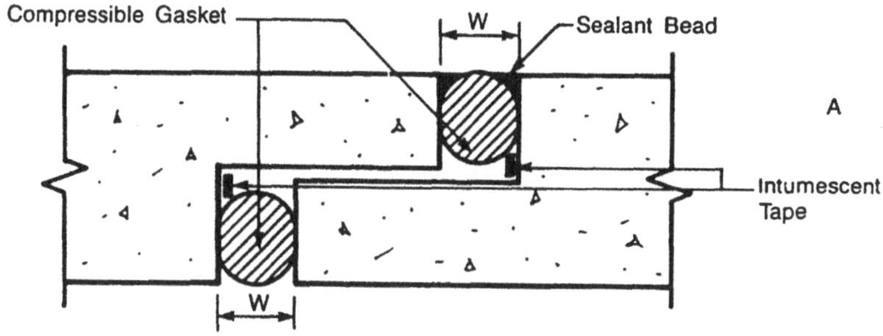

EXTERIOR WALL SECTION
(TYPICAL EXAMPLE)

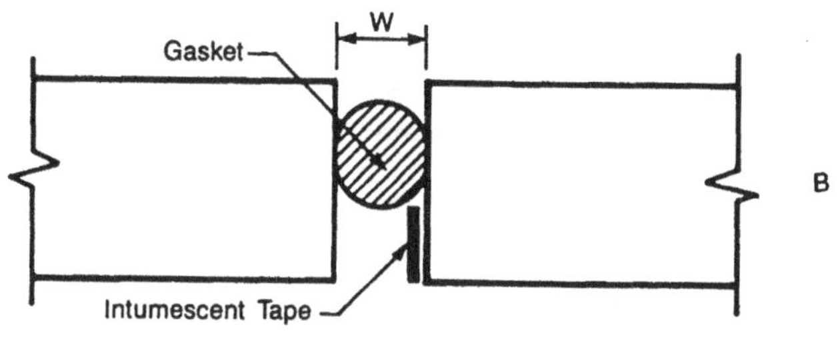

for solid concrete or masonry should not be used for a gypsum wallboard cavity wall or floor-ceiling assembly unless permitted by the approved listing.

The use of intumescent materials is a relatively new innovation in the field of fire protection. It is the direct result of the concern over the penetrations, the subject of the Chapter 7 code changes discussed in Article 8 of this Guide.

An intumescent material, as used in connection with fire-resistive assemblies, is a material that will, on exposure to high temperature, foam up to create a fire-resistant barrier. The barrier acts in much the same way that char does for wood or foamed insulation does in clothing and as a building insulation. The materials come in various forms, including tapes, foam boards and paste format. The most common materials are manufactured by such firms as Minnesota Mining and Dupont. The materials are listed in the Underwriters Laboratories, Inc. *Building Materials Directory*.

Use of intumescent materials must be based on

- the width of the gap required for the movement anticipated,
- the thickness of intumescent material required at ambient temperature to close that gap,
- the fire-resistive time period for the wall or floor element and
- the compatibility of the intumescent material with the materials to which it is attached.

In many instances the intumescent material needs a substantial backing material against which to expand. Thus, an intumescent material recommended for use in concrete or masonry, with wide surfaces against which to act, should not be used in a $\frac{5}{8}$-inch Type X gypsum wallboard gap without some other devices provided to assure the presence of sufficient resistance to allow the intumescent material to expand under heat.

SECTION 708 — FIRE BLOCKS AND DRAFT STOPS

708.1 General. In combustible construction, fireblocking and draftstopping shall be installed to cut off all concealed draft openings (both vertical and horizontal) and shall form an effective barrier between floors, between a top story and a roof or attic space, and shall subdivide attic spaces, concealed roof spaces and floor-ceiling assemblies. The integrity of all fire blocks and draft stops shall be maintained.

708.2 Fire Blocks.

708.2.1 Where Required. Fireblocking shall be provided in the following locations:

1. In concealed spaces of stud walls and partitions, including furred spaces, at the ceiling and floor levels and at 10-foot (3048 mm) intervals both vertical and horizontal. See also Section 803, Item 1.

   EXCEPTION: Fire blocks may be omitted at floor and ceiling levels when approved smoke-actuated fire dampers are installed at these levels.

2. At all interconnections between concealed vertical and horizontal spaces such as occur at soffits, drop ceilings and cove ceilings.
3. In concealed spaces between stair stringers at the top and bottom of the run and between studs along and in line with the run of the stairs if the walls under the stairs are unfinished.
4. In openings around vents, pipes, ducts, chimneys, fireplaces and similar openings that afford a passage for fire at ceiling and floor levels, with non-combustible materials.
5. At openings between attic spaces and chimney chases for factory-built chimneys.
6. Where wood sleepers are used for laying wood flooring on masonry or concrete fire- resistive floors, the space between the floor slab and the

underside of the wood flooring shall be filled with noncombustible material or fire blocked in such a manner that there will be no open spaces under the flooring that will exceed 100 square feet (9.3 m^2) area and such space shall be filled solidly under all permanent partitions so that there is no communication under the flooring between adjoining rooms.

EXCEPTIONS: 1. Fire blocking need not be provided in such floors when at or below grade level in gymnasiums.

2. Fire blocking need be provided only at the juncture of each alternate lane and at the ends of each lane in a bowling facility.

708.2.2 Fire block construction. Except as provided in Item 4 above, fireblocking shall consist of 2 inches (51 mm) nominal lumber or two thicknesses of 1-inch (25 mm) nominal lumber with broken lapjoints or one thickness of $\frac{23}{32}$-inch (18.3 mm) wood structural panel with joints backed by $\frac{23}{32}$-inch (18.3 mm) wood structural panel or one thickness of $\frac{3}{4}$-inch (19.1 mm) Type 2-M particleboard with joints backed by $\frac{3}{4}$-inch (19.1 mm) Type 2-M particleboard.

Fire blocks may also be of gypsum board, cement fiber board, batts or blankets of mineral or glass fiber, or other approved materials installed in such a manner as to be securely retained in place. Loose-fill insulation material shall not be used as a fire block unless specifically tested in the form and manner intended for use to demonstrate its ability to remain in place and to retard the spread of fire and hot gases.

Walls having parallel or staggered studs for sound-transmission control shall have fire blocks of batts or blankets of mineral or glass fiber or other approved flexible materials.

708.3 Draft Stops.

708.3.1Where required. Draftstopping shall be provided in the locations set forth in this section:

708.3.1.1 Floor-ceiling assemblies.

708.3.1.1.1 Single-family dwellings. When there is usable space above and below the concealed space of a floor-ceiling assembly in a single-family dwelling, draft stops shall be installed so that the area of the concealed space does not exceed 1,000 square feet (93 m^2) Draftstopping shall divide the concealed space into approximately equal areas.

708.3.1.1.2 Two or more dwelling units and hotels. Draft stops shall be installed in floor-ceiling assemblies of buildings having more than one dwelling unit and in hotels. Such draft stops shall be in line with walls separating individual dwelling units and guest rooms from each other and from other areas.

708.3.1.1.3 Other uses. Draft stops shall be installed in floor-ceiling assemblies of buildings or portions of buildings used for other than dwelling or hotel occupancies so that the area or the concealed space does not exceed 1,000 square feet (93 m^2) and so that the horizontal dimension between stops does not exceed 60 feet (18 288 mm).

EXCEPTION: Where approved automatic sprinklers are installed within the concealed space, the area between draft stops may be 3,000 square feet (279 m^2) and the horizontal dimension may be 100 feet (30 480 mm).

708.3.1.2 Attics

708.3.1.2.1 Two or more dwelling units and hotels. Draft stops shall be installed in the attics, mansards, overhangs false fronts set out from walls

and similar concealed spaces of buildings containing more than one dwelling unit and in hotels. Such draft stops shall be above and in line with the walls separating individual dwelling units and guest rooms from each other and from other uses.

EXCEPTIONS: 1. Draft stops may be omitted along one of the corridor walls, provided draft stops at walls separating individual dwelling units and guest rooms from each other and from other uses, extend to the remaining corridor draft stop.

2. Where approved sprinklers are installed, draftstopping may be as specified in the exception to Section 708.3.1.2.2

708.3.1.2.2 Other Uses. Draft stops shall be installed in attics, mansards, overhangs, false fronts set out from walls and similar concealed spaces of buildings having uses other than dwellings of hotels so that the area between draft stops does not exceed 3,000 square feet (279 m^2) and the greatest horizontal dimension does not exceed 60 feet (18 288 mm).

EXCEPTION: Where approved automatic sprinklers are installed within the concealed space, the area between draft stops may be 9,000 square feet (836 m^2) and the greatest horizontal dimension may be 100 feet (30 480 mm).

708.3.1.3 Draft stop construction. Draftstopping materials shall not be less than $\frac{1}{2}$-inch (12.7 mm) gypsum board, $\frac{3}{8}$-inch (9.5 mm) wood structural panel, $\frac{3}{8}$-inch (9.5 mm) Type 2-M particleboard or other approved materials adequately supported.

Openings in the partitions shall be protected by self-closing doors with automatic latches constructed as required for the partitions.

Ventilation of concealed roof spaces shall be maintained in accordance with Section 1505.

708.4 Draft Stops or Fire Blocks in Other Locations. Fireblocking of veneer on noncombustible walls shall be in accordance with Section 708.2.1, Item 1.

For fireblocking ceilings applied against noncombustible construction, see Section 803, Item 1.

This section provides the mandatory locations for draftstopping and fire blocking in wood-framed buildings. The term "draftstopping" refers to the prevention of the free flow of air in stud wall and ceiling cavities by means of a barrier material, such as $\frac{1}{2}$-inch gypsum wallboard or $\frac{3}{8}$-inch wood structural panel (plywood) or particleboard. Fire blocking, on the other hand, must also provide some degree of fire-resistant capability. Thus, the material has to be of more substantial dimension, such as 2-inch thick wood or one of the equivalent built-up assembly of materials.

In both instances, the intent is to slow the spread of fire by blocking the draft or by placing a fire barrier in its path.

The designer should be aware that all too often these hidden elements of construction are frequently so poorly installed as to be ineffective or simply left out during construction. This is usually the case when double-studded walls are constructed. The designer should provide details or notes on the design drawings calling out both the location and the form of the draft stops and fire blocks to use.

The location of draft stops in attics of multifamily buildings is required at the tenant separation walls. In other than residential buildings, there are to be draft stops at no more than 60-foot intervals and creating not more than 3000 square feet in each subdivided space. These provide draft barriers to fire's rapid spread in attics.

Note also that Section 1505 requires attic ventilation be provided. Thus, each compartment formed by the draft stops must have separate ventilation means without relying on the adjacent space; otherwise the intent of the draft stop is negated.

Where fire sprinklers are provided in the attic, the size of the area and the maximum spacing of the draft stops may be increased substantially. Note that this does not require that the entire building be sprinklered.

> Sprinklers in concealed spaces such as attics should be used with great caution and only in extraordinary circumstances. Since the sprinklers are completely hidden, they are prone to neglect and lack of maintenance. If the sprinkler system leaks or a head goes off for any reason, the ceiling is likely to become saturated by water and may fail, leading to major repairs or a hazardous condition.

Section 1505 and Sections 601.5.4, 803 and 3102.7.13 have substituted the terms "fire block," "fire blocks" and "fire blocking" for the terms "firestop" and "firestopping" used in prior codes. These substitutions occur when the intent of the code relates to those uses generally in frame construction using materials comparable in size to the studs or such equivalent acceptable materials as provided for in the various sections.

The new terminology eliminates the conflict in the meaning of the terms in the prior codes, when the intent of the use of firestop and firestopping differed between various sections of the code. Since the publication of the 1991 UBC, the term "firestop" has related solely to fire-resistive assemblies.

SECTION 709—WALLS AND PARTITIONS

709.3.2 Vertical Fire Spread at Exterior Walls.

709.3.2.1 General. The provisions of this section are intended to restrict the passage of smoke, flame and hot gases from one floor to another at exterior walls. See Section 4305 for floor penetrations.

709.3.2.2 Interior. Where fire-resistive floor or floor-ceiling assemblies are required, voids created at the intersection of the exterior wall assemblies and such floor assemblies shall be sealed with an approved material. Such material shall be securely installed and capable of preventing the passage of flame and hot gases sufficient to ignite cotton waste when subject to U.B.C. Standard No. 43-1 time-temperature fire conditions under a minimum positive pressure differential of 0.01 inches of water column for the time period at least equal to the fire resistance rating of the floor assembly.

709.3.2.3 Exterior. Where openings in an exterior wall are above and within 5 feet (1524 mm) laterally of an opening in the story below, such openings shall be separated by an approved flame barrier extending 30 inches (762 mm) beyond the exterior wall in the plane of the floor or by approved vertical flame barriers not less than 3 feet (914 mm) high measured vertically above the top of the lower opening. Flame barriers shall have a fire resistance of not less than three-fourths hour.

EXCEPTIONS: 1. Flame barriers are not required in buildings equiped with an approved automatic sprinkler system throughout.

2. This subsection shall not apply to buildings two stories or less in height.

3. Flame barriers are not required on Group S, Division 4 Occupancies.

These exterior wall provisions apply to all buildings that are more than two stories in height and that are not sprinklered. Therefore, the requirements do not apply to

- high-use buildings complying with Section 403,
- Group R, Division 1 Occupancy buildings complying with Section 904.2.9,
- Group H, Division 1, 2, 3 and 7 Occupancy buildings and
- any other building that is sprinklered throughout, regardless of the reason.

The primary concerns of these provisions are

- to seal the floor-exterior wall intersection and
- to provide flame barriers at the exterior wall to restrict floor-to-floor fire spread on the exterior wall surface.

Section 709.3.2.2 addresses the first concern by requiring that voids at the building exterior wall and floor be filled with approved materials. These are commonly referred to as fire safing by manufacturers.

Section 709.3.2.3 addresses the second concern regarding openings in the exterior wall that are above and within 5 feet of an opening in the floor below. (See Figure 8-9.) The hazard of the spread of fire can be reduced by providing either a $\frac{3}{4}$-hour fire-resistive flame barrier in the form of a 3-foot-high spandrel or a 30-inch wide "eyebrow."

This is the first time fractional hourly ratings have been permitted for wall assemblies. No $\frac{3}{4}$-hour fire-resistive wall assemblies are presently listed in the UBC or have Evaluation Reports.

> It is the authors' opinion that until such time as these Evaluation Reports are made available, the designer should use 1-hour fire-resistive assemblies.

The spandrel or eyebrow requirement is the result of the major fire losses in Los Angeles and Las Vegas that had substantial degree of fire spread via the exterior wall openings.

709.4 Parapets.

709.4.1 General. Parapets shall be provided on all exterior walls of buildings.

EXCEPTIONS: A parapet need not be provided on an exterior wall when any of the following conditions exist:

1. The wall is not required to be of fire-resistive construction.
2. The wall, due to location on property, may have unprotected openings.
3. The building has an area of not more than 1,000 square feet (93 m^2) on any floor.
4. Walls which terminate at roofs of not less than two-hour fire-resistive construction or roofs constructed entirely of noncombustible materials.
5. One-hour fire-resistive exterior walls may terminate at the underside of the roof sheathing, deck or slab, provided:
   - 5.1 Where the roof-ceiling elements are parallel to the walls, such framing and the elements supporting such framing shall be of not less than one-hour fire-resistive construction for a width of 5 feet on the interior side of the wall for group M and R Occupancies and 10 feet for all other occupancies.
   - 5.2 Where roof-ceiling framing elements are not parallel to the wall, the entire span of such framing and elements supporting such framing shall not be of less than one-hour fire-resistive construction.

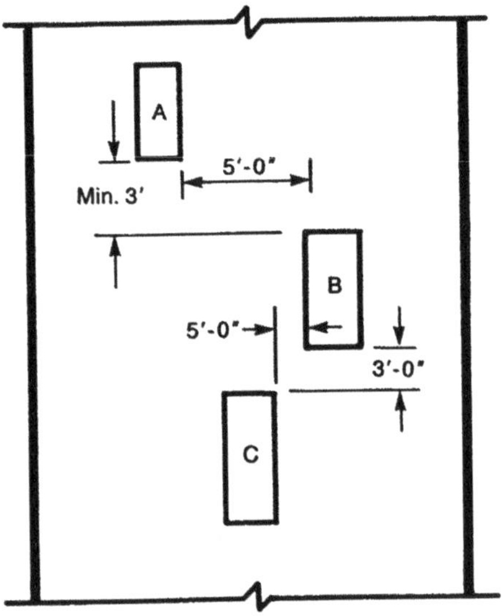

BUILDING ELEVATION
PARTIAL

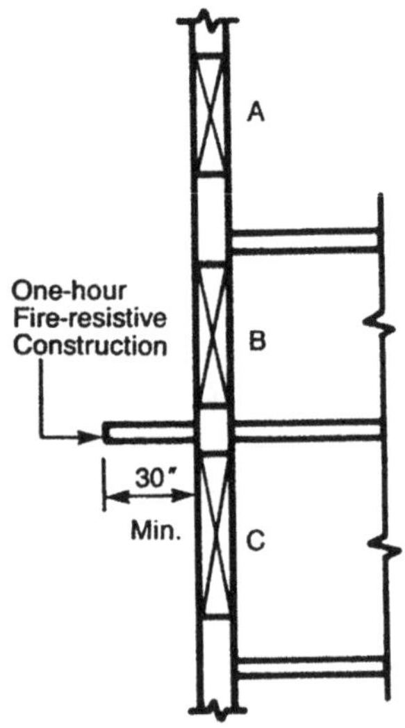

Exterior Wall Section

GIVEN:

Building is not sprinklered.
Window A is more then 5' laterally from window B.
Window C is either less than 5' laterally from window B, or less than 3' below window B, or both conditions apply.

If window A were less than 5' from window B, and there were room for a 3' high one-hour spandrel between windows A and B; that would meet Section 709.3.2.3 requirements. Otherwise, window A as shown does not require any special protection because it is more than 5' from window B.

Window C does not have sufficient room for a 3' height of one-hour spandrel. It is less than 5' from window B, therefore a one-hour "eyebrow" must be provided. The "eyebrow" must project at least 30" from the exterior wall.

REFERENCE: SECTION 709.3.2

FIGURE 8-9 VERTICAL FLAME SPREAD AT EXTERIOR WALLS-FLAME BARRIER

5.3 **Openings in the roof shall not be within 5 feet (1524 mm) of the one-hour fire-resistive exterior wall for Groups R and U Occupancies and 10 feet (3048 mm) for all other occupancies.**

5.4 **The entire building shall be provided with not less than a Class B roof assembly.**

The parapet requirements for all buildings are contained in this section. The exceptions generally cover a substantial number of buildings including most single-family dwellings. Exception 5 is an attempt to reduce the construction costs and problems associated with parapet construction. The exception does this without sacrificing the fire containment intent of the parapet provision.

The provisions of Exception 5 are somewhat similar to the provisions of Section 504.6.4 for the omission of parapets on area separation walls. However, because the concern is to assure that fire does not spread readily across a property line, the criteria for omitting the parapet are more restrictive than for the area separation wall.

A parapet can be omitted under Exception 5 only when the exterior wall is of not more than 1-hour fire-resistive construction. Thus, the exception does not apply to a building unless the exterior wall is permitted to be so constructed per Table 5-A. In some instances this would apply only when the buildings were set back as much as 40 feet from the property line.

Example: Group A (Public Assembly), Division 2.1 Occupancy.

Another requisite is that the roof must be at least Class B roof assembly. This requirement takes precedence over the other permissive roofing provisions of the code and the locality. Thus, a Class C or an unrated roof would not be permitted where the exception 5 provisions apply. This requirement was made a part of the exception so that the top surface of the roof-ceiling assembly would not readily be ignited from either

- an exterior fire brand falling on the roof or
- from a fire inside the building extending up through a skylight some distance from the exterior wall.

A Class B roofing assembly has substantially slower flame-spreading characteristics and uses larger brands in the tests required to obtain its rating than does a Class C roofing assembly. An unrated roofing assembly provides virtually no such protection.

The 1-hour fire-resistive roof-ceiling assembly requirements in Exception 5 are substantially more restrictive than those in Section 504.6.4 for area separation walls, except for Group R and U Occupancies, where they are comparable. The following are major differences for all occupancies, except Group R and U occupancies:

1. The 1-hour fire-resistive construction for the roof-ceiling assembly and the supports for the roof-ceiling assembly is to extend 10 feet from the exterior wall for framing parallel to that exterior wall.
2. The 1-hour fire-resistive construction is to extend for the entire span of the framing elements that are perpendicular to the exterior wall. The supports for the roof-ceiling assembly are also to be of not less than 1-hour fire-resistive construction.
3. Openings in the roof-ceiling assemblies for skylights are not to be within 10 feet of the exterior wall.

As with the supports for the roof-ceiling assembly adjacent to an area separation wall, the 1-hour fire-resistive construction applies to the amount of roof-ceiling assembly involved based on the direction of the framing. (See Figure 8-10.)

The openings in the roof are permitted based on the distance of the opening to the exterior wall on which the parapet is to be omitted. The intent of this provision was based on the assumption that the building was on, or immediately adjacent to, the property line as shown in Figure 8-10.

However, as seen in Table 5-A, many occupancies require a 1-hour wall without openings or with protected openings, when the exterior wall is 10 feet or more from the property line. In such instances, the roof openings will be at least 20 feet from the property line: The distance the exterior wall is from the property line plus the 10 feet the opening is set back from the exterior wall as required in Exception 5.3.

709.4.2 Construction. Parapets shall have the same degree of fire resistance required for the wall upon which they are erected and on any side adjacent to a roof surface shall have noncombustible faces for the uppermost 18 inches (457 mm), including counterflashing and coping materials. The height of the parapet shall be not less than 30 inches (762 mm) above the

point where the roof surface and the wall intersect. Where the roof slopes toward a parapet at slopes greater than 16.7% slope, the parapet shall extend to the same height as any portion of the roof that is within the distance where protection of wall openings would be required, but in no case shall the height be less than 30 inches (762 mm).

This section requires that a parapet have the same degree of fire resistance as the wall on which it is erected. As the walls can be area separation walls, the parapets that surmount them must have 1-hour, 2-hour or 4-hour construction.

Sections 504.6.5 and 709.4.2 require that the noncombustible surface of the parapet need only be provided for the upper 18 inches on both sides when above an area separation wall and on the roof side for other parapets. The intent of this provision is to prevent, through use of noncombustible surfacing materials, the spread of fire from one side of the area separation wall to the other and to require the roof covering to be effectively flashed. (See Figure 8-11.)

709.5 Nonsymetrical Wall Construction. Walls and partitions of nonsymetrical construction shall be tested with both faces exposed to the furnace, and the assigned fire-resistive rating will be the shortest duration obtained from the two tests conducted in conformance with UBC Standard 7-1. When evidence is furnished to show that the wall tested with the least fire-resistive side exposed to the furnace, subject to acceptance of the building official, the wall need not be subjected to tests from the opposite side.

The designer is urged to avoid the use of this section since it is unlikely that the designer and the building official will agree about the potential source of fire in the proposed building. It will be up to the designer to fully substantiate his or her position regarding the fire source and, in an obvious manner, convince the building official that the design is correct. Unless the designer is sure that this can be done, avoiding the use of this section may be the best course of action.

709.6 Through Penetrations.

709.6.1 General. Through penetrations of the fire-resistive walls shall comply with Section 709.6.2 or 709.6.3.

EXCEPTIONS: Where the penetrating items are steel, ferrous or copper pipes or steel conduits, the annular space shall be permitted to be protected as follows:

1. In concrete or masonry walls where the penetrating items are a maximum 6-inch (152 mm) nominal diameter and the opening is a maximum 144 square inches (92 903 mm^2) concrete, grout or mortar shall be

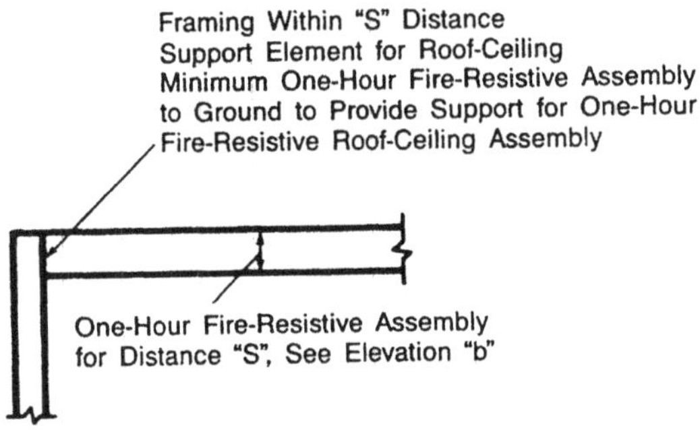

SECTION A-A

S = 5 feet for Group M and R Occupancies
= 10 feet for All Other Occupancies

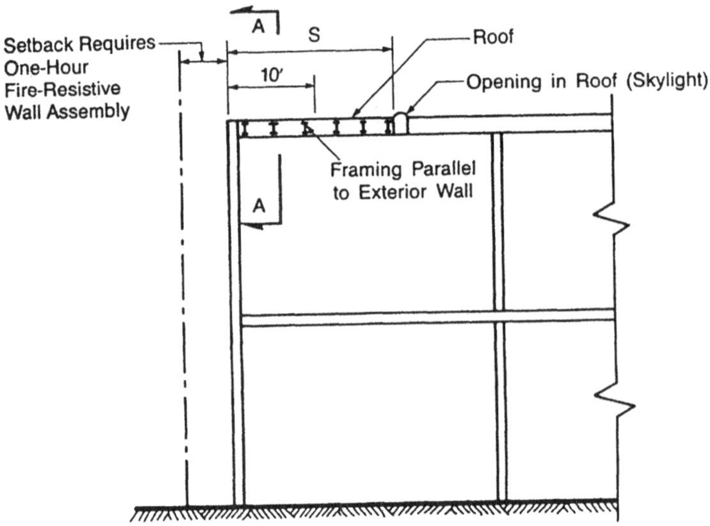

ELEVATION (b)

NOTE: Parapet may be omitted only when exterior wall is of one-hour fire-resistive construction.

REFERENCE: SECTION 709.4.1, EXCEPTION 5 AND TABLE 5-A

FIGURE 8-10 OMISSION OF PARAPETS AT EXTERIOR WALLS INCLUDING AT PROPERTY LINES FOR BUILDINGS WITH ONE-HOUR FIRE-RESISTIVE EXTERIOR WALL ASSEMBLIES

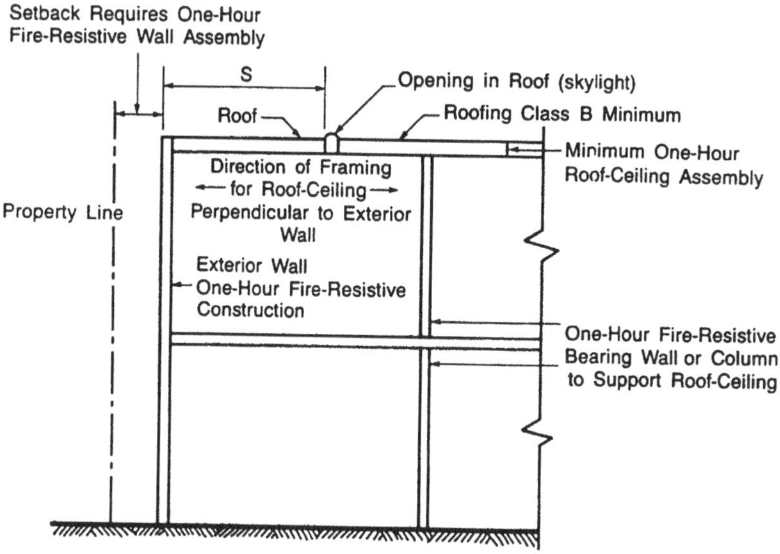

ELEVATION (a)

permitted when installed the full thickness of the wall or the thickness required to maintain the fire rating, or

2. The material used to fill the annular space shall prevent the passage of flame and hot gasses sufficient to ignite cotton waste when subjected to UBC Standard 7-1 time-temperature fire conditions under a minimum positive pressure differential of 0.01 inch of water column (2.5 Pa) at the location of the penetration for the time period equivalent to the fire rating of the construction penetrated.

709.6.2 Fire-rated assembly. Penetrations shall be installed as tested in the approved UBC Standard 7-1 rated assembly.

709.6.3 Penetration firestop system. Penetrations shall be protected by an approved penetration firestop system installed as tested in accordance with UBC Standard 7-5 and shall have an F rating of not less than the required rating of the wall penetrated.

709.7 Membrane Penetrations Membrane penetrations of the fire-resistive walls shall comply with Section 709.6

EXCEPTIONS: 1. Steel electrical boxes that do not exceed 16 square inches (10 323 mm^2) in area, provided that the area of each of such openings does not exceed 100 square inches for any 100 square feet (694 mm^2/m^2) of wall area. Outlet boxes on opposite sides of the wall shall be separated by a horizontal distance of not less than 24 inches (610 mm). Membrane penetrations for electrical outlet boxes of any material are permitted, provided that such boxes are tested for use in fire-resistive assemblies and installed in accordance with the tested assembly.

2. The annular space created by the penetration of a fire sprinkler shall be permitted to be unprotected, provided such space is covered by a metal escutcheon plate.

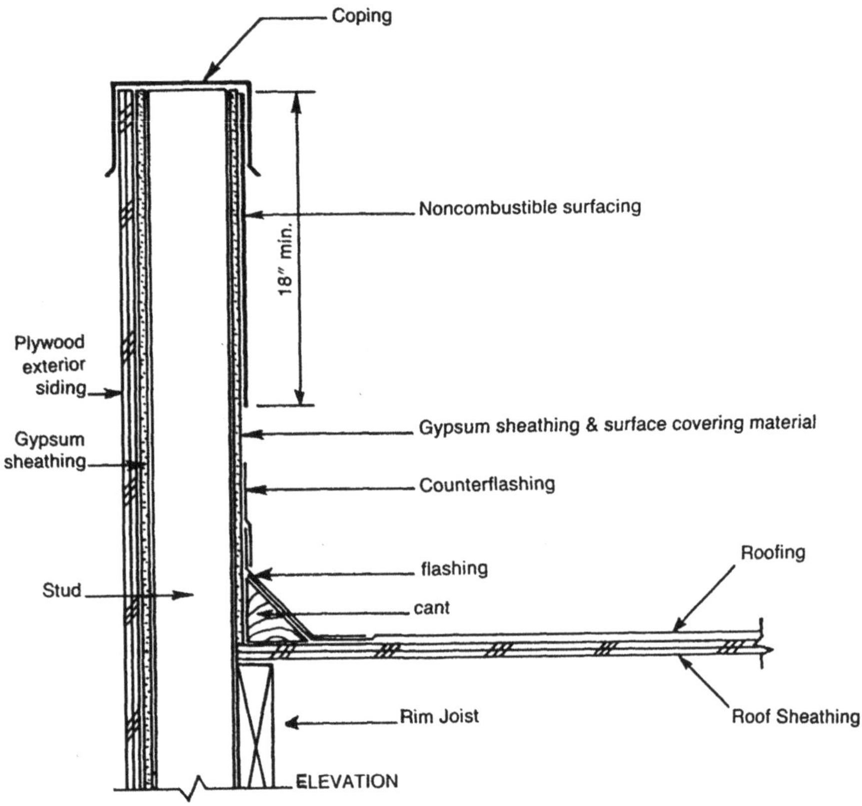

NOTES:
1. Coping can be part of non-combustible surfacing.
2. Where parapet is part of an area separation wall, the non-combustible surface must be on both sides of the parapet.

REFERENCE: SECTION 709.4.2 AND 504.6.4

FIGURE 8-11 PARAPET CONSTRUCTION DETAILS

Noncombustible penetrating items shall not be connected to combustible materials on both sides of the membrane unless it can be confirmed that the fire-resistive integrity of the wall is maintained in accordance with UBC Standards 7-1.

709.8 Joints. The protection of joints shall comply with the requirements of Section 706.

Section 709 has been substantially revised over the last three code cycles to reflect the concept of penetration fire stops. The prior code provisions appeared to permit penetrations of fire-resistive walls and partitions by steel or copper items without specific need for protection. The only provision relating to protection was the requirement for filling the space between the penetrating item and the wall surface. The present code provisions require a through-penetration fire stop for all such penetrations, except at special sited locations. Note that the noncombustible penetrating item referred to in the exception applies to any part of the connection between the penetrating item and the internal system, if present, such as a vertical riser.

The code provides a performance criteria for the space filler around a penetration. This provision alone does not solve the problems of penetrations or inclusions. It does, however, aid in establishing the physical characteristics essential for such sealant materials, namely that they must prevent passage of flame or hot gasses through the seal.

The listed devices referred to in Figure 8-12, as an example, meet both of these criteria.

The use of plastic piping, conduit and ducts in fire-resistive assemblies must require approved penetration devices be provided in accordance with these sections. There are approved penetration devices and installation procedures for PVC electrical raceways and components. It is expected that other devices will be approved for use with other plastic materials.

If the designer does not want to provide the penetration devices, these materials should be installed in nonfire-resistive locations instead of within fire-resistive walls.

SECTION 710—FLOOR CEILINGS OR ROOF CEILINGS

710.1 General. Fire-resistive floors, floor-ceiling or roof-ceiling assemblies shall be assumed to have the fire-resistance ratings set forth in Table 7-C. When materials are incorporated into an otherwise fire-resistive assembly that may change the capacity for heat dissipation, fire test results or other substantiating data shall be made available to the building official to show that the required fire-resistive time period is not reduced.

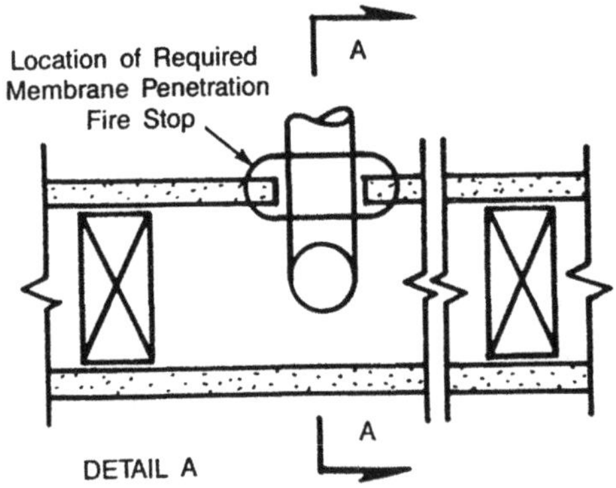

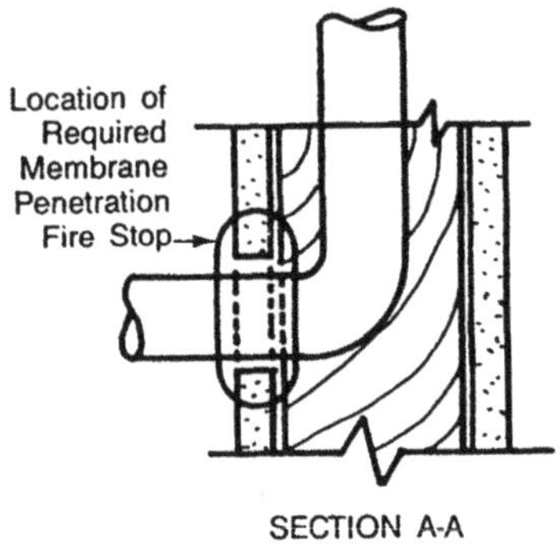

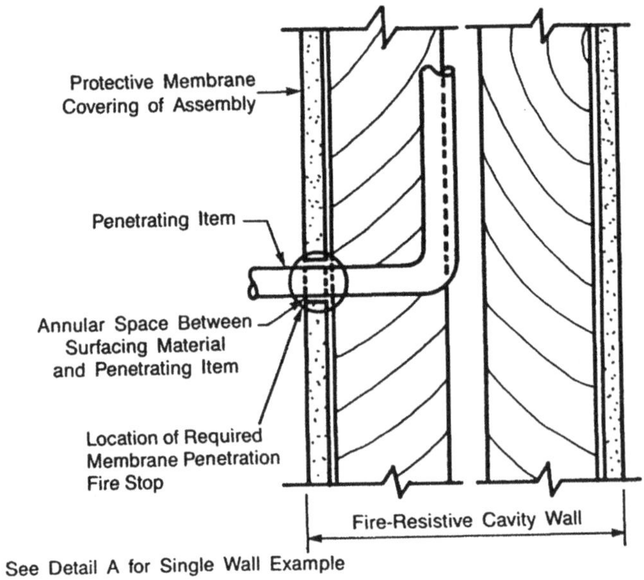

NOTES:
1. See Section 709.7, Exception 2
2. The annular space around the membrane penetrations shall be not more than 1/8-inch wide unless a greater width is permitted by the approved listing.
3. Note #2 also applies to penetrations of plates.

REFERENCE: SECTION 709.7

FIGURE 8-12 ILLUSTRATION OF THE USE OF A PENETRATION FIRE STOP

Where the weight of lay-in ceiling panels used as part of fire-resistive floor-ceiling or roof-ceiling assemblies is not adequate to resist the upward force of 1 pound per square foot (0.048 kN/m^2), wire holddowns or other approved devices shall be installed above the panels to prevent vertical displacement under such upward force.

710.2 Through Penetrations.

710.2.1 General. Through penetrations of fire-resistive horizontal assemblies shall be enclosed in fire-resistive shaft enclosures in accordance with Section 711.1 or shall comply with Section 710.2.2 or 710.2.3.

EXCEPTIONS: 1. Steel, ferrous or copper conduits, pipes, tubes, vents, concrete, or masonry penetrating items that penetrate a single fire-rated floor assembly where the annular space is protected with materials that prevent the passage of flame and hot gases sufficient to ignite cotton waste when subjected to UBC Standard 7-1 time-temperature fire conditions under a minimum positive pressure differential of 0.01 inch of water column (2.5 Pa) at the location of the penetration for the time period equivalent to the fire-resistive rating of the construction penetrated. Penetrating items with a maximum 6-inch (152 mm) nominal diameter shall not be limited to the penetration of a single-fire-resistive floor assembly, provided that the area of the penetration does not exceed 144 square inches in any 100 square feet (100 000 mm^2 in 10 m^2) of floor area.)

2. Penetrations in a single concrete floor by steel, ferrous or copper conduits, pipes, tubes and vents with a maximum 6-inch (152 mm) nominal diameter provided concrete, grout or mortar is installed the full thickness required to maintain the fire-resistive rating. The penetrating items with a maximum 6-inch (152 mm) nominal diameter shall not be limited to the penetration of a single concrete floor, provided that the area of the penetration does not exceed 144 square inches (92 903 mm^2).

3. Electrical outlet boxes of any material are permitted provided that such boxes are tested for use in fire-resistive assemblies and installed in accordance with the tested assembly.

710.2.2 Fire-rated assemblies. Penetrations shall be installed as tested in the approved UBC Standard 7-1.

710.2.3 Penetration firestop system. Penetration shall be protected by an approved penetration firestop system installed as tested in accordance with UBC Standard 7-5. The system shall have an F rating and a T rating of not less than one hour but not less than the required rating of the floor penetrated.

EXCEPTION: Floor penetrations contained and located within the cavity of a wall do not require a T rating.

710.3 Membrane Penetrations. Penetrations of membranes that are part of a fire-resistive horizontal assembly shall comply with Section 710.2.

EXCEPTIONS: 1. Membrane penetrations of steel, ferrous or copper conduits, electrical outlet boxes, pipes, tubes, vents, concrete, or masonry penetrating items where the annular space is protected in accordance with Section 709.6 or 710.2 or is protected to prevent the free passage of flame and the products of combustion. Such penetrations shall not exceed an aggregate area of 100 square inches an any 100 square feet (694 mm^2/m^2) of ceiling area in assemblies tested without penetrations.

2. Membrane penetrations for electrical outlet boxes on any material are permitted, provided that such boxes are tested for use in fire-resistive assemblies and installed in accordance with the tested assembly.

3. The annular space created by the penetration of a fire sprinkler shall be permitted to be unprotected, provided such space is covered by a metal escutcheon plate.

710.6 Joints. The protection of joints in fire-resistive floors and roofs shall comply with the requirements of Section 706.

The primary use of the through-penetration fire stop and membrane penetration fire stop are for penetrations of fire-resistive walls and floors. Section 710.2 contains provisions for these penetrations. The requirements for walls (walls and partitions) and floors (floor-ceiling or roof-ceilings) are contained in two separate code sections although much of the language is the same. In addition to the wall and floor regulations in these sections, the requirements for roofs, wiring in plenums and the requirements for construction joints and the exterior wall-floor intersection are also present.

Section 710.1 specifically requires that when, in the judgment of the enforcement official, a material is made part of a fire-resistive assembly and may change the assembly's performance, the user must provide substantiation that the fire-resistive time period is not affected.

This provision establishes the authority and responsibility of the enforcement official in assuring proper construction of fire-resistive assemblies. Failure to obtain such valid substantiating data can result in a 50 percent reduction of a fire-resistive assembly's rating, based on full-scale fire tests.

The burden of providing that data for the proposed use rests with the applicant. The enforcement official should obtain these data before permitting the job to proceed, in the same way the official would require structural data for the use of a new truss system.

Note that the through-penetration fire stop must have an F rating for any penetration of a floor, but need only have a T rating when the item is outside a wall where it penetrates the floor or the item exceeds the minimum allowed sizes for exemption.

The wall-floor intersection, and construction joints in general, have presented serious fire spread problems over the years. In many high-rise fires, this has been a primary means of fire spread from floor to floor. Although some enforcement agencies regulate this area of a building by requiring that the fire-resistive requirement of the floor be maintained, there was not a specific code provision for officials to cite. Prior enforcement was based on the logic of the continuity of fire-resistive construction.

With this section in the code, officials can readily insist that continuity of fire resistance rating be demonstrated on the drawings. The designer should provide an adequate number of details to cover the building's wall-floor and other construction joint conditions. Often at the exterior wall-floor intersection there will be an exterior column and spandrel located in this area. The details should provide for these intersections as well.

> In the authors' opinion, three-dimensional representations should be used to assure the closure intended by this provision.

Section 710.2.1, Exceptions, clarifies the permissible noncombustible penetration items that previously were not limited in size. In particular, the space around any such penetration must be filled with noncombustible material meeting specific performance criteria.

A common violation found in the field is a hole drilled through a floor slab to install a new telephone outlet. The cables may be run in the concealed space of the story below. If a fire resistance rating is required for the floor, an unprotected penetration is not permitted. Such an opening violates that fire rating because it would permit fire, smoke and gases to enter the floor above in less than the rated time period. (See Figure 8-6.)

Intumescent and other materials or devices may be useful in these installations. The UL Fire Resistance Directory and ICBO Evaluation Reports should be used to determine the best material and arrangement for a particular application. The designer should not rely on the contractor how best to restore the integrity of holes or penetrated areas in floors.

SECTION 711—SHAFT ENCLOSURES

711.1 General. Openings through floors shall be enclosed in a shaft enclosure of fire-resistive construction having the time period set forth In Table No. 6-A for "Shaft Enclosures" except as permitted in Sections 711.3, 711.5 and 711.6. See also Section 304.6 for shafts in Group B Occupancies, Section 306.6 for shafts in Group F Occupancies, Sections 307.6 and 307.11.2.3 for shafts in Group H Occupancies, Section 309.6 for shafts in Group M occupancies and Section 311.6 for shafts in Group S Occupancies.

711.2 Extent of Enclosures. Shaft enclosures shall extend from the lowest floor opening through successive floor openings and shall be enclosed at the top and bottom.

EXCEPTIONS: 1. Shafts extending through or to the underside of the roof sheathing, deck or slab need not be enclosed at the top.

2. Shafts need not be enclosed at the bottom when protected by fire dampers conforming to approved recognized standards, installed at the lowest floor level within the shaft enclosure.

Shaft enclosures shall be constructed to continuously maintain the required fire-resistive integrity.

711.3 Special Provisions. In other than Group I Occupancies, openings which penetrate only one floor and are not connected with openings communicating with other stories or basement and which are not concealed within the building construction need not be enclosed.

Exit enclosures shall conform to the applicable provisions of Section 1005.3.3.

In one- and two-story buildings of other than Group I Occupancies, gas vents, ducts, piping and factory-built chimneys which extend through not more than two floors need not be enclosed, provided the openings around the penetrations are fire stopped at each floor.

EXCEPTION: BW gas vents installed in accordance with their listing.

Gas vents and factory-built chimneys shall be protected as required by the Mechanical Code.

Walls containing gas vents or noncombustible piping which pass through three floors or stories need not provide the fire-resistance rating specified in Table No. 6-A for "Shaft Enclosures," provided the annular space around the vents or piping is filled at each floor or ceiling with noncombustible materials.

EXCEPTION: BW gas vents installed in accordance with their listing.

Openings made through a floor for penetrations such as cables, cable-trays, conduit, pipes or tubing which are protected with approved through-penetration firestops to provide the same degree of fire-resistance as the floor construction need not be enclosed. For floor-ceiling assemblies see Section 710.

711.4 Protection of Openings. Openings into a shaft enclosure shall be protected by self-closing or automatic-closing fire assembly conforming to Section 713 and having a fire-protection rating of one-hour for openings through one-hour walls and one and one-half hours through two-hour fire-resistive walls.

EXCEPTIONS: 1. Openings to the exterior may be unprotected when permitted by Table No. 5-A.

2. Openings protected by through-penetration fire stops to provide the same degree of fire resistance as the shaft enclosure. See Sections 709 and 710.

3. Noncombustable ducts, vents or chimneys used to convey vapors, dusts or combustion products may penetrate the enclosure at the bottom.

711.5 Rubbish and Linen Chute Termination Rooms. In other than Group R, Division 3 Occupancies, rubbish and linen chutes shall terminate in rooms separated from the remainder of the building by an occupancy separation having the same degree of fire resistance as required for the shaft enclosure,

but not less than one-hour. Openings into chutes and chute termination rooms shall not be located in exit corridors or stairways. For sprinklers, see Section 904.2.2.

711.6 Chute & Dumbwaiter Shafts. In buildings of Type V construction, chutes and dumbwaiter shafts with a cross-sectional area of not more than 9 square feet (.084 m^2) may be either of approved fire-resistive wall construction or may have the inside layers of the approved fire-resistive assembly replaced by a lining of not less than 0.019-inch (0.48 mm) No. 26 galvanized sheet gage metal with all joints locklapped. The outside layers of the wall shall be as required for the approved construction. All openings into any such enclosure shall be protected by not less than a self closing solid wood door 1⅜ inches (35 mm) thick or equivalent.

This section has been extensively revised, primarily editorially, from the previous code additions with some material transferred to the appropriate occupancy classifications in Chapter 3. This was done when the UBC was reformatted to be consistent with the "common code format." This will be explored in more detail in the discussion of shaft and exit enclosures.

This section provides the exceptions to the general requirement of Table 6-A that shafts be enclosed with walls of fire-resistive construction.

The provisions of Section 711 are comparable to the provisions in Section 1005.3.3 dealing with stairways. Both sets of provisions require the enclosures except when the openings are through only two adjacent floors.

Section 711.6 describes small shafts, less than 9 square feet in cross-sectional area, in Type V buildings only, which may have lesser construction than would be required for a fire-resistive wall assembly. (See Figure 8-13.)

The intent of this item is to facilitate the construction of small cross-sectional area shafts, the interiors of which workers cannot finish as required for fire-resistive assemblies.

The requirements for elevator shafts are also located in Chapter 30.

SECTION 712—USABLE SPACE UNDER FLOORS

Usable space under the first story shall be enclosed, and such enclosure, when constructed of metal or wood, shall be protected on the side of the usable space as required for one-hour fire-resistive construction. Doors shall be self-closing, tightfitting of solid-wood construction 1⅜ inches (35 mm) in thickness or self-closing, tightfitting doors acceptable as a part of an assembly having a fire-protection rating of not less than 20 minutes when tested in accordance with Part II of UBC Standard 7-2.

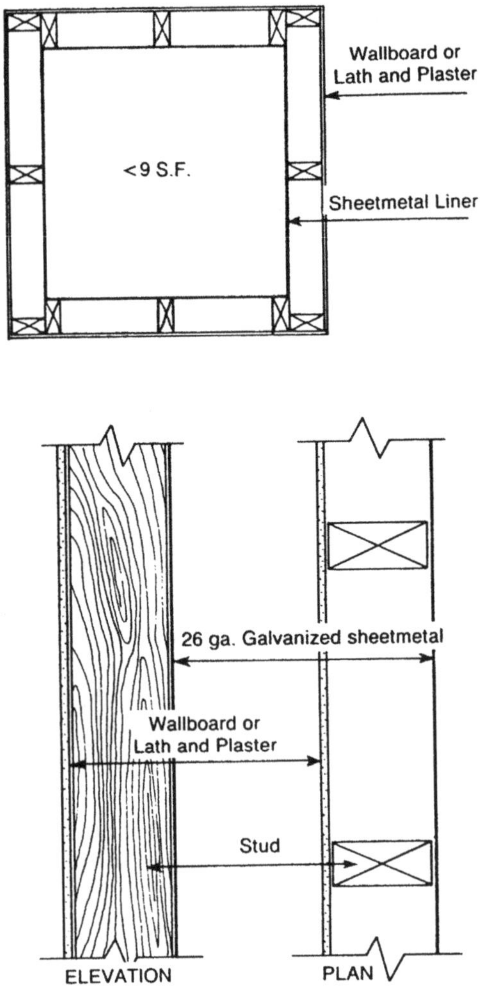

SMALL SHAFTS < 9 S.F.

NOTE: Openings to have metal or metal clad-doors, jambs, casings or frames.

REFERENCE: SECTION 711.6

FIGURE 8-13 SMALL SHAFT WALL CONSTRUCTION-TYPE V BUILDINGS

EXCEPTIONS: 1. Group R, Division 3 and Group U Occupancies.
2. Basements in single-story Group S, Division 3 repair garages where 10 percent or more of the area of the floor-ceiling is open to the first floor.
3. Underfloor spaces protected by an automatic sprinkler system.

This section permits the omission of certain fire protection for the usable space under the first floor. The designer is cautioned to consider this provision together with the definition of "story" and be sure that the design provides a reasonable level of code compliance. These two code provisions, Section 712 and the story definition, present a conflict.

If the space below the first floor meets the following criteria, i.e., if the height above grade exceeds

- 6 feet average for more than 50 percent of the perimeter or
- 12 feet at any point,

by definition that space is a story.

> In the authors' opinion, whether the space is usable or not, the space should be protected in the same manner as the rest of the building. A fire in that space could cause collapse of the building unless the surfaces enclosing the space are protected.

The term "usable space" is often a transient concept; that is, the space may be unused today and used tomorrow. The designer should be aware of this possibility and the tendency of individuals to use all available space. The designer should consider providing the built-in protection.

The conflict between what the code allows and what, logically, should be done has concerned many building and fire officials. However, at present there exists no code change proposal that would resolve the conflict.

SECTION 713—FIRE-RESISTIVE ASSEMBLIES FOR PROTECTION OF OPENINGS

713.1 General. Where required by this code for fire protection of openings, fire assemblies shall meet the requirements of this section.

This section contains the requirements for fire-resistive openings, i.e., doors and windows. When fire doors are installed in corridors, they are often used by designers as part of the air-handling system for the corridor of the floor. This has been the case particularly in apartment houses and hotels. This misuse of fire doors is a violation of the integrity of the corridor fire doors.

The basic document on which fire doors are tested and installations controlled, aside from the UL standard fire test for doors, the National Fire Protection Association NFPA Standard 80 for fire doors and windows. In that NFPA standard is the following clear statement:

> **Fire doors equiped with automatic louvers shall be used only when the opening is not in an exit or otherwise located so that products of combustion flowing through the opening could jeopardize the use of exits prior to operation of the louver.**

In the Uniform Mechanical Code (UMC), Section 601.1.1 contains the following prohibition:

> **Corridors shall not be used to convey air to or from rooms if the corridor is required to be of fire-resistive construction by Section 1005 of the Building Code.**

The prohibition of louvers in corridor fire doors has its corollary in the UMC provisions prohibiting the openings or undercutting of fire doors to exhaust air from a corridor into a guest room or dwelling unit as part of the corridor air-handling system.

The intent is manifest: If the corridor is used as part of the air-handling system and smoke is in the corridor, the smoke will be brought into the apartments and the guest rooms. Not only will the corridor be untenable in such a situation, but all dwelling units will also be made untenable. There will be no way for occupants to escape the smoke and gases.

Therefore, the corridor walls are to be maintained as smoke and fire barriers. In fact Section 1004.3.4.3.2.1 requires a 20-minute door to be "a tight-fitting smoke and draft-control assembly." This smoke and draft-control door should provide protection to the dwelling units and guest rooms in the event the occupants cannot exit through the corridor.

As an extension of this rationale, the designer should avoid specifying excessive undercutting of the corridor fire doors for clearing carpets or other floor covering. The designer should note the imposed limitation of the $\frac{3}{4}$ inch for such undercuts in Section 2-5.4 of the NFPA 80.

713.2 Definitions.

FIRE ASSEMBLY is the assembly of a fire door, fire windows or fire damper, including all required hardware, anchorage, frames and sills.

FIRE ASSEMBLY, AUTOMATIC CLOSING, is a fire assembly that may remain in an open position and that will close automatically when subjected to one or the other of the following:

1. An increase in temperature.

Unless otherwise specified, the closing device shall be one rated at a maximum temperature of 165°F (74°C).

2. Actuation of a smoke detector.

The closing device shall operate by the activation of an approved listed smoke detector. Smoke detectors shall be installed and maintained as set forth in the approved nationally recognized standards.

FIRE ASSEMBLY, SELF-CLOSING, is a fire assembly that is kept in a normally closed position and is equiped with an approved device to ensure closing and latching after having been opened for use.

These definitions describe two types of fire door closing methods, the automatic-closing and the self-closing.

> In the authors' opinion, although both are legal in most locations where fire doors are required, the self-closing door is more reliable.

However, an automatic-closing door activated by a smoke detector release device could be as reliable as the self-closing door.

The reason the authors favor the self-closing mode of operation is that automatic-closing doors are all too often accidently, or deliberately, blocked open. These doors normally remain open and not are recognized as providing the necessary closure in emergencies. Furthermore, the automatic door is permitted to have a temperature-activated release device, usually a fusible link. These devices are slow activating and allow considerable quantities of smoke and toxic gases through the opening before activating.

The self-closing door, on the other hand, it is expected to operate in the same way in an emergency. It is normally in the closed position, thereby preventing the smoke and toxic gases from passing through the opening during the early stages of a fire. The self-closing door is therefore more reliable as a fire assembly.

713.6 Hardware.

713.6.1 Closing devices. Every fire assembly shall be provided with a closing device as follows:

1. Fire assemblies required to have a three-hour fire-protection rating shall be automatic-closing fire assemblies. Automatic-closing fire assemblies to be activated by an increase in temperature shall have one heat-activating device installed on each side of the wall at the top of the opening and one on each side of the wall at the ceiling height where the ceiling is more than 3 feet (914 mm) above the top of the opening.

2. Fire assemblies required to have a one- and one-half-hour, one-hour or three-fourths-hour fire-protection rating shall be either automatic- or self-closing fire assemblies. Automatic-closing fire assemblies to be activated by an increase in temperature shall have heat-activating devices located as required in Item 1 or by a single fusible link in the opening incorporated in the closing device.

3. Fire door assemblies required to have fire-protection rating, which are installed across a corridor, shall be automatic-closing fire assemblies. Such fire assemblies shall be activated by a smoke detector. All hold-open devices shall be listed for the purpose and shall release or close the door in the event of a power failure at the device.

4. Fire assemblies required by provisions of Chapter 10 shall have closing devices as specified in Chapter 10.

5. Doors that are a part of an automobile ramp enclosure shall be equiped with automatic-closing devices.

Fire doors that are automatic closing by smoke detection shall not have a closing or reclosing delay of more than 10 seconds.

The designer should consider the installation of the smoke-detector-activated hold-open devices of item 3 for any stairway used by the building occupants on a regular basis, such as those in hospitals and schools. Hospital employees often use the stairs when the number of service elevators is inadequate or when they need to rush from floor to floor without delay.

Smoke is the primary hazard in any occupancy. Reliance on fusible links to activate stairway door closures is a poor practice because a substantial amount of smoke could enter before the closer activates. A smoke-detector-operated release device is strongly recommended even though they are not mandated for stairway doors in the present code. They afford considerably greater protection at a nominal cost increase.

The designer is also advised to consider the use of smoke-detector-activated hold-open devices for all locations where it is believed that a door may constitute a nuisance barrier to the free flow of traffic. In such instances, the occupants tend to wedge the door open. The designer would be exercising good professional judgment if the design were to incorporate a reliable method of holding the door open; one which would still afford the desired protection in the event of a fire.

713.8 Fire Window Size. Fire windows required to have a three-fourths-hour fire-protection rating for protection of openings in exterior walls shall have an area not greater than 84 square feet (7.8 m²) with neither width nor height exceeding 12 feet (3658 mm) and for protection of openings in interior walls shall be limited in area and size to that tested.

This section establishes the size limitation for $\frac{3}{4}$-hour fire windows. The designer is reminded of the glazing materials discussed under Section 713.9 below, which have recently become available. These materials enable the installation of clear glass fire windows—having no internal wires—which have been tested and labeled for 1-hour fire resistance. These are expensive at present but in certain locations the costs will decrease. When that time comes, these windows will provide the designer with additional flexibility in design.

713.9 Glazing. Glazing materials and glass block assemblies shall be qualified by tests in accordance with UBC Standard 7-2 (for fire doors) or UBC Standard 7-4 (for fire windows) as appropriate for the use, and they shall be labeled for the required fire-protection rating and installed in accordance with their listing. Glazing in fire door assemblies and in fire window assemblies subject to human impact in hazardous locations as indicated in Section 2406.4 shall comply with Section 2406.3.

This section contains the glazing requirements for glass used in fire doors and windows. The prior codes permitted generic wired glass for such glazing. The code now requires that all glazing be tested, labeled and listed and installed in accordance with the listing. In general, all glazing in fire assemblies must be installed using ferrous frames and retainers. The designer can cover the steel frame of the window with any material desired to make the window more aesthetically acceptable.

713.10 Smoke Dampers. Not less than Class II, 250°F (121°C) smoke dampers complying with approved recognized standards (see Chapter 35, Part IV) shall be installed and be accessible for inspection and servicing in the following ducted or unducted air openings at:

1. Penetrations of area or occupancy separation walls.

2. Penetrations of the fire-resistive construction of horizontal exit walls or corridors serving as a means of egress.

EXCEPTION: Openings for steel ducts penetrating the required fire-resistive construction of corridors are not required to have smoke dampers when such ducts are of not less than 0.019-inch (0.48 mm) thickness (No. 26 galvanized sheet steel gage) and have no openings serving the corridor.

3. Penetrations of shaft enclosures.

4. Penetrations of smoke barriers.

5. Penetrations of elevator lobbies required by Section 3002.

6. Penetrations of areas of refuge.

EXCEPTION: Ventilation systems specifically designed and protected to supply outside air to these areas during an emergency.

The locations requiring smoke dampers are listed in Section 713.10. Prior to the 1994 UBC, smoke dampers were specifically required only in Group E and I occupancies in what are now Sections 305.2.2 and 308.2.2.

713.11 Fire Dampers. Fire dampers complying with the requirements of approved recognized standards (see Chapter 35, Part IV) shall be installed and be accessible for inspection and servicing in the following ducted air openings at:

1. Penetrations through area separation walls or occupancy separations.

2. Penetrations of the fire-resistive construction of horizontal exit walls or corridors serving as a means of egress.

EXCEPTION: Openings for steel ducts penetrating the required fire-resistive construction of corridors are not required to have smoke dampers when such ducts are of not less than 0.019-inch (0.48 mm) thickness (No. 26 galvanized sheet steel gage) and have no openings serving the corridor.

3. Penetrations of shaft enclosures.

EXCEPTIONS: 1. Duct penetrations by steel exhaust air subducts extending vertically upward at least 22 inches (559 mm) above the top of the opening in a vented shaft where the airflow is upward.

2. Penetrations of a fire-resistive floor forming the base of a shaft enclosure may be protected by fire dampers listed for installation in the horizontal position.

4. Penetrations of the ceiling of fire-resistive floor-ceiling or roof-ceiling assemblies shall be protected in accordance with Section 710.3.

5. Penetrations of an atrium enclosure element.

6. Penetrations of the building exterior required to have protected openings by Section 503.

7. Penetrations of areas of refuge.

EXCEPTION: Ventilation systems specifically designed and protected to supply outside air to these areas during an emergency.

A fire damper is not required where fire tests have demonstrated that fire dampers are not required to maintain the fire resistance of the construction.

The operating temperature of the fire-damper actuating device shall be approximately 50°F (27.8°C) above the normal temperature within the duct system, but not less than 160°F (71°C). The operating temperature of the actuating device may be increased to not more than 286°F (141°C) when located in a smoke-control system complying with Chapter 9.

The requirements for fire dampers can be summarized as follows:

WHERE REQUIRED:

1. Through occupancy separations,
2. through area separation walls,
3. horizontal exit walls,
4. through shaft enclosures,
5. through fire-resistive floor-ceiling assemblies,
6. through fire-resistive elements of corridor walls,
7. atrium enclosure elements,
8. building exterior required to have protected openings by Section 503 and
9. areas of refuge.

WHERE EXCEPTED:

1. Where subducts are used in shafts,
2. where there are horizontal fire dampers immediately above them in shafts,
3. in corridors where steel ducts without corridor openings are used and
4. where tests have demonstrated that fire dampers are not required.

The substantive changes to this section are:

1. The addition of another exception to item 3. This permits the omission of a vertical fire damper on one floor provided there is a horizontal fire damper in the shaft above the location. (See Figure 8-14.)
2. The cross-reference in item 4 to the Section 710.3 provisions.

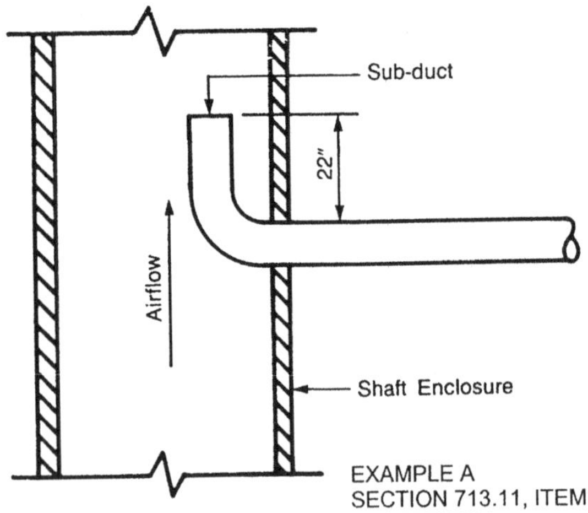

EXAMPLE A
SECTION 713.11, ITEM 3
EXCEPTION 1

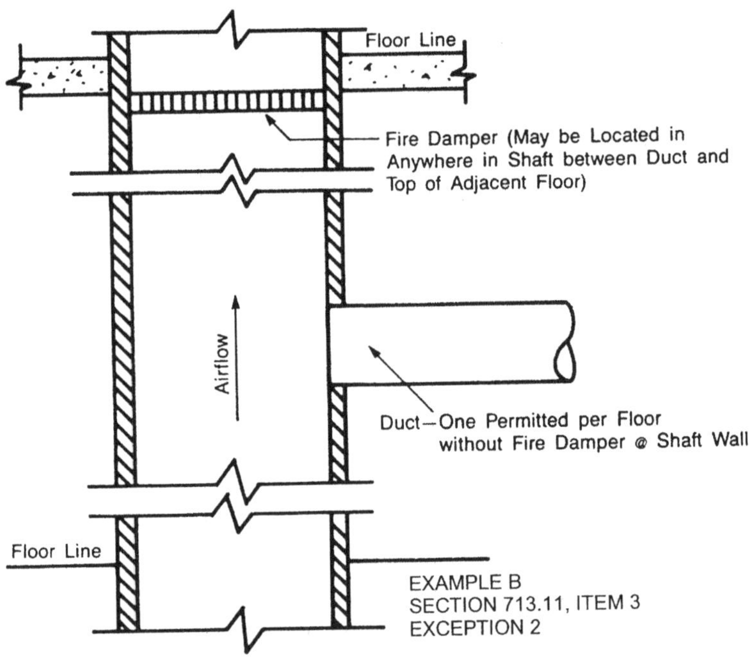

EXAMPLE B
SECTION 713.11, ITEM 3
EXCEPTION 2

REFERENCE: SECTION 713.11

FIGURE 8-14 PERMISSIBLE OMISSION OF FIRE DAMPER FOR SHAFTS WITH DUCT PENETRATIONS

SECTION 714—THROUGH-PENETRATION FIRE STOPS

Through-penetration fire stops required by this code shall have an F or T rating as determined by tests conducted in accordance with UBC Standard 7-5.

Through-penetration fire stops may be used for membrane penetrations.

The F rating shall apply to all through penetrations and shall not be less than the required fire-resistance rating of the assembly penetrated.

The T rating shall apply to those through-penetration locations required to have T ratings as specified in Section 710.3 and shall not be less than the required fire-resistance rating of the assembly penetrated.

Where sleeves are used, the sleeves shall be securely fastened to the assembly penetrated. All space between the item contained in sleeve and the sleeve itself and any space between the sleeve and the assembly penetrated shall be protected. Insulation and coverings on the penetrating item shall not penetrate the assembly unless the specific materials used have been tested as part of the assembly.

EXCEPTION: Fire damper or combination fire damper/smoke damper sleeves shall be installed in accordance with their listing.

Although this section is located toward the end of Chapter 7, it forms the basis for the through-penetration fire-stop performance requirements. The test standard is based on ASTM E814. For a discussion of the difference between the two standards, see Technical Appendix TA4.

The test provision for qualifying membrane penetration fire stops is UBC Standard 7-5.

The common requirement for all penetration fire stops is that they must at least meet the F rating of the assembly penetrated. Thus, if the area separation wall is of 2-hour fire-resistive construction, the F rating of the penetration fire stop through that wall must be at least 2 hours.

Where a T rating is required in Section 710.3, that rating must also be not less than the fire-resistive rating of the assembly penetrated. (See Figure 8-14.)

Table 7-B Item 18: The description of construction no longer makes reference to "or $\frac{3}{8}$-inch exterior-type plywood." This was deleted in a previous edition of the UBC. This change resulted from the finding that the original listing of the plywood assembly in the 1967 UBC was not based on actual fire test data. Recent full-scale fire tests have proven that the plywood assembly did not meet the 1-hour fire test criteria.

Designers desiring to use plywood-surfaced exterior walls can still do so provided the wall assembly complies with an approved 1-hour fire-resistive wall. (See Figure 8-15.) One such assembly

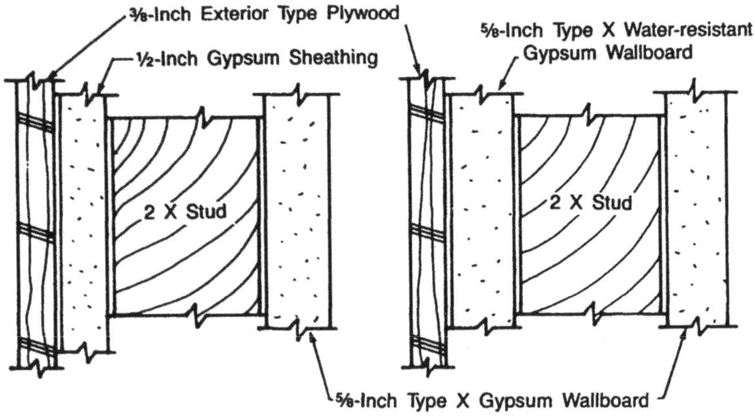

DETAIL "A"

ASSEMBLY DELETED FROM TABLE FORMERLY PART OF ITEM 75

DETAIL "B"

ACCEPTABLE ASSEMBLY

The plywood assembly with 1/2-inch gypsum sheathing, which was contained in Item 75 of prior codes, has been deleted. There are alternative systems that can provide the required one-hour fire resistance ratings. These are one-hour assemblies that are listed in Table 7-B for interior use and which, when placed under the plywood weatherboarding can make an acceptable assembly.

One such material to take the place of the 1/2-inch gypsum sheathing could be 5/8-inch water-resistant Type X gypsum wall board per Item 17 in Table 7-B.

REFERENCE: SECTION 703.2 AND TABLE 7-B

FIGURE 8-15 EXTERIOR PLYWOOD SURFACED ONE-HOUR FIRE-RESISTIVE WALL, TABLE 7-B MATERIALS CHANGE

could be a typical $\frac{5}{8}$-inch Type X gypsum wallboard assembly similar to Item 17-1.3 in Table 7-B.

With the use of water-resistant gypsum wallboard or backing board and the $\frac{3}{8}$-inch minimum exterior plywood covering, the assembly should satisfy both fire and water resistance requirements of the code.

In Section 703.3 of the code, reference is made to the method for calculating the fire resistance of materials or assemblies. These are found in Standard 7-7, UBC Volume 3.

In recent years considerable effort has gone to reduce the cost of fire testing by using existing data, the physical and thermal characteristics of materials and computers to establish mathematical models of performance. These have been done primarily for steel protected by coverings such as wallboard, concrete and spray-applied fire protection materials and for concrete walls, floors roofs, columns and beams.

The provisions for calculating fire ratings for these two basic materials were added to the UBC Standards in 1985. The standards now include material to assist in determining fire rating for some wood-based assemblies in Part III of that standard.

UBC Standard 7-7
Methods of Calculating Fire Resistance

Part V: Methods for Calculating Fire-Resistive Ratings of Wood-Framed Walls Floors and Roofs (See Section 703.3, Uniform Building Code)

SECTION 7.721—SCOPE

This part establishes acceptable calculation methods for determining the fire-resistive classification of structural parts, walls and partitions and floor-ceiling and roof-ceiling assemblies. It is intended for use in cases where fire test results specified in UBC Standard 7-1 are not available and the specific assembly of materials is not among those listed in Tables 7-A, 7-B and 7-C.

Wood-framed Walls, Floors and Roofs

SECTION 7.722—GENERAL

These procedures apply to both load-bearing and nonbearing construction. The calculated fire-resistive ratings shall only apply to one hour construction. When the wall construction is nonsymetrical, the provisions of Section 709.5 of the Building Code apply.

SECTION 7.723—PROCEDURES

The fire-resistive rating of wood-framed construction is equal to the sum of the time assigned to the membrane on the fire-exposed side (Table 7-7-W-A), the time assigned to the framing members (Table 7-7-W-C), and the time assigned for other protective measures, such as insulation (Table 7-7-W-D). The membrane on the unexposed shall not be included in determining the fire resistance of the assembly. When more than one membrane is installed on the wall surface exposed to fire, ratings of each membrane may be added.

SECTION 7.724—WALLS AND PARTITIONS

Table 7-7-W-A lists the time of fire resistance accredited to the materials used on the fire-exposed side of walls and partitions.

SECTION 7.725—ROOF-CEILING AND FLOOR-CEILING ASSEMBLIES

Table 7-7-W-B specifies the various acceptable membranes and limits the structural frame to wood joists installed on no more than 16-inch spacing (406 mm) spacings. Ratings for roof-ceiling and floor-ceiling assemblies are based on the membranes listed in Table 7-7-W-A being installed on the fire-exposed side in combination with membranes listed in Table 7-7-W-B being installed on the side not exposed to furnace temperatures.

SECTION 7.726—MEMBRANE FASTENING

Fastening the membrane to the supporting construction shall be as specified in Tables 7-B, 7-C and 23-II-B-1 of the Building Code for corresponding membrane materials.

For brevity, only the opening text of the wood provisions in this standard has been reproduced here. This discussion will relate only to wood assemblies.

The designer desiring to use this method of determining the fire resistance of a system is directed to the complete text of the standard in Volume 3 of the 1997 UBC.

An example can best illustrate the procedure used to determine calculated fire rating for a wood-based assembly. This method of determining the fire resistance is permitted by Section 703.3. Tables 7-7-W-A, 7-7-W-C and 7-7-W-D are required to determine the times attributed to the various components of an assembly.

TABLE NO. 7-7-W-A—Time Assigned to Wallboard Membranes (Partial)

Description of Finish	Time (min)
$\frac{1}{2}$-inch fiberboard	5
$\frac{1}{2}$-inch exterior glue plywood	10
$\frac{3}{8}$-inch gypsum wallboard	10[a]
$\frac{1}{2}$- + $\frac{3}{8}$-inch gypsum wallboard	35

[a]Membrane rating combined with stud rating is 25.

TABLE NO. 7-7-W-C—Time Assigned for Contribution of Wood Frame (Partial)

Description of Frame	Time Assigned to Frame (min)
Wood studs 16 inches o.c.	20

Selected items from these tables are reproduced below for the following calculations. The designer is referred to the complete tables for other possible combinations of materials.

We have assumed that a 1-hour fire rating is required for the wall illustrated in Figure 8-16. Using these tables for the existing wall assembly shown in Figure 8-16, detail (a) provides the following calculated ratings, based on whether the measurement is for the right or left half of the assembly:

For fire exposure on right side:

$\frac{3}{8}$-inch wallboard	10 minutes/25 minutes w/stud
$\frac{1}{2}$-inch fiberboard	5 minutes/5 minutes w/stud
Wood studs @ 16 inch o.c.	20 minutes/—
	Total 35 minutes/30 minutes w/stud

Fire exposure on left side:

$\frac{3}{8}$-inch wallboard	10 minutes/25 minutes w/stud
$\frac{1}{2}$-inch plywood w/exterior glue	10 minutes/10 minutes w/stud
Wood studs @ 16 inch o.c.	20 minutes/—
	Total 40 minutes /35 minutes w/stud

In both instances the wall is deficient in the required 1-hour rating. It would be upgraded using the tables as shown below.

The right side is deficient by 30 minutes, based on the combined wallboard and stud time computation; the left side is deficient by 25 minutes. In combination with the other elements on that side of the wall, the following would be the results if one layer of $\frac{1}{2}$-inch regular wallboard was placed over the $\frac{3}{8}$-inch wallboard presently in place:

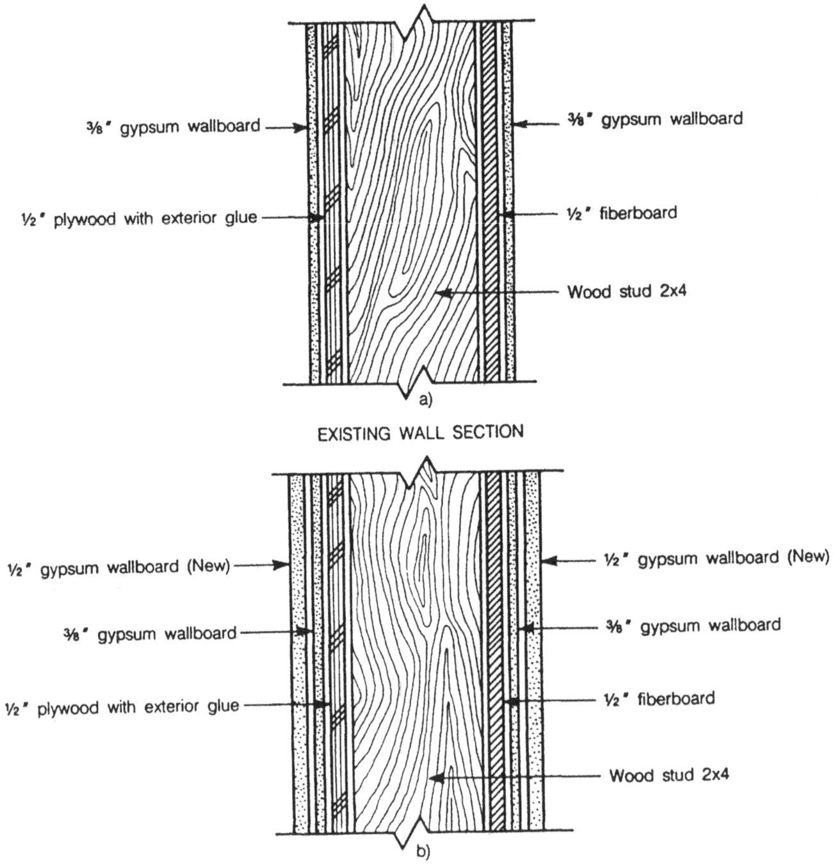

UPGRADED WALL SECTION EQUIVALENT TO 1-HOUR RATING

ASSUME: EXISTING WALL REQUIRED TO BE UPGRADED TO A MIN. 1-HOUR RATING

REFERENCE: UBC STANDARD 7-7 AND SECTION 703.3

FIGURE 8-16 FIRE RATING CALCULATION EXAMPLE, WOOD STUD ASSEMBLY

For fire exposure on the right side:

$\frac{1}{2}$-inch + $\frac{3}{8}$-inch wallboard	35 minutes
$\frac{1}{2}$-inch fiberboard	05 minutes
Wood studs @ 16 inch o.c.	20 minutes
	Total 60 minutes

For fire exposure on the left side:

$\frac{1}{2}$-inch + $\frac{3}{8}$-inch wallboard	35 minutes
$\frac{1}{2}$-inch fiberboard	10 minutes
Wood studs @ 16 inch o.c.	20 minutes
	Total 65 minutes

This proposed method of correction—by adding wallboard to each side of the present wall—will thus permit the building official to calculate the wall rating and except the wall based on Section 703.3.

NOTE: The provisions of Section 7.723 require that the calculation of the fire rating of the assembly be made without the membrane on the unexposed side included. Earlier we pointed out that there was no 1-hour wallboard.

This does not mean that one-sided assemblies are permitted by either the standards or Section 703.3 of the code. There must be no confusion generated by the method required for calculating the fire rating of an assembly by the procedure outlined in this standard and our comments in this Guide.

For example, using the standard for the calculation of the fire rating of $\frac{5}{8}$-inch Type X gypsum wallboard on wood studs at 16 inches o.c., a 40-minute rating is assigned to the wallboard and 20 minutes to the stud space, for a total of 60 minutes. This calculation satisfies the 1-hour requirement. However, the calculation applies to only one side of the assembly being exposed to a fire. Because the designer does not know the direction of fire exposure of an assembly, the wallboard must be on both faces of the stud. This, however, is not stated in the standards, and the designer should not be misled.

Our reasons for the above statement are as follows:

For wallboard to be allowed the designation Type X, it must be tested on both sides of a 2 × 4 stud wall under the ASTM E-119 procedure. The criteria for passing this test were discussed earlier in this chapter. A one-sided assembly would not pass these criteria.

Furthermore, a one-sided assembly with exposed studs would lead to rapid burning of the studs due to the presence of unlimited air supply. A failure would occur in considerably less than the 1-hour period.

The calculation methods in this standard are useful tools, but as with all tools one must be knowledgeable about how to use them, the limitations of their use and their attendant hazards.

Chapter 8 Interior Finishes

The provisions of Chapter 8 regulate the surface burning characteristics of materials used to decorate, sound deaden or insulate the walls and ceiling of a room or space in a building. The puprose of these regulations is to control the rate of fire spread along the surface of the material.

The Chapter 8 regulations trace their roots back to the early 1940s when the tragic Boston Coconut Grove fire claimed over 400 lives. A major cause of those deaths was traced to the wall and ceiling coverings. The covering materials permitted the fire to spread rapidly, cutting off access to exits. The subsequent investigations resulted in Underwriter's Laboratories, Inc. developing a test procedure for surface burning characteristics.

The 1952 UBC contained the first flame-spread regulations. The regulations were based on the test procedure, UBC Standard 8-1 (ASTM E-48), commonly called the tunnel test.

Materials used for floor coverings, other than in toilet compartments and showers (see Section 807), are not presently regulated in the UBC. However, under state and federal regulations, certain occupancies such as hospitals are so regulated. It is the authors' opinion that within 5 to 10 years such regulations will be included in the building code for most occupancies. Flooring materials, where they are presently regulated, are tested using an evaluation procedure that differs from the tunnel test.

In the tunnel test, a sample of material 20 inches wide and 24 feet long is placed at the top surface of a "tunnel" that is 12 inches high, 18 inches wide and 25 feet long. The sample is exposed to a $4\frac{1}{2}$-foot flame tongue at one end with a prescribed air flow, gas supply and pressure. The test period for the burn is 10 minutes. The furnace is initially calibrated with asbestos cement board and red oak samples before testing the particular material.

A row of glass view ports along one side of the furnace allows the flame front's rate of progress for the two calibration samples to be observed and noted during the test period. The rate of flame spread for the asbestos cement board and red oak is rated 0 and 100, respectively.

The flame front of the red oak sample should reach a point $19\frac{1}{2}$ feet from the end of the ignition flame in $5\frac{1}{2}$ minutes. The asbestos cement board does not produce a spread of flame past the end of the ignition flame tongue. The unknown material is then placed in the tunnel furnace and exposed to the same flame tongue and test conditions. The time and extent of the flame front is noted and the relative flame-spread value is calculated from the data observed during the test.

Thus, the flame-spread value is a relative number, being compared to the two calibration materials. A material with a flame spread of 25 can be considered as having a rate of surface burning (flame spread) one quarter that of red oak, while one with a 200 value has a flame spread twice that of red oak.

Two other characteristics are measured in the tunnel test:

1. smoke density and
2. fuel contributed.

The data for these characteristics are obtained during the same test period from a photoelectric cell and thermocouple placed at the exhaust end of the furnace. The resultant data are compared to that of the red oak standard. The red oak value is set for each of these characteristics at 100.

Knowing the background of the test procedure should assist the reader in understanding the philosophy of the provisions of Chapter 8.

SECTION 801—GENERAL

801.1 Scope. Interior wall and ceiling finish shall mean the exposed interior surfaces of buildings including, but not limited to, fixed or moveable walls and partitions, interior wainscoting, paneling or other finish applied structurally for decoration, acoustical correction, surface insulation, sanitation,

structural fire resistance or similar purposes. Requirements for finishes in this chapter shall not apply to trim defined as picture molds, chair rails, baseboards and handrails; or to doors and windows or their frames; or to materials that are less than $\frac{1}{28}$ inch (0.9 mm) in thickness applied directly to the surface of walls or ceilings.

Foam plastics shall not be used as interior finish except as provided in Section 2602. For foam plastic trim, see Section 601.5.5.

See Section 1403 for veneer.

The types of materials regulated by the code are large expanse covering materials, not trim and other small or isolated items of decoration. Thin materials essentially made of paper, such as wallpaper, are not subject to regulation. However, vinyl wallcovering is regulated since its burning characteristics, particularly that of smoke generation (smoke density), are considerably greater than those of paper.

The designer is cautioned to avoid materials that could exceed the permissible flame-spread values. Often these fire considerations are overlooked when choosing materials, particularly when a materials representative, in extolling the benefits of a new surfacing product, emphasizes ease of maintenance over the material's burning characteristics.

SECTION 803—APPLICATION OF CONTROLLED INTERIOR FINISH

Interior finish materials applied to walls and ceilings shall be tested as specified in Section 802 and regulated for purposes of limiting surface-burning characteristics by the following provisions:

1. When walls and ceilings are required by any provision in this code to be of fire-resistive or noncombustible construction, the finish material shall be applied directly against such fire-resistive or noncombustible construction or to furring strips not exceeding $1\frac{3}{4}$ inches (44 mm) applied directly against such surfaces. The intervening spaces between such furring strips shall be filled with inorganic or Class I material or shall be fire blocked not to exceed 8 feet (2438 mm) in any direction. See Section 708 for fireblocking.

2. Where walls and ceilings are required to be of fire-resistive or noncombustible construction and walls are set out or ceilings are dropped distances greater than specified in paragraph 1 of this section, Class I finish materials shall be used except where the finish materials are protected on both sides by automatic sprinkler systems or are attached to a noncombustible backing or to furring strips installed as specified in paragraph 1. The hangers and assembly members of such dropped ceilings that are below the main ceiling line shall be of noncombustible materials except that in Types III and V construction, fire-retardant-treated wood may be used. The construction of each set-out wall shall be of fire-resistive construction as required elsewhere in this code. See Section 708 for fire blocks and draft stops.

3. Wall and ceiling finish materials of all classes as permitted in this chapter may be installed directly against the wood decking or planking of Type IV

heavy-timber construction, or to wood furring strips applied directly to the wood decking or planking installed and fire blocked as specified in item 1.

4. An interior wall or ceiling finish that is less than $\frac{1}{4}$ inch (6.4 mm) thick shall be applied directly against a noncombustable backing.

EXCEPTIONS: 1. Class I materials.

2. Materials where the qualifying tests were made with the material suspended or furred out from the noncombustable backing.

This section regulates the installation of interior finishes. The main concern expressed in the several provisions is the furring out of the finish material because the space behind the finish can cause problems such as the following:

- Fire can spread in the cavity formed by the building surface and finish material.
- The finish material can burn through from the room side of the finish material and burn simultaneously on both sides at a greater rate than is tested, thus spreading the fire faster than permitted in that location.
- The rate of heat release of the finish material may greatly exceed that of the finish as tested.

The designer must be sure that the drawings reflect code-complying filling or fire blocking of any such cavities.

There are two changes in this section; the first is one of several changes made for the previously used term "firestopping," replacing it with fire blocking, as discussed in Section 708.

Item 4 allows two types of materials, such as a Class I material, to be unblocked or a material of any thickness provided it was tested in an unbacked condition. Thus, ceiling tile that is usually thicker than $\frac{1}{4}$ inch can qualify provided it passes the appropriate fire testing or is a Class I material. Such is the case for tile that is part of a fire-resistive floor-ceiling assembly.

SECTION 804—MAXIMUM ALLOWABLE FLAME SPREAD

804.1 General. The maximum flame-spread class of finish materials used on interior walls and ceilings shall not exceed that set forth in Table 8-B.

EXCEPTIONS: 1. Except in Group I Occupancies and in enclosed vertical exits, Class III may be used in other means of egress and rooms as wainscoting extending not more than 48 inches (1219 mm) above the floor and for tack and bulletin boards covering not more than 5 percent of the gross wall area of the room.

2. When a sprinkler system complying with UBC Standards 9-1 or 9-3 is provided, the flame-spread classification rating may be reduced one

classification, but in no case shall materials having a classification greater than Class III be used.

3. The exposed faces of Type IV-H.T. structural members, and Type IV-H.T., decking and planking, where otherwise permissible under this code, are excluded from flame-spread requirements.

Table 8-B provides the regulatory flame-spread values for all occupancies and specific locations within an occupancy. There is a general concept behind this table: The more important the location is along the exit path from a room or area within the building to the street, the lower the flame-spread value (the "safer material") required for the materials forming the wall and ceiling coverings.

The materials permitted within a room or area are generally allowed to have a flame spread of up to 200, double that of red oak. These materials would include most wood products and plywoods. However, a qualifying provision in Section 803 Item 4, regarding the use of thin materials such as plywood, reads:

4. An interior wall or ceiling finish that is less than $\frac{1}{4}$ inch (6.4 mm) thick shall be applied directly against a noncombustable backing.

EXCEPTIONS: 1. Class I materials.

2. Materials where the qualifying tests were made with the material suspended or furred out from the noncombustable backing.

This means that all interior wall or ceiling finishes other than Class I material, which is less than $\frac{1}{4}$ inch thick, must be applied directly against a noncombustable backing unless the qualifying tests were made with the material suspended from the noncombustable backing. The reason for this qualifying provision is that thin materials can burn through at a point of weakness in the material. When this occurs in a material that is not solidly backed, the burning will spread very rapidly on both the front and back sides of the material.

In tunnel tests of backed and unbacked samples, a $\frac{3}{16}$-inch thick plywood sample when tested

- burned for 8 feet of its length in 10 minutes with a backing against it and
- burned for its entire 24-foot length in less than 10 minutes when not backed.

Plywood inner plies are permitted to have a certain amount of "holidays" or unfilled holes. The inner plies are not necessarily laid up with tight butt joints and may have gaps, splits or unfilled knot holes. Thin sheets of plywood usually have only three plies, two face veneers and a core ply. The face veneers of plywood less than $\frac{1}{4}$ inch thick are only 0.083 inch (one-twelfth inch) thick. As a result, thin plywood can burn through very quickly.

> In the authors' opinion, backing should be provided for any plywood less than $\frac{1}{2}$ inch thick. Use of $\frac{1}{2}$-inch thick gypsum wallboard as the backing is an economical solution. (See Figure 8-17.)

As one progresses along an exit path in the exit corridor, the permissible flame-spread drops from 200, allowed in rooms, to 75. Materials meeting this rating include fire-retardant wood and plywood. Few untreated organic materials will have a flame-spread value below 75. Gypsum wallboard has a flame spread value of 25. That low flame-spread is a result of the treated paper covering the gypsum core. Paint or similar finishes on such wallboard generally do not result in a higher flame-spread value.

The most restrictive flame-spread limitation applies to enclosed vertical exit ways, i.e., exit stairways, smoke towers and their exit passageways, for the following reasons:

- They serve as the primary path of exiting.
- They provide access for the fire-fighting activities for the upper floors of a building and thus must be kept functional.
- They are vertical shafts and thus have a more rapid spread of fire along the wall surfaces due to stack effect, draft and other sources of air movement.

For these reasons the flame spread of materials in the vertical exit ways is limited to 25. (See Figure 8-18.)

One resource for flame-spread values is the Underwriters Laboratories, Inc. *Building Materials Directory;* another is the ICBO Evaluation Reports. The designer is urged to inquire, in regard to any material considered for wall and ceiling materials, into the flame-spread and smoke density values for the materials.

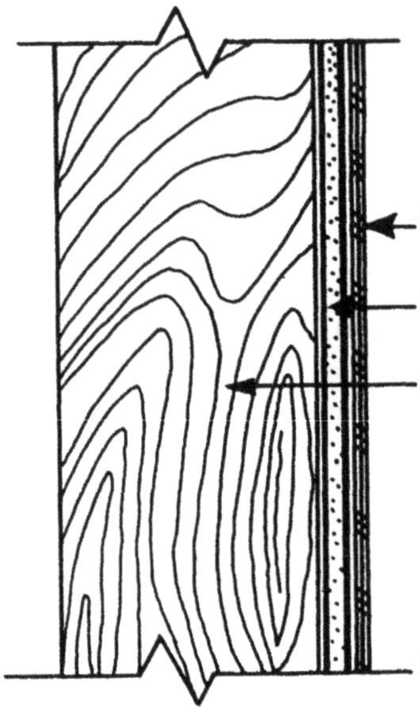

The use of thin combustible finish material requires noncombustible backing per Section 803. Gypsum wall board can be used for such backing. Testing has shown that the minimum thickness of combustible finish that should be backed is material less than ½-inch thick if a Class 3 finish material.

Recommendation: Use backing behind any class 3 interior finish material ≤ ½" thickness.

REFERENCE: SECTION 803, ITEM 4

FIGURE 8-17 INTERIOR FINISH REQUIREMENT-THIN SURFACE MATERIALS, BACKING

The manufacturer, and not the designer, has the burden of having the listing information available and in a form acceptable to the jurisdiction. As previously indicated in Article 1 of this Guide, if job delays are to be avoided, the designer should avoid specifying a material unless it has been previously submitted by the manufacturer or its representative and accepted by the jurisdiction.

TABLE 8-A—FLAME-SPREAD CLASSIFICATION

MATERIAL QUALIFIED BY:	
Class	Flame-spread Index
I	0-25
II	26-75
III	76-200

TABLE 8-B—MAXIMUM FLAME-SPREAD CLASS[1]

OCCUPANCY GROUP	ENCLOSED VERTICAL EXITWAYS	OTHER EXITWAYS[2]	ROOMS OR AREAS
A	I	II	II[3]
B	I	II	III
E	I	II	III
F	II	III	III
H	I	II	III[4]
I-1.1, I-1.2, I-2	I	I[5]	II[6]
I-3	I	I[5]	I[6]
M	I	II	III
R-1	I	II	III
R-3	III	III	III[7]
S-1, S-2	II	II	III
S-3, S-4, S-5	I	II	III
U	NO RESTRICTIONS		

[1]Foam plastics shall comply with the requirements specified in Section 2602. Carpeting on ceilings and textile wall coverings shall comply with the requirements specified in Sections 804.2 and 805, respectively.
[2]Finish classification is not applicable to interior walls and ceilings of exterior exit-access balconies.
[3]In Group A, Divisions 3 and 4 Occupancies, Class III may be used.
[4]Over two stories shall be of Class II.
[5]In Group I, Divisions 2 and 3 Occupancies, Class II may be used.
[6]Class III may be used in administrative spaces.
[7]Flame-spread provisions are not applicable to kitchens and bathrooms of Group R, Division 3 Occupancies.

REFERENCE: TABLE 8-A, 8-B

FIGURE 8-18 FLAME SPREAD VALUES BY LOCATION

ARTICLE 9
MISCELLANEOUS CODE PROVISIONS

SECTION 304–REQUIREMENTS FOR GROUP B OCCUPANCIES
SECTION 307–REQUIREMENTS FOR GROUP H OCCUPANCIES
SECTION 310–REQUIREMENTS FOR GROUP R OCCUPANCIES
SECTION 311–REQUIREMENTS FOR GROUP S OCCUPANCIES
SECTION 602–TYPE I FR BUILDINGS
SECTION 604–TYPE III BUILDINGS
Including
BUSINESS and RESIDENTIAL OCCUPANCY
& HIGH-RISE BUILDING REQUIREMENTS

This article of the Guide reviews certain miscellaneous Uniform Building Code (UBC) occupancy provisions that, for a designer, either have frequent application or can cause problems. In Article 10 the provisions in certain additional UBC chapters will be reviewed. The provisions in these two articles are reviewed to supplement those discussed in Articles 3 through 8 herein.

304.6 Shaft and Exit Enclosures. Exits shall be enclosed as specified in Chapter 10.

Elevator shafts, vent shafts and other openings through floors shall be enclosed, and the enclosure shall be as specified in Section 711.

In buildings housing Group B Occupancies equipped with automatic sprinkler systems throughout, enclosures shall not be required for escalators where the top of the escalator opening at each story is provided with a draft curtain and automatic fire sprinklers are installed around the perimeter of the opening within 2 feet (610 mm) of the draft curtain. The draft curtain shall enclose the perimeter of the unenclosed opening and extend from the ceiling downward at least 12 inches (305 mm) on all sides. The spacing between sprinklers shall not exceed 6 feet (1829 mm).

NOTE: This provision is one part of several code provisions relating to penetrations of fire-resistive wall, floor-ceiling and shaft wall assemblies. See discussions in Sections 709.6, 710.2 and 711 in Article 8 of this Guide regarding penetrations.

This unique code latitude addresses a need in Group B and M Occupancies such as department stores; however, it is inconsistent with the general code provision for shaft enclosures. Fortunately, fire experience in Group B and M Occupancies has been good and the provision has been used successfully at least since 1949.

307.6 Shaft and Exit Enclosures. Exits shall be enclosed as specified in Chapter 10.

Elevator shafts, vent shafts and other openings through floors shall be enclosed, and the enclosure shall be as specified in Section 711.

Doors which are part of an automobile ramp enclosure shall be equipped with automatic-closing devices.

For Group H, Division 6 Occupancies, see Section 307.11.2.3.

NOTE: This provision is one of several code provisions relating to penetrations of fire-resistive wall, floor-ceiling and shaft wall assemblies.

310.1 Group R Occupancies Defined. Group R Occupancies shall be:

Division 1. Hotels and apartment houses.
Congregate residences (each accommodating more than 10 persons)
Division 2. Not used.
Division 3. Dwellings and lodging houses.
Congregate residences (each accommodating 10 persons or less).

For occupancy separations, see Table 3-B.

A complete code for construction of detached one- and two-family dwellings is in Appendix Chapter 3, Division III, of this code. When adopted, as set forth in Section 101.3, it will take precedence over the other requirements set forth in this code.

This occupancy group was expanded to establish a new category of housing. The new provisions recognize the extreme housing pressures, particularly in urban areas of the country. The new category is referred to as congregate residence.

Congregate residences include such traditional multiple housing as monasteries and convents, but expand into the unconventional or nontraditional housing for students or persons with no binding relationships such as a family. Because there is no family, the prior code definitions would not cover these new forms of house-sharing practices.

Numerous code changes were made for this new concept of housing, essentially deleting the terms for monasteries, convents and dormitories and adding the term congregate residence whenever dwelling unit or similar reference is made to assure application of the requirement to the congregate residence form as well.

310.2 Construction, Height and Allowable Area.
310.2.2 Special Provisions. Walls and floors separating dwelling units in the same building, or guest rooms in Group R, Division 1 hotel occupancies, shall be not less than one-hour fire-resistive construction.

Group R, Division 1 Occupancies more than two stories in height or having more than 3000 square feet (279 m^2) of floor area above the first story shall not be of less than one-hour fire-resistive construction throughout except as provided in Section 601.5.2.2.

Storage or laundry rooms that are within Group R. Division 1 Occupancies that are used in common by tenants shall be separated from the rest of the building by not less than one-hour fire-resistive occupancy separation.

For Group R, Division I Occupancies with a Group S, Division 3 parking garage in the basement or first story, see Section 311.2.2.

For attic space partitions and draft stops, see Section 708.

Section 310.2 requires that all dwelling units be separated, one from another, by not less than a 1-hour fire-resistive assembly. If there are openings in the separation, the code does not indicate the required fire rating for the opening assembly. This will be discussed later.

Even where the code allows a building to be constructed as a Type II-N, III-N or V-N structure based on floor area, height and occupancy, the dwelling units must be separated by rated construction.

Because of the importance of this provision and the lack of clarifying details, an intensive examination of the implications follows.

Effect of the Dwelling Unit Separation (DUS) Requirement

a) Application to Group R, Division 1 and R, Division 3 Occupancies

The code provision is not limited to Group R, Division 1 Occupancy. It applies to Group R, Division 3, two-dwelling-unit building as well. See Figure 9-1.

b) Group R, Division 3 Occupancy Buildings

The provisions also affect the two-family Group R, Division 3 Occupancy. The terminology used in the provision refers only to "walls and floors separating dwelling units in the same building."

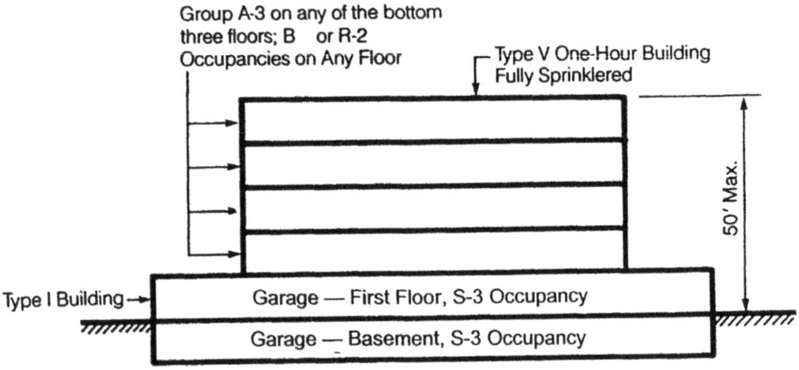

A Type V One-Hour building may be constructed on top of a Type I garage, (Group S, Division 3 Occupancy) building

The overall height of the Type V building is limited by Table 5-B to 50'. If the upper structure were of Type III construction, the height to the top of the upper structure could be 65' above grade.

The upper building may contain Group A, Division 3, Group B or Group R, Division 1 Occupancies, or a mix of all three occupancies. Table 5-B provides the story location limitations for the various occupancies. Thus, the Group A, Division 3 Occupancy in a Type V one-Hour building cannot be above the second floor of the building if the building were not sprinklered or may be on the third floor as it is sprinklered.

REFERENCE: SECTION 304.2.1 AND TABLE 5-B

FIGURE 9-1 GROUP A, DIV. 3, B, AND R, DIV. 1 OCCUPANCIES OVER GARAGE

Because Section 310.2.1 General refers to the Group R Occupancy in general, and as Section 310.2.2 is not limited to Group R, Division 1 Occupancy, the conclusion that one must reach is that the DUS applies wherever there are adjacent dwelling units. (See Figures 9-2 and 9-5.)

c) Support of DUS

The code provision requires that there be a 1-hour DUS provided. Note that the type of separation is not specifically designated as either an occupancy separation or an area separation as defined in Chapters 2 and 3.

Therefore, the support provision of Section 302.2 for an occupancy separation is not directly applicable. However, the designer is cautioned that it would be poor practice to provide a design such that a rated separation would occur over an unprotected support. Liability may occur if the designer permitted this situation. Therefore, the authors' believe that whether or not the code requires the separation to be supported by construction of equivalent fire resistance, this fire rating should be provided in all instances.

d) Applicability of Type V-N Construction for Multiple-Dwelling-Unit Buildings

The designer should recognize that with this code requirement the simple Type V-N construction for a multifamily residential building is no longer permitted. In its place will be a form of hybrid construction.

A considerable portion of the Type V-N building must be of 1-hour fire-rated construction, as mandated by this code provision. The authors suggests that the designer consider whether it would be best for the entire building to be a Type V 1-hour building at the outset. This would provide the benefits of increased area and height and would satisfy the separation requirements. Otherwise, the expenditures required to provide for the DUS will not be compensated by any credits given in the code.

e) Consideration for Upgrade to One-hour Construction to Satisfy New Requirements

The impact of this provision should be brought to the attention of the owner/developer in the early stages of the design. If the owner/

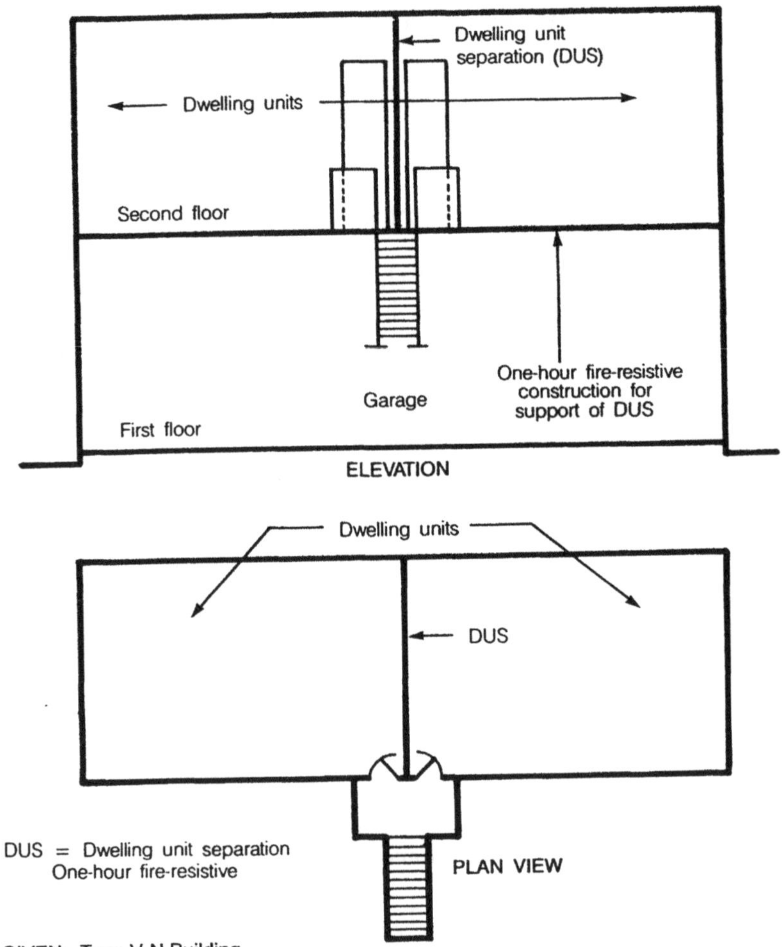

GIVEN: Type V-N Building
Group R-Div. 3 Occupancy on the 2nd floor
Group U (garage) on 1st level

Per Section 302.4 Exception 3, the garage/dwelling unit separation need be surfaced only on the garage side as for a one-hour fire resistant floor-ceiling assembly. However, per Section 310.2.2, the DUS between the dwelling units must be at least one-hour fire-resistive construction.

Thus, the supports for that DUS, as provided by the floor-ceiling assembly of the second floor over the garage, should be at least a complete one-hour fire-resistive assembly and not simply the surfacing layer of same.

REFERENCES: SECTIONS 302.4, EXCEPTION 3 AND 310.2.2

FIGURE 9-2 DWELLING UNIT SEPARATION REQUIREMENTS-TYPE V-N BUILDING, GROUP R, DIV. 3 OVER GARAGE

developer decides on a 1-hour building throughout, the benefits of such a building can be readily integrated into that design.

f) Double-Loaded Corridor and DUS Requirements

With the new DUS provisions an ambiguous condition occurs in a double-loaded corridor. Although the corridor may be interpreted as providing a form of the required DUS from one dwelling unit to another across the corridor from it, this interpretation is not stated in the code text. Although this is a common type of corridor arrangement, it is not readily evaluated by a reading of the code provision.

The corridor wall must be 1-hour fire rated under the provisions of Section 1007.6.1 when the occupant load is 10 or more. The openings therein are permitted to have 20-minute smoke- and draft-control doors per Section 1004.3.4.3.2.1.

With this in mind, we can make some general assumptions as to what code provisions would apply for the corridor walls forming the separation between the dwelling units:

1. Occupant load in corridor less than 10

When the occupant load is less than 10, the walls of the double-loaded corridor are permitted to be of nonrated construction with the openings therein unprotected, i.e., nonrated doors. The 1-hour DUS requirement is not satisfied, therefore, by this minimal nonrated code-complying construction. Because the doors in such nonrated walls can have only a 6-minute fire resistance rating (a hollow-core door), the net protection from unit to unit across the corridor could be only about 12 to 15 minutes instead of the 1-hour separation required by the code. See Figure 9-3.

A. The two nonrated corridor walls would probably provide the equivalence of the 1-hour separation. This conclusion is reached by assuming there is $\frac{1}{2}$-inch regular gypsum wallboard on both sides of a wood stud. The two layers of wallboard are credited with a 15-minute fire resistance time period, as noted in Table 7-7-W-A of UBC Standard 7-7 (as discussed in Article 8 of this Guide).

The studs are given 20-minute ratings in that standard; thus, each wall assembly will have about a

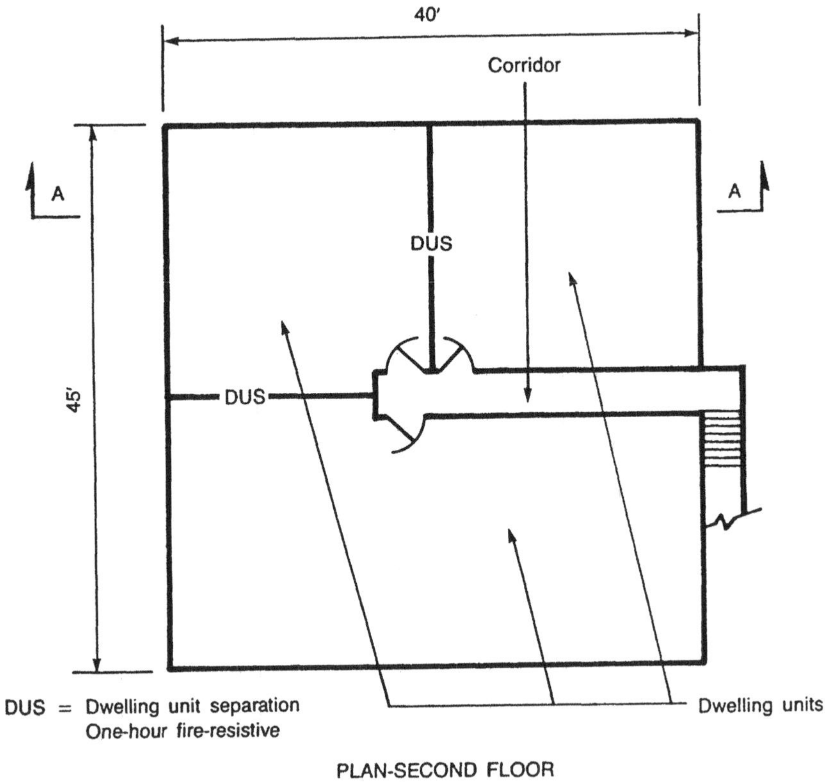

GIVEN: Type V-N Building
Group R Div.1 Occupancy - 2 stories
3 dwelling units on 2nd floor w/double loaded corridor
2 dwelling units on 1st floor

Per Section 1001.1 the occupant load on the 2nd floor is 1800/200 = 9

However, per Section 312.2.2, a one-hour DUS is required between the dwelling units on the second floor. The corridor is part of that separation. Therefore, the two corridor walls are required to provide the aggregate equivalence of one-hour fire-resistive construction with the openings protected at least with three-quarter hour assemblies. The fire assemblies should also meet the smoke- and draft-control requirements of Section 1004.3.4.3.2.1.

REFERENCE: SECTIONS 321.2.2, 1001.1 and 1004.3.4.3.2.1 AND TABLE 10-A

FIGURE 9-3 DWELLING UNIT SEPARATION (DUS) REQUIREMENTS TYPE V-N BUILDING, GROUP R, DIVISION 1

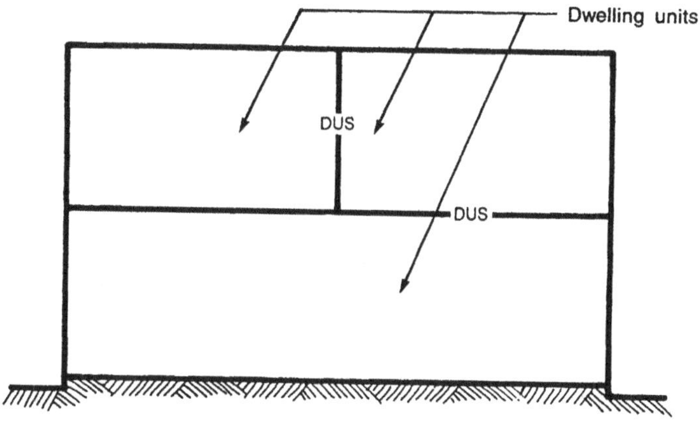

SECTION A-A

35-minute rating. The pair of walls on both sides of the corridor can, therefore, be considered equivalent to the 1-hour separation because it can be demonstrated from the UBC Book of Standards that these walls will calculate to a net fire-resistive time period of 70 minutes.

B. The nonrated doors are the problem in the less-than-10-occupant load corridor. They can provide as little as a 12-minute fire rating. Openings in the 1-hour separation should have a fire resistance rating of at least $\frac{3}{4}$ hour. This opening-to-barrier ratio is the accepted standard, except where a greater time requirement is specifically cited in the code.

Therefore, in such a double-loaded corridor situation, the authors' believe that the doors should be not less than 20-minute, self-closing, smoke- and draft-control assemblies. This installation would provide a total of at least 40 minutes for two doors, if located directly opposite each other on the corridor. See Figure 9-4.

The 5 minutes needed to reach 45 minutes may reasonably be assumed, given the width of the corridor and the time for a fire to traverse that width to attack the second door are considered. In the opinion of the authors', this would be a reasonable interpretation of equivalence, to the extent that the interpretation is

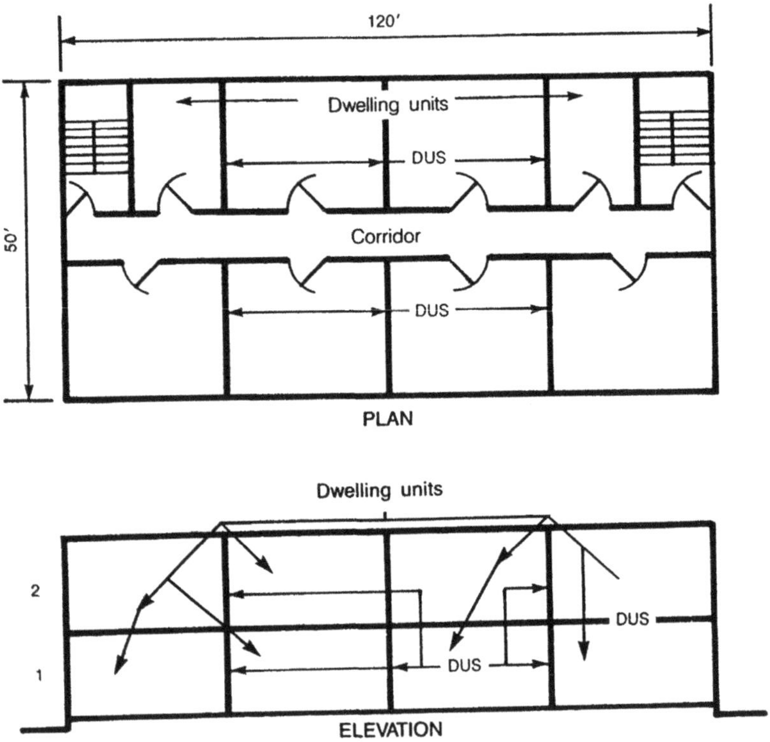

GIVEN: Type V-N Building
Group R Div. 1 Occupancy, 4 units per floor
Double loaded exit corridor

DUS = Dwelling Unit Separation
One-hour fire-resistive

The requirements for the dwelling unit separations (DUS) in subject building require that virtually all elements of the building be of one-hour fire-resistive construction. The corridor must be of one-hour construction per Section 1004.3.4.3. The 20 minute smoke and draft control doors can be used to provide the one-hour protection of the openings in the DUS across the corridor.

REFERENCE: SECTIONS 312.2, 1001.1, 1004.3.4.3.2.1 AND TABLE 10-A

FIGURE 9-4 DWELLING UNIT SEPARATIONS—TYPE V-N BUILDING, GROUP R, DIVISION 1 OCCUPANCY, DOUBLE-LOADED ONE-HOUR EXIT CORRIDOR

limited to the separation requirement due to the newness of same and the need for an interpretive resolution of the ambiguity.
2. Occupant load in corridor of 10 or more.

When the occupant load is 10 or more, the corridor walls are required by Section 1007.6.1 to be of 1-hour fire-resistive construction. The walls, therefore, obviously satisfy the minimal DUS requirement. The doors, which are required by Section 1004.3.4.3.2.1 to be 20-minute self-closing smoke- and draft-control doors, are the "weak link." With regard to the less-than-10-occupant-load corridor, by the absence of specific requirements in the DUS provision for this very common condition in most multistoried multifamily occupancy buildings, we can infer that probably the doors required in Section 1004.3.4.2.1 would be acceptable. (See Figure 9-5.)

g) Garage Separation in Group R, Division 3, When Supporting a DUS

In two-story, two-dwelling-unit Group R, Division 3 buildings with a garage on the ground floor under the residential portion, the separation between the garage and the residential units is usually required to have the ceiling surface of a 1-hour floor-ceiling assembly by Section 302.4, Exception 3. (See Figure 9-2.)

However, that floor-ceiling assembly should be constructed as a full 1-hour fire-resistive assembly in most instances because it provides the support for the required 1-hour vertical separation between the dwelling units.

h) Sprinkler Substitution for DUS, Section 508

The use of fire sprinklers in lieu of 1-hour fire-resistive construction is provided for in Section 508. The code contains a prohibited Item 4 in the list of items where sprinkler trade-offs are not allowed. Item 4 was added to the code the year after the DUS was added, even though there had not been time to use the original provision.

Item 4 is "Dwelling unit separations per Section 310.2.2."

i) Preliminary Plan Check

In the preliminary plan check, using the DUS provision, the designer should contact the local building official and clear with that

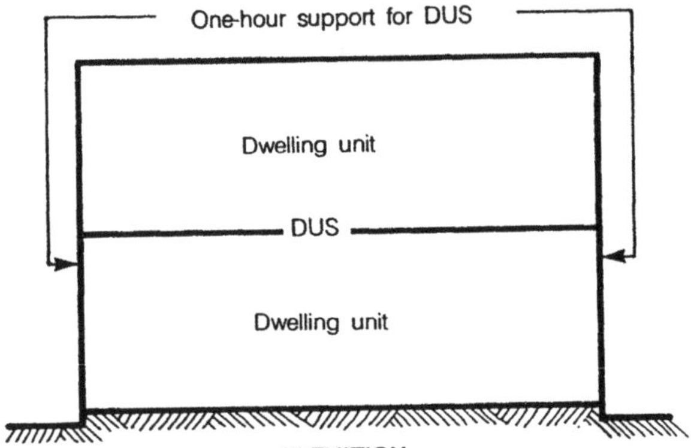

ELEVATION
2 STORIES

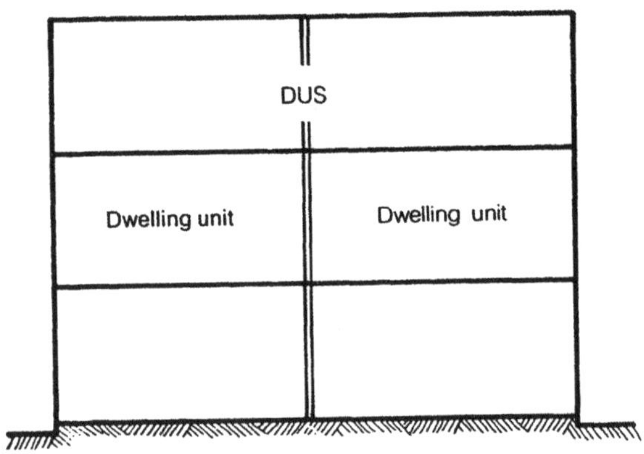

ELEVATION
3 STORIES
(Townhouse)

DUS = Dwelling unit separation
One-hour fire-resistive

GIVEN: Type V-N Building
Group R, Div. 3 Occupancy
Two dwelling units
2 or 3 story

REFERENCE: SECTION 312.2

FIGURE 9-5 DWELLING UNIT SEPARATION REQUIREMENTS—GROUP R, DIVISION 3 OCCUPANCY (TWO FAMILY DWELLING) 2 OR 3 STORIES

office the method and construction to be employed in the project. Make use of the confirmation procedures discussed in this Guide.

j) Summary of Recommendations

In summary, therefore, the following are the authors' recommendations:

- A designer should consider whether an N-rated type of construction serves the best interests of the client in view of the DUS requirements.
- The code requirements apply to both the vertical and horizontal separations between adjacent dwelling units. A floor-ceiling assembly serving as a DUS must be of at least 1-hour fire-resistive construction, in accordance with Table 43-C of the code.
- In cases where the 1-hour DUS is not supported by fire-rated construction, the designer should provide at least 1-hour fire-resistive protection for the support elements. See Figure 9-2.
- All openings into double-loaded exit corridors, regardless of the occupant load served, should be not less than 20-minute self-closing smoke- and draft-control doors. See Figures 9-3 and 9-4.
- In two-story, two-dwelling-unit Group R Division 3 buildings with a garage on the ground floor level under the residential portion, the separation between the garage and the residential units is usually required to have only the ceiling surface of a 1-hour floor-ceiling assembly by Section 302.4, Exception 3. See Figure 9-2. However, that floor-ceiling assembly should be constructed as a full 1-hour fire-resistive assembly in most instances because it provides the support for the required 1-hour vertical separation between the two dwelling units.

This provision, with its considerable effect on the nonrated type of building, will generate both controversy and interpretive problems for all concerned. The authors' recommend that both the designer and the enforcement official apply conservative and prudent judgments until such time as experience with the provisions develops accepted interpretations. There may well be need for possible modifications of the DUS provisions to clarify the present uncertainties.

Section 310.2.2 relates to dwelling units and guest rooms in Group R, Division 1 Occupancies (apartment houses, hotels and similar multiple unit residential uses). The second paragraph states that an R-1 Occupancy building must be 1-hour fire-resistive throughout when either

- the second floor is greater than 3000 square feet or
- the building is three or more stories in height.

The floor area measurement must meet the definition of floor area in Chapter 2. That definition requires that all parts of the floor, except vent shafts and courts, be included in the calculation. Thus, stairways, corridors, balconies and landings must be included in the calculation.

> In the authors' opinion, where there is a mezzanine in the second floor that does not qualify as a separate story, the area of the mezzanine must also be included in the area of the second floor.

The area criterion that invokes the 1-hour fire-resistive requirement should not be confused with the area criterion that invokes the two exit provision of Section 1003.2.2 (Table 10-A); 2000 square feet for an apartment or hotel occupancy (10 occupants × 200 square feet per occupant). (See Figure 9-6.)

310.4 Access and Means of Egress Facilities and Emergency Escapes. Means of egress shall be as specified in Chapter 10. (See also Section 1007.6.2 for exit markings.)

Access to, and egress from, buildings required to be accessible shall be provided as specified in Chapter 11.

Basements in dwelling units and every sleeping room below the fourth story shall have at least one operable window or door approved for emergency escape or rescue which shall open directly onto a street, a public alley, a yard or an exit court. The emergency door or window shall be operable

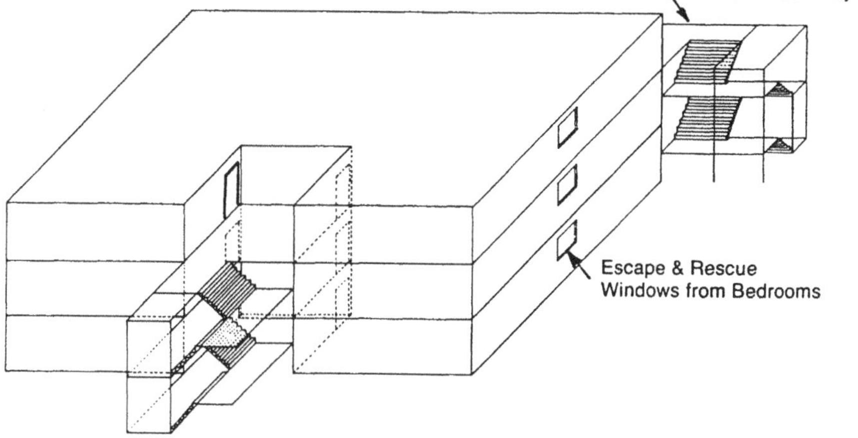

If 2nd floor > 3,000 S.F. - minimum One-hour throughout
If 3 or more stories - minimum One-hour throughout and 2 exits required 3rd floor
If area of 2nd floor + ½ area of 3rd floor ÷ 200 ≥ 10, 2 exits required 2nd floor

Escape and rescue widows are required from every bedroom. These are NOT exits, but are additional openings for building four stories or less in height essentially for fire department rescue. These windows must open onto a street or public alley, yard or exit court.

Escape and rescue windows must be openable and of the minimum size as specified in Section 1204 to facilitate their use.

REFERENCE: SECTIONS 310.2.2, 310.4, 1004.2.3 AND TABLE 10-A

FIGURE 9-6 HEIGHT, AREA AND EGRESS RELATIONSHIPS—GROUP R, DIV. 1 OCCUPANCY

from the inside to provide a full clear opening without the use of separate tools.

EXCEPTION: The window or door may open into an atrium complying with Section 402 provided the window or door opens onto an exit-access balcony and the dwelling unit or guest room has an exit or exit-access doorway that does not open into the atrium.

Escape or rescue windows shall have a minimum net clear openable area of 5.7 square feet (0.53 m²). The minimum net clear openable height dimension shall be 24 inches (610 mm). The minimum net clear openable width dimension

shall be 20 inches (508 mm). When windows are provided as a means of escape or rescue, they shall have a finished sill height not more than 44 inches (1118 mm) above the floor.

Escape and rescue windows with a finished sill height below the adjacent ground elevation shall have a window well. Window wells at escape or rescue windows shall comply with the following:

1. The clear horizontal dimensions shall allow the window to be fully opened and provide a minimum accessible net clear opening of 9 square feet (0.84 m^2), with a minimum dimension of 36 inches (914 mm).

2. Window wells with a vertical depth of more than 44 inches (1118 mm) shall be equipped with an approved permanently affixed ladder or stairs that are accessible with window in the fully open position. The ladder or stairs shall not encroach into the required dimensions of the window well by more than 6 inches (152 mm).

Bars, grilles, grates or similar devices may be Installed on an emergency escape or rescue windows or doors, provided:

1. The devices are equiped with approved release mechanisms which are openable from the inside without the use of a key or special knowledge or effort; and

2. The building is equipped with smoke detectors installed in accordance with Section 310.9.

Article 7 of this Guide indicates that Section 310.4 contains the requirements for the escape and rescue windows in any Group R Occupancy and in all sleeping rooms below the fourth floor of a building with such an occupancy.

There were several changes made to Section 310.4 (1991 UBC Section 1204) from prior codes. Three changes were made in the escape or rescue window provisions:

1. In the third paragraph, the intent of the escape or rescue window or door is stated. This is an important clarification. These escape or rescue windows or doors must be directly accessible to a public space and by the fire service.

   The author has encountered buildings in which bedrooms have had openings, i.e., windows, onto interior stairway landing areas. There were no other accessible openings to the exterior of the building for these bedrooms. (See Figure 9-7.) These bedrooms clearly violate the intent of the code, but due to the lack of clear language in this section at the time of construction, the enforcement official permitted these rooms. They subsequently had to be corrected at considerable cost.

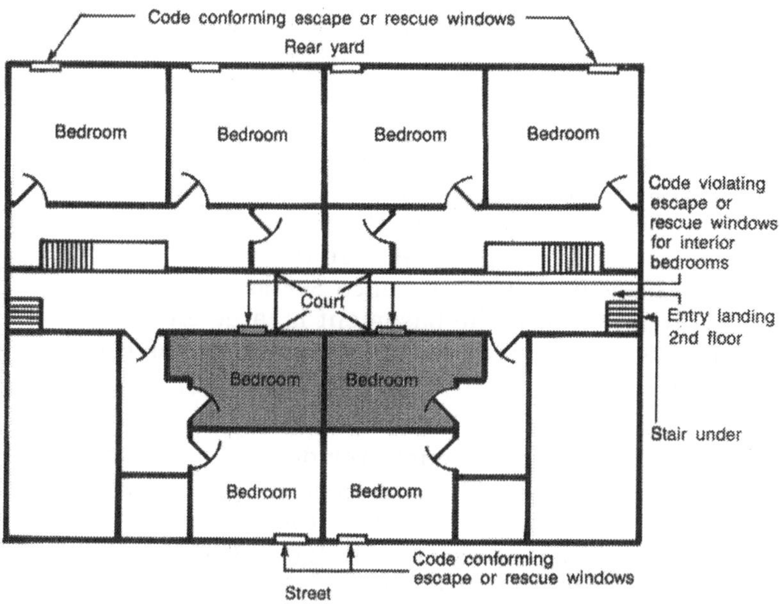

PLAN - 2ND FLOOR

Escape and rescue windows must be openable and of the minimum size as specified in Section 310.4 to facilitate their use.

The two bedrooms shown shaded which open onto the corridor within the building do NOT meet the requirements for an escape and rescue window.

REFERENCE: SECTION 310.4

FIGURE 9-7 ESCAPE OR RESCUE WINDOWS, CODE CONFORMING AND NON-CONFORMING EXAMPLES

2. In the fourth paragraph of this section, the term "operable" was corrected to "openable." This change reflects the code intent that these windows must not simply be operable but openable to facilitate escape or rescue.
3. A requirement added to the third paragraphs stating that basements must also have escape or rescue windows. The intent of this provision involves the realization that, in residential buildings, sleeping rooms are often located in basements. To ignore this fact and not provide the escape or rescue windows at the time of construction creates a code enforcement problem. Problems occur when the sleeping room is installed subsequent to the building's construction and is then discovered by the enforcement agency.

   By requiring the provision of the windows during the construction phase, regardless of whether the basement is intended for use as a sleeping room at that time, the enforcement problem is obviated. (See Figure 9-8.)

   Note that the windows for the unfinished basement may be located anywhere because there is no sleeping room to be served. The reference Section 10042.3.2 requires only that if the basement is large enough to require two such windows, the windows be separated from each other.

Escape and rescue windows must provide access to and from a public space such as a street. Windows opening only to the interior of the building and causing one to rely on the interior exits for the escape are not acceptable as escape windows. A fire blocking the exit path from that interior space would also block the escape and rescue path for the window. The escape window must be a separate facility that does not rely on any of the required exits.

The escape and rescue window is to be provided in addition to all required exits. It cannot be made a substitute for any exit. The escape window must be

- no smaller than the minimum size and
- no higher than the height above the floor set by the UBC.

This is to facilitate the windows' use in an emergency by firefighters or occupants within the bedroom. Each sleeping room must

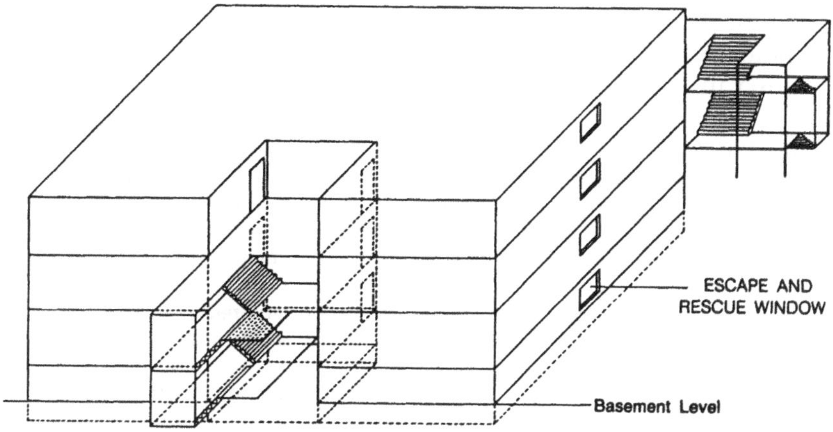

ASSUME:
GROUP R OCCUPANCY BUILDING ≤ 4 STORIES

Escape and rescue widows are required from every bedroom and from basements of dwelling units. These are NOT exits, but are additional openings for building four stories or less in height essentially for fire department rescue. These windows must open onto a street or public alley, yard or exit court.

The requirement for basement is not dependent on whether there is a bedroom located there. The window is required if the basement is in a dwelling unit.

Escape and rescue windows must be openable and of the minimum size as specified in Section 310.4 to facilitate their use.

REFERENCE: SECTION 310.4, 3RD PARAGRAPH

FIGURE 9-8 ESCAPE OR RESCUE WINDOWS INCLUDING BASEMENT LEVEL

have its own escape window: A window in another sleeping room cannot be used to meet this provision.

The window must open to the required width. Jalousie or louvered-type windows are not permitted. Grilles used over the windows must be openable from inside without special knowledge or tools. All too often, grilles and other devices installed to secure against burglary have trapped occupants who could not open them or have hampered firefighting efforts. (See Figure 9-6.)

310.5. Light, Ventilation and Sanitation. Light and ventilation shall be as specified in Chapter 12. The number of plumbing fixtures shall not be less than specified in Section 2902.6.

The following sections are referenced in Section 310.5. (The provisions for light, ventilation and sanitation for all occupancies are contained in the .5 sections of Chapter 3.)

1203.1 Light. For the purpose of determining the light or ventilation for Group Occupancies required by this section, any room may be considered as a portion of an adjoining room when one half of the area of the common wall is open and unobstructed and provides an opening of not less than one tenth of the floor area of the interior room or 25 square feet (2.3 m^2), whichever is greater.

Exterior openings for natural light or ventilation required by this section shall open directly onto a public way or a yard or court as set forth in Section 1203.4.

EXCEPTIONS: 1. Required exterior openings may open into a roofed porch where the porch:

1.1 Abuts a public way, yard or court;

1.2 Has a ceiling height of not less than 7 feet (2134 mm); and

1.3 Has a longer side at least 65 percent open and obstructed.

2. Skylights

1203.2 Light. Guest rooms and habitable rooms. Guest rooms and habitable rooms within a dwelling unit or congregate residence shall be provided with natural light by means of exterior glazed openings with an area not less than one tenth of the floor area of such rooms with a minimum of 10 square feet (0.93 m^2).

EXCEPTION: Kitchens in Group R Occupancies may be provided with artificial light.

Residential occupancies require a minimum level of natural light and ventilation. The amount of available openings is arbitrarily set in Section 1203.2. These amounts have been in effect for many years with only slight variations to develop uniformity with the other model codes. This lack of uniformity will change with the publication of the UBC in the year 2000.

1203.3 Ventilation. Guest rooms and habitable rooms within a dwelling unit or congregate residence shall be provided with natural ventilation by means of openable exterior openings with an area of not less than 1/20 of the floor area of such rooms with a minimum of 5 square feet (0.46 m^2).

In lieu of required exterior openings for natural ventilation, a mechanical ventilation system may be provided. Such system shall be capable of providing two air changes per hour in guest rooms, dormitories, habitable rooms and in public corridors with a minimum of 15 cubic feet per minute (7 L/s) of outside air per occupant during such time as the building is occupied.

Bathrooms, water closet compartments, laundry rooms and similar rooms shall be provided with natural ventilation by means of openable exterior openings with an area of not less than 1/20 of the floor area of such rooms with a minimum of $1\frac{1}{2}$ square feet (0.14 m^2).

EXCEPTION: Laundry rooms in Group R, Division 3 Occupancies.

In lieu of required exterior openings for natural ventilation in bathrooms containing a bathtub, shower or combination thereof; laundry rooms; and similar rooms, a mechanical ventilation system connected directly to the outside capable of providing five air changes per hour shall be provided. Such systems shall be connected directly to the outside, and the point of discharge shall be at least 3 feet (914 mm) from any opening that allows air entry into occupied portions of the building. Bathrooms that contain only a water closet, lavatory or combination thereof and similar rooms may be ventilated with an approved mechanical recirculating fan or similar device designed to remove odors from the air.

An alternative means of providing the ventilation is contained in Section 1203.3, i.e., mechanical systems.

Natural light and ventilation are to be obtained from exterior openings that are directly on a street or other public space. The exceptions permit the opening to be onto a roofed porch under specific conditions.

Skylights are another acceptable means for that light. Skylights have been generally accepted by many local jurisdictions for this purpose. Such skylights must comply with Section 2409 provisions.

When using a skylight for the light requirement, the clear area of the glazing must be used because skylights frequently have heavier supports than wall-mounted glazing.

In the authors' opinion, when the skylight is a domed or other type of skylight that is not in the plane of the roof, the area of the glazing to be used to determine the area being furnished should be the plane area of the skylight.

The required area for light is set forth in Section 1203.3 as a minimum of 10 square feet. The light requirement can be met by adding the amount of wall and skylight areas furnished.

When it is intended to use the skylight to provide the required ventilation per Section 1203.3, the skylight must be operable from a convenient floor-level location. Thus, the operating mechanism should be a readily accessible device that can open the skylight at least to the required minimum area. The need for ready access is to make a skylight, which is otherwise an inaccessible exterior opening, comparable to a wall opening.

The provisions of Sections 1203.2 and 1203.3 do not state that the openings must be accessible. Logic must be used when a requirement states that the openings must be "operable."

> It is the authors' opinion, for example, that clerestory windows can be used for ventilation only when the operating mechanism is extended so that it is operable from the floor level of the room.

310.8 Shaft and Exit Enclosures. Exits shall be enclosed as specified in Chapter 10.

Elevator shafts, vent shafts, dumbwaiter shafts, clothes chutes and other vertical openings shall be enclosed and the enclosure shall be as specified in Section 711.

In nonsprinklered Group R, Division 1 Occupancies, corridors serving an occupant load of 10 or more shall be separated from corridors and other areas on adjacent floors by not less than approved fixed wire glass set in fixed steel frames or by 20-minute smoke- and draft-control assemblies, which are automatic closing by smoke detection.

NOTE: Fire sprinklers axe requited in some Group R, Division 1 buildings. The requirements are in Section 904.2.9 and will be discussed under that provision in this Guide.

Cross references to particular shaft enclosures are contained in the first two paragraphs of this section.

The last paragraph of this section is important both for its intent and for the change in a basic philosophical provision of the code that it represents.

This provision requires that in a two-story Group R, Division 1 Occupancy building (apartment house, hotel or motel) with corridors serving occupant loads greater than 10 (i.e., floor areas greater than 2000 square feet), the corridors are to be separated from corridors and other areas of the adjacent floor. This requirement applies only to unsprinklered buildings. Therefore, if the building is sprinklered for any reason, the separation required by this section would not apply.

The separation does not need to be of 1-hour fire-resistive construction but may be a 20-minute smoke- and draft-stop assembly. Thus, a door and equivalent construction for the surrounding wall can be used. (See Figure 9-9.)

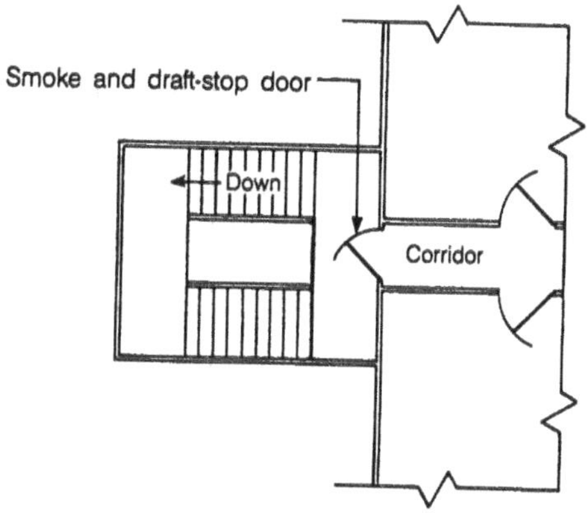

EXAMPLE #1

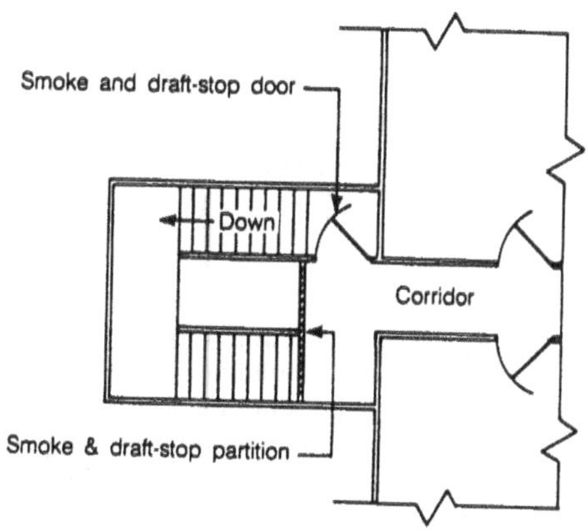

EXAMPLE #2

PARTIAL PLAN VIEWS-2ND FLOOR

REFERENCE: SECTION 310.8, 3RD PARAGRAPH

FIGURE 9-9 TWO STORY GROUP R, DIVISION 1 BUIDLING, NON-SPRINKLERED, SMOKE STOP BARRIERS

In Article 8 of this Guide, our discussion of the provisions of Standard 7-7 and Figure 8-15 illustrate methods of achieving fractional wall ratings.

This provision is the result of three fires occurring between 1978 and 1981 that involved two-story motels. Multiple deaths occurred in two of the fires and multiple injuries occurred in the third. In each instance the fire started on the first floor. The code intent is to provide isolation of the individual levels of the building, so that fire or smoke from the lower level will not trap people on the second floor.

This provision is a major one, because it negates the general provision that two adjacent floors may be unenclosed. (See Section 711 and Sections 1003.3.3 and 1003.3.4.) In particular, two-story buildings generally had no requirement for enclosed stairways.

Although this change applies only to Group R, Division 1 Occupancy buildings and does not require fully complying enclosures, it still achieves the effect of enclosures. It will require, where it is the designer's intent to have open railings, walls and the types of aesthetic openness usually found in such buildings, that the separation be provided by some form of smoke- and draft-stop enclosure or separation. The actual method for providing the separation is left to the designer.

310.9 Smoke Detectors and Sprinkler Systems.
310.9.1 Smoke Detectors.

.
.
.

310.9.1.3 Power source. In new construction, required smoke detectors shall receive their primary power from the building wiring when such wiring Is served from a commercial source and shall be equipped with a battery backup. The detector shall emit a signal when batteries are low. Wiring shall be permanent and without a disconnecting switch other than those required for overcurrent protection. Smoke detectors may be solely battery operated when installed in existing buildings, or in buildings without commercial power, or in buildings which undergo alterations, repairs or additions regulated by Section 310.9.1.2.

310.9.1.4 Location within dwelling units. In dwelling units, a detector shall be installed in each sleeping room and at a point centrally located in the corridor or area giving access to each sleeping area. When the dwelling unit has more than one story and in dwellings with basements, a detector shall be installed on each story and in the basement. In dwelling units where a story or basement is split into two or more levels, the smoke detector shall be installed on the upper level, except that when the lower level contains a sleeping area, a detector shall be installed on each level. When sleeping

rooms are on an upper level, the detector shall be placed at the ceiling of the upper level in close proximity to the stairway. In dwelling units where the ceiling height of a room open to the hallway serving bedrooms exceeds that of the hallway by 24 inches (610 mm) or more, smoke detectors shall be installed in the hallway and in the adjacent room. Detectors shall sound an alarm audible in all sleeping areas of the dwelling unit in which they are located.

Section 310.9 provides the requirements for smoke detectors in Group R, Division 1 Occupancy buildings. Over the past several years these devices have proven to be one of the key life-saving tools in residential buildings. The failure of the detector is usually due to battery failure. For this reason, in new buildings the detectors must be hard wired into the building wiring. However, to account for a possible power failure, a battery backup is required together with a warning signal when the battery loses strength.

The change to Section 310.9.1.9 contains two performance criteria for the smoke detector required in existing dwelling units in Group R, Division 1 Occupancy buildings:

1. The detectors must have an integral battery backup.
2. The detectors shag have the capability of giving a warning signal when the backup battery runs low.

Smoke detectors with these capabilities are presently available.

There is no requirement that the batteries be rechargeable or that the detector have recharging capability.

The AC–DC type of wired-in detector can use standard carbon zinc, alkaline or other low-cost batteries. The intent of the code provision is to provide a low-cost method of obtaining an emergency backup in the event of a fire-caused power failure in the unit or building.

In Section 310.9.1.4, the detector locations have been increased to include placement of detectors within the sleeping rooms. The purpose is to provide a warning device to room occupants of a fire initiating within the room, e.g., someone smoking in bed and falling asleep. Note that this provision of additional detectors will be triggered in existing buildings when work is done in excess of the Section 310.9.1.2 dollar valuation. These detectors will also be required in some communities where the provisions of Section 310.9 are triggered on sale of a property.

310.10 Fire Alarm Systems. Group R, Division 1 Occupancies shall be provided with a manual and automatic fire alarm system in apartment houses

three or more stories in height or containing 16 or more dwelling units, in hotels three or more stories in height or containing 20 or more guest rooms and in congregate residences three or more stories in height or having an occupant load of 20 or more. A fire alarm and communication system shall be provided in Group R, Division 1 Occupancies located in a highrise building.

EXCEPTIONS: 1. A manual fire alarm system need not be installed in buildings not over two stories in height when all individual dwelling units and contiguous attic and crawl spaces are separated from each other and from public or common areas by at least one-hour fire-resistive occupancy separations and each individual dwelling unit or guest room has an exit direct to a public way, exit court or yard.

2. A separate fire alarm system need not be provided in buildings which are protected throughout by an approved supervised fire sprinkler system having a local alarm to notify all occupants.

The alarm signal shall be a distinctive sound that is not used for any other purpose other than the fire alarm. Alarm-signaling devices shall produce a sound that exceeds the prevailing code equivalent sound level in the room or space by 15 decibels minimum, or exceeds any maximum sound level with a duration of 30 seconds minimum by 5 decibels minimum, whichever is louder. Sound levels for alarm signals shall be 120 decibels maximum.

For the purpose of this section, area separation walls shall not define separate buildings.

The last paragraph, which relates to the area-separation-wall-(ASW-)divided building, removes a credit provided through the use of an ASW. This provision is more restrictive, because the number of dwelling units or guest rooms will be the aggregate of such units or rooms in the entire structure rather than just the number of such units or rooms in one part of the building as separated by an ASW.

Of greater concern to the designer should be the portent of this type of change.

The concept behind the ASW provision, Section 504.6, is that it creates separate buildings. That concept is in conflict with this provision. It will require diligence on the part of enforcement officials and designers to avoid enacting more restrictive code changes aimed at removing the credits previously warranted by the ASW-divided building.

311.2 Construction, Height and Allowable Area.

311.2.1 General. Buildings or parts of buildings classed as Group S Occupancy because of the use or character of the occupancy shall be limited to the types of construction set forth in Tables No. 5-B. Such occupancies shall not exceed, in area or height, the limits specified in Sections 504, 505 and 506.

311.2.2 Special Provisions

311.2.2.1 Group S, Division 3 with Group A, Division 3; Group B; Group M or R, Division 1 Occupancy above. Other provisions of this code notwithstanding, a basement or first story of a building may be considered as a separate and distinct building for the purposes of area limitations, limitation of number of stories and type of construction when all of the following conditions are met:

1. The basement or first story is of Type I construction and is separated from the building above with a three-hour occupancy separation. See Section 302.3.
2. The building above the three-hour occupancy separation contains only Group A, Division 3, Group B, or Group M or R, Division 1 Occupancies.
3. The building below the three-hour occupancy separation is a Group S, Division 3 Occupancy used exclusively for the parking and storage of private or pleasure-type motor vehicles.

    EXCEPTION: 1. Entry lobbies, laundry rooms and mechanical rooms and similar uses incidental to the operation of the building.

    2. Group A, Division 3 and Group B office, drinking and dining establishments and Group M retail occupancies in addition to those incidental to the operation of the building (including storage areas) provided the entire structure below the three-hour occupancy separation is protected throughout by an automatic sprinkler system.

4. The maximum building height in feet shall not exceed the limits set forth in Table 5-B for the least type of construction involved.

The provisions in Section 311.2.2.1 describe a concept that permits one type of construction to support a different and lesser type of construction.

The intent of this concept is that if the base structure can be constructed to simulate the same degree of safety as if it was ground, then separate structures could be built on the base structure. These structures would be considered distinct buildings and could be constructed of any type of construction without the base structure being downgraded to that type of construction.

Thus, a Type I garage could be built with Type V buildings on top of the garage. There is no limit to the size of the base structure or to the number of individual buildings that can be built on top of the base provided the limitations in Section 311.2.2.1 are met. (See Figure 9-1.)

The changes to Section 311.2.2.1 second paragraph from the prior code [Section 702(a), 1991 UBC] include adding the Group S, Division 3, Group A, Division 3 and Group M or R, Division 1 Occupancy to those permitted to be above a Type I or II-FR structure housing a Group B Occupancy. In addition, the basement or first story may contain offices or retail stores as well as the garage. These changes increase the flexibility of this concept whereby the lower segment and the upper segment of the building are each considered as separate structures. These identical provisions have been in use in San Francisco in the Embarcadero Center area for more than 20 years without problems. (See Figure 9-1.)

The Group A, Division 3 Occupancy includes restaurants, conference rooms and senior citizen centers. Such Group A, Division 3 Occupancies are commonly needed in conjunction with the Group B, Division 2 Occupancy and Group R, Division 1 Occupancy uses. The new provision will accommodate that need without creating code difficulties.

Proper occupancy separations, per Table 3-B, must be provided between the various occupancies.

602.5 Roofs. Group M or S, Division 1 Occupancies and in Group H Occupancies, roofs and their members, other than the structural frame may be of unprotected noncombustible materials when every part of the roof framing, including the structural frame, is 25 feet (7620 mm) or more above the floor, balcony or gallery immediately below. Heavy-timber members in accordance with Section 605.6 may be used for such unprotected members in one-story buildings.

Except in retail sales and storage areas classified as Group M or S, Division 1 Occupancies and in Group H Occupancies, roofs and their members, other than the structural frame may be of unprotected noncombustible materials when every part of the roof framing, including the structural frame, is 25 feet (7620 mm) or more above the floor, balcony or gallery immediately below. Heavy-timber members in accordance with Section 605.6 may be used for such unprotected members in one-story buildings.

When every part of the structural framework of the roof of a Group A or E Occupancy or of an atrium is not less than 25 feet (7620 mm) above any floor, balcony or gallery, fire protection of all members of the roof construction, including those of the structural frame, may be omitted. Heavy-timber members in accordance with Section 605.6 may be used for such unprotected members in one-story buildings.

Roofs of unprotected noncombustible or Heavy-timber construction conforming to Section 605.4.6 may be less than 25 feet (7620 mm) above any floor, balcony or gallery of a Group A, Division 2.1 Occupancy having an occupant load of 10,000 or more when all of the following conditions are met:

1. The building is not more than one story in height, except for multi-level areas located under the roof and used for locker rooms, exiting, concession stands, mechanical rooms and others accessory to the assembly room.

2. The area in which the roof clearance is less than 25 feet (7620 mm) does not exceed 35 percent of the area encompassed by the exterior walls.

3. An approved supervised automatic sprinkler system shall be installed throughout.

Where every part of the structural steel framework of the roof of a Group A or E Occupancy is more than 18 feet (5486 mm) and less than 25 feet

(7610 mm) above any floor, balcony or gallery, the roof construction shall be protected by a ceiling of not less than one-hour fire-resistive construction.

Roof coverings shall be as specified in Chapter 15.

604.5 Roofs. Roof coverings shall be as specified in Chapter 15.

Except in retail sales and storage areas classified as Group M or S, Division 1 Occupancies and in Group H Occupancies, roofs and their members, other than the structural frame may be of unprotected noncombustible materials when every part of the roof framing, including the structural frame, is 25 feet (7620 mm) or more above the floor, balcony or gallery immediately below. Heavy-timber members in accordance with Section 605.6 may be used for such unprotected members in one-story buildings.

Section 602.5 prohibits the reduction of the fire resistance of a high roof assembly for retail sales and storage areas classified as Group B, Division 2 Occupancy or Group H Occupancy. The prior codes allowed all occupancies to make use of the nonrated roof construction provisions of then Section 1806 when there was a minimum height of the roof above the floor. The concern expressed for the change was related to high piled storage and the highly flammable materials in sales and storage areas.

A second change requires that the roof and the structural frame be at least 25 feet above the floor, balcony or gallery. This requirement for the structural frame was added even though the structural frame must have the required fire resistance in accordance with Table 6-A.

As seen above, there is a comparable provision to Section 602.5 in Section 604.5 for the roofs of Type III buildings.

Section 403–Special Provisions for Group B Office Buildings and Group R, Division 1 Occupancies

These high-rise life safety provisions apply only to Group B and Group R, Division 1 Occupancies, when they have an occupancy floor more than 75 feet above grade. This provision is not discussed in detail because this section is limited to high-rise buildings, which are a specialized area of design.

The high-rise life safety requirements include those that provide alternatives for some conventional code requirements and greater safety than the conventional provisions. The items comprising the life safety fire-sprinkler-based package include

- sprinklers throughout,
- elevator recall,

- communications,
- emergency power,
- smoke control and
- central control station.

The recent code changes to the high-rise provisions include

- elimination of the use of compartmentation as an alternative to sprinklering,
- the permissive use of the elevator lobby for exit corridor passage and
- changes to use of natural ventilation as an alternative to mechanical smoke control.

403.1 Scope. This section applies to all Group B, Division 2 office buildings and Group R, Division 1 Occupancies, each having floors used for human occupancy located more than 75 feet above the lowest level of fire department access. Such buildings shall be of Type I or II-F.R. construction and shall be provided with an approved automatic sprinkler system in accordance with Section 403.2.

403.2 Automatic Sprinkler System.

403.2.1 System Design. The automatic sprinkler system shall be provided throughout the building as specified by UBC Standard 9-1, and shall be designed in accordance with that standard and the following: The sprinkler system shall be designed using the parameters set forth in UBC Standard No. 38-1 and the following:

1. Shutoff valves and a water-flow device shall be provided for each floor. The sprinkler riser may be combined with the standpipe riser.

2. In Seismic Zones 2, 3 and 4, in addition to the main water supply, a secondary on-site supply of water equal to the hydraulically calculated sprinkler design demand plus 100 gallons per minute (378.5 L/m) additional for the total standpipe system shall be provided. This supply shall be automatically available if the principal supply falls and shall have a duration of 30 minutes.

403.2.2 Modifications. The following modifications of code requirements are permitted:

1. In buildings of Type 1 construction, the fire-resistive time periods set forth in Table 6-A may be reduced by one hour for interior bearing walls, exterior bearing and nonbearing walls, roofs and the beams supporting roofs, provided they do not frame into columns. In buildings of Type II-F.R. construction, the fire-resistive time period reduction set forth in Table 6-A may be reduced by one hour for interior-bearing, exterior-bearing and nonbearing walls, but no reduction is allowed for roofs. The fire-resistive time period as specified herein shall not apply to exterior bearing and nonbearing walls whose fire-resistive rating is less than four hours.

Shafts other than stairway enclosures and elevator shafts may be reduced to one hour when sprinklers are installed within shafts at alternate floors.

2. Except for corridors In Group B, offices and Group R, Division 1 Occupancies and partitions separating dwelling units or guest rooms, all interior nonbearing partitions required to be one-hour fire-resistive construction by Table 6-A may be of noncombustible construction without a fire-resistive time period.

3. Fire dampers, other than those needed to protect floor-ceiling assemblies to maintain the fire resistance of the assembly, are not required.

4. Emergency windows required by Section 310.4 are not required.

In the 1988 UBC, the compartmentation option was deleted from the high-use life safety provisions of Section 1807.

The design problems associated with the compartmentation concept presented formidable and rigorous requirements that had to be met.

403.4 Smoke Control. A smoke-control system meeting the requirements of Chapter 9 shall be provided.

SECTION 905–SMOKE CONTROL

905.1 Scope and Purpose. This section applies to mechanical and passive smoke-control systems when they are required by other provisions of this code. The purpose of this section is to establish minimum requirements for the design, installation and acceptance testing of smoke-control systems that are intended to provide a tenable environment for the evacuation or relocation of occupants. These provisions are not intended for the preservation of contents or for assistance in fire-suppression or overhaul activities. Smoke-control systems need not comply with the requirements of Section 609 in the Mechanical Code unless their normal use would otherwise require compliance. Nothing in these requirements is intended to apply when smoke control is not otherwise required by this code. Smoke-control systems are not a substitute for sprinkler protection.

Section 403.4 of the high-rise requirements requires smoke control. The provisions of Section 905 require a "designed" smoke control system, whether it be mechanical or passive.

> The authors recommend that a qualified fire protection or mechanical engineer be retained when a smoke control system is required.

403.7 Elevators. Elevators and elevator lobbies shall comply with the provisions of Chapter 30 and the following:

NOTE: A bank of elevators is a group of elevators or a single elevator controlled by a common operating system; that is, all those elevators which

respond to a single call button constitute a bank of elevators. There is no limit on the number of cars which may be in a bank or group but there may be not more than four cars within a common hoistway.

1. Elevators on all floors shall open into elevator lobbies which are separated from the remainder of the building, including corridors and other exits, by walls extending from the floor to the underside of the fire-resistive floor or roof above. Such walls shall be of not less than one-hour fire-resistive construction. Openings through such walls shall conform to Section 1004.3.4.3.2.

EXCEPTIONS: 1. The main entrance level elevator lobby in office buildings.

2. Elevator lobbies located within an atrium complying with the provisions of Section 402.

3. In fully sprinklered office buildings, corridors may lead through enclosed elevator lobbies if all areas of the building have access to at least one required exit without passing through the elevator lobby.

2. Each elevator lobby shall be provided with approved smoke detector(s) installed in accordance with their listings. When the detector is activated, elevator doors shall not open and all cars serving the lobby are to return to the main floor and be under manual control only. If the main floor detector or a transfer floor detector is activated, all cars serving the main floor or transfer floor shall return to a location approved by the fire department and building official and be under manual control only. The detector may serve to close the lobby doors, additional doors at the hoistway opening allowed in Section 3007 and smoke dampers serving the lobby.

3. Elevator hoistways shall not be vented through an elevator machine room. Each elevator machine room shall be treated as a separate smoke-control zone.

The primary intent of this section of the high-rise life safety provisions is to prevent smoke migration by stack effect through the elevator shafts onto the upper floors of the building. This is achieved by requiring the upper elevator lobbies to have enclosed lobbies. The enclosures are to be smoke- and draft-tight.

The addition of Exception 3 is an important change involving the exit corridors and elevator lobbies in high-use life safety buildings.

In the development of the high-use life safety provisions of Section 1807 in 1973, one of the primary concerns was the smoke migration induced by the stack effect in high-rise buildings, as well as the piston or pumping action of an elevator running in a shaft. For this reason, the requirement for separation of the elevator lobby from the corridors was added.

The 1973 high-rise requirement resulted in a need to redesign the exit corridor arrangements of Group B, and Group R, Division 1 high-rise buildings, so that the exit corridors no longer passed through the elevator lobbies. This separation of elevator lobbies from corridors resulted in considerable loss of usable, rentable space. In particular, in a central core-type Group B office building, the redesign usually necessitated a corridor running almost completely around the core.

The present provision permits the exit corridor to use the elevator lobby as part of the exiting path. It allows passage through the one-hour smoke- and draft-stop separation when the specific requirements of Exception 3 are met:

- The building must be sprinklered per Section 403 of the high-rise requirements. The compartmentation option, which was deleted, would not be acceptable. In the event the locality retains the compartmentation alternative, the elevators still must be separated from the exit corridors.
- The exit passage using the elevator lobby must also provide access to at least one required exit without going through that elevator lobby.

Thus, a corridor with a stair at one end and the other end, traversing the elevator lobby and then leading to another stairway satisfies this requirement.

(See Figures 9-10 and 9-11 for examples of the provisions for a Group B, and Group R, Division 1 Occupancy, respectively.)

Figure 9-12 illustrates the conditions in a Group R, Division 1 Occupancy with only two elevators and a small elevator lobby. Floor plan (a) shows a typical arrangement for the present elevator/corridor separation requirements. Note that to provide the separation in floor plan (a) and the separation from the two doors to the units opposite the lobby, the elevator lobby must be set off from the corridor.

Floor plan (b) meets the intent of the new code provisions. The arrangement of cross-corridor smoke- and draft-barrier doors, together with similar doors for the two units opposite the elevators, satisfies the two criteria stated above. This arrangement was the common one found in pre-high-rise buildings and in many low-rise buildings.

The designer should note that when the floor areas involved are large enough to result in occupant loads in the corridor of 50 or more, the requirements of Section 1003.3.1.5 apply, i.e., the exit doors must swing in the direction of exit travel. In such instances, the elevator lobby doors may have to be paired so that one leaf swings in one direction and the other in the opposite direction. (See

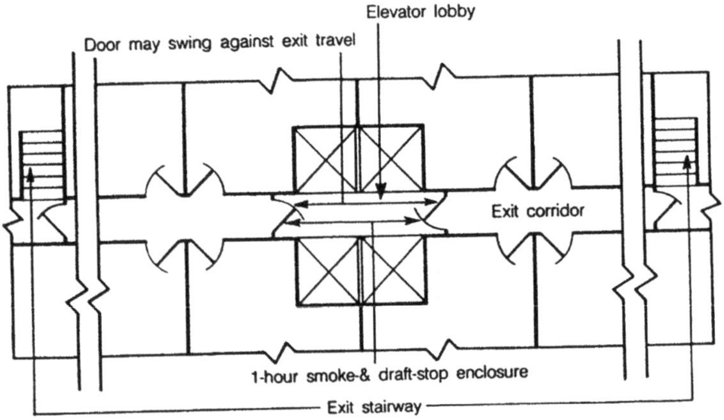

TYPICAL FLOOR WITH OCCUPANT LOAD <50 ON EACH SIDE OF ELEVATOR LOBBY

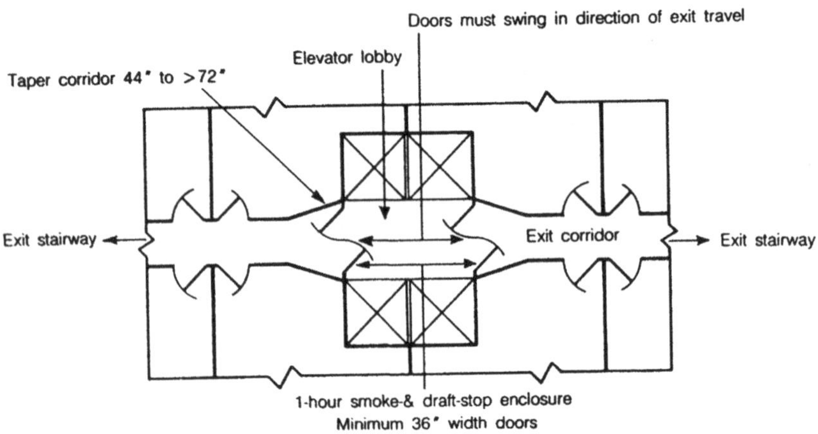

TYPICAL FLOOR WITH OCCUPANT LOAD ≥ 50 ON EACH SIDE OF ELEVATOR LOBBY

REFERENCE: SECTION 403.7 & 1003.3.1.5

FIGURE 9-10 EXIT CORRIDOR THROUGH ELEVATOR LOBBY, GROUP R, DIVISION 1 OCCUPANCY HIGH RISE BUILDING

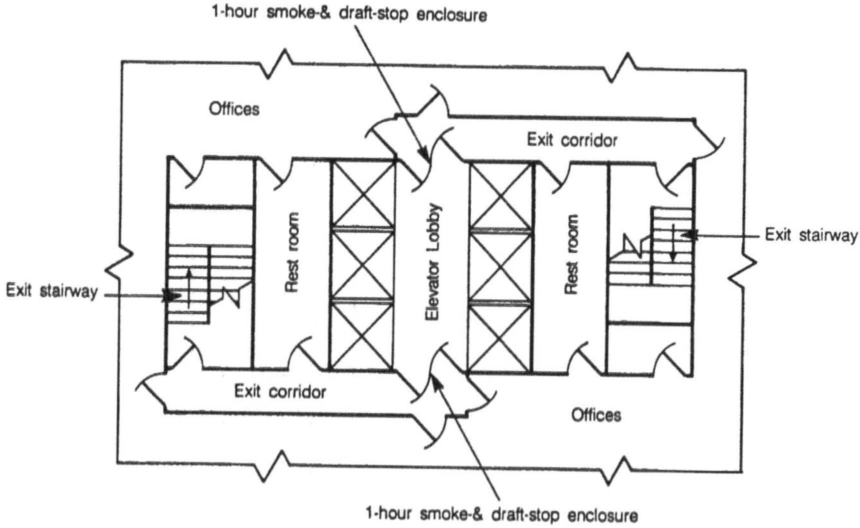

PARTIAL TYPICAL FLOOR PLAN, B OCCUPANCY, HIGH RISE BUILDING W/CENTRAL SERVICE CORE

ASSUME: GROUP B OCCUPANCY, HIGH RISE BUILDING OCCUPANT LOAD >50 ON EACH SIDE OF ELEVATOR LOBBY

NOTE: If 1-hour smoke & draft stop enclosure placed across the exit corridors, the corridors must be of sufficient width to permit two 3' wide exit doors to be installed, each swinging in a direction of exit travel.

REFERENCE: SECTION 403.7 & 1003.3.1.5

FIGURE 9-11 EXIT CORRIDOR THROUGH ELEVATOR LOBBY, GROUP B OCCUPANCY HIGH RISE BUILDING

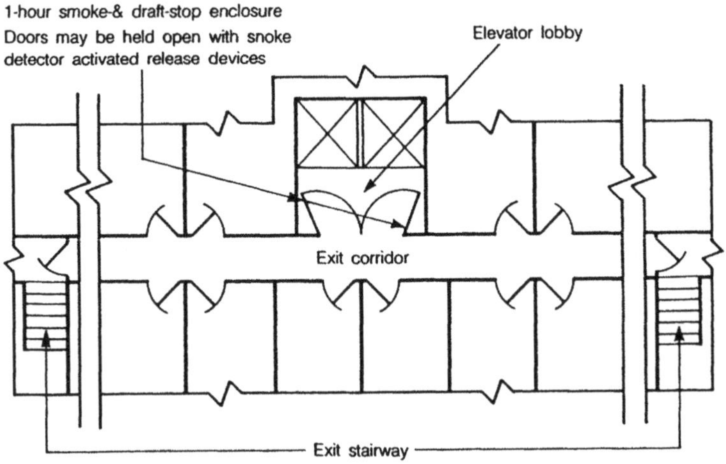

Floor Plan (a)

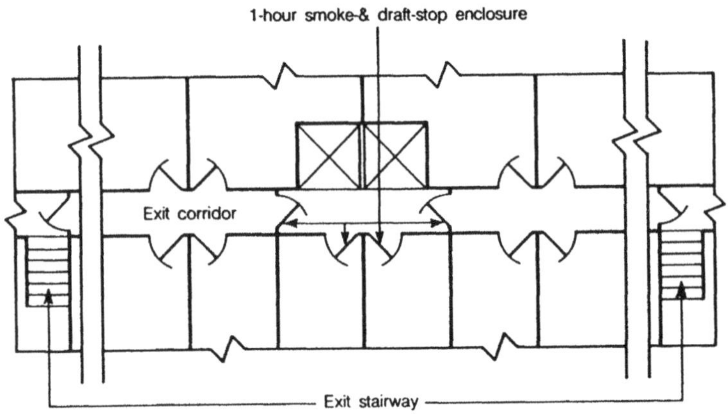

Floor Plan (b)

REFERENCE: SECTION 403.7 & 1003.3.1.5

FIGURE 9-12 ELEVATOR/CORRIDOR SEPARATION COMPARISON, GROUP R, DIVISION 1 OCCUPANCY WITH & WITHOUT LOBBY

Figure 9-12 for an example.) This requirement will ensure that occupant loads of 50 or more on either side of the elevator lobby can exit through the lobby by doors swinging in the direction of exit travel.

The doors to the elevator lobby may be left in the open position by using smoke-detector-activated release devices. The designer must provide for the required width of the corridor/elevator lobby for the pair of doors in the circumstance described above. A smooth transition should be made between the normal width of the corridor and the widened section. (See Figure 9-12.)

When pairs of doors are required, each swinging in an opposite direction, they should be arranged so that the like-swinging directions are on the same side of the elevator lobby. This is recommended to prevent the occupant from entering the lobby and seeking to enter the other exit corridor, only to find that the door does not swing in the direction of exit travel.

NOTE: As discussed in regard to Section 403.7, Item 1, Exception 3, the code requirement for separation of the elevator lobby from the exit corridors applies only to high-rise buildings under Section 1004.3.4.5. No prior code provision mandated such separation for any other building prior to the high-rise changes (1973 UBC).

ARTICLE 10

MISCELLANEOUS CODE PROVISIONS CHAPTERS 7, 8, 11, 12, 15, 23, 25, 26 AND 35 INCLUDING ACCESSIBILITY, INTERIOR ENVIRONMENT, SPRINKLER PROVISIONS AND STANDARDS

This article of the Guide reviews certain miscellaneous Uniform Building Code (UBC) provisions that, for a designer, either have frequent application or can cause problems. In Article 9, the provisions in certain other UBC chapters were reviewed. The provisions in these two articles are intended to supplement those discussed in Articles 3 through 8 herein.

SECTION 708—FIRE BLOCKS AND DRAFT STOPS

708.1 General. In combustible construction, fireblocking and draftstopping shall be installed to cut off all concealed draft openings (both vertical and horizontal) and shall form an effective barrier between floors, between a top story and a roof or attic space, and shall subdivide attic spaces, concealed roof spaces and floor-ceiling assemblies. The integrity of all fire blocks and draft stops shall be maintained.

708.2 Fire Blocks.

708.2.1 Where Required. Fireblocking shall be provided in the following locations:

1. In concealed spaces of stud walls and partitions, including furred spaces, at the ceiling and floor levels and at 10-foot (3048 mm) intervals both vertical and horizontal. See also Section 803, Item 1.

   EXCEPTION: Fire blocks may be omitted at floor and ceiling levels when approved smoke-actuated fire dampers are installed at these levels.

2. At all interconnections between concealed vertical and horizontal spaces such as occur at soffits, drop ceilings and cove ceilings.

3. In concealed spaces between stair stringers at the top and bottom of the run and between studs along and in line with the run of the stairs if the walls under the stairs are unfinished.

4. In openings around vents, pipes, ducts, chimneys, fireplaces and similar openings that afford a passage for fire at ceiling and floor levels, with noncombustible materials.

5. At openings between attic spaces and chimney chases for factory-built chimneys.

6. Where wood sleepers are used for laying wood flooring on masonry or concrete fire-resistive floors, the space between the floor slab and the underside of the wood flooring shall be filled with noncombustible material or fire blocked in such a manner that there will be no open spaces under the flooring that will exceed 100 square feet ($9.3\ m^2$) area and such space

shall be filled solidly under all permanent partitions so that there is no communication under the flooring between adjoining rooms.

EXCEPTIONS: 1. Fire blocking need not be provided in such floors when at or below grade level in gymnasiums.

2. Fire blocking need be provided only at the juncture of each alternate lane and at the ends of each lane in a bowling facility.

708.2.2 Fire block construction. Except as provided in Item 4 above, fireblocking shall consist of 2 inches (51 mm) nominal lumber or two thicknesses of 1-inch (25 mm) nominal lumber with broken lapjoints or one thickness of $\frac{23}{32}$-inch (18.3 mm) wood structural panel with joints backed by $\frac{23}{32}$-inch (18.3 mm) wood structural panel or one thickness of $\frac{3}{4}$-inch (19.1 mm) Type 2-M particleboard with joints backed by $\frac{3}{4}$-inch (19.1 mm) Type 2-M particleboard.

Fire blocks may also be of gypsum board, cement fiber board, batts or blankets of mineral or glass fiber, or other approved materials installed in such a manner as to be securely retained in place. Loose-fill insulation material shall not be used as a fire block unless specifically tested in the form and manner intended for use to demonstrate its ability to remain in place and to retard the spread of fire and hot gases.

Walls having parallel or staggered studs for sound-transmission control shall have fire blocks of batts or blankets of mineral or glass fiber or other approved flexible materials.

708.3 Draft Stops.

708.3.1 Where required. Draftstopping shall be provided in the locations set forth in this section:

708.3.1.1 Floor-ceiling assemblies.

708.3.1.1.1 Single-family dwellings. When there is usable space above and below the concealed space of a floor-ceiling assembly in a single-family dwelling. draft stops shall be installed so that the area of the concealed space does not exceed 1,000 square feet (93 m^2). Draftstopping shall divide the concealed space into approximately equal areas.

708.3.1.1.2 Two or more dwelling units and hotels. Draft stops shall be installed in floor-ceiling assemblies of buildings having more than one dwelling unit and in hotels. Such draft stops shall be in line with walls separating individual dwelling units and guest rooms from each other and from other areas.

708.3.1.1.3 Other uses. Draft stops shall be installed in floor-ceiling assemblies of buildings or portions of buildings used for other than dwelling or hotel occupancies so that the area or the concealed space does not exceed 1,000 square feet (93 m^2) and so that the horizontal dimension between stops does not exceed 60 feet (18 288 mm).

EXCEPTION: Where approved automatic sprinklers are installed within the concealed space, the area between draft stops may be 3,000 square feet (279 m^2) and the horizontal dimension may be 100 feet (30 480 mm).

708.3.1.2 Attics

708.3.1.2.1 Two or more dwelling units and hotels. Draft stops shall be installed in the attics, mansards, overhangs, false fronts set out from walls and similar concealed spaces of buildings containing more than one dwelling unit and in hotels. Such draft stops shall be above and in line with the walls

separating individual dwelling units and guest rooms from each other and from other uses.

EXCEPTIONS: 1. Draft stops may be omitted along one of the corridor walls, provided draft stops at walls separating individual dwelling units and guest rooms from each other and from other uses, extend to the remaining corridor draft stop.

2. Where approved sprinklers are installed, draftstopping may be as specified in the exception to Section 708.3.1.2.2

708.3.1.2.2 Other Uses. Draft stops shall be installed in attics, mansards, overhangs, false fronts set out from walls and similar concealed spaces of buildings having uses other than dwellings of hotels so that the area between draft stops does not exceed 3,000 square feet (279 m²) and the greatest horizontal dimension does not exceed 60 feet (18 288 mm).

EXCEPTION: Where approved automatic sprinklers are installed within the concealed space, the area between draft stops may be 9,000 square feet (836 m²) and the greatest horizontal dimension may be 100 feet (30 480 mm).

708.3.1.3 Draft stop construction. Draftstopping materials shall not be less than ½-inch (12.7 mm) gypsum board, ⅜-inch (9.5 mm) wood structural panel, ⅜-inch (9.5 mm) Type 2-M particleboard or other approved materials adequately supported.

Openings in the partitions shall be protected by self-closing doors with automatic latches constructed as required for the partitions.

Ventilation of concealed roof spaces shall be maintained in accordance with Section 1505.

708.4 Draft Stops or Fire Blocks in Other Locations. Fireblocking of veneer on noncombustible walls shall be in accordance with Section 708.2.1, Item 1.

For fireblocking ceilings applied against noncombustible construction, see Section 803, Item 1.

This section provides the mandatory locations for draft stopping and fire blocking in wood-framed buildings. The term "draft stopping" refers to the prevention of the free flow of air in stud wall and ceiling cavities by means of a barrier material, such as ½-inch gypsum wallboard or a ⅜-inch wood structural panel (plywood) or particleboard. "Fire blocking," on the other hand, must also provide some degree of fire-resistant capability. Thus, the material must be of more substantial dimension, such as 2-inch thick wood or one of the equivalent built-up assembly of materials. In both instances, the intent is to slow the spread of fire by blocking the draft or by placing a fire barrier in its path.

The designer should be aware that all too often these hidden elements of construction are frequently so poorly installed as to be ineffective or simply left out during construction. This is usually the case when double-studded walls are constructed. The designer should provide details or notes on the design drawings calling out both the location and the form of the draft stops and fire blocks to use.

The location of draft stops in attics of multifamily buildings is required at the tenant separation walls. In other than residential buildings, there are to be draft stops at no more than 60-foot intervals and creating not more than 3000 square feet in each subdivided space. These provide draft barriers to prevent fire's rapid spread in attics.

Note also that Section 1505.3 requires attic ventilation be provided. Thus, each compartment formed by the draft stops must have separate ventilation means without relying on the adjacent space; otherwise the intent of the draft stop is negated.

Where fire sprinklers are provided in the attic, the size of the area and the maximum spacing of the draft stops may be increased substantially. Note that this does not require that the entire building be sprinklered.

> Sprinklers in concealed spaces such as attics should be used with great caution and only in extraordinary circumstances. Since the sprinklers are completely hidden, they are prone to neglect and lack of maintenance. If the sprinkler system leaks or a head goes off for any reason, the ceiling is likely to become saturated by water and may fail, leading to major repairs or a hazardous condition.

This section and Sections 601.5.4, 803 and 3102.7.13 have substituted the terms "fire block," "fire blocks" and "fire blocking" for the terms "fire stop" and "fire stopping" used in prior codes. These substitutions occur when the intent of the code relates to those uses generally in frame construction using materials comparable in size to the studs or such equivalent acceptable materials as provided for in the various sections.

The new terminology eliminates the conflict in the meaning of the terms in the prior codes, when the intent of the use of fire stop and fire stopping differed between various sections of the code. Since the publication of the 1991 UBC the term "fire stop" has related solely to fire-resistive assemblies.

Chapter 8 Interior Finishes

Sanitary Finishes; for fire-related finishes see Article 8.

SECTION 807—SANITATION

807.1 Floors and Walls in Water Closet Compartment and Showers

807.1.1 Floors. In other than dwelling units, toilet room floors shall have a smooth, hard nonabsorbent surface such as portland cement, concrete, ceramic tile or other approved material that extends upward onto the walls at least 5 inches (127 mm).

807.1.2 Walls. Walls within 2 feet (610 mm) of the front and sides of urinals and water closets shall have a smooth, hard non-absorbent surface of portland cement, concrete, ceramic tile or other smooth, hard non-absorbent surface to a height of 4 feet (1219 mm) and except for structural elements, the materials used in such walls shall be of a type that is not adversely affected by moisture. See Section 2512 for other limitations.

EXCEPTIONS: 1. Dwelling units and guest rooms.

2. Toilet rooms that are not accessible to the public and that have not more than one water closet.

807.1.3 Showers. Showers in all occupancies shall be finished as specified in Sections 807.1.1 and 807.1.2 to a height of not less than 70 inches above the drain inlet. Materials other than structural elements used in such walls shall be of a type that is not adversely affected by moisture. See Section 2512 for other limitations

SECTION 2512—USE OF GYPSUM IN SHOWERS AND WATER CLOSETS

When gypsum is used as a base for tile or wall panels for tub, shower or water closet compartment walls (see Sections 807.1.1 and 807.1.3), water-resistant gypsum backing board shall be used. Regular gypsum wallboard is permitted under tile or wall panels in other wall and ceiling areas when installed in accordance with Table 25-G. Water-resistant gypsum board shall not be used in the following locations:

1. Over a vapor barrier.
2. In areas subject to continuous high humidity, such as saunas, steam rooms or gang shower rooms.
3. On ceilings where frame spacing exceeds 12 inches (305 mm) on center.

In addition to regulating such things as fire safety and exiting, the code addresses other health and safety issues such as sanitation. This section sets out the requirements for floor and wall surfaces in toilet and bathing facilities. While residential occupancies and single accommodation toilets are exempt from these requirements, the designer should consider providing similar sanitation measures in all toilet facilities. Note also that shower requirements apply to all occupancies without exception. Verify that wall materials specified (including backing materials) meet the requirements of moisture resistance noted in the code. The code-mandated restrictions on the use of certain materials in certain applications are usually based on historical instances of poor performance of systems. In this case the restrictions on the use of water-resistant gypsum come from problems that have been prevalent enough or troublesome enough to warrant mention in the code.

Sections 807.1.3 and 2512 illustrate another lesson in code usage. The designer should always read any section cross referenced in another code section to verify that there is not an added requirement or an exception that may apply to a specific project.

Chapter 9 Fire Protection Systems

904.2 Automatic Fire-extinguishing Systems

904.2.9 Group R Division 1 Occupancies. An automatic sprinkler system shall be installed throughout every apartment house three or more stories in height or containing 16 or more dwelling units, every congregate residence three or more stories in height or having an occupant load of twenty or more, and every hotel three or more stories in height or containing 20 or more guest rooms. Residential or quick response standard sprinkler heads shall be used in the dwelling units and guest room portions of the building.

This sprinkler requirement for Group R, Division 1 apartment houses and hotels is in addition to

- the 1-hour fire-resistive construction required by Section 310.2.2,
- the smoke detector requirements of Section 310.9.1 and
- the fire alarm requirements in Section 310.10.

The form of the requirement is identical to the fire alarm requirement, i.e., the sprinklers will be required in the same size building. Therefore, whenever a fire alarm is required, there also must be fire sprinklers throughout. The sprinkler system must be tied to the fire alarm system, so that a flow in the sprinklers will initiate the fire alarm.

In some buildings the requirements for tying the two systems together may be modified to allow for a "silent alarm," provided the fire department approves such a system. This will usually require a 24-hour staffed location that will receive the silent alarm and will have the capability of verifying the reason for same before initiating the fire alarm signal.

In buildings that require the sprinkler system throughout, the provisions of Section 508 for fire-resistive substitution may not be applicable. That section specifically restricts the use of sprinklers as a trade-off for fire-resistive construction to situations where the sprinklers are not otherwise required throughout the building.

The code stipulates that either a residential sprinkler head or a quick-response standards sprinkler head be used within the dwelling unit or guest room. The inference, therefore, is that in the public areas of the building, which include the corridors, stairways, lobbies, service closets and other rooms not specifically considered dwelling units or guest rooms, standard heads will be used.

As can readily be seen, the growing use of sprinkler systems mandated by the code continues unabated. By adding this level of requirement to residential buildings, lives will be saved. However, omitting any cost offsets or trade-offs for the additional requirements is unfortunate. The reader is directed to Section 403.2.2, where the concept of trade-offs, an integral part of the sprinkler requirements in high-rise buildings, is discussed.

Chapter 11 Accessibility Including Appendix Chapter 11

The basic accessibility requirements in the UBC have been developed jointly with the two other model code agencies through the Board for the Coordination of Model Codes (BCMC). This chapter has been extensively revised over the course of the last two code adoption cycles. The designer must be aware that many states have significantly different locally developed accessibility requirements, in some cases rewriting Chapter 11 completely. These basic UBC provisions should be reviewed carefully against state and local amendments. The likelihood of significant and extensive local variation from the basic UBC is higher for this chapter than any other in the code. The designer must be certain to use the correct accessibility code for a specific project.

Making buildings accessible to persons with disabilities is an increasingly important design requirement. It has become an even greater issue since the passage of the Americans with Disabilities Act (ADA) in 1990. The model codes have incorporated requirements for accessibility that are intended to be coordinated with the requirements of the ADA. However, the designer must remember that plan review by the building official is done for compliance only with the provisions of the building code. The model code is not considered equivalent to the ADA and compliance with the UBC is no guarantee of compliance with the ADA. No designer should rely solely on this code to determine access compliance requirements. Every project should also be carefully reviewed against the provisions of the ADA [or the Federal Fair Housing Act (FFHA) for housing] to assure compliance with federal law. A detailed discussion of the relationship of ADA or FFHA requirements to those of the UBC is beyond the scope of this book. Using these new UBC sections and the related scoping documents will start the designer in the proper direction, but review of the ADA or FFHA is necessary as well.

SECTION 1101—SCOPE

1101.1 General. Buildings or portions of buildings shall be accessible to persons with disabilities as required by this chapter.

See also Appendix Chapter 11 for requirements governing the provision of accessible site facilities not regulated by this chapter. See Section 101.3 for applicability of appendix.

Note that the scope definition shows a reference to the Appendix. This begs the question of what is the extent of the code scope if the appendix is not formally adopted by the jurisdiction. This is especially true for existing buildings. If Division II of Appendix Chapter 11 is not adopted, then both the designer and the building official are left with no guidance regarding criteria for existing buildings, an untenable position.

> The authors believe that it is essential that the Appendix chapter be adopted. An increasing number of building projects involve existing buildings. The ADA requires that altered buildings incorporate accessibility and the UBC must be in accord with those ADA requirements.

Because of the interrelationship of new and existing scoping provisions, the problems with nonadoption of the Appendix and the volume of existing building design work, the authors will assume that the existing building provisions of the Appendix will be adopted and treat Chapter 11 as containing both the body of the code and the Appendix.

The designer must verify the status of the Appendix in the jurisdiction where a project is located. Check the adoption of local amendments and appendices with the local building official before beginning design. Both the basic code and the appendix should be read together to ascertain their applicability of provisions to existing buildings.

1101.3 Design. The design and construction of accessible buildings and building elements shall be in accordance with this chapter and CABO/ANSI A117.1-1992. For a building to be considered accessible, it shall be designed and constructed to the minimum provisions of this chapter and CABO/ANSI A117.1.

The detailed dimensional requirements for design are contained in the referenced standard, CABO/ANSI A117.1. The provisions of Chapter 11 are to set "scoping." This chapter tells the designer and building official where provisions are to apply and in what quantities. For example, scoping sets forth such items as the number of required accessible rooms in accessible hotel accommodations. The dimensions and technical requirements for such accessible hotel rooms are contained in A117.1. The designer *must* have a current copy of CABO/ANSI A117.1 to use for reference to be able to comply with the access requirements of the UBC. Designers must familiarize themselves with the detailed requirements of CABO/ANSI A117.1. We will touch on only small areas of that standard here. The designer should read the standard thoroughly.

CABO/ANSI A117.1 has a strong resemblance to the Americans with Disabilities Act Access Guidelines (ADAAG), but they are not currently identical. Again, the designer should consult both the code and the ADA to be certain of compliance. There is currently a movement to coordinate A117.1 and ADAAG so this may be less of a potential coordination problem in the future.

The fundamental basis of clearance and reach range requirements for persons with disabilities is for persons with mobility impairments who use wheelchairs. It is important to remember that the definition of disability also includes sensory and cognitive impairments, not just mobility impairments. The other major groups of persons that a designer must accommodate are persons with visual impairments and persons with hearing impairments. Provision of access for mobility impaired persons will accommodate most disabilities, but the designer must also be certain to accommodate other disabled groups as well in a coordinated fashion. A design solution for one group of disabilities must not adversely impact another group.

SECTION 1102—DEFINITIONS

For the purpose of this chapter, certain terms are defined as follows:

ACCESSIBLE describes a site, building, facility or portion thereof that complies with this chapter and that can be approached, entered and used by persons with physical disabilities.

ACCESSIBLE MEANS OF EGRESS is a path of travel, usable by a mobility-impaired person, that leads to a public way.

ACCESSIBLE ROUTE is a continuous path connecting accessible elements and spaces in a building or facility that is usable by persons with disabilities.

ADAPTABILITY is the capability of altering or adding to certain building spaces and elements, such as kitchen counters, sinks and grab bars, to accommodate the needs of persons with and without disabilities, or to accommodate the needs of persons with different types or degrees of disability.

AREA OF REFUGE is an area with direct access to an exit or an elevator where persons unable to use stairs can remain temporarily in safety to await instructions or assistance during emergency evacuation.

The basis of accessible design is the idea of an "accessible route." The definition of accessible route uses the words "continuous" and "connecting." Any usable path for persons with disabilities must not trap them or cut them off from the spaces or elements of the building that they have a right to use. This route is also referred to in other documents as the "path of travel." The intent is that persons with disabilities may enter a building, get into and out of spaces where desired functions occur and then exit the building. It is also necessary that functions such as toilets, telephones and drinking fountains be accessible. The goal is the integration of persons with disabilities into the full function of a facility with a minimum of atypical treatment: such as provision of special routes or auxiliary aids such as wheelchair lifts. The concept of "universal design" is useful to keep in mind. The goal of universal design is to make facilities accessible to the widest possible range of persons, regardless of mobility, physical ability, size, age or cognitive skills.

The designer should keep in mind all types of disabilities when designing accessible routes. Projections may effect persons with visual impairments and of course changes in grade such as ramps or steps impact persons in wheelchairs. Ramps with slope equal to or shallower than 1:12 complying with the technical requirements of CABO/ANSI A117.1 are acceptable for use in accessible routes. A sloped surface shallower than 1:20 is not considered a ramp. It is acceptable, indeed desirable, to use such shallower slopes in accessible routes if level landing areas are provided at doors or changes in direction, as required by CABO/ANSI A117.1. (Note that the ADA Accessibility Guidelines, Section 4.8.2, states that "the least possible slope shall be used for any ramp." This is just one example of why the designer must be familiar with ADA requirements and review the design for compliance with the ADA as well as the UBC.)

The requirements for areas of refuge recognize that getting persons with disabilities into a building under normal conditions may not allow them to exit under emergency circumstances. These areas are to allow persons with disabilities a relatively safe haven to await evacuation assistance. It is worth noting here that the definition for areas of refuge notes that these are to be areas for "temporary" use. The title "refuge" may imply a level of safety that is not consistent with the idea that these are temporary havens. The provisions for areas of refuge will be discussed in detail in a later section.

Definitions and requirements for Type A and Type B dwelling units have been incorporated into the code to bring the code requirements in line with the Federal Fair Housing Act Guidelines (FFHA). The designer has the option under given conditions of providing fully accessible units per CABO/ANSI A117.1 (Type A) or "adaptable" units (Type B) in residential projects. The scoping requirements for these dwelling units are contained in Section 1103.1.9. The plan dimension requirements are the same for both types of units, as clearances must be provided for accessibility in adaptable units. Certain accessibility features such as grab bars, lowered counters and clear space under cabinets may be provided later. Construction feature such as convertible cabinetry and wall blocking for grab bars are necessary so that the conversion to an accessible units may be made readily, without remodeling the spaces.

The requirements for both types of units apply to a broad category of residential units. These requirements have significantly changed the space requirements for single-level multifamily housing and multiple-level buildings where elevators are provided. The scoping requirements of 1103.1.9 should be studied carefully by designers of R Occupancies. Note also that while these code revisions are intended to conform to the Federal Fair Housing requirements, those requirements should be reviewed as well, so that the designer may ensure compliance with both federal and local requirements.

SECTION 1103—BUILDING ACCESSIBILITY

1103.1.1 Where required.

1103.1 General. Accessibility to temporary or permanent buildings, or portions thereof, shall be provided for all occupancy classifications except as modified by this chapter. See also Appendix Chapter 11.

EXCEPTIONS: 1. Floors or portions of floors not customarily occupied, including, but not limited to elevator pits; observation galleries used primarily for security purposes; elevator penthouses; nonoccupiable spaces accessed only by ladders, catwalks, crawl spaces or freight elevators; piping and equipment catwalks; and machinery, mechanical and electrical equipment rooms.

2. Subject to the approval of the building official, areas where work cannot reasonably be performed by persons having a severe impairment (mobility, sight or hearing) need not have specific features which provide accessibility to such persons.

3. Temporary structures, sites and equipment directly associated with the construction process such as construction site trailers, scaffolding, bridging or material hoists are not required to be accessible. This exception does not include walkways or pedestrian protection required by Chapter 33.

When dealing with accessibility requirements, especially for new buildings, the designers first assumption should be that all areas and all functions used by the public should be accessible. It is also a prudent assumption that all employee areas should be accessible to persons with disabilities except for specific areas not occupied by either the public or employees. Examples of these exempt areas are listed in Exception 1. Exception 2 should be used with extreme caution and very infrequently. Remember that any approval by the building official has no bearing on the applicability of the ADA. There are few spaces that would not fall under the meaning of Exception 1 for which access should not be provided.

> Accessibility to buildings is monitored closely by a large number of advocacy groups. They review the provision of or lack of access to buildings on an ongoing basis. Any decision that leads to a lack of access is subject to scrutiny over the life of the project. Our advice is: When in doubt about the applicability of accessibility requirements, the designer should provide the access.

Note that Exception 3 applies to temporary structures associated with construction. Other temporary facilities, such as tents or temporary public-use facilities are not exempt from access requirements.

1103.1.2 Group A Occupancies. Group A Occupancies shall be accessible as provided in this chapter.

EXCEPTION: In the assembly area of dining and drinking establishments that are located within nonelevator buildings, when the area of mezzanine seating is not more than 25 percent of the total seating, an accessible means of vertical access to the mezzanine is not required, provided the same services are provided in an accessible space.

The provision of various access elements such as path of travel, wheelchair seating or assistive listening devices are contained in CABO/ANSI A117.1. The exception allows the use of nonaccessible mezzanines in buildings without elevator access to the mezzanine. This exception should be used with caution due to the ambiguous interpretations possible of the term "same services." The intent of the exception is that the same experiences of environmental character, service and food be available to all patrons, regardless of disability. The designer must be certain that not only the physical character of the space, but the operation of the establishment will not result in segregation of persons with disabilities.

See the requirements of Section 1105.4.8 for specific scoping provisions for accessible seating and for assistive listening systems. A key factor to remember in providing wheelchair spaces in assembly areas is the requirement for dispersal of seating throughout various sight lines, ticket costs and locations in the seating area to allow persons with disabilities the same range of choices as other patrons. The accessible seating areas should have companion seating available and may be filled with temporary seating if not required for persons with disabilities during an event. The quantities of required seats are noted in Table 11-A.

Assistive listening devices are required for all spaces where audio-amplification systems are installed. The best guidelines is that if amplification is provided for some it should be provided for all. It is often possible with current technology to provide portable systems to comply with these requirements . The designer should coordinate with the future operator of any assembly facility to determine what are the anticipated uses of amplification and the size of audiences in various spaces. With this information the facility requirement for assistive listening systems can be determined and responsibility for meeting those requirements assigned to a defined party; the owner, the operator or the designer.

1103.1.3 Group B Occupancies. Group B Occupancies shall be accessible as provided in this chapter.

1103.1.4 Group E Occupancies. Group E Occupancies shall be accessible as provided in this chapter.

1103.1.5 Group F Occupancies. Group F Occupancies shall be accessible as provided in this chapter.

1103.1.6 Group H Occupancies. Group H Occupancies shall be accessible as provided in this chapter.

1103.1.7 Group I Occupancies. Group I Occupancies shall be accessible in public-use, common-use and employee-use areas, and shall have accessible patient rooms, cells, and treatment or examination rooms as follows:

1. In Group I, Division 1.1 patient-care units within hospitals that specialize in treating conditions that affect mobility, all patient rooms, including associated toilet rooms and bathrooms.

2. In Group I, Division 1.1 patient-care units within hospitals that do not specialize in treating conditions that affect mobility, at least one in every 10 patient rooms, or fraction thereof, including associated toilet rooms and bathrooms.

3. In Group I, Divisions 1.1 and 2 nursing homes and long-term care facilities, at least one in every two patient rooms, or fraction thereof, including associated toilet rooms and bathrooms.

4. In Group I, Division 3 mental health occupancies, at least one in every 10 patient rooms, or fraction thereof, including associated toilet rooms and bathrooms.

5. In Group I, Division 3 jail, prison and similar occupancies, at least one in every 20 rooms or cells, or fraction thereof, including associated toilet rooms and bathrooms.

6. In Group I Occupancies, all treatment and examination rooms shall be accessible.

1103.1.8 Group M Occupancies. Group M Occupancies shall be accessible as provided in this chapter.

1103.1.10 Group S Occupancies. Group S Occupancies shall be accessible as provided in this chapter.

1103.1.11 Group U Occupancies. Group U, Division 1 Occupancies shall be accessible as follows:

1. Private garages and carports that contain accessible parking.

2. In Group U, Division 1 agricultural buildings, access need be provided only to paved work areas and areas open to the general public.

The list of occupancies is provided to make it clear that all occupancies are required to have some level of accessibility. Certain occupancies such as I and R have increased requirements. For example, Group I occupancies have higher requirements for Group I, Division 1.1 patient care units that treat conditions that affect mobility. These facilities are required to provide access to all patient rooms. Paragraph 6 requires all treatment and examination rooms in all I Occupancies to be accessible. Where accessible patient rooms or cells are required, the accompanying toilets and bathrooms are to be accessible as well.

Note that in Group U occupancies a private garage or carport containing accessible parking is required to be accessible. This requires an accessible garage to connect to the accessible route leading to other building functions.

1103.1.9 Group R Occupancies.

1103.1.9.1 General. Group R Occupancies shall be accessible as provided in this chapter. Rooms and spaces available to the general public and spaces available for the use of residents that serve Group R, Division 1 Occupancy accessible dwelling units shall be accessible.

Where recreational facilities are provided serving accessible dwelling units, 25 percent, but not less than one of each type in each group of such facilities, shall be accessible. All recreational facilities of each type on a site shall be considered to determine the total number of each type that are required to be accessible.

The intent of the Group R requirements is that hotels, motels and multifamily dwellings be accessible to the maximum extent that is practical and in quantities that will serve the anticipated demand by persons with disabilities. The determination of the quantities required is not always empirically based, but the designer must use the scoping given by the code to design the facility. Common use and recreational facilities are to be accessible with access provided to 25 percent, or a minimum of one, of each type of recreational facility.

1103.1.9.2 Hotels, lodging houses and congregate residences. In hotels, lodging houses and congregate residence occupancies containing six or more guest rooms, multibed rooms or spaces for more than six occupants, one for the first 30 guest rooms or spaces and one additional for each additional 100 guest rooms or spaces, or fraction thereof, shall be accessible. In hotels with more than 50 sleeping rooms or suites, roll-in-type showers shall be provided in one half, but not less than one, of the required accessible sleeping rooms or suites.

In addition to the accessible guest rooms required above, guest rooms for persons with hearing impairments shall be provided in accordance with Table 11-B. Guest rooms for persons with hearing impairments shall be provided with visible and audible alarm-indicating appliances, activated by both the in-room smoke detector and the building fire protective signaling system.

The trigger for various scoping requirements in these occupancies is the number of sleeping spaces. Access requirements are triggered in facilities with more than 6 spaces. A percentage of each type of facility must be accessible with the number and the diversity of the types of accommodations increasing with the size of the facility. For example, roll-in showers are to be provided in certain rooms in addition to stall showers in hotels with more than 50 sleeping rooms.

Note also that accommodations must be provided for persons with other than mobility impairments. The code indicates that accommodations for persons with hearing impairments are to be provided in addition to the rooms for persons with mobility impairments, i.e., in separate rooms than the accessible rooms for mobility impaired persons.

1103.1.9.3 Multi-unit dwellings. In Group R, Division 1 Occupancy apartments containing four or more dwelling units and Group R, Division 3 Occupancies where there are four or more dwelling units in a single structure, all dwelling units shall be Type B dwelling units. In Group R, Division 1 apartment occupancies containing more than 20 dwelling units, at least 2 percent, but not less than one, of the dwelling units shall be Type A dwelling units. All dwelling units on a site shall be considered to determine the total number of accessible dwelling units.

As noted in the discussion regarding definitions, Section 1103.1.9.3 introduces the concept of two types of dwelling unit: Type A, fully accessible, or Type B, adaptable. All units in R-1 apartments of four or more dwelling units or R-3 dwelling units with four of more units in a single structure shall be Type B dwelling units. In buildings containing more than 20 dwelling units 2 percent, but not less than one unit, shall be Type A dwelling units.

EXCEPTIONS: 1. Where no elevator service is provided in a building, Type B dwelling units need not be provided on floors other than the ground floor.

2. Where no elevator service is provided in a building and the ground floor does not contain dwelling units, only those dwelling units located on the first floor of either Group R, Division 1 apartment occupancies or Group R, Division 3 Occupancies need comply with the requirements of this section.

3. A multistory dwelling unit not provided with elevator service is not required to comply with requirements for Type B dwelling units. Where a multistory dwelling unit is provided with elevator service to only one floor, the floor provided with elevator service shall comply with the requirements for a Type B dwelling unit, and a toilet facility shall be provided on that floor.

4. The number of Type B dwelling units provided in multiple nonelevator buildings on a single site may be reduced to a percentage of the ground floor units that is equal to the percentage of the entire site having grades, prior to development, that are 10 percent or less; but in no case shall the number of Type B units be less than 20 percent of the ground floor dwelling units on the entire site.

5. The required number of Type A and Type B dwelling units shall not apply to a site where the lowest floor or the lowest structural building members is required to be at or above the base flood elevation resulting in:

5.1 A difference in elevation between the minimum required floor elevation at the primary entrances and all vehicular and pedestrian arrival points within 50 feet (15 240 mm) exceeding 30 inches (762 mm).

5.2 A slope exceeding 10 percent between the minimum required floor elevation at the primary entrances and all vehicular and pedestrian arrival points within 50 feet (15 240 mm).

The exceptions deal with provision of Type B units where elevators are not provided or where site grades preclude building an accessible site path of travel to ground-floor units. In buildings without elevators only the units on the ground floor need be Type B units. Also, multistory dwelling units ("townhouses") are not required to be Type B units unless they have elevator access to the floors. Where elevator access is provided to only one floor, that floor shall meet the Type B requirements and a toilet facility shall be provided on that floor.

> To meet the intent of accessibility provisions we recommend that the ground floor of townhouses that are on an accessible route be made adaptable and that an adaptable (or fully accessible) powder room be provided for use by guests of the townhouse.

Exceptions 4 and 5 apply to sites where steep grades or flood control measures preclude provision of accessible routes to certain dwelling units. The overall code intent is that a certain portion, at least 20 percent, of ground-floor units be adaptable, Type B units.

1103.2 Design and Construction.

1103.2.1 General. When accessibility is required by this chapter, it shall be designed and constructed in accordance with this chapter and CABO/ANSI A117.1.

EXCEPTION: Type B dwelling units shall comply with Section 1106.

1103.2.2 Accessible route. When a building, or portion of a building, is required to be accessible, an accessible route shall be provided to all portions of the building, to accessible building entrances, connecting accessible pedestrian walkways and the public way.

EXCEPTION: In other than the offices of health-care providers, transportation facilities, airports and Group M Occupancies with five or more tenants, floors above and below accessible levels that have an aggregate area of not more than 3,000 square feet (278.7 m^2) need not be served by an accessible route from an accessible level.

When floor levels are required to be connected by an accessible route, and an interior path of travel is provided between the levels, an interior accessible route between the levels shall be provided. When only one accessible route is provided, it shall not pass through kitchens, storage rooms, toilet rooms, bathrooms, closets or other similar spaces.

EXCEPTION: A single accessible route may pass through a kitchen or storage room in a Type A dwelling unit.

When more than one building or facility is located on a site, accessible routes shall be provided connecting accessible buildings and accessible site facilities.

Again the standards of CABO/ANSI A117.1 are cited as the design criteria for access. An accessible route is to be provided in buildings with the exception of small facilities of less than 3000 square feet that are not offices of health care providers or small shopping center type M Occupancies. Note the requirement that paths of access be equal; if an interior route is provided, then an interior accessible route must be provided as well. Accessible facilities must be provided on the accessible route even in such small buildings. If a toilet room is provided on the inaccessible levels above or below the accessible level, then an accessible toilet must be provided on the accessible level as well. In such buildings the designer should consider providing just these accessible facilities on the accessible route to avoid duplication of facilities on multiple levels.

1103.2.3 Accessible entrances. Each building and structure, and each separate tenancy within a building or structure, shall be provided with at least one entrance that complies with the accessible route provisions of CABO/ANSI A117.1. At least 50 percent of all entrances shall be accessible.

EXCEPTIONS: 1. Entrances used exclusively for loading and service.

2. Entrances to spaces not required to be accessible as provided for in Section 1103.

When a building or facility has entrances that normally serve accessible parking facilities, transportation facilities, passenger loading zones, taxi stands, public streets and sidewalks, or accessible interior vertical access, at least one of the entrances serving each such function shall comply with the accessible route provisions of CABO/ANSI A117.1.

The primary entrance to either a Type A or Type B dwelling unit shall be located on an accessible route from public or common areas. The primary entrance to the dwelling unit shall not be to a bedroom.

The basic intent of the requirements for accessible entrances are that one main entrance be accessible and that the accessible route inside the building connect to all of the tenant spaces. Site facilities should be on an accessible route. The code allows some latitude for service entrances and for site conditions as noted in the provisions for site grading in 1103.2. The code does require that one half of all entrances be accessible. Where possible the designer should endeavor to make all public entrances accessible.

Designers should pay particular attention to door clearance and landing requirements contained in CABO/ANSI A117.1. The requirements for clear and level landings and clearances at the latch side of doors depend on the direction of approach to the door by persons with mobility impairments. The provision of space in the floor plan for these clearances is essential during the initial design phases of a project. The designer should consider the approach configuration and the side of approach to determine which criteria to apply. If these clearances are not provided at the outset of planning, it will be very difficult to provide such clearances later without major revisions to the floor plans. It is essential that such clearance criteria for doors and for Type A and B dwelling units be understood early and incorporated into the plans. Study the diagrams in CABO/ANSI A117.1 to understand the criteria for provision of these clearances. The clearances are to allow wheelchairs to clear door swings, to allow maneuvering around obstacles and to allow wheelchairs to pivot and turn. It is acceptable to demonstrate alternative means of providing such maneuvering room, but the designer must understand wheelchair movements and design criteria in the same way one understands how a car moves through a parking lot or a truck approaches a loading dock. The same understanding should be gained of reach ranges for persons seated in wheelchairs to allow the designer to correctly place operating switches or equipment.

1103.2.4 Signs.

1103.2.4.1 International symbol of accessibility. The following elements and spaces of accessible facilities shall be identified by the international symbol of accessibility:

1. Accessible parking spaces, except where the total parking spaces provided are five or less.
2. Accessible areas of refuge.
3. Accessible passenger loading zones.
4. Accessible toilet and bathing facilities.

1103.2.4.2 Other signs. Inaccessible building entrances, inaccessible public toilets and bathing facilities, and elevators not on an accessible route shall be provided with directional signage indicating the route to the nearest similar accessible element.

In assembly areas, a sign notifying the general public of the availability of assistive listening systems shall be provided at ticket offices or similar locations.

Each door to an exit stairway shall have a tactile sign, including raised letters and Braille, stating EXIT and shall comply with CABO/ANSI A117.1.

At exits and elevators serving a required accessible space, but not providing an approved accessible means of egress, signs shall be installed indicating the location of accessible means of egress.

In addition to the international symbol of accessibility, each unisex toilet or bathing room shall be identified by a tactile sign including raised letters and Braille. Directional signage shall be provided at all separate-sex toilet or bathing facilities indicating the location of the nearest unisex room.

Signage must be provided indicating the existence and location of accessible routes and also to guide persons with disabilities away from inaccessible routes to accessible ones. Exits and paths of travel that abut an accessible route but that do not provide accessible egress should be clearly marked to avoid misguiding persons with disabilities into what could effectively be a dead-end corridor for them in an emergency.

SECTION 1104—EGRESS AND AREAS OF REFUGE

1104.1 Means of Egress.

1104.1.1 General. All required accessible spaces shall be provided with not less than one accessible means of egress. When more than one exit or exit-access door is required from any accessible space, each accessible portion of the space shall be served by not less than two accessible means of egress. The maximum travel distance from any accessible space to an area of refuge shall not exceed the travel distance set forth in Chapter 10.

Each accessible means of egress shall be continuous from each required accessible occupied area to a public way and shall include accessible routes, ramps, exit stairs, elevators, horizontal exits or smoke barriers.

The original thrust of accessibility criteria was to get persons with disabilities into buildings to allow them to use the facilities in normal circumstances. Now there is an increasing recognition that persons with disabilities must also be able to exit these buildings in an emergency. The requirements for means of egress for persons with disabilities recognize that elevators may be a part of that means of egress for multiple-story buildings. This is in sharp contrast to the way elevators are treated in Chapter 10. While the use of elevators for egress is not allowed under Chapter 10, this chapter may actually require an elevator for disabled egress in some cases.

This section requires at least one accessible means of egress from each accessible route. Where more than one exit is required from an accessible space, then two exits must be provided. For larger areas that may require more than two exits, there are still only two accessible exits required. This allows persons with disabilities a second way out if an exit is blocked in an emergency, but also recognizes that the percentage of such persons will be lower than the overall occupant load, which generated the requirement for multiple exits.

1104.1.2 Stairways. When an exit stairway is part of an accessible means of egress, the stairway shall have a clear width of not less than 48 inches (1219 mm) between handrails. The stairway shall either incorporate an area of refuge within an enlarged story-level landing or shall be accessed from an area of refuge complying with Section 1104.2 or a horizontal exit.

EXCEPTIONS: 1. Exit stairways serving a single dwelling unit or guest room.

2. Exit stairways serving buildings protected throughout by an approved automatic sprinkler system.

3. The clear width of 48 inches (1219 mm) between handrails is not required for exit stairways accessed from a horizontal exit.

4. Areas of refuge are not required in open parking garages.

Stairways may be considered as part of an accessible means of egress when they have a clear width of not less than 48 inches between handrails. Note that this is a different clearance requirement and different clearance measurement criteria than used in Chapter 10. These requirements supersede those of Chapter 10, and wider stairs must be provided if they are required for accessible egress. It is very unclear whether the exceptions to the stair section are meant to apply to the stair width requirements, the area of refuge requirements, or both. Section 1104.2.4 dealing with construction requirements for areas of refuge is silent about the requirements for areas of refuge in fully sprinklered buildings. (See Figures 10-1 and 10-2)

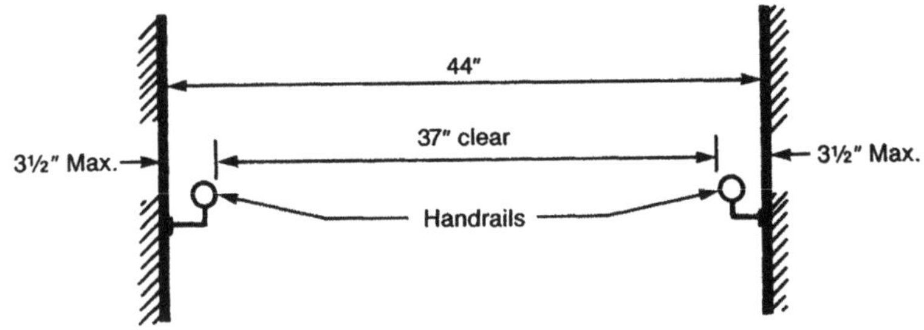

Exit Stair Width Measurement
per Section 1003.3.3.2

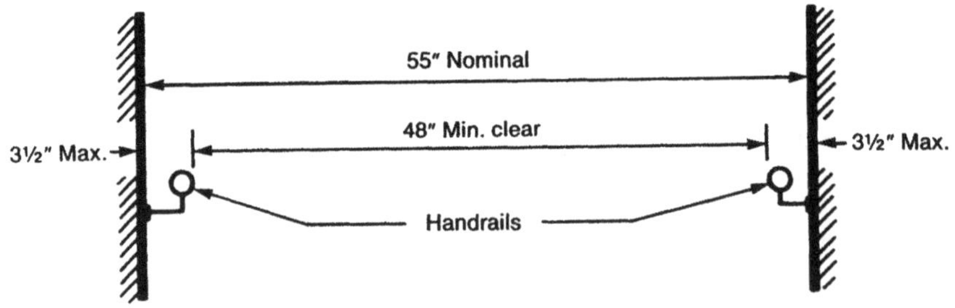

Exit Stair Width Measurement
per Section 1104.1.2

The provisions in Section 1104.1.2 take precedence over the stair width provisions in Section 1003.3.3.2 where accessibility requirements apply. The key difference is that the minimum widths are measured in different manners. Where the accessibility provisions apply, the width is based on the clear dimension of 48 inches between the handrails. Thus, if the handrails project the permitted 3½ inches from the wall of the stairs, the overall width of the stairway must be not less than 55 inches.

The minimum width of 44 inches per Section 1003.3.3.2 is based on the gross dimension for the stair overall, i.e., without considering the handrails. Because the handrails may project 3½ inches into the stairway, the net clear dimension is allowed to be 37 inches.

REFERENCE: SECTION 1003.3.3.2 & 1104.1.2

FIGURE 10-1 STAIR WIDTH COMPARISON, HANDRAILS GROSS VS. NET WIDTH

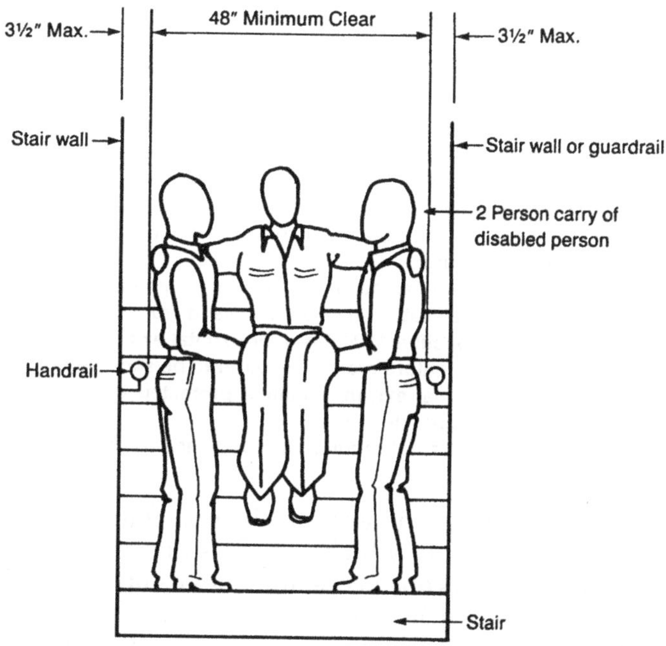

EVACUATION OF DISABLED PERSON DOWN STAIR TWO PERSON CARRY

This illustration shows the basis of the minimum clear width requirement of Section 1104.1.2. The provisions of Section 1104.1.2 supersede the minimum provisions of Section 1003.3.3.2 because the minimum requirement in Section 1104.1.2 are greater than that in Section 1003.3.3.2. The intent of these two sections is also different. Section 1003.3.3.2 was based on the gross width of the stairwell assuming handrails projecting not more than 3½" from the wall. This would allow a net width between handrails of 37" and a gross width of stairway of 44" minimum. Section1104.1.2 is based on a net width between the handrails. This will result in a nominal 55" wide stairway as the minimum.

REFERENCE: SECTION 1104.1.2

FIGURE 10-2 MINIMUM WIDTH OF STAIRWAY BASED ON TWO PERSONS CARRYING OF DISABLED PERSON DOWN STAIRWAY

> It is the authors' opinion that areas of refuge and the accompanying wider stairs are not required in fully sprinklered buildings. This interpretation should be verified by the designer with the building official before undertaking any project where these provisions may apply.

1104.1.3 Elevators. When an accessible floor is four or more stories above or below the level of exit discharge serving that floor, at least one elevator shall serve as one required accessible means of egress.

EXCEPTION: In fully sprinklered buildings, the elevator need not be provided to floors provided with a horizontal exit and located at or above the level of exit discharge.

When an elevator is part of an accessible means of egress, standby power shall be provided. The elevator shall be accessed from either an area of refuge complying with Section 1104.2 or a horizontal exit.

EXCEPTIONS: 1. Elevators are not required to be accessed by an area of refuge or a horizontal exit in buildings protected throughout by an approved automatic sprinkler system.

2. Areas of refuge are not required in open parking garages.

In buildings where an accessible floor is four or more stories above or below the level at which the exits discharge to the street, an elevator is to serve as one accessible means of egress. The elevator must be provided with standby power and should be accessed from an area of refuge or a horizontal exit. Again there is an exception reducing the requirements for this access in fully sprinklered buildings, which furthers the confusion of when areas of refuge are to be provided.

1104.2 Areas of Refuge.

1104.2.1 Access. Required areas of refuge shall be accessible from the space served by an accessible means of egress. Required areas of refuge shall have direct access to a stairway or an elevator complying with Section 1104.1.

1104.2.2 Pressurization. When an elevator lobby is used as an area of refuge, the elevator shaft and lobby shall be pressurized in accordance with the requirements of Section 905.

EXCEPTION: When elevators are in an area of refuge formed by a horizontal exit or smoke barrier.

1104.2.3 Size. Each area of refuge shall be sized to accommodate one wheelchair space not less than 30 inches by 48 inches (762 mm by 1219 mm) for each 200 occupants, or portion thereof, based on the occupant load of the area of refuge and areas served by the area of refuge.

Wheelchair spaces shall not reduce the required exit width or interfere with access to or use of fire department hose connections and valves. Access to required wheelchair spaces in an area of refuge shall not be obstructed by more than one adjoining wheelchair space.

1104.2.4 Construction. Each area of refuge shall be separated from the remainder of the story by a smoke barrier having at least a one-hour fire-resistance rating. Smoke barriers shall extend to the roof or floor deck above. Doors in the smoke barrier shall be tightfitting smoke- and draft-control assemblies having a fire-protection rating of not less than 20 minutes. Doors shall be self-closing or automatic closing by smoke detection. An approved damper designed to resist the passage of smoke shall be provided at each point a duct penetrates the smoke barrier.

EXCEPTION: Areas of refuge located within a stairway enclosure.

1104.2.5 Two-way communication. Areas of refuge shall be provided with a two-way communication system between the area of refuge and a central control point. If the central control point is not constantly attended, the area of refuge shall also have controlled access to a public telephone system. Location of the central control point shall be approved by the fire department.

EXCEPTION: Buildings four stories or less in height.

1104.2.6 Instructions. In areas of refuge that have a two-way emergency communication system, instructions on the use of the area under emergency conditions shall be posted adjoining the communications system. The instructions shall include:

1. Directions to find other exits,
2. Advice that persons able to use the exit stairway do so as soon as possible, unless they are assisting others,
3. Information on planned availability of assistance in the use of stairs or supervised operation of elevators and how to summon such assistance, and
4. Directions for use of the emergency communications system.

1104.2.7 Identification. Each area of refuge shall be identified by a sign stating AREA OF REFUGE and the international symbol of accessibility. The sign shall be located at each door providing access to the area of refuge. The sign shall be illuminated as required for exit signs when exit sign illumination is required. Tactile signage shall be located at each door to an area of refuge.

Areas of refuge, where required, are to be constructed to the criteria listed in this section. The area is to be sized to accommodate one wheelchair for each 200 building occupants. The areas are to be located immediately adjacent to stairs or elevators, with 1-hour walls and should be pressurized or treated in some fashion to prevent the entry of smoke. Two-way communications must be provided to allow persons awaiting rescue assistance in the area of refuge to let someone know they are in the area. Instructions on the purpose and use of the area of refuge is to be provided to the occupants. Signs should also indicate the location of the area of refuge and have the international symbol of accessibility along with tactile identification of the space. As discussed in the definition section above, these areas are for "temporary" use to await rescue. They are not intended for long-term use for the occupants to wait out the duration of an emergency. (See Figures 10-3 and 10-4)

> The requirements and interpretation of the scope of the requirements for areas of refuge and for stair widths has been the source of great controversy over the past several years. Numerous code revisions have been proposed to attempt to clarify the stair and area of refuge requirements with little success. This section and these requirements should be carefully reviewed by the designer with the local authority having jurisdiction early in the design process. The designer must get a clear indication from the local building official of how this section is interpreted locally since varying interpretations can result in major design impacts. The ADAAG exempts fully sprinklered buildings from the requirements for areas of refuge, but this is still very unclear in the UBC.

SECTION 1105—FACILITY ACCESSIBILITY

1105.1 General. When buildings or portions of buildings are required to be accessible, building facilities shall be accessible as provided in this section.

Building facilities or elements required by this section to be accessible shall be designed and constructed in accordance with CABO/ANSI A117.1.

EXCEPTION: Type B dwelling units shall comply with Section 1106.

This section sets the scoping provisions for the technical requirements of CABO/ANSI A117.1 for permanent building facilities that are regulated by the building code. Quantities, relationships to accessible route and other facilities are set forth. It is important to understand the distinction between a basic requirement and a requirement for access to features if they are provided. For example, toilet rooms are to be provided and are to be accessible. On the other hand, drinking fountains "where provided" must have at least 50 percent of the drinking fountains accessible. It is not required that accessible drinking fountains be provided, only that a reasonable number be accessible if they are provided.

SECTION 1106—TYPE B DWELLING UNITS

1106.1 General. Type B dwelling units, when required, shall comply with this section.

EXCEPTION: Type B dwelling units designed and constructed as Type A dwelling units.

This section defines the requirements for "adaptable" dwelling units. It is intended to bring the UBC into conformance with the basic requirements of the Federal Fair Housing Act Guidelines for adaptable units. This is more than just a scoping provision. There are a number of specific technical requirements that are meant to work in concert with CABO/ANSI A117.1. There are many specific references to specific sections of A117.1 that define several alternative provisions that may apply to Type B units. The goal of these units is to provide the physical space for adaptability in the basic floor plan layout, while allowing certain elements such a grab bars to be deferred until needed by a disabled occupant. The intent is that the units not typically appear to be fully accessible units, but be readily convertible for access, with minimal effort or expense.

Appendix Chapter 11, Division I—SITE ACCESSIBILITY
SECTION 1107—ACCESSIBLE EXTERIOR ROUTES

1107.1 General. Accessible exterior routes shall be provided from public transportation stops, accessible parking and accessible passenger loading zones and public sidewalks to the accessible building entrance they serve.

When more that none building or facility is located on a site, at least one accessible route shall connect accessible elements, facilities and buildings that are on the same site. The accessible route between accessible parking accessible building entrances shall be the most practical direct route.

SECTION 1108—PARKING FACILITIES

1108.1 Accessible Parking Required. When parking lots or garage facilities are provided, accessible parking spaces shall be provided in accordance with Table A-11-A except for the following occupancies:

1. For Group I, Divisions 1.1 and 2 medical care occupancies specializing in the treatment of persons with mobility impairments, 20 percent of the parking spaces provided shall be accessible.

2. For Group I, Divisions 1.1 and 1.2 and Group B Occupancies providing outpatient medical care facilities, 10 percent of the parking spaces shall be accessible.

3. For Group R, Division 1 apartment buildings containing accessible or adaptable dwelling units where parking is provided, 2 percent of the parking

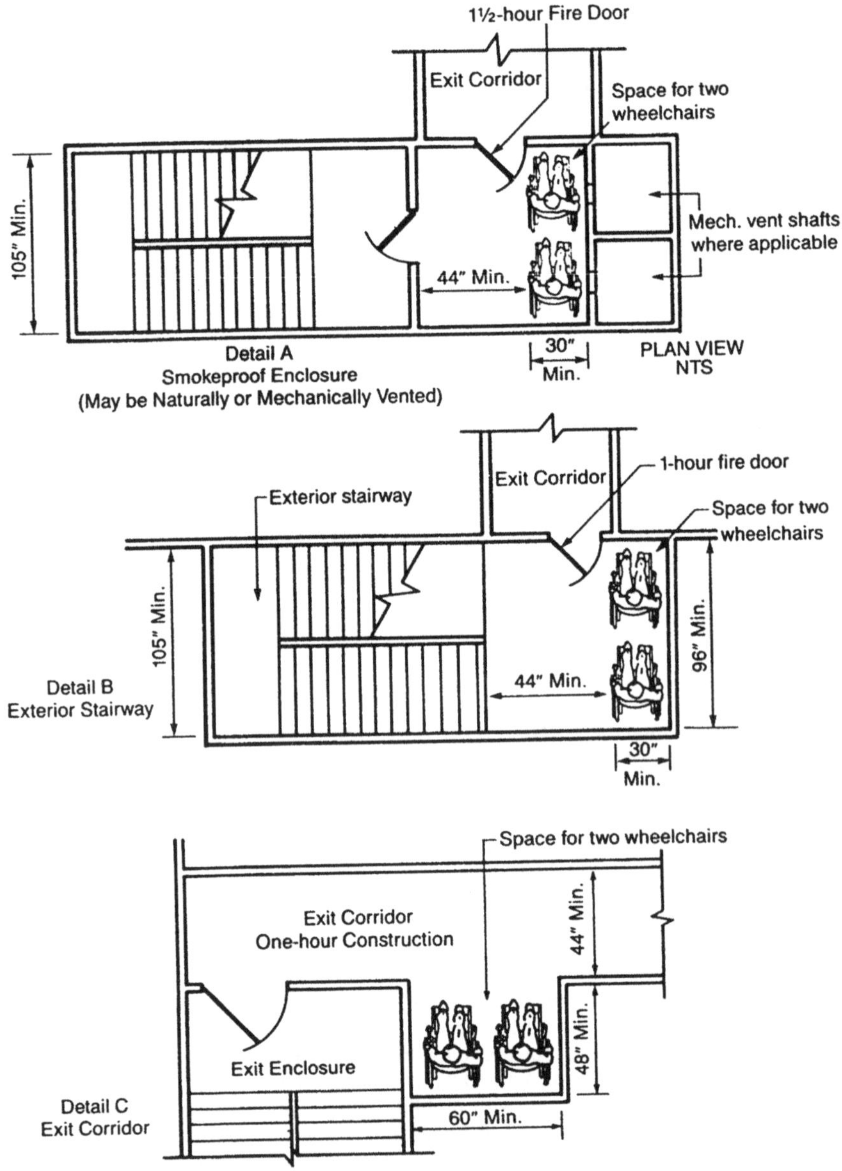

REFERENCE: SECTION 1104.2

FIGURE 10-3 AREAS OF EVACUATION ASSISTANCE-EXAMPLES

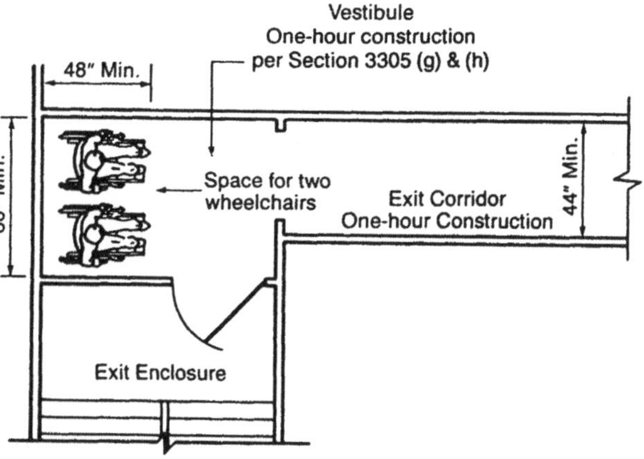

Detail D
Vestibule to Exit Enclosure

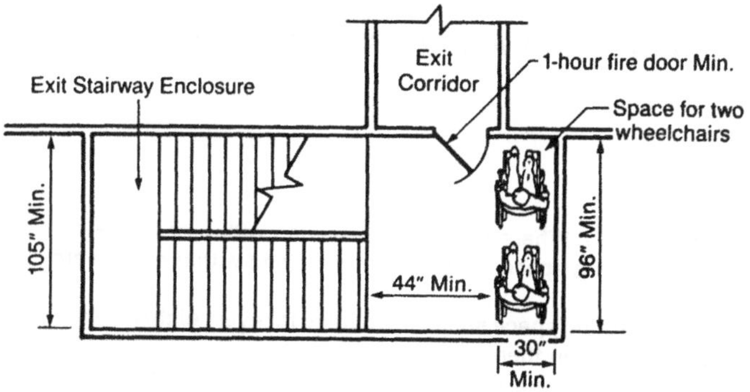

Detail E
Exit Stairway Enclosure

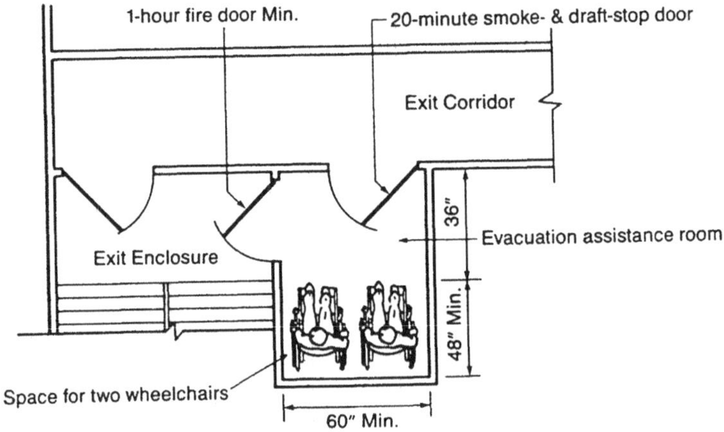

DETAIL F
Evacuation Assistance Room

Evacuation assistance rooms must have fire-resistive construction as for an exit access into which it opens per Section 1004.3.4.3.2.1 The door into an exit must conform to the requirements of Section 1005.3.3.5 and be at least of one-hour rating.

The room must have a telephone connected to the primary entry area. See Section 1104.2.5.

The room should have emergency lighting; see Section 1003.2.9.

REFERENCE: SECTION 1104.3.3.5, 1004.3.4.3.2.1 & 1104.2.5.

FIGURE 10-4 AREA OF EVACUATION ASSISTANCE ROOM

spaces shall be accessible. Where parking is provided within or beneath a building, accessible parking space shall also be provided within or beneath the building.

One van accessible parking space shall be provided for every eight accessible parking spaces, or faction thereof.

Accessible parking spaces shall be located on the shortest possible accessible route from adjacent parking to an accessible building entrance. In facilities with multiple accessible building entrances with adjacent parking, accessible parking space shall be dispersed and located near the accessible entrances.

TABLE A-11-A—NUMBER OF ACCESSIBLE PARKING SPACES

TOTAL PARKING SPACES IN LOT OR GARAGE	MINIMUM REQUIRED NUMBER OF ACCESSIBLE SPACES
1–25	1
26–50	2
51–75	3
76–100	4
101–150	5
151–200	6
201–300	7
301–400	8
401–500	9
501–1,000	2% of total spaces
Over 1,000	20 spaces plus 1 space for every 100 spaces, or fraction thereof, over 1,000

Site elements such as parking space and provision of accessible routes from bus stops and loading zones are contained in this section. As noted previously the designer should confer with the local jurisdiction to determine the status of adoption of this appendix. Table A-11-A details the scoping requirements for the number of accessible parking spaces required.

Appendix Division II—ACCESSIBILITY FOR EXISTING BUILDINGS

SECTION 1110—SCOPE

The provisions of this division apply to renovations, alterations and additions to existing buildings, including those identified as historic buildings. This division includes minimum standards for removing architectural barriers, and providing and maintaining access to existing buildings and facilities for persons with disabilities.

SECTION 1111—DEFINITIONS

For the purpose of this division, certain terms are defined as follows:

ALTERATION is any change, addition or modification in construction or occupancy.

TECHNICALLY INFEASIBLE is an alteration of a building or facility that has little likelihood of being accomplished because existing structural conditions would require removing or altering a load-bearing member that is an essential part of the structural frame, or because existing physical or site constraints prohibit modification or addition of elements, spaces or features that are in full and strict compliance with the minimum requirements for new construction and which are necessary to provide accessibility.

SECTION 1112—ALTERATIONS

1112.1 General.

1112.1.1 Compliance. Alterations to existing buildings or facilities shall comply with this section. Alterations shall not reduce or have the effect of reducing accessibility or usability of a building, portion of a building, or facility. If compliance with this section is technically infeasible, the alteration shall provide access to the maximum extent technically feasible.

EXCEPTION: Alterations to Group R, Division 1 apartment occupancies need not comply with this section.

1112.1.2 Existing Elements: If existing elements, spaces, essential features or common areas are altered , each such altered element, space, feature or area shall comply with the applicable provisions in Division I of this appendix chapter and CABO/ANSI A117.1.

EXCEPTION: Accessible means of egress required by Section 1004 need not be provided in alterations of existing buildings and facilities.

When an alteration is to a an area of primary function, the accessible route to the altered area shall be made accessible. The accessible route to the primary functions area shall include toilet facilities or drinking fountains serving the area of primary function.

EXCEPTIONS: 1. The costs of providing the accessible route need not exceed 20 percent of the costs of the alterations affecting the area of primary function.

2. Alterations to windows, hardware, operating controls, electrical outlets and signs.

3. Alterations to mechanical systems or electrical systems, installation or alteration of fire-protection systems, and abatement of hazardous materials.

4. Alterations undertaken for the primary purpose of increasing the accessibility of an existing building, facility or element.

1112.2 Modifications.

1112.2.1 General. Modifications set forth in this section may be used for compliance when the required standard is technically infeasible.

Appendix Chapter 11, Division II contains definitions for alteration and technical infeasibility. The definition of alteration is essentially the same at that in Chapter 2. It is worth noting that a change in occupancy is considered an alteration and will trigger the same requirements to comply with current codes as would an addition or physical alteration. Moving a new use into an existing structure, which may require no physical alterations may trigger accessibility (and other) code upgrade requirements.

The definition of technical infeasibility is an invitation to negotiate with the building official. When the designer opts to use this definition to justify exclusion of an accessible element that would otherwise be required in new construction, the designer should seek the concurrence of the building official during the plan review process of this interpretation. This will assure the designer that this does not become an issue during field inspection of the project.

It is much easier to amend documents or justify an interpretation during the design process than it is to alter already built work or justify an interpretation under the time pressures always present during construction.

The intent of the alterations section is that provision of accessibility occur to the maximum extent feasible. The extent of these requirements are directly related to their proximity to the area of alteration. Accessibility should be provided throughout the structure to the maximum extent feasible. There is a cost cap of 20 percent assignable to the cost of providing an accessible route. This cost cap can be construed in two ways. One is that the cost of access is 20 percent of the total cost of the project with a total cost of 100 percent for the project. However, the text states that the cost of providing an accessible route shall not exceed 20 percent of the cost of alterations. If the cost of alterations is x, then the total budget for the work would be x plus 20 percent of x, or 120 percent of the budget for the work, exclusive of the accessible route. The interpretation of this section should be verified with the local authorities while the budget is being established.

> Since most owners do not initially consider the cost of providing access elements when setting their budgets, it is wise for the designer to use the 120 percent rule when establishing the initial construction budget.

Note that Section 1112 lists a series of modifications of elements that may be used in specific instances when provision of access is deemed to be technically infeasible. These provisions should not be used without the prior approval of the building official and concurrence that technically infeasible conditions exist that necessitate the use of these modifications.

> Implicit in the definition of technically infeasible is the assumption that this must be determined in concert with the building official. Accessibility is far too important an issue for the designer to be making such determinations alone.

SECTION 1114—HISTORIC PRESERVATION

Accessibility provisions of this division shall be applied to historic buildings and facilities as defined in Section 3403.5 of this code.

The building official, after consulting with the appropriate historic preservation officer, shall determine whether provisions required by this division for accessible routes, ramps, entrances, toilets, parking or signage would threaten or destroy the historic significance of the building or facility.

If it is determined that any of the accessibility requirements listed above would threaten or destroy the historic significance of a building or facility, the modifications of Section 1112.2 for that feature may be utilized.

As noted above, use of Section 1111 requires consultation with the building official to determine what is technically infeasible to perform in a building. This is further complicated if the facility is a qualifying historical building. In addition to the structural determinations made under the definition of technical infeasibility, the designer and the building official must confer regarding the impact of accessible elements on the historic fabric of the building. It is essential to understand that the fact that a building has historical significance is not enough to justify not providing accessibility. Any determinations regarding provision of less than full access under the doctrine of technical infeasibility or historical impact must be verified by the building official. Such determinations should be rendered in writing and kept on file by the jurisdiction, the designer and the building owner.

Chapter 12 Interior Environment

SECTION 1201—GENERAL

Buildings and portions thereof shall provide occupants with light and ventilation as set forth in this chapter. For ventilation of hazardous vapors or fumes, see Section 306.5 and the Mechanical Code.

The "light and ventilation" sections of the occupancy chapters have been moved to this newly reformatted chapter. These were the "05" sections of the old, pre-1994 code occupancy chapters. The regulations are divided into two parts, one related to residential occupancies and one for all others. The residential requirements are an outgrowth of the deplorable conditions in multifamily tenement buildings built in cities during the industrial revolution. These conditions resulted in the development of health standards for light and ventilation in various rooms and requirements for how the rooms relate to each other. Requirements for exterior plan elements that provide light and air, such as yards and courts are also contained in this chapter. These exterior design requirements thus relate to providing a minimum level of air and light to dwellings to provide for healthful living conditions. The requirements for other occupancies are based on those for residential occupancies with special provisions for hazardous conditions in various other occupancies.

SECTION 1204—EAVES

Where eaves extend over required windows, they shall project not closer than 30 inches (762 mm) to any side or rear property line. Se also Sections 503.2 and 705.

Section 1204 is an "orphan" provision in this chapter related to the relationship of eave projections at "required windows." This is really related to fire protection requirements found in Chapters 5 and 7 and probably belongs in one of those chapters. It seems it is in this chapter because a "required" window is somehow related to ventilation or light requirements. The intent of the section is that eaves at these windows be no closer than 30 inches to a property line to prevent spread of fire to adjacent properties.

The long-term intent for this chapter is that as regulations for indoor air quality are developed they will also be located in this chapter.

Chapter 15 Roofs and Roof Structures

SECTION 1505–ATTICS: ACCESS, DRAFT STOPS AND VENTILATION

505.1 Access. An attic access opening shall be provided to attics of buildings with combustible ceiling or roof construction.

EXCEPTION: Attics with a maximum vertical height of less than 30 inches (762 mm).

The opening shall be not less than 22 inches (559 mm) by 30 inches (762 mm) and shall be located in a corridor, hallway or other readily accessible location. Thirty-inch-minimum (762 mm) unobstructed headroom in the attic space shall be provided at or above the access opening.

The attic access provision does not refer to fire-resistive roof-ceiling assemblies. Often, the lack of code references to fire-resistive assemblies leads designers to ignore the general requirements set forth in Chapter 7. As we discussed in Article 8 of this Guide with regard to Section 710.3, the code has a requirement that membrane

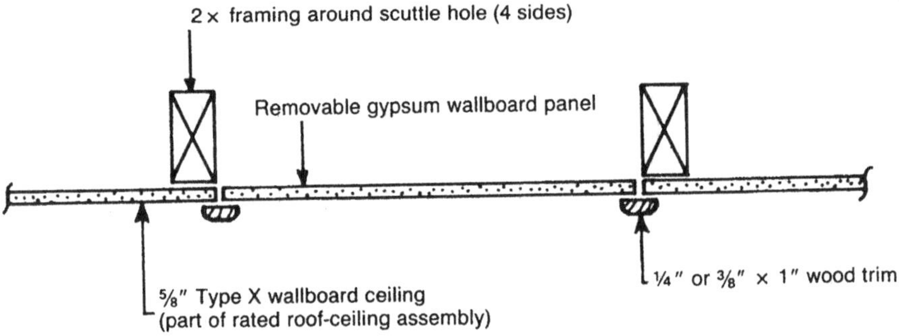

REFERENCE: SECTIONS 703.2 and 1505

FIGURE 10-5 ATTIC ACCESS, NON-CONFORMING DETAIL

penetrations through a portion of a fire-rated assembly must be fire-resistive horizontal assemblies. (See Figure 10-5.)

The usual attic access is through a scuttle, made by cutting an opening in the ceiling between two joists. The closure is made with a piece of wallboard supported by thin wooden trim. This construction does not meet the intent of Section 710.3 when used in ceilings that are required to be fire rated.

The installation of an approved access door will require a labeled frame properly attached to the adjacent framing. The essential point is that the required fire resistivity of the ceiling membrane must be maintained.

Chapter 23 Wood

Division II—GENERAL REQUIREMENTS
PART I—REQUIREMENTS APPLICABLE TO ALL DESIGN METHODS
SECTION 2306–DECAY AND TERMITE PROTECTION

2306.9 Wood Supporting Roofs and Floors. Wood structural members supporting moisture permeable floors or roofs that are exposed to the weather, such as concrete or masonry slabs, shall be approved wood of natural resistance to decay or treated wood unless separated from such floors or roofs by an impervious moisture barrier.

This section requires that floors and roofs supporting "moisture permeable" surfaces be constructed of

- decay-resistant wood,
- treated wood or
- wood separated from the permeable surface by an impervious membrane.

Often overlooked is the fact that concrete is a pervious, hygroscopic material, usually containing hairline cracks. It is not inherently impervious or waterproof. Therefore, concrete must be separated from wood by an impervious membrane. This membrane cannot simply be an impervious material, such as plastic sheeting, laid down with lapped, open joints. The joints between adjacent sheets must be sealed to provide continuity, and the edges or ends of the membrane area must be finished properly to prevent moisture from entering under the membrane. (See Figure 10-6.)

The authors have encountered numerous constructions where:

- the membrane was omitted,
- individual sheets of plastic were laid down without regard to the joints other than lapping them or
- the edge details, or lack thereof, permitted water entry under the membrane.

Pervious materials include concrete, deck surfacing materials and lightweight fills used for sound-deadening and fire-resistive purposes.

WOOD (Excerpts from Chapter 23)

2320.13 Exit Facilities. In Seismic Zones 3 and 4, exterior exit balconies, stairs and similar exit facilities shall be positively anchored to the primary structure at not over 8 feet (2438 mm) on center or shall be designed for lateral forces. Such attachment shall not be accomplished by use of toenails or nails subject to withdrawal.

Section 2320.13 reiterates the intent of Chapter 23 that all structures have proper anchorage or design for lateral forces, including those structures built under the "Conventional Light-frame Construction Provisions" of Section 2320.

The use of Section 2320 does not permit the designer to disregard proper structural design as set forth in Chapter 23, particularly for those essential life safety elements such as exit ways.

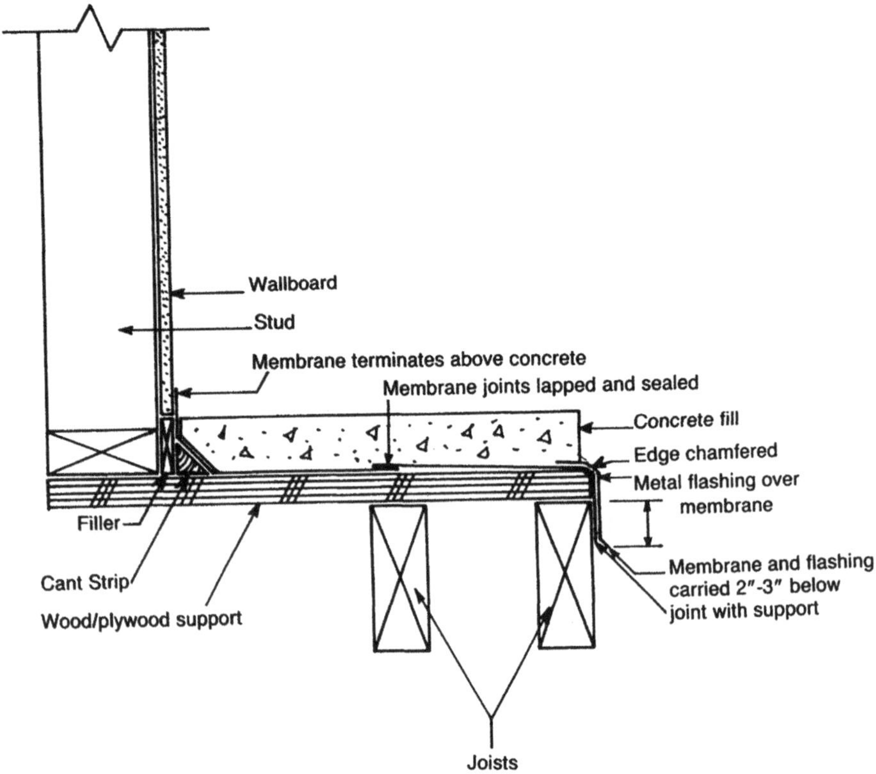

SUGGESTED METHOD OF MEETING SECTION 2306
AND PREVENTING WIND-DRIVEN WATER ENTRY

REFERENCE: SECTION 2306

FIGURE 10-6 CONCRETE/MASONRY ON WOOD SUPPORTS

In the authors' opinion, particularly for seismic zones 3 and 4, the use of "conventional construction" is adequate for vertical load-bearing considerations. But for seismic force resistance, the design must be in accordance with all of the other provisions of Chapter 23. We recommend avoiding sole reliance on conventional details when there is a likelihood of severe seismic activity. The modern light-frame building does not have inherent seismic resistance. If there is any doubt, perform seismic analysis, or obtain help from a consultant experienced in this type of light-frame construction.

TABLE 25-I–ALLOWABLE SHEAR FOR WIND OR SEISMIC FORCES IN POUNDS PER SQUARE FOOT FOR VERTICAL DIAPHRAGMS OF LATH AND PLASTER OR GYPSUM BOARD FRAME WALL ASSEMBLIES

Footnote 1: These vertical diaphragms shall not be used to resist loads imposed by masonry or concrete construction. See Section 2513.2. Values shown are for short-term loading due to wind or due to seismic loading. Values shown must be reduced 25 percent for normal loading. The values shown in Items 2, 3 and 4 shall be reduced 50 percent for loading due to earthquake in Seismic Zones 3 and 4.

The last sentence in Footnote 1 is of major importance in seismic zones 3 and 4.

This requirement in Table 25-I results from testing done in California involving both repetitive loading and full reversals of loads. This approach to the evaluation of shear panels under seismic loading is more realistic than the unidirectional, single such ASTM test standard. The test findings indicated a substantial reduction in the lateral load-carrying capability of gypsum board panels.

It is the authors' opinion that similar reductions must be made to other brittle-type materials used in seismic design. Also, great care and careful attention to detailing must be used when relying on gypsum board or plaster walls to resist lateral forces. The adequacy of the lateral resistance performance of such brittle diaphragms under actual earthquake loadings is open to question.

Chapter 26 Plastic

SECTION 2602—FOAM PLASTIC INSULATION

2602.1 General. The provisions of this section shall govern the requirements and uses of foam plastic insulation in buildings and structures. For trim, see 601.5.5.

2602.3 Surface-burning Characteristics. Foam plastic insulation used in building construction shall have a flame-spread rating of not more than 75 and smoke-developed rating of not more than 450 when tested in accordance with UBC Standard 8-1 in the maximum thickness intended for use.

2602.4 Thermal Barrier. The interior of the building shall be separated from the foam plastic insulation by an approved thermal barrier having an index of 15 when tested in accordance with UBC Standard 26-2. The thermal barrier shall be installed in such a manner that it will remain in place for the time of its index classification based on approved diversified tests.

EXCEPTION: The thermal barrier is not required:

1. For siding backer board, provided the foam plastic insulation is not of more than 2,000 Btu per square foot (22.7 MJ/m^2) as determined by UBC Standard 26-1 and when it is separated from the interior of the building by not less than 2 inches (51 mm) of mineral fiber insulation or equivalent, or applied as re-siding over existing wall construction.

2602.5.2.1 One-story buildings. Foam plastic insulation may be used in exterior walls of one-story buildings where exterior walls are required to be of noncombustible construction subject to the following:

1. The building is protected throughout with automatic sprinklers.
2. Foam plastic insulation, tested in the maximum thickness and density intended for use, has a flame spread rating of 25 or less and a smoke developed rating of 450 or less in accordance with UBC Standard 8-1.
3. The foam plastic insulation has a maximum 4-inch thickness (102 mm).
4. The thermal barrier may be omitted when the foam plastic insulation is covered by not less than 0.032-inch-thick (0.8 mm) aluminum or corrosion-resistant sheet steel, having a base metal thickness of 0.0160 (0.4 mm) inch.

2602.5.2.2 Buildings of any height. Except for foam plastic insulation in masonry or concrete construction complying with Section 2602.4, Exception 3, assemblies employing foam plastic insulation in or on exterior walls of buildings where the exterior walls are required to be of noncombustible construction shall comply with the following:

1. When the wall is required to have a fire-resistive rating, data based on tests conducted in accordance with UBC Standard 7-1 are provided to substantiate that the fire-resistive rating is maintained.
2. The foam plastic insulation is separated from the interior of the building by a thermal barrier having an index of 15 unless specifically approved under Section 2602.6.
3. Combustible content of foam plastic insulation in any portion of the wall or panel does not exceed 6,000 Btu per square foot (68.2 MJ/m^2) of wall area as determined by tests in accordance with UBC Standard 26-1.
4. Foam plastic insulation, exterior coatings and facings tested separately shall each have a flame-spread rating of 25 or less and a smoke-developed

rating of 450 or less in accordance with UBC Standard 8-1. The foam plastic shall be tested in the thickness intended for use.

Section 2602 governs the installation of exterior insulation and finish systems (EIFS) and of aluminum composite panels. This section responds to the increasing use of new and innovative materials. Exterior insulation and finish (EIFS) systems and composite panels have been in use outside of the UBC territory for a number of years. These sections were developed to allow the use of these systems under controlled conditions with verifiable criteria.

The code is an inherently conservative document that responds slowly to new methods and construction practices. Sections such as these may take several rounds of code adoption before they are finalized. As technology is refined and performance experience gathered as new technologies are used in construction, code provisions may change based on experience. Thus it is not wise to try and memorize code provisions. There may be subtle, or major, changes in code language from edition to edition and memorized knowledge is likely to be erroneous.

Initially, when new systems such as EIFS come into use in the UBC territory, each proposed use requires interpretation of requirements under the "alternate materials and methods section" of the code, Section 104.2.8. Use of this section requires submission of product data, interpretation of potentially applicable code sections and negotiation with the building official to obtain approval. As use of a new system increases, it becomes in the best interest of the industry representatives and code officials to agree upon code criteria for use of such systems to obtain uniform interpretations and enforcement from jurisdiction to jurisdiction. As a new product gains acceptance, the volume of test and field data grows and predictions of performance become the basis for code provisions.

EIF systems employ foam insulation covered with synthetic stucco that forms a weather barrier. The systems use materials that are combustible alone, but the fire performance of the system is better than the individual parts. The testing protocols that are set out in the standards referenced in the code help the designer to understand the level of expected performance and to use the products with confidence in their performance.

> Careful attention must be paid to water proofing and flashing details when using EIFS. Any break in the membrane of the system can lead to water intrusion and deterioration of the substrates of the system and of the building structure. Provisions must also be made for venting or for allowing the escape of moisture in the system that may enter the building through breaks in the membrane.

Manufacturers should be able to provide literature on code compliance and detailing for products such as EIFS assemblies or for other products such as composite aluminum and plastic wall panels. Be certain to verify the applicability of systems to the intended use and to verify the compatibility of manufacturer's details with specific job conditions such as building structure and weather conditions. Also be certain that various components are those tested and listed in code compliance literature. It is not acceptable to randomly mix and match components of fire-rated assemblies and still be certain of code compliance of assemblies.

2603.6 Roof Panels. Approved plastic roof panels may be installed in roofs of buildings not required to have a fire-resistive rating, subject to the following limitations:

1. Individual roof panels or units shall be separated from each other by distances of not less than 4 feet (1219 mm) measured in a horizontal plane.

2. Roof panels or units shall not be installed within that portion of a roof located within a distance to the property line or public way where openings in exterior walls are prohibited or required to be protected, whichever is most restrictive.

2603.7 Skylights.

2603.7.1 General. Skylight assemblies may be glazed with approved plastic materials in accordance with the following provisions:

6. Skylight units shall be separated from each other by a distance of not less than 4 feet (1219 mm) measured in a horizontal plane.

Exceptions: 1. Except for Groups A, Divisions 1 and 2; I, Divisions 1.1, 1.2 and 2: and H, Divisions 1 and 2 Occupancies, the separation is not required where the skylights are:

1.1 Serving as a fire venting system complying with this code; or

1.2 Used in a building completely equipped with an approved automatic sprinkler system complying with UBC Standard 9-1 or 9-3.

2. Multiple skylights located above the same room or space with a combined area not exceeding the limits set forth in Section 2603.7.1, Item 4.

7. Skylights shall not be installed within that portion of a roof located within a distance to property line or public way where openings in exterior walls are prohibited or required to be protected, whichever is most restrictive.

These sections provide the regulations for the installation of roof panels and skylights in buildings. The concern is twofold:

1. The prevention of fire entry into a building from flying brands from an adjacent building, thus preventing the spread of fire and
2. The prevention of fire spreading from a building to an adjacent structure via an opening in the roof that may be close to the property line.

The intent is to permit unprotected roof openings when they are located the same distance from the property line or public way that would allow unprotected exterior openings. (See Figure 10-7.)

Appendix Chapter 29 Minimum Plumbing Fixtures

SECTION 2905—GENERAL

Each building shall be provided with sanitary facilities, including provisions for accessibility in accordance with Chapter 11. Plumbing fixtures shall be provided to the type of building occupancy with the minimum numbers as shown in Table A-29-A. The number of fixtures are the minimum required as shown in Table A-29-A and are assumed to be based on 50 percent male and 50 percent female. The occupant load factors shall be as shown in Table A-29-A.

EXCEPTION: Where circumstances dictate that a different ratio is needed, the adjustment shall be approved by the building official.

Hopefully your local building jurisdiction will adopt this appendix section into the body of the code. This section regulates the number of plumbing fixtures to be provided in buildings based upon their occupancy. The determination of the number of fixtures is a design-related decision and as such belongs in the building code, not in the plumbing code. The plumbing code determines such things as the size of drain lines and vent sizes, it is a detailed engineering design document. The fixture counts are related to architectural planning and as such belong in the building code.

The appendix chapters are not considered a part of the code unless they are specifically adopted by the authorities having jurisdiction into the body of the code by amendment.

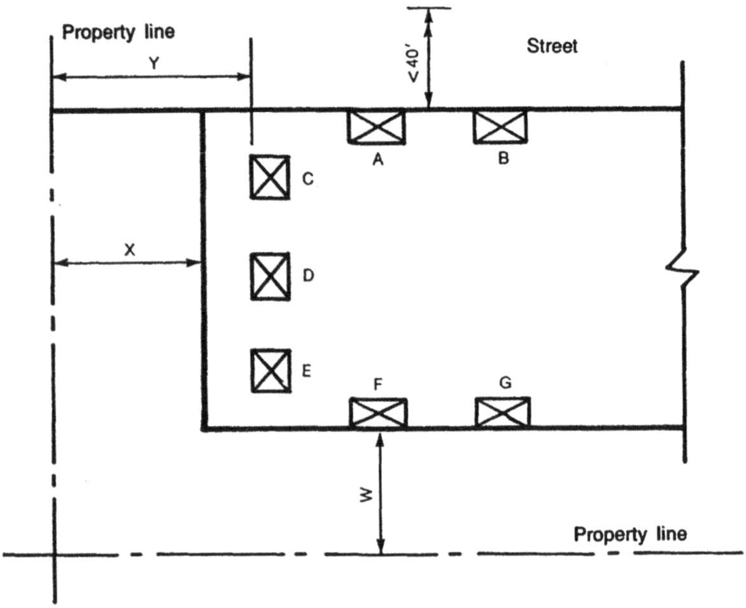

GIVEN: Type III-N building
Group B Occupancy

Per Section 2603.6 and 2603.7:

a) When X = 5', no openings are permitted in the exterior wall. If Y = 5', no roof openings are permitted.
b) When 5' ≤ X , 20', protected openings are allowed on the exterior wall. If 5' ≥ Y ≤ 20', no roof openings are permitted. Roof openings C, D, and E can only be located so that the closest edge of the opening is at least 20 feet from the property line.
c) When X, Y or W > 20', unprotected openings are permitted on the exterior wall. Roof openings are permitted as well; openings F & G are permitted when the closest edge is more than 20' from the property line.

REFERENCE: SECTIONS 604.3, 2603.6 and 2603.7

FIGURE 10-7 LOCATION CRITERIA FOR ROOF OPENINGS AS RELATED TO EXTERIOR WALL OPENINGS

> Even if the Uniform Plumbing Code (UPC), which has its own table of fixture counts, is in effect in your jurisdiction, the designer should validate the fixture counts with Table A-29-A. It is a more rationally based chart and relates better to the new occupancy classifications in the new code format than does the older format of the UPC. Any such analysis can then be discussed with the building official as a basis for a favorable interpretation of the applicability of fixture counts to a specific project.

Chapter 35 Uniform Building Code Standards

This chapter lists the categories and cross references for standards of testing and installation that are adopted by reference into the code. Note that these standards become a legal part of the code because of their adoption by reference. While detailed knowledge of the contents of the standards is not usually required of the designer, it is essential that the designer know of the existence of these standards. If is also essential to know that the building design and construction must comply with these standards since they are a part of the code by reference even though not printed out in their entirety. The distinctions of the four "parts" of the chapter are related to adoption deal mostly with adoption procedures. For all practical purposes the designer should consider the standards in all four parts to be on an equal and interrelated footing. It is worthwhile to remember that specifying code compliance for products will bring these standards into play since they are legally part of the code.

Part 1—General
SECTION 3501—UBC STANDARDS
The Uniform Building Code Standards referred to in various parts of this code, which are also listed in Part II of this chapter, are hereby declared to be part of this code and are referred to in this code as a "UBC standard".

The standards in Part II of the chapter have been formally adopted by the International Conference of Building Officials (ICBO) as recognized standards. Many of these standards have been developed by other organizations such as the American Society for Testing and Materials (ASTM) as national test standards to establish performance criteria for use by industry. They are usually technical requirements such as ASTM E-119-83 for fire tests of building construction components, which is referenced as UBC Standard 7-1. Another example are the sprinkler installation standards set forth by the National Fire Protection Association (NFPA) as NFPA 13, which is referenced as UBC Standard 9-1. References in the code are to the UBC Standard. It is necessary to look in Chapter 35 to determine the source document for the standard.

SECTION 3502—ADOPTED STANDARDS

The standards referred to in various parts of the code, which are listed in Part III of this chapter, are hereby declared to be part of this code.

These standards are adopted by reference to specific standards by other bodies and are referred to by name in the body of the code. Some are developed by broad national coalitions of experts to set standards for national issues. A prime example is the standard for accessible design referenced in Chapter 11: CABO/ANSI A117.2-1992. Other examples are specifications and standards developed by industry trade groups to control the quality of products made by a specific industry. An example of this type of standards are the National Design Specification for Wood Construction developed by the American Forest and Paper Association.

SECTION 3503—STANDARD OF DUTY

The standard of duty established for the recognized standards listed in Part IV of this chapter is that the design, construction and quality of materials of buildings and structures be reasonably safe for life, limb health, property and public welfare.

SECTION 3504—RECOGNIZED STANDARDS

The standards listed in Part IV of this chapter are recognized standards. Compliance with these recognized standards shall be prima facie evidence of compliance with the standard of duty set forth in Section 3503.

Note that Section 3503 repeats the purpose of the code as stated in Section 101.2. These standards are to be followed to ensure that the building meets the minimum standards for health, safety and welfare. These are broader standards, often related to performance of systems rather than to test criteria. A good example of this is the adoption of ventilation standards for Chapter 12 contained in ANSI/ASHRAE 62-1989. This standard is itself a book as big as a substantial portion of the code.

ARTICLE 11
LEGAL IMPLICATIONS OF THE CODE

The code is frequently viewed as a hurdle to be surmounted by the designer, the contractor and others involved in the building process. Some can gracefully maneuver over the obstacle; some ignore its presence and try to bulldoze through it; others try to circumvent it.

Unfortunately, we are living in an increasingly litigious society. Because the code is an ordinance or law, enacted by a jurisdiction, it is as much the law as any other law on the books. Violation of the code is a violation of the law and can result in financial or personal loss to the individual or firm committing the violation.

Contractor and the Code

The authors' have occasionally used, with appropriate modifications, a nationally circulated contract document that indicates that the contractor is not required to know the code but need only follow the drawings that are part of the contract. In many states this is not true. Contractor licensing laws require the contractor to abide by all laws and ordinances. To obtain a contractor's license, the contractor must know the codes in effect in the locality in which the contractor intends to operate.

In fact, the contractor may have a much greater familiarity with the different types of construction and code problems than many designers. It is incumbent on the contractor, in the review and in estimating a job for the materials and methods intended to be used in the project, to pay special attention to those areas found at variance with the locally applicable code. When these areas are encountered, the contractor should notify the designer, in writing, of the findings. The correspondence should state that the contractor will not be liable for what may happen if the suspected violation remains uncorrected.

By writing about these findings to the designer, and by clearly delineating any future noninvolvement with that issue, the contractor may sidestep future liability in that case. The designer must be attentive to those areas of the contract documents the contractor identifies.

Designer and the Code

Under the professional licensing provisions in each state, the designer is also subject to the legal requirement for code compliance.

A substantial number of projects have come to the authors' attention where contractors and designers committed code violations either knowingly or unknowingly.

The frequency of these cases indicates that all too often the participants place too great an emphasis on obtaining the permit and consider the building official to be the sole enforcer of the law. They assume that after the permit has been obtained, the code hurdle is successfully negotiated and there need be no further concerns.

Many unusual determinations have come to the authors' attention. These involve interpretations by local officials that are totally at variance with the accepted views of the design profession, the International Conference of Building Officials (ICBO) and enforcement officials generally and the definitions in the Uniform Building Code (UBC).

The designers had experience in other jurisdictions and should have known better than to follow the misinterpretations of the enforcement officials. In one instance, the designer did what was proper and ignored the ruling of the enforcement official. In the others, the designers followed the bad advice and designed buildings in violation of the UBC. The irony was that the enforcement officials, when the matter was brought to their attention, chose to place themselves above the code, i.e., the law in their own jurisdiction. Such posturing does not serve the public nor the design profession.

The designer should follow the code when faced with a determination made at the local level that is knowingly contrary to the code and accepted practice in the profession. The choice of a more restrictive reading of the code cannot be overruled by the official. One can always exceed the minimum standards in the code. By so doing, the designer will avoid the trap of taking responsibility for the code violation that the official inadvertently set up. Remember that the code provides an "out" for the official via Section 106.4.3; there is no similar one for the designer.

Building Officials Legal Responsibility and Resources

As indicated in this Guide, many years of statutory liability face the designer, the contractor and others party to the construction. In an article published in ICBO's Building Standards Monthly, the Guide's original author indicated concern with the increasing tendency of some building officials to fail to exercise their responsibilities. The locality, in accepting the permit and plan check fees, is obliged to provide the services those fees are meant to procure and to protect the public by means of its checking and inspection fimctions.

Several resources are available to the building official when a design is so complex or unusual that the official's time or level of knowledge may not be adequate to review the design documents properly. The nearest resources are larger jurisdictions or design professionals who have had experience in plan checking and who may be retained to review the drawings and other design documents for the complex project. This type of assistance can augment the technical capacities of the locality and reduce the possibility of the building official becoming a party to potential code violations.

A second resource is the staff of the ICBO in Whittier, California, and its regional offices. The staff is experienced in plan checking. The plan-checking services conducted by the ICBO can provide the building official with a written review of the permit documents. After a line of communication has been opened with the ICBO, questions that occur after the plan check can be resolved with the ICBO staff assistance.

The building official can also obtain assistance by making inquiry to the ICBO regarding a particular arrangement, configuration or material. The resources of the ICBO are available to the building official, and written responses enable the official to arrive at equitable solutions to complex questions.

The enforcement official who chooses to ignore the code (see The Designer and the Code above) places both the jurisdiction and the official in serious jeopardy. Cases have ruled that both the individual and the jurisdiction can sustain liability if the action by the official was knowingly wrong. The official should obtain maximum assistance from the cited sources rather than incur such liability. The public is ill served by officials who choose to ignore the law they are to enforce.

Standard of Care

Another issue that usually arises in litigation is the question of what constitutes the prevailing standard of care in a particular locality because construction and design practices vary according to the locality.

The acceptance of substandard drawings from several designers does not establish a standard level of acceptance in that locality.

If that standard results in drawings that are incomplete for proper construction, in litigation the designer will answer to the courts. It is foolish to hope the courts will rule that the continued presence of inadequate drawings will, over a period of time, establish that level of performance as the professional standard in the locality.

If a building official has made an erroneous interpretation and maintains that misinterpretation when responding to similar inquiries from other design professionals, that repetition of error does not establish a legal basis for violating the code. The designer must know and comply with the code, just as the driver of a car is required to know the speed limits, comply with them and not rely on the traffic cop to verify them.

A court decision in California (*Huang v. Garner*) found, among other rulings, that violation of the code was negligence on the part of the designer. It further found the failure of the contractor/developer to comply with the Uniform Building Code, which creates potential risks to future purchasers. Moreover, the court indicated that the standard of care required of designers and engineers may, in fact, be the standard for the profession as a whole.

Thus, the local community may not be equivalent to the community at issue. The *Huang v. Gamer* case is having a strong impact on litigation. Its message is clear, and its meaning should warn everyone of the dangers involved in committing code violations.

Decision-Making Process and Pressures

In the code development process at the committee levels and at the annual business meeting, during which the code changes are finally discussed and voted on, even well-informed individuals differ in their interpretations of provisions. When inexperienced officials attempt to make decisions on complex provisions of the code and do so without the background necessary to formulate those decisions, the day-today pressures placed on them by their jobs and by the individuals seeking those decisions increase the likelihood that errors will be made.

It is better for the building official to use the services of the ICBO. The official can direct an inquiry to the ICBO staff, and, after receiving a reply, the official will have a clear-cut understanding of the code's intent. The resultant interpretation will be prepared by personnel impartial yet experienced in code and code development.

If there are doubts about the propriety of a decision, it is best to have the decision evaluated through the ICBO or to have the backing of a local chapter of the ICBO. These chapters are made up of building officials and others interested in the code. The problem can be brought before the group and discussed, so that the best available expertise in the locality can assist the official.

When a locality adopts a new edition of the code or other ordinances, it provides an opportunity for the design professional and others in the building process to resolve locally recognized code problem areas. This resolution can be accomplished either by adopting a local amendment to the code or by establishing an appeal procedure whereby interpretations or rulings on the code can be made within the locality. As previously stated, if an appeal board for such issues does not exist, one should be established with interested and knowledgeable members of the building industry as active members.

Summary

When errors are made, the public suffers and the individuals involved in the decision are placed in legal jeopardy. Although the code hurdle may apparently have been overcome successfully, one finds, years later, that it was not truly overcome. Instead, it had been simply pushed ahead to a future date at which point it suddenly looms up, much more difficult to conquer, and placing much more at stake. Many of the parties originally involved are no longer around, and the circumstances of the original decision-making process are no longer pressing or even known.

In such situations, when dispassionate evaluations can take place, the design professional, the contractor and the building official can find themselves under the scrutiny of the law. The public will want to know why they supported and allowed noncompliance with the laws of the locality.

The authors' hope that this Guide will assist the designer and others involved with the building process in avoiding the much tougher legal hurdle by providing methods for avoiding unwitting code violations and by promoting an understanding of the code process and intent.

ARTICLE 12
APPLICABILITY OF CODES

An area of code enforcement causing considerable problems for the building official, the designer and the attorney is the determination of what code applies to an existing building. It is important to determine just what codes applied at various tines during a building's life. The building may now be the subject of litigation due to alleged defects involving the original construction as well as subsequent alterations.

General Definitions, Parameters and Approach

To provide guidance in resolving this type of situation, we must first establish certain parameters and define terms.

Definition of Terms

Code at Time of Original Construction: The building code adopted by the jurisdiction prior to the date of the original construction.

Retroactivity: The application of a requirement in a code, ordinance or other regulation to an existing building. The application is not dependent on whether the owner desires to comply or do any work and is mandatory on the owner. Failure of the owner to comply results in the full force of the enforcement process by the local jurisdiction.

Building Code Appendix: As stated in this Guide, the Appendix must be specifically adopted by the local jurisdiction. If not so adopted, it does not apply. Any adopted part of the Appendix has the same force of law as does the rest of the code.

Certain provisions in the Appendix have retroactive intent. In the present code these are Appendix Chapter 34, Division I and Division II. In prior editions of the Uniform Building code (UBC), the retroactive provisions may have different chapter designations.

The key terminology is the reference to "existing buildings" in the opening sections of the Appendix provisions. This terminology gives the intent for application of the requirements to all existing buildings. See Section 3406.1 of Appendix Chapter 34, Division I for example.

Prime Criteria

A building must always comply with the code in effect at the time of its original construction.

Building codes are not retroactive.

Retroactive regulations apply only to specific areas of buildings and to buildings that were built either when less-restrictive provisions were in effect or when there was no code in effect in the locality.

Parameters of Application

Retroactive code provisions are aimed at correcting existing conditions that are now deemed to be deficiencies in buildings. The deficiencies were not considered as such under the codes in effect at the time of the original construction. These deficiencies include such conditions as the presence of unenclosed exit stairways or lack of a second exit.

Retroactivity involves constitutional issues as well as economic impacts on the owner and building occupants. The enactment of retroactive provisions requires very careful consideration of the issues involved, the details of the provisions to be invoked and the methods permitted for satisfying them, so that the regulations are not excessive.

It was not until after World War II that enclosed stairways were mandated for all new buildings three or more stories in height. Thus, any building built prior to that period would be subject to retroactive provisions of Appendix Chapter 34, Division I, if such were adopted by the locality.

Sometimes the state adopts retroactive provisions and mandates them for enforcement by the local jurisdiction. Such state action preempts the option of the local jurisdiction to determine whether it wants to have such regulations. The decision is made for the jurisdiction by the state legislature.

When the edition of the building code adopted by a jurisdiction contains provisions of equal or greater restrictiveness than a retroactive requirement, all buildings built after the adoption of that edition must exceed that retroactive provision. The retroactive provisions would apply only to buildings built prior to that edition.

If the original construction did not meet the requirements of the code in effect at the time of the original construction, then under the code in effect at that time there are requirements that apply. These are the provisions in Chapters 1 and 34 requiring that the building must be brought into compliance with the code in effect at the time of original construction. Any permit issued or finaled does not validate noncompliance with that code.

Since before 1950 all editions of the UBC have had provisions similar to those in Sections 104(i) and 302(c) of the 1949 UBC. In the 1997 UBC these same provisions are contained in Sections 108 and 3402.

Code provisions contained in codes in effect at the time of original construction that exceed the restrictiveness of the retroactive provisions always take precedence over the retroactive provisions. In such buildings, the retroactive provisions of the Appendix do not apply.

Application of the Definitions and Parameters

To provide the reader with a methodology for applying the above definitions and parameters to a variety of conditions, we will assume a broad range of possible situations regarding regulations in effect and evaluate how a given building would be affected in each circumstance. To aid in this evaluation, the conditions and evaluation will be discussed both in text and by several figures.

Main Assumption:	PC = Building built before adoption of local code. See Figure 12-1. AC = Building built after adoption of local code. See Figure 12-2.
Secondary Assumptions:	Locality adopted Appendix provisions comparable to Chapter 34, Division I. Locality did not adopt Appendix. Locality or state-adopted Uniform Housing code (UHC) or other housing code. Locality adopted later edition of UBC. Locality adopted special regulations regarding conversion of condominiums.

NOTE: The applicablility of a particular ordinance is shown by the heavy vertical line extending from the top of the chart and intersecting the bar representing the life history of the particular building. For example, the adoption of the Appendix intersecting the "A" bar. As of that time, all existing buildings would have had to comply with the Appendix provision of the UBC edition cited as well as any prior UBC edition in effect at the time of original construction.

The UBC in effect at the time the alteration work is done applies only to the specific alteration work, unless the Appendix had also been adopted for the first time.

FIGURE 12-1 CODE/ORDINANCE TIME HISTORY & APPLICATION TO EXISTING BUILDING BUILT PRIOR TO ANY UBC ADOPTION

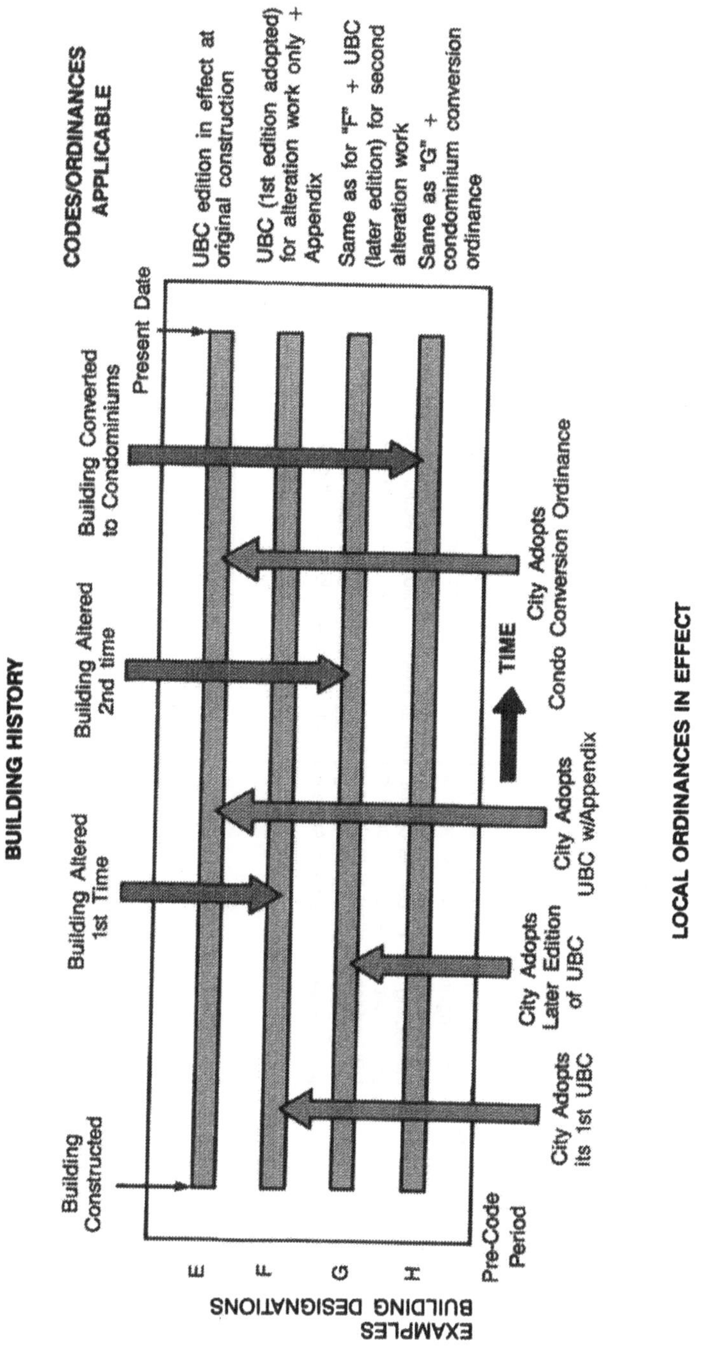
BUILDING HISTORY
Building Constructed
Building Altered 1st Time
Building Altered 2nd time
Building Converted to Condominiums
Present Date
CODES/ORDINANCES APPLICABLE
UBC edition in effect at original construction
UBC (1st edition adopted) for alteration work only + Appendix
Same as for "F" + UBC (later edition) for second alteration work
Same as "G" + condominium conversion ordinance
EXAMPLES BUILDING DESIGNATIONS
E
F
G
H
Pre-Code Period
City Adopts its 1st UBC
City Adopts Later Edition of UBC
City Adopts UBC w/Appendix
TIME
City Adopts Condo Conversion Ordinance
LOCAL ORDINANCES IN EFFECT

NOTE: The applicablility of a particular ordinance is shown by the heavy vertical line extending from the top of the chart and intersecting the bar representing the life history of the particular building. For example, the adoption of the Appendix intersecting the "E" bar. As of that time, all existing buildings would have had to comply with the Appendix provision of the UBC edition cited as well as any prior UBC edition in effect at the time of original construction.

The UBC in effect at the time the alteration work is done applies only to the specific alteration work, unless the Appendix had also been adopted for the first time.

FIGURE 12-2 CODE/ORDINANCE TIME HISTORY & APPLICATION TO EXISTING BUILDING BUILT AFTER A UBC ADOPTION

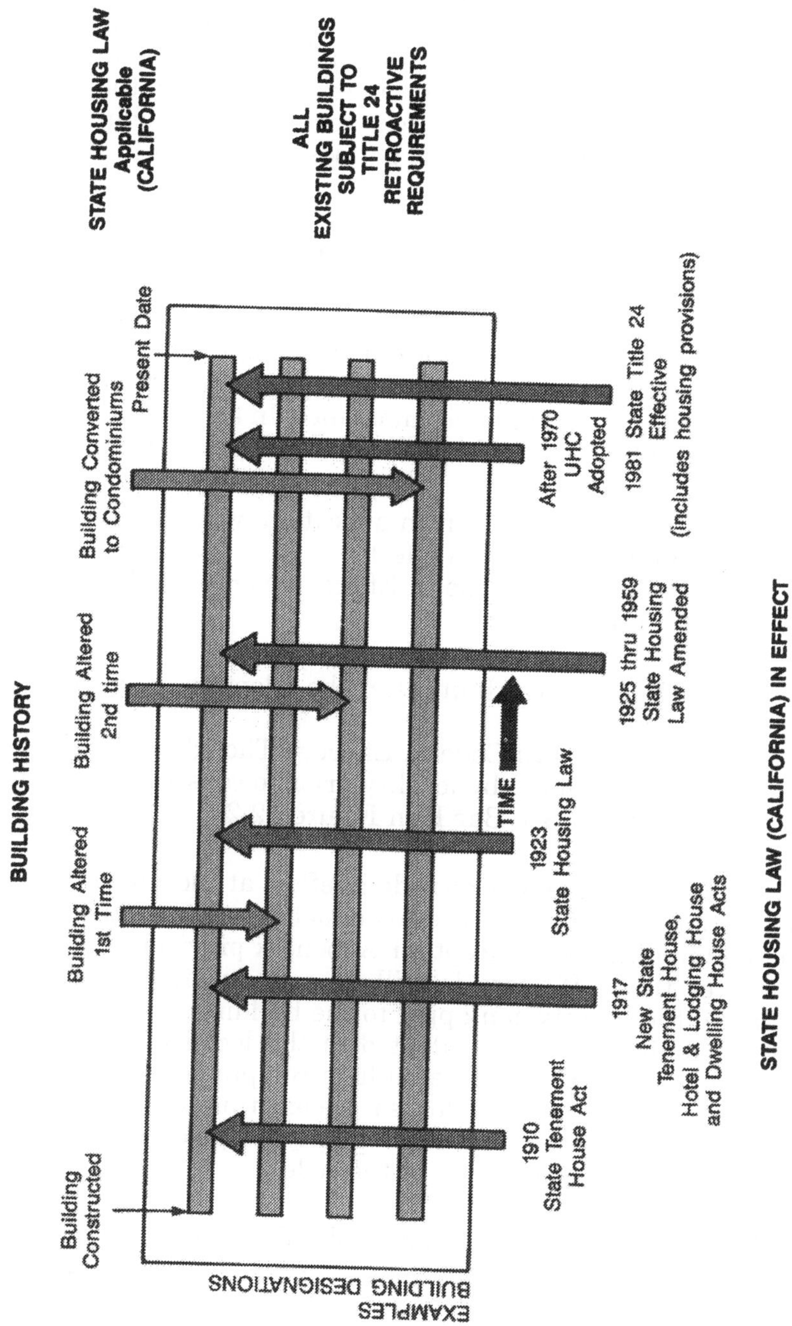
BUILDING HISTORY
Building Constructed
Building Altered 1st Time
Building Altered 2nd time
Building Converted to Condominiums
Present Date
STATE HOUSING LAW Applicable (CALIFORNIA)
ALL EXISTING BUILDINGS SUBJECT TO TITLE 24 RETROACTIVE REQUIREMENTS
EXAMPLES BUILDING DESIGNATIONS
TIME
1910 State Tenement House Act
1917 New State Tenement House, Hotel & Lodging House and Dwelling House Acts
1923 State Housing Law
1925 thru 1959 State Housing Law Amended
After 1970 UHC Adopted
1981 State Title 24 Effective (includes housing provisions)
STATE HOUSING LAW (CALIFORNIA) IN EFFECT

Finally, we will examine the effect of one or more of the assumptions on a three-story building with multifamily Occupancy Group R, Division 1. See Figure 12-4 for an example of how the assumptions and the evaluations apply to determine the code in effect on the original building at different periods and events in the building's life.

Rationale in Determining Code in Effect

To determine the code in effect we will progress from the simpler assumptions to the more complex. This technique will enable the reader to use the same rationale for other assumptions that may be applicable to a particular circumstance. In all cases, the evaluation of the condition should parallel the analyses herein.

I. Building PC was built in a location where there is no local building code in effect.
   1. Building PC: Code in Effect = None. See Bar A in Figure 12-1.

II. Building AC was built after the adoption of the local building code.
   2. Building AC: Code in Effect = The edition of the UBC adopted by locality prior to construction of the building. See Bar E in Figure 12-2.

Discussion: If there was no code in effect at the time of original construction of building PC, there cannot be any retroactive application of a building code (except for Appendix provisions adopted at some later time). If there is still no code in effect, there is no regulation the locality can apply to the building.

After a building code is adopted in the locality, all buildings, such as building AC, must be built in compliance with that code or a later edition when so adopted. Preexisting buildings, such as building PC, are not subject to the newly adopted code, except for any work done after adoption of the code.

III. Assume locality has adopted UBC with Appendix provision applicable to existing residential buildings.
   3. Building PC: Code in Effect = Appendix provisions. See Bar A in Figure 12-1.

4. Building AC: Code in Effect = Appendix provision unless the UBC provisions at the time of original construction exceeded the requirements of the Appendix. The most restrictive provision applies. See Bar E in Figure 12-2.

Discussion: The adoption of the Appendix means the locality has established that all buildings must meet certain minimum standards regardless of whether they were built in conformance to a prior code or built when there was no code in effect in the locality. Those buildings, such as building PC, that do not meet or exceed the requirements in the Appendix for the areas specifically covered therein must be brought up to compliance with the minimum provisions of the Appendix.

Those buildings, such as building AC, that were built when the codes in effect in the locality exceeded the requirements of the Appendix must meet the requirements of the more restrictive UBC editions because a prime criterion is that a building as a minimum must meet the requirements of the code in effect at the time of original construction.

IV. Assume for both buildings that the locality has updated its code to a later edition of the UBC.

5. Building PC: Code in Effect = The Appendix. See Row A in Figure 12-1.
6. Building AC: Code in Effect = The prior UBC edition in effect at time of original construction and/or the Appendix, depending on which provisions are more restrictive. See Bar F in Figure 12-2.

   Assume that alterations are contemplated in both buildings.
7. Building PC: Code in Effect = Code in effect at the time of the alterations for the work done for the alterations only. If the Appendix was applicable, it also applies. See Row B in Figure 12-1.
8. Building AC: Code in Effect = Code in effect at the time of the alterations for the work done for the alterations only. The rest of the building must still comply with the code in effect at the time of original

construction. If the Appendix is applicable, it also applies. See Column F in Figure 12-2.

Discussion: A locality periodically updates the building code it uses by adopting a more recent edition or latest edition of the UBC. If it had adopted the Appendix in a prior edition, it usually did so as part of the update adoption.

Whenever a later edition of the UBC is adopted, it applies to all work done thereafter whether it is new construction or alterations. If alteration work, only the area subject to the alterations is subject to the new code. As before, the building must always meet the prime criterion of being in compliance with the code in effect at the time of original construction. Where the Appendix provision applies it must also be complied with.

The alteration work must comply with the code in effect at the time the alteration work is done, even if the building was built prior to any code being adopted in the locality.

V. Assume that the locality or the state has adopted the UHC.

9. Building PC: Code in Effect = Same as item 7 plus the UHC. See Figure 12-3.
10. Building AC: Code in Effect = Same as item 8 plus the UHC. See Figure 12-3.

Discussion: At times, due to local, state or federal pressures, the state or locality enacts ordinances or adopts the UHC to require that all residential buildings under their jurisdiction be brought up to and maintained to a specified set of standards, including many provisions not found in the building code under which they were originally constructed. Housing codes are retroactive.

Uniform Housing Code provisions include many of the following: freedom from rubbish, vermin and insect infestation; minimum lighting levels in public corridors; minimum electrical requirements; carpeting regulations; painting and wall covering criteria.

These UHC or other similar housing regulations are retroactive to all residential buildings, subject to the jurisdiction of that regulation, regardless of when they were constructed. Failure to comply with the housing code can result in condemnation action against the building and its demolition.

NOTE: We have not covered the following variations of codes in effect:

- those localities that enforce state-adopted building codes,
- those jurisdictions that have local adoption of codes and when either state law preempts certain of the local codes for specific occupancies or
- when state law is retroactive for specific occupancies.

When there are state-mandated codes enforced by the locality, they have the same authority insofar as which code is applicable at different times in a building's life, as did the locally adopted codes in our discussion. In Figures 12-1 and 12-2, replace chart designation "Local codes in effect" by "State codes in effect."

When there is local adoption of codes and state law as well, as in California, both sets of laws must be considered and applied. For that reason, in Figure 12-3 we have noted that the requirements of Figure 12-3 should be superimposed on Figures 12-1 and 12-2 because both sets of requirements apply.

For other states, the designer and enforcement official must check the various applicable laws and create their own charts similar to Figure 12-3.

VI. Assume the locality has adopted regulations applicable to the conversion of existing buildings into condominiums.

11. Building PC: Code in Effect = Appendix plus the UBC in effect for alterations plus UHC and the minimum requirements of the condominium conversion regulations. See Bar D in Figure 12-1.
12. Building AC: Code in Effect = UBC in effect at time of original construction plus the Appendix, if it is more restrictive than the UBC at time of original construction, plus the UBC in effect for alterations plus UHC and the minimum requirements of the condominium conversion regulations. See Bar G in Figure 12-2.

Discussion. The trend in recent years for converting apartment buildings into condominiums has resulted in the enactment of condominium conversion ordinances by local jurisdictions. These ordinances are aimed at protecting the buyer and the locality from the effects of the conversion.

The buyer is purchasing a unit in a building that was built in the past and, therefore, may have unknown defects. The conversion

Where state law applies in the locality as in California, the chart representing the state laws versus time should be superimposed on the localities chart of ordinance adoption to determine the total legislation applicable to a particular existing building. See Figures 12-1 and 12-2.

The state regulations establish minimum standards for new construction and alterations. The Tenement House Act and Housing laws, the Uniform Housing Code (UHC) and Title 24 (State Building Code) all contain provisions that affect existing buildings and are retrocative; i.e., those provisions are mandatory for all existing buildings as a minimum requirement.

FIGURE 12-3 STATE HOUSING LAW (CALIFORNIA) TIME HISTORY AND APPLICATION TO EXISTING BUILDING

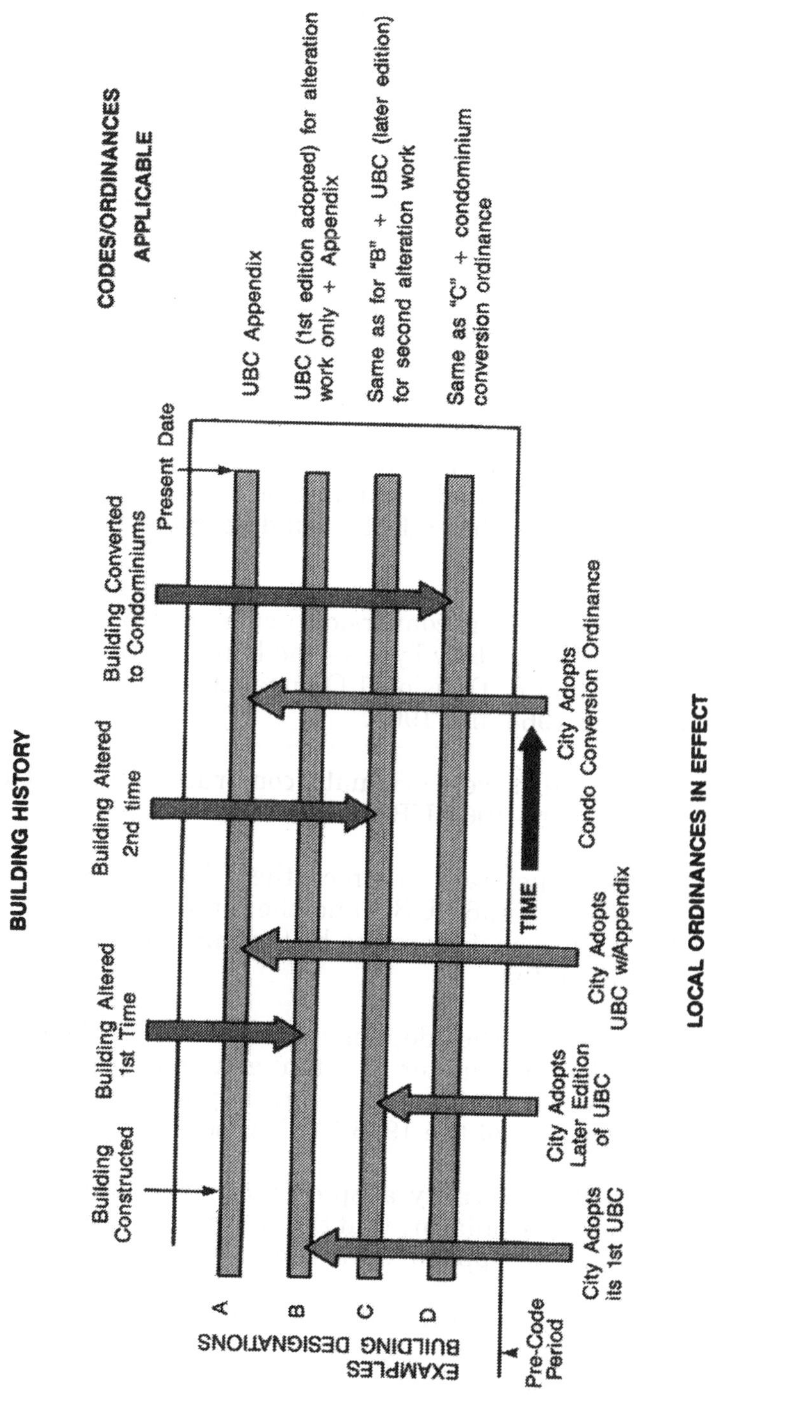
BUILDING HISTORY
Building Constructed
Building Altered 1st Time
Building Altered 2nd time
Building Converted to Condominiums
Present Date
CODES/ORDINANCES APPLICABLE
UBC Appendix
UBC (1st edition adopted) for alteration work only + Appendix
Same as for "B" + UBC (later edition) for second alteration work
Same as "C" + condominium conversion ordinance
EXAMPLES BUILDING DESIGNATIONS
A
B
C
D
Pre-Code Period
City Adopts its 1st UBC
City Adopts Later Edition of UBC
City Adopts UBC w/Appendix
TIME
City Adopts Condo Conversion Ordinance
LOCAL ORDINANCES IN EFFECT

ordinance usually requires that the defects be divulged in public record and be corrected. The ordinance can require that some lower-cost housing, additional parking and so forth also be provided.

At no time can the conversion ordinance replace or nullify the application of the prior adopted local codes and ordinances of the locality or state. These prior codes and ordinances include the UBC, UHC, Appendix and other enacted regulations. The condominium conversion ordinance is simply another requirement to be met in *addition to* all the other requirements.

Illustrative Example

The following simplified example is a composite of conditions in several condominium complexes. The authors' purpose is to demonstrate the sort of misinterpretations and misrepresentations that can occur due to faulty understanding of the code intent and the other legal documents that affect a building over its life.

Given:

1. The condominium conversion occurs in 1975 and involves a group of three-story Type V-One-hour apartment buildings with Group R, Division 1 Occupancies designed and built between 1963 and 1965.

2. The buildings were originally constructed in a jurisdiction that had the 1961 UBC in effect.

3. In 1968, the state in which these buildings are located adopted the 1967 UBC and the Uniform Housing Code. The UBC was declared to be the minimum code in effect in that state.

4. In 1969, with the adoption of the 1967 UBC, the Appendix provisions of Chapter 13 of that edition were also adopted. That Appendix Chapter is virtually identical to Chapter 1, Division 1 of the 1988 UBC Appendix.

5. In 1972 the locality adopted a condominium conversion ordinance stipulating that the minimum requirement to be met was the Appendix provision of the local building code.

6. Alterations had been done in 1967 and 1970.

7. The building areas exceed the allowables in the code in effect at the time of original construction and require area separation walls (ASWs). The buildings have exit stairways that exit through garages at the ground level of the building.

8. Investigations disclose that the ASWs were not constructed correctly and the buildings are not 1-hour rated throughout. The required exits are not provided, the exit paths are not properly protected and other violations of the code in effect at the time of original construction exist.

From the details provided for this example, the following are the minimum requirements mandated by the original construction, the subsequent alterations, the state law and the condominium ordinance: (The dates of effective ordinances and the work done on this particular building have been superimposed in Figure 12-1 and are shown in Figure 12-4.

Evaluation

Minimum building code: the 1961 UBC, which was the code in effect at the time of original construction.

Alterations should have complied with the edition in effect in 1967 and 1970. Because the state adopted the 1967 UBC in 1968, that would have been the minimum code in effect in 1970 for the locality as well.

The Appendix provisions of the 1967 UBC and the provisions of the 1967 UHC are less restrictive than the 1961 UBC requirements. Therefore, *they do not take precedence over the 1961 UBC as the minimum code requirements.*

The requirement invoking the Appendix in the condominium conversion ordinance does not replace the prime criterion; i.e., the building must conform to the minimum requirements of the code in effect at the time of the original construction.

Conclusion

Unfortunately, given the above circumstances and findings, the locality invoked only the Appendix requirements of the 1967 UBC as part of the condominium conversion considerations. This was

Minimum building code: The 1961 UBC which was the code in effect at the time of the original construction.

Alterations should have complied with the edition in effect in 1967 and 1970. Since the state had adopted the 1967 UBC in 1968, that would have been the minimum code in effect in 1970 for the locality as well.

The Appendix provisions of the 1967 UBC are less restrictive than the 1961 UBC requirements, therefore the Appendix does not take precedence over the 1961 UBC as the minimum code requirements.

The condominium conversion ordinance invoking the Appendix does not replace the prime criterion. i.e.:

1. The building must conform to the minimim requirements of the code in effect at the time of the original construction.
2. The subsequent alterations must be in compliance with the UBC editions under which that work was done.
3. Any retroactive state requirements are superimposed on the earlier codes. Local conversion ordinance cannot supercede these state requirements or the earlier codes.

FIGURE 12-4 EXAMPLE OF APPLICATION OF CODE/ORDINANCE TIME HISTORY TO A SPECIFIC BUILDING

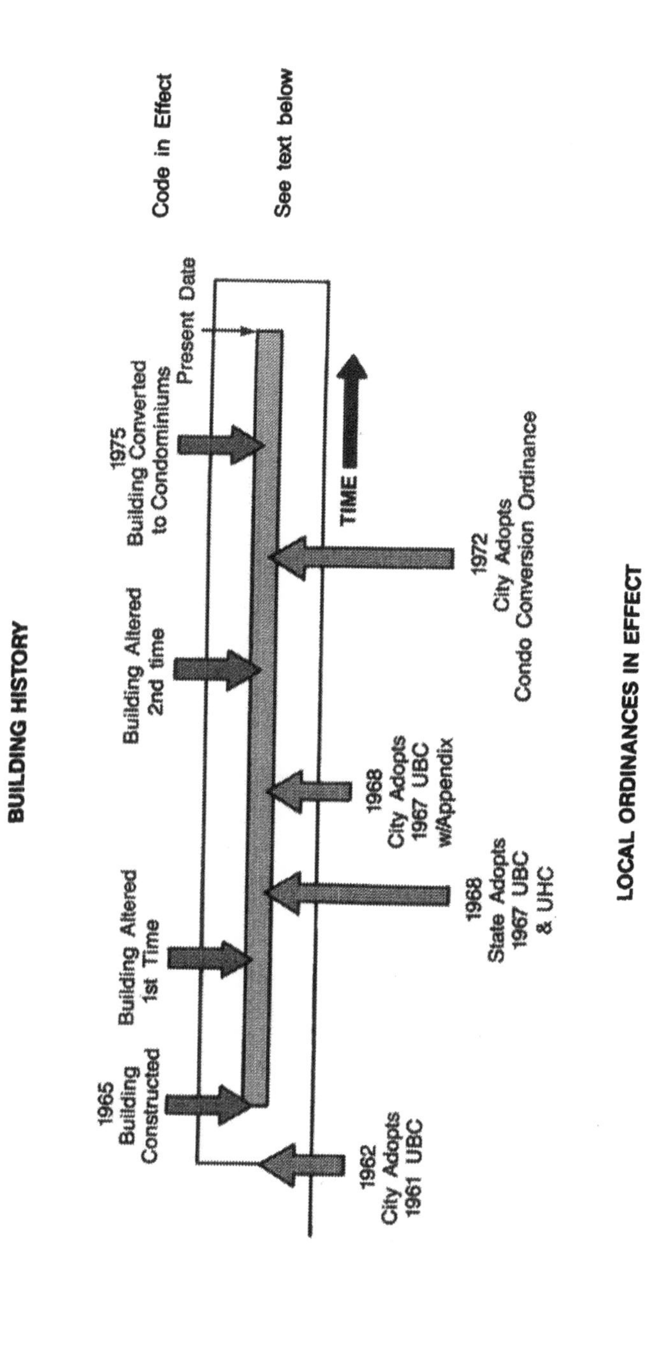
BUILDING HISTORY
1965 Building Constructed
Building Altered 1st Time
Building Altered 2nd time
1975 Building Converted to Condominiums
Present Date
Code in Effect
See text below
TIME
1962 City Adopts 1961 UBC
1968 State Adopts 1967 UBC & UHC
1968 City Adopts 1967 UBC w/Appendix
1972 City Adopts Condo Conversion Ordinance
LOCAL ORDINANCES IN EFFECT

done obviously through ignorance of the application of the codes as herein discussed.

The enforcement officials participated in that decision and did not point out that the 1961 UBC should have been the minimum standard applied. The developer who made the conversion came off very well indeed; but occupants of the buildings are denied the minimum safety to which they were entitled.

APPENDIX A-1
TYPICAL PERMIT PROCESS

The following description of the permit process is provided for illustration only. It does not represent an actual permit process in any particular city or section of the country or define how a jurisdiction should review plans or issue building permits. The intent of Appendix A-1 is to illustrate

- the various steps involved in such a process,
- the reason for each step,
- the degree of detail required for a proper review and
- the interaction of the several jurisdictional agencies on a project.

Readers should note that although their local jurisdiction may have a more or less sophisticated process, the essential elements are generally similar. For this example assume that there exists an industrial park in which a company has facilities. The company intends to construct a new building housing an H-6 occupancy on a corner of its property.

Prepermit Application Phase

At this stage the project's general size, schematic layout and building type are known and the questions of code impact need to be determined before detailed design is begun. A meeting should be scheduled with the jurisdiction's planning agency for its review of the zoning code and planning requirements, including, but not limited to, parking, truck loading and traffic impacts.

A separate meeting should be scheduled with the building inspection and fire department to review the building and fire code requirements. Since only schematic drawings are available at this time, the items to be discussed will be related to

- type of construction,
- height of building,
- the different occupancies in the building,
- area of each occupancy,
- the overall size of the building and
- the general exit requirements.

As we emphasized in Article 1, all decisions made at these meetings should be confirmed with the jurisdiction to establish mutual concurrence, and thus minimize misunderstandings. An example of such a letter is found in Appendix A-3. There may be several such meetings with the local departments as the plans are refined.

Filing the Building Permit Application

The jurisdiction will have a building permit application form that must be completed and submitted when filing for the permit. This application usually requires the following minimum information:

1. The address of the proposed building or other identification of the location,
2. the name of the owner, contractor and design professional,
3. the type of construction to be used, the floor area of each story, the gross floor area of the building and the number of stories and
4. the building's proposed occupancies, by classification.

Other information may be required, such as small-scale site plan, utilities (sewer, water, gas and electricity) size and location, and location of streets.

The permit application may come in multiple copies. Two sets of plans and specifications are required to be filed with the application. At this time a plan check fee is usually required, based on the estimated cost of the building as determined by the jurisdiction, using standard costs for the type of construction, occupancy, number of stories and various add-ons such as air conditioning, elevators, etc. Some jurisdictions also check plans for electrical, plumbing and mechanical requirements. This may require additional plans and fees.

Processing the Permit Application

The local jurisdiction's internal review of the permit application usually involves the following minimal steps:

1. The first review checks for conformance with the planning and zoning code. This review could reveal the need for special variances where General Plan changes

may have imposed new criteria that were not in effect at the time the site was originally obtained.

2. The next review is usually made by the building inspection agency to check for compliance with the building and other codes under its jurisdiction. In some localities the fire service review may be included within the office of the building department. However, in most jurisdictions the fire review is a separate step.

   In this review it is not unusual for additional information or clarifications to be requested by the checker. Many jurisdictions use a plan review list and will not contact the permit applicant until the review is completed, at which point the check list and noted deficiencies are provided. In some instances, the plan checker will go over the list with the applicant and discuss the findings.

   The purpose of the check and the deficiencies list is to bring the design documents into code compliance. Any differences in agreement or understanding should be presented, in a meeting, to the person responsible for the checking operation. The meeting's decisions should be documented and confirmed to establish the grounds for either changes to the plans or possible appeal.

3. The fire department review usually follows that of the building department. A similar procedure should be followed with regard to its checker's comments. In some jurisdictions the comments of all the locality's agencies will be collected into a master list of deficiencies. The designer should carefully evaluate the several concerns shown on that list. Contact is recommended with the various agency checkers whose conclusions differ from those of the designer, and from whom clarifications are needed.

4. In many jurisdictions, depending on local and state laws, there may be review of the application by
   a. an environmental agency responsible for water, sewer and/or air pollution control,
   b. the health department, which may review the plans if there is to be a food service facility in the building,
   c. the department of public works, or a similar agency, charged with traffic controls or encroachment on

public right-of-ways, to determine the acceptability of driveway entrances and exits and

d. other agencies, or a department within one previously discussed, that may need to review
   - handicapped access,
   - energy conservation,
   - sound control,
   - hazardous waste disposal,
   - security provisions,
   - building design architectural review,
   - landscaping and
   - requirements for historical buildings or districts.

Once the first review has been completed, it is the responsibility of the submitter to revise the plans or otherwise indicate how the deficiencies are to be corrected or eliminated. A revised set of documents should be submitted to the jurisdiction. The review process to validate the resolution of the cited deficiencies will then be a faster repeat of the original review.

Issuance of the Building Permit

When a reviewing agency is satisfied that its codes and other requirements have been met, a representative of that agency will sign and approve the application. When all required approvals are on the application, the applicant is notified that the permit is ready to be issued. The issuance of the permit occurs after the various fees levied by the jurisdiction are paid. These fees may include, but not be limited to, the following:

- the building permit fee (to cover the field inspection of the construction),
- the sewer and water connection fees and
- a fee to cut the curb for the driveways.

Some jurisdictions require that the plumbing and electrical permits be obtained at the same time as the building permit.

The building permit will be issued and provided to the applicant along with one copy of the approved application, one set of the approved plans, and other documents submitted with the application. These documents are of extreme value and importance. Every effort should be made to store them safely and, at the completion of construction, to file them together with a complete record of all correspondence and other communication between the designer and the local agencies as a record of the project. These documents are permanent records of value.

Summary

This outline of the permit process also applies to alterations and additions to existing facilities; although the detail and time involved in the review will vary considerably with the extent and complexity of the proposed work. The legal review requirements apply regardless of whether the work is new construction or the alteration of an existing facility.

The reader is urged to become familiar with

- the local jurisdiction's requirements and procedures,
- appeals boards,
- departmental structure of the review agencies and
- other agencies at a regional or state level with requirements for construction in the locality.

The responsibility for obtaining such knowledge, and for meeting the various agencies' requirements, rests with the applicant. A little time spent in learning the twists and turns of the permit process in a jurisdiction will be time well spent.

APPENDIX A-2
INTERNATIONAL CODE COUNCIL CODE DEVELOPMENT PROCESS

Appendix A-2 discusses the code development process of the International Code Council (ICC). The International Conference of Building Officials (ICBO) suspended all code development activities for the Uniform Building Code (UBC), as well as the other ICBO codes, with the completion of the 1996 code development cycle (1997 editions of the Uniform Codes).

The ICC was developed by ICBO, the Building Officials and Code Administrators International (BOCA) and the Southern Building Code Congress International (SBCCI). BOCA previously published the National Building Code, SBCCI the Standard Building Code. These organizations have also suspended work on their respective codes in favor of the International Codes.

Origin of the International Code Council

On December 9, 1994, the International Code Council (ICC) was established as a nonprofit organization dedicated to developing a single set of comprehensive and coordinated national codes. Since the early part of this century, BOCA, ICBO and SBCCI have developed the three sets of model codes used throughout the United States.

Although regional code development has been effective and responsive to our country's needs, technical disparities among the codes do exist. As such, it has been difficult for professionals in the building industry to move or expand into different regions within the United States, much less into an international environment. The nation's three model code groups responded by creating the ICC to develop a complete set of construction codes without regional limitations–the International Codes. These include the International Building Code (IBC), International Plumbing Code (IPC) and the International Mechanical Code (IMC).

The process for development of the IBC, while generally similar to that of the UBC, has some major differences. The following description of the ICC Code Development Process details all aspects of the procedures for submitting a code change to any ICC code. The major differences in this process is the manner in which the proposed changes are dealt with by the code development committees. These committees play a larger role in the consideration of changes; primarily due to the method of voting by the three code organizations.

The ability to effectively lobby for changes to the recommendations of the code development committees at the annual meetings of the three organizations is limited. (Refer to Tables A2-A and A2-B.) This makes participation at the code development committee public hearings important for effectively impacting the resultant changes to the codes.

ICC Code Change Process

The components of the ICC code change process are as follows:

- Proposed changes can be made by any party.
- Proposed changes processed by secretariat staff (number assigned and analysis developed).
- Suggested revisions published.
- Code development committees hold hearings. Withdrawals (allowed up until committee action).
  Committees take action.
  Assembly may take action.
- Report of the public hearing published.
  Unchallenged items forwarded to code change sessions at annual meetings of BOCA, ICBO and SBCCI.
- Challenge may be made by any party; processed by secretariat staff.
- Challenge agenda published.
- Code change sessions held at the annual meetings of BOCA, ICBO and SBCCI.
  Consent on unchallenged items.
  Consideration of challenges.
- Items approved or approved as modified published in supplement or new edition of code.

ICC Code Change Hearings

After consideration of proposed code changes, the code development committees make a recommendation. This will either be for approval as submitted (AS), approval as amended (AM) or denied (D). The assembly may take action, by two-thirds vote, to revise a committee recommendation. *This is the prime reason why attendance at the code development committee meetings is important in affecting the outcome of the code change process.*

Submittal of Code Change Proposals

Any interested person, persons or group may submit a code change proposal. Each proposal is submitted separately and be complete in itself, including the following information:

1. *Proponent.* Name, title mailing address and telephone number.
2. *Code Reference.* The proposal shall relate to the applicable code section(s) in the latest edition of the code and any supplement thereto.
3. *Text Presentation.* The text proposal shall be presented in the specific wording desired with deletions shown struck out with a single line and additions shown underlined with a single line.
4. *Supporting Information.* Each code change proposal shall include sufficient supporting information to indicate how the proposal is intended to affect the intent and application of the code, including:
   a. Purpose of the proposal, i.e., clarify the code.
   b. Stating the reasons, i.e., stating why the proposal is superior to the current provisions of the code.
   c. Cost Impact. Statement regarding anticipated cost impact of proposed change.
   d. Substantiation. The burden of providing substantiating material rests with the proponent.
   e. Copyright release.

Public Hearing

The work of the code development committees is conducted at public hearings. The intent of the public hearing is to permit interested parties to present their views on the code change proposals on the published agenda for the meeting.

At the code development committee meetings, the moderator of the committee will place each code change proposal before the hearing for discussion. The order of discussion is as follows:

1. The moderator asks the proponent and others in support for comments.
2. After discussion by those in support of the proposal, those opposed have the opportunity to present their views.
3. The proponents shall then have the opportunity to rebut the points raised by the opponents.
4. Opponents have the opportunity to respond to the proponents rebuttal.

Modifications to proposals may be suggested from the floor by any person participating in the public hearing.

Following the floor discussion of each code change proposal, a motion is made and seconded by members of the committee to

1. approve the code change proposal as submitted (AS) or
2. approve the code change proposal as modified with specific modifications (AM) or
3. disapprove the code change proposal (D).

Discussion on this motion is limited to code development committee members. The committee shall vote on each motion with the majority dictating the committee's action. Each committee vote is supported by a reason.

At the conclusion of the committee's action on a code change proposal and before the next code change proposal is called to the floor, the moderator asks for a motion from the public hearing attendees who may object to the committee's action. If a motion is not made from the floor, the results on the code change proposal are established by the committee's action.

If an objection is made, it is followed by a motion to

1. approve the code change proposal as submitted (ASF) or
2. disapprove the code change proposal (DF).

To revise the committee's action as a result of a motion from the floor, the assembly action shall be in accordance with the following majorities based on the number of votes cast by eligible voters. Only active members of BOCA, Class A member designees of ICBO and active member representatives of SBCCI shall be permitted to vote on any motion.

Table A2-A summarizes this process.

TABLE A2-A—ICC Change Process

	Desired Assembly Action	
Committee Action	**ASF**	**DF**
AS	—	Majority
AM	$\frac{2}{3}$	Majority
D	$\frac{2}{3}$	—

Challenges

Any interested person or group may submit a challenge to the results of the public hearing. Each challenge to a code change proposal is to be submitted separately and include the following information:

1. Name, title, mailing address and telephone number of the challenger. If a group, organization or committee submits a challenge, an individual with prime responsibility shall be indicated. If a challenge is submitted on behalf of a client, group, organization or committee, the name and mailing address shall be indicated.
2. The name of the code to which the challenge is directed, the code change proposal number and the results of the public hearing being challenged.
3. The desired final action as one of the following:
   a. approve the code change proposal (AS) or
   b. approve the code change proposal as modified (AM) by the code development committee or
   c. disapprove the code change proposal.

Final Action Consideration

The purpose of the final action consideration is to make a final determination of all code change proposals that have been considered in the code development cycle. The final action on each challenged public hearing result is accomplished by a vote cast by eligible voters (see discussion above) after interested parties have had the opportunity to present their views.

All public hearing results that have not been challenged shall be placed before the assembly with a single motion for final action in accordance with the results of the public hearing. The vote shall be taken with no testimony being allowed.

Upon completion of the final action consent vote, all proposed changes that have been challenged shall be placed before the assembly with a standing motion to sustain the results of the hearing for each proposal. When the standing motion has been seconded, the question will be divided to permit individual consideration of each challenge.

At the conclusion of all challenges to each proposal, each person eligible to vote shall complete a written ballot reflecting their vote on each challenged result of the public hearing. The vote will be to sustain the results of the public hearing or to revise the results of the public hearing and approve the code change proposal as submitted (AS) or to approve the code change proposal as modified (AM) by the code development committee or to disapprove the code change proposal (D).

The final action on all challenged proposals shall be determined by the results of the public hearing unless the required majority is received to revise the final action in accordance with a requested challenge. The final action on all challenged proposals is based on the aggregate count of all ballots received in accordance with the majorities shown in Table A2-B.

TABLE A2-B—ICC Challenge Process

	Challenger's Desired Final Action		
Public Hearing Results	AS	AM	D
AS or ASF	—	$\frac{2}{3}$	Majority
AM	$\frac{2}{3}$	—	Majority
D or DF	$\frac{2}{3}$	$\frac{2}{3}$	—

APPENDIX A-3
SUMMARIZING MEETING WITH BUILDING OFFICIAL SAMPLE LETTER

The following is a sample of a confirmation letter that should be sent to the local building official after each plan check meeting in which the elements of a project were discussed.

In this sample letter, not only are the main items covered, but the sense of the discussion regarding the question of the setback dimension for the H-2 and H-3 occupancies per Table 5-A is covered as well. Mentioning this discussion item in the letter will establish the time when this matter was brought up and will indicate that, although consideration was given to a different interpretation, the dimension specifically agreed to was from the perimeter walls of the H-2 and H-3 areas. The inclusion of the matter in this confirmation letter should preclude it from being raised as a "new" problem after final plans are submitted for permit.

This record of the meeting should include as much information as possible to avoid raising issues later and to provide a record of the decision-making process. Copies of the letter should go to all the meeting participants, even though the final decision rests with building and fire officials. These courtesy copies will allow others to comment to the officials and to speed up the response.

John J. Jones, Building Official
City of Anywhere
123 Main Street
Anywhere, Any State 00000

Re: Meeting on May 7, 1995
New Building w/H-6 Occupancy
Confirmation of Discussion Items

Dear Mr. Jones:

The purpose of this letter is to confirm the discussion at the meeting held in your office on May 7, 1995, regarding the proposed new Group H, Division 6 occupancy building in the Blank Industrial Park. At that meeting the following persons were also present: Mr.

Smith, your plan checker; Fire Marshal Flamb; and Mr. Trace of my office.

Please find attached a copy of the preliminary site plan we presented at the meeting showing the following:

- the relationship of the building to the property lines,
- the preliminary arrangement of the different occupancies in the building and
- the proposed type of construction.

The proposed design is based on the 1997 UBC.

We are proposing to use Type III One-Hour construction for the one-story building. The floor area will be 100,000 square feet. The building will be fully sprinklered. The main use will be H-6, although there will also be small areas of A-3, B, H-2 and H-3 in the building. The H-2 and H-3 Occupancies exceed 1500 square feet in area.

You indicated that the proposed construction type and siting was acceptable for the one-story building, with the exception of the setback requirement for the H-2 and H-3 Occupancies, which are required to be not less than 30 feet from adjacent property lines per Table 5-A. To meet this requirement you will note that we have relocated the building to provide the 30-foot setback from both exterior walls of the H-2 and H-3 areas.

Fire Marshal Flamb was concerned with the interpretation of Table 5-A for the H-2 and H-3 Occupancies and whether the entire building should have the 30-foot setback. It was your opinion that the provisions of Table 5-A are met by the distances of the required setback from the perimeter walls of the H-2 and H-3 areas. This was our position as well, and your concurrence is appreciated.

We will provide the occupancy separations between the several occupancies as required in Table 5-B.

You indicated that, in the event we decide to construct a two-story structure with these same occupancies, at least one area separation wall must be provided to bring the areas within the code allowables. We will consider this matter further and, if the two-story concept is to be used, will return to discuss this item. In the meantime we will proceed with the schematic drawings for the interior arrangement of the occupancies, exitways and service corridors. We will contact your office to arrange another meeting when we have completed this preliminary interior design to be sure we are in code compliance before we commence final drawings.

Please confirm in writing this summary of the May 7th discussions. In the event you find that your understanding of the conclusions differ, please advise me as to the particulars. Your earliest response will assist me in moving forward with this project.

Very truly yours,

John Doe

Attachments: 3
copy: Fire Marshal Flamb
Plan Checker Smith

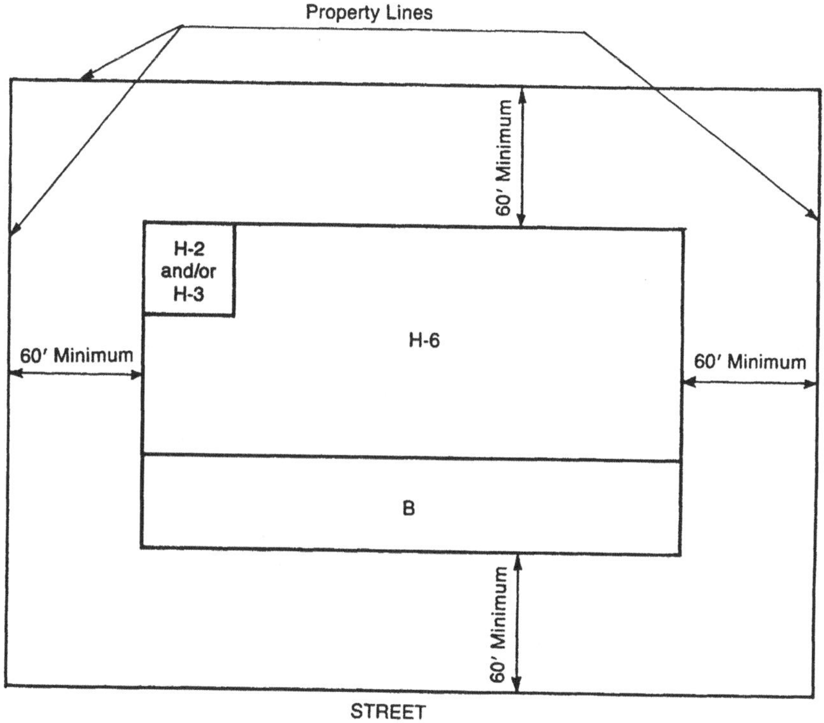

An H-2 or H-3 building or a mixed occupancy building (as shown) with H-2 or H-3 as one of the occupancies is required to be 30 feet from all property lines and streets or public ways, when the area of the H-2 or H-3 exceeds 1,500 square feet.

The method for measuring the setback as shown above assumes that the building cannot be closer than 30 feet to these lines. In the author's opinion, the measurements for the H-2 and H-3 Occupancies to the property line should be made from the boundary lines of these H Occupancies and not from the exterior walls of the overall building. See Figure A3-2.

REFERENCE: SECTION 504.3

FIGURE A3-1 SITE REQUIREMENT-GROUP H, DIV. 2 OCCUPANCY

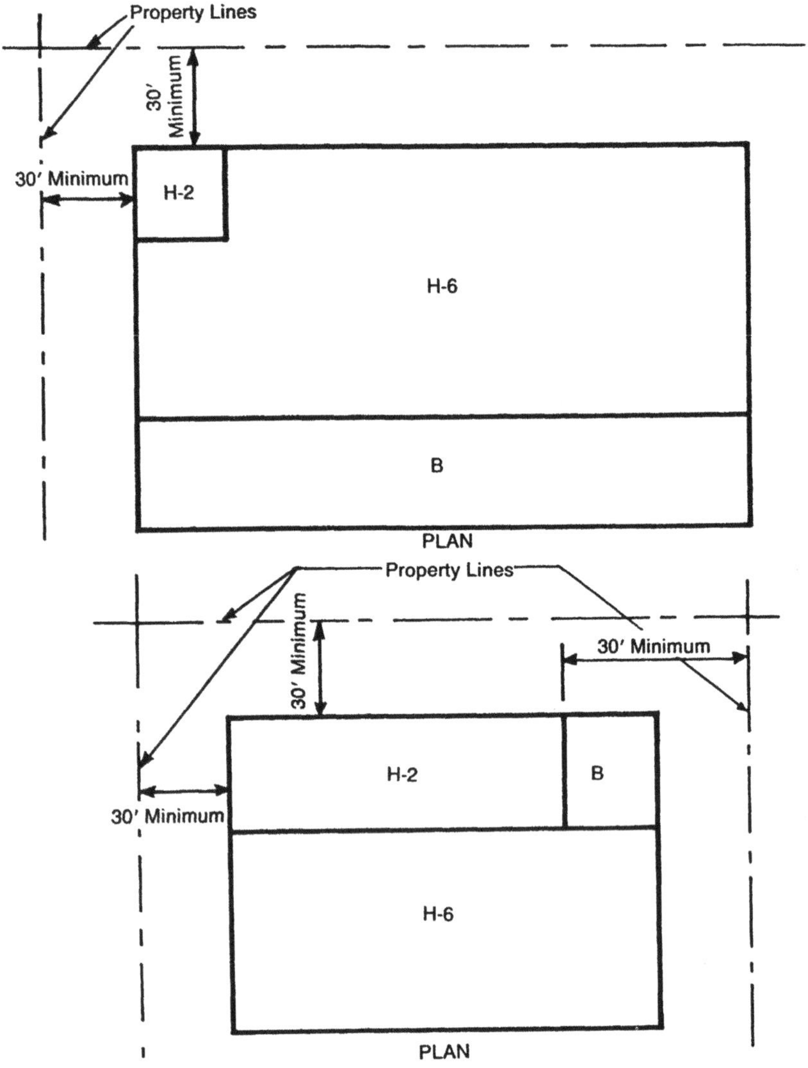

An H-2 Occupancy building or mixed occupancy building containing an H-2 occupancy (as shown) requires that all walls of the H-2 Occupancy be at least 30 feet from property lines, streets and public ways when the area of the H-2 Occupancy exceeds 1,000 square feet.

The H and B Occupancy provisions are based on the Sections 304, 307 and Table 5-A.

REFERENCE: SECTION 503, 503.4.5, ITEM 2, 504.3 AND TABLE 5-A

FIGURE A3-2 SITE REQUIREMENT-GROUP H DIV. 3 AND DIV. 6 OCCUPANCIES

APPENDIX A-4

INADEQUACIES IN DESIGNS OR COMMON DESIGNER OMISSIONS

The authors have been requested to provide a checklist of the areas often overlooked or improperly understood by designers. Over the years these areas have formed a common thread in many litigation cases.

The purpose of such a checklist is to assist the designer and the enforcement official by providing a review source on key items for use on a job-by-job basis and a cross reference to the detailed discussion within this Guide. If one of the subjects is not discussed elsewhere in this Guide, it will be discussed in this appendix.

Each of the listed items below will be discussed and referenced to the appropriate chapter in this Guide.

1. Measurement of floor area,
2. Area separation walls:
   a. inadequate details for project conditions,
   b. improper fire-rating conditions,
   c. interchanging terminology with "party walls" and
   d. improper wall termination at roof in lieu of parapet,
3. complex designations of wall/ceiling construction,
4. Multiple lengths of fasteners in multiple-layer fire-rated assemblies and
5. protection of openings below and adjacent to exterior stairways.

1. Measurement of Floor Area. See Article 4.

Areas to be included in the floor area computation include covered balconies, decks, entry landings and stairways. Mechanical areas, shafts and similar nonhabitable spaces are also to be included.

2. Area Separation Walls (ASW). See Article 5.
a. Inadequate details for project conditions.

This subject includes the innumerable variations that a particular project may present to the designer. When deciding to use an ASW, it is important for the designer to understand exactly how the project's unique conditions may affect the construction and extent of the ASW. The designer must not rely on the plan check to find deficiencies that may exist.

b. Improper fire-rating determination.

The minimum fire-rating of an ASW per Section 504.6.2 is 2 hours, not 1 hour.

c. Interchanging terminology with "party walls."

Whenever terms are used without careful discrimination, confusion and inappropriate design may occur. Frequently tenant party walls are referred to instead of either a true property line wall or an area separation wall. Tenant separation walls are also confused with both property line and area separation walls. The designer must understand the specific code terminology and, whenever possible, use that terminology on the contract documents.

Tenant separation walls, the new dwelling unit separation or ASWs will be within a building. It is very unlikely that there would be a property line wall. Regardless of how condominium units may have been sold, property line walls would not be within a building.

d. Improper wall termination at roof in lieu of parapet.

The provisions of Section 504.6.4 must be followed whenever the ASW will not have a parapet. The designer must not go by local tradition of construction, particularly in this regard. In most instances, local tradition may be no more than the continuation of misinterpretations by designers and contractors.

A good example of this misguided approach is the use of sheet metal over the roof sheathing, or the placement of wallboard directly under the roof sheathing in lieu of the 1-hour roof-ceiling assembly required by the code.

3. Complex Designations of Wall/Ceiling Construction. See Article 8.

The designer's concern with meeting the minimum code requirements can result in the contract documents generating an almost assured field deficiency. In some projects, the wallboard required by the drawings were

- $\frac{1}{2}$-inch regular gypsum wallboard for walls and ceiling coverage of nonrated construction,
- $\frac{1}{2}$-inch Type C gypsum wallboard for the ceiling coverage within 5 feet of an ASW to provide that portion of a 1-hour roof-ceiling assembly and
- $\frac{5}{8}$-inch Type X gypsum wallboard for the ASW construction.

The designer should be aware that such complex requirements on a drawing do not reflect the field problems faced by the contractor in trying to carry them out. It is unrealistic to expect three types of wallboard either to be on hand or to be properly located and installed. To obtain the desired result, careful field observation by the designer's personnel is required.

Inevitably an error will occur in this situation. In one project, all surfaces were found to be covered by $\frac{1}{2}$-inch regular wallboard, including the two layers on the ASW.

4. Multiple Lengths of Fasteners in Multiple-Layer Fire-Rated Assemblies

Frequently the designer sites, as part of the description of the minimum construction for multiple-layer fire-rated assemblies, the description from the code or from an evaluation report. Such an assembly will usually describe two different lengths of fasteners. For example, a 2-hour wall assembly would have 2 layers of $\frac{5}{8}$-inch Type X gypsum wallboard on each side of the wall. The inner layer, per Item 17.1-5 of Table 7-B, is required to have 6d nails, and the outer layer, 8d nails. The longer nails in the outer layer are required to assure that the wallboard is fastened to the studs, not just to the inner layer of wallboard.

If the outer layer was nailed with the shorter 6d nails, there would be only a $\frac{3}{4}$-inch penetration into the stud instead of the required $1\frac{1}{4}$-inch minimum required. Such an inadequate embedment would cause the assembly to be disqualified as a 2-hour wall; the wall would fail in less time due to the pullout of the outer layer nails shortly after the start of the fire test, as the wallboard undergoes dimensional changes.

In the construction of real buildings, and not simply test samples, a carpenter usually carries only one size nail at a time, not nails with minor differences in their size. If the carpenter has only one size nail—the size commonly to be used that day—it is usually the

6d nail, because most wallboard the carpenter installs is in a single layer application. The result, therefore, of having only one length of nail is that the second, or outer layer, of a two-layer assembly may be fastened with only the 6d nails. Unfortunately, this occurs in many projects.

The authors recommend that where a project has multiple-layer fire-rated assemblies, the designer should specify only one nail length to be used for any installation, including single-layer installations. That nail should be the larger of the two nails required for the multiple-layer installation, i.e., the 8d nail in the example cited.

Furthermore, the designer should place emphasis on this change from the standard length nail either on the drawings or in the specifications. This will alert the contractor that special care need be taken for the wall installations.

5. Protection of Openings Below and Adjacent to Exterior Exit Stairways. See Article 7.

Included in the range of openings to be protected are the entry door, windows, vents, air inlets, exhausts, and any other opening to the interior normally found near a stairway.

TECHNICAL APPENDIX TA-1
UBC CHAPTER 5
GENERAL BUILDING LIMITATIONS

This technical appendix is provided to aid in understanding the mixed occupancy provisions of Section 504.3 for allowable floor area determination. The two criteria or rules contained in Section 504.3 are

1. the unity rule and
2. the 10 percent rule.

To facilitate the explanation of these mixed occupancy provisions, the following examples will be used:

Building:
- Type II-N one story
- Sprinklered throughout
- 60-foot separations all around.

Case A Occupancies	• Group S, Div. 3	100,000 sq.ft.
	• Group A, Div. 3	5,000 sq.ft.
	• Group H, Div. 3	3,000 sq.ft.
Case B Occupancies	• Group S, Div. 3	65,000 sq.ft.
	• Group A, Div. 3	3,000 sq.ft.
	• Group H, Div. 3	2,000 sq.ft.
Case C Occupancies	• Group S, Div. 3	45,000 sq.ft.
	• Group A, Div. 3	1,000 sq.ft.
	• Group H, Div. 3	4,000 sq.ft.

Several questions are usually raised by the mixed-occupancy provisions. Some occur because of the presentation order of the code requirements; others occur because of the wording of the provisions.

The first requirement is stated in the second paragraph: the unity rule. Because the other provisions are exceptions to the unity rule, it is the primary rule for mixed occupancies.

The other rule together with its key stipulation is in the third paragraph: the 10 percent rule and the basic allowable area limitation. In the authors' opinion, this third paragraph is really an exception to the unity rule in the second paragraph. For instance, the use of the 10 percent rule, limited only by the basic allowable area in Table 5-B, can result in minor use areas that will not satisfy the unity rule.

In the Case B example an illustration of this can be seen because the aggregate minor use area is 5000 square feet. This is less than 10 percent of the floor area of the building. If the unity rule is also applied, the following would be the calculations:

$$\overset{\text{S-3}}{\frac{65{,}000}{12{,}000 \times 6}} + \overset{\text{H-3}}{\frac{2{,}000}{7{,}500 \times 2}} + \overset{\text{A-3}}{\frac{3{,}000}{9{,}100 \times 6}} = 0.90 + 0.13 + 0.05 = 1.08$$

Not OK

In the Group B area increases to near the maximum allowed by Table 5-B, including the increases for sprinklers and separations, the allowable areas for the minor uses are substantially reduced. This would be contrary to the intent of the 10 percent rule because that provision considers a small minor use as presenting no unusual hazard to the major use.

Finally, the code considers that when the minor uses are less than 10 percent of the floor area, the major use will determine the occupancy classification of that floor. This provision runs counter to the second paragraph, where the first sentence states that each portion of the building must conform to the occupancy requirements therein.

Thus, the conclusion reached by the authors is that when the 10 percent rule and the basic allowable area stipulation are both satisfied the unity rule does not apply. This makes the second paragraph of Section 504.3 an exception to the first paragraph. This determination is important to the designer and to the enforcement official.

Specific Questions of the Intent of the Provisions

Questions are raised that need to be addressed regarding the mixed occupancy provisions. For example:

a. Should the area increases permitted in Sections 505.1 and 505.3 apply to the basic allowable areas referred to in the third paragraph? Both the unity and 10 percent rules? Why?

b. Do both rules apply to each building situation?
c. How do the rules apply when the unlimited area permitted in Section 505.2 is involved?
d. How are the allowable areas for an unlimited area building to be calculated when a mixed occupancy is involved?
e. How are the relative hazards assessed when the minor use is of a greater hazard than the major use?

The following discussion of the answers is provided both to resolve the questions and to stimulate debate, which possibly will lead to clarification of the mixed-occupancy provisions presently in the code. Answers will be presented in the same order as the five questions were posed.

a. For the calculation of the 10 percent rule and the related stipulation, the Section 505 increases for separations and sprinklers are not to be added to the Table 5-B basic allowable areas. The intent of this code provision is to keep the minor uses to a small percentage of the total floor area.

If the Section 505.1 and 505.3 increases were to be permitted for the calculation of the basic allowable area in the stipulation attendant to the 10 percent rule, that basic allowable area could then be as large as 54,600 square feet for the Group A, Division 3 Occupancy, as in our Case A example. This size is achieved by adding the sprinkler credits for a one-story building and the credit for four separations to the basic allowable area.

The area of the Group B Occupancy is 100,000 square feet. This large of a "minor-use" basic allowable area would not be in keeping with the intent of the code regarding a minor use. Only the 9100 square feet basic allowable area in Table 5-B should be used.

If the Section 505.2 provisions for unlimited area (infinite size) were allowed to be used for the major use in the calculation of the 10 percent rule, the minor areas would also be allowed to be "infinite" as well because 10 percent of infinity is still infinity. This interpretation would be grossly in conflict with the intent of limiting the size of the minor uses. Using only the 10 percent rule is obviously inadequate in limiting the size of the minor use. Some absolute limit to the size of the minor use is needed. That limit is the basic allowable area stipulation based on Table 5-B.

The second paragraph with the unity rule does not refer to the basic allowable area, whereas the third paragraph does refer to basic allowable area when referring to allowable areas. Instead, the second paragraph refers to the total allowable area. The total allowable area includes the Table 5-B areas and the increases allowed by Section 505.

> In the authors' opinion, for these reasons only the unity rule should be calculated based on the Table 5-B areas plus the applicable increases of Section 505.

b. Whether both the unity and the 10 percent rules apply to all buildings involves the order of consideration of the code provisions, as discussed earlier. The 10 percent rule should always be checked first to determine whether it can be met.

If the 10 percent rule is applied and satisfied, the code requirements in Section 504.3 are met. With the basic allowable also satisfied, it is the authors' opinion that the unity rule need not be applied. As stated earlier, the third paragraph is considered to be an exception to the second paragraph, which contains the unity rule. Therefore, the unity rule in the second paragraph should not be used in this case.

If, however, the 10 percent rule is not met, i.e., the sum of minor-use areas exceeds 10 percent of that floor of the building, or if the area for the minor uses is greater than the basic allowable area permitted by Table 5-B, then the unity rule must be applied because the "exception" of the third paragraph does not apply.

The code does not provide the necessary guidance to lead to the order in which the second and third paragraphs are to be evaluated. Just as we found it necessary to avoid using the infinite area for the Group B Occupancy determination in applying the 10 percent rule, the order of consideration is an unstated criteria; that is, when the 10 percent rule is not met, the unity rule must apply.

For the Case A example, the basic allowable areas from Table 5-B are

Group A, Division 3 = 9100 square feet and
Group H, Division 3 = 7500 square feet.

Because the actual areas proposed for our Case A example are less than these basic allowable areas, and because the 8000 square feet aggregate area of the two major uses is less than 10 percent of the floor area of the building, the 10 percent rule is satisfied. Thus, the unity rule does not apply.

In summary, the 10 percent rule and the basic allowable area provision should always be applied as a first trial. If the 10 percent rule is also satisfied, there is no need to meet the unity rule. If the 10 percent rule is not satisfied, i.e., the aggregate areas of the minor uses exceed 10 percent of the floor area of the building, then the unity rule must be used and satisfied.

c. For the unlimited area building permitted by Section 505.2 with a mixed occupancy (e.g., the building described in Case A of this discussion), it would not be reasonable to use only the infinite allowable area to determine whether the 10 percent rule is satisfied. As previously stated, 10 percent of infinity is still infinity and, thus, of no assistance in determining whether the 10 percent rule is met. In these buildings the controlling finite limitation is the basic allowable area provision in the second paragraph.

When there is more than one minor use or occupancy in an unlimited area building, it is not obvious how to determine whether the basic allowable areas are exceeded. It is not sufficiently simply to take each such minor use and compare it to its Table 5-B basic allowable area. If this was done and there were several different minor uses, the aggregate of these minor uses would quickly mount up and not be a controlling factor.

> In the authors' opinion, the method of handling multiple minor uses in determining whether the aggregate exceeds the intent of the code for the basic allowable area limitation is similar to that of the unity rule calculation. If there was only one use involved, the basic allowable area and the actual allowable area permitted would be the same, or the ratio of the actual over the allowable would be unity.

Thus, for the evaluation of whether the minor-use areas meet the basic allowable area intent of the code, where there is more than one minor use, the sum of the ratios of the various actual floor areas for each use, divided by the basic allowable area for that use, cannot exceed one (1).

In Case A example:

$$\overset{\text{A-3}}{\frac{5000}{9100}} + \overset{\text{H-3}}{\frac{3000}{7500}} = 0.55 + 0.4 = 0.95 < 1.0 \qquad \text{OK}$$

Because the basic allowable area limitation is met, the 10 percent rule is satisfied and the unity rule does not apply.

d. In the application of the unity rule, the unlimited allowable area for the Group S Occupancy from Section 505.2 is used. For the minor uses, the total allowable areas are used. The reason for using the Section 505.2 provisions in the unity rule calculation only is as follows:

If the building contained only the S-3 Occupancy, the application of the unity rule would be

$$\frac{\text{Actual Area (S-3)}}{\text{Total allowable area (S-3)}} \leq 1.0$$

Per Section 505.2, the total allowable area for the S Occupancy may be infinite. That denominator is, therefore, unlimited or infinite; no matter what the numerator is, the equation will always be satisfied, even if the numerator was infinite.

If any other denominator was used, i.e., assuming Section 505.2 was not allowed to apply as the denominator for the allowable area, then the numerator, which is permitted to be infinite by Section 505.2, would result in a fraction greater than 1.0 and the unity rule would not be satisfied. The fraction would be

$$\frac{\text{Infinity}}{\text{Any infinite number}} = \text{Infinity} > 1.0 \qquad \text{Not OK}$$

Therefore, the only logical denominator for the unity rule application to the major area where Section 505.2 applies is infinity. Because the denominator of the ratio calculation is to be the total allowable area, each minor occupancy area is to be calculated with the allowable increases of Sections 505.1 and 505.3 added.

Thus, in the unlimited area building the unity equation 5-1 (see page 109) becomes:

$$\frac{a_1}{A_1} + \frac{a_2}{A_2} + \cdots + \frac{a_n}{A_n} \leq 1.0 \tag{5-2}$$

where a_1 = area of one use
a_2 = area of a second use
a_n = area of any other use
A_1 = maximum allowable area of first use per Table 5-B and allowable increases
A_2 = maximum allowable area of second use per Table 5-B or infinity if Section 505.2 applies
A_n = maximum allowable area of any other use per Table 5-B and allowable increases

For Case A this becomes

$$\frac{\text{Actual (A-3)}}{\text{Total allowable (A-3)}} + \frac{\text{Actual (H-3)}}{\text{Total allowable}} + \frac{\text{Actual (S-3)}}{\text{Infinity (S-3)}} \leq 1.0$$

As has been shown, the control for Case A is the 10 percent rule stipulation regarding basic allowable area limitation. The unity rule does not control and need not apply.

We can see this rule applies by examining this equation and the equation for determining the basic allowable areas criteria for multiple minor uses. They are identical in regard to the minor uses, with the exception of the added divisor in the denominator when the unity rule is calculated. In the unlimited area building, most occupancies will have increased allowable areas for the separations—in many uses the sprinkler increases as well. Thus, the denominators will have a multiplier of 2 or more times the basic allowable area from Table 5-B.

If the basic allowable area calculations and the 10 percent rule are satisfied, the unity rule need not be tested; it will undoubtedly also be satisfied.

NOTE: As shown in Figure TA1-1, if the other use is located on an exterior wall of the unlimited area building, the requirement

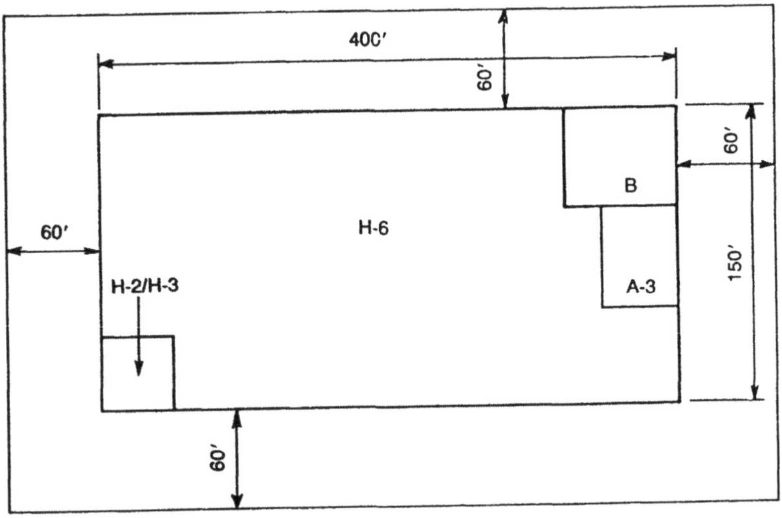

Given:
Type II 1-Hour, 2 Story Building—60,000 s.f. overall
Fully Sprinklered; 60′ clear all around building (4 separations)

Group H-6 space	=	50,000 s.f.
Group H-2/H-3 space	=	1,500 s.f.
Group B space	=	5,500 s.f.
Group A-3 space	=	3,000 s.f.
		60,000 s.f.

(Note: Arrangement of Occupancies within building shown schematically only.)

Allowable Areas

	Basic Allowable (Table No. 5-C)		Sprinkler Increase		Separation Increase*		Gross Allowable Area
H-6	18,000	×	2	×	2	=	72,000
H-2/H-3	5,600	×	-	×	2	=	11,200
B	18,000	×	2	×	2	=	72,000
A-3	13,500	×	2	×	2	=	54,000

*Separation increase for 60′ all around = (60 − 20) × 2.5% = 100%

Mixed Occupancy Calculation Per Sec. 503 (a)

$$\frac{\text{Actual Area}}{\text{Allowable Area}} \leq 1.0$$

$$\underset{\text{H-6}}{\frac{50{,}000}{72{,}000}} + \underset{\text{H-2/H-3}}{\frac{1{,}500}{11{,}200}} + \underset{\text{B}}{\frac{5{,}500}{72{,}000}} + \underset{\text{A-3}}{\frac{3{,}000}{54{,}000}} \leq 1.0$$

$$0.69 + 0.13 + 0.08 + 0.06 = 0.96 < 1.0 \quad \text{O.K.}$$

REFERENCE 504.3

FIGURE TA1-1 MIXED OCCUPANCY EXAMPLE

of Section 505.2 for the Group B Occupancy to have a 60-foot separation all around is violated.

> In the authors' opinion, an unlimited area building must meet the Section 506 (b) criteria as stated. There is no latitude on the part of the enforcement official to waive adherence with those criteria.

e. When a minor use is more hazardous than the major use, i.e., the relative hazard of an H-3 Occupancy exceeds that of the B, the question arises of whether that greater hazard affects the use of the two rules for mixed occupancies.

As the higher hazard actual areas increase in a building, the ratio for that occupancy's contribution to the basic allowable area evaluation increases as well. This will effectively limit the increase of the high-hazard minor use area. For example, consider the H-3 ratio in the example shown in item (c) above:

Assume H-3 = 3000 sq. ft. $\dfrac{3000}{7500} = 0.40$

And if H-3 = 5000 sq. ft. $\dfrac{5000}{7500} = 0.67$

By checking the calculations for the basic allowable area limitation, we see that a small increase in the H-3 area would result in this limit being exceeded because the sum of the ratios was already at 0.95 as calculated in item (c) above, without being the maximum basic allowable area allowed.

As was shown in item (a) above, even if there was only one minor use in the building, for instance, an H-3 Occupancy in the Case A example without the A-3 Occupancy, the maximum area allowed for the H-3 Occupancy would be its basic allowable area from Table 5-B and not the area resulting from the use of the 10 percent rule.

If the building was smaller in the overall area than the Case A example, for instance, with an aggregate area of 45,000 square feet, and if the H-3 Occupancy was more than 10 percent of that area, 5000 square feet, the unity rule could be applied without consideration of the relative hazards. On the other hand, in an unlimited area building, the unity rule would not control the higher hazard. Thus, there must be another controlling requirement. The code provides no guide to this controlling criteria in such buildings.

> In the authors' opinion, the direct means of dealing with this unlimited area condition in a manner consistent with the overall intent of this section of the code is to require that the unlimited area building unity equation (5-2) not use infinity for the denominator of the major use.

Therefore, when the Section 505.2 provisions are used for a mixed-occupancy building that does not exceed the total allowable area for the major use, the unity equation should be calculated using the total allowable area in determining the ratio of that major use and not the unlimited or infinite total allowable area.

By doing this, the relative hazard as well as the relative sizes of the spaces would be reflected in the evaluation, and excessively large hazardous uses would be avoided.

In the Case C example, the basic allowable area calculation for the minor areas is

$$\overset{\text{A-3}}{\frac{1000}{9100}} + \overset{\text{H-3}}{\frac{4000}{7500}} = 0.1 + 0.53 = 0.63 \qquad \text{OK}$$

The united rule calculation is

$$\frac{1{,}000}{54{,}600} + \frac{4{,}000}{15{,}000} + \frac{45{,}000}{72{,}000} = 0.02 + 0.27 + 0.62 + 0.91 \qquad \text{OK}$$

The unity rule is satisfied. Note that even small increases in the size of either minor-use area would have a considerable effect and possibly lead to the unity requirement being exceeded. (See Figure TA1-2.)

Summary of the mixed occupancies provisions and rules:

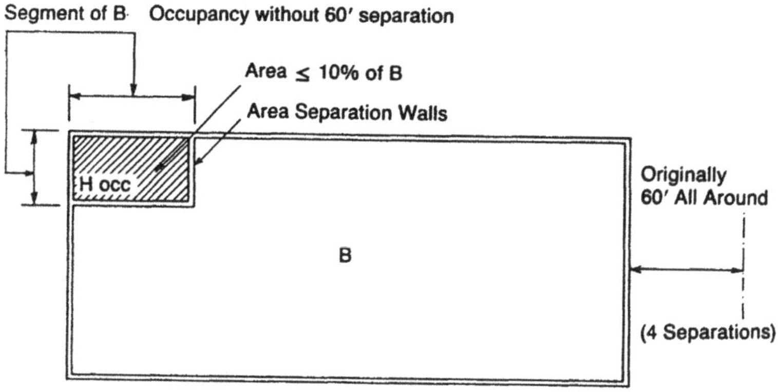

The addition of the small H Occupancy, into an unlimited area B Occupancy building, results in the revocation of the "unlimited" area permitted under Section 504.2 since the B Occupancy no longer has 60-foot separation all around it.

REFERENCE: SECTION 504.2

FIGURE TA1-2 UNLIMITED AREA BUILDING WITH H OCCUPANCY ADDED

1. Check for whether the aggregate area of the minor uses is less than 10 percent of that floor area of the building.
2. Check whether the basic allowable areas meet the Table 5-B allowables. Use the sum of the ratios when there is more than one minor use involved; this must be equal or less than 1.0.
3. If items 1 and 2 above are satisfied, there is no need to go further except in unlimited area buildings.
4. If the aggregate area of the minor uses exceeds 10 percent, check the unity rule, equation 5-1.
5. If the building design uses the unlimited area provisions of Section 505.2, use equation 5-2 to check the unity rule.
6. If the building design uses the unlimited area provisions of Section 505.2 and the aggregate area of the building is less than the total allowable area of the major use, use the unity rule equation 5-2 with, as the denominator of the major use, the total allowable area of that major use and not infinity.

TECHNICAL APPENDIX TA-2
TYPE OF CONSTRUCTION ANALYSIS
TABLE 6-A

This technical appendix discusses the provisions of Table 6-A regarding the types of construction and the relationship of the provisions therein.

Type V Construction

Starting with the least fire-resistive type of building construction, the Type V-N building in Table 6-A, no building elements other than shaft enclosures require hourly fire ratings. A check of Section 711.3 indicates that there are exceptions to this requirement for the following situations:

- In other than Group I Occupancies, openings that penetrate only one floor and are not connected with other openings communicating with other stories or basements need not be enclosed.
- In one- and two-story buildings other than Group I Occupancies, gas vents, piping and factory-built chimneys that extend through not more than two floors need not be enclosed.

In the review of the concepts of Table 6-A, we will address only the major requirements and not those special items whose exceptions are cross referenced to other parts of the code, as with the Type V shaft enclosures.

The Type V-N building is assigned the lowest allowable area, number of floors and building height in Table 5-B for each occupancy group. Thus, the least fire-resistive building has the smallest allowable areas and the lowest allowable heights. These limitations mean that a fire in such a building would affect only a limited number of stories and occupants.

Type II-N and III-N Construction

Presumably, the other two nonfire-rated building types, Types II-N and III-N, would have similar restrictive heights and areas per Chapter 5. This, however, is not the case. The Table 6-A requirements—and the character of the buildings these two types of construction represent—will be discussed in light of the two main fire spread criteria of the code concept.

All Type II buildings are required to be constructed of noncombustible materials; i.e., the structure will not provide fuel to a fire. With the noncombustible requirement satisfied, the allowable area, but not the number of stories of the Type II-N building, is permitted to be increased. A comparison of these two types of construction with the Type V-N building, using Table 5-B, shows the greater allowable area afforded to Type II buildings as a result of their noncombustible construction materials.

The noncombustible characteristics theoretically will limit the intensity of the fire and thus reduce the overall conflagration potential. Therefore, the allowable area for the Type II-N building is increased over that allowed for the Type V-N building. However, the lack of fire separations and protection for building support members within the building permits fire spread from floor to floor or collapse, if a bearing member were attacked by a fire. Thus, the number of allowable stories remains the same in the Type II-N buildings as in the Type V-N building for all occupancies except for H-6 and H-7.

The Type III-N building, however, has fire-resistive requirements for the exterior walls of the building. Although this type of building can be constructed internally of any type of material, combustible or noncombustible, the exterior wall has to be noncombustible.

The fire-resistive requirements of the exterior wall elements will assist considerably in limiting conflagration potential from a fire either within the structure or from another building. Accordingly, the Type III-N building is considered on a par with the Type II-N building for allowable area. However, the exterior wall protection does not provide any additional safety within the building from either the fire spread or internal collapse if interior support members are attacked by a fire. The number of stories for the Type III-N building is therefore the same as the Type II-N and V-N buildings, again, with the exception of the H-6 and H-7 occupancies.

Type II One-hour, III One-hour and V One-hour Construction

The three building types having at least a minimum 1-hour fire-resistive requirement, Types II One-hour, III One-hour and V One-hour, are substantially more fire resistive than nonfire-rated types.

The Table 5-B provisions indicate that both the conflagration hazard and the internal fire spread or collapse hazard are mitigated by the 1-hour construction requirement.

Accordingly, their allowable areas are greater than for the comparable nonfire-rated buildings. The three types of 1-hour buildings are not considered equal to one another in their limitation of the conflagration hazard. The Type V One-hour building has neither the degree of exterior wall protection required for the Type III One-hour building nor the limitation of combustibility for the materials used to construct the Type II One-hour building. Therefore, the Type V One-hour building is permitted a lesser allowable floor area than the other two 1-hour building types.

Type I and II-FR Construction

The component of the Type I and II-FR buildings are required to have substantially greater fire-resistive ratings than those of the 1-hour buildings. Except for the roof and the interior nonbearing partitions, all the fire-resistive ratings for the Type II-FR buildings are for the most part double those of the 1-hour structures. The allowable area is generally at least double those allowed for the 1-hour buildings.

The hazard of interior fire spread or collapse is sharply reduced due to the minimum 2-hour requirement for the floors, structural and interior bearing walls. As a result, for many of the occupancies the allowable number of stories for the Type II-FR building is greatly increased over that allowed for the 1-hour buildings. The danger to the occupants and fire fighters in such a building is reduced because more time is available for evacuation and fire fighting.

The Type I building represents the highest type of fire-resistive construction because the fire rating for the entire structural support system is raised to 3 or 4 hours. The resultant reduction of the building collapse hazard is considerable. The code allows unlimited area and height of the Type I building for almost all occupancies because of the substantial fire resistance of the building.

The only exception to this unlimited allowable area applies to the Group H-1 and H-2 Occupancies. The code considers that the hazards associated with the H-1 and H-2 Occupancies could be such that even the fire-resistive requirements of the Type I building are insufficient to permit more than a 15,000-square-foot basic allowable area.

Type IV Construction

The remaining type of construction, Type IV, is an anomaly insofar as our prior rationale is concerned. This building is also known as a Heavy Timber, or HT type. It represents a construction type common for factories at the turn of the century: the mill building. This was a structure built with exterior walls of masonry and exterior openings protected by steel shutters. The interior was all wood of very heavy and substantial dimensions. The columns, beams and girders were massive timbers. The floors, because they had to support a heavy load of equipment or storage, were of heavy planking usually at least 3 inches thick and tightly joined.

The fire experience with these buildings indicated that a fire was usually contained within the structure. In most instances the heavy floor members helped slow the fire's spread from floor to floor and allowed evacuation and fire fighting to proceed. The massive columns and beams were slow to burn through and cause collapse. For these reasons, the Type IV or HT building is permitted the same allowable areas and stories as the Type II and III One-hour buildings.

However, the system of establishing fire-resistive ratings using the ASTM standard E-119 fire test procedure does not equate HT with 1-hour construction, nor does the code. In this instance we are guided by experience rather than scientific rationale.

TECHNICAL APPENDIX TA-3
RESTRAINED VS. UNRESTRAINED ASSEMBLIES
CHAPTER 7

The concept of restraint as it applies to fire-resistive assemblies will be discussed in this technical appendix. The code citations are in Section 703.2.

In the general discussion in Chapter 7, it was indicated that the temperature of the structural elements such as columns, beams and girders is used to determine the endpoint of the test. This became a generally required condition for horizontal structural elements after it was noted that several tests had been deemed successful even though they had "structurally" failed. An evaluation of the many fire tests conducted in the 1950s and 1960s clearly indicates that the main structural members in these tests had expanded under the heat of the furnace and were subjected to very high compressive thermal restraint from the test furnace.

The horizontal fire test furnace has two heavy steel beams enclosing the top of the furnace, which form a box-shaped ring that resists the forces that occur when a floor system expands during a test. These heavy furnace beams are capable of exerting sufficient reaction to the expansion of the test assembly to cause, shortly after the start of the fire test, what originally was to be a simple beam, i.e., a pin-ended member, to become a fixed-ended member. The fire test protocol requires that the member must be loaded to produce stresses comparable to the field conditions. When the end support and fixity conditions of the structural member change, the loading condition no longer meets that test criteria. The change from pin-end to fixed-ended conditions substantially reduces the test loading condition, particularly the maximum bending moment.

The solution to this fire test problem was to establish a two-track system of rating an assembly based on one fire test.

1. The first method uses the endpoint temperatures of 1100–1300°F as previously discussed. This method and the resultant test value is called the unrestrained value for the assembly. It is a conservative value, independent of how the assembly is installed in the field.
2. The second method allows a restrained or higher hourly rating to apply but requires that the method of providing the thermal restraint of the assembly in the actual

building be certified by the structural designer as meeting the conditions attendant to such assemblies in the standard.

One further comment is necessary regarding the latter test condition of passage. The restraint that develops in the fire test and for which the structural design must provide evidence is not the restraint associated with continuous members or similar standard structural restraint. The fire test restraint is thermally induced and therefore will exist in addition to any structural design values that result from the normal design calculations. The structural designer should be aware of this difference and how to deal with it.

In the authors' opinion, unless the designer is confident that both the design and field installations can be satisfied, the unrestrained fire resistance ratings should be used.

TECHNICAL APPENDIX TA-4
FIRE TESTING PROCEDURES CHAPTER 7

This technical appendix will discuss the fire test procedures cited in Chapter 7 that form the basis of acceptance of fire-resistive assemblies.

The standard fire test is a severe performance requirement. It provides a means of comparing different configurations of materials and constructions under standardized test conditions. The ASTM E-119 test has its counterparts in other countries. They use similar fire exposure time-temperature curves. The test requires a minimum 100-square-foot sample for walls and 180-square-foot sample for floor and roof.

The fire test procedure originated in the early 1900s. Early tests consisted of measuring the amount, by weight, of the usual combustibles found in various occupancies. Duplicates of furnishings and other combustible loadings were placed in instrumented rooms that were then ignited. The time-temperature curves in these burn-outs were plotted, with repeated testing for confirmation. (See Figure TA4-1.)

Eventually, the replicas of the furnishings and other combustibles were replaced by wooden pallets that contained fuel loads equivalent to the materials found in real rooms. A wood pallet loading equivalent to 10 pounds of fuel per square foot was comparable to the furnishings in a room that would provide a 1-hour fire exposure as measured by the time-temperature curve: 20 pounds per square foot for 2 hours.

To avoid needing a large room in which to make these tests, and to provide better control of the test procedure, the wood pallets were later replaced by gas burners. In the present tests, thermocouples are positioned in the furnace so that the time-temperature curve can be accurately duplicated by varying the rate of gas being consumed at a given moment.

The test sample is placed in close proximity to the burners with an orientation either horizontal or vertical, depending on whether it is material for a wall, roof, beam or column. Separate furnaces are used for floor-ceiling and roof-ceiling assemblies including beams and trusses.

In the vertical tests, the furnace burners are arranged vertically facing the test assembly. (See Figure TA4-2.) In the horizontal tests, the burners are situated below the test sample. Columns are subjected to fire from burners placed on all four sides.

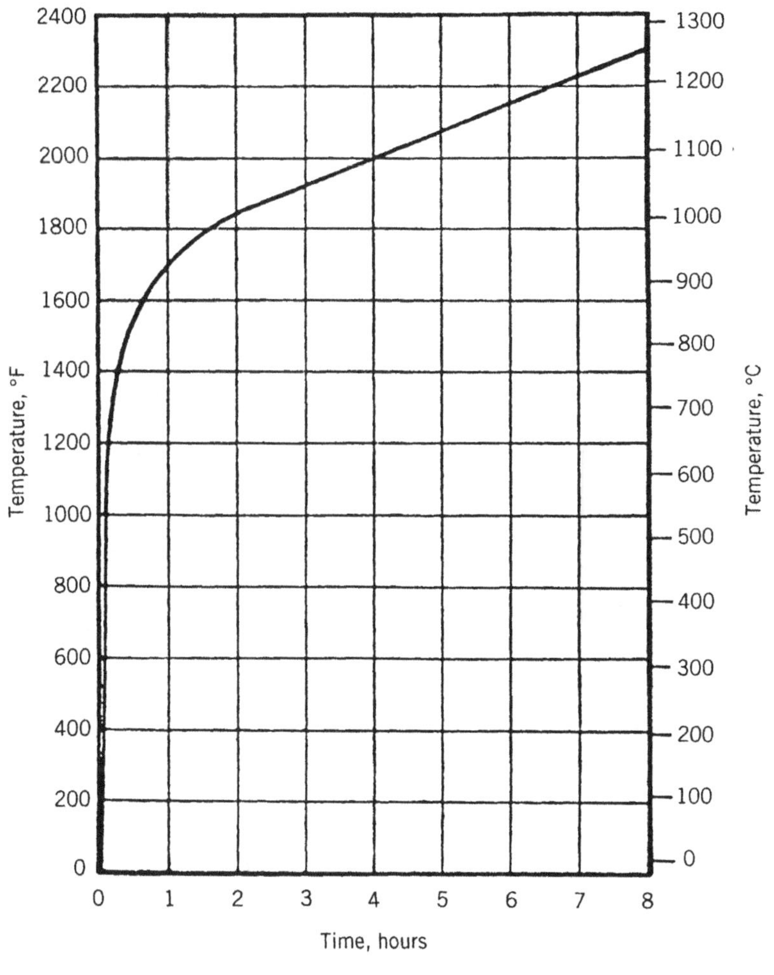

REFERENCE: UBC STANDARD 7-1, FIGURE 7-1-1
ASTM E-119

FIGURE TA4-1 STANDARD FIRE TEST TIME-TEMPERATURE CURVE

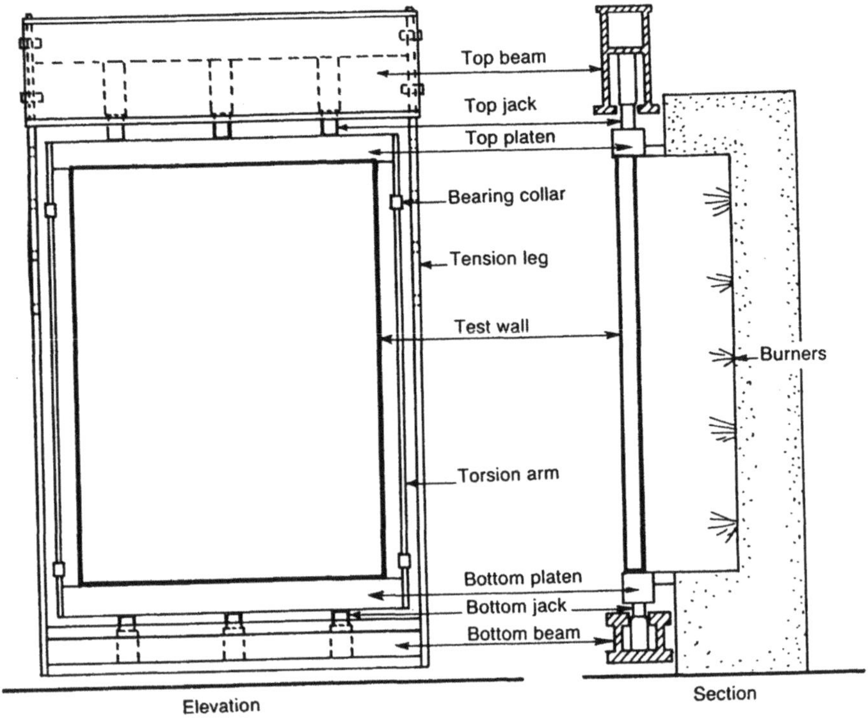

Specimen size must be minimum 100 S.F. The test can be either load-bearing or non-load bearing. Thermocouples are located within the furnace space, within the wall (if hollow) and on the non-fire side.

REFERENCE: SECTION 703.2, UBC STANDARD 7-1

FIGURE TA4-2 STANDARD WALL FIRE TEST FURNACE

The purpose of the test procedures is to evaluate the ability of the assembly to withstand exposure to the fire and to prevent the fire from breaching the barrier the assembly presents or to cause a collapse if the sample is a load-bearing member. To standardize these criteria, conditions of passage have been set up as part of the test protocol. These conditions establish the time or point in the fire test that an assembly "fails." These test endpoints are

1. For wall and floor systems (See Figures TA4-3, TA4-4 and TA4-5):
   - There should be no flame penetration.
   - The temperature of all thermocouples on the side away from the fire shall not exceed an average of 250°F above the initial room temperature (ambient).
   - The temperature on a single thermocouple shall not exceed 325°F above ambient within the time period sought for the assembly.
   - Cotton waste applied to any point on the unexposed surface should not ignite.

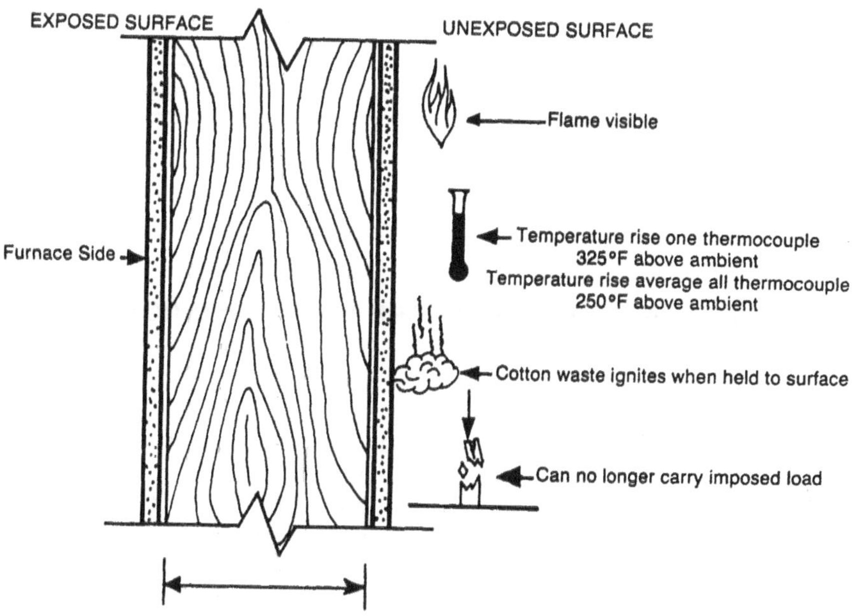

REFERENCE: UBC STANDARD 7-1

FIGURE TA4-3 WALL FIRE TEST—CONDITIONS OF PASSAGE

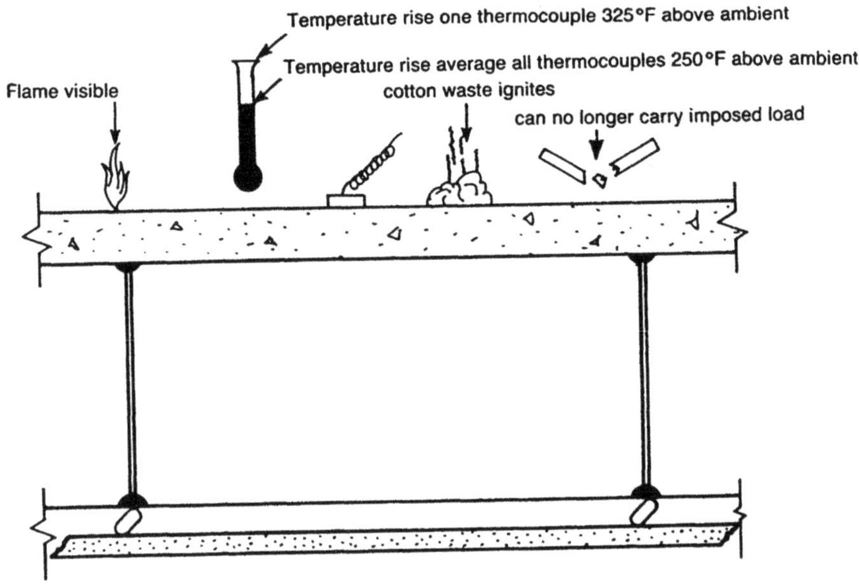

REFERENCE: UBC STANDARD 7-1

FIGURE TA4-4 FLOOR OR ROOF FIRE TEST—CONDITIONS OF PASSAGE

- If the assembly is load bearing, the load must be carried for the rating time period.

2. For columns, the endpoint is based on the critical surface temperatures at any cross section, dependent on the materials used. (See the general discussion hereafter.)
3. For beams and girders, the critical temperatures are dependent on the end restraint of the members. This subject will be covered in detail in the following general discussion.

When the fire-resistive assembly involved in a proposed fire test is load bearing, it is often considered too dangerous to subject the member to load during the test because collapse could damage the test facility. It is also impractical to attempt to load large members, such as heavy columns and girder sections, because their design

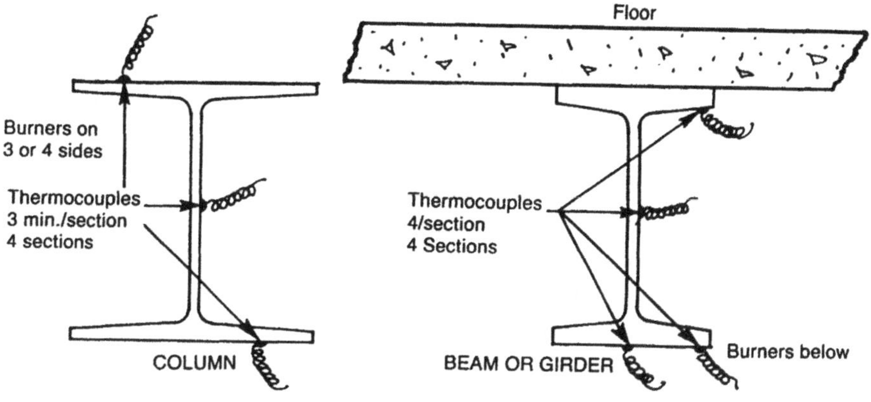

EITHER:
1. Carry applied load for rating period, or
2. a) Maximum temperature at any one thermocouple < 1200°F
   b) Average temperature at any level of 4 sets of thermocouples <1000°F

UNRESTRAINED BEAM/GIRDER
1. The specimen shall have sustained the applied load during the classification period.
2. For steel beams the temperature of the steel shall not have exceeded 1300°F at any location during the classification period nor shall the average temperature recorded by four thermocouples at any section have exceeded 1100°F during this period.
3. For conventionally designed concrete beams, the average temperature of the tension steel at any section shall not have exceeded 800°F for cold-drawn prestressing steel or 1100°F for reinforcing steel during the classification period.

RESTRAINED BEAM/GIRDER
1. The specimen shall have sustained the applied load during the classification period.
2. The specimen shall have achieved a fire-endurance classification on the basis of the temperature criteria specified below of one half the classification of the assembly or one hour, whichever is the greater.
3. For specimens employing steel structural members (beams, open-web steel joists, etc.) spaced more than 4 feet on centers, the temperature of the steel shall not have exceeded 1300°F at any location during the classification period nor shall the average temperature recorded by four themocouples at any section have exceeded 1100°F during the classification period.
4. For specimens employing steel structural members (beams, open-web steel joists, etc.), spaced 4 feet or less on center, the average temperature recorded by all joist or beam thermocouples shall not have exceeded 1100°F during the classification period.

REFERENCE: UBC STANDARD 7-1

FIGURE TA4-5 COLUMN, BEAM OR GIRDER FIRE TEST, CONDITIONS OF PASSAGE

conditions may involve hundreds of tons. Therefore, for these building elements, a set of conditions of passage takes into account the effect of elevated temperatures on the material being used.

For example, structural steel's ultimate strength at temperatures above 1000°F is substantially reduced to the range of its yield and design stresses. At these elevated temperatures the load-carrying capacity of a steel member may no longer be able to support the load for which it was designed without serious distortion or collapse. Because the furnace temperature for a 1-hour rating will reach 1700°F at the end of that time period, the fireproofing of the steel must be effective in preventing the steel from reaching temperatures above 1000°F. (See Figure TA4-6.)

The test conditions for columns are explicit. A failure condition is reached when there is an average temperature of 1000°F on any cross section of the member being tested or when any individual thermocouple reaches 1200°F.

Beams and girders are rated by one of two methods, either

- by use of endpoint temperatures as described for columns but with 1100 and 1300°F as the respective temperature limits or
- by using a variation that takes into account the thermal restraint provided for the member.

In the restrained test condition, the conditions of passage require the temperature limits be used only for 1-half the desired hourly rating period, or one hour, whichever is the lesser time.

> In the authors' and others opinion, the restrained values are difficult to regulate or control in practical application. The designer is therefore urged to consider using only unrestrained values in any design for a building.

For a further detailed discussion of the restrained/unrestrained test values, see Technical Appendix 3.

Strength of Structural Steel Under Fire Exposure

NOTE THAT ULTIMATE STRENGTH IN COMPRESSION AT 1000°F APPROACHES USUAL DESIGN STRESS FOR STEEL.

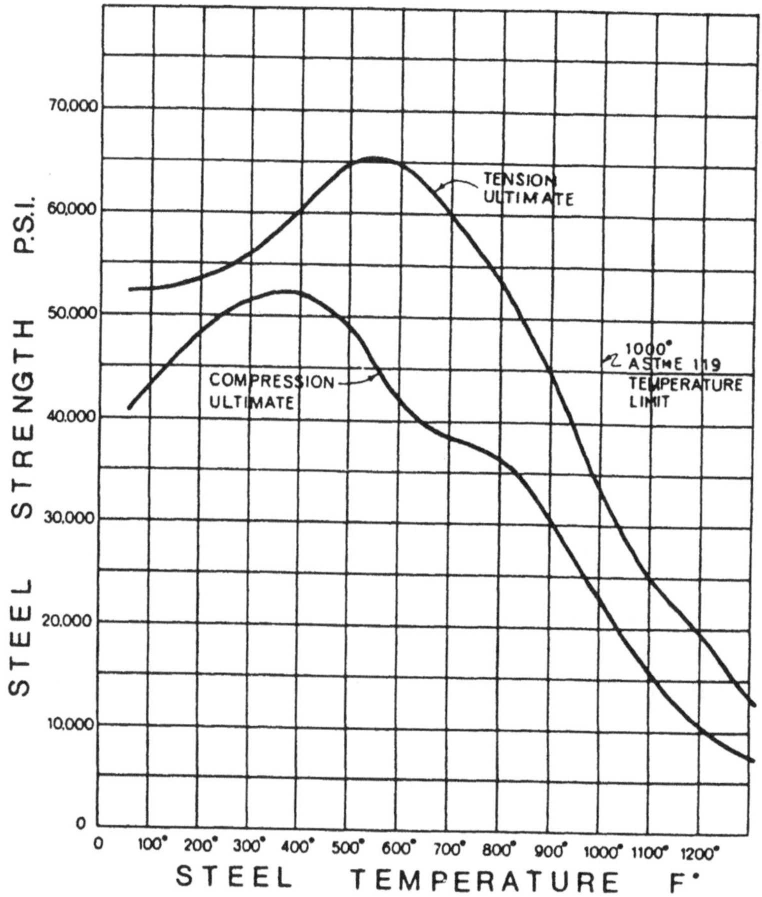

The graph indicates the values for A-36 structural steel. Other steels have similar relationships.

REFERENCE: SECTION 703.2

FIGURE TA4-6 STRENGTH VS. TEMPERATURE-STRUCTURAL STEEL

Ferrous materials other than structural steel have comparable endpoint temperatures:

- For prestressed steel, the value is 800°F.
- For reinforcing steel, the value is 1100°F.

Fire doors and windows are subjected to fire tests similar to those for walls. However, their conditions of passage are not as stringent as those for the fire-resistive assemblies because endpoint temperature limitations are either not applicable or apply to certain fire doors and then only for the first 30 minutes of the test.

Fire doors and windows are subject to fire tests similar to those for walls. However, their conditions of passage are both more severe and less stringent in certain regards. The doors and windows are mandatorily subject to a fire hose stream impact test immediately after the fire test. In the ASTM E-119 fire tests when hose streams are required, they can be imposed either on the test sample after the full time period of the test or to a replica of the sample tested for one-half the test period.

On the other hand, the door and window test conditions of passage are not as restrictive in that openings are allowed in the plane at right angles to the plane of the door or window. Thus, from a direct view of the sample there is no visible flame, but there can be openings due to bowing at right angles to that plane. In addition, endpoint temperature limitations are either not applicable or apply to certain fire doors and then only for the first 30 minutes of the test.

INDEX

Printed and bound by CPI Group (UK) Ltd, Croydon, CR0 4YY
16/09/2026
14963456-0002